KT-294-785

The goal of the *Handbook of Creativity* is to provide the most complete, definitive, and authoritative single-volume review available in the field of creativity. To this end, the book contains 22 chapters covering a wide range of issues and topics in this field, all written by distinguished leaders. The chapters are intended to be accessible to all readers with an interest in creative thinking. Although the authors are leading behavioral scientists, people in all disciplines will find the coverage of creativity in the arts and sciences to be of interest. The volume's first part sets out the major themes and reviews the history of thinking about creativity. Subsequent parts deal with methods, origins, self and environment, special topics, and conclusions.

Robert J. Sternberg is IBM Professor of Psychology and Education at Yale University. He is a Fellow of the American Academy of Arts and Sciences, and has served as President of the Divisions of General Psychology and Educational Psychology in the American Psychological Association. His work has been honored by the Early Career and McCandless Awards of the APA and the Research Review, Outstanding Book, and Sylvia Scribner Awards of the American Educational Research Association. His recent books include *Cupid's Arrow: The Course of Love Through Time*, *Thinking Styles*, and *Intelligence, Heredity, and Environment* (coedited with Elena Grigorenko).

6

J8

Handbook of Creativity

Edited by ROBERT J. STERNBERG

CAMBRIDGE
UNIVERSITY PRESS

PUBLISHED BY THE PRESS SYNDICATE OF THE UNIVERSITY OF CAMBRIDGE
Pitt Building, Trumpington Street, Cambridge CB2 1RP, United Kingdom

CAMBRIDGE UNIVERSITY PRESS
The Edinburgh Building, Cambridge CB2 2RU, UK
40 West 20th Street, New York, NY 10011-4211, USA
477 Williamstown Road, Port Melbourne, VIC 3207, Australia
Ruiz de Alarcón 13, 28014 Madrid, Spain
Dock House, The Waterfront, Cape Town 8001, South Africa

http://www.cambridge.org

© Cambridge University Press 1999

First published 1999
Reprinted 2000 (twice), 2002 (twice)

Printed in the United States of America

Typeset in New Caledonia 9/11 QuarkXPress ™[BB]

A catalog record for this book is available from the British Library.

Library of Congress Cataloging-in-Publication data available
Handbook of creativity / edited by Robert J. Sternberg.
p. cm.
Includes indexes.
ISBN 0-521-57285-1. –ISBN 0-521-57604-0 (pbk.)
1. Creative ability.   2. Creative thinking.   I. Sternberg, Robert J.
BF408.H285   1999
153.3'5–DC   2198-35205
                                         CIP

ISBN 0 521 57285 1 hardback
ISBN 0 521 57604 0 paperback

Contents

v

Contributors

Robert S. Albert
Pitzer College
1050 N. Mills
Claremont, CA 91711

Teresa M. Amabile
Graduate School of Business
Harvard University
Soldier's Field Road
Boston, MA 02163

Margaret A. Boden
School of Cognitive and Computing
    Sciences
University of Sussex
Brighton BN1 9QH
United Kingdom

Mary Ann Collins
Department of Psychology
Spring Hill College
4000 Dauphin Street
Mobile, AL 36608

Mihaly Csikszentmihalyi
Department of Psychology
University of Chicago
Chicago, IL 60637

Gregory J. Feist
Department of Psychology
College of William and Mary
P.O. Box 8795
Williamsburg, VA 23187

David Henry Feldman
Department of Child Study
Tufts University
Medford, MA 02155

Ronald A. Finke
Department of Psychology
Texas A&M University
College Station, TX 77843-4235

Howard Gardner
Graduate School of Education
Harvard University
Longfellow Hall, Appian Way
Cambridge, MA 02138-3752

Howard E. Gruber
Teachers College
Columbia University
525 West 120th Street
New York, NY 10027-6625

Michael J. A. Howe
Department of Psychology
University of Exeter
Washington Singer Laboratories
Perry Road
Exeter EX4 4QG
United Kingdom

Todd I. Lubart
Laboratoire de Psychologie Differentielle
Université René Descartes
28 rue Serpente
Paris 75006
France

Charles J. Lumsden
Institute of Medical Science
Medical Sciences Building
University of Toronto
Toronto, Ontario M5S 1A8
Canada

Colin Martindale
Department of Psychology
Clarence Cook Little Hall
University of Maine
Orono, ME 04469-0140

Richard E. Mayer
Department of Psychology
University of California at Santa Barbara
Santa Barbara, CA 93106

Raymond S. Nickerson
Department of Psychology
Paige Hall
Tufts University
Medford, MA 02155

Linda A. O'Hara
Department of Psychology
Yale University
P.O. Box 208205
New Haven, CT 06520-8205

Jonathan A. Plucker
5766 Shibles Hall
University of Maine
Orono, ME 04469-5766

Emma Policastro
Graduate School of Education
Harvard University
Longfellow Hall, Appian Way
Cambridge, MA 02138-3752

Joseph S. Renzulli
Department of Psychology
University of Connecticut
362 Fairfield Road U-7
Storrs, CT 06267-2007

Mark A. Runco
California State University EC 105
Fullerton, CA 92634

Shawn Okuda Sakamoto
Institute for the Academic Advancement of
   Youth

Johns Hopkins University
3400 N. Charles Street
Baltimore, MD 21218

Dean Keith Simonton
Department of Psychology
University of California at Davis
Davis, CA 95616

Steven M. Smith
Department of Psychology
Texas A&M University
College Station, TX 77843-4235

Robert J. Sternberg
Department of Psychology
Yale University
P. O. Box 208205
New Haven, CT 06520-8205

Doris B. Wallace
Teachers College
Columbia University
525 West 120th Street
New York, NY 10027-6625

Thomas B. Ward
Department of Psychology
Texas A&M University
College Station, TX 77843-4235

Robert W. Weisberg
Department of Psychology
Temple University
Philadelphia, PA 19122

Wendy M. Williams
Human Development and Family Studies
Martha Van Rensselaer Hall
Cornell University
Ithaca, NY 14853

Lana T. Yang
Columbia University Law School
435 West 116 St.
New York, NY 10027

Preface

The goal of the *Handbook of Creativity* is to provide the most comprehensive, definitive, and authoritative single-volume review available in the field of creativity. To this end, the book contains 22 chapters covering a wide range of issues and topics in this field.

The chapters are intended to be accessible to all individuals with an interest in creative thinking. Although the authors are leading behavioral scientists and most readers are likely to have an interest in behavioral sciences, those involved in the natural sciences and humanities will find much that appeals to them in the volume, especially because so many of the examples and even case studies draw on the natural sciences and humanities.

The volume is divided into six parts, each dealing with a different aspect of creativity and its investigation. Part I, the introduction, sets out the volume's major themes. It reviews the history of thinking about creativity in general and the field of creativity in particular. Part II characterizes some of the main ways in which creativity can be investigated. Part III looks at how creativity originates and develops, both over the course of historical time and over the course of an individual's life span. Part IV considers the relation between the self and the environment in the nature and development of creativity. Part V deals with a wide variety of topics in the study of creativity that are outside the mainstream but that are nevertheless important to the field. Part VI, the conclusion, contains one essay that summarizes the chapters that precede it.

I am grateful to Julia Hough for her support of this project and for the support given by the Javits Program, Grant R206R50001 of the U.S. Office of Educational Research and Improvement, in funding my own research on creativity and backing this volume. Sai Durvasula was instrumental in the preparation of the manuscripts.

Handbook of Creativity

PART I

Introduction

1   The Concept of Creativity: Prospects and Paradigms

ROBERT J. STERNBERG AND TODD I. LUBART

If one wanted to select the best novelist, artist, entrepreneur, or even chief executive officer, one would most likely want someone who is creative. Indeed, today many CEOs are selected not for their pleasant personalities (it's hard to be perceived as pleasant when you may have to fire 20% of the company) or their learning and memory skills (they use computers or subordinates to remember the details for them), but for their creative vision of how to turn a company around.

Creativity is the ability to produce work that is both novel (i.e., original, unexpected) and appropriate (i.e., useful, adaptive concerning task constraints) (Lubart, 1994; Ochse, 1990; Sternberg, 1988a; Sternberg & Lubart, 1991, 1995, 1996). Creativity is a topic of wide scope that is important at both the individual and societal levels for a wide range of task domains. At an individual level, creativity is relevant, for example, when one is solving problems on the job and in daily life. At a societal level, creativity can lead to new scientific findings, new movements in art, new inventions, and new social programs. The economic importance of creativity is clear because new products or services create jobs. Furthermore, individuals, organizations, and societies must adapt existing resources to changing task demands to remain competitive.

CREATIVITY AS A NEGLECTED RESEARCH TOPIC

As the first half of the twentieth century gave way to the second half, Guilford (1950), in his APA Presidential Address, challenged psychologists to pay attention to what he found to be a neglected but extremely important attribute, namely, creativity. Guilford reported that less than 0.2% of the entries in *Psychological Abstracts* up to 1950 focused on creativity.

Interest in creativity research began to grow somewhat in the 1950s, and a few research institutes concerned with creativity were founded. However, several indicators of the volume of work on creativity show that it remained a relatively marginal topic in psychology, at least until recently. We analyzed the number of references to creativity in *Psychological Abstracts* from 1975 to 1994. To conduct this analysis, we searched the computerized PsychLit database of journal articles using the database keywords of *creativity, divergent thinking,* and *creativity measurement.* These terms are assigned by the database to articles whose content concerns primarily the subject of creativity. We also identified additional entries that contained the word stem *creativ*-somewhere in the title or abstract of the article but were not indexed by one of the keywords for creativity. We examined a random subset of these additional entries and found that they did not concern creativity to any notable extent and were best excluded from the set of articles on creativity. The result of our analysis is that approximately 0.5% of the articles indexed in *Psychological Abstracts* from 1975 to 1994 concerned creativity. For comparative purposes, articles on reading accounted for approximately 1.5% of the entries in *Psychological Abstracts* during the same 20-year period.

3

If we look at introductory psychology textbooks as another index, we find that creativity is barely covered. Whereas intelligence, for example, gets a chapter or a major part of one, creativity gets a few paragraphs, if that. Major psychology departments rarely offer courses on creativity, although such courses are sometimes offered in educational psychology programs.

In terms of academic positions, there are virtually no listings in departments of psychology for positions in the study of creativity. Departments are typically not organized into a division for the study of creativity (unlike, say, divisions studying cognitive, social, or clinical psychology). At the American Psychological Association convention, research on creativity is either placed under "Psychology and the Arts" (Division 10) or can be found scattered among cognitive, social, or clinical divisions. However, it is important to note that the APA has recently begun to give this domain some attention by sponsoring a conference on creativity in 1995 and featuring research on creativity in the *APA Monitor* in August 1995.

With regard to research journals, there are no journals on creativity at the top of most-cited journal lists (unlike, say, perception, learning and memory, interpersonal relations, or personality). There are two less widely circulating psychology journals devoted to creativity. The *Journal of Creative Behavior* was founded in 1967, when interest grew in teaching people to be more creative. An analysis of this journal's content shows that nonempirical articles exceeded empirical ones and creativity enhancement and education were the most frequent topics (Feist & Runco, 1993). The *Creativity Research Journal,* which has a research focus, began only in 1988.

Creativity is important to society, but it traditionally has been one of psychology's orphans. Why? We believe that, historically, the study of creativity has faced at least six major roadblocks: (a) the origins of the study of creativity in a tradition of mysticism and spirituality, which seems indifferent or even possibly counter to the scientific spirit; (b) the impression conveyed by pragmatic, commercial approaches to creativity that its study lacks a basis in psychological theory or verification through psychological research; (c) early work on creativity that was theoretically and methodologically apart from the mainstream of theoretical and empirical psychology, resulting in creativity sometimes being seen as peripheral to the central concerns of the field of psychology as a whole; (d) problems with the definition of and criteria for creativity that seemed to render the phenomenon either elusive or trivial; (e) approaches that have tended to view creativity as an extraordinary result of ordinary structures or processes, so that it has not always seemed necessary to have any separate study of creativity; (f) unidisciplinary approaches to creativity that have tended to view a part of creativity as the whole phenomenon, often resulting in what we believe is a narrow vision of creativity and a perception that creativity is not as encompassing as it truly is.

In this chapter, we will discuss these six roadblocks and, in the course of discussing them, review six approaches, or paradigms, that have been used to understand creativity – mystical, psychoanalytic, pragmatic, psychometric, cognitive, and social-personality. Of course, these approaches do not exhaust all the approaches to creativity, nor is it possible in a short chapter to do full justice even to the six approaches considered. But we believe that the survey of these approaches covers some of the major highlights. We also believe that there is a seventh approach that is likely to be particularly fruitful in future work – that of confluence theories – which we shall also review. These theories utilize various multidisciplinary approaches to creativity and combine some of the elements of, and derive from, uniperspective views.

MYSTICAL APPROACHES TO THE STUDY OF CREATIVITY

The study of creativity has always been tinged – some might say tainted – with associations to mystical beliefs. Perhaps the earliest accounts of creativity were based on divine intervention. The creative person was seen as an empty vessel that a divine being would fill with inspiration. The individual would then pour out the inspired ideas, forming an otherworldly product.

In this vein, Plato argued that a poet is able to create only that which the Muse dictates, and even today people sometimes refer to their own Muse as a source of inspiration. In Plato's view, one person might be inspired to create choral songs, another, epic poems (Rothenberg & Hausman, 1976). Often, mystical sources have been suggested in creators' introspective reports (Ghiselin, 1985). For example, Rudyard Kipling (1937/1985) referred to the "Daemon" that lives in the writer's pen: "My Daemon was with me in the Jungle Books, Kim, and both Puck books, and good care I took to walk delicately, lest he should withdraw. . . . When your Daemon is in charge, do not think consciously. Drift, wait, and obey" (p. 162).

The mystical approaches to the study of creativity have probably made it harder for scientific psychologists to be heard. Many people seem to believe, as they do about love (see Sternberg, 1988a, 1988b), that creativity is something that just doesn't lend itself to scientific study, because it is a spiritual process. We believe that it has been hard for the scientific approach to shake the deep-seated view of some people that, somehow, scientific psychologists are treading where they should not.

PRAGMATIC APPROACHES TO THE STUDY OF CREATIVITY

Equally damaging to the scientific study of creativity, in our view, has been the takeover of the field, in the popular mind, by those who follow what might be referred to as a pragmatic approach. Those taking this approach have been concerned primarily with developing creativity, secondarily with understanding it, but almost not at all with testing the validity of their ideas about it.

Perhaps the foremost proponent of this approach is Edward De Bono, whose work on lateral thinking and other aspects of creativity has had what appears to be considerable commercial success (e.g., De Bono, 1971, 1985, 1992). De Bono's concern is not with theory, but with practice. For example, he suggests using a tool that focuses on the aspects of an idea that are pluses, minuses, and interesting (such as PMI). Or he suggests using the word *po*, derived from hypothesis, suppose, possible, and poetry, to provoke rather than judge ideas. Another tool, that of "thinking hats," has individuals metaphorically wear different hats, such as a white hat for data-based thinking, a red hat for intuitive thinking, a black hat for critical thinking, and a green hat for generative thinking, in order to stimulate seeing things from different points of view.

DeBono is not alone in this enterprise. Osborn (1953), based on his experiences in advertising agencies, developed the technique of brainstorming to encourage people to solve problems creatively by seeking many possible solutions in an atmosphere that is constructive rather than critical and inhibitory. Gordon (1961) also attempted to stimulate creative thinking by a method called synectics, which primarily involves analogies.

More recently, authors such as Adams (1974/1986) and von Oech (1983) have suggested that people often construct a series of false beliefs that interfere with creative functioning. For example, some people believe that there is only one right answer and that ambiguity must be avoided whenever possible. People can become creative by identifying and removing these mental blocks. Also, von Oech (1986) has suggested that we need to adopt the roles of explorer, artist, judge, and warrior in order to foster our creative productivity.

These approaches have had considerable public visibility, in much the way that Leo Buscaglia has given visibility to the study of love. And they may well be useful. From our point of view as psychologists, however, these approaches lack any basis in serious psychological theory, as well as serious empirical attempts to validate them. Of course, techniques can work in the absence of psychological theory or validation. But the effect of such approaches is often to leave people associating a phenomenon with commercialization and to see it as less than a serious endeavor for psychological study.

PSYCHODYNAMIC APPROACHES TO THE STUDY OF CREATIVITY

The psychodynamic approach can be considered the first major twentieth-century theoretical approach to the study of creativity. Based on the idea that creativity arises from the tension between conscious reality and unconscious drives, Freud (1908/1959) proposed that writers and artists produce creative work as a way to express their unconscious wishes in a publicly acceptable fashion. These unconscious wishes may concern power, riches, fame, honor, or love (Vernon, 1970). Case studies of eminent creators, such as Leonardo da Vinci (Freud, 1910/1964), were used to support these ideas.

Later, the psychoanalytic approach introduced the concepts of adaptive regression and elaboration for the study of creativity (Kris, 1952). Adaptive regression, the primary process, refers to the intrusion of unmodulated thoughts in consciousness. Unmodulated thoughts can occur during active problem solving, but often occur during sleep, intoxication from drugs, fantasies or daydreams, or psychoses. Elaboration, the secondary process, refers to the reworking and transformation of primary process material through reality-oriented, ego-controlled thinking. Other theorists (e.g., Kubie, 1958) have emphasized that the preconscious, which falls between conscious reality and the encrypted unconscious, is the true source of creativity because thoughts are loose and vague but interpretable. In contrast to Freud, Kubie claimed that unconscious conflicts actually have a negative effect on creativity because they lead to fixated, repetitive thoughts. Recent work has recognized the importance of both primary and secondary process (Noy, 1969; Rothenberg, 1979; Suler, 1980; Werner & Kaplan, 1963).

Although the psychodynamic approach may have offered some insights into creativity, psychodynamic theory was not at the center of the emerging scientific psychology. The early-twentieth-century scientific schools of psychology, such as structuralism, functionalism, and behaviorism, were devoting practically no resources at all to the study of creativity. The Gestaltists studied a portion of creativity – insight – but their study never went much beyond labeling, as opposed to characterizing, the nature of insight.

Further isolating creativity research, the psychodynamic approach and other early work on creativity relied almost exclusively on case studies of eminent creators. This methodology has been criticized because of the difficulty of measuring proposed theoretical constructs (such as primary process thought) and the amount of selection and interpretation that can occur in a case study (Weisberg, 1993). Although there is nothing a priori wrong with case-study methods, the emerging scientific psychology valued controlled, experimental methods. Thus, both theoretical and methodological issues served to isolate the study of creativity from mainstream psychology.

PSYCHOMETRIC APPROACHES TO THE STUDY OF CREATIVITY

When we think of creativity, eminent artists or scientists such as Michelangelo or Einstein immediately come to mind. However, these highly creative people are rare and difficult to study in the psychological laboratory. In his APA address, Guilford (1950) noted that the rarity of these individuals had limited research on creativity. He proposed that creativity could be studied in everyday subjects and with a psychometric approach, using paper-and-pencil tasks. One of these was the Unusual Uses Test, in which an examinee thinks of as many uses for a common object (such as a brick) as possible. Many researchers adopted Guilford's suggestion, and "divergent-thinking" tasks quickly became the main instruments for measuring creative thinking. The tests were a convenient way of comparing people on a standard "creativity" scale.

Building on Guilford's work, Torrance (1974) developed the Torrance Tests of Creative Thinking. These tests consist of several relatively simple verbal and figural tasks that involve divergent thinking plus other problem-solving skills. The tests can be scored for fluency (total number of relevant responses), flexibility (number of different categories of relevant responses), originality (the statistical rarity of the responses), and elaboration (amount of detail in the responses). Some of the subtests from the Torrance battery include the following:

1. Asking questions: The examinee writes out all the questions he or she can think of, based on a drawing of a scene.
2. Product improvement: The examinee lists ways to change a toy monkey so that children will have more fun playing with it.
3. Unusual uses: The examinee lists interesting and unusual uses of a cardboard box.
4. Circles: The examinee expands empty circles into different drawings and titles them.

The psychometric revolution of measuring creativity had both positive and negative effects on the field. On the positive side, the tests facilitated research by providing a brief, easy-to-administer, objectively scorable assessment device. Furthermore, research was now possible with everyday people (i.e., noneminent samples). On the negative side, first, some researchers criticized brief paper-and-pencil tests as trivial, inadequate measures of creativity (see essays in Sternberg, 1986); more significant productions, such as actual drawings or writing samples, should be used in addition or, better, instead. Second, other critics suggested that fluency, flexibility, originality, and elaboration scores failed to capture the concept of creativity (see Amabile, 1983). In fact, the definition and criteria for creativity are a matter of ongoing debate, and relying on the objectively defined statistical rarity of a response with regard to all the responses of a subject population is only one of many options. Other possibilities include using a consensus of judges regarding a product's creativity. Third, some researchers rejected the assumption that noneminent samples could shed light on eminent levels of creativity, which was the ultimate goal of many studies of creativity. Thus, a certain malaise developed and continues to accompany the paper-and-pencil assessment of creativity. Some psychologists, at least, avoided this measurement quagmire in favor of less problematic research topics.

COGNITIVE APPROACHES TO THE STUDY OF CREATIVITY

The cognitive approach to creativity seeks to understand the mental representations and processes underlying creative thought. There have been studies with both human subjects and computer simulations of creative thought. Approaches based on the study of human subjects are perhaps prototypically exemplified by the work of Finke, Ward, and Smith (1992; see also contributions to Smith, Ward, & Finke, 1995; Sternberg & Davidson, 1995). Finke and his colleagues have proposed what they call the Geneplore model, according to which there are two main processing phases in creative thought: a generative phase and an exploratory phase. In the generative phase, an individual constructs mental representations referred to as preinventive structures, which have properties promoting creative discoveries. In the exploratory phase, these properties are used to come up with creative ideas. A number of mental processes may enter into these phases of creative invention, including the processes of retrieval, association, synthesis, transformation, analogical transfer, and categorical reduction (i.e., mentally reducing objects or elements to more primitive categorical descriptions). In a typical experimental test based on the model (see, e.g., Finke, 1990), subjects will be shown parts of objects, such as a circle, a cube, a parallelogram, and a cylinder. On a given trial, three parts will be named, and subjects will be asked to imagine combining the parts to produce a practical object or device. For example, subjects might imagine a tool, a weapon, or a piece of furniture. The objects thus produced are then rated by judges for their practicality and originality.

Weisberg (1986, 1993) proposes that creativity involves essentially ordinary cognitive processes yielding extraordinary products. Using case studies of eminent creators and laboratory research, such as studies with Duncker's (1945) candle problem, which requires subjects to attach a candle to a wall using only objects available in a picture (candle, box of tacks, and book of matches), Weisberg attempts to show that the insights depend on subjects using conventional cognitive processes (such as analogical transfer) applied to knowledge already stored in memory.

Computer simulation approaches, reviewed by Boden (1992, 1994), have as their goal the production of creative thought by a computer in a manner that simulates what people do. Langley, Simon, Bradshaw, and Zytkow (1987), for example, developed a set of programs that rediscover basic scientific laws. These computational models rely on heuristics – problem-solving guidelines – for searching a data set or conceptual space and finding hidden relationships between input variables. The initial program, called BACON, uses heuristics such as "If the value of two numerical terms increase together, consider their ratio" to search data for patterns. One of BACON's accomplishments has been to examine observational data available to Kepler on the orbits of planets and to rediscover Kepler's third law of planetary motion. Further programs have extended the search heuristics, the ability to transform data sets, and the ability to reason with qualitative data and scientific concepts. There are also models concerning an artistic domain. For example, Johnson-Laird (1988) developed a jazz improvisation program in which novel deviations from the basic jazz chord sequences are guided by harmonic constraints (or tacit principles of jazz) and random choice when several allowable directions for the improvisation exist.

SOCIAL-PERSONALITY APPROACHES TO THE STUDY OF CREATIVITY

Developing in parallel with the cognitive approach, work in the social-personality approach has focused on personality variables, motivational variables, and the sociocultural environment as sources of creativity. Researchers such as Amabile (1983), Barron (1968, 1969), Eysenck (1993), Gough (1979), and MacKinnon (1965) have noted that certain personality traits often characterize creative people. Through correlational studies and research contrasting high- and low-creativity samples (at both eminent and everyday levels), a large set of potentially relevant traits has been identified (Barron & Harrington, 1981). These traits include independence of judgment, self-confidence, attraction to complexity, aesthetic orientation, and risk taking.

Proposals regarding self-actualization and creativity can also be considered within the personality tradition. According to Maslow (1968), boldness, courage, freedom, spontaneity, self-acceptance, and other traits lead a person to realize his or her full potential. Rogers (1954) described the tendency toward self-actualization as having motivational force and being promoted by a supportive, evaluation-free environment.

Focusing on motivation for creativity, a number of theorists have hypothesized the relevance of intrinsic motivation (Amabile, 1983; Crutchfield, 1962; Golann, 1962), need for order (Barron, 1963), need for achievement (McClelland, Atkinson, Clark, & Lowell, 1953), and other motives. Amabile (1983; Hennessey & Amabile, 1988) and her colleagues have conducted seminal research on the importance of intrinsic motivation. Studies using motivational training and other techniques have manipulated motivation and observed effects on creative performance tasks, such as writing poems and making collages.

Creativity may not only require motivation, but also generate it. Research has shown that when creative students are taught and their achievements are then assessed in a way that values their creative abilities, their academic performance improves (Sternberg, Ferrari, Clinkenbeard, & Grigorenko, 1996). Given the chance to be creative, students who might otherwise lose interest in school instruction might find that it instead captures their interest.

Finally, the relevance of the social environment to creativity has also been an active area of research. At the societal level, Simonton (1984, 1988, 1994a, 1994b) has conducted numerous studies in which eminent levels of creativity over large spans of time in diverse cultures have been statistically linked to environmental variables such as cultural diversity, war, availability of role models, availability of resources (such as financial support), and number of competitors in a domain. Cross-cultural comparisons (e.g., Lubart, 1990) and anthropological case studies (e.g., Maduro, 1976; Silver, 1981) have demonstrated cultural variability in the expression of creativity. Moreover, they have shown that cultures differ simply in the amount that they value the creative enterprise.

The cognitive and social-personality approaches have each provided valuable insights into creativity. However, if you look for research that investigates both cognitive and social-personality variables at the same time, you will find only a handful of studies. The cognitive work on creativity has tended to ignore or downplay the personality and social system, and the social-personality approaches have tended to have little or nothing to say about the mental representations and processes underlying creativity.

This disciplinary subsumption may have been due, at least in part, to the organizational structure of psychology departments and psychology journals. In many psychology departments, cognitive and social psychologists seek to maintain their separate identities because of resource considerations (e.g., funding and faculty positions). Furthermore, apart from the two journals specializing in creativity research, most of the prominent journals are unidisciplinary in approach. Cognitive psychology journals take cognitive work and social psychology journals take research with social-personality variables.

Looking beyond the field of psychology, Wehner, Csikszentmihalyi, and Magyari-Beck (1991) examined 100 recent doctoral dissertations on creativity. They found a "parochial isolation" of the various studies concerning creativity. There were relevant dissertations from psychology, education, business, history, history of science, and other fields, such as sociology and political science. However, the different fields tended to use different terms and to focus on different aspects of what seemed to be the same basic phenomenon. For example, business dissertations used the term *innovation* and tended to look at the organizational level, whereas psychology dissertations used the term *creativity* and looked at the level of the individual. Wehner, Csikszentmihalyi, and Magyari-Beck (1991) describe the situation with creativity research in terms of the fable of the blind men and the elephant: "We touch different parts of the same beast and derive distorted pictures of the whole from what we know: 'The elephant is like a snake,' says the one who only holds its tail; 'The elephant is like a wall,' says the one who touches its flanks" (p. 270).

Were it the case that an understanding of creativity required a multidisciplinary approach, the result of a unidisciplinary approach might be that we would view a part of the whole as the whole, but at the same time, have an incomplete explanation of the phenomenon we are seeking to explain, leaving dissatisfied those who do not subscribe to the particular discipline doing the explaining. We believe that traditionally this has been the case for creativity.

Recently, theorists have begun to develop confluence approaches to creativity, which we will now discuss.

CONFLUENCE APPROACHES TO THE STUDY OF CREATIVITY

Many recent works on creativity hypothesize that multiple components must converge for creativity to occur (Amabile, 1983, 1996; Csikszentmihalyi, 1988; Gardner, 1993; Gruber, 1989; Lubart, 1994; Mumford & Gustafson, 1988; Perkins, 1981; Simonton, 1988; Sternberg, 1985a, 1985b, 1996; Sternberg & Lubart, 1991, 1995; Weisberg, 1993; Woodman & Schoenfeldt, 1989). Sternberg (1985b), for example, examined laypersons' and experts' conceptions of the creative person. People's implicit theories contain a combination of cognitive and personality elements, such as "connects ideas," "sees similarities and differences," "has flexibility," "has aesthetic taste," "is unorthodox," "is motivated," "is inquisitive," and "questions societal norms."

At the level of explicit theories, Amabile (1983) describes creativity as the confluence of intrinsic motivation, domain-relevant knowledge and abilities, and creativity-relevant skills. The creativity-relevant skills include (a) a cognitive style that involves coping with complexities and breaking one's mental set during problem solving, (b) knowledge of heuristics for generating novel ideas, such as trying a counterintuitive approach, and (c) a work style characterized by concentrated effort, an ability to set aside problems, and high energy.

Gruber and his colleagues (1981, 1988; Gruber & Davis, 1988) have proposed a developmental evolving-systems model for understanding creativity. A person's purpose, knowledge, and affect grow over time, amplify deviations that an individual encounters, and lead to creative products. Developmental changes in the knowledge system have been documented in cases such as Charles Darwin's thoughts on evolution. Purpose refers to a set of interrelated goals, which also develop and guide an individual's behavior. Finally, the affect or mood system encompasses the influence of joy or frustration on the projects undertaken.

Csikszentmihalyi (1988, 1996) takes a different "systems" approach and highlights the interaction of the individual, domain, and field. An individual draws upon information in a domain and transforms or extends it via cognitive processes, personality traits, and motivation. The field, consisting of people who control or influence a domain (e.g., art critics and gallery owners), evaluates and selects new ideas. The domain, a culturally defined symbol system, preserves and transmits creative products to other individuals and future generations. Gardner (1993) has conducted case studies which suggest that the development of creative projects may stem from an anomaly within a system (e.g., tension between competing critics in a field) or moderate asynchronies between the individual, domain, and field (e.g., unusual individual talent for a domain).

A final confluence theory considered here is Sternberg and Lubart's (1991, 1992, 1995, 1996) investment theory of creativity, according to which creative people are ones who are willing and able to "buy low and sell high" in the realm of ideas (see also Rubenson & Runco, 1992, for use of concepts from economic theory). Buying low means pursuing ideas that are unknown or out of favor but that have growth potential. Often, when these ideas are first presented, they encounter resistance. The creative individual persists in the face of this resistance and eventually sells high, moving on to the next new or unpopular idea.

Preliminary research within the investment framework has yielded support for this model (Lubart & Sternberg, 1995). This research has used tasks such as (a) writing short stories with unusual titles (e.g., "The Octopus' Sneakers"), (b) drawing pictures with unusual themes (e.g., the Earth from an insect's point of view), (c) devising creative advertisements for boring products (e.g., cuff links), and (d) solving unusual scientific problems (e.g., how we could tell if someone had been on the moon within the past month). This research showed creative performance to be moderately domain-specific and to be predicted by a combination of certain resources, as described next.

According to the investment theory, creativity requires a confluence of six distinct but interrelated resources: intellectual abilities, knowledge, styles of thinking, personality, motivation, and environment.

Three intellectual abilities are particularly important (Sternberg, 1985a): (a) the synthetic ability to see problems in new ways and to escape the bounds of conventional thinking, (b) the analytic ability to recognize which of one's ideas are worth pursuing and which are not, and (c) the practical-contextual ability to know how to persuade others of – to sell other people on – the value of one's ideas. The confluence of these three abilities is also important. Analytic ability used in the absence of the other two abilities results in powerful critical but not creative thinking. Synthetic ability in the absence of the other two results in new ideas that are not subjected to the scrutiny required, first, to evaluate their promise and, second, to make them work. And practical-contextual ability in the absence of the other two may result in the transmittal of ideas not because the ideas are good, but rather because they have been well and powerfully presented.

With regard to knowledge, on the one hand, one needs to know enough about a field to move it forward. One cannot move beyond where a field is if one doesn't know where it is. On the other hand, knowledge about a field can result in a closed and entrenched perspective, leading to a person's not moving beyond the way in which he or she has seen problems in the past (Frensch & Sternberg, 1989).

With regard to thinking styles, a legislative style is particularly important for creativity (Sternberg, 1988, 1997), that is, a preference for thinking in novel ways of one's own choosing. This preference needs to be distinguished from the ability to think creatively: Someone may like to think along new lines, but not think well, or vice versa. To become a major creative thinker, it also helps if one is able to think globally as well as locally, distinguishing the forest from the trees and thereby recognizing which questions are important and which ones are not.

Numerous research investigations (summarized in Lubart, 1994, and Sternberg & Lubart, 1991, 1995) have supported the importance of certain personality attributes for creative functioning. These attributes include, but are not limited to, self-efficacy and a willingness to overcome obstacles, take sensible risks, and tolerate ambiguity. In particular, buying low and selling high typically means defying the crowd, so that one has to be willing to stand up to conventions if one wants to think and act in creative ways.

Intrinsic, task-focused motivation is also essential to creativity. The research of Amabile (1983, 1996) and others has shown the importance of such motivation for creative work, and has suggested that people rarely do truly creative work in an area unless they really love what they are doing and focus on the work rather than on the potential rewards.

Finally, one needs an environment that is supportive and rewarding of creative ideas. One could have all of the internal resources needed in order to think creatively, but without some environmental support (such as a forum for proposing those ideas), the creativity that one has might never be displayed.

With regard to the confluence of components, creativity is hypothesized to involve more than a simple sum of a person's attained level of functioning on each component. First, there may be thresholds for some components (e.g., knowledge) below which creativity is not possible, regardless of the levels attained on other components. Second, partial compensation may occur in which a strength on one component (e.g., motivation) counteracts a weakness on another component (e.g., environment). Third, interactions may also occur between components, such as intelligence and motivation, in which high levels on both could multiplicatively enhance creativity.

In general, confluence theories of creativity offer the possibility of accounting for diverse aspects of creativity (Lubart, 1994). For example, analyses of scientific and artistic achievements suggest that the median creativity of work in a domain tends to fall toward the lower end of the distribution and that the upper (high-creativity) tail extends quite far. This pattern can be explained as the need for simultaneous multiple components in order for the highest levels of creativity to be achieved. As another example, the partial domain-specificity of creativity, which is often observed, can be explained through the mixture of some relatively domain-specific components for creativity, such as knowledge, and other more domain-general components, such as the personality trait of perseverance.

CONCLUSION

Few resources have been invested in the study of creativity, relative to its importance both to the field of psychology and to the world. We have sought to understand what we perceive as a serious underinvestment and suggest several reasons why this underinvestment might have occurred:

1. The origins of the study of creativity were based in a tradition of mysticism and spirituality, which has seemed indifferent and possibly runs counter to the scientific spirit.
2. Pragmatic approaches to creativity have given some the impression that the study of creativity is driven by a kind of commercialism that, while it may be successful in its own way, lacks a basis in psychological theory and verification through psychological research.
3. Early work on creativity was theoretically and methodologically adrift from the mainstream of scientific psychology, resulting in creativity sometimes being seen as peripheral to the central concerns of the field of psychology as a whole.
4. Problems with the definition of and criteria for creativity caused research difficulties. Paper-and-pencil tests of creativity resolved some of these problems but led to criticisms that the phenomenon had been trivialized.
5. Single approaches have tended to view creativity as an extraordinary result of ordinary structures or processes, so that it has not always seemed necessary to have any separate study of creativity. In effect, these approaches have subsumed creativity under them, as a special case of what is already being studied.
6. Unidisciplinary approaches to creativity have tended to view a part of the phenomenon (e.g., the cognitive processes of creativity, the personality traits of creative persons) as the whole phenomenon, often resulting in what we believe is a narrow, unsatisfying vision of creativity.

NOTE

The work reported herein was supported under the Javits Act program (Grant R206R50001) as administered by the Office of Educational Research and Improvement, U.S. Department of Education. The findings and opinions expressed in this report do not reflect the positions or policies of the Office of Educational Research and Improvement or the U.S. Department of Education. This chapter draws in part on Sternberg and Lubart (1996).

REFERENCES

Adams, J. L. (1986). *Conceptual blockbusting* (3rd ed.). New York: Addison-Wesley. (Original work published 1974)
Amabile, T. M. (1983). *The social psychology of creativity*. New York: Springer-Verlag.
Amabile, T. M. (1996). *Creativity in context*. Boulder, CO: Westview.
Barron, F. (1963). *Creativity and psychological health*. New York: Van Nostrand.
Barron, F. (1968). *Creativity and personal freedom*. New York: Van Nostrand.
Barron, F. (1969). *Creative person and creative process*. New York: Holt, Rinehart, & Winston.
Barron, F., & Harrington, D. M. (1981). Creativity, intelligence, and personality. *Annual Review of Psychology, 32*, 439–476.
Boden, M. (1992). *The creative mind: Myths and mechanisms*. New York: Basic.
Boden, M. (Ed.). (1994). *Dimensions of creativity*. Cambridge, MA: MIT Press.
Crutchfield, R. (1962). Conformity and creative thinking. In H. Gruber, G. Terrell, & M. Wertheimer (Eds.), *Contemporary approaches to creative thinking* (pp. 120–140). New York: Atherton.

Csikszentmihalyi, M. (1988). Society, culture, and person: A systems view of creativity. In R. J. Sternberg (Ed.), *The nature of creativity* (pp. 325–339). Cambridge University Press.

Csikszentmihalyi, M. (1996). *Creativity.* New York: HarperCollins.

De Bono, E. (1971). *Lateral thinking for management.* New York: McGraw-Hill.

De Bono, E. (1985). *Six thinking hats.* Boston: Little, Brown.

De Bono, E. (1992). *Serious creativity: Using the power of lateral thinking to create new ideas.* New York: HarperCollins.

Duncker, K. (1945). On problem solving. *Psychological Monographs, 68* (5), whole no. 270.

Eysenck, H. J. (1993). Creativity and personality: A theoretical perspective. *Psychological Inquiry, 4,* 147–178.

Feist, G. J., & Runco, M. A. (1993). Trends in the creativity literature: An analysis of research in the *Journal of Creative Behavior* (1967–1989). *Creativity Research Journal, 6* (3), 271–286.

Finke, R. (1990). *Creative imagery: Discoveries and inventions in visualization.* Hillsdale, NJ: Erlbaum.

Finke, R. A., Ward, T. B., & Smith, S. M. (1992). *Creative cognition: Theory, research, and applications.* Cambridge, MA: MIT Press.

Frensch, P. A., & Sternberg, R. J. (1989). Expertise and intelligent thinking: When is it worse to know better? In R. J. Sternberg (Ed.), *Advances in the psychology of human intelligence* (Vol. 5, pp. 157–158). Hillsdale, NJ: Erlbaum.

Freud, S. (1964). *Leonardo da Vinci and a memory of his childhood.* New York: Norton. (Original work published in 1910)

Freud, S. (1908/1959). The relation of the poet to day-dreaming. In *Collected papers* (Vol. 4, pp. 173–183). London: Hogarth.

Gardner, H. (1993). *Creating minds.* New York: Basic.

Ghiselin, B. (Ed.). (1985). *The creative process: A symposium.* Berkeley: University of California Press.

Golann, S. E. (1962). The creativity motive. *Journal of Personality, 30,* 588–600.

Gordon, W. J. J. (1961). *Synectics: The development of creative capacity.* New York: Harper & Row.

Gough, H. G. (1979). A creativity scale for the Adjective Check List. *Journal of Personality and Social Psychology, 37,* 1398–1405.

Gruber, H. (1981). *Darwin on man: A psychological study of scientific creativity* (2nd ed.). Chicago: University of Chicago Press. (Original work published 1974)

Gruber, H. E. (1988). The evolving systems approach to creative work. *Creativity Research Journal, 1,* 27–51.

Gruber, H. E. (1989). The evolving systems approach to creative work. In D. B. Wallace & H. E. Gruber (Eds.), *Creative people at work: Twelve cognitive case studies* (pp. 3–24). New York: Oxford University Press.

Gruber, H. E., & Davis, S. N. (1988). Inching our way up Mount Olympus: The evolving-systems approach to creative thinking. In R. J. Sternberg (Ed.), *The nature of creativity* (pp. 243–270). Cambridge University Press.

Guilford, J. P. (1950). Creativity. *American Psychologist, 5,* 444–454.

Hennessey, B. A., & Amabile, T. M. (1988). The conditions of creativity. In R. J. Sternberg (Ed.), *The nature of creativity* (pp. 11–38). Cambridge University Press.

Johnson-Laird, P. N. (1988). Freedom and constraint in creativity. In R. J. Sternberg (Ed.), *The nature of creativity* (pp. 202–219). Cambridge University Press.

Kipling, R. (1937/1985). Working-tools. In B. Ghiselin (Ed.), *The Creative Process: A Symposium* (pp. 161–163). Berkeley: University of California Press. (Original article published in 1937)

Kris, E. (1952). *Psychoanalytic exploration in art.* New York: International Universities Press.

Kubie, L. S. (1958). *The neurotic distortion of the creative process.* Lawrence: University of Kansas Press.

Langley, P., Simon, H. A., Bradshaw, G. L., & Zytkow, J. M. (1987). *Scientific discovery: Computational explorations of the creative process.* Cambridge, MA: MIT Press.

Lubart, T. I. (1990). Creativity and cross-cultural variation. *International Journal of Psychology, 25,* 39–59.

Lubart, T. I. (1994). *Product-centered self-evaluation and the creative process.* Unpublished doctoral dissertation, Yale University, New Haven, CT.

Lubart, T. I., & Sternberg, R. J. (1995). An investment approach to creativity: Theory and data. In S. M. Smith, T. B. Ward, & R. A. Finke (Eds.) *The creative cognition approach* (pp. 269–302). Cambridge, MA: MIT Press.

MacKinnon, D. W. (1965). Personality and the realization of creative potential. *American Psychologist, 20,* 273–281.

Maduro, R. (1976). Artistic creativity in a Brahmin painter community. Research monograph 14, Berkeley: Center for South and Southeast Asia Studies, University of California.

Maslow, A. (1968). *Toward a psychology of being.* New York: Van Nostrand.

McClelland, D. C., Atkinson, J. W., Clark, R. A., & Lowell, E. L. (1953). *The achievement motive.* New York: Appleton-Century-Crofts.

Mumford, M. D., & Gustafson, S. B. (1988). Creativity syndrome: Integration, application, and innovation. *Psychological Bulletin, 103,* 27–43.

Noy, P. (1969). A revision of the psychoanalytic theory of the primary process. *International Journal of Psychoanalysis, 50,* 155–178.

Ochse, R. (1990) *Before the gates of excellence: The determinants of creative genius.* Cambridge University Press.

Osborn, A. F. (1953). *Applied imagination* (rev. ed.). New York: Scribner's.

Perkins, D. N. (1981). *The mind's best work.* Cambridge, MA: Harvard University Press.

Rogers, C. R. (1954). Toward a theory of creativity. *ETC: A Review of General Semantics, 11,* 249–260.

Rothenberg, A. (1979). *The emerging goddess.* Chicago: University of Chicago Press.

Rothenberg, A., & Hausman, C. R. (Eds.). (1976). *The creativity question.* Durham, NC: Duke University Press.

Rubenson, D. L., & Runco, M. A. (1992). The psychoeconomic approach to creativity. *New Ideas in Psychology, 10* (2), 131–147.

Silver, H. R. (1981). Calculating risks: The socioeconomic foundations of aesthetic innovation in an Ashanti carving community. *Ethnology, 20* (2), 101–114.

Simonton, D. K. (1984). *Genius, creativity, and leadership.* Cambridge, MA: Harvard University Press.

Simonton, D. K. (1984). Age and outstanding achievement: What do we know after a century of research? *Psychological Bulletin, 104,* 251–267.

Simonton, D. K. (1994a). *Greatness.* New York: Guilford.

Simonton, D. K. (1994b). Individual differences, developmental changes, and social context. *Behavioral and Brain Sciences, 17,* 552–553.

Smith, S. M., Ward, T. B., & Finke, R. A. (Eds.). (1995). *The creative cognition approach.* Cambridge, MA: MIT Press.

Sternberg, R. J. (1985a). *Beyond IO: A triarchic theory of human intelligence.* Cambridge University Press.

Sternberg, R. J. (1985b). Implicit theories of intelligence, creativity, and wisdom. *Journal of Personality and Social Psychology, 49,* 607–627.

Sternberg, R. J. (1986). *Intelligence applied: Understanding and increasing your intellectual skills.* San Diego: Harcourt, Brace, Jovanovich.

Sternberg, R. J. (1988). *The triarchic mind: A new theory of human intelligence.* New York: Viking.

Sternberg, R. J. (Ed.). (1988a). *The nature of creativity: Contemporary psychological perspectives.* Cambridge University Press.

Sternberg, R. J. (1988b). *The triangle of love.* New York: Basic.

Sternberg, R. J. (1996). *Successful intelligence.* New York: Simon & Schuster.

Sternberg, R. J. (1997). *Thinking styles.* Cambridge University Press.

Sternberg, R. J., & Davidson, J. E. (Eds.). (1995). *The nature of insight.* Cambridge, MA: MIT Press.

Sternberg, R. J., Ferrari, M., Clinkenbeard, P., & Grigorenko, E. L. (1996). Identification, instruction, and assessment of gifted children: A construct validation of a triarchic model. *Gifted Child Quarterly, 40,* 129–137.

Sternberg, R. J., & Lubart, T. I. (1991). An investment theory of creativity and its development. *Human Development, 34,* 1–32.

Sternberg, R. J., & Lubart, T. I. (1992). Buy low and sell high: An investment approach to creativity. *Current Directions in Psychological Science, 1* (1), 1–5.

Sternberg, R. J., & Lubart, T. I. (1995). *Defying the crowd: Cultivating creativity in a culture of conformity.* New York: Free Press.

Sternberg, R. J., & Lubart, T. I. (1996). Investing in creativity. *American Psychologist, 51,* 677–688.

Suler, J. R. (1980). Primary process thinking and creativity. *Psychological Bulletin, 88,* 144–165.

Torrance, E. P. (1974). *Torrance Tests of Creative Thinking.* Lexington, MA: Personnel Press.

Vernon, P. E. (Ed.). (1970). *Creativity: Selected readings.* Baltimore, MD: Penguin.

von Oech, R. (1983). *A whack on the side of the head.* New York: Warner.

von Oech, R. (1986). *A kick in the seat of the pants.* New York: Harper & Row.

Wallach, M. A., & Kogan, N. (1965). *Modes of thinking in young children: A study of the creativity–intelligence distinction.* New York: Holt, Rinehart, & Winston.

Wehner, L., Csikszentmihalyi, M., & Magyari-Beck, I. (1991). Current approaches used in studying creativity: An exploratory investigation. *Creativity Research Journal, 4* (3), 261–271.

Weisberg, R. W. (1986). *Creativity, genius, and other myths.* New York: Freeman.

Weisberg, R. W. (1993). *Creativity: Beyond the myth of genius.* New York: Freeman.

Werner, H., & Kaplan, B. (1963). *Symbol formation.* Hillsdale, NJ: Erlbaum.

Woodman, R. W., & Schoenfeldt, L. F. (1989). Individual differences in creativity: An interactionist per-
    spective. In J. A. Glover, R. R. Ronning, & C. R. Reynolds (Eds.), *Handbook of creativity* (pp. 77–92).
    New York: Plenum.

2   A History of Research on Creativity

ROBERT S. ALBERT AND MARK A. RUNCO

The title we have given this chapter is meant to signal to readers that we recognize that the history we describe is one among other possible histories of the same subject. This chapter truly presents a and not *the* history of research on creativity.

Our attempt to describe the broad and extended historical changes in the concept of creativity can be easily contrasted with efforts to describe the narrower historical changes in actual creativity. Bullough, Bullough, and Mauro (1981), Gray (1966), Kroeber (1944, 1956), Martindale (1992), Naroll et al. (1971), and Sorokin (1947) compared specific historical eras in terms of various indices of creativity. Bullough et al., for instance, compared eighteenth-century Scotland with fifteenth-century Italy. Historical differences in content and abstractness are also implied in studies of *Zeitgeist;* these assume that there is a "spirit" that is unique to creative eras (Boring, 1929; Simonton, in press).

Additional historical perspectives are involved in studies of eminent creators' developmental background and careers. Although they may not have influenced the meeting of *research* and *creativity,* investigations of eminent persons have contributed chiefly to the way we think about creativity (see, e.g., Albert, 1975; Gardner, 1994; Ochse, 1990; Roe, 1952). Our own perspective directed us to the work of eminent individuals (e.g., Francis Bacon, Darwin, Galton, Malthus, and Adam Smith) who had particular impact on the clarification and eventual meeting of the concepts of research and creativity.

Our assumption is that history is the medium in which ideas and events build up and arrive, with some significant effects rarely going away. (This is history seen as a slow boil.) In this chapter we take the position that the early conceptualizations of creativity and research were in themselves exceptional creative acts, as was the eventual bridging of these concepts through deliberately applying research methods. These methods were essential not only to the meaning and significance of creativity in human experience, but to how and why historical events were set in motion. Understanding this should help us appreciate three aspects of creativity within history. The first is that the significance of historical processes lies as much in their timing as in their content. "When" determines "what" will be important. Second, institutions and identifiable groups are critical in selecting and giving coherence to the important strands of possibilities already in the work and minds of creative persons. Third, the relevance of ideas and events becomes apparent only when there is a group of engaged articulate persons deeply concerned with the same question, problem, or set of possibilities. This implies that (a) a critical mass of information and interest must coexist and be in place and (b) significance and meaning are not only abstract but, as William James pointed out, come from consequences, not all of which are predictable. Seen in this light, history is experimental.

Some of the most evident creativity in Western history can therefore be found by tracing evolving concepts of research and creativity through the past 2,000 years and by examining their eventual linkage in the late nineteenth century after centuries of being apart. The necessary first step in doing research was to have the concept of research in mind, which more or less required its invention. The next step was nearly as difficult, but no less important. This was to believe that research regarding human nature was important and as feasible as doing research on physical nature, rather than speculating about it. The history of research on creativity began with the recognition that research constitutes an effective and practical way of learning about and understanding the world around us.

It is important to recognize that the concept of creativity has its own history, taking an intellectual path that was for two centuries independent of the institutionalization and conceptualization of research. At their beginnings and during most of their histories of development, research and creativity were not viewed as related to one another; therefore, if there was to be creativity research, the pairing of creativity and research had to go through several major intellectual transformations and a deliberate extension in how scientific research was defined and could be applied. As it was, it took another 150 years after research was a recognized and widely encouraged institutional undertaking before the concept of creativity was sufficiently sculpted out of the many debates regarding the meaning and eventual separation of such competing ideas as imagination, originality, genius, talent, freedom, and individuality (Engell, 1981; Gruber, 1996; Kaufman, 1926; Singer, 1981–1982). As we will show in detail, the invention of research was the outgrowth of long-standing questions about the nature of physical laws and the belief that it was possible for men and women to understand the physical world without divine intervention. The conceptualization of creativity, on the other hand, grew out of discussion and argument regarding the basic nature of man when released from institutional doctrine. Early on these debates involved only a slight interest in how this could be investigated. The main issue was freedom.

As important as is understanding the nature of man and the meaning by which creativity expresses it in a number of ways, we are surprised to find how small a proportion of professional interest there has been devoted to the topic.

Until recently there have been a very small number of professional articles and books specifically devoted to creativity (Albert, 1969; Feist & Runco, 1993; Guilford, 1950). In the words of Feist and Runco (1993):

One of the most widely cited statements from Guilford's article is that out of the 121,000 titles listed in *Psychological Abstracts* from the late 1920's to 1950, only 186 dealt with creativity. This is fewer than 2 articles out of 1,000. We recently discovered that the figure for more recent creativity research is roughly five times higher. . . . The percentage of articles dealing with creativity in the *Psychological Abstracts* has grown from .002% in the 1920's to approximately .01% in the 1980's. From the late 1960's until 1991, almost 9,000 creativity references have been added to the literature. (p. 272)

Yet nearly every major twentieth-century psychologist (e.g., Freud, Piaget, Rogers, and Skinner) has taken creativity seriously and explored what it means to be creative, and at present the field can only be described as explosive. It has been noted that the maturing of a professional interest can be seen in the growth of its professional journals. Creativity research now has its own scholarly journal (*Creativity Research Journal*) and creativity is attracting increasing attention in the media and popular press. In 1996 alone, three articles on creativity or creativity research appeared in the *American Psychologist* (Eisenberger & Cameron, 1966; Schneider, 1996; Sternberg & Lubart, 1966).

CONCEPTIONS OF CREATIVITY

Pre-Christian Views of Creativity

Long before the Christian view of creativity had begun to emerge, there were efforts to grasp the meaning for humanity of what we now recognize as creativity.

The pre-Christian understanding, and a view that has influenced our thinking throughout the centuries, is the concept of genius, which was originally associated with mystical powers of protection and good fortune. When the Greeks placed emphasis on an individual's Daimon (guardian spirit) the idea of genius became mundane and was progressively associated with an individual's abilities and appetites, some of which were destructive as well as constructive. Creativeness took on a social value and, by the time of Aristotle, an association with madness and frenzied inspiration, a view that reappeared during most of the nineteenth and the first half of the twentieth centuries. When we examine the succeeding Roman view of genius, we find two additional characteristics given to it. It eventually was seen as an illustrious male's creative power that could be passed on to his children. At this point creativity was a male capacity. Giving birth was the exception.

Early Western View of Creativity

Scholars agree that the earliest Western conception of creativity was the biblical story of the Creation given in Genesis, from which came the idea of the artisan doing God's work on Earth (Boorstin, 1992; Nahn, 1956). Boorstin (1992) wrote:

> For man's awareness of his capacity to create, the Covenant was a landmark. It declared that a people become a community through their belief in a Creator and His Creation. They confirmed their creative powers through their kinship, their sharing qualities of God, their intimate and voluntary relationship to a Creator – God. (p. 42)

This view of creativity persisted until the second century A.D., after which it was debated and weakened by a number of early Christian writers and replaced by Saint Augustine's (354–430) doctrine set forth in his *City of God*. By turning our eyes to the future, "Christianity . . . played a leading role in the discovery of our power to create" (p. 55).

This belief reflects a significant difference between Western and Eastern thinking about the goal of creativity and the participants' role in the process. For the Hindus (1500–900 B.C.), Confucius (c. 551–479 B.C.), and the Taoists and Buddhists, creation was at most a kind of discovery or mimicry. The early Taoists and Buddhists emphasized natural cycles, harmony, regularity, and balance, therefore "the idea of the creation of something ex nihilo (from nothing) had no place in a universe of the yin and yang" (Boorstin, 1992, p. 17). Plato felt that nothing new was possible, and art in his time was an effort to match or mimic ideal forms. Originality, which has become a contemporary marker of creativity, was not an early attribute of creativity during early history (Child, 1972; Dudek, in press).

These assumptions were not seriously challenged for nearly 1200 years. During the Middle Ages the idea emerged that special talent or unusual ability by an individual (almost always a male) was the manifestation of an outside spirit for which this individual was a conduit. Early in the Renaissance a significant change in this view took place. At this historical moment the divine attribute of great artists and artisans was recognized and often emphasized as manifestly their own and not of divine origin. Furthermore, this change in perspective was not isolated, but part of a broader set of social transformations that included "the decline of serfdom, the triumph of the English language, the rise of the judicial and medical professions, and the growth of religious nonconformity" (Wilson-Given, 1996, p.3).

These changes were quite subtle until the Renaissance was clearly under way (approximately 1500 to 1700). Even though Chaucer used the word *create* as early as 1393, the conceptual outline of creativity remained relatively faint and, at times, was even lost sight of until most of the major philosophers (e.g., Hobbes [1588–1679], Locke [1632–1704]) of the

Enlightenment were able to move beyond a concern with imagination, individual freedom, and society's authority in human affairs.

The Invention of Research

Throughout most of the years of the Renaissance and the many philosophical discussions that took place, scientific works were known for their power of discovery and disruption of cultural and religious paradigms. Three of the Western world's greatest scientists – Copernicus (1473–1543), Galileo (1564–1642), and Newton (1642–1727) – had given proof of this. Yet it took more than their example. It required a widespread change to perceiving the laws of the physical world working in the here and now and a recognition of how this lawfulness related to human existence (the meaning of which scientific knowledge produced) and, just as important, the social purposes it could serve (Shapin, 1996).

In the eighteenth century, two profound intellectual perspectives concerning reason and individualism shaped Western thought: The Enlightenment became an identifiable and coherent intellectual philosophy, the clearest expression of which was the intellectual attacks on what was believed to be unwarranted authority emanating from a variety of (dogmatic) nonscientific sources. While the Enlightenment was reaching its own critical mass, Natural Science as an institutionalized philosophy and methodology was taking shape (Bronowski & Mazlish, 1960). What made this primarily an English intellectual movement was that although parts of the Enlightenment did occur in continental Europe, they did so primarily among poets and artists. Those Continental scientists who were interested were "speculative." This growing interest in science is evidenced by the fact that the word *research*, meaning deliberate scientific inquiry, entered English in 1639, soon after the appearance of the word *researcher* in 1615.

Just how profound these *changes* were for Western culture can be gauged by the transformed status of the Bible, no less. For hundreds of years it had been a divine source of wisdom and morality, but by the late eighteenth century it had become a secular model of literature. Prickett (1996) tells us that

during the late 18th century the Bible underwent a shift in interpretation so radical as to make it virtually a different book from what it had been 100 years earlier. Even as historical criticism suggested that, far from being divinely inspired or even a rock of certainty in a world of flux, its text was neither stable nor original, the new notion of the Bible as a cultural artifact became a paradigm of all literature. While formal religion declined, the prestige of the Bible as a literary and aesthetic model rose to new heights. (p. ii)

Knowing the depth, power, and range of the Enlightenment's resistance to divine authority and religion's "wisdom," we should not be at all surprised that another kind of freedom would become a part of the paradigmatic shift, and it did. This was the individual's right to explore his or her world without institutional permission and divine guidelines or intervention.

Although ideas related to creativity had been relatively unchanged between the years 1500 and 1700, the other changes taking place were exceptionally fertile grounds for the idea of research. It is around this time that science and scientific thinking took form as the preeminent instruments of discovery and models for thinking about the physical world. So complete were the changes that evolved from this merger of scientific model and technique that many writers believe this was the beginning of a distinctive, modern Western civilization, "from a world of things ordered according to their ideal nature to a world of *events* running in a steady mechanism of before and after" (Bronowski, 1951, italics added).

Institutional and Philosophical Antecedents to Research on Creativity

At the same time that a more far reaching intellectual revolution, known as the English Enlightenment, was gathering persuasive force and an increasing coherence of new attitudes and concerns was emerging, Francis Bacon's (1605) *Advancement of Learning* became an accepted argument for the importance of empirical investigation. The Enlightenment's widespread philosophical and social opposition to authority (e.g., religion, monarchies, and political oppression) grew in parallel to science's own opposition to the ideas of these authorities. These arguments included an ever-increasing belief in the necessity of such freedom as speech, the press, and the life of the individual. Freedom, so it was argued, was essential because of the individual's basic rationality, which daily – so it seems – was being confirmed by and in science. The conclusion from all this was that people had no need for artificial authority and social restraint.

As these ideas were being openly championed, the institution that was to embody them and drive the argument home through the seventeenth and eighteenth centuries rapidly took shape. Science and scientific research were institutionalized when the Royal Society was chartered by Charles II in 1662, with John Locke (1632–1704) one of its early members. The fact that there were already two similar academies in France and Italy with none of the influence of the Royal Society tells us just how good a fit there was between science and England. At this point research had acquired the purpose of discovery. It is not simply that the Royal Society quickly became a meeting place for otherwise scattered (and often rancorous) scientists and mathematicians of historical eminence that is significant, but that the Royal Society institutionalized recognition of their work. Among the Royal Society's formal requirements was that a scientist's peers review the presentation of his work. Members were expected not only to publish their scientific work, but to do so only in the Society's *Philosophical Transactions*. Private papers were no longer to be circulated. Furthermore, it was stated, if others were to understand and be able to use individual scientists' work, then other rules would have to be followed. Personal idiosyncratic language was to be avoided, or at least minimized (Bronowski & Mazlish, 1960). The form of presentation, the symbolism, and the system of notation used by a member would have to be made comprehensible to other scientists.

Of all its requirements, probably the most influential was the obligation to publish one's results in the Society's *Transactions*, which soon gave the Royal Society a great influence over the reputations of the members. Just how important this influence on reputation was, was illustrated in the Society's mediation of the prolonged and bitter debate between Robert Hooke and Isaac Newton. The expectation to "publish for merit," while driven primarily by individuals' motivation, at least early on, was itself institutionalized by the Society in two ways: by the Society's sense of responsibility to science as an institution, and by its emphasis on the publication of scientific results. This requirement accompanied a second goal, which was to make evident the power and practicality of science.

Two practical consequences resulted from these institutional requirements (vestiges of which remain). One was the reduced individuality shown in published papers. While encouraging individual originality and genius, as they were understood at the time, the Royal Society had installed a set of requirements that effectively stripped scientific communication of many signs of individuality. (These expectations operate to this day in scientific journals, although in somewhat modified form.) The second consequence was to shift the Society's early concern with individuality – which, ironically, some seventeenth- and eighteenth-century writers believed was the sine qua non of genius and creativity – to the Royal Society's explicit emphasis on the lawfulness of nature and the discovery of practical benefits from science. These benefits, so it was thought, underscored the validity of natural laws and the importance of scientific experimentation in the physical world (i.e., nature). Early debates and speculation on the question of where "ideas" for this program came from were soon overshadowed by a growing confidence in the inventive power of empirical methods and natural science's apparent infinite capacity to produce practical benefits. Although physical nature was accepted as science's prime source of knowledge and man was accepted as a part of nature, the scientific investigation of *human* nature was not yet seriously considered during this period.

The Great and Nearly Endless Debate

Several further intellectual developments would take place before a concept of creativity could develop. During the last half of the eighteenth century, natural science's belief in natural law became widely accepted. Everyday justification for an unshakable confidence was seen all around in the practical inventions that natural science was credited for putting into the English economy – the spinning machine and the steam engine – inventions that were accelerating the Industrial Revolution and England's own lead in manufacturing and business over foreign competition.

On a somewhat more speculative level, for English and European artists, poets, writers, and philosophers there remained two questions that had been endlessly discussed throughout the eighteenth century: What were the limits to freedom of thought? What was the social and political significance of such freedom? These questions reflected the abiding issues throughout the century. As we know now, until they were answered, there could be no clear understanding of what creativity was, much less what it could do.

The most significant distinctions made in the mid-1700s were between the idea of creativity and those of genius, originality, talent, and formal education. At the heart of these debates were efforts to clarify the legitimate sphere of individual freedom, as distinguished from social and political restraints. Society's laws and the somewhat arbitrary limitations imposed by authority were naturally in opposition against "original" genius and constituted a pernicious barrier to people's freedom and originality (Addison 1711/1983). But perhaps there was nothing as influential in propelling the history of creativity as the concerted efforts to understand the differences between talent and original genius. By the end of the eighteenth century, it was concluded that whereas many persons may have talent of one sort or another and that this talent would be responsive to education, original genius was truly exceptional and by definition was to be exempt from the rules, customs, and obligations that applied to the talented. This was not an abstract argument. As Kaufman (1926) and Engell (1981) make clear, these prolonged debates regarding the relationships and differences among genius, originality, exceptionality, innate ability, and freedom eventually came together in the eighteenth century doctrine of individualism (with the American and French Revolutions just around the corner). But still no concept of creativity existed at this time.

Hobbes (1588–1679) was the first major figure to recognize how important imagination was in human thought and planning and how constructive it could be, an idea that reappeared as a starting point of discussions during the Enlightenment (Braun, 1991; Singer, 1981–1982).

To appreciate how difficult it was to develop the concept of creativity, remember it had taken several generations of writers, philosophers, and artists to come close to the concept.

Their difficulty can be seen in the fact that their discussions of imagination led as early as the 1730s to the phrase "the creative imagination." And by the late 1700s, "imagination itself" was accepted as governing artistic creativity (Engell, 1981, pp. vii–viii).

As tedious and tangential as they were at times, the debates through the eighteenth century nevertheless eventually came to four fundamental acceptable distinctions, which were to become the bedrock of our present-day ideas about creativity: (a) Genius was divorced from the supernatural; (b) genius, although exceptional, was a potential in every individual; (c) talent and genius were to be distinguished from one another; and (d) their potential and exercise depend on the political atmosphere at the time. (For the reader who believes these matters are settled, similar issues of separation and distinctions [i.e., discriminant validity] can be seen in recent research on domain-specificity [Albert, 1980; Baer, 1995; Bloom, 1985; Gardner, in press; Runco, 1986].)

By the end of the eighteenth century, it was widely accepted that neither genius nor talent could survive in repressive societies. When freedom did exist, according to Duff, one of the century's most prolific and convincing writers on genius and talent (Kaufman, 1926), spontaneity and genius would be "irresistible" because they reflected an innate predisposition and needed no education, a belief soon shared by Rousseau and later Romantics. On a practical level the arguments over these distinctions were important in helping to define the differences between the exceptional and unpredictable force of genius and the less extraordinary, more predictable talent seen everyday. By the end of the century it was concluded that whereas many people had talent that could respond to education, genius was original, manifested in someone seeming to come out of nowhere, out of reach or need of education, and immune from the rules and obligations appropriate for talent. (It is interesting and politically significant that Rousseau saw genius in every man with the same exemptions.)

The Influence of Unintended and Unanticipated Consequences

By now there were two models that incorporated many of the important arguments and practical observations related to research and creativity. One of these models – of Rational Science – bears on science's power and the practical use of research, which has been pretty much covered. The other model can be called the Ideology of Creativity. It had to do with the social significance and potential dangers of originality and individualism in the context of compliance to authority and maintenance of social order.

The Rational Science model has always been formal in its arguments and can appear moderately removed from the day-to-day consequences of research. On the other hand, while there have been much older discussions about the religious and secular significance of creativity, creativity acquired an ideology because of its relevance in defining human nature and sociopolitical conditions.

While natural science and practical inventors such as Arkwright and Watt were busy demonstrating what human reason and English inventiveness could do, it was numerous practical inventions and their ever-increasing power that eventually led to unforeseen and unintended dire consequences. Rapid population shifts of farmers off the land and laborers out of villages and into increasingly dirty sprawling cities and regimented impersonal factories soon alarmed many persons. Interestingly, while science was still busy demonstrating what rational human reason could do, there now arose a growing parallel concern regarding the ultimate effect of these results, especially in terms of social and political stability.

It was not long before an increasing number of people, especially among the upper middle class and gentry, were having second thoughts about individualism, its alleged irresistible spontaneity, and the unrestricted use of science. What they were witnessing was clearly not the efficient machine-driven society envisioned early in the Industrial Revolution. The rapidity and threat that characterized this change became one of the most important influences in the development of social sciences. The unpredicted widespread dislocations resulting from natural science was too obvious to overlook in spite of natural science's century-old belief that physical nature was governed by rational and intelligible laws. "Unintended and unanticipated consequences" – more and more threatening and poorly understood – were entering the social world, and with them came calls for political movements and social action. The spreading doctrine of individualism, which motivated the unrest, quickly became the accepted explanation for, and source of fear over, these consequences. In order to understand one of these consequences, we need to recognize that they were not new; they had been an intractable concern during most of Adam Smith's lifetime (1723–1790). He knew that consequences that were unintended and unanticipated happened often (as did his Swiss contemporary Jean-Jacques Rousseau).

From the mid-1700s there was almost constant turmoil in England and Europe. The many dislocations from the Industrial Revolution led to two very diverse but equally influential responses. One was Adam Smith's rational argument, which is discussed later, and the other was Jean-Jacques Rousseau's (1712–1778) Romanticism, which, among other social consequences, became the source of an artistic counterthrust to scientific rationalism. This part of Romanticism's response to the industrialization of Europe was expressed in artists' emphasis on inner feelings as a natural and therefore democratic source of wisdom and artistic inspiration. The conflict was soon identified as one between intellect and feeling, which in turn was personified as one between the overly rational scientist and the artist as the misunderstood genius. In 100 years this new identity, which marked artists' sense of deviance and their deliberate defiance of middle-class society, would be used by charlatans such as Lombroso as justification to denigrate artists in general and genius and creativity specifically. Although both reactions occurred at the same time, their consequences for research and creativity had different timetables, which were not to be coordinated until the end of the nineteenth century, through the achievements of Galton and Freud.

Adam Smith was one of the first to recognize the need for a science of human behavior. His *Wealth of Nations* (1776) was a deliberate effort to bring together the many reasons for a social science; it is "almost an encyclopedia of the effects of unintended consequences in human affairs. . . . The *consequences* of action are often different from the *intentions* which motivate the actors" (quoted in Muller, 1995, p. 85). His argument was free of blame and pontification. His point was that not all consequences were either good or bad, but they were often unintended and unanticipated. One undeniable unanticipated consequence he pointed to was the dramatic and frightening population and industrial upheaval, and one of its consequences, he believed, was the American Revolution, to which Smith devoted extensive attention. Because of such consequences, Smith and others argued that it was imperative to develop a science much like Natural Science, based on systematic, political, and social knowledge. It was thought that such a social science would help anticipate social change before it got out of hand.

Eight years after Smith's death, there occurred a major intellectual and empirical development that contributed to the establishment of a social science – the publication of Malthus's *Essay on Population* (1798). Not simply an argument (there were enough of them), it documented with exhaustive empirical evidence (rudimentary statistics) the apparent uncontrolled growth and social disorganization in the English population, predicting unanticipated consequences if social and political action were not taken.

The importance of Malthus's work is twofold. His research was as empirical as nonphysical science research would be until Galton. And 40 years later a phrase in *Essay on Population* that he used to explain the social disruptions – "the struggle for existence" – provided Darwin (1859) with the explanation for natural selection that he was trying to articulate. This particular idea helped organize Darwin's efforts, and *The Origin of Species* added new evidence that human existence was indeed precarious, subject to unintended and unanticipated shifts and demands of natural selection. It did not move according to any individual's wishes or plans, or embody any morality or purpose. Natural selection was blind.

The intellectual breakthrough of the late nineteenth and early twentieth centuries' understanding of creativity was implied in the role that Darwin gave to adaptation in survival. Freud, who read Darwin and met Galton, was later to incorporate this idea in his psychodynamic theory of defenses and creativity (Albert, 1996; Ellenberger, 1970; S. Freud, 1900/1953, 1908/1958).

Adaptation, Diversity, and Natural Selection: Darwin's Empirical Formula for Creativity

From the time it was first discussed, creativity has been enclosed in abstract questions and connected to issues larger than itself (e.g., What is individualism and why do we need individual freedom?). It was only after Darwin worked out the processes underlying natural selection that several basic characteristics of creativity were brought into sharp focus, especially its value in adaptation. One important role that creativity has had since Darwin has been in solving problems and in leading to "successful" adaptations that are individual in character.

We can understand this by recognizing both that evolutionary theory's basic principles are diversity and adaptation and that they are related to each other and to natural selection: "The generation of adaptations and the generation of diversity . . . [are] different aspects of a single complex phenomenon, and the unifying insight, [Darwin] claimed, was not the idea of evolution, but 'the principle of natural selection.'" Furthermore, Darwin argued, "natural selection would inevitably produce *adaptation*" (Dennett, 1995, pp. 42–43). The idea that was the most difficult for many persons to accept was the most counterintuitive of all. Because evolution occurs without foresight, "adaptations get their start as fortuitous [unintended, we must note,] – effects that get opportunistically picked up by selective forces in the environment" (Dennett, 1995, p. 248). At this time what was laid before us was the possibility of research on creativity if we try to observe adaptations in controlled everyday conditions (see Campbell, 1960).

The Transfer from Darwin to Galton

The intellectual bridge from Darwin to Galton was built early in Galton's career through steady correspondence and visits between the two, up to Darwin's death. The content of their exchanges was more often than not about evolution. Early in their relationship Galton proposed his own version of heredity and evolution, but soon became convinced of the validity and greater explanatory power of Darwin's model as it centered on natural selection and on the necessity of diversity and the role of adaptation in natural selection. However, it was natural that in Galton's hands diversity would become a problem of measurement. To solve that problem he operationalized diversity as individual differences within an environment of known dimensions (Galton, 1874, 1883). This environment consisted of what was measurable by instruments, most of which were designed by Galton. Thus, one of Galton's significant contributions directly to psychological research and indirectly to creativity was the operational definition of broad evolutionary diversity as manifested in specific individual differences that could be measured.

Galton had two compelling interests that tied together much of his career. One was the study of individual differences. The second was a deliberate program of Eugenics, which he believed was needed to increase British talent scientifically. Whether or not he was aware of it, Galton was following in Adam Smith's and Malthus's footsteps in his wish to protect society from unintended social consequences. Eugenics was Galton's program to minimize the uncertainty in natural selection as it might specifically affect Britain. These two research interests led to Galton's most direct contribution to research on creativity – his choice of eminence-achieving families as examples of hereditary ability. Out of this came the selection of eminent persons as subjects of obvious creativity (although some researchers will argue the point) and the practical use of statistics, some of which Galton developed. It is here that we see another of Galton's lasting contributions. Earlier we described "the great and nearly endless debate" that occurred during the eighteenth century, out of which came four important distinctions. It seems to us that, intentionally or not, Galton gave us evidence for the ideas that genius was divorced from the supernatural and, although exceptional, was a potential in every individual, because ability is distributed throughout populations.

From Galton to the Present

The reader might wonder if Galton was the only person interested in creativity at this time. The answer is absolutely not. But he was the strongest force in applying empirical methods in the selection of subjects and the measurement of their individual differences. Sternberg and Lubart (1996) have suggested that one impediment to research on creativity over the years was the tie between creativity and mysticism, in the sense that creativity might have mystical origins. This mistake could no longer be made after Galton. The magnitude of Galton's achievement is apparent when we learn of others who were interested in the same problems around the same time.

After her review of the nineteenth-century research, Becker (1995) concluded that in spite of the differences in the characteristics of the authors and articles, the themes of that century were not dissimilar to the those of the twentieth century. She stated that a number of nineteenth-century authors concentrated on five basic questions: What is creativity? Who has creativity? What are the characteristics of creative people? Who should benefit from creativity? Can creativity be increased through conscious effort? No one doubts that these are important questions for understanding creativity, but at the time only Galton made real progress in suggesting how they could be answered. It is not so much to ask these questions, which all have some merit, but to ask how one goes about answering them. This is what matters the most in science. We have two illustrations of this.

As early as 1837, Bethune was interested in the ability to "originat[e] new combinations of thought" and felt that creative genius could "store away ideas for future combinations" (see Becker, 1995, p. 220). Becker suggested that Bethune foresaw some of Freud's thinking, arguing that those future combinations would be conscious only "when the chain of association is regained" (p. 220). Actually, quite a few writers anticipated elements of Freud's thinking without putting them together as Freud did.

In 1877, Jevons defined genius as "essentially creative" and manifest when there is a "divergence from the ordinary grooves of thought and action" (Becker, 1995, p. 225). Some may see this as anticipating Guilford (1950), Mednick (1963), and Wallach and Kogan (1965), who would make much of the concept of divergent thinking.

It is not until we read William James that we see an appreciation of research and empirical fact to match Galton's earlier appreciation of empiricism. The depth of James's understanding is seen in his 1896 public lectures, in which he demolishes the "wild" assertions then being made by untrained self-appointed social critics and medical experts regarding exceptional mental states (James 1896/1992).

The idea of divergent thinking, or at least the possibility of complex ideation, was formulated by William James (1880), who understood the rarity of ideational complexity:

Instead of thoughts of concrete things patiently following one another in a beaten track of habitual suggestion, we have the most abrupt cross-cuts and *transitions* from one idea to another . . . the most unheard-of *combinations* of elements, the subtlest associations of *analogy*; in a word, we seem suddenly introduced into a seething caldron of ideas . . . where partnerships can be joined or loosened in an instant, treadmill routine is unknown, and the unexpected seems the only law. (Quoted in Becker, 1995, p. 222, italics added)

It is not easy to know just when and where Galton's influence ends. Most of it seems to have been assimilated in the ongoing interests and research by the end of the nineteenth century. We know that by 1879 Galton had developed the earliest laboratory in which to measure individual differences in sensory functioning, and that this research was related to the assumption that sensory discrimination was positively associated with intelligence. And by 1883 he had concluded that "creative products" came largely from "general ability," which in *Hereditary Genius* (1869) he stated was one of the essential capacities for genius (Albert, 1975; Cropley, 1966). But by the 1900s, measuring individual differences in intelligence had become a research interest of many psychologists. In fact by 1904 Binet and Spearman were doing their empirical investigations on intelligence tests with Binet's test including items that he believed required imagination and what is now called divergent thinking (Brody, 1992; Willerman, 1986). Terman was among this group, revising the Binet-Simon test; although the IQ test was his research instrument of choice, the conceptual framework came from Galton (Terman, 1924).

Even though Galton's work no longer stood out, his influence continued. Terman was the earliest U.S. psychologist to take a research interest in genius. His profound and deep interest in genius (and that of twentieth-century research) can be seen in the titles and dates of his work (Terman, 1906, 1917, 1924; Terman & Chase, 1920), including his five-volume *Genetic Studies of Genius,* (1925, 1926, 1930, 1947, 1954). This research was important not only for its methodological challenge, but also for its educational and social implications. Both Galton and Terman worried about their nations' futures and how to safeguard them. (We hope the reader sees the concern connecting Adam Smith, Malthus, Galton, and Terman.) Terman has been criticized at times because of what we sometimes see as his narrow focus on IQ as constituting giftedness, to the exclusion of creativity and nonacademic achievement. As true as this is, the course of Terman's research was always guided by his wish to help make "an American society based on the principles of meritocracy" (Minton, 1988, p. 139). To do this required identifying individual differences in ability and bestowing upon children with high native ability (IQ) the appropriate educational opportunities. What is significant is that Terman's research program ran counter to the intellectual changes taking place in Europe, which were to some degree a return of Rousseauian philosophy. These changes were antimaterialism, antielitism, antipositivism, and antirationality. With them came a rediscovery, by Bergson, Freud, and Marx (Barron, 1995; Hughes, 1953), of the power and validity of subjective, intuitive, and preconscious thought.

Guilford (1970) astutely observed that, over the years, Terman's project was directed toward being able to scale people along a dimension (much as Galton and some German experimentalists had done with mixed success). His method was relatively simple, whereas creativity was too complex, mentalistic, and removed from educational performances for the same treatment. Catherine Cox's dissertation (directed by Terman) documented a study that was an extension of Terman's (1917) own method of estimating Galton's IQ to a sample of individuals that achieved eminence between 1450 and 1850. But more important than its methodology was its developmental goal, which was to determine if Galton's conclusions concerning genius (Galton, 1869, p. 43) would apply to children who would later achieve eminence. A subtext to Cox's research, which is not usually recognized, is that Terman and Cox were aware of Lombroso's fraudulent methods and conclusions and wished to test their validity empirically (Cox, 1926, pp. 14–15).

Although there were limits to its perspective and emphasis on "practical" results, it is through Terman's interest in Galton that the latter had so much influence on Cox's research (1926). Galton's (1869) research was both a stimulus and the model for her monumental study of 300 historically eminent men. Like Galton, Cox never questioned what she too assumed was the high positive correlation between eminent achievement and "very high abilities." In fact, all three – Galton, Terman, and Cox – took for granted that achievement was a valid measure of "mental capacity," which helps explain why Terman and Cox start their research where Galton's ended – believing creativity to be an integral part of intelligence. Both Galton's and Cox's subjects were no longer alive and were selected from archives, but Cox improved on Galton's work in several important ways. Her sample was much broader, larger, and objectively selected. Cox used experts' ratings for her criteria of eminence. (Expert judgment has been used ever since. It was used extensively at the Institute of Personality Assessment and Research, for example, by Barron, Helson, and MacKinnon.) Another of her improvements over Galton was in her deliberate use of biographical, autobiographical, and sociocultural information – all exhaustively coded – from which she and several other psychologists estimated subjects' IQs and their childhood traits. This made her subjects more alive and their "stories" plausible, not reduced to mere numbers, and this gave her conclusions personal relevance and made them more easily acceptable. Other than her sample having an average IQ of 154, the most quoted conclusion of Cox's (1926) findings on creativity research is that "youths who achieved eminence are characterized not only by high intellectual traits, but also by persistence of motive and effort, confidence in their abilities, and great strength or force of character" (p. 218). Note that this *configuration* of particular traits, which she carefully documented (pp. 177–213), varied according to subjects' areas of achievement, indicating domain-specificity. It is no accident that these traits figure in Cox's conclusions. Like other similarities between Galton and Cox, there is the recognition that intrinsic motivation, described earlier by Galton (1869), is "one of the vital 'qualities of intellect and disposition' and acts as an inherent stimulus" (from Runco, 1993, p. 6). Just how valid Cox's conclusions are is attested to by the contemporary emphasis and evidence on persistence, intrinsic motivation, and autonomy (Albert & Runco, 1989; Amabile, in press; MacKinnon, 1963, 1970).

It is difficult to think of any other research on creativity up to World War II equal to Cox's (1926) contributions. Nor should we overlook the fact that she chose a historiometric method of investigation because she understood that creativity research concerned a problem common to both psychology and history. This was "the application to historical data of the criteria of standardized measures of the mental ability of children" (Cox, 1926, p. 21). This methodology is still being used (e.g., Albert, 1994, 1998; Simonton, in press). Another aspect of Cox's contribution derives from the timing of her work.

Cox's research in the mid-1920s coincided with the development of ego psychology. The configuration of childhood traits characteristic of some of her eminent subjects fit the ego psychology's growing interest in mastery, confidence, and persistence – the basic ego drives. This suggested that creativity was not primarily unconsciously driven. Moreover, the small differences in the subjects' IQ and the diversity of traits that Cox described argued for caution in overemphasizing IQ's influence on creativity. The combination of Cox's work and ego psychology's orientation demonstrated that creativity is not simply one type of behavior (psychopathology), nor does it originate on only one level of dynamics (the unconscious), nor does it express just one (or a dominant) trait of the individual (antisocial behavior), nor has it just one adaptive purpose. This view of creativity fit the psychoanalytic proposition that creativity, like all behavior, was overdetermined (i.e., multivariate), and this has led to recent definitions of creativity as a complex (Albert & Runco, 1989) or syndrome (MacKinnon, 1970; Mumford & Gustafson, 1988). Cox's results reinforced the importance that ego psychology saw in the interdependence of personal identity and conscious processes of adaptation (Erikson, 1950; Kubie, 1961; Vaillant, 1977). Soon after World War II, the focus of research would increasingly center on the personalities, values, talents, and IQs of exceptionally creative men and women, as well as compare exemplars with their more average counterparts (see e.g., Barron, 1953, 1955; Helson, 1968, 1971; MacKinnon, 1963, 1970, 1992; Roe, 1953). This body of work confirmed that, of all their differences, the most influential factors of individuals were developmental and family differences. A difference in IQ was not one of the significant differences. Above IQ 115, creativity and IQ constitute two more or less independent sets of abilities from late childhood on (see e.g., Albert & Runco, 1989; MacKinnon, 1963, 1970; Wallach, 1983).

Helson (1996) has reviewed the decade of the 1950s and the research on the creative personality then going on. She reminds us that during the 1950s and 1960s, the creative personality was the hot new topic. Whether they knew it or not, researchers on creativity were in the avant garde of a new version of individualism. Creative people of all types became our culture's heroes. What Helson observed was a change in perspective, but not a paradigmatic shift of the type we have attempted to track in this history of research on creativity.

Soon afterward, interests widened even more. Other researchers shifted the emphasis to creative types or styles, and still other researchers, such as Dudek and Hall (1991), described comparison participants with as much respect as they did their creative counterparts, achieving a depth of portrayal at times absent from early studies, which would exaggerate less creative persons' deficiencies. Over the past 50 years, research on creativity has merged an interest in creative persons with empirical methods and a feeling for the humanity and dignity of subjects, out of which has come respect for unambiguous as well as everyday creativity (e.g., Runco & Richards, in press). MacKinnon (1963) noted:

The history of the concepts of ego and self has been a long and confused one, but there is today rather general agreement upon the sense in which each is to be used in psychological theory. In a functionalist psychology of personality, the ego is conceived to be a system of regulating functions – reality testing, decision-making, etc. – which serve to integrate the subsystems of personality. On the other hand, it permits the individual to express himself in creative actions, which change the environment and contribute to the actualization of himself through the development and expression of his potentialities. (pp. 252–253)

When we look back at Darwin and think over MacKinnon's (1963) observation, we can only marvel how deep historical questions and our efforts to make sense of them may come together in time with profound implications for research.

Now to close the circle. We have observed over its history that research on creativity is able to progress as science when, at times blind to the next step, it is empirical, as Bacon (1605) told us science should be.

REFERENCES

Addison, J. (1983). On genius. In R. S. Albert (Ed.), *Genius and eminence* (pp. 3–5). Oxford: Pergamon. (Original work published 1711)

Albert, R. S. (1969). The concept of genius and its implications for the study of creativity and giftedness. *American Psychologist, 24,* 743–753.

Albert, R. S. (1975). Toward a behavioral definition of genius. *American Psychologist, 30,* 140–151.

Albert, R. S. (1980). Genius. In R. H. Woody (Ed.), *Encyclopedia of clinical assessment* (vol. 2). San Francisco: Jossey-Bass.

Albert, R. S. (1994). The contribution of early family history to the achievement of eminence. In N. Colangelo, S. G. Assouline and D. I. Ambroson (Eds.) *Talent development* (pp. 311–360). Dayton: Ohio Psychological Press.

Albert R. S. (1996, Fall). Some reasons why creativity often fails to make it past puberty and into the real world. *New Directions in Child Development*, no. 72, 43–56.

Albert, R. S. (1998). Mathematical giftedness and mathematical genius. In A. Steptoe (Ed.), *Genius and the mind* (pp. 111–140). Oxford: Oxford University Press.

Albert, R. S. (in press). The achievement of eminence as an evolutionary strategy. In M. A. Runco (Ed.), *Creativity research handbook* (Vol. 2). Cresskill, NJ: Hampton.

Albert, R. S., & Runco, M. A. (1989). Independence and cognitive ability in gifted and exceptionally gifted boys. *Journal of Youth and Adolescence, 18*, 221–230.

Amabile, T. M. (in press). In M. A. Runco & R. S. Albert (Eds.), *Theories of creativity* (rev. ed.). Cresskill, NJ: Hampton.

Bacon, F. (1605). *Advancement of learning.* Oxford: Oxford University Press.

Baer, J. (1995). Generality of creativity across performance domains. *Creativity Research Journal, 4*, 23–39.

Barron F. (1953). Complexity–simplicity as a personality dimension. *Journal of Abnormal and Social Psychology, 48*, 163–172.

Barron, F. (1955). The disposition toward originality. *Journal of Abnormal and Social Psychology, 51*, 478–485.

Barron, F. (1995). *No rootless flower: An ecology of creativity.* Cresskill, NJ: Hampton.

Becker, M. (1995). Nineteenth century foundations of creativity research. *Creativity Research Journal, 8*, 219–229.

Bloom, B. S. (1985). *Developing talent in young people.* New York: Ballantine.

Boorstin, D. J. (1992). *The creators: A history of heroes of the imagination.* New York: Random House.

Boring, E. G. (1929). *A history of experimental psychology.* New York: Century.

Braun, E. T. H. (1991). *The world of imagination.* Savage, MD: Rowman & Littlefield.

Brody, N. (1992). *Intelligence* (2d ed.). New York: Academic.

Bronowski, J. (1951). *The common sense of science.* London: Methuen.

Bronowski, J., & Mazlish, B. (1960). *The Western intellectual tradition.* London: Hutchinson.

Bullough, V., Bullough, B., & Mauro, M. (1981). History and creativity: Research problems and some possible solutions. *Journal of Creative Behavior, 15*, 102–116.

Campbell, D. T. (1960). Blind variation and selective retention in creative thought as in other knowledge processes. *Psychological Review, 67*, 380–400.

Child, I. L. (1972). Esthetics, *Annual Review of Psychology, 23*, 669–694.

Cox, C. M. (1926). *Genetic studies of genius: Vol. 2. The early mental traits of three hundred geniuses.* Stanford, CA: Stanford University Press.

Cropley, A. J. (1966). Creativity and intelligence. *British Journal of Educational Psychology, 36*, 259–266.

Darwin, C. (1859). *On the origin of species by means of natural selection.* London: Murray.

Dennett, D. C. (1995). *Darwin's dangerous idea.* New York: Touchstone.

Dudek, S. Z. (in press). Art and aesthetics. In M. A. Runco (Ed.), *Creativity research handbook* (vol. 2). Cresskill, NJ: Hampton.

Dudek, S. Z., & Hall, W. (1991). Personality consistency: Eminent architects 25 years later. *Creativity Research Journal, 4*, 213–232.

Eisenberger, R., & Cameron, J. (1996). Detrimental effects of rewards: Reality or myth? *American Psychologist, 51*, 1153–1166.

Ellenberger, H. F. (1970). *The discovery of the unconscious.* New York: Basic.

Engell, J. (1981). *The creative imagination: Enlightenment to romanticism.* Cambridge, MA: Harvard University Press.

Erikson, E. (1950). *Childhood and society.* New York: Norton.

Feist, G. J., & Runco, M. A. (1993). Trends in the creativity literature: An analysis of research in the *Journal of Creativity Behavior* (1967–1989). *Creativity Research Journal, 6*, 271–286.

Freud, S. (1953). *The interpretation of dreams* (vols. 4–5 in the Standard Edition.) London: Hogarth. (Original work published 1900)

Freud, S. (1958). The relation of the poet to day-dreaming. In B. Nelson (Ed.), *On creativity and the unconscious* (pp. 44–54). New York: Harper & Row. (Original work published 1908)

Freud, S. (1961). *The ego and the id* (vol. 19 of the Standard Edition). London: Hogarth. (Original work published 1923)

Freud, S. (1953). *Leonardo da Vinci and a memory of his childhood* (vol. 2 in the Standard Edition). London: Hogarth. (Original work published 1910)

Galton, F. (1869). *Hereditary genius*. New York: Macmillan.

Galton, F. (1874). *English men of science: Their nature and nurture*. London: Macmillan.

Galton, F. (1883). *Inquiries into human faculty*. London: Macmillan.

Gardner, H. (1994). *Creating minds*. New York: Basic.

Gardner, H. (in press). Is there a moral intelligence? An essay in honor of Howard Gruber. In M. A. Runco, R. Keegan, & S. Davis (Eds.), *Festschrift for Howard Gruber*. Cresskill, NJ: Hampton.

Gray, C. E. (1966). A measurement of creativity in Western civilization. *American Anthropologist, 68*, 1384–1417.

Gruber, H. E. (1996). The life space of a scientist: The visionary function and other aspects of Jean Piaget's thinking. *Creativity Research Journal, 9*, 251–265.

Guilford, J. P. (1950). Creativity. *American Psychologist, 5*, 444–454.

Guilford, J. P. (1970). Creativity: Retrospect and prospect. *Journal of Creative Behavior, 5*, 77–87.

Helson, R. (1968). Generality of sex differences in creative style. *Journal of Personality, 36*, 33–48.

Helson, R. (1971). Women mathematicians and the creative personality. *Journal of Consulting and Clinical Psychology, 36*, 210–220.

Helson, R. (1996). In search of the creative personality. *Creativity Research Journal, 9*, 295–306.

Hughes, H. S. (1953). *Consciousness and society*. New York: Vintage.

James, W. (1992). William James on exceptional mental states: The 1896 Lowell lecture. In R. S. Albert (Ed.), *Genius and eminence* (2d ed., pp. 41–52). Oxford: Pergamon. (Original work published 1896)

Kaufman, P. (1926). *Essays in memory of Barrett Wendell*. Cambridge, MA: Harvard University Press.

Kroeber, A. (1944). *Configurations of cultural growth*. Berkeley: University of California Press.

Kubie, L. S. (1961). *Neurotic distortion of the creative process*. New York: Noonday.

MacKinnon, D. W. (1963). Creativity and images of the self. In R. W. White (Ed.), *The study of lives* (pp. 251–278). New York: Atherton.

MacKinnon, D. W. (1970). The personality correlates of creativity: A study of American architects. In P. E. Vernon (Ed.), *Creativity* (pp. 289–311). Harmondsworth: Penguin.

MacKinnon, D. W. (1992). The highly effective individual. In R. S. Albert (Ed.), *Genius and eminence* (2d ed., pp. 179–193). Oxford: Pergamon.

Martindale, C. (1992). *The clockwork muse*. New York: Basic.

Mednick, S. A. (1962). The associative basis of the creative process. *Psychological Review, 69*, 202–232.

Minton, H. L. (1988). Charting life history: Lewis M. Terman's study of the gifted. In J. G. Morawski (Ed.), *The rise of experimentation in American psychology* (pp. 138–160). New Haven, CT: Yale University Press.

Muller, J. Z. (1995). *Adam Smith in his time and ours*. Princeton, NJ: Princeton University Press.

Mumford, M. D., & Gustafson, S. G. (1988). Creativity syndrome: Integration, application, and innovation. *Psychological Bulletin, 103*, 27–43.

Nahn, M. (1956). *The artist as creator*. Baltimore: Johns Hopkins University Press.

Naroll, R., Benjamin, E. C., Fohl, F. K., Fried, R. E., Hildreth, R. E., & Schaefer, J. M. (1971). Creativity: Cross-historical pilot study. *Journal of Cross-Cultural Psychology, 2*, 181–188.

Ochse, R. (1990). *Before the gates of excellence. The determinants of creative genius*. Cambridge University Press.

Pearson, K. (1930). *The life, letters, and labours of Francis Galton* (vols 1–3). Cambridge University Press.

Prickett, S. (1996). *Origins of narrative: The Romantic appropriation of the Bible*. Cambridge University Press.

Roe, A. (1952). *The making of a scientist*. New York: Dodd, Mead.

Roe, A. (1970). A psychologist examines sixty-four eminent scientists. In P. E. Vernon (Ed.), *Creativity* (pp. 43–51). Harmondsworth: Penguin.

Runco, M. A. (1986). Divergent thinking and creative performance in gifted and nongifted children. *Educational and Psychological Measurement, 46*, 375–384.

Runco, M. A. (1993). Operant theories of insight, originality, and creativity. *American Behavioral Scientist, 37*, 54–67.

Runco, M. A., & Albert, R. S. (1986). The threshold hypothesis regarding creativity and intelligence: An empirical test with gifted and nongifted children. *Creative Child and Adult Quarterly, 11*, 212–218.

Runco, M. A., & Richards, R. (in press). *Eminent creativity, everyday creativity, and health*. Norwood, NJ: Ablex.

Schneider, S. F. (1996). Random thoughts on leaving the fray. *American Psychologist, 51*, 715–721.

Shapin, S. (1996). *The scientific revolution*. Chicago: University of Chicago Press.

Simonton, D. K. (in press). In M. A. Runco & R. S. Albert (Eds.), *Theories of creativity* (rev. ed.). Cresskill, NJ: Hampton.

Singer, J. L. (1981–1982). Towards the scientific study of imagination. *Imagination, Cognition and Personality, 1*, 5–28,

Sorokin, P. A. (1947). Society, culture, and personality. New York: Cooper Square.

Sternberg, R. J., & Lubart, T. I. (1996). Investing in creativity. *American Psychologist, 51*, 677–688.

Terman, L. M. (1906). Genius and stupidity: A study of the intellectual processes of seven "bright" and seven "stupid" boys. *Pedagogical Seminary, 13*, 307–373.

Terman, L. M. (1917). The intelligence quotient of Francis Galton in childhood. *American Journal of Psychology, 28*, 209–215.

Terman, L. M. (1924). The mental tests as a psychological method. *Psychological Review, 31*, 93–117.

Terman, L. M., & Chase, J. M. (1920). The psychology, biology, and pedagogy of genius. *Psychological Bulletin, 17*, 397–409.

Vaillant, G. E. (1977). *Adaptation to life.* Boston: Little, Brown.

Wallach, M. A. (1983). What do tests tell us about talent? In R. S. Albert (Ed.), *Genius and eminence* (pp. 99–113). Oxford: Pergamon.

Wallach, M. A., & Kogan, N. (1965). *Modes of thinking in young children.* New York: Holt, Rinehart, & Winston.

Willerman, L. (1986). *The psychology of individual and group differences.* San Francisco: Freeman.

Wilson-Given, C. (1996). *An illustrated history of the late medieval England.* Manchester: Manchester University Press.

PART II

Methods for Studying Creativity

3 · Psychometric Approaches to the Study of Human Creativity

JONATHAN A. PLUCKER AND JOSEPH S. RENZULLI

The study of human creativity, although historically extensive, is in the midst of a second golden age as the century comes to a close. Authors and researchers from a variety of backgrounds publish hundreds of articles and books on creativity every year, conferences that cross disciplines frequently include sessions on creativity, and programs for increasing the creative productivity of young people and adults are introduced on a regular basis. And while several distinct approaches are used to examine creative phenomenon, a majority of work dealing with creativity relies on psychometric methods – the direct measurement of creativity and/or its perceived correlates in individuals.

Indeed, practically all current work on creativity is based upon methodologies that either are psychometric in nature or were developed in response to perceived weaknesses of creativity measurement. As such, the psychometric studies of creativity conducted in the past few decades form the foundation of current understandings of creativity. Yet the psychometric approach is significantly more complex and comprehensive than its critics (and many of its proponents) would have us believe, and alternatives to the psychometric approach are wrought with many of the same difficulties posed during the direct measurement of creativity. A thorough review of psychometric techniques for the study of creativity benefits both those individuals attempting to measure creativity and those individuals studying creativity via other techniques.

Our purpose is to analyze critically the development, characteristics, strengths, and weaknesses of the psychometric approach in order to inform future research efforts using this and other approaches. With that in mind, this chapter is composed of several sections. First, an overview of the psychometric approach's historical development and main characteristics is presented. Second, comparisons are made to other approaches to the study of creativity. Third, major areas of psychometric work are examined in detail. Fourth, an area of study upon which the psychometric approach often focuses – the relationship between creativity and other cognitive constructs such as intelligence and giftedness – is analyzed. Fifth, criticisms of the psychometric approach are considered. Finally, the implications of past psychometric work for future creativity study, both psychometrically and through other methodologies, are discussed.

DEVELOPMENT OF THE PSYCHOMETRIC APPROACH

The predominance of the psychometric perspective is surprising considering the widely held lay belief that creativity is undefinable and unmeasureable (Callahan, 1991; Khatena, 1982). Attempts to explain the influence of psychometric methods usually focus on parallels between the development of creativity study and the development of the study of intelligence (Gardner, 1988b, 1993a). While the dominance of psychometric techniques in the study of both constructs is obvious, the parallel is a bit overused. For example, the anthropometric techniques that dominated early phases of intelligence research have never held considerable importance in creativity research. The primary cause of the predominance of psychometric perspectives is probably that the researchers who first became interested in creativity were already approaching other cognitive phenomenon from the psychometric perspective and continued with their methodological habits as they began to investigate creativity (see Cramond, 1993; Gardner, 1993a).

Regardless of the causes, psychometric approaches date from well before J. P. Guilford's 1950 APA Presidential Address, which is traditionally considered the formal starting date of scientific creativity research. The 1883 publication of Galton's *Inquiries into Human Faculty* called attention to the measurement of creativity (Taylor & Barron, 1963a), resulting in several investigations into creativity and imagination in the next couple of decades. Torrance (1982) found evidence of significant efforts by Whipple around the turn of the century (i.e., tests of imagination and invention) and in the Human Engineering Laboratories during the 1930s and 1940s, while Barron and Harrington (1981) note that divergent thinking tests were developed by Binet and Henri before 1900. Several investigations into the creativity–intelligence relationship between 1898 and 1950 are also noted by Guilford (1967a). However, in part due to the advent of behaviorism, this work received little lasting scientific scrutiny and was not appreciably influential.

In contrast to the relatively infrequent (and forgotten) work in the first half of this century, the 25 years after Guildford's call to arms were marked by extensive study of creativity (the first golden age of creativity research; see Taylor & Barron, 1963a). Nearly all of this work was conducted under the aegis of the psychometric perspective. Cases in point are the collective proceedings from the National Science Foundation–sponsored Utah Conferences on the Identification of Creative Scientific Talent (C. W. Taylor, 1964; Taylor & Barron, 1963b; Taylor & Williams, 1966), which served collectively as a focal point for creativity research in the late 1950s and early 1960s.

Summarizing the work of this period, Torrance (1979) noted that the psychometric study of creativity was essentially dichotomous:

Creativity tests tend to be of two types – those that involve cognitive-affective skills such as the *Torrance Tests of Creative Thinking . . .* and those that attempt to tap a personality syndrome such as the *Alpha Biological Inventory. . . .* Some educators and psychologists have tried to make an issue of whether creativity is essentially a personality syndrome that includes openness to experience, adventuresomeness, and self-confidence and whether the cognitive processes of rational and logical thinking in creative thinking are precisely the same as those used by high-IQ children. (p. 360)

Based in large part upon the work of Amabile (1983), Torrance (1979), and researchers and theorists who have promoted more encompassing systems theories of creative development (e.g., Csikszentmihalyi, 1988; Walberg, 1988), psychometric approaches to the study of creativity have grown beyond the traditional cognitive and personality perspectives mentioned by Torrance. While a few individuals dominated the psychometric work on creativity for decades (e.g., J. P. Guilford, E. P. Torrance, and C. W. Taylor), the diversity of current psychometric approaches is matched only by the diversity of philosophical and empirical perspectives of the researchers conducting the investigations.

For example, in the past 15 to 20 years, researchers have used psychometric methods to measure the creativity of products (see e.g., Besemer & O'Quin, 1986; Reis & Renzulli, 1991), to investigate the environmental characteristics that are associated with creativity (Amabile, Conti, Coon, Lazenby, & Herron, in press), to refine measures of idea generation and evaluation (Runco, 1991; Runco & Mraz, 1992), and to develop new measures of personality characteristics associated with creative and inventive behavior (Colangelo, Kerr, Hallowell, Huesman, & Gaeth, 1992). But many other studies in this period have been characterized by other methodologies, some of which differ substantially from the psychometric approach.

Nearly all creativity studies can be classified into five categories: psychometric, experimental, biographical, historiometric, and biometric. Since all but biometric methods are described in significant detail elsewhere in this volume, the emphasis in this section is on comparisons between these approaches and the psychometric perspective.

The *experimental approach* is quite similar to the psychometric approach in that experimental researchers use many of the same instruments used by psychometricians to measure creativity. For example, experimental methods have been used to investigate the effect of transfer strategies on problem-solving performance (Cramond, Martin, & Shaw, 1990), the effect of exposure to uncommon solutions on problem solving (Maltzmann, Brooks, Bogartz, & Summers, 1958), and the impact of external evaluation on the creativity of student products (Amabile, 1979, 1983; Amabile, Hennessey, & Grossman, 1986). The major difference between the two approaches lies in the research design employed. While psychometricians utilize correlational and causal-comparative designs, quasi-experimental and experimental designs are used by researchers favoring experimental investigations. Therefore, the limitations of nonexperimental designs and the added logistical and financial costs of experimental designs dominate comparisons between the two approaches.

Another significant difference between experimental and psychometric methodologies is that experimentalists tend to isolate cognitive, problem-solving, and, to a lesser extent, product aspects of creativity for manipulation during experiments, while psychometricians, as will be described in detail in the next section, focus on personality and environmental correlates of creativity in addition to creative processes and products.

The *historiometric approach* is best characterized in the prolific work of Simonton, who substantially refined the methodology that was used for several decades in studies of eminence (e.g., Cattell, 1963; Dennis, 1956; Lehman, 1953; Roe, 1952). Like the psychometric approach, historiometry involves the measurement of creativity. But unlike psychometric methods, in which aspects of creativity are measured in the present or recent past, historiometricians draw quantitative data almost exclusively from historical documentation (e.g., Ludwig, 1992; Root-Bernstein, Bernstein, & Garnier, 1995) with little reliance upon the self-report measures commonly administered in psychometric research. Simonton has applied historiometric methods to the study of creativity and leadership (1988a), invention and discovery (1979), creativity and age (1984a), musical creativity (1984b), and eminence (1986a, 1994), among other areas.

Another distinction between psychometric and historiometric approaches is the concern with the creator's role of gaining acceptance for his or her creative products as an area of creativity investigation (Simonton, 1988a). While theoretical musings on the role of creative persuasion have an appreciable history (Albert, 1975; Amabile, 1983; Plucker, 1993; Stein, 1974, 1975), empirical investigations of persuasion as applied during creative production are predominantly limited to historiometric (and to a minor degree, biographical) methodologies.

Perhaps the approach most similar to the psychometric perspective is characterized by the recent work being done in biometry as it relates to cognition. Gardner (1993a) described the value of creativity analysis at the "subpersonal" level, suggesting that

little is known about the genetics and the neurobiology of creative individuals. We know neither whether creative individuals have distinctive genetic constitutions, nor whether there is anything remarkable about the structure or functioning of their nervous systems. Yet, any scientific study of creativity will ultimately need to address these biologically oriented questions, and I expect that such study will soon be undertaken. (p. 36; see expanded discussion in Gardner, 1988b)

While some critics (e.g., Plucker, 1994a) questioned the usefulness and reality of a *biometric approach* to creativity research, the publication of recent investigations into the relationship between brain function and specific types of cognitive functioning (and the development of technology allowing such comparisons) in the scientific literature (Haier & Benbow, 1995; Haier, Siegel, Tang, Abel, & Buchsbaum, 1992; Larson, Haier, & Hazen, 1995; O'Boyle, Benbow, & Alexander, 1995; Shaywitz et al., 1995) and resulting coverage in the popular press (Begley, 1995) have piqued the interests of scientists, educators, and the public at large. Briefly, these techniques involve the monitoring of an individual's glucose metabolism in the brain while he or she performs certain cognitive tasks (e.g., attempting to solve mathematical problems). Since glucose metabolism is a measure of brain activity, researchers can pinpoint and measure activity in certain areas of the brain as each area is used during the cognitive activity. While a "neurometric" approach may be hindered by problems similar to those faced by traditional psychometric approaches (e.g., defining a "creative" task, precision of measurement), this extension of the psychometric approach holds promise for the future study of creativity.

The approach most distinct from the psychometric approach is the *biographical* or *case study approach,* in which researchers construct case studies of eminent creators using qualitative research methodology (Gedo & Gedo, 1992; Gruber & Davis, 1988). In addition to the advantages and limitations of qualitative inquiry, biographical methods are also unique to creativity research in their reliance upon eminent (i.e., indisputable) instances of creativity (e.g., Gruber, 1981; Wallace & Gruber, 1989). This highly exclusive definition of creativity helps biographical researchers avoid the problems and issues surrounding the definition of creativity faced by investigators adhering to most other methodological approaches.

Gardner (1988a, 1993a) and his colleagues (Feldman, Csikszentmihalyi, & Gardner, 1994; Gardner & Nemirovsky, 1991) recently proposed and modeled a sixth technique that they believe combines the biographical and historiometric approaches. As this methodology is still in its infancy, comparisons to other approaches are premature. However, distinguishing this new approach in practice from examples of biographical work is difficult, suggesting that comparisons to the psychometric approach are similar to those between biographical and psychometric methods.

In summary, while the various approaches to the study of creativity share many features, fundamental differences separate them from one another. The most significant differences involve the research designs commonly used (i.e., correlational and causal-comparative vs. qualitative and experimental), the specific areas focused on by researchers (person, product, process, environment, persuasion), and the time frame in which data are collected.

SPECIFIC AREAS OF PSYCHOMETRIC STUDY

The four specific areas in which psychometric methods are applied to creativity research include investigations into creative processes, personality and behavioral correlates of creativity, characteristics of creative products, and attributes of creativity-fostering environments. This section includes reviews of seminal and recent work in each of these areas and concludes with a comparison of the specific areas of psychometric investigation. Readers will not find a detailed listing of the hundreds of creativity tests, instruments, and rating scales that have been developed in recent decades and are referred elsewhere for these reviews (Callahan, 1991; Davis, 1971, 1989; Hocevar, 1981; Hocevar & Bachelor, 1989; Houtz &

Krug, 1995; Hunsaker & Callahan, 1995; Kaltsounis, 1971, 1972; Kaltsounis & Honeywell, 1980).

Creative Processes

The quest to quantify the creative process, primarily through the use of divergent thinking batteries, has been a lightning rod for the psychometric study of creativity. A majority of criticisms and adverse reactions directed at creativity measures are primarily (but not exclusively) directed at "creativity tests." At the same time, both researchers and educators have used tests of the creative process extensively for decades, and divergent thinking tests remain a popular measure of creative process and potential. The predominance of divergent-thinking tests is especially evident in our schools (Hunsaker & Callahan, 1995).

Divergent-thinking tests require individuals to produce several responses to a specific prompt, in sharp contrast to most standardized tests of achievement or ability that require one correct answer. This emphasis upon fluency, also referred to as ideational fluency or simply ideation, is seen as a key component of creative processes, although it is clearly not the only component. Among the first tests of divergent thinking were Guilford's (1967b) Structure of the Intellect (SOI) divergent production tests, Torrance's (1962, 1974) Tests of Creative Thinking (TTCT), and those by Wallach and Kogan (1965) and Getzels and Jackson (1962). Almost all of these tests remain in wide use in creativity research and education. While space does not permit a detailed description of each test and battery, a brief description of the most widely cited instruments is provided.

The SOI battery (as summarized in Guilford, 1967b) consists of several tests on which subjects are asked to exhibit evidence of divergent production in several areas, including that of semantic units (e.g., listing consequences of people no longer needing to sleep), of figural classes (finding as many classifications of sets of figures as is possible), and of figural units (taking a simple shape such as a circle and elaborating upon it as often as possible). The entire SOI divergent production battery consists of several dozen such tests corresponding to the various divergent-thinking components of Guilford's SOI model. Factors representing several types of fluency, flexibility, originality, and elaboration of ideas have been established for the SOI tests. Meeker (1969) and colleagues (Meeker & Meeker, 1982; Meeker, Meeker, & Roid, 1985) developed a version of the SOI, the Structure of the Intellect–Learning Abilities Test (SOI-LA) to diagnose weaknesses in divergent thinking (among other areas), which are then addressed by remedial services.

The TTCT, which is based on many aspects of the SOI battery, is by far the most commonly used test of divergent thinking and continues to enjoy widespread international use. As with the SOI, students provide multiple responses to either figural or verbal prompts that are scored for fluency (or number of ideas), flexibility with respect to the variety of perspectives represented in the ideas, originality (or statistical infrequency), and elaboration of ideas beyond that required by the prompt. Over the past several decades, Torrance (1974) refined the administration and scoring of the TTCT, which may account for its enduring popularity.

Both Getzels and Jackson (1962) and Wallach and Kogan (1965) developed divergent thinking batteries that are very similar to the SOI tests. For example, the Instances Test requires that students list as many things that move on wheels (things that make noise, etc.) as possible (Wallach & Kogan, 1965), and on variations of the Uses Test students provide responses to prompts such as "Tell me all the different ways you could use a chair" (newspaper, knife, of tire [Wallach & Kogan, 1965, p. 31] or bricks, pencils, and toothpicks [Getzels & Jackson, 1962]). Other tests in each battery include word association, embedded figures, story completion, and problem construction tasks (Getzels & Jackson, 1962) and similarity, pattern interpretation, and line interpretation problems (Wallach & Kogan, 1965). The most appreciable difference between the batteries lies in the conditions in which students take the tests. Wallach and Kogan (1965) supported gamelike, untimed administration of divergent thinking tasks, which they believed allows creativity to be measured distinctly from intelligence due to the creation of "a frame of reference which is relatively free from the coercion of time limits and relatively free from the stress of knowing that one's behavior is under close evaluation" (p. 24). This constraint-free administration is in contrast to the testlike, timed procedures used with most other divergent thinking measures.

The fact that divergent-thinking tests have changed very little since their inception may be an indication that this line of research is not inexhaustible. While evidence of reliability for the SOI, TTCT, Wallach and Kogan, Getzels and Jackson, and similar tests (e.g., Cline, Richards, & Abe, 1962; Eisen, 1989; Hoepfner & Hemenway, 1973; Torrance, 1981c; Torrance, Khatena, & Cunnington, 1973; Williams, 1979, 1980) is fairly convincing, the predictive and discriminant validity of divergent-thinking tests enjoys mixed support (cf. Bachelor, 1989; Clapham, 1996; Cooper, 1991; L. H. Fox, 1985; Renzulli, 1985; Rosen, 1985; Thompson & Anderson, 1983). The debate centers around the predictive validity of the tests[1] and the apparent susceptibility of divergent thinking tests to administration, scoring, and training effects.

For example, the homogeneity of the sample with respect to achievement or ability may influence results, since somewhat improved psychometric properties are generally associated with samples of gifted or high-achieving children (Runco, 1985, 1986b; Runco & Albert, 1985; see Runco, 1986a, for an exception). In addition, the conditions under which tests are administered (e.g., gamelike vs. testlike, timed vs. untimed, individual vs. group, specific instructions to "be creative" vs. generic instructions) appear to influence student originality and/or fluency scores (Chand & Runco, 1992; Harrington, 1975; Hattie, 1980; Renzulli, Owen, & Callahan, 1974; Runco, 1986c; Runco & Okuda, 1991; Torrance, 1971). Critics occasionally note that scores on divergent production tests are susceptible to training and intervention effects (see evidence presented by Clapham, 1996; Feldhusen & Clinkenbeard, 1986; Torrance, 1972a, 1988). Since many of these tests are frequently applied in educational settings, the lack of a stable creativity quotient (CQ) should be viewed as an advantage. Since considerable reliability evidence exists for most popular divergent-thinking tests, the concern over stability may be better addressed by studying the development of divergent-thinking ability over time.

Researchers have conducted several longitudinal studies of creativity since the late 1950s, with a majority relying at least in part on data gathered with divergent-thinking tests (Cropley, 1972; Howieson, 1981; Kogan & Pankove, 1974). Implications for the predictive validity of divergent-thinking measures are discussed later in this chapter, but studies that follow students over the course of several years also provide information about the *fourth grade slump* in creativity (Torrance, 1968). Torrance (1962, 1965, 1968), as a result of his numerous cross-sectional and longitudinal studies, discovered that students' TTCT scores decreased for a high percentage of students in fourth grade yet rebounded almost completely by fifth grade (completely in the cases of originality and elaboration). Other researchers and theorists perceive a longer general decline in creative performance through the late elementary grades. Possible causes include socialization and changes in school climate as students enter those grades, although success in correcting the effects of the slump through focused classroom treatment (Torrance & Gupta, 1964) suggest the latter cause. Unfortunately, decreases in ideational-thinking performance in the middle to late elementary grades have been the subject of few significant research efforts in the past 20 years, and these investigations produced conflicting results (Baer, 1996; Johnson, 1985).

Analyses of various scoring systems for divergent-thinking tests provide evidence that alternatives to the traditional frequency tabulations of fluency, flexibility, originality, and elaboration should be considered (e.g., Torrance, 1972d). These alternatives include the calculation of summative scores (i.e., totaling fluency, flexibility, and originality scores), uncommon scores (answers given by less than 5% of participants), weighted fluency scores, percentage scores, and scores based on the entire body of each subjects' answers as opposed to scoring individual responses in a list of ideas (Hocevar & Michael, 1979; Runco & Mraz, 1992; Runco, Okuda, & Thurston, 1987).

A measurement dilemma unique to divergent-thinking tests is the possibility of fluency acting as a contaminating factor, especially on originality scores (Hocevar, 1979c, 1979; Runco & Albert, 1985). Hocevar (1979a, 1979c), after parceling fluency effects out of other divergent-thinking test scores, found little evidence of reliability for originality and flexibility scores. But this work has significant empirical (Runco & Albert, 1985) and theoretical limitations (e.g., the role of associative hierarchies in creative individuals; see Mednick, 1962; Milgram & Rabkin, 1980).[2] A case in point is the effort by Runco and Albert (1985) to utilize both verbal and nonverbal tasks, since Hocevar (1979a, 1979c) used only verbal tests. Runco and Albert (1985) found that originality scores produced evidence of reliability after removing fluency effects on the nonverbal tasks, with significant differences among groups based on achievement (i.e., gifted vs. nongifted students). Collectively, this work suggests that the role of fluency is more complex than originally thought.

While several problems hinder the proper administration and interpretation of divergent thinking tests, the obstacles are not insurmountable and should be addressed in the near future. However, divergent-thinking tests historically occupy nearly the entire creative process spotlight. Since the ability to generate ideas is only one aspect of the creative process (see, e.g., Runco & Okuda, 1988, in their discussion of the componential theory of creativity), its predominance devalues the integral role of creativity in the solving of problems (Davis, 1973; Dombroski, 1979; Rickards, 1994; Speedie, Treffinger, & Houtz, 1976; Sternberg & Davidson, 1992). Professing a viewpoint widely held by other researchers (Basadur, Wakabayashi, & Graen, 1990; Osborn, 1963; Parnes, Noller, & Biondi, 1977; Simonton, 1988b; Torrance, 1976), Runco (1991) observes, "The evaluative component of the creative process has received very little attention. This is surprising because it is a vital constituent of the creative process, and is required whenever an individual selects or expresses a preference for an idea or set of ideas" (p. 312). The movement toward psychometric research involving aspects of creative problem solving other than divergent production, such as problem identification (Runco & Okuda, 1988; Wakefield, 1985) and evaluative thinking (Okuda, Runco, & Berger, 1991; Runco, 1991; Runco & Chand, 1994), is slowly gathering steam.

A corollary to the psychometric study of problem solving involves tests of insight. Historically, the relationship between insight and creativity received little theoretical and empirical attention (see Mayer, 1995, for some exceptions), although detailed examinations have been recently published (Dominowski & Dallob, 1995; Finke, 1995). For example, Martinsen (1993, 1995) is pursuing a line of research in which cognitive styles are compared with the ability to solve insight problems. To date, the research has produced support for the position that the necessary level of experience for solving problems varies based on an individual's cognitive style.

Researchers investigating aspects of insight should exhibit caution when designing their research. Many of the commonly used insight problems have enjoyed considerable exposure in textbooks, as parlor games, in magazines, and through other forms of dissemination. Especially when working with older students and adults, researchers should take precautionary steps to ascertain whether subjects have been previously exposed to the problems. Isaak and Just (1995) and Mayer (1995) provide detailed lists of frequently used insight problems.

The Creative Person

The second major area of psychometric study involves attempts to measure facets of creativity associated with creative people. Measures focusing on characteristics of the person are diverse, with a variety of self-reports and teacher/external ratings of past behavior, personality, and attainments.

Instruments designed to measure personality correlates of creative behavior are generally designed by studying highly creative individuals and determining their common personality characteristics. These traits are then compared with those of other children and adults under the assumption that individuals who compare favorably are predisposed to creative accomplishment. Such measures are quite common in creativity research and include the Group Inventory for Finding Talent and the Group Inventory for Finding Interests (see Davis, 1989), What Kind of Person Are You? (Torrance & Khatena, 1970), work undertaken at the Institute of Personality Assessment and Research (Hall & MacKinnon, 1969; Helson, 1971; MacKinnon, 1965, 1975, 1978), and specific scoring dimensions of the Adjective Check List (Domino, 1970, 1994; Gough, 1979; Smith & Schaefer, 1969) and the Sixteen Personality Factor Questionnaire (Cattell & Butcher, 1968, chap. 15; Cattell, Eber, & Tatsuoka, 1970). After analyzing the results of research in which these and several other related instruments were used, Davis (1992, pp. 69–72) concluded that personality characteristics of creative people include awareness of their creativity, originality, independence, risk taking, personal energy, curiosity, humor, attraction to complexity and novelty, artistic sense, open-mindedness, need for privacy, and heightened perception.

Tolerance for ambiguity is often mentioned as a personality characteristic of creative individuals (Dacey, 1989; MacKinnon, 1978; Sternberg, 1988a). For example, when taking the Barron-Welsh Art Scale (Welsh & Barron, 1963), individuals report their preferences for drawings that are either complex and asymmetrical or simple and symmetrical. Studies suggest that creative individuals generally prefer the complex figures. Several other scales have been developed to measure aesthetic sensitivity (see Frois & Eysenck, 1995, for a review) or – more generally – tolerance for ambiguity (Kirton, 1981).

In addition to personality traits, past behavior of creative individuals has been studied to determine if certain experiences are associated with creative production. As a result, self-reports are the methodology of choice when researchers wish to collect information about an individual's activities and accomplishments that may reflect creative potential and achievement. Based on the assumption that "the best predictor of future creative behavior may be past creative behavior" (Colangelo et al., 1992, p. 158), several investigators have developed self-report biographical and activity inventories such as the Alpha Biological Inventory (Taylor & Ellison, 1966, 1967), Creative Behavior Inventory (Hocevar, 1979b), and other checklists (Anastasi & Schaefer, 1969; Holland & Nichols, 1964; Holland & Richards, 1965; James, Ellison, Fox, & Taylor, 1974; Milgram & Hong, 1994; Milgram & Milgram, 1976; Runco, 1987a; Runco, Noble, & Luptak, 1990; Runco & Okuda, 1988; Schaefer & Anastasi, 1968; Wallach & Wing, 1969). Colangelo et al. (1992), based on their work with inventors, constructed an inventive inventory that combines the personality characteristic and attainment approaches. These instruments generally require respondents to report past accomplishments, but several instruments include items relating, either to current activities or to both past and current activities. Hocevar (1981; Hocevar & Bachelor, 1989) and Wallach (1976) believe self-reports of activities and attainments to be the preferable technique with which to measure creativity.

Two clarifications are necessary with respect to the widespread use of activity checklists and biographical inventories. First, self-reported attainments and activities can technically be interpreted as creative products. They are discussed in light of the creative personality because this particular type of product is usually not directly observed or measured. Techniques for rating creative products, which are discussed later in this chapter, involve direct observation and judgment of a product. Second, psychometric applications of biographical and activity inventories differ from historiometric uses of similar instruments in the former's reliance upon data gathered about recent behavior and activities as opposed to the historical accomplishments of eminent and/or highly accomplished individuals.

The administration of self-report scales may not be logistically feasible, as in the case of very young children or a schoolwide screening program for giftedness. In response to this need, several instruments have been developed to allow parents, teachers, other adults, and even peers to assess personality and past behavior correlates of creativity (Pearlman, 1983; Runco, 1984, 1987b, 1989b; Torrance, 1962; Wasik, 1974). Popular instruments include the Preschool and Kindergarten Interest Descriptor (Rimm, 1983) and the Scales for Rating the Behavioral Characteristics of Superior Students (SRBCSS; Renzulli, Hartman, & Callahan, 1981). The SRBCSS is frequently included in gifted education screening procedures (Hunsaker & Callahan, 1995). Judgments of the validity of ratings by people familiar with an individual are inconclusive concerning creativity and talent in general, with the evidence supporting both the presence of validity (Renzulli et al., 1981; Runco, 1984) and a lack thereof (Hocevar & Bachelor, 1989; Holland, 1959; Pegnato & Birch, 1959).

ATTITUDES. The measurement of attitudes toward creativity is important because, as Basadur and Hausdorf (1996) describe in their attitude research within the business community,

it identifies managers' attitudes related to skills in innovation. . . . Managers with more positive attitudes could be encouraged to participate in activities where these views can be optimized for the company. Alternatively, managers with less positive attitudes could participate in training to improve their attitudes and skills. Thus, the understanding and measurement of these attitudinal concepts provides a pathway to increasing managers' and companies' success. (p. 23)

Additionally, theoretical and empirical support exist for a connection between ideational attitudes and ideational thinking (Basadur & Finkbeiner, 1985). While attempts to measure creative attitudes have not been widespread, considerable effort is being expended on the creation of attitude measures for the purpose of evaluating attitude interventions in business (Basadur, Graen, & Scandura, 1986; Basadur, Wakabayashi, & Graen, 1990; Runco & Basadur, 1993) and identifying individuals who are predisposed to innovation or adaptation (Kirton, 1976, 1992; Kirton & McCarthy, 1988). One of the more advanced research programs in this area is that of Basadur and colleagues (Basadur & Finkbeiner, 1985; Basadur & Hausdorf, 1996), who are developing a series of scales to measure attitudes in five areas (i.e., preference for ideation, tendency to [not] make premature critical evaluations of ideas, valuing new ideas, stereotypes of creative individuals, being too busy for new ideas). Creative attitude research within education and psychology are limited, perhaps because of the perceived lack of application.

IMPLICIT THEORIES. An interesting and fairly recent application of person-oriented psychometric methods is the measurement of implicit theories of creativity. Implicit theories are generally defined as the conceptions that laypeople hold about certain constructs. For example, investigations of implicit intelligence theories are especially prominent in the literature (e.g., Lynott & Woolfolk, 1994; Sternberg, 1985a, 1985b; Sternberg, Conway, Ketron, & Bernstein, 1981). Sternberg (1993) provides a rationale for the study of implicit theories: "In studying implicit theories, one is trying to find out what the stereotypes are, to find out how people process the information. It is important to know this, in part so that one can know where interventions should be made" (p. 16; see Sternberg, 1987 for a detailed discussion of the usefulness of implicit theories). Researchers believe that knowledge of implicit theories regarding creativity will facilitate both the planning and evaluation of efforts to foster creativity.

As with other exploratory areas within the psychometric tradition, only a few studies of implicit creativity theories are available in the literature. Runco, Johnson, and Bear (1993), confirming the results of previous research efforts (Runco, 1984, 1989b; Runco & Bahleda, 1986), provide evidence that the implicit creativity definitions of teachers and parents are similar, with characteristics such as being active, adventurous, artistic, curious, enthusiastic, and imaginative used by both groups to describe creative children. Additionally, Runco et al. (1993) report that teachers use social characteristics (e.g., being cheerful, friendly, easygoing), while parents list intrapersonal characteristics (e.g., being self-confident, resourceful, industrious).

In studies involving college students' implicit theories of creativity, wisdom, and intelligence, Sternberg (1990) found that creativity definitions were characterized by nonentrenchment, integration and intellectuality, aesthetic taste and imagination, decisional skill and flexibility, perspicacity, drive for accomplishment and recognition, inquisitiveness, and intuition. These characteristics are quite different than those provided for definitions of intelligence (e.g., practical problem-solving ability, goal orientation and attainment, fluid thought) and wisdom (e.g., reasoning ability, sagacity, judgment). The results of these studies suggest that implicit theories of creativity generally match explicit theories, with some between-group differences, and that implicit theories of creativity are distinct from implicit theories of other psychological constructs.

Creative Products

MacKinnon (1978) argued that "the starting point, indeed the bedrock of all studies of creativity, is an analysis of creative products, a determination of what it is that makes them different from more mundane products" (p. 187). A decade later, Runco (1989a) noted that analysis of creative products[3] may address the measurement problems caused by the inconsistent psychometric quality of divergent thinking tests and adult rating scales. A significant number of researchers and educators share MacKinnon's and Runco's belief in the importance of the creative product (e.g., D. W. Taylor, 1960; Treffinger & Poggio, 1972; Wallach, 1976). Indeed, the importance of the creative product emerged in response to perceived needs for external criteria to which researchers could compare other methods of measuring creativity for the purposes of establishing validity. However, an absolute and indisputable criterion of creativity is not readily available, hence the criterion problem (McPherson, 1963; Shapiro, 1970).

Given that the importance of creative products is generally acknowledged and that theoretical musings regarding creative products have been commonplace for decades (Besemer & Treffinger, 1981; Ghiselin, 1963; Guilford, 1957; Jackson & Messick, 1965), the psychometric study of product ratings has been surprisingly limited. Product analyses range from rather straightforward rating scales (Besemer & O'Quin, 1993; Hargreaves, Galton, & Robinson, 1996; Treffinger, 1989) to conceptually complex consensual assessment techniques (Amabile, 1983; Hennessey & Amabile, 1988a). By far the most common method for the measurement of creative products utilizes the ratings of external judges, an approach that can be further categorized into teacher and parent ratings and ratings by experts.

For obvious reasons, teacher ratings receive the most attention in educational circles, with serious efforts put forth by Besemer and O'Quin (1986; O'Quin & Besemer, 1989), Reis and

Renzulli (1991), and Westberg (1991) during the past decade. Each of these instruments requires educators to rate specific characteristics of students' products. For example, the Creative Product Semantic Scale (Besemer & O'Quin, 1993) allows raters to judge the novelty, problem resolution, and elaboration and synthesis attributes of products, and the Student Product Assessment Form (Reis & Renzulli, 1991), designed to serve as an evaluation instrument in gifted programs, provides ratings of nine product traits (e.g., problem focusing, appropriateness of resources, originality, action orientation, audience). Westberg (1991) designed an instrument to evaluate student inventions, with analyses producing evidence of originality, technical goodness, and aesthetic appeal factors. Each of these instruments is associated with evidence of reliability, although validity issues remain to be addressed. In the one available comparison of teachers' and parents' ability to evaluate children's ideas, the two groups were similarly successful, with number of children and adult divergent thinking test scores positively and moderately correlated with evaluative skill (Runco & Vega, 1990).

The second area of product ratings, those provided by expert judges, is marked by an interesting dichotomy. When relying upon expert ratings, researchers occasionally provide judges with rating categories not unlike those developed by Besemer and O'Quin and Reis and Renzulli. These categories serve as guides for the judges as they evaluate creative products. For example, Csikszentmihalyi and Getzels (1971) asked artists and art critics to rate drawings by art students on the basis of craftsmanship, originality, and aesthetic value, with mixed reliability and validity results.

In contrast, other researchers ask experts to rate products' creativity with little additional guidance (e.g., MacKinnon, 1962). This methodology was refined by Amabile (1979, 1982, 1983) in her development of the Consensual Assessment Technique (CAT). The CAT addresses a perceived weakness of guided product assessments when they are applied to social psychology investigations of creativity: Through reliance on provided definitions or criteria of creativity, traditional product assessments accent domain-specific skills (and, therefore, individual differences) and decrease the ability to detect environmental effects upon creativity. By utilizing an amorphous definition of creativity, "a product or response is creative to the extent that appropriate observers independently agree it is creative" (Amabile, 1982, p. 1001), criterion problems are avoided, individual differences are muted, and environmental influences on the creative process can be examined. Theoretically, CAT adherents believe the approach to be more valid than traditional creativity assessments due to the accent on real-world definitions of creativity: People know creativity when they see it (Amabile, 1982; Baer, 1994b). This view is at least partially validated by the studies of implicit creativity theories and definitions discussed earlier. As evidence of reliability mounts and the technique is applied to a broader array of creative products (Amabile, 1996; Baer, 1994b; Hennessey & Amabile, 1988a, 1988b), research applications of the CAT are becoming quite common (e.g., Baer, 1993a; Sternberg & Lubart, 1991). The CAT is even being applied as a measure of creative process (Hennessey, 1994) and as an individual differences measure of creativity (Amabile, 1996).

However, the use of expert judges is not without its problems. Determining the necessary level of expertise for judges depends on a variety of factors, including the skill of the subjects, the target domain, and purpose of the assessments (Amabile, 1996; Runco, McCarthy, & Svenson, 1994; Runco & Smith, 1992). Runco and Chand (1994) also suggest that experts who can judge their own products effectively do not necessarily possess the ability to evaluate the creative products of other individuals. And while progress is being made in applying consensual techniques to the measurement of individual differences in creativity (Amabile, 1996), procedures for making between-group comparisons (when different sets of judges rate each group's products) are not yet perfected (Baer, 1994b). Comparisons between consensual assessment and more traditional psychometric techniques (Amabile, Phillips, & Collins, 1994; Runco, 1989a) have yet to produce definitive conclusions, yet the comparisons between the different methods will add to the knowledge base of each set of techniques. Runco et al. (1994) and Amabile (1996) and her colleagues report moderate relationships between self-ratings and expert ratings of products. In general, individuals evaluate their work more highly than judges, with similar rank orderings of products and moderate correlations between the two groups.

Creative Environments and Environment–Person Interactions

The study of the context in which creativity occurs, while enjoying some precedence in the fields of technology transfer and management of innovation (e.g., Mahajan & Peterson, 1985; Rogers, 1983; Tushman & Moore, 1988), has only recently gained significant academic attention in psychology, education, and other social sciences. Amabile's work (1983, 1996) on the social psychology of creativity opened the academic door for other "systems" approaches of creativity, such as Sternberg and Lubart's (1991, 1992, 1995) investment theory, Rubenson and Runco's psychoeconomic theory (Rubenson, 1990; Rubenson & Runco, 1992), Kasof's (1995) attributional perspective, and Amabile's (1988) own work with innovation management in organizations. The common characteristic of systems approaches is the emphasis on the environment in which creativity occurs. The implications for creativity education are substantial, and researchers are beginning to investigate the ways that systems approaches can be used to develop creativity-fostering environments in educational settings (Plucker, 1994b).

Given the recent development of contextual investigations of creativity, the relative lack of psychometric investigations in this area is not surprising. Researchers currently seek to determine environmental variables that are related to creative productivity, with the hope that measurement of these contextual factors will facilitate the design and implementation of environments that promote creative achievement more efficiently than those in our school and businesses. Based on several years of research on management and organizational creativity (see Amabile et al., in press; Witt & Beorkrem, 1989), Amabile and her colleagues (Amabile et al., in press; Amabile & Gryskiewicz, 1989) are developing a work environment inventory that provides various scores related to workers' perceptions of climate conditions that stimulate or deter creativity (e.g., supervisory encouragement, freedom to choose and work on assignments, sufficient resources, workload pressure, organizational impediments). Amabile et al. (in press) report preliminary evidence of reliability and validity and plan to conduct additional validity studies. Siegel and Kaemmerer (1978) and Hill (1991) conducted similar research on classroom environments, although this work has not yet progressed beyond the original research.

Context investigations also involve comparison of workers' motivational orientations (i.e., intrinsic and extrinsic) to their creativity-related personality characteristics and the creativity of their products. This line of inquiry is not unlike Gardner's (1993b) theorizing about the relationship between multiple intelligences profiles and work preferences (see also Zuboff, 1988). Amabile, Hill, Hennessey, and Tighe (1994), in a psychometric study of the Work Preference Inventory, found moderate positive correlations between intrinsic motivation scores and certain measures of creative personality and creative products. Negative or nonsignificant correlations were found between the creativity measures and extrinsic motivation scores. Oldham and Cummings (1996), in a comparison of personality traits, environmental characteristics, and product ratings, found evidence that people with specific personality traits (i.e., as judged by Gough's [1979] Creative Personality Scale) produced creative products when challenged by their work and supervised in a supportive "noncontrolling fashion"

(p. 607). Like other areas of creative environment investigation, this work is in its nascent stages. As the psychometric quality of environment-related instruments improves, our understanding of creative environment–person–product–process interactions will correspondingly increase.

Comparisons Among the Specific Areas

Reviewing the diverse techniques used to measure creativity reinforces the difficulty encountered when attempting to describe psychometric efforts as a collective entity. Further evidence of the disparate nature of psychometric creativity investigations is found in the frequent criticism of divergent thinking tests by proponents of other psychometric approaches. For example, Amabile (1982) and Baer (1993b, 1994c) criticize divergent thinking measures due to their perceived lack of validity, and instead recommend expert ratings and consensual assessment techniques. In response, Cramond (1994) argues that expert ratings also possess considerable limitations and recommends the use of different types of creativity measures in concert. Hocevar (1981) and Wallach (1976) endorse the measure of attainments, yet Torrance (1995) holds strong reservations about their use in educational settings. Several other psychometricians suggest that one type of assessment is not inherently better than any other (e.g., Davis, 1992), and a few researchers believe that combinations of the various techniques hold the most promise (e.g., Cooper, 1991; Wakefield, 1991). In the end, one is left with the impression that psychometric approaches to the study of creativity are incredibly diverse and not easily characterized as a group.

RELATIONSHIPS TO OTHER COGNITIVE CONSTRUCTS

Psychometric methods for the study of creativity are generally used to address two specific types of research problems. In the first, of which major themes are described earlier in this chapter, researchers attempt to learn more about creativity. In the second, researchers examine the relationship between creativity and other cognitive constructs. Intelligence is by far the construct with which a majority of researchers concern themselves, in part because intelligence was the dominant cognitive construct during the advent of creativity testing, and in part to address theoretical questions regarding the link or lack thereof between creativity and intelligence. The creativity–intelligence relationship also has considerable implications for creativity training and education (Gowan, 1971), hence another reason for the dozens of studies in this area.

The dominant view of the relationship between intelligence and creativity is characterized by the *threshold effect,* in which a minimum of intelligence is required for an individual to exhibit creative problem-solving behaviors such as problem finding, divergent thinking, remote associations, and convergent thinking (Guilford, 1967b). Empirical evidence for the threshold effect ranges from enthusiastic support (Getzels & Jackson, 1962; Guilford & Christensen, 1973; Guilford & Hoepfner, 1966; Torrance, 1962) to qualified reserve (Fuchs-Beauchamp, Karnes, & Johnson, 1993; Tannenbaum, 1983; Yamamoto & Chimbidis, 1966) to refutation and rejection (Fox, 1981; Mednick & Andrews, 1967; Runco & Albert, 1985, 1986; Runco & Pezdek, 1984; Wallach & Kogan, 1965; Ward, 1968). In general, research on the distinction or lack thereof between creativity and intelligence produces widely varying results (Horn, 1976; Torrance, 1967; Wallach & Wing, 1969).

Callahan (1991) attributes the mixed results of research on the creativity–intelligence distinction to extraneous factors such as the population studied, the conditions under which the tests are given, the specific instruments used to measure intelligence and creativity, and other extraneous factors. A few researchers even suggest that the statistical methods employed to analyze creativity and intelligence data have a direct impact on the outcome (Cronbach, 1968; Hattie & Rogers, 1986).

However, the apparent confusion surrounding the creativity–intelligence relationship is not as troubling as it first appears. Theories and instruments created to assist in the exploration of cognitive constructs are not static objects, and instruments and theory related to creativity and intelligence are certainly not exceptions to that rule (Anastasi & Schaefer, 1971). As intelligence and creativity theories become more complex (e.g., Ceci, 1990; Gardner, 1983; Sternberg, 1988b), measures for the resulting constructs similarly evolve into successively complex techniques. For example, early investigations support the threshold theory (Guilford & Hoepfner, 1966; Torrance, 1962), while recent studies provide evidence that creativity–intelligence relationships are more complex than previously thought (Hattie & Rogers, 1986; Runco & Albert, 1986). The question is no longer one of whether creativity and intelligence are related, but in what ways they are related and in what ways they are distinct. Consumers of intelligence–creativity research should be aware of the conditions under which the research is performed, including construct definitions, instrumentation, administration, sampling, and statistical analysis.

CRITICISMS OF THE PSYCHOMETRIC APPROACH

Taylor and Holland (1964), in their generally favorable review of psychometric work conducted prior to the mid-sixties, noted "a great need in creativity research for predictive (longitudinal) studies which use a very wide variety of potential predictors, and then, after a suitable follow-up period, utilize good external criteria of creativity" (p. 48). Similarly, as Cattell and Butcher (1968) remark:

> Seldom has psychology been asked to undertake so ambitious a task as that of defining the creativity criterion. If getting a reliable criterion for "success as a bus driver" has its difficulties, it will be evident that obtaining a criterion score on "creativity" to check the predictive power of our tests is going to present formidable conceptual and practical problems. (pp. 285–286)

After over 30 years of investigation in this area, the criterion problem, although discussed herein only in terms of creative products (i.e., the most commonly used criterion), is still the major stumbling block for the advance of psychometric creativity research. For example, critics believe that evidence of discriminant and predictive validity, and criterion validity in general, is still lacking (Gardner, 1988b, 1993a; Kogan & Pankove, 1974; Wallach, 1976). Weisberg (1993) uses this point to criticize tests of remote association, intuition, personality, and divergent thinking, commenting that the latter "do not measure either creative thinking or the capacity to become creative" (p. 61). Wallach (1976), in a widely cited review of psychometric creativity research, stated that "subjects vary widely and systematically in their attainments – yet little if any of that systematic variation is captured by individual differences on ideational fluency tests" (p. 60).

Suggested reasons for the lack of predictive validity vary widely. While some discount psychometric methods in their entirety (Gardner, 1988b; Weisberg, 1993), others suggest that divergent thinking tests are susceptible to coaching, testing conditions, and related administration issues (Hattie, 1980; Wallach, 1976), that longitudinal studies are generally too short and should be at a minimum more than 7 or even 12 years in duration (Torrance, 1972b, 1979), that quality of creative accomplishment is usually overlooked in favor of quantity (Runco, 1986b), or that initial socioeconomic conditions and intervening life events (e.g., the fourth grade slump, military service) make prediction of adult creative achievement solely on the basis of ideational-thinking test scores difficult if not impossible (Cramond, 1993, 1994).

Regardless of the criticisms of psychometric methods, specifically divergent-thinking tests, Torrance (1969, 1972b, 1972c, 1981a, 1981b; Torrance & Safter, 1989; Torrance, Tan, & Allman, 1970; Torrance & Wu, 1981) and others (Howieson, 1981; Milgram & Hong, 1994; Milgram & Milgram, 1976; Rotter, Langland, & Berger, 1971; Runco, 1986b; Yamada & Tam, 1996) conducted several studies that provide at least limited evidence of discriminant validity and of relationships between divergent-thinking test scores and various criteria, including adult creative accomplishment. Several researchers now believe that predictive validity for divergent-thinking tests is highest for intellectually gifted and high-achieving students (Runco, 1986c), and only then when predicting achievement in specific content areas (Hocevar, 1981; Milgram & Milgram, 1976; Runco, 1986b). Gardner (1988b) notes a reliance on self-report measures of creative behavior in this work, but Torrance and Ball (1984) and Runco (1986b) addressed this perceived weakness in their work with little apparent change in their conclusions.

A criticism that has emerged in the past decade is the role of task specificity in creativity measurement. Baer (1994a) strongly cautions educators against reliance upon divergent thinking tests for several reasons, the most serious of which is the perceived task-specific nature of creativity (Baer, 1993a, 1993b). Baer's research, however, utilizes alternative assessment techniques similar to those of Amabile (1983, 1996). Given the task specificity generally associated with alternative assessments (Baxter, Shavelson, Goldman, & Pine, 1992; Dunbar, Koretz, & Hoover, 1991; Linn & Burton, 1994; Linn, Burton, DeStefano, & Hanson, 1996), the preliminary nature of other research occasionally cited in support of task-specific theories of creativity (Runco, 1987a, 1989a), and evidence of generality across various domains (Hocevar, 1976), conclusions regarding the general or content-specific nature of creativity are not yet warranted.

Another serious criticism is that psychometric approaches to creativity research have added little to the educational and research communities (Gardner, 1993a). For example, Weisberg (1993) believes that study of personality correlates of creative production reveals only intuitive information about creative personalities. However, any observation of creative practices reveals this argument to be rather shallow with respect to educational implications. More than any other approach to the study of creativity, investigations utilizing psychometric methods provide the foundation for the ways in which creativity is approached in our schools and businesses, including creative problem-solving programs (Basadur, Graen, & Green, 1982; Isaksen & Treffinger, 1985), creativity training programs (Renzulli, 1976), remediation programs (Meeker, 1969; Meeker & Meeker, 1982), and whole school, talent development models (Renzulli, 1994; C. W. Taylor, 1988). The methodology may be far from perfect, but criticisms that psychometric creativity work has had little impact on psychological or classroom practice must be taken with a grain of salt.

Indeed, a great deal of the criticism directed at psychometric approaches to creativity study may be the social science equivalent of throwing the baby out with the bathwater. Many complaints regarding psychometric approaches are standard postmodern criticisms of quantitative methodology, and many of the same criticisms are directed at psychometric approaches to the study of intelligence. While several of the critics' finer points – such as incorrect interpretation of inferential statistics and poor research design – hold significant merit, suggested alternatives to the psychometric approach are fraught with equally serious problems. For example, investigations that rely upon examination of relatively indisputable examples of creative achievement may avoid the criterion problem, but are faced with problems of generalizability like those faced by other qualitative and small-sample research techniques. Rather than reject one or more methodologies in favor of another, which is admittedly par for the course in the history of human inquiry, people interested in studying creativity should understand the merits and limitations of the available methods and the type of information that each method is best suited to provide about creativity.

THE FUTURE OF PSYCHOMETRIC CREATIVITY STUDY

Nicholls (1983) mused:

Yamamoto (1965) accounted for the confusion in creativity research by likening researchers to blind men and creativity to the proverbial elephant. This simile, however, is too simple. There are, in fact, a variety of genuine elephants, and the blind men have in many cases coped with this pretty well. A major source of confusion, however, is the unacknowledged collection of domestic pets that accompany the blind men into the elephant compound. (p. 276)[4]

The challenge to creativity researchers, especially those employing psychometric methods, is to distinguish between the elephants (various conceptualizations of creativity) and the domestic pets (barely relevant constructs and extraneous factors influencing creative productivity). Surprisingly, after almost 50 years of research and development, this distinction is still often blurred. While the following suggestions are by no means exhaustive, they may help researchers strengthen psychometric contributions to the study of creativity.

First, longitudinal studies of predictive validity rarely account for the predictive power of creativity–intelligence interactions. This observation may be due to the fact that most major longitudinal studies have relied almost strictly upon bivariate correlational analyses, which is not surprising considering that these investigations generally occurred several decades ago. Given that the creativity–intelligence distinction remains a conundrum, researchers who neglect the interaction of these constructs – however they are measured – may be missing significant pieces of the predictive validity puzzle.

Second, much of the literature on creativity occurred decades ago, when statistical techniques were less powerful (i.e., were less able to detect group differences) and more limited in their application. Reanalysis of previously published data using recent developments in statistical analysis, such as structural equation modeling, will allow more stringent and parsimonious evaluation of psychometric creativity research. This is especially the case with the numerous longitudinal, predictive validity, and creativity–intelligence distinction studies.

Third, with the advent of comprehensive systems theories of creativity, psychometric analysis of creativity solely within a specific area (e.g., process, person, product, or context) is less defensible than in previous eras. Research on interactions among the four areas of traditional psychometric research, such as the person–product–environment work of Oldham and Cummings (1996) and climate–product research recommended by MacKinnon (1978), has much greater potential for unearthing valuable information about the psychology of creativity than more myopic perspectives. A broader approach may also increase work in relatively neglected areas, such as creative classroom environments, creative attitudes, and the role of motivation in creative production. As Renzulli (1991) noted:

New research in the 1990's and in the century ahead must begin to focus on that elusive "thing" that is left over when everything explainable has been explained. This "thing" is the true mystery of our common interest in creative productivity, and the area that might represent a new frontier for research in the Twenty-First Century. . . . [For example,] what we know about world famous creative producers . . . is certainly a compass point on our journey toward understanding this mysterious phenomenon, but my concern is with how we can promote a disposition toward creative productivity in today's classrooms. This kind of creative productivity, in most cases, will never be recorded in the annals of eminence, but if we can create a modus operandi for such productivity in larger and larger numbers of young people, then we may actually be contributing to the encouragement and development of Nobel Prize winners in the Twenty-First Century. (p. 2)

The elusive "thing" will only be found if traditional boundaries, both within and outside of the psychometric perspective, are crossed by creativity researchers.

Finally, researchers should strongly consider the criticisms of psychometric methods as applied to creativity and even research in general. Perhaps the most important critique in this regard is that psychometric conceptions of creativity have been far too narrow, focusing only within specific areas (as mentioned earlier) and on certain types of creative process and achievement (e.g., the concern with divergent thinking at the expense of convergent thinking). While the psychometric study of creativity will certainly have a lasting legacy, whether the legacy is one of activity or passivity is yet to be determined. After all, the Latin language has a lasting legacy but survives no more. Researchers electing to measure creativity must adapt their methods to address the serious and often accurate criticisms of psychometric approaches to avoid the creation of a dead methodology.

NOTES

The authors thank several researchers, including Mark A. Runco, Teresa M. Amabile, and Robert J. Sternberg, for providing access to their work. All interpretations and opinions expressed in this chapter, however, are solely those of the authors.

1 Issues surrounding the predictive validity of divergent-thinking tests are discussed with other criticisms of psychometric methods in a later section.

2 The measurement of associative processes forms an important foundation for much of the current psychometric work in creativity. However, interest in this aspect of creative process has waned recently, and the main instrument in this area (Mednick and Mednick's [1967] Remote Associates Test) is no longer published. Readers are referred to discussions in Mednick (1962), Mendelsohn (1976), Merten (1995), and Runco and Chand (1995) for detailed discussions of associative thinking from a creativity perspective and Snow and Yalow (1982) for an analysis of associative abilities from an education and intelligence perspective.

3 Again, psychometric analysis of creative products versus historiometric study of products differ primarily on the age of the product being studied. For example, a psychometric perspective might be used to create a rating scale for creative products for use by classroom teachers (e.g., Besemer & O'Quin, 1986), while a historiometric analysis of products might entail the analysis of historical documentation of patents or notebooks to attempt the reconstruction of an inventor's creative experiences. Of course, historiometric methods are used to examine other areas that overlap with those frequently studied by psychometricians (e.g., personality; Simonton, 1986b).

4 The metaphor of the elephant and blind men is quite common in creativity literature. For example, see Starko (1995), p. 327.

REFERENCES

Albert, R. S. (1975). Toward a behavioral definition of genius. *American Psychologist 30*, 140–151.

Amabile, T. M. (1979). Effects of external evaluation on artistic creativity. *Journal of Personality and Social Psychology, 37*, 221–233.

Amabile, T. M. (1982). Social psychology of creativity: A consensual assessment technique. *Journal of Personality and Social Psychology, 43*, 997–1013.

Amabile, T. M. (1983). *The social psychology of creativity.* New York: Springer-Verlag.

Amabile, T. M. (1988). A model of creativity and innovation in organizations. In B. M. Staw & L. L. Cummings (Eds.), *Research in organizational behavior* (Vol. 10, pp. 123–167). Greenwich, CT: JAI Press.

Amabile, T. M. (1996). *Creativity in context: Update to the social psychology of creativity.* Boulder, CO: Westview.

Amabile, T. M., Conti, R., Coon, H., Lazenby, J., & Herron, M. (in press). Assessing the work environment for creativity. *Academy of Management Journal.*

Amabile, T. M., & Gryskiewicz, N. (1989). The Creative Environment Scales: The Work Environment Inventory. *Creativity Research Journal. 2*, 231–254.

Amabile, T. M., Hennessey, B. A., & Grossman, B. S. (1986). Social influences on creativity: The effects of contracted-for reward. *Journal of Personality and Social Psychology, 50*, 14–23.

Amabile, T. M., Hill, K. G., Hennessey, B. A., & Tighe, E. M. (1994). The work preference inventory: Assessing intrinsic and extrinsic motivational orientations. *Journal of Personality and Social Psychology, 66*, 950–967.

Amabile, T. M., Phillips, E., & Collins, M. A. (1994). Person and environment in talent development: The case of creativity. In N. Colangelo, S. G. Assouline, & D. L. Ambroson (Eds.), *Talent development: Proceedings from the 1993 Henry B. and Jocelyn Wallace National Research Symposium on Talent Development* (pp. 265–277). Unionville, NY: Trillium.

Anastasi, A., & Schaefer, C. E. (1969). Biographical correlates of artistic and literary creativity in adolescent girls. *Journal of Applied Psychology, 53,* 267–273.

Anastasi, A., & Schaefer, C. E. (1971). Note on the concepts of creativity and intelligence. *Journal of Creative Behavior, 5,* 113–116.

Bachelor, P. (1989). Maximum likelihood confirmatory factor-analytic investigation of factors within Guilford's Structure-of-Intellect model. *Journal of Applied Psychology, 74,* 797–804.

Baer, J. (1993a). *Divergent thinking and creativity: A task-specific approach.* Hillsdale, NJ: Erlbaum.

Baer, J. (1993b, December/January). Why you shouldn't trust creativity tests. *Educational Leadership,* 80–83.

Baer, J. (1994a). Divergent thinking is not a general trait: A multi-domain training experiment. *Creativity Research Journal, 7,* 35–36.

Baer, J. (1994b). Performance assessments of creativity: Do they have long-term stability? *Roeper Review, 17,* 7–11.

Baer, J. (1994c, October). Why you *still* shouldn't trust creativity tests. *Educational Leadership,* 72–73.

Baer, J. (1996). Does artistic creativity decline during elementary school? *Psychological Reports, 78,* 927–930.

Barron, F., & Harrington, D. M. (1981). Creativity, intelligence, and personality. *Annual Review of Psychology, 32,* 439–476.

Basadur, M. S., & Finkbeiner, C. T. (1985). Measuring preference for ideation in creative problem-solving training. *Journal of Applied Behavioral Science, 21* (1), 37–49.

Basadur, M. S., Graen, G. B., & Green, S. G. (1982). Training in creative problem solving: Effects on ideation and problem finding in an applied research organization. *Organizational Behavior and Human Performance, 30,* 41–70.

Basadur, M. S., Graen, G. B., & Scandura, T. A. (1986). Training effects on attitudes toward divergent thinking among manufacturing engineers. *Journal of Applied Psychology, 71,* 612–617.

Basadur, M., & Hausdorf, P. A. (1996). Measuring divergent thinking attitudes related to creative problem solving and innovation management. *Creativity Research Journal, 9,* 21–32.

Basadur, M. S., Wakabayashi, M., & Graen, G. B. (1990). Individual problem solving styles and attitudes toward divergent thinking before and after training. *Creativity Research Journal, 3,* 22–32.

Baxter, G. P., Shavelson, R. J., Goldman, S. R., & Pine, J. (1992). Evaluation of procedure-based scoring for hands-on science assessment. *Journal of Educational Measurement, 29,* 1–17.

Begley, S. (1995, March 27). Gray matters. *Newsweek,* pp. 48–54.

Besemer, S. P., & O'Quin, K. (1986). Analyzing creative products: Refinement and test of a judging instrument. *Journal of Creative Behavior, 20,* 115–126.

Besemer, S. P., & O'Quin, K. (1993). Assessing creative products: Progress and potentials. In S. G. Isaksen, M. C. Murdock, R. L. Firestien, & D. J. Treffinger (Eds.), *Nurturing and developing creativity: The emergence of a discipline* (pp. 331–349). Norwood, NJ: Ablex.

Besemer, S. P., & Treffinger, D. J. (1981). Analysis of creative products: Review and synthesis. *Journal of Creative Behavior, 15,* 158–178.

Callahan, C. M. (1991). The assessment of creativity. In N. Colangelo & G. A. Davis (Eds.), *Handbook of gifted education* (pp. 219–235). Boston: Allyn & Bacon.

Cattell, R. B. (1963). The personality and motivation of the researcher from measurements of contemporaries and from biography. In C. W. Taylor & F. Barron (Eds.), *Scientific creativity: Its recognition and development* (pp. 119–131). New York: Wiley.

Cattell, R. B., & Butcher, H. (1968). *The prediction of achievement and creativity.* Indianapolis, IN: Bobbs-Merrill.

Cattell, R. B., Eber, H. W., & Tatsuoka, M. M. (1970). *Handbook for the Sixteen Personality Questionnaire (16 PF).* Champaign, IL: Institute for Personality and Ability Testing.

Ceci, S. J. (1990). *On intelligence . . . more or less: A bio-ecological treatise on intellectual development.* Englewood Cliffs, NJ: Prentice-Hall.

Chand, I., & Runco, M. A. (1992). Problem finding skills as components in the creative process. *Personality and Individual Differences, 14,* 155–162.

Clapham, M. M. (1996). The construct validity of divergent scores in the Structure-of-Intellect Learning Abilities Test. *Educational and Psychological Measurement, 56,* 287–292.

Cline, V. B., Richards, J. M., Jr., & Abe, C. (1962). The validity of a battery of creativity tests in a high school sample. *Educational and Psychological Measurement, 22,* 781–784.

Colangelo, N., Kerr, B., Hallowell, K., Huesman, R., & Gaeth, J. (1992). The Iowa Inventiveness Inventory: Toward a measure of mechanical inventiveness. *Creativity Research Journal, 5,* 157–163.

Cooper, E. (1991). A critique of six measures for assessing creativity. *Journal of Creative Behavior, 25,* 194–204.

Cramond, B. (1993). The Torrance Tests of Creative Thinking: From design through establishment of predictive validity. In R. F. Subotnik & K. D. Arnold (Eds.), *Beyond Terman: Contemporary longitudinal studies of giftedness and talent* (pp. 229–254). Norwood, NJ: Ablex.

Cramond, B. (1994, October). We *can* trust creativity tests. *Educational Leadership*, 70–71.

Cramond, B., Martin, C. E., & Shaw, E. L. (1990). Generalizability of creative problem solving procedures to real-life problems. *Journal for the Education of the Gifted, 13,* 141–155.

Cronbach, L. J. (1968). Intelligence? Creativity? A parsimonious reinterpretation of the Wallach-Kogan data. *American Educational Research Journal, 5,* 491–511.

Cropley, A. J. (1972). A five-year longitudinal study of the validity of creativity tests. *Developmental Psychology, 6,* 119–124.

Csikszentmihalyi, M. (1988). Society, culture, and person: A systems view of creativity. In R. J. Sternberg (Ed.), *The nature of creativity: Contemporary psychological perspectives* (pp. 325–339). Cambridge University Press.

Csikszentmihalyi, M., & Getzels, J. W. (1971). Discovery-oriented behavior and the originality of creative products: A study with artists. *Journal of Personality and Social Psychology, 19,* 47–52.

Dacey, J. S. (1989). *Fundamentals of creative thinking.* Lexington, MA: Lexington Books.

Davis, G. A. (1971). Instruments useful in studying creative behavior and creative talent. Part 2, Noncommercially available instruments. *Journal of Creative Behavior, 5,* 162–165.

Davis, G. A. (1973). *Psychology of problem solving: Theory and practice.* New York: Basic.

Davis, G. A. (1989). Testing for creative potential. *Contemporary Educational Psychology, 14,* 257–274.

Davis, G. A. (1992). *Creativity is forever* (3rd ed.). Dubuque, IA: Kendall/Hunt.

Dennis, W. (1956). Age and productivity among scientists. *Science, 123,* 724–725.

Dombroski, T. W. (1979). *Creative problem-solving: The door to progress and change.* Hicksville, NY: Exposition.

Domino, G. (1970). Identification of potentially creative persons from the Adjective Check List. *Journal of Consulting and Clinical Psychology, 35,* 48–51.

Domino, G. (1994). Assessment of creativity with the ACL: An empirical comparison of four scales. *Creativity Research Journal, 7,* 21–33.

Dominowski, R. L., & Dallob, P. (1995). Insight and problem solving. In R. J. Sternberg & J. E. Davidson (Eds.), *The nature of insight* (pp. 33–62). Cambridge, MA: MIT Press.

Dunbar, S. G., Koretz, D. M., & Hoover, H. D. (1991). Quality control in the development and use of performance assessment. *Applied Measurement in Education, 4,* 289–303.

Eisen, M. L. (1989). Assessing differences in children with learning disabilities and normally achieving students with a new measure of creativity. *Journal of Learning Disabilities, 22,* 462–464.

Feldhusen, J. F., & Clinkenbeard, P. R. (1986). Creativity instructional materials: A review of research. *Journal of Creative Behavior, 20,* 153–182.

Feldman, D. H., Csikszentmihalyi, M., & Gardner, H. (1994). *Changing the world: A framework for the study of creativity.* Westport, CT: Praeger.

Finke, R. A. (1995). Creative insight and preinventive forms. In R. J. Sternberg & J. E. Davidson (Eds.), *The nature of insight* (pp. 255–280). Cambridge, MA: MIT Press.

Fox, L. H. (1985). Review of Thinking Creatively with Sounds and Words. In J. V. Mitchell, Jr. (Ed.), *Ninth mental measurements yearbook* (pp. 1622–1623). Lincoln: University of Nebraska Press.

Fox, M. N. (1981). Creativity and intelligence. *Childhood Education, 57,* 227–232.

Frois, J. P., & Eysenck, H. J. (1995). The Visual Aesthetic Sensitivity Test applied to Portuguese children and fine arts students. *Creativity Research Journal, 8,* 277–284.

Fuchs-Beauchamp, K. D., Karnes, M. B., & Johnson, L. J. (1993). Creativity and intelligence in preschoolers. *Gifted Child Quarterly, 37,* 113–117.

Gardner, H. (1983). *Frames of mind: The theory of multiple intelligences.* New York: Basic.

Gardner, H. (1988a). Creative lives and creative works: A synthetic scientific approach. In R. J. Sternberg (Ed.), *The nature of creativity: Contemporary psychological perspectives* (pp. 298–321). Cambridge University Press.

Gardner, H. (1988b). Creativity: An interdisciplinary perspective. *Creativity Research Journal, 1,* 8–26.

Gardner, H. (1993a). *Creating minds.* New York: Basic.

Gardner, H. (1993b). *Multiple intelligences: The theory in practice.* New York: Basic.

Gardner, H., & Nemirovsky, R. (1991). From private intuitions to public symbol systems: An examination of the creative process in Georg Cantor and Sigmund Freud. *Creativity Research Journal, 4,* 1–21.

Gedo, J. E., & Gedo, M. M. (1992). *Perspectives on creativity: The biographical method.* Norwood, NJ: Ablex.

Getzels, J. W., & Jackson, P. W. (1962). *Creativity and intelligence: Explorations with gifted students.* New York: Wiley.

Ghiselin, B. (1963). Ultimate criteria for two levels of creativity. In C. W. Taylor & F. Barron (Eds.), *Scientific creativity: Its recognition and development* (pp. 30–43). New York: Wiley.

Gough, H. G. (1979). A creative personality scale for the Adjective Check List. *Journal of Personality and Social Psychology, 37*, 1398–1405.

Gowan, J. C. (1971). The relationship between creativity and giftedness. *Gifted Child Quarterly, 15*, 239–244.

Gruber, H. E. (1981). *Darwin on man: A psychological study of scientific creativity* (2d ed.). Chicago: University of Chicago Press.

Gruber, H. E., & Davis, S. N. (1988). Inching our way up Mount Olympus: The evolving-systems approach to creative thinking. In R. J. Sternberg (Ed.), *The nature of creativity: Contemporary psychological perspectives* (pp. 243–270). Cambridge University Press.

Guilford, J. P. (1957). Creative abilities in the arts. *Psychological Review, 64*, 110–118.

Guilford, J. P. (1967a). Creativity: Yesterday, today, and tomorrow. *Journal of Creative Behavior, 1*, 3–14.

Guilford, J. P. (1967b). *The nature of human intelligence.* New York: McGraw-Hill.

Guilford, J. P., & Christensen, P. R. (1973). The one-way relation between creative potential and IQ. *Journal of Creative Behavior, 7*, 247–252.

Guilford, J. P., & Hoepfner, R. (1966). Creative potential is related to measures of IQ and verbal comprehension. *Indian Journal of Psychology, 41*, 7–16.

Haier, R. J., & Benbow, C. P. (1995). Sex differences and lateralization in temporal lobe glucose metabolism during mathematical reasoning. *Developmental Neuropsychology, 11*, 405–414.

Haier, R. J., Siegel, B., Tang, C., Abel, L., & Buchsbaum, M. S. (1992). Intelligence and changes in regional cerebral glucose metabolic rate following learning. *Intelligence, 16*, 415–426.

Hall, W., & MacKinnon, D. W. (1969). Personality inventory correlates of creativity among architects. *Journal of Applied Psychology, 53*, 322–326.

Hargreaves, D. J., Galton, M. J., & Robinson, S. (1996). Teachers' assessments of primary children's classroom work in the creative arts. *Educational Research, 38*, 199–211.

Harrington, D. M. (1975). Effects of explicit instructions to "be creative" on the psychological meaning of divergent thinking test scores. *Journal of Personality, 43*, 434–454.

Hattie, J. (1980). Should creativity tests be administered under testlike conditions? An empirical study of three alternative conditions. *Journal of Educational Psychology, 72*, 87–98.

Hattie, J., & Rogers, H. J. (1986). Factor models for assessing the relation between creativity and intelligence. *Journal of Educational Psychology, 78*, 482–485.

Helson, R. (1971). Women mathematicians and creative personality. *Journal of Consulting and Clinical Psychology, 36*, 210–220.

Hennessey, B. A. (1994). The Consensual Assessment Technique: An examination of the relationship between ratings of product and process creativity. *Creativity Research Journal, 7*, 193–208.

Hennessey, B. A., & Amabile, T. M. (1988a). The conditions of creativity. In R. J. Sternberg (Ed.), *The nature of creativity: Contemporary psychological perspectives* (pp. 11–38). Cambridge University Press.

Hennessey, B. A., & Amabile, T. M. (1988b). Story-telling: A method for assessing children's creativity. *Journal of Creative Behavior, 22*, 235–246.

Hill, K. (1991). *An ecological approach to creativity and motivation: Trait and environmental influences in the college classroom.* Unpublished Ph.D. dissertation, Brandeis University, Waltham, MA.

Hocevar, D. (1976). Dimensionality of creativity. *Psychological Reports, 39*, 869–870.

Hocevar, D. (1979a). A comparison of statistical infrequency and subjective judgment as criteria in the measurement of originality. *Journal of Personality Assessment, 43*, 297–299.

Hocevar, D. (1979b, April). *The development of the Creative Behavior Inventory.* Paper presented at the annual meeting of the Rocky Mountain Psychological Association. (ERIC Document Reproduction Service No. ED 170 350)

Hocevar, D. (1979c). Ideational fluency as a confounding factor in the measurement of originality. *Journal of Educational Psychology, 71*, 191–196.

Hocevar, D. (1979d). The unidimensional nature of creative thinking in fifth grade children. *Child Study Journal, 9*, 273–277.

Hocevar, D. (1981). Measurement of creativity: Review and critique. *Journal of Personality Assessment, 45*, 450–464.

Hocevar, D., & Bachelor, P. (1989). A taxonomy and critique of measurements used in the study of creativity. In J. A. Glover, R. R. Ronning, & C. R. Reynolds (Eds.), *Handbook of creativity* (pp. 53–75). New York: Plenum.

Hocevar, D., & Michael, W. B. (1979). The effects of scoring formulas on the discriminant validity of tests of divergent thinking. *Educational and Psychological Measurement, 39*, 917–921.

Hoepfner, R., & Hemenway, J. (1973). *Test of Creative Potential.* Hollywood, CA: Monitor.

Holland, J. L. (1959). Some limitations of teacher ratings as predictors of creativity. *Journal of Educational Psychology, 50,* 219–223.

Holland, J. L., & Nichols, R. C. (1964). Prediction of academic and extracurricular achievement in college. *Journal of Educational Psychology, 55,* 55–65.

Holland, J. L., & Richards, J. M., Jr. (1965). Academic and nonacademic accomplishment: Correlated or uncorrelated? *Journal of Educational Psychology, 56,* 165–174.

Horn, J. L. (1976). Human abilities: A review of research and theory in the early 1970s. *Annual Review of Psychology, 27,* 437–485.

Houtz, J. C., & Krug, D. (1995). Assessment of creativity: Resolving a mid-life crisis. *Educational Psychological Review, 7,* 269–300.

Howieson, N. (1981). A longitudinal study of creativity – 1965–1975. *Journal of Creative Behavior, 15,* 117–134.

Hunsaker, S. L., & Callahan, C. M. (1995). Creativity and giftedness: Published instrument uses and abuses. *Gifted Child Quarterly, 39,* 110–114.

Isaak, M. I., & Just, M. A. (1995). Constraints on thinking in insight and invention. In R. J. Sternberg & J. E. Davidson (Eds.), *The nature of insight* (pp. 281–325). Cambridge, MA: MIT Press.

Isaksen, S. G., & Treffinger, D. J. (1985). *Creative problem-solving: The basic course.* Buffalo, NY: Bearly Limited.

Jackson, P. W., & Messick, S. (1965). The person, the product, and the response: Conceptual problems in the assessment of creativity. *Journal of Personality, 33,* 309–329.

James, L. R., Ellison, R. L., Fox, D. G., & Taylor, C. W. (1974). Prediction of artistic performance from biographical data. *Journal of Applied Psychology, 59,* 84–86.

Johnson, L. D. (1985). Creative thinking potential: Another example of U-shaped development? *Creative Child and Adult Quarterly, 10,* 146–159.

Kaltsounis, B. (1971). Instruments useful in studying creative behavior and creative talent. Part 1, Commercially available instruments. *Journal of Creative Behavior, 5,* 117–126.

Kaltsounis, B. (1972). Additional instruments useful in studying creative behavior and creative talent. Part 3, Non-commercially available instruments. *Journal of Creative Behavior, 6,* 268–274.

Kaltsounis, B., & Honeywell, L. (1980). Additional instruments useful in studying creative behavior and creative talent. Part 4, Noncommercially available instruments. *Journal of Creative Behavior, 14,* 56–67.

Kasof, J. (1995). Explaining creativity: The attributional perspective. *Creativity Research Journal, 8,* 311–366.

Khatena, J. (1982). Myth: Creativity is too difficult to measure! *Gifted Child Quarterly, 26,* 21–23.

Kirton, M. J. (1976). Adaptors and innovators: A description and measure. *Journal of Applied Psychology, 61,* 622–629.

Kirton, M. J. (1981). A reanalysis of two scales of tolerance to ambiguity. *Journal of Personality Assessment, 45,* 407–414.

Kirton, M. J. (Ed.). (1992). *Adaptors and innovators: Styles of creativity and problem solving.* London: Routledge.

Kirton, M. J., & McCarthy, R. (1988). Cognitive climate and organizations. *Journal of Occupational Psychology, 61,* 175–184.

Kogan, N., & Pankove, E. (1974). Long-term predictive validity of divergent-thinking tests: Some negative evidence. *Journal of Educational Psychology, 66,* 802–810.

Larson, G. E., Haier, R. J., & Hazen, K. (1995). Evaluation of a "mental effort" hypothesis for correlations between cortical metabolism and intelligence. *Intelligence, 21,* 267–278.

Lehman, H. C. (1953). *Age and achievement.* Princeton, NJ: Princeton University Press.

Linn, R. L., & Burton, E. (1994). Performance-based assessment: Implications of task specificity. *Educational Measurement: Issues and Practices, 13*(1), 5–8, 15.

Linn, R. L., Burton, E., DeStefano, L., & Hanson, M. (1996). Generalizability of New Standards Project 1993 pilot study tasks in mathematics. *Applied Measurement in Education, 9,* 201–214.

Ludwig, A. M. (1992). The Creative Achievement Scale. *Creativity Research Journal, 5,* 109–124.

Lynott, D. J., & Woolfolk, A. E. (1994). Teachers' implicit theories of intelligence and their educational goals. *Journal of Research and Development in Education, 27,* 253–264.

MacKinnon, D. W. (1962). The nature and nurture of creative talent. *American Psychologist, 17,* 484–495.

MacKinnon, D. W. (1965). Personality correlates of creativity. In M. J. Aschner & C. E. Bish (Eds.), *Productive thinking in education* (pp. 159–171). Washington, DC: National Education Association.

MacKinnon, D. W. (1975). IPAR's contribution to the conceptualization and study of creativity. In I. A. Taylor & J. W. Getzels (Eds.), *Perspectives in creativity* (pp. 60–89). Chicago: Aldine.

MacKinnon, D. W. (1978). *In search of human effectiveness: Identifying and developing creativity.* Buffalo, NY: Creative Education Foundation.

Mahajan, V., & Peterson, R. A. (1985). *Models for innovation diffusion.* Newbury Park, CA: Sage.

Maltzmann, I., Brooks, L., Bogartz, W., & Summers, S. (1958). The facilitation of problem-solving by prior exposure to uncommon responses. *Journal of Experimental Psychology, 56,* 399–406.

Martinsen, Ø. (1993). Insight problems revisited: The influence of cognitive styles and experience on creative problem solving. *Creativity Research Journal, 8,* 291–298.

Martinsen, Ø. (1995). Cognitive styles and experience in solving insight problems: Replication and extension. *Creativity Research Journal, 6,* 435–447.

Mayer, R. E. (1995). The search for insight: Grappling with Gestalt psychology's unanswered questions. In R. J. Sternberg & J. E. Davidson (Eds.), *The nature of insight* (pp. 3–32). Cambridge, MA: MIT Press.

McPherson, J. H. (1963). A proposal for establishing ultimate criteria for measuring creative output. In C. W. Taylor & F. Barron (Eds.), *Scientific creativity: Its recognition and development* (pp. 24–29). New York: Wiley.

Mednick, M. T., & Andrews, F. M. (1967). Creative thinking and level of intelligence. *Journal of Creative Behavior, 1,* 428–431.

Mednick, S. A. (1962). The associative basis for the creative process. *Psychological Review, 69,* 220–232.

Mednick, S. A., & Mednick, M. T. (1967). *Remote Associates Test examiner's manual.* Boston: Houghton Mifflin.

Meeker, M. (1969). *The Structure-of-Intellect: Its interpretation and uses.* Columbus, OH: Charles & Merrill.

Meeker, M., & Meeker, R. (1982). *Structure-of-Intellect Learning Abilities Test: Evaluation, leadership, and creative thinking.* El Segundo, CA: SOI Institute.

Meeker, M., Meeker, R., & Roid, G. H. (1985). *Structure-of-Intellect Learning Abilities Test (SOI-LA) manual.* Los Angeles: Western Psychological Services.

Mendelsohn, G. A. (1976). Associational and attentional processes in creative performance. *Journal of Personality, 44,* 341–369.

Merten, T. (1995). Factors influencing word-association responses: A reanalysis. *Creativity Research Journal, 8,* 249–263.

Milgram, R. M., & Hong, E. (1994). Creative thinking and creative performance in adolescents as predictors of creative attainments in adults: A follow-up study after 18 years. In R. F. Subotnik & K. D. Arnold (Eds.), *Beyond Terman: Contemporary longitudinal studies of giftedness and talent* (pp. 212–228). Norwood, NJ: Ablex.

Milgram, R. M., & Milgram, N. A. (1976). Creative thinking and creative performance in Israeli students. *Journal of Educational Psychology, 68,* 255–259.

Milgram, R. M., & Rabkin, L. (1980). Developmental test of Mednick's associative hierarchies of original thinking. *Developmental Psychology, 16,* 157–158.

Nicholls, J. G. (1983). Creativity in the person who will never produce anything original or useful. In R. S. Albert (Ed.), *Genius and eminence* (pp. 265–279). Oxford: Pergamon.

O'Boyle, M. W., Benbow, C. P., & Alexander, J. E. (1995). Sex differences, hemispheric laterality, and associated brain activity in the intellectually gifted. *Developmental Neuropsychology, 11,* 415–443.

Okuda, S. M., Runco, M. A., & Berger, D. E. (1991). Creativity and the finding and solving of real-world problems. *Journal of Psychoeducational Assessment, 9,* 45–53.

Oldham, G. R., & Cummings, A. (1996). Employee creativity: Personal and contextual factors at work. *Academy of Management Journal, 39,* 607–634.

O'Quin, K., & Besemer, S. P. (1989). The development, reliability, and validity of the revised creative product semantic scale. *Creativity Research Journal, 2,* 267–278.

Osborn, A. A. (1963). *Applied imagination* (3rd ed.). New York: Scribner's.

Parnes, S. J., Noller, R. B., & Biondi, A. M. (1977). *Guide to creative action.* New York: Scribner's.

Pearlman, C. (1983). Teachers as an informational resource in identifying and rating student creativity. *Education, 103,* 215–222.

Pegnato, C. W., & Birch, J. W. (1959). Locating gifted children in junior high schools: A comparison of methods. *Exceptional Children, 25,* 300–304.

Plucker, J. A. (1993). *Gaining acceptance for creativity: A general framework of articulation.* Unpublished manuscript.

Plucker, J. A. (1994a). *Creating minds* [book review]. *Gifted Child Quarterly, 38,* 49–51.

Plucker, J. A. (1994b). Reconceptualizing creativity education. *Gifted Education Press Quarterly, 8(1),* 7–12. (Available from Gifted Education Press, P. O. Box 1586, Manassas, VA 20108)

Reis, S. M., & Renzulli, J. S. (1991). The assessment of creative products in programs for gifted and talented students. *Gifted Child Quarterly, 35,* 128–134.

Renzulli, J. S. (1976). *New directions in creativity.* New York: Harper & Row.

Renzulli, J. S. (1985). Review of Thinking Creativity in Action and Movement. In J. V. Mitchell, Jr. (Ed.), *Ninth mental measurements yearbook* (pp. 1619–1621). Lincoln: University of Nebraska Press.

Renzulli, J. S. (1991). *A general theory for the development of creative productivity through the pursuit of ideal acts of learning.* Paper presented at the biennial meeting of the World Congress for the Gifted and Talented, The Hague, the Netherlands.

Renzulli, J. S. (1994). *Schools for talent development: A practical plan for total school improvement.* Mansfield Center, CT: Creative Learning Press.

Renzulli, J. S., Hartman, R. K., & Callahan, C. M. (1981). Teacher identification of superior students. In W. B. Barbe & J. S. Renzulli (Eds.), *Psychology and education of the gifted* (3rd ed., pp. 151–156). New York: Irvington.

Renzulli, J. S., Owen, S. V., & Callahan, C. M. (1974). Fluency, flexibility, and originality as a function of group size. *Journal of Creative Behavior, 8,* 107–113.

Rickards, T. J. (1994). Creativity from a business school perspective: Past, present, and future. In S. G. Isaksen, M. C. Murdock, R. L. Firestien, & D. J. Treffinger (Eds.), *Understanding and recognizing creativity: The emergence of a discipline* (pp. 331–368). Norwood, NJ: Ablex.

Rimm, S. B. (1983). *Preschool and Kindergarten Interest Descriptor.* Watertown, WI: Educational Assessment Service.

Roe, A. (1952). The psychologist examines 64 eminent scientists. *Scientific American, 187*(5), 21–25.

Rogers, E. M. (1983). *Diffusion of innovations* (3rd ed.). New York: Free Press.

Root-Bernstein, R. S., Bernstein, M., & Garnier, H. (1995). Correlations between avocations, scientific style, work habits, and professional impact of scientists. *Creativity Research Journal, 8,* 115–137.

Rosen, C. L. (1985). Review of Creativity Assessment Packet. In J. V. Mitchell, Jr. (Ed.), *Ninth mental measurements yearbook* (p. 1621). Lincoln: University of Nebraska Press.

Rotter, D. M., Langland, L., & Berger, D. (1971). The validity of tests of creative thinking in seven-year-old children. *Gifted Child Quarterly, 4,* 273–278.

Rubenson, D. L. (1990). The accidental economist. *Creativity Research Journal, 3,* 125–129.

Rubenson, D. L., & Runco, M. A. (1992). The psychoeconomic approach to creativity. *New Ideas in Psychology, 10,* 131–147.

Runco, M. A. (1984). Teachers' judgments of creativity and social validation of divergent thinking tests. *Perceptual and Motor Skills, 59,* 711–717.

Runco, M. A. (1985). Reliability and convergent validity of ideational flexibility as a function of academic achievement. *Perceptual and Motor Skills, 61,* 1075–1081.

Runco, M. A. (1986a). The discriminant validity of gifted children's divergent thinking test scores. *Gifted Child Quarterly, 30,* 78–82.

Runco, M. A. (1986b). Divergent thinking and creative performance in gifted and nongifted children. *Educational and Psychological Measurement, 46,* 375–384.

Runco, M. A. (1986c). Maximal performance on divergent thinking tests by gifted, talented, and nongifted children. *Psychology in the Schools, 23,* 308–315.

Runco, M. A. (1987a). The generality of creative performance in gifted and nongifted children. *Gifted Child Quarterly, 31,* 121–125.

Runco, M. A. (1987b). Interrater agreement on a socially valid measure of students' creativity. *Psychological Reports, 61,* 1009–1010.

Runco, M. A. (1989a). The creativity of children's art. *Child Study Journal, 19,* 177–189.

Runco, M. A. (1989b). Parents' and teachers' ratings of the creativity of children. *Journal of Social Behavior and Personality, 4,* 73–83.

Runco, M. A. (1991). The evaluative, valuative, and divergent thinking of children. *Journal of Creative Behavior, 25,* 311–319.

Runco, M. A., & Albert, R. S. (1985). The reliability and validity of ideational originality in the divergent thinking of academically gifted and nongifted children. *Educational and Psychological Measurement, 45,* 483–501.

Runco, M. A., & Albert, R. S. (1986). The threshold theory regarding creativity and intelligence: An empirical test with gifted and nongifted children. *Creative Child and Adult Quarterly, 11,* 212–218.

Runco, M. A., & Bahleda, M. D. (1986). Implicit theories of artistic, scientific, and everyday creativity. *Journal of Creative Behavior, 20,* 93–98.

Runco, M. A., & Basadur, M. (1993). Assessing ideational and evaluative skills and creative styles and attitudes. *Creativity & Innovation Management, 2,* 166–173.

Runco, M. A., & Chand, I. (1994). Problem finding, evaluative thinking, and creativity. In M. A. Runco (Ed.), *Problem finding, problem solving, and creativity* (pp. 40–76). Norwood, NJ: Ablex.

Runco, M. A., & Chand, I. (1995). Cognition and creativity. *Educational Psychology Review, 7,* 243–267.

Runco, M. A., Johnson, D. J., & Bear, P. K. (1993). Parents' and teachers' implicit theories of children's creativity. *Child Study Journal, 23,* 91–113.

Runco, M. A., McCarthy, K. A., & Svenson, E. (1994). Judgments of the creativity of artwork from students and professional artists. *Journal of Psychology, 128,* 23–31.

Runco, M. A., & Mraz, W. (1992). Scoring divergent thinking tests using total ideational output and a creativity index. *Educational and Psychological Measurement, 52,* 213–221.

Runco, M. A., Noble, E. P., & Luptak, Y. (1990). Agreement between mothers and sons on ratings of creative activity. *Educational and Psychological Measurement, 50,* 673–680.

Runco, M. A., & Okuda, S. M. (1988). Problem finding, divergent thinking, and the creative process. *Journal of Youth and Adolescence, 17,* 211–220.

Runco, M. A., & Okuda, S. M. (1991). The instructional enhancement of the flexibility and originality scores of divergent thinking tests. *Applied Cognitive Psychology, 5,* 435–441.

Runco, M. A., Okuda, S. M., & Thurston, B. J. (1987). The psychometric properties of four systems for scoring divergent thinking tests. *Journal of Psychoeducational Assessment, 2,* 149–156.

Runco, M. A., & Pezdek, K. (1984). The effect of television and radio on children's creativity. *Human Communications Research, 11,* 109–120.

Runco, M. A., & Smith, W. R. (1992). Interpersonal and intrapersonal evaluations of creative ideas. *Personality and Individual Differences, 13,* 295–302.

Runco, M. A., & Vega, L. (1990). Evaluating the creativity of children's ideas. *Journal of Social Behavior and Personality, 5,* 439–452.

Schaefer, C. E., & Anastasi, A. (1968). A biographical inventory for identifying creativity in adolescent boys. *Journal of Applied Psychology, 52,* 42–48.

Shapiro, R. J. (1970). The criterion problem. In P. E. Vernon (Ed.), *Creativity* (pp. 257–269). New York: Penguin.

Shaywitz, B. A., Shaywitz, S. E., Pugh, K. R., Constable, R. T., Skudlarski, P., Fulbright, R. K., Bronen, R. A., Fletcher, J. M., Shankweiler, D. P., Katz, L., & Gore, J. C. (1995). Sex differences in the functional organization of the brain for language. *Nature, 373* (6515), 607–609.

Siegel, S. M., & Kaemmerer, W. F. (1978). Measuring the perceived support for innovation in organizations. *Journal of Applied Psychology, 63,* 553–562.

Simonton, D. K. (1979). Multiple discovery and invention: Zeitgeist, genius, or chance? *Journal of Personality and Social Psychology, 37,* 1603–1616.

Simonton, D. K. (1984a). Creative productivity and age: A mathematical model based on a two-step cognitive process. *Developmental Review, 4,* 77–111.

Simonton, D. K. (1984b). Melodic structure and note transition probabilities: A content analysis of 15,618 classical themes. *Psychology of Music, 12,* 3–16.

Simonton, D. K. (1986a). Biographical typicality, eminence, and achievement style. *Journal of Creative Behavior, 20,* 14–22.

Simonton, D. K. (1986b). Presidential personality: Biographical use of the Gough Adjective Check List. *Journal of Personality and Social Psychology, 51,* 1–12.

Simonton, D. K. (1988a). Creativity, leadership, and chance. In R. J. Sternberg (Ed.), *The nature of creativity: Contemporary psychological perspectives* (pp. 386–426). Cambridge University Press.

Simonton, D. K. (1988b). *Scientific genius: A psychology of science.* Cambridge, MA: Harvard University Press.

Simonton, D. K. (1994). *Greatness: Who makes history and why.* New York: Guilford.

Smith, J. M., & Schaefer, C. E. (1969). Development of a creativity scale for the Adjective Check List. *Psychological Reports, 34,* 755–758.

Snow, R. E., & Yalow, E. (1982). Education and intelligence. In R. J. Sternberg (Ed.), *Handbook of human intelligence* (pp. 493–585). Cambridge University Press.

Speedie, S. M., Treffinger, D. J., & Houtz, J. C. (1976). Classification and evaluation of problem solving tasks. *Contemporary Educational Psychology, 1,* 52–75.

Starko, A. J. (1995). *Creativity in the classroom: Schools of curious delight.* New York: Longman.

Stein, M. (1974). *Stimulating creativity,* vol. 1. New York: Academic.

Stein, M. (1975). *Stimulating creativity,* vol. 2. New York: Academic.

Sternberg, R. J. (1985a). *Beyond IO.* Cambridge University Press.

Sternberg, R. J. (1985b). Implicit theories of intelligence, creativity, and wisdom. *Journal of Personality and Social Psychology, 49,* 607–627.

Sternberg, R. J. (1987). Implicit theories: An alternative to modeling cognition and its development. In J. Bisanz, C. J. Brainerd, & R. Kail (Eds.), *Formal methods in developmental psychology* (pp. 155–192). New York: Springer-Verlag.

Sternberg, R. J. (1988a). A three-facet model of creativity. In R. J. Sternberg (Ed.), *The nature of creativity* (pp. 125–147). Cambridge University Press.

Sternberg, R. J. (1988b). *The triarchic mind: A new theory of human intelligence.* New York: Penguin.

Sternberg, R. J. (1990). Wisdom and its relation to intelligence and creativity. In R. J. Sternberg (Ed.), *Wisdom* (pp. 142–159). Cambridge University Press.

Sternberg, R. J. (1993). The concept of 'giftedness': A pentagonal implicit theory. In G. R. Bock & K. Ackrill (Eds.), *The origins and development of high ability* (pp. 5–21). New York: Wiley.

Sternberg, R. J., Conway, B. E., Ketron, J. L., & Bernstein, M. (1981). People's conception of intelligence. *Journal of Personality and Social Psychology, 41,* 37–55.

Sternberg, R. J., & Davidson, J. E. (1992). Problem solving. In M. C. Aikin (Ed.), *Encyclopedia of educational research* (Vol. 3, pp. 1037–1045). New York: Macmillan.

Sternberg, R. J., & Lubart, T. I. (1991). An investment theory of creativity and its development. *Human Development, 34,* 1–31.

Sternberg, R. J., & Lubart, T. I. (1992). Buy low and sell high: An investment approach to creativity. *Current Directions in Psychological Science, 1,* 1–5.

Sternberg, R. J., & Lubart, T. I. (1995). *Defying the crowd: Cultivating creativity in a culture of conformity.* New York: Free Press.

Tannenbaum, A. J. (1983). *Gifted children: Psychological and educational perspectives.* New York: Macmillan.

Taylor, C. W. (1964). Widening horizons in creativity. New York: Wiley.

Taylor, C. W. (1988). Various approaches to and definitions of creativity. In R. J. Sternberg (Ed.), *The nature of creativity: Contemporary psychological perspectives* (pp. 99–121). Cambridge University Press.

Taylor, C. W., & Barron, F. (1963a). Preface. In C. W. Taylor & F. Barron (Eds.), *Scientific creativity: Its recognition and development* (pp. xiii–xix). New York: Wiley.

Taylor, C. W., & Barron, F. (Eds.). (1963b). *Scientific creativity: Its recognition and development.* New York: Wiley.

Taylor, C. W., & Ellison, R. L. (1966). *Alpha Biological Inventory.* Salt Lake City, UT: Institute for Behavioral Research.

Taylor, C. W., & Ellison, R. L. (1967). Predictors of scientific performance. *Science, 155,* 1075–1079.

Taylor, C. W., & Holland, J. (1964). Predictors of creative performance. In C. W. Taylor (Ed.), *Creativity: Progress and potential* (pp. 15–48). New York: McGraw-Hill.

Taylor, C. W., & Williams, F. E. (Eds.). (1966). *Instructional media and creativity.* New York: Wiley.

Taylor, D. W. (1960). Thinking and creativity. *Annals of the New York Academy of the Sciences, 91,* 108–127.

Thompson, B., & Anderson, B. V. (1983). Construct validity of the divergent production subtests from the Structure-of-Intellect Learning Abilities Test. *Educational and Psychological Measurement, 43,* 651–655.

Torrance, E. P. (1962). *Guiding creative talent.* Englewood Cliffs, NJ: Prentice-Hall.

Torrance, E. P. (1965). *Rewarding creative behavior.* Englewood Cliffs, NJ: Prentice-Hall.

Torrance, E. P. (1967). The Minnesota Studies of Creative Behavior: National and international extensions. *Journal of Creative Bahavior, 1,* 137–154.

Torrance, E. P. (1968). A longitudinal examination of the fourth grade slump in creativity. *Gifted Child Quarterly, 12,* 195–199.

Torrance, E. P. (1969). Prediction of adult creative achievement among high school seniors. *Gifted Child Quarterly, 13,* 223–229.

Torrance, E. P. (1971). Stimulation, enjoyment, and originality in dyadic creativity. *Journal of Educational Psychology, 62,* 45–48.

Torrance, E. P. (1972a). Can we teach children to think creatively? *Journal of Creative Behavior, 6,* 114–143.

Torrance, E. P. (1972b). Career patterns and peak creative achievements of creative high school students 12 years later. *Gifted Child Quarterly, 16,* 75–88

Torrance, E. P. (1972c). Predictive validity of the Torrance Tests of Creative Thinking. *Journal of Creative Behavior, 6,* 236–252.

Torrance, E. P. (1972d). Predictive validity of "bonus" scoring for combinations on repeated figures tests of creative thinking. *Journal of Psychology, 81,* 167–171.

Torrance, E. P. (1974). *Torrance Tests of Creative Thinking: Norms-technical manual.* Lexington, MA: Ginn.

Torrance, E. P. (1976). Creativity testing in education. *Creative Child and Adult Quarterly, 1,* 136–148.

Torrance, E. P. (1979). Unique needs of the creative child and adult. In A. H. Passow (Ed.), *The gifted and talented: Their education and development.* 78th NSSE Yearbook (pp. 352–371). Chicago: National Society for the Study of Education.

Torrance, E. P. (1981a). Empirical validation of criterion-referenced indicators of creative ability through a longitudinal study. *Creative Child and Adult Quarterly, 6,* 136–140.

Torrance, E. P. (1981b). Predicting the creativity of elementary school children (1958–1980) – and the teacher who "made a difference." *Gifted Child Quarterly, 25,* 55–62.

Torrance, E. P. (1981c). *Thinking creatively in action and movement.* Bensenville, IL: Scholastic Testing Service.

Torrance, E. P. (1982). Misperceptions about creativity in gifted education: Removing the limits on learning. In S. N. Kaplan, A. H. Passow, P. H. Phenix, S. M. Reis, J. S. Renzulli, I. S. Soto, L. H. Smith, E. P. Torrance, & V. S. Ward, *Curriculum for the gifted: Selected proceedings of the first national conference on curricula for the gifted/talented* (pp. 59–74). Ventura, CA: Office of the Ventura County Superintendent of Schools.

Torrance, E. P. (1988). The nature of creativity as manifest in its testing. In R. J. Sternberg (Ed.), *The nature of creativity: Contemporary psychological perspectives* (pp. 43–75). Cambridge University Press.

Torrance, E. P. (1995). Insights about creativity: Questioned, rejected, ridiculed, ignored. *Educational Psychology Review, 7,* 313–322.

Torrance, E. P., & Ball, O. E. (1984). *Torrance Tests of Creative Thinking: Revised manual.* Bensenville, IL: Scholastic Testing Services.

Torrance, E. P., & Gupta, R. K. (1964). *Programmed experiences in creative thinking, Final report on Title VII Project to the U.S. Office of Education.* Minneapolis: Bureau of Educational Research, University of Minnesota.

Torrance, E. P., & Khatena, J. (1970). What kind of person are you? *Gifted Child Quarterly, 14,* 71–75.

Torrance, E. P., Khatena, J., & Cunnington, B. F. (1973). *Thinking creatively with sounds and words.* Bensenville, IL: Scholastic Testing Service.

Torrance, E. P., & Safter, H. T. (1989). The long range predictive validity of the Just Suppose Test. *Journal of Creative Behavior, 23,* 219–223.

Torrance, E. P., Tan, C. A., & Allman, T. (1970). Verbal originality and teacher behavior: A predictive validity study. *Journal of Teacher Education, 21,* 335–341.

Torrance, E. P., & Wu, T. H. (1981). A comparative longitudinal study of the adult creative achievement of elementary school children identified as highly intelligent and as highly creative. *Creative Child and Adult Quarterly, 6,* 71–76.

Treffinger, D. J. (1989). *Student Invention Evaluation Kit: Field test edition.* Sarasota, FL: Center for Creative Learning.

Treffinger, D. J., & Poggio, J. P. (1972). Needed research on the measurement of creativity. *Journal of Creative Behavior, 6,* 253–267.

Tushman, M. L., & Moore, W. L. (Eds.). (1988). *Readings in the management of innovation* (2d ed.). New York: HarperBusiness.

Wakefield, J. F. (1985). Towards creativity: Problem finding in a divergent-thinking exercise. *Child Study Journal, 15,* 265–270.

Wakefield, J. F. (1991). The outlook for creativity tests. *Journal of Creative Behavior, 25,* 184–193.

Walberg, H. J. (1988). Creativity and talent as learning. In R. J. Sternberg (Ed.), *The nature of creativity: Contemporary psychological perspectives* (pp. 340–361). Cambridge University Press.

Wallace, D. B., & Gruber, H. E. (Eds.). (1989). *Creative people at work.* New York: Oxford University Press.

Wallach, M. A. (1976, January–February). Tests tell us little about talent. *American Scientist,* 57–63.

Wallach, M. A., & Kogan, N. (1965). *Modes of thinking in young children: A study of the creativity–intelligence distinction.* New York: Holt, Rinehart, & Winston.

Wallach, M. A., & Wing, C. W., Jr. (1969). *The talented student: A validation of the creativity–intelligence distinction.* New York: Holt, Rinehart, & Winston.

Ward, W. C. (1968). Creativity in young children. *Child Development, 39,* 737–754.

Wasik, J. L. (1974). Teacher perceptions of behaviors associated with creative problem solving performance. *Educational and Psychological Measurement, 34,* 327–341.

Weisberg, R. W. (1993). *Creativity: Beyond the myth of genius.* New York: Freeman.

Welsh, G. S., & Barron, F. (1963). *Barron-Welsh Art Scale.* Palo Alto, CA: Consulting Psychologists Press.

Westberg, K. L. (1991). The effects of instruction in the inventing process on students' development of inventions. *Dissertation Abstracts International, 51.* (University Microfilms No. 9107625)

Williams, F. E. (1979). Assessing creativity across William's "cube" model. *Gifted Child Quarterly, 23,* 748–756.

Williams, F. E. (1980). *Creativity assessment packet.* Buffalo, NY: DOK Publishers.

Witt, L. A., & Beorkrem, M. N. (1989). Climate for creative productivity as a predictor of research use-fulness and organizational effectiveness in an R&D organization. *Creativity Research Journal, 2,* 30–40.

Yamada, H., & Tam, A. Y.-W. (1996). Prediction study of adult creative achievement: Torrance's longi-tudinal study of creativity revisited. *Journal of Creative Behavior, 30,* 144–149.

Yamamoto, K., & Chimbidis, M. E. (1966). Achievement, intelligence, and creative thinking in fifth-grade children: A correlational study. *Merrill-Palmer Quarterly, 12,* 233–241.

Zuboff, S. (1988). *In the age of the smart machine.* New York: Basic.

4 Experimental Studies of Creativity

MARK A. RUNCO AND SHAWN OKUDA SAKAMOTO

Creativity is among the most complex of human behaviors. It seems to be influenced by a wide array of developmental, social, and educational experiences, and it manifests itself in different ways in a variety of domains. The highest achievements in the arts are characterized by their creativity, as are those in the sciences. Creativity is also quite common in a wide range of everyday activities (Runco, 1996; Runco & Richards, 1998). Theories of creativity have attempted to recognize the inherent complexity by defining creativity as a syndrome (MacKinnon, 1983; Mumford & Gustafson, 1988) or even a complex (Albert & Runco, 1986).

The complex nature of creativity suggests that meaningful research must take multiple influences and diverse forms of expression into account. Experimental research on creativity is useful precisely for this reason. Experimental methods utilize various controls to reduce complexity to a manageable level. They deal with complexity by manipulating one or a set of independent variables, controlling (and thereby minimizing the effects of) confounding or nuisance variables and measuring changes in the dependent variables. These dependent variables are the components, traits, or indicators of creativity. The independent variables are the developmental, social, educational, cognitive, and emotional influences.

Manipulation and control are the defining characteristics of experimental research. As Hyman (1964) described it, experimentation focuses on "*induced changes* in performance . . . [creativity is] something which can change or be changed within an individual rather than [being] something that varies among individuals" (p. 70). This distinguishes experimental work from psychometric work; the latter focuses on the individual differences that exist without experimental manipulation.

Experimental techniques reduce the complexity surrounding creativity and thereby allow reliable measurement and sound inferences about causality. There is, however, a trade-off. This is because manipulation may elicit "induced changes" that may not be all that indicative of behavior that occurs in the natural environment. This trade-off between control, or *internal validity*, and generalizability, or *external validity*, is inherent in all experimental research, but the problem is especially acute in studies of creativity. That is because creativity may depend on spontaneity, which is contrary to control. In addition to spontaneity, creativity is also by definition novel. This implies unpredictability, which can be contrasted with the accuracy of predictions that is often used to gauge the success of experimental research (Skinner, 1975).

Issues of internal and external validity are not the only concerns for experimental research on creativity. For the present purposes, they may not even be the most important concerns. After all, the research reviewed in this chapter first appeared in peer-reviewed journals, implying a systematic preselection. Research that is accepted for publication is probably at least adequate in its internal validity; otherwise it would not be published.

The most important criterion for evaluating the experimental research on creativity concerns the representativeness of the behaviors sampled. This is why we started this chapter with a brief discussion about creativity being defined as a complex. The key question for experimental research is, How well does it capture the range of influences and the diverse expressions of creativity? This question is especially important because it is not something that can be addressed in individual experiments. It can be addressed only in a comprehensive overview. Individual investigations often exercise control by focusing on one aspect of the creativity complex; but in this chapter we are able to stand back from the individual investigations and consider the larger issue of representativeness.

A reliance on traditional experimental criteria and conventional assumptions about internal validity could work against efforts to conduct studies that are representative of the creativity complex. Traditional criteria could dictate that only certain parts of the creativity complex are studied. In psychometric terms this is the issue of *content validity,* which is a consideration when a test or assessment contains questions that reflect only the material about which questions can easily be written. When a test does not contain a sufficiently representative sample of questions, it has dubious content validity. The parallel in the experimental research arises when only certain components and traits from the creativity complex are investigated. These may not be the most important components and traits; they might instead be the easiest to justify, operationalize, and test.

As Hyman (1964) described it, experimental work should emphasize

> *immediate* rather than remote *determinants* of creative performance. Although I believe that dispositions, personality traits, and stable, long-term factors are important, I also believe that we may be wise to see first how much we can change creative performance by proximate controls as "hints," "directions," "sets," and other instructional and task variables. Only after we know the range within which we can change performance by these more immediate inputs can we adequately study the contributions of the more remote factors. (p. 70)

Following Hyman (1964), this chapter focuses on proximate, contiguous, immediate influences on creativity. Hyman's own work on instructional manipulations gives us a good place to begin. We then review the experimental research on perception and imagery, then on affect, and then on arousal and attention. The two last sections of the chapter review the relevant operant research and the experimental research on intrinsic motivation. In the conclusion to this chapter we revisit the issue of representativeness, address the limitations of the experimental approach, recommend some specific directions and topics for future research, and offer suggestions about collaborations between experimental research and several other approaches (i.e., the psychometric and the cognitive) that should maximize our understanding of creativity.

MANIPULATIONS OF INFORMATION AND STRATEGIES

Many experiments manipulate the information given to experimental subjects before they solve problems or complete some sort of creativity tasks. Apparently such informational manipulations can facilitate divergent thinking, insight, intuition, and creative problem solving. The manipulation is usually in the form of directions given orally, textually, or even through audio and video media.

Instructions with Open-Ended Tasks

Hyman (1964) manipulated the instructions and information given to individuals before they received open-ended problems. In one study Hyman administered an open-ended Tourist Problem, which was essentially a kind of realistic divergent thinking task, to 166 college students. The students were asked to generate various means for increasing the number of European tourists to the United States. Subsamples of students also received information about either four common solutions or four uncommon solutions. Other subsamples were asked to devote 20 minutes to (a) constructive criticism (i.e., identifying the strengths, or "good features," of the four sample solutions), (b) critical criticism (identifying weaknesses), or (c) a syllogism. This last subsample was the nonexperimental (control) group. After generating their own ideas, the students were asked to evaluate "various ideas that were relevant to the Tourist problem" (p. 72). Finally they received two additional open-ended tasks to assess transfer. This last assessment was useful as a check of the generalizability of findings. Recall in this regard the question mentioned earlier about external validity and the generalizability of experimental results.

Only slight differences were found among effectiveness ratings of the solutions given by the various subsamples of students. What difference existed indicated that the students who spent their 20 minutes constructively criticizing the sample solutions tended to give the most effective solutions. Yet content analyses suggested that examinees in this same instructional condition tended to imitate the solutions given as samples. The solutions given by the students who were asked to identify weaknesses reflected more originality. This is very important because originality is probably the most widely respected trait in the creativity complex (Barron, 1995; Runco & Charles, 1993). It is also important because differences between the constructive and critical experimental conditions may have reflected changes in the attitudes of the students and not just the information received in the course of the experiment. Davis (1992, p. 294) proposed that attitudes are the easiest facet of the creativity complex to change (see also Basadur, Wakabayashi, & Graen, 1990; Runco & Basadur, 1993). Davis was referring to changes resulting from education or training, but attitudes may be similarly amenable to experimental manipulation.

Hyman (1964) expressed some surprise about the performance of the subsample asked to be critical and identify weaknesses. Earlier he had asked a group of engineers to "design an automatic Warehousing system" (Hyman, 1961), and group differences were more obvious (and statistically significant) than they were when the students tackled the Tourist Problem. The engineers in the constructive condition supplied more creative solutions to the Warehousing Problem and on subsequent problems given to assess transfer. Hyman explained the more significant difference between the informational conditions in terms of the fit of the Warehousing Problem with the interests of the engineers. This explanation is consistent with the recent theories that describe the importance of realism for problem-solving efforts (Baltes, Staudinger, Maercker, & Smith, 1995; Runco & Chand, 1994) and of problem ownership (Basadur, 1994). It also suggests that experimental research should take individual differences into account. In this case the individual differences might explain the fit of the problem with the research participants.

In later research Harrington (1975) confirmed that explicit information can be communicated by task instructions to increase originality scores on divergent thinking tests. Runco (1985) extended this by demonstrating that flexibility scores could be increased independently of originality scores, which suggests that the two represent distinct cognitive processes. It also suggests that flexible ideation does not guarantee that original ideas will be found (see also Runco & Okuda, 1991). Runco, Eisenman, and Harris (1997) used informational manipulations and uncovered differences between explicit instructions focusing on the originality of ideas and instructions focusing on the appropriateness of solutions. These particular instructions were suggested by the numerous definitions of creativity as requiring some index of appropriateness to go along with originality. For a review of the research on explicit instructions targeting creativity, see Runco and Nemiro (1996).[1]

The efficacy of informational manipulations has been demonstrated with several different samples of subjects, in addition to college students (Chand & Runco, 1992; Harrington, 1975; Hyman, 1964). Kramer, Tegan, and Knauber (1970) and Pesut (1990), for example, examined effects in a sample of nurses; Martinsen and Kaufmann (1991) employed military personnel; Hyman (1961) worked with engineers; and Runco (1986) compared effects with gifted and nongifted children. All groups seemed to benefit from the information supplied, though some benefited more than others.

Runco's (1986) comparison indicated that it was the nongifted children who benefited the most from the explicit information provided by the informational manipulations. Runco suggested that this may have occurred because the gifted children were already using the strategies supplied by the information, so the presented information was of little use. This finding is consistent with the results from Davidson and Sternberg's (1983) comparison of gifted and nongifted children who solved problems that were designed to facilitate the selective encoding, selective combination, or selective comparisons of information. Results indicated that nongifted children benefited the most from the manipulation and the preselection of key information by the experimenters. As was the case in Runco's (1986) investigation, there was a possible confounding by "regression toward the mean," but the groups may have differed because the gifted children were selective even without the experimental manipulations.

Other individual differences were suggested by Martinsen and Kaufmann's (1991) investigation of analytic and exploratory problem-solving strategies. In this research four experimental groups were selected from 148 members of the Norwegian military corps. Each group was given explicit instructions. In particular, they were requested to (a) analyze and think verbally, (b) analyze and think in pictures, (c) explore and think verbally, or (d) explore and think in pictures. *Exploration* was defined for the subjects as using trial and error, and *analysis* was defined as applying known principles to find solutions. Subjects were presented with the Two-String Problem and the Hat Rack Problem, both insight tasks. Subjects also received a questionnaire to identify *assimilator–explorer* cognitive styles, a spatial ability test, the vocabulary subtest of the WAIS, and a verbal analogies test. The measure of cognitive style was predicated on the idea that assimilators tend to extend a problem-solving approach as far as possible, while explorers vary their problem-solving strategies, even when the task does not require a shift. Results revealed that instructions to use an exploratory strategy contributed to success at solving the problems. More important was the statistical interaction between the type of instruction and the assimilator–explorer scores. This indicated that assimilators benefited from instructions to explore and visualize, and explorers benefited from instructions to analyze and verbalize.

Summary

Martinsen and Kaufmann's (1991) findings suggest that cognitive style represents a potentially very important dimension of individual differences. This particular dimension can be taken into account in experimental studies. Their finding that assimilators will "most likely follow the implicit instructions that are part of the problem formulation" (meaning that they are most likely to respond well to explicit instructions) might apply to all research on explicit instructions. Other important dimensions of individual differences will be highlighted throughout this chapter.

The experimental research just reviewed indicates that information is vital for creative thinking and creative performance. This idea is compatible with the research on strategies, for strategies depend on procedural knowledge (Davidson & Sternberg, 1983; Gruber, 1988; Keegan, 1996; Root-Bernstein, Bernstein, & Garnier, 1993). It is also compatible with suggestions from case studies that creative persons tend to be immersed in their fields (Albert, 1994) and that there is a minimum of 10 years of work necessary for expertise to develop

(Simon & Chase, 1973). Immersion would likely allow the individual to acquire an exceptionally large amount of information about his or her area of expertise.

The irony is that it is possible that too much information can lead to a kind of rigidity, and rigidity, like fixity, makes original thinking very difficult, if not impossible. That possibility was suggested by Martinsen's (1995) empirical demonstration that there is an optimal level of experience for creative work. It is also suggested by the experimental comparisons of video, audio, and textual information that will be described in the next section.

MANIPULATIONS OF PROBLEMS

The research just reviewed focused on informational manipulations that pertained to the solution of problems – how solutions are found and how they are recognized as viable solutions. It is also possible, however, to manipulate an individual's perception of the problem itself. This line of work is potentially very important because creative achievements often result from *problem finding* (Getzels, 1975) rather than just problem solving, and problem finding often requires *problem definition*, which is often just a restructuring of the problem (Runco, 1994b). As we shall see, manipulations of problem perception also allow tests of media effects and of the Gestalt proposition that insight and solution are found quickly (rather than gradually) after a problem is restructured or redefined.

Manipulations of Audio, Video, and Text Information

Meline (1976), Runco and Pezdek (1984), and Greenfield, Geber, Beagles-Roos, Farrar, and Gat (1981) compared audio, video, and text presentations of problems. The assumption was that a video presentation is indicative of what is experienced when someone watches television; an audio presentation is indicative of listening to the radio; and text is indicative of reading. These studies were, in that light, comparing television with two other media. What is most significant for the present purposes is that video information is the most explicit of the three media; it provides visual and auditory information, with plenty of detail. For this reason this line of research is relevant to the question of the effects of explicit information given to individuals when they solve problems.

In the investigation by Greenfield et al. (1981), schoolchildren were allowed to watch (or listen or read) a story. The story was stopped before it was completed, and they were asked how it might end. Greenfield et al. found differences in the way the three media influenced the conclusions to the stories generated by the children. The video elicited low originality scores. The differences were not easy to interpret, however, because the plot of the story might have compelled the children to finish it using the existing plot lines. That, in turn, could have minimized the number of alternatives, and thereby the originality of the stories. With this in mind Runco and Pezdek (1984) replicated the earlier study but asked their examinees about alternatives only after the story (again, presented via video, audio, or text) was completed. Their questions were more hypothetical, which should have allowed more alternatives to be considered. In fact, the questions posed in this research were similar to those found on a common test of divergent thinking called the "what if" test (Torrance, 1974). Unlike Greenfield et al. (1981), Runco and Pezdek (1984) found no differences in the originality of the conclusions elicited by the various media.

The overarching problem with this line of work is that the subjects had only a short exposure to the various media. The animated stories presented via video, for example, lasted less than 10 minutes. For this reason the findings from the research may not apply well to the natural environment. In the natural environment children watch 20–30 hours of television each week, and this may very well inhibit originality (cf. Singer & Singer, in press; Sneed & Runco, 1992). The research comparing different media does raise the question of potential drawbacks to information. Television and video may be too explicit. They may present too much detail, contain too few gaps, and minimize opportunities for viewers to creatively construct their own interpretations of experience. The research on insight, described next, addresses a parallel issue, namely the conditions of fixity.

Insight

Weisberg and Alba (1981) tested the idea that insight problems are difficult because subjects experience rigidity, or a kind of *fixity,* when faced with certain problems, and this in turn limits the search for solutions. Weisberg and Alba used the nine-dot problem, which contains a 3 × 3 symmetrical matrix of dots; the objective is to connect all nine with four straight connected lines. (Solutions with just three and even one line were presented by Adams, 1979.) Fixation in the nine-dot problem keeps one's search within the boundaries implied by the perimeter dots. Solutions require that lines be drawn outside of the perimeter. Weisberg and Alba (1981) gave hints to subjects (after the subjects had failed to solve the problem), suggesting that they draw lines outside the boundaries. Not even 25% of the subjects solved the problem after they had received the hints, leading Weisberg and Alba to reject the Gestalt prediction about fixity and sudden insights. Other investigations of insight and restructuring were reported by Burnham and Davis (1969) and Epstein (in press).

Baker-Sennett and Ceci (1996) were convinced that creative thinking requires some sort of "leap." They tested this idea by comparing perceptual and verbal problems about which varying amounts of information were given. The perceptual information was given in images that had been scanned into a computer, some with significant portions of information omitted, some with very little information omitted. The linguistic information was in the form of common words with letters omitted. Subjects were asked to determine what the image represented or which word was listed, using as few cues (as little information) as they could. Baker-Sennett and Ceci (1996) found that the pattern of cue usage by subjects was related to success on the insight problems. The subjects who "leaped" and needed few cues earned higher scores on the insight problems. Baker-Sennett and Ceci also reported a drop in the efficiency of cue usage by elementary-school-age children. Later in this chapter we review experimental research on intuition (e.g., Bowers, Regehr, Balthazard, & Parker, 1990) and feelings of warmth (Jausovec, 1989, 1994; Jausovec & Bakracevic, 1995; Metcalfe, 1986), each of which fits well with Baker-Sennett and Ceci's (1996) findings about leaps.

Manipulations of Features and Structures

Presumably the problem restructuring required by the insight problems in the research just reviewed is indicative of underlying cognitive restructuring by the experimental participants. Such restructuring may play a role in other kinds of creative thinking, in addition to insight.

Baughman and Mumford (1995) examined restructuring as an influence on categorical and conceptual thought. They asked college students to use presented category exemplars to generate a new category that would account for all exemplars. Three manipulations were used: One varied the degree of interrelatedness among the original exemplar categories. The second varied the instructions given with tasks that were interspersed among the category tasks. Instructions "were intended to induce active application of the operations held to underlie the combination and reorganization process, prior to generating the new category." These operations included the active searching for and mapping of features (see Hyman, 1964). The third manipulation required that students in a particular group elaborate on the categories they themselves had generated.

Baughman and Mumford (1995) used category and exemplar quality and originality as dependent measures. Both were derived from ratings given by trained judges using a modified consensual assessment. Analyses of covariance allowed Baughman and Mumford to control individual differences in general reasoning, divergent-thinking ability, and problem-finding ability. Results demonstrated that the manipulations intended to elicit feature searches "influenced originality [but] only if they occurred in tandem." Apparently, the "effective application of search and mapping operations can proceed in two ways: either by (a) inclusion, where shared unusual features are used to construct the new category, or (b) exclusion, where mundane features shared by the stimulus categories are eliminated as a basis for constructing a new category" (Baughman & Mumford, 1995). Category elaboration had only a limited effect.

This line of work is important in part because it did not rely on insight problems. Insight problems have long been used in problem-solving research, and insight does seem to be very important for particular creative performances (see, e.g., Davidson & Sternberg, 1983; Gruber, 1988). Yet many insight problems are closed rather than open ended, and it can be difficult to be original on tasks that are not open ended. Problems like the nine-dot problem, for example, have limited solutions, and in this sense they may tap more convergent than divergent thinking (Guilford, 1968; Runco, 1992a). The dependent measures used by Baughman and Mumford (1995), on the other hand, were open ended and examinees could be original when solving them. Such open-ended tasks also have an advantage in that they rely on skills that are probably indicative of those necessary for creative performances in the natural environment. This suggests that research results like Baughman and Mumford's (1995) have some degree of external validity.

Intuition

Many eminent creators have reported following a hunch of some sort when doing their work (see Gardner, 1994; Schaffner, 1994). This suggests that creative insights and ideas, like problems, may themselves be ill defined, at least at first. In a word, they may begin as some sort of intuition.

Bowers et al. (1990) defined intuition as "a preliminary perception of coherence (pattern, meaning, structure) that is at first not consciously represented, but which nevertheless guides thought and inquiry toward a hunch or hypothesis about the nature of the coherence in question" (p. 74). To examine it empirically, they asked college students to solve a set of nonverbal and verbal tasks. In each task the students were to identify the coherent pattern, and if they were uncertain, they were asked to guess. Bowers et al. very carefully examined the guesses, assuming them to be indicative of accurate intuitive hunches. And indeed, the guesses often were related to the correct solutions. This led Bowers et al. (1990) to conclude that individuals can "respond discriminatively to coherences that they could not identify" (p. 72) and that tacit understandings of such coherences "guided people gradually to an explicit representation of it in the form of a hunch or hypothesis" (p. 72).

Summary

It is very important that different kinds of problems and tasks are used in the experimental research on creativity. We already contrasted divergent- and convergent-thinking tasks, but it is also important that nonverbal kinds of creativity have been examined by Baker-Sennett and Ceci (1996) and Bowers et al. (1990). There are other data supporting a distinction between verbal and nonverbal creativity (Runco & Albert, 1985; Smith, Michael, & Hocevar, 1990; Wallach & Kogan, 1965) and good reason to suspect that particular skills (e.g., verbal or nonverbal) are requisite for creative work in certain fields (Gardner, in press; Li, in press). Thus, what we learn about verbal creativity may not apply to nonverbal creativity, and experimental research must investigate each if it is to understand the range of skills and preferences within the creativity complex.

A similar line of reasoning has led researchers to study the preverbal processes that underlie creativity. As we will see in the next section, preverbal processes play a role in perception, imagery, and several kinds of mental synthesis.

MENTAL SYNTHESIS, IMAGERY, AND PERCEPTION

Preverbal processes are difficult to manipulate and assess, precisely because they are preverbal. Verbal processes can be manipulated with verbal instructions and informational manipulations, but how do you manipulate preverbal processes? Several answers are suggested by the experimental research.

Rothenberg (1991; Rothenberg & Hausman, in press) described a series of investigations testing *Janusian* and *homospatial* processes and their relationship to creativity. The former was named after the Roman god Janus, who "had faces that simultaneously looked in diametrically opposite directions" (Rothenberg, 1991, p. 183). Homospatial processes were defined as "actively conceiving two or more discrete entities or elements occupying the same mental space, a conception leading to the articulation of new identities" (Rothenberg & Hausman, in press). Homospatial thinking was experimentally manipulated via slides, which were superimposed for writers and other artists who participated in the research. The superimposition was intended to facilitate homospatial insights. Expert judgments confirmed that metaphors suggested by the superimposed images were more creative than those elicited by other slide presentations, which were designed to facilitate finding metaphors via analogical, associational, and gestalt processes.

Finke (1990) argued that *preinventive forms* are useful for invention. Preinventive forms are ideas and images used by the individual before he or she actually conceptualizes a specific product. To examine them Finke and Slayton (1988) gave subjects 3 randomly chosen parts from a group of 15 basic geometric forms and alphabets. Subjects were asked to imagine combining the parts to create a pattern. A large number of creative patterns were produced in this manner, many of which would have been difficult to predict. In a subsequent investigation, Finke (1990) instructed subjects to use three-dimensional shapes and simple object parts to construct a useful and "practical object" or "device." Additionally, subjects were asked to be flexible and to construct objects using diverse object categories. The subjects responded by producing a number of inventions, which were judged for their practicality and originality. Significantly, Finke found that the subjects produced a larger number of creative inventions when both the parts and the object category had been randomly selected at the beginning of each session.

What would happen if the subjects were asked to generate images and forms using the parts and components, but did not know the particular kind of object that the final product would represent? To test this Finke's (1990) next experiment required participants to formulate images using object parts, and they were told that these preinventive forms should be "interesting and potentially meaningful." The subjects were given a randomly chosen object category, after they imagined and designed their preinventive form, and were then told to interpret their forms as a practical object or device. Finke found that these subjects produced significantly more creative inventions, compared with the subjects who had been given an object category prior to the generation of their preinventive forms.

The practicality of this line of work is suggested by the strategies recommended by Finke (in press; also see Weber, 1996). Finke argued, for instance, that creative inventions may be generated by first producing a preinventive image, and then evaluating its utility and application. This parallels the fundamental premise of *brainstorming* in the sense that judgment is postponed. Like other types of strategies (Runco, 1992a, 1992b), there may be tactics that dictate what to do and others that dictate what not to do, but as Finke and Slayton (1988) cautioned, subjects "might never have had any of these visual discoveries without explicit, guiding instructions for how to imagine combining the parts . . . [but] the artificial constraints that such instructions impose may severely restrict the subjects' ability to make *creative* discoveries" (p. 252). Surely certain kinds of instructions can inhibit creative thought, either by misdirecting the individual toward unproductive lines of thought or by eliciting emotional and attitudinal blocks and rigidity. More will be said about attentional blocks in the section of this chapter devoted to affect and motivation.

First the experimental technique developed by Smith (1990; Smith & Van der Meer, 1994, in press) should be reviewed. It too involves creative perception and imagery, or what Smith calls percept-genesis. This process is assessed with the Identification Task, wherein subjects view a monitor on which a face is flashed. The face is intentionally ambiguous and includes subliminal verbal descriptors, which allow "the experimenter . . . to manipulate the projected identification" (Smith, 1990, p. 162) by the experimental subject and with the person whose face is projected. Smith and Van der Meer (1994) claimed that the subliminal message "prepares the viewer for the face and influences how it is perceived" (p. 162). The second part of Smith's percept-genesis technique is the Creative Functioning Test (CFT). It also uses tachistoscope presentations, but in it simple stimuli (e.g., a bowl and bottle) are presented. The presentation begins with very brief exposures (0.01 second) of the stimulus, which gradually increase. Subjects are asked to describe what they think they have seen, and they are encouraged to share impressions even if they are not certain about the object. The assumption of this test is that creative persons are extraordinarily open to subjective impressions, alternatives, and insights. This assumption is frequently made in theories of creativity (see Martindale, Anderson, Moore, & West, 1996). The stimuli and the exposure times are manipulated using the CFT. Smith reported that individuals who form impressions on the CFT (especially in reaction to the very brief and therefore ambiguous stimulus presentations) tend to report positive interpretations of the faces on the Identification Task, even if they had subliminal verbal messages about illness superimposed on them. Subjects are ostensibly counteracting the subliminal manipulation. Creative persons also use more emotional words in the Identification Test (see Hoppe & Kyle, 1990).

Summary

Several different kinds of preverbal processes have been investigated. Some, like those described by Rothenberg and Hausman (in press) and the strategies recommended by Finke (in press), reflect the intentional efforts of individuals. Other processes, like those examined by Smith et al. (1990), are less intentional – and perhaps more spontaneous. This connection to spontaneity may be very important because it implies that there is some generalizability to creativity in the natural environment, where creative efforts are typically self-initiated. Other very important unintentional processes have been investigated in the research on creativity and affect.

AFFECT AND CREATIVITY

Some experimental research has been designed to compare and contrast specific affective states in terms of their relationships to creativity (Isen, Daubman, & Nowicki, 1987; Isen, Johnson, Mertz, & Robinson, 1985; Vosburg, in press). Other experimental work has focused on underlying influences on those states, including arousal and attention (Martindale & Greenough, 1973; Mendelsohn & Griswold, 1964, 1966).

Feelings of Warmth

Metcalfe (1986) investigated the emotions that individuals may experience as they make progress toward solving a problem. She collected data by asking subjects to report, at regular intervals, how close they felt they were to solving (i.e., completing) a problem. Metcalfe referred to the reports as feelings of warmth (FoW). These suggested differences between insight and noninsight problems, with the former showing more abrupt changes in FoW than the latter.

Jausovec (1989, 1994; Jausovec & Bakracevic, 1995) collected FoW data, along with physiological data (i.e., heart rate) and information about creative problem-solving performance. In one of his experiments the heart rate of subjects was monitored as they solved four different kinds of problems. FoW reports were collected every 15 seconds. For controls, Jausovec and Bakracevic conducted the experiment in a soundproof room with the temperature of the setting and the time of day held constant. Analyses showed a continual increase in heart rate when subjects solved so-called *interpolation problems* (which were essentially convergent-thinking problems), but a sudden increase when they solved insight problems. Significantly, changes in heart rate were consistent with the subjects' own FoW ratings, at least on some of the problems. Heart rate during the solving of open-ended divergent-thinking problems both increased and decreased, which Jausovec and Bakracevic (1995) interpreted as indicative of a hypothesis-testing problem-solving strategy. The finding that the physiological states were related to cognitive performance and to the self-reported descriptions of affective states may be taken as a kind of validation of the FoW techniques, but these same techniques do have their problems (see Weisberg, 1992).

Manipulations of Anxiety and Conflict

Hoppe and Kyle (1990) manipulated affective states by asking various samples of subjects, including a subsample of commissurotomy patients, to view a brief film containing various symbols of personal loss and mourning. The symbols were both visual (e.g., an empty crib) and musical. No words were used in the film. Experimental subjects saw the film four times. EEGs were recording during the viewings, and written and spoken data were collected after each viewing. Subjects were, for example, asked to write down four sentences about the film and to answer a series of questions about the same. In contrast to control subjects (matched for handedness, sex, age, and linguistic and ethnic background), the commissurotomy subjects used few affect-laden words in their sentences. They "applied adjectives sparsely, revealing a speech that was dull, uninvolved, flat, and lacking in color and expressiveness" (p. 151). They also "tended not to fantasize about, imagine, or interpret the symbols." They focused on the circumstances and ignored their feelings. Hoppe and Kyle concluded that it was *alexithymia,* a paucity of affect, that kept the commissurotomy patients from being imaginative. Based on their work with various groups, Hoppe and Kyle hypothesized that many relatively uncreative persons may have the same trouble, although not resulting from surgery. This was labeled a *functional commissurotomy.*

Smith et al. (1990) compared several sets of test-taking directions, one of which was intended to induce test anxiety, in terms of its effect on performance on creativity measures.[2] First a group of 132 students was divided into experimental and control groups. Creativity was assessed with verbal, mathematical, and figural (visual) divergent-thinking tests. The directions that were intended to induce test anxiety did so in several ways: First, they emphasized that the tests were to be "strictly graded." Examinees were told to ensure that each answer was the "absolute best" they could give. Second, examinees were constrained in that they were told not to go back and rework any ideas or responses. Third, competition was introduced by promising that cash would be given to the "top three scorers." Fourth, examinees were timed (2 minutes per task), told about the time limits, and even shown the stopwatch. The control group, on the other hand, was told to relax, have fun, and work however they wanted (e.g., going back and forth among tasks). Comparisons indicated that only the mathematical fluency scores were significantly inhibited by the induced anxiety. To explain this effect, Smith et al. cited a theory of *cognitive interference* and *attentional capacity* (Tobias, 1985), the basic idea being that anxiety can interfere with retrieval processes, and this in turn can inhibit ideation. With limited attentional capacity, anxiety may force examinees to divide their attention between the task and their concerns about competition and high scores (see Kasof, in press). Other demonstrations of the inverse relationship between constraint and creativity (Amabile, in press; Finke & Slayton, 1988; Wallach & Kogan, 1965) suggest that the impact of anxiety and constraint may be even more profound than Smith et al. (1990) found. Surely replications are in order, especially given the practical implications of the findings. Several implications for educational settings are explored in the discussion section of this chapter.

James (1995) used less obtrusive methods and focused on the affect associated with conflict. This work was unobtrusive in the sense that the subjects experienced the conflict only vicariously: They simply read about it. Nonetheless, results supported the hypotheses. Many individuals reacted with original ideation to the essay that described conflict, but there were significant individual differences. Those reacting in the most original fashion had a social orientation and those not reacting in an original fashion tended toward an instrumental orientation.

Earlier we pointed out that an optimal level of information is related to creative thinking, and beyond the optimum, gains may actually inhibit creativity. Heinzen (1989) presented data sugesting that there is also an optimal level of affect that is most conducive to original thinking. Using a brief realistic divergent-thinking task, he found that moderate challenge elicited the most original problem solving. Very likely this conclusion about optimal levels applies to other kinds of affect as well.

Summary

Hoppe and Kyle (1990) and Smith et al. (1990) demonstrated that affect can influence creative performances. Other research has pinpointed conflict and challenge as influences (Heinzen, 1989; James, 1995; Sheldon, 1995) and suggested that there are physiological correlates of affect that may play a role in some creative problem solving (Jausovec & Bakracevic, 1995).

Obviously it would be advantageous to determine experimentally exactly how affect exerts its influence. It may be that certain emotions selectively inhibit or facilitate critical stages in the creative process (e.g., depression facilitating the criticism of one's own work). It is also possible that the impact of affect is a result of the arousal or shift in attention that may accompany certain emotional states. We explore these possibilities in the next section.

AROUSAL AND ATTENTION

Arousal is often defined in physiological terms. *Attention,* on the other hand, is typically defined in terms of the allocation of cognitive resources.

Arousal

Martindale and Greenough (1973) examined the impact of arousal on creative thinking by manipulating noise levels during problem solving. Three experimental conditions were compared: low, medium, and high arousal. Eighty male undergraduates were assigned to one of six groups, two for each experimental condition. One group was given the Remote Associates Test (RAT), and the other was given the Similarities Test of divergent thinking. The low- and medium-arousal groups did not differ significantly in their RAT scores. The medium-arousal group, however, had significantly higher RAT scores than the high-arousal group. On the Similarities Test, there was no difference between the high and medium groups, but the high-arousal group gave significantly more responses than the low-arousal group. These findings generally support the idea that arousal is associated with performance on tests of creative thinking. Subsequent research using noise has produced less consistent results (Kasof, in press; Toplyn & Maguire, 1991; Voss, 1977).

Martindale and Armstrong (1974) used cortical activation as an index of arousal. The undergraduate students in their experiment were tested for creative potential, and then EEG measurements of cortical activity were taken. The first EEG trial was a baseline recording of alpha. Subjects were told that a tone they would hear during the trials was activated by a particular mental state. During the next trial, the tone sounded, and the trial treated as an index of habituation. The next three trials were alpha enhancement trials. In the final trial, subjects were asked to try to keep the tone off. Analyses indicated that subjects with higher scores on the divergent-thinking test and the RAT exhibited lower alpha and larger decrements in alpha when the stimulus was introduced. These same subjects showed a more immediate acquisition of control during the alpha enhancement trials, but they demonstrated little improvement across trials. The low-scoring subjects, on the other hand, showed continual improvement, and they eventually reached the level of control of the subjects who earned high scores on the RAT and divergent-thinking measure. Subjects from the high-scoring group were noticeably better at alpha suppression in the final trial. These results suggest that highly creative subjects have fairly good short-term control of alpha, and they demonstrate control in a short period of time. Interestingly, Martindale and Armstrong (1974) attributed this last finding to a sensitivity to internal cues associated with alpha control (see Martindale et al., 1996). The idea of sensitivity is noteworthy because it is consistent with the openness to subliminal impressions that Smith and Van der Meer (1994, in press) found to characterize creative persons. Although they attributed the lack of improved alpha control across trials to boredom with the experiment, Martindale and Armstrong did acknowledge the possibility of a "genuine losing of control." Still they concluded that creative subjects are sometimes better able to focus attention than other persons, and they suggested that this is related to the ability to escape into secondary process states. This explanation is consistent with existing theories of secondary process (e.g., Eysenck, 1993; Kris, 1952; Rothenberg, 1991) and with other research on attention (e.g., Kasof, in press; Toplyn & Maguire, 1991).

Martindale and Hasenfus (1978) conducted two experiments to further examine the relationship between EEG alpha and creativity. In the first, 12 subjects from an undergraduate creative-writing class were asked to think of the plot for a fantasy story and then to write out the story. The formulation of a plot was thought to be indicative of the inspirational stage of the creative process. The writing was taken to be indicative of the elaboration stage. (For a discussion of stage theories of creative thinking, see Runco [1994b] and Wallas [1926].) The participants were placed into a creative or uncreative group based on their instructor's ratings. Comparisons indicated that the creative group operated at a low level of arousal during the inspiration stage. During the inspiration stage, creative subjects demonstrated higher alpha than did the less creative subjects.

In the second experiment, subjects were asked to free-associate (using random words) during the inspiration stage. During the elaboration stage, they were asked to tell a fantasy story. Thirty-two subjects were chosen from a larger group based on scores from the Shipley Vocabulary Test, the RAT, and the Alternate Uses test. These tests were used to match subjects for verbal ability and then place them into one of four groups representing high and low levels of performance on the alternate uses test and the RAT. Half of the subjects were given instructions to be as original as possible and the other half were given instructions with no reference to being original. EEGs were taken. The highly creative subjects who received instructions demonstrated slightly less alpha during the inspiration than during the elaboration phase. The other groups showed even less alpha during inspiration than during elaboration.

Attention

Three experimental investigations have manipulated attention with noise (Kasof, in press; Martindale & Greenough, 1973; Toplyn & Maguire, 1991). Presumably noise can significantly influence attention, and attention can then influence creative thinking. In the most recent of these investigations, Kasof assessed creativity by asking subjects to compose a poem while sitting in a quiet setting. Later some of the research participants were asked to compose another poem, but at this point the manipulation was introduced: These individuals experienced either predictable or unpredictable noise (intended to narrow their attention), the contents of which was either unintelligible or intelligible. The control group wrote their second poem while sitting in the quiet setting. Judgments of the creativity of the poems were significantly but moderately correlated with *breadth of attention,* which was assessed with a self-report. Noise seemed to inhibit creativity. This inhibition was especially obvious with the unpredictable and intelligible noise and for participants who had wide trait breadth of attention. Kasof suggested that both broad attentional capacity and the capacity for parallel processing are useful for writing poems and that these can be impaired by noise.

Summary

The research using noise can be interpreted in the light of the associative theories that posit that original ideas are remote. Remote ideas are found at the end of a chain of associations (Mednick, 1962). When solving problems or thinking divergently, obvious ideas are generated first, and when these are exhausted more remote associations are found. The capacity for broad attention may allow very remote ideas and associations to be found. The experimental manipulation of attention confirms that broad attentional capacities are associated with the generation of a large number of ideas and divergent associations (Kasof, in press; Mendelsohn, 1976; Mendelsohn & Lindholm, 1972; Toplyn & Maguire, 1991; Wallach, 1970). The effects of arousal may be explained in a similar way. Arousal may induce a temporary broadening of attentional capacity.

Kasof (in press) defined what we just called "broad attentional capacity" as a trait variable, the assumption being that broad attention reflects a stable characteristic. Other extracognitive tendencies may lead an individual to search for and consider remote and original ideas. One that has received a great deal of attention is intrinsic motivation, the benefits of which have been demonstrated in a large number of investigations. These are reviewed next.

INTRINSIC MOTIVATION

Intrinsic motivation has long been recognized as one of the most prevalent traits in studies of the creative personality (e.g., MacKinnon, 1965). The experimental research suggests that intrinsic motivation is tied to the creative process as well as the creative personality. In this sense it has a logical and functional association with creative work, as well as a post hoc empirical one.

Amabile, Goldfarb, and Brackfield (1990) investigated *coaction* (defined by the presence of other persons) and *surveillance* (expected evaluation by experts) as possible influences on intrinsically motivated and creative work. The dependent variables in this research involved a verbal task (American haiku) and a collage. The manipulation was essentially informational – what the subjects were told – but the information was supported by props. When told that they would be working with others (and to test coaction), for example, subjects worked in a room with chairs placed such that they suggested imminent use. For the evaluation treatment, subjects were informed that their haiku would be judged by hand-writing professionals and the collages by professional artists. Results indicated that the expectation of evaluation influenced both the poetry and the collages. They were, however, very specific, influencing originality but not the technical quality of the creative products. Post-treatment questions indicated that subjects were relatively dissatisfied with their work in the expected evaluation conditions. This supports the interpretation that the work was neither intrinsically motivated nor satisfying in terms of personal standards. Note that the evaluation was expected – no audience was present in the evaluation condition. (In fact, the effects of surveillance were explained in terms of implied evaluation.) The effects may have differed if an audience was in fact present. Amabile et al. found only ambiguous effects of coaction.

Hennessey (1989), Howe (1992), and Stohs (1992) extended this line of work. Hennessey, for example, examined the effects of extrinsic factors on the creativity of children as they worked on computers. She manipulated the source of the evaluation (human vs. computer) and confirmed that both can inhibit the creativity of children's work on computers. Moreover, both reward and evaluation had similar inhibitive effects. Younger children were less sensitive to the effects than the older children (age range 7–13 years). Howe (1992) manipulated evaluative feedback with a computer and compared the graphic designs of undergraduate students who worked on a computer with those who did not. Designs from the former were judged more positively than those from the latter, especially along dimensions that described the designs as *organic* and *well crafted.* Judgments of the *logic* or *value* of the designs did not differ significantly. Curiously, judgments of *originality* also did not differ significantly.

Like Amabile et al. (1990) and Hennessey (1989), Howe (1992) relied on ratings from judges who were asked to use their own personal definitions of creativity. Judges were not given more specific criteria or definitions.[3] This is an important point because, from the experimental perspective, such latitude may undermine experimental control. Who knows what judges actually think about when examining the products? Why not give them precise information to ensure that they are using the same features in their judgments? The assumption is that asking judges to use their own opinions allows them to be more consistent and reliable. And when Howe (1992), Hennessey (1989), and Amabile et al. (1990) scrutinized the reliability of the judges' ratings, which is where the subjectivity would be most apparent, the reliabilties seemed to be adequate. These were, however, adjusted reliabilites, and as Nunnally (1976) described them, they are really estimates and hypothetical. Such adjusted reliabilities should not be used as substitutes for actual indices of interjudge agreement.

Summary

The experimental research suggests that various conditions (e.g., coaction, survelliance, evaluation) can undermine the intrinsic motivation that contributes to creative efforts. The effect has been found when evaluations are given by various sources (including computers), though the impact is somewhat selective. In one study, originality was inhibited but technical quality was not.

Admittedly, there are some questions about the explanatory power of the concept of intrinsic motivation (Runco, 1994a, 1994c), but these do not suggest that creative persons are not intrinsically motivated. They offer cognitive explanations for what underlies intrinsic motivation (Lazarus, 1991). For the present purposes, intrinsic motivation is an adequate label for a useful dependent variable.[4]

Recall here that Hennessey (1989) found evaluation and rewards to have inhibitive effects. This would seem to contradict research showing that reinforcement is associated with increased originality and divergent thinking (e.g., Holman, Goetz, & Baer, 1977; Moran & Liou, 1982; Ward, Kogan, & Pankove, 1972). This brings us to the experimental research that uses operant techniques.

OPERANT EXPERIMENTATION

It may come as a slight surprise that there is operant research to review in a chapter on creativity. After all, the operant perspective emphasizes overt behavior, and we have already proposed that affect, attitude, and other subjective processes may be vital aspects of the creativity complex. That being said, the operant research has developed several methods that are applicable to creative behaviors, and from a traditional experimental perspective the research designed and conducted with operant assumptions is among the best there is. What the operant researchers have done is to target reliable behavioral indicators, such as novelty and several kinds of flexibility. Novelty is especially important because it can be defined in very reliable and even observable terms (as uniqueness), and it is very clearly tied to originality. Novel behavior is unique and therefore original.

Pryor, Hoag, and O'Reilly (1969) manipulated the novel behaviors of dolphins. They reinforced specific swimming and leaping responses that were novel for each particular training session. A novel response was reinforced continuously within a session, but never reinforced in any other sessions. As a result, the dolphins became progressively faster at emitting novel behaviors in each new session.

Epstein, Kirshnit, Lanza, and Rubin (1984) used differential reinforcement to condition pigeons to (a) push a small box toward a colored spot on the floor of the chamber, and (b) climb on a box in order to peck a banana-shaped object that was hanging from a string. These behaviors were conditioned separately and at different times. However, after the conditioning was complete, the pigeons were placed in a situation where they had to push the box before they could climb on it and reach the banana-shaped object. In this new situation, the pigeons did indeed spontaneously integrate the two behaviors. The result was a chain of behaviors never before emitted – that is, novel behavior. The explanation is that novel behaviors result from the *spontaneous integration of previously learned responses*. Epstein (in press) described several demonstrations of the integration of three and later even five discrete behaviors.

Pushing a box is not a behavior that is typical for a pigeon – after all, they have no arms. It was, however, analogous to tasks presented to chimpanzees by Kohler (1925), the implication being that higher-order insight behavior observed in a chimpanzee can be explained in terms of operant principles and the spontaneous integration of previously learned responses. Admittedly, this approach does not explain the actual integration. Epstein demonstrated how discrete behaviors of a hungry pigeon can be controlled with "pigeon chow," but the integration of those behaviors occurs somewhere, and one obvious explanation is that it reflects a kind of cognition that is similar to the associative processes so often used to describe creative insights (Mednick, 1962, Runco, 1985). There is also some question that the "spontaneous integration" that occurs in the insight of pigeons may not generalize to humans.

Epstein's (in press) *generativity theory* applies more directly to human behavior. It retains the operant focus on measurable behavior, but defines behavior as novel, fluid, and probabilistic. The probabilistic nature of behavior reflects the large number of options available and the transformation functions that influence responses. (These are thought to have a neurophysiological basis.) Computer simulations of problem solving as influenced by such functions are in progress.

Most important for the present purposes are the operant investigations employing human subjects. These usually parallel the work of Pryor et al. (1969) in their reliance on differential reinforcement: Reinforcers are selectively given for novel behavior. Glover and Gary (1976), for example, manipulated reinforcement, the amount of practice, and instructions given to subjects. In one experimental condition, eight 4th- and 5th-grade children had 10 minutes to "list all possible uses" for an object that was listed on the chalkboard of their classroom. During the five-day baseline portion of the study, reinforcement was given to each student. The experimental treatment was presented on the sixth day of the study. It involved (a) discussion of the different kinds of divergent thinking (i.e., fluency, flexibility, elaboration, and originality), and (b) competition between two groups (the two halves of the class) for the best uses. The team that scored the most points was reinforced with early recess and milk and cookies. On days 7 through 25, one of the four indices was chosen. The groups were to focus their efforts on that one index, and they again competed with one another. Not surprisingly, findings indicated that each of the indices increased when reinforcement was directed at that particular index. This was especially true of the elaboration index (which indicates that details are added to one line of thought) and least true of the originality index (which indicates unusual or unique ideas). Fluency and flexibility (the number of ideas and their variety, respectively) showed moderate changes in their respective instructional conditions.

This investigation is yet another demonstration of the efficacy of explicit instructions. Yet with the experimental design used by Glover and Gary (1976), the unique contribution of the instructions cannot be inferred. This is because the treatment used in this study was tripartite. It involved reinforcement, instructions, and practice. Glover and Gary seemed to be interested primarily in whether or not these standardized indices of creativity were susceptible to treatment, rather than in which part of treatment was most effective.

In related research Goetz and Salmonson (1972) demonstrated the efficacy of reinforcement given for the number of forms used in children's paintings. This is directly relevant to discussions of creativity because painting is an unambiguously creative domain and because the number of forms used in the paintings may be indicative of a kind of flexibility, which, like originality, is a common index of creative potential (Runco, 1985). Goetz and Baer

(1973) demonstrated the effectiveness of reinforcement given to preschool children for their building with blocks. Their *diversity of block-building* dependent variable is also probably indicative of flexibility.

In two very important experiments, Holman et al. (1977) evaluated the *generalization* and *maintenance* (stability) of the conditioned tendency to emit novel behavior. The first experiment gave two preschool boys access to an easel, three colors of paint, and three paint brushes. Each boy worked alone and was allowed to paint as long as he liked. After each painting session, the boy received a token and a toy. Each child also had sessions of block building, with a token and toys given after all blocks were used. No reinforcement was given during the sessions. After a baseline of three sessions, one of the boys received six sessions in which verbal encouragement was administered for using new forms in the paintings. Five baseline sessions followed (without reinforcement) and then eight more treatment conditions with reinforcement, again contingent on new forms. The second child received a similar ABAB reversal design (i.e., baseline, treatment, baseline, treatment), although the number of sessions in his baseline was different from that of the first child, as was the number of sessions wherein reinforcement was given.

Both painting and block building were scored for *form diversity* (the number of forms used, relative to a predetermined category of acceptable forms) and *new forms* (the number of novel forms). Results indicated that the reinforcement led to increased form diversity and new forms. One child reacted by using approximately 7 forms for each painting during the baseline, and between 9 and 12 in the treatment conditions. The other child used 8–12 forms in the treatment conditions, up at least 5 from the baseline. Just as important is the fact that the effect of the reinforcement generalized to block building. Even though the children were not specifically encouraged to use diverse forms in block building, their form diversity scores reflected the treatment of the ABAB design. The new forms scores for painting also increased with reinforcement and followed the reversal design, but unlike form diversity scores, effects did not generalize to block building. Holman et al. (1977) suggested that the reinforcement of form diversity might be used in educational settings, but the reinforcement of new forms might not result in generalized effects. Because Holman et al. studied only preschool children, their conclusions and recommendations presumably apply directly only to that level.

The second experiment presented by Holman et al. (1977) applied operant procedures to Lego block building and felt-pen drawing. This allowed Holman et al. to determine if the generalization of new forms would occur if the nonreinforced task was topographically similar to the reinforced task (i.e., blocks to Lego, painting to drawing). Results supported this prediction, although the effects were only moderate. The evidence for the maintenance of the effects, however, was very convincing. That is, reinforcement resulted in lasting and durable changes in behavior.

Individual differences moderate the impact of the operant manipulations. In one demonstration of this, Moran and Liou (1982) gave college students the Wide Range Vocabulary Test and Raven's Standard Progressive Matrices, and four groups were defined: high-ability/reward, high-ability/no reward, low-ability/reward, low-ability/no reward. Two divergent-thinking tests were administered, with the two (experimental) rewarded groups told that they could earn monetary rewards if they did well on the divergent-thinking tasks. (Unfortunately Moran and Liou did not report how long after the tests the rewards were administered. This may be a critical point because a great deal of research in other areas has demonstrated that the closer a consequence is to a behavior, the more effective it will be as reinforcer or punisher.) Results indicated that there was a significant interaction between reward and level of ability. High-ability subjects in the reward condition had lower scores than high-ability subjects in the no-reward condition, and low-ability subjects in the reward condition had higher scores than those in the no-reward condition. This was true of the three separate divergent-thinking indices as well as the total score. On the vocabularly and matrices tests, main effects for reward were not significant.

Summary

The operant research reviewed in this section exemplifies the power of experimental methods and provides convincing demonstrations of how reinforcers can be causally related to novel, original, and varied (e.g., new forms) behaviors.[5] Note that the research suggests a *causal* relationship. Typically this term is avoided because causality is not guaranteed by research showing associations; but the designs used in the operant research are typically powerful enough for us to be confident about the causal relationships between the independent variables (e.g., reinforcement) and the dependent variables (e.g., novel behavior).

A second virtue of the operant research is what Stokes and Baer (1977) termed the *technology for generalization and maintenance.* This technology was originally developed for clinical treatment – to ensure that behaviors acquired during treatment would be maintained and would generalize to the natural environment – but Holman et al. (1977) demonstrated that it could be applied to issues of enhancement and education. Given the concern about external validity throughout the experimental literature, it would behoove others investigating creativity to follow the lead of Holman et al. (1977) and routinely examine the generalization and maintenance of experimental manipulations.

What external validity already exists in the research can be seen when findings have direct applications in the classroom, the home, or the organizational setting. More will be said in the following section of this chapter about implications for those settings. In the next section we also highlight limitations of the experimental research and, as promised, revisit the questions about the coverage and representativeness of the dependent variables used in the experimental research on creativity.

DISCUSSION

Although most empirical research on creativity exercises some sort of control, only experimental work *manipulates* and controls. The manipulation is the unique feature in the experimental research. It is impossible in archival research and many case studies (e.g., Albert, 1994, in press; Davis, Keegan, & Gruber, in press; Ludwig, 1995; Simonton, in press; Wallace & Gruber, 1989) and is nothing short of anathema to naturalistic observations and survey research (e.g., Saracho, 1992). In naturalistic studies manipulation is obtrusive and precludes the external validity that is the salient virtue of all kinds of nonexperimental research. Nonexperimental research does exercise control, but it is typically statistical or ex post facto and not the kind of active manipulation that characterizes the experimental investigations.

Does the Experimental Research Cover the Creativity Complex?

What exactly does the experimental research suggest about the creativity syndrome? Given the length of this review it might be useful to highlight some of the specific findings:

- Explicit instructions are often used as manipulations and can provide an individual with knowledge and strategies and thereby facilitate original and flexible ideation and insight. Both procedural and declarative information can be given to subjects via explicit instructions.
- Individual differences have been found to moderate the reactions to explicit instructions. In other words, some individuals benefit more than others from explicit information. Individual differences probably moderate a wide range of experimental effects.
- Information from directions or experience can contribute to creative problem solving, but

the effects may be more gradual than predicted by Gestalt theory and models of sudden insight.

- There seems to be an optimal level of knowledge for creative work; more is not necessarily better for creativity.
- Imagery can be manipulated to maximize the creativity of subsequent insights about inventions.
- Intuition manifests itself in a reliable manner on both verbal and nonverbal tasks. People detect coherent information (Bowers et al., 1990), have accurate feelings of knowing (Jausovec, 1989; Metcalfe, 1986), and sometimes leap from partial information to a solution or insight (Baker-Sennett & Ceci, 1996).
- Creative persons are sensitive to subjective interpretations and subliminal, preconscious, internal cues, as well as preverbal information. These may be related to the intuitions, feelings of knowing, and leaps of insight.
- Creative individuals are able to control alpha states and can do so in a short period of time (Martindale et al., 1996).
- Creative thinking seems to be associated with a broad attentional capacity, which may be influenced by levels of arousal. Individual differences are suggested by what Kasof (in press) called trait breadth of attention.
- Both intrinsic motivation and contingencies have been associated with certain kinds of novel behavior and original work. Again, individual differences have been identified; here they indicate that contingencies are moderated by ability levels (Moran & Liou, 1982).
- Certain kinds of affect, including conflict or tension, are associated with creative problem solving. Positive affect may be associated with creativity on other kinds of problems, and for both negative and positive affect there seems to be an optimum level. The dictim "moderation in all things" applies well to (all) influences on creative work.
- Different kinds of problems may be differentially related to creativity and may elicit performances that vary in their generalizability.

Most significant may be the experimental studies of percept genesis (Smith 1990; Smith & Van der Meer, in press), preinventive forms (Finke, in press), intuition (Bowers et al., 1990), and affect (Jausovec, 1989; Jausovec & Bakracevic, 1995; Metcalfe, 1986). If any bias was to be expected within the experimental research and against any facet of the creativity complex, it would have been against such preconscious, affective, preverbal processes.

There are several notable parallels and points of agreement among the experimental findings. The finding of short-term control of alpha, for example, and the conclusion that creative persons are sensitive to internal cues (Martindale & Armstrong, 1974) fits very well with Smith's (1990; Smith & Van der Meer, 1997) results about subliminal processing and with case studies showing some creators to be sensitive (e.g., Wallace, 1992). There is also some convergence about optima: When important determinants or contributions to creativity are identified, it is often the case that the benefit is greatest at an optimal (not maximal) level. This holds true of information, experience, arousal, and conflict – and probably much more. Runco and Sakamoto (1996) found clear support for optima in psychometric, cognitive, developmental, educational, and psychoeconomic research on creativity. Too much of just about anything tends to be detrimental.

These points of agreement do not indicate that the specific findings from the experimental studies fit nicely together in a theoretically comprehensive fashion. This is to be expected, however, because there is no one model of creativity that accounts for the complicated etiology and diverse expressions of creativity. Moreover, the various studies were conducted by independent experimenters. Many different components of the creativity complex have been examined, but few investigations take more than one or two components into account. True multivariate research that examines cognitive process, affect, attitude, and perhaps even physiological states is needed. Ideally this would allow the construction of a general model that would in turn lead to theoretically grounded predictions for additional experimental work.

Replications

Replications might also be helpful. Replications are of course an integral part of traditional experimental research. They are, however, much less common in the creativity research than they are in the hard sciences. Moreover, replication in the hard sciences tends to be exacting; the procedures used in the original experiment are duplicated, the sole intent being validation through replication. In the creativity research (and, to our reading, in most of the social and behavioral sciences), replications are rarely conducted. The closest to a replication that occurs is an extension of the original experiment, which begins with a partial duplication of a previous experiment and then goes on to extend the earlier work. Replications may be rare because they are contrary to the push for originality that is understandably prevalent in creativity research (Runco, 1996). After all, if creativity is valuable enough to study, originality is likely to be valued as well. Replications do offer an important kind of validation and should be treated more seriously in creativity research, especially if findings from the research are to be used for decisions about education or organizational structures. Perhaps replications could be conducted as part of the multiple study experiments that have become so popular (and publishable). Alternatively, they could be published as short research notes (e.g., Heinzen, 1989; James, 1995; Martinsen, 1995; Sheldon, 1995) or in a journal devoted to replications.

One kind of extension is fairly common in creativity research. This involves the extension of a particular technique to a new population. Experimental research has sampled young children (Hennessey, 1989; Okuda, Runco, & Berger, 1991; Runco, 1986; Runco & Pezdek, 1984), secondary school students (Smith et al. 1990), managers (Basadur, 1994; Runco & Basadur, 1993), the elderly (Wikstrom, Ekvall, & Sandstrom, 1994),[6] the military (Martinsen & Kaufmann, 1991), health-care providers (Gendrop, 1996), and college students (Baughman & Mumford, 1995; Harrington, 1975; Hyman, 1964; Kasof, in press; Mumford, Mobley, Uhlman, Reiter-Palmon, & Doares, 1991; Mumford, Reiter-Palmon, & Redmond, 1994). There is in this light a kind of cross-validation of many of the experimental findings. Procedural information supplied by informational manipulations, for example, seems to have a benefit in various samples.

There is one population that has been essentially ignored in experimental studies. We are referring to eminently creative persons. These persons do receive a great deal of attention in the larger creativity literature, and for good reason. They represent "unambiguous creativity." There is no question about their creativity; they have demonstrated it, often repeatedly so, and frequently their work has stood the test of time. In experimental terms, there is no question of the validity of the kind of creativity that is demonstrated by eminent persons. There is a wide consensus about it. But again, eminent creators are virtually ignored in the experimental research. Again using the vernacular, this omission suggests a sampling bias.

Issues of Enhanced Control

Without doubt research in the hard sciences utilizes more comprehensive control than does the experimental work on creativity. A prototypical experiment in the hard sciences might hold constant or eliminate a large number of potential confounding variables by virtue of the (laboratory) setting and sampling. The control of confounding variables in creativity research usually involves only matching subjects, taking care with their sampling, perhaps collecting (and covarying) information about their background, and so on. Control occasionally involves the experimental setting (e.g., Jausovec & Bakracevic, 1995; Ward, 1969), but in general the control is not all that robust. True laboratory investigations rarely control for noise, light, and other sensory distractions. Most experimental research on creativity is probably most accurately described as quasi-experimental.

Experimental studies of creativity might be designed with additional control. This would, however, require reconsideration of the trade-off between internal and external validity that we mentioned in the introduction to this chapter. This is because true creativity probably requires some spontaneity on the part of the individual. Intrinsic motivation, personal choice, and extended periods of time may each also be required (Gruber, 1981, 1988; Runco, Johnson, & Gaynor, in press), and each of these may be precluded by extensive control. Perhaps creativity cannot be studied in a highly controlled experimental setting. Extreme control may take the creativity out of the behavior being investigated. Experimenters must therefore choose either extreme control or the spontaneity and intrinsic motivation that may be required for creative efforts. The moderate (i.e., not comprehensive) control currently prevalent in the experimental research probably reflects the desire to avoid precluding spontaneous creative efforts.

The most extreme control in the existing experimental research on creativity has been exercised by the research we classified as operant. This is precisely why we suggested earlier that the investigations manipulating novel and observable behavior (e.g., Pryor et al., 1969) might be the most respectable from the traditional experimental perspective. These experiments not only focused on observable and novel behavior, with novelty defined objectively and statistically; they also used traditional experimental designs. Multiple baselines were employed, for example, and these allow for great confidence in the inferences drawn. It is still possible that critics will question the actual creativity of the novel behaviors.

As a matter of fact the most common question throughout the experimental research focuses on the dependent variables and their predictive validity. How are the dependent variables – the indicators of creativity – related to the creativity that is found in the natural environment? The optimistic view is that creativity is made up of these indicators: They may be the components of the creativity complex or at least indicators of creative *potential,* the assumption being that the right circumstances will allow the potential to be fulfilled and eventually expressed in actual creative performance. The pessimistic view is that the dependent variables are indicative of a kind of creativity that is found only in the laboratory and that it is unlikely that the same behaviors would be displayed or have any utility in the natural environment. This pessimistic view posits that the experimental research on creativity exerts too much control and that results lack external validity.

The realistic divergent-thinking problems used by Hyman (1964), Chand and Runco (1992), and Runco and Basadur (1993) were developed to assess behaviors that would be similar to those found in the natural environment (also see Baltes & Smith, 1990; Heinzen, 1989). Certainly more could be done in the experimental research to boost the external validity of the results. This is why earlier we recommended the technology of generalization and maintenance.

Informational Manipulations and Problem Solving

Much of the experimental research relies on some sort of informational manipulation. Explicit instructions manipulate information, for example, as do the cues, clues, hints, and strategies targeted in various experimental manipulations. In the research on conflict (James, 1995; Sheldon, 1995) experimental and control groups were defined on the basis of the unique information given to each. Even the intelligibility of the noise used as manipulation in the research on attention (Kasof, in press) was intelligible precisely because it contained sensical and interpretable information. The popularity of informational manipulations suggests that it is necessary to understand informational effects as well as possible.

It is possible that many interventions are informational because there is a high premium placed on objectivity in the experimental research and because manipulations of information lend themselves to tenable assessments. After all, when information is given, predictions about the effects of manipulation are easy to compose and justify. Subjects would be expected to know more, and changes in behavior can be explained in a direct and parsimonious way by pointing to the new knowledge. (This would include declarative and factual knowledge and procedural knowledge, or know-how.) This is in direct contrast to interventions that do not use explicit information. When the manipulation is not information that can be easily articulated, it can be difficult to predict, assess, and explain effects. Studies manipulating conflict, for instance, may put persons in a tense situation, and then assess the impact. The effects may be emotional, and an experimenter may find him- or herself in the situation where a verbal assessment must be developed to assess nonverbal results, or where the only chance to explain effects is to draw weak inferences – inferences that go far beyond the objective facts. Recall here that when affect is investigated, underlying processes (e.g., arousal, attention) are often considered in an effort to explain what is really going on. The point is that there may be so much research using informational manipulations because they are entirely compatible with the assumptions of experimental methods. This could be a serious limitation for studies of creativity, at least for the understanding of whether creativity relies on nonverbal (or preverbal) processes (e.g., Smith, 1990; Tweney, 1996).

The best examples of research using manipulations that do not rely on the presence or absence of information may be the studies of art as intervention (Wikstrom et al., 1994) and the work on percept genesis (Smith, 1990; Smith & Van der Meer, 1994). Even in these areas of research we might infer the contribution of some kind of nonverbal, preverbal, or symbolic information within the interventions, but the effects are probably much better understood in terms of the emotions experienced.

These studies of art as intervention are also important because they represent the only research approaching creativity as the independent variable. It may be that creativity results from certain conditions and affective states – look back at all the studies that have used some index of creativity as their dependent measures – but it is also true that certain affective states can result from creativity (Rothenberg, 1990; Runco & Richards, 1998). This position is almost absent from the research, with the possible exception being the studies that examines the effects of artwork.

In addition to the potential bias toward research using an informational manipulation, there is the tendency to focus on dependent measures that require problem solving by the research participant. The most commonly used dependent measures in the experimental research on creativity seem to involve some kind of problem solving, perhaps because when problems are administered it is relatively easy to operationalize success. Frequently, problems are designed such that the quality and quantity of solutions and responses can be reliably assessed. There is reason to be concerned, however, given the need for adequate sampling of behaviors across the creativity complex and if we are correct that problem-solving assessments may be overrepresented in the creativity research. We alluded to this issue early in the chapter as a parallel to the question of content validity. Just as poor written examinations contain only questions concerning material that is easily described in writing, so too poor experimental research examines only the kinds of creativity that are easy to assess (e.g., problem solving) and ignores the other expressions of creativity.

Problem solving is related to certain kinds of creative work, but creativity may not always require problem solving, and creative problem solving should be distinguished from other kinds of problem solving. Jausovec and Bakracevic (1995), Metcalfe (1986), and Runco and Albert (1985) all found significant differences among various kinds of problems, and if different types of problems differ significantly in the demands they place on the cognition, affect, and physiology of the individual, or if they vary in their structure or lack thereof, they may very well differ in their relationship to creativity. For this reason not all work on problem solving will be equally applicable to studies of creativity.

In general, creative problem solving is most likely when the task is open ended and allows originality. Divergent-thinking tests were developed with this in mind, and they are very frequently used in the creativity research (e.g., Guilford, 1968; Runco, 1991, 1992a). Certainly, divergent-thinking tests are far from perfect measures of true creativity. They are instead useful estimates of the potential for creative thinking, and the emphasis should be on *estimates* and *potential*. (Incidentally, this is a good way to describe the indicators targeted in the experimental research: They define potential and estimate what is possible in the natural environment. Whether or not it actually occurs in the natural environment is another question.)

Since not all problems require creativity for their solution, we can say that not all creativity involves problem solving. Problem solving may be a special kind of creativity, or creativity may be a special kind of problem solving. Both views can be found in the literature (Runco, 1994b). The first perspective, that problem solving is one of several kinds of creativity, is supported by research that creativity may be a kind of self-actualization or self-expression (Maslow, 1971; Rogers, 1961; Runco, Ebersole, & Mraz, 1991). The rebuttal to this view is that these expressions of creativity still involve problems, even if they are personal problems. These views differ in how they define *problem* (Runco, 1994b). An artist, for example, may be experimenting and strategically following deviations of some theme or technique. He or she may not be working on an issue, hurdle, or obstacle that others would acknowledge, but it may be an obstacle nonetheless. If an obstacle is being eliminated somehow through the artwork, it is a kind of problem solving. (The notion that some problems are personally defined is yet another way of saying that individual differences, intrinsic motivation and idiosyncratic interpretations of experience are significant.)

Other support for the idea that creativity is more than problem solving comes from the research on problem *finding* (Jay & Perkins, in press; Runco, 1994b). The logic here is that creative insights often occur when a problem is discovered or defined, rather than just when solutions are formed. Many anecdotal reports point in this direction, and numerous research efforts have successfully defined problem generation (Chand & Runco, 1992), problem construction (Mumford et al., 1994), problem posing (Moore, 1994), and problem discovery (Csikszentmihalyi, in press). Each of these precedes the solving of the problem. Empirical evidence for the distinctiveness of problem finding and problem solving was provided by Chand and Runco (1992) and Csikszentmihalyi (in press). Getzels (1975) went as far as to predict that the creativity of a solution depends on the creativity of the problem being solved.

Complementary Experimental and Nonexperimental Research

Even if experimental methods cannot be used with certain components and traits from the creativity complex, it is still possible that a comprehensive picture of the complex can be derived. We say this because there are many ways in which the experimental research on creativity complements the nonexperimental research – and vice versa. Here are a few of the more obvious examples of how experimental findings complement nonexperimental research on creativity:

- The experimental work on instructions and contingencies fits easily with educational, cognitive, and developmental research. Hennessey and Zbikowski (1993), for example, demonstrated that children can be "immunized" such that the negative effects of reward are minimized. This immunization involved discussion and modeling to demonstrate how to "distance oneself from reward contingencies" and to focus on intrinsic motives (p. 297).

- The experimental research on insight is in some ways compatible with the case studies reported by Gruber (1988; see also Davis et al., in press; Wallace & Gruber, 1989) and with computer simulations (see Holmes, 1996). Gruber's (1981) examination of historically significant discoveries, for example, are consistent with the experimental findings from Weisberg and Alba (1981). Gruber also found gradual, rather than sudden improvements, suggestive of traditional learning and information acquisition. In Gruber's (1981) terms, insights are not sudden but instead are *protracted* and require much thought, experience, and incubation (also see Wallace, 1992).
- The experimental research that uses realistic problems can be cited again, for it complements the psychometric research on individual differences. As noted earlier, certain individual differences will moderate the use of information presented via explicit instructions. The cognitive research on the benefits of *situated cognition* (Greeno, 1989) also complements both the psychometric and experimental work on realistic problems.
- The broad attention that seems to lead to divergent and thus original ideation has been supported by experimental research (Kasof, in press) but also by the self-reports of creative scientists (Ghiselin, Rompel, & Taylor, 1964). Self-reports suggest that it is critical to take a broad view and do a bit of scanning in the early stages of problem solving. In those terms it sounds a bit like brainstorming, where all options are considered, which suggests yet another body of complementary research (Rickards & deCock, in press). Observational research suggests that children's divergent thinking benefits from a rich environment (Ward, 1969), and this benefit would be possible only if they direct their attention in various and diverse directions.
- The research on stress is relevant to explicit instructions because the provided information can have different influences on different persons. Individuals will construct their own interpretations of the information, just as they do potential stressors. (This explains why there can be significant differences between objective events and "hassles" and perceived or subjective stress.) Other useful individual difference measures are suggested by the research on cognitive style (Martinsen, 1995; Martinsen & Kaufmann, 1991) and the trait measures used by Kasof (in press).

Implications of the Experimental Research and Future Research

Several practical implications of the experimental research have already been mentioned. Explicit instructions, for instance, have obvious application in education. The effects of these instructions have been demonstrated with several populations, and appropriate controls suggest that the effects are specific to particular dimensions of creative thinking, such as ideational fluency, originality, or flexibility (Runco & Okuda, 1991). Certain individual and group differences need to be taken into account (see Houtz, Jambor, Cifone, & Lewis, 1989; Runco, 1986), but it appears that educators would be well advised to supply procedural knowledge and strategies and to target students' knowledge bases and thereby increase the probability that those students will solve problems in an original fashion.

Future research should be conducted to isolate the attitudinal effects of instructions (see Hyman, 1964; Runco & Basadur, 1993). It is possible that informational manipulations supply subjects with procedural knowledge and strategies for problem solving, but it is also quite possible that the manipulations change the attitude of the subjects toward creativity and that these attitudinal changes in turn influence the performances of the subjects more than the information does. Such a global impact of experimental manipulations (called the Hawthorne effect; Rosnow & Rosenthal, 1997) is not uncommon and is a real possibility in this area of research because, as mentioned earlier, attitudes may be the most sensitive and malleable of all facets of the creativity complex (Davis, 1992). Research could be conducted to determine if instructional effects are the result of changes in knowledge, attitudes, or both. Field research would suggest that the both are involved (Basadur et al., 1990; Runco

& Basadur, 1993), but this is precisely the kind of multivariate question that experimental research can best answer.

Surely educators should also be aware of the impact of constraint and stress on creative thinking (Hennessey, 1989; Smith et al., 1990). Practical concerns within a classroom may lead educators to time assignments, but they should be aware of the potential impact on creative thinking. Related to this is the concept of optimization (Runco & Sakamoto, 1996): Constraint and excessive structure may inhibit creative thinking, but educators should not go to the opposite extreme either.

There are also clear implications of operant research. Indeed, some of this experimental research was with children and used meaningful target behaviors. Admittedly, incentives and consequences can distract the individual, forcing him or her to think about the contingencies and not about the product or the process that can lead to the product, but it may be a matter of which comes first: If the individual is intrinsically motivated to create something, those working with this individual – parents, teachers, supervisors – need not take a chance on undermining that drive. But if there is no intrinsic motivation, it may make more sense to attempt to encourage novel behavior, or simply effort, by administering reinforcers. This either/or description would explain the varied results from the experimental studies, though of course in the natural environment both intrinsic and extrinsic motives probably influence creative behaviors (Rubenson & Runco, 1992; Runco, 1993, 1994c).[7]

There are yet other implications of the research comparing audio, video, and text. The experiments on the three media were in fact designed to inform television studies, and the best-designed studies demonstrate that video information may minimize the options for independent and creative thinking. This in turn suggests that parents should watch television with their children, discussing what is being viewed and perhaps monitoring the number of hours spent watching television. In addition to a potential narrowing of options, television viewing is a concern because it displaces children from other healthful activities (Sneed & Runco, 1992).

Conclusions

Some of the experimental research on creativity may seem unconventional even by quasi-experimental guidelines. The subject matter is, however, creativity, and it is therefore reasonable to experiment some with experimental methods and to avoid shying away from breaking tradition or adapting the methods for the subject matter. Recall also that experimental findings supply only one of several perspectives on the topic. We mentioned several specific parallels between experimental findings and results from nonexperimental research on creativity. This field will certainly continue to evolve if it can accept complementarity of perspectives. A deep understanding can be developed from the diverse perspectives offered by very different methods. We also suggested that more emphasis be given to replications in the experimental research on creativity. In this light many of the more quasi-experimental investigations can be treated as exploratory, with confirmation to be obtained in more conventional experimentation. It seems to us that the experimental research on creativity has been directed to a respectable range of traits and components from the creativity complex, but surely there is much more work to be done.

NOTES

1 The information given to examinees when they receive a test are probably best labeled *directions* rather than the much more common *instructions*. Of course, if the information is procedural, the lat-

ter may apply as well. The difference is in the meaning of the information. Does it actually instruct examinees, as implied by the term *instructions?*

2 It is only for shorthand that we will refer to the assessments in the research as "creativity tests" or "creativity measures." We are well aware that this assumes that the tests or measures are valid indicators of actually creativity or that the behavior elicited by the test is itself creative. If nothing else, that assumption could be questioned because the behavior is elicited and not spontaneous. This is another part of the issue of the external validity discussed elsewhere in this chapter.

3 There is some debate about what judges should be told (Runco, 1989) and about how judges should be selected. As Murray (1959) put it, who is to judge the judges? And the judges of the judges? There is even controversy about the need for agreement (and reliability) among judges. Csikszentmihalyi and Getzels (1970) proposed that some disagreement is useful for it indicates that the judges are covering various perspectives. The problem is that any disagreement will lower estimates of reliability.

4 It may be that emotions can exist without a cognitive basis (Zajonc, 1980), and in that light the experienced emotions may not convey information. Then again emotions may reflect a kind of information, even if not of the kind that can be verbalized. Or it could be that emotions are not really understood until they are cognitively processed and interpreted (Lazarus, 1991; Runco, 1994c).

5 For years there was discussion about the *criterion problem* (Shapiro, 1970) plaguing the creativity research. Note that it was singular, rather than the *problem of criteria*, as the contemporary definitions of a creativity syndrome would dictate.

6 One interesting feature of this research is that the creative work is the intervention. In most of the research reviewed in this chapter, creativity was *assessed* – it was treated as a dependent variable. In other work, like that of Wikstrom et al. (1994) and Pennebaker, Kiecolt-Glaser, and Glaser (1997) the interest is in the effects of creative efforts. And there are dramatic effects. Pennebaker, for example, reported significant improvements in immune functioning resulting from regular writing.

7 Perhaps the same can be said for other disagreements about creativity. Competition was, for example, used to elicit creative work in the operant research (Glover & Gary, 1976), but it was also used to inhibit creative work by inducing stress and test anxiety (Smith et al., 1990). And that stress may indeed inhibit some creative efforts, but then again some creators seem to be challenged by it (Mumford, 1984). So just as both intrinsic and extrinsic motives may contribute to creativity in that natural environment, so too might competition and stress both have the potential to contribute to or inhibit creativity, depending on the recipient and the context.

REFERENCES

Adams, J. (1979). *Conceptual blockbusting* (2nd ed.). New York: Norton.

Albert, R. S. (1978). Observations and suggestions regarding giftedness, familial influence, and the achievement of eminence. *Gifted Child Quarterly, 22,* 201–211.

Albert, R. S. (1994). The contribution of early family history to the achievement of eminence. In N. Colangelo, S. Assouline, & D. L. Ambroson (Eds.), *Talent development* (Vol. 2, pp. 311–360). Dayton: Ohio Psychology Press.

Albert, R. S. (in press). What the study of eminence can teach us. *Creativity Research Journal.*

Albert, R. S., & Runco, M. A. (1986). The achievement of eminence: A model of exceptionally gifted boys and their families. In R. J. Sternberg and J. E. Davison (Eds.), *Conceptions of giftedness* (pp. 332–357). Cambridge University Press.

Amabile, T. M. (in press). Within you, without you: Towards a social psychology of creativity, and beyond. In M. A. Runco & R. S. Albert (Eds.), *Theories of creativity* (rev. ed.). Cresskill, NJ: Hampton.

Amabile, T. M., Goldfarb, P., & Brackfield, S. C. (1990). Social influences on creativity: Evaluation, coaction, and surveillance. *Creativity Research Journal, 3,* 6–21.

Baker-Sennett, J., & Ceci, S. (1996). Clue-efficiency and insight: Unveiling the mystery of inductive leaps. *Journal of Creative Behavior, 30,* 153–172.

Baltes, P., Staudinger, U. M., Maercker, A., & Smith, J. (1995). People nominated as wise: A comparative study of wisdom-related knowledge. *Psychology and Aging, 10,* 155–166.

Barron, F. (1995). *No rootless flower: An ecology of creativity.* Cresskill, NJ: Hampton. (Original work published 1963).

Basadur, M. (1994). Managing the creative process in organizations. In M. A. Runco (Ed)., *Problem solving, problem finding, and creativity* (pp. 237–268). Norwood, NJ: Ablex.

Basadur, M., Wakabayashi, M., & Graen, G. B. (1990). Individual problem solving styles and attitudes toward divergent thinking before and after training. *Creativity Research Journal, 3,* 22–32.

Baughman, W. A., & Mumford, M. D. (1995). Process analytic models of creative capacities: Operations influencing the combination and reorganization process. *Creativity Research Journal, 8,* 37–62.

Bowers, K. S., Regher, G., Balthazard, C., & Parker, K. (1990). Intuition in the context of discovery. *Cognitive Psychology, 22,* 72–110.

Burnham, C. A., & Davis, K. G. (1969). The 9-dot problem: Beyond perceptual organization. *Psychonomic Science, 17,* 321–323.

Chand, I., & Runco, M. A. (1992). Problem finding skills as components in the creative process. *Personality and Individual Differences, 14,* 155–162.

Csikszentmihalyi, M. (in press). The domain of creativity. In M. A. Runco & R. S. Albert (Eds.), *Theories of creativity* (rev. ed.). Cresskill, NJ: Hampton.

Csikszentmihalyi, M., & Getzels, J. W. (1970). Concern for discovery: An attitudinal component of creative production. *Journal of Personality, 38,* 91–105.

Davidson, J. E., & Sternberg, R. J. (1983). The role of insight in intellectual giftedness. *Gifted Child Quarterly, 28,* 58–64.

Davis, G. A. (1992). *Creativity is forever* (3rd ed.). Dubuque, IA: Kendall/Hunt.

Davis, S., Keegan, R., & Gruber, H. E. (in press). Creativity as purposeful work: The evolving systems approach. In M. A. Runco (Ed.), *Creativity research handbook* (Vol. 2) Cresskill, NJ: Hampton.

Elbert, T., Pantev, C., Wienbruch, C., Rockstroh, B., & Taud, E. (1995, October 13). Increased cortical representation of the fingers of the left hand in string players. *Science, 270,* 305–307.

Epstein, R. (in press). Generativity theory and creativity. In M. A. Runco & R. S. Albert (Eds.), *Theories of creativity* (rev. ed.). Cresskill, NJ: Hampton.

Epstein, R., Kirshnit, C., Lanza, R. P., & Rubin, L. (1984). Insight in the pigeon: Antecedents and determinants of an intelligence performance. *Nature, 308,* 61–62.

Eysenck, H. (1993). Creativity and personality: Suggestions for a theory. *Psychological Inquiry, 4,* 147–178.

Finke, R. A. (1990). *Creative imagery: Discoveries and inventions in visualization.* Hillsdale, NJ: Erlbaum.

Finke, R. A. (in press). *Mental Imagery and Visual Creativity* In M. A. Runco (Ed.), *Creativity research handbook* (Vol. 1, pp. 183–202). Cresskill, NJ: Hampton.

Finke, R. A., & Slayton, K. (1988). Explorations of creative visual synthesis in mental imagery. *Memory and Cognition, 16,* 252–257.

Gardner, H. (1994). More on private intuitions and public symbol systems. *Creativity Research Journal, 7,* 265–275.

Gardner, H. (in press). Is there a moral intelligence? *Creativity Research Journal.*

Gendrop, S. (1996). Effect of an intervention in synectics on the creative thinking of nurses. *Creativity Research Journal, 9,* 11–19.

Getzels, J. W. (1975). Problem finding and the inventiveness of solutions. *Journal of Creative Behavior, 9,* 12–18.

Ghiselin, B., Rompel, R., & Taylor, C. (1964). A creative process checklist: Its development and validation. In C. Taylor (Ed.), *Widening horizons in creativity* (pp. 19–33). New York: Wiley.

Glover, J., & Gary, A. L. (1976). Procedures to increase some aspects of creativity. *Journal of Applied Behavior Analysis, 9,* 79–84.

Goetz, E. M., & Baer, D. M. (1973). Social control of form diversity and the emergence of new forms in children's blockbuilding. *Journal of Applied Behavior Analysis, 6,* 209–217.

Goetz, E. M., & Salmonson, M. M. (1972). The effects of general and descriptive reinforcement of creativity in easel painting. In G. B. Semb (Ed.), *Behavior analysis in education* (pp. 53–61). Lawrence: University of Kansas Press.

Greenfield, P., Geber, B., Beagles-Roos, J., Farrar, D., & Gat, I. (1981, April). *Television and radio experimentally compared: Effects of the medium on imagination and transmission of content.* Paper presented at the meeting of the Society for Research in Child Development, Boston, MA.

Greeno, J. G. (1989). A perspective on thinking. *American Psychologist, 44,* 134–141.

Gruber, H. E. (1981). On the relation between "aha" experiences and the construction of ideas. *History of Science, 19,* 41–59.

Gruber, H. E. (1988). The evolving systems approach to creative work. *Creativity Research Journal, 1,* 27–51.

Guilford, J. P. (1968). *Creativity, intelligence, and their educational implications.* San Diego, CA: EDITS/Knapp.

Harrington, D. M. (1975). Effects of explicit instructions to be creative on the psychological meaning of divergent test scores. *Journal of Personality, 43,* 434–454.

Heinzen, T. (1989). On moderate challenge increasing ideational creativity. *Creativity Research Journal, 2,* 223–226.

Hennessey, B. A. (1989). The effect of extrinsic constraint on children's creativity when using a computer. *Creativity Research Journal, 2,* 151–168.

Hennessey, B. A., & Zbikowski, S. M. (1993). Immunizing children against the negative effects of reward: A further examination of intrinsic motivation training techniques. *Creativity Research Journal, 6,* 297–307.

Holman, J., Goetz, E. M., & Baer, D. M. (1977). The training of creativity as an operant and an examination of its generalization characteristics. In B. C. Etzel, J. M. LeBlanc, & D. M. Baer (Eds.), *New developments in behavioral research: Theory, method, and application* (pp. 441–447). New York: Wiley.

Holmes, F. (1996). Research trails and the creative spirit: Can historical case studies integrate the short and long timescales of creative activity? *Creativity Research Journal, 9,* 239–249.

Hoppe, K., & Kyle, N. (1990). Dual brain and creativity. *Creativity Research Journal, 3,* 146–157.

Houtz, J. C., Jambor, S. O., Cifone, A., & Lewis, C. D. (1989). Locus of evaluation control, task directions, and type of problem effects on creativity. *Creativity Research Journal, 2,* 118–125.

Howe, R. (1992). Uncovering the creative dimensions of computer-based graphic design products. *Creativity Research Journal, 5,* 233–243.

Hyman, R. (1961). On prior information and creativity. *Psychological Reports, 9,* 151–161.

Hyman, R. (1964). Creativity and the prepared mind: The role of information and induced attitudes. In C. W. Taylor (Ed.), *Widening horizons in creativity* (pp. 69–79). New York: Wiley.

Isen, A. M., Daubman, K. A., & Nowicki, G. P. (1987). Positive affect facilitates creative problem solving. *Journal of Personality and Social Psychology, 52,* 1122–1131.

Isen, A. M., Johnson, M. M., Mertz, E., & Robinson, G. F. (1985). The influence of positive affect on the unusualness of word associations. *Journal of Personality and Social Psychology, 48,* 1413–1426.

James, K. (1995). Goal conflict and originality of thinking. *Creativity Research Journal, 8,* 285–290.

Jausovec, N. (1989). Affect in analogical transfer. *Creativity Research Journal, 2,* 255–266.

Jausovec, N. (1994). Metacognition in creative problem solving. In M. A. Runco (Eds.), *Problem solving, problem finding, and creativity* (pp. 77–95). Norwood, NJ: Ablex.

Jausovec, N., & Bakracevic, K. (1995). What can heart rate tell us about the creative process? *Creativity Research Journal, 8,* 11–24.

Jay, E., & Perkins, D. (in press). Creativity's compass: A review of problem finding. In M. A. Runco (Ed.), *Creativity research handbook* (vol. 1). Cresskill, NJ: Hampton.

Kasof, J. (in press). Creativity and breadth of attention. *Creativity Research Journal.*

Keegan, R. T. (1996, Summer). Creativity from childhood to adulthood: A difference of degree and not kind. *New Directions for Child Development* (No. 71, pp. 57–66). San Francisco: Jossey-Bass.

Kohler, W. (1925). *The Mentality of apes.* London: Rootledge & Kegan Paul.

Kramer, M., Tegan E., & Knauber, J. (1970). The effect of presets on creative problem solving. *Nursing Research, 19,* 303–310.

Kris, E. (1952). *Psychoanalytic explorations in art.* New York: International Universities Press.

Lazarus, R. S. (1991). Cognition and motivation in emotion. *American Psychologist, 46,* 352–367.

Li, J. (1997). Creativity in horizontal and vertical domains. *Creativity Research Journal, 10,* 103–132.

Ludwig, A. (1995). *The price of greatness.* New York: Guilford.

MacKinnon, D. (1965). Personality and the realization of creative potential. *American Psychologist, 20,* 273–281.

MacKinnon, D. (1983). The highly effective individual. In R. S. Albert (Ed.), *Genius and eminence: A social psychology of creativity and exceptional achievement* (pp. 114–127). Oxford: Pergamon. (Original work published 1960)

Martindale, C., Anderson, K., Moore, K., & West, A. N. (1996). Creativity, oversensitivity, and rate of habituation. *Personality and Individual Differences, 20,* 423–427.

Martindale, C., & Armstrong, J. (1974). The relationship of creativity to cortical activation and its operant control. *Journal of Genetic Psychology, 124,* 311–320.

Martindale, C., & Greenough, J. (1973). The differential effect of increased arousal on creative and intellectual performance. *Journal of Genetic Psychology, 123,* 329–335.

Martindale, C., & Hasenfus, N. (1978). EEG differences as a function of creativity, stage of the creative process, and effort to be original. *Biological Psychology, 6,* 157–167.

Martinsen, O. (1995). Cognitive styles and experience in solving insight problems: Replication and extension. *Creativity Research Journal, 8,* 291–298.

Martinsen, O., & Kaufmann, G. (1991). Effect of imagery, strategy and individual differences in solving insight problems. *Scandinavian Journal of Educational Research, 35,* 69–76.

Maslow, A. H. (1971). *The farther reaches of human nature.* New York: Viking.

Mednick, S. A. (1962). The associative basis for the creative process. *Psychological Review, 69,* 200–232.

Meline, C. W. (1976). Does the medium matter? *Journal of Communication, 26,* 81–89.

Mendelsohn, G. (1976). Associative and attentional processes in creative performance. *Journal of Personality, 44,* 341–369.

Mendelsohn, G., & Griswold, B. (1964). Differential use of incidental stimuli in problem solving as a function of creativity. *Journal of Abnormal and Social Psychology, 68,* 431–436.

Mendelsohn, G., & Griswold, B. (1966). Assessed creative potential, vocabulary level, and sex as predictors of the use of incidental cues in verbal problem solving. *Journal of Personality and Social Psychology, 4,* 423–431.

Mendelsohn, G., & Lindholm, E. (1972). Individual differences and the role of attention in the use of cues in verbal problem solving. *Journal of Personality, 40,* 226–241.

Metcalfe, J. (1986). Feeling of knowing in memory and problem solving. *Journal of Experimental Psychology: Learning, Memory, and Cognition, 12,* 288–294.

Moore, M. (1994). In M. A. Runco (Ed.), *Problem finding, problem solving, and creativity* (pp. 3–39). Norwood, NJ: Ablex.

Moran, J. D., & Liou, E. Y. (1982). Effects of reward on creativity in college students at two levels of ability. *Perceptual and Motor Skills, 54,* 43–48.

Mumford, M. D. (1984). Age and outstanding occupational achievement: Lehman revisited. *Journal of Vocational Behavior, 25,* 225–244.

Mumford, M. D., & Gustafson, S. B. (1988). Creativity syndrome: Integration, application, and innovation. *Psychological Bulletin, 103,* 27–43.

Mumford, M. D., Mobley, M. I., Uhlman, C. E., Reiter-Palmon, R., & Doares, L. (1991). Process analytic models of creative thought. *Creativity Research Journal, 4,* 91–122.

Mumford, M. D., Reiter-Palmon, R., & Redmond, M. R. (1994). Problem construction and cognition: Applying problem representations in ill-defined domains. In M. A. Runco (Ed.), *Problem finding, problem solving, and creativity* (pp. 3–39). Norwood, NJ: Ablex.

Mumford, M. D., Supinski, E. P., Baughman, W. A., Costanza, D. P., & Threlfall, K. V. (in press). Process-based measures of creative problem-solving skills. Part 5, Overall prediction. *Creativity Research Journal.*

Murray, H. A. (1959). Vicissitudes of creativity. In H. H. Anderson (Ed.), *Creativity and its cultivation* (pp. 203–221). New York: Harper.

Nunnally, J. C. (1976). *Psychometric theory* (2nd ed.). New York: McGraw-Hill.

Okuda, S. M., Runco, M. A., & Berger, D. E. (1991). Creativity and the finding and solving of real-world problems. *Journal of Psychoeducational Assessment, 9,* 45–53.

Pennebaker, J. W., Kiecolt-Glaser, J. K., & Glaser, R. (1997). Disclosure of trauma and immune functioning: Health implications for psychotherapy. In M. A. Runco & R. Richards (Eds.), *Eminent creativity, everyday creativity, and health* (pp. 287–302). Norwood, NJ: Ablex.

Pesut, D. J. (1990). Creative thinking as a self-regulatory metacognitive process: A model for education, training and further research. *Journal of Creative Behavior, 24,* 105–110.

Pryor, K. W., Hoag, R., & O'Reilly, J. (1969). The creative porpoise: Training for novel behavior. *Journal of the Experimental Analysis of Behavior, 12,* 653–661.

Rickards, T., & deCock, C. (in press). Understanding organizational creativity: Towards a multiparadigmatic approach. In M. A. Runco (Ed.), *Creativity research handbook* (vol. 2). Cresskill, NJ: Hampton.

Rogers, C. R. (1961). *On becoming a person.* Boston, MA: Houghton Mifflin.

Root-Bernstein, R. S., Bernstein, M., & Garnier, H. (1993). Identification of scientists making long-term, high-impact contributions, with notes on their methods of working. *Creativity Research Journal, 6,* 320–343.

Rosnow, R. L., & Rosenthal, R. (1997). *People studying people.* New York: Freeman.

Rothenberg, A. (1990). Creativity, health, and alcoholism. *Creativity Research Journal, 3,* 179–202.

Rothenberg, A., & Hausman, C. (in press). Metaphor and creativity. In M. A. Runco (Ed.), *Creativity research handbook* (Vol. 2). Cresskill, NJ: Hampton.

Rubenson, D. L., & Runco, M. A. (1992). The psychoeconomic approach to creativity. *New Ideas in Psychology, 10,* 131–147.

Runco, M. A. (1985). Reliability and convergent validity of ideational flexibility as a function of academic achievement. *Perceptual and Motor Skills, 61,* 1075–1081.

Runco, M. A. (1986). Maximal performance on divergent thinking tests by gifted, talented, and nongifted children. *Psychology in the Schools, 23,* 308–315.

Runco, M. A. (1989). The creativity of children's art. *Child Study Journal, 19,* 177–189.

Runco, M. A. (1991). *Divergent thinking.* Norwood, NJ: Ablex.

Runco, M. A. (1992a). Children's divergent thinking and creative ideation. *Developmental Review, 12,* 233–264.

Runco, M. A. (1992b). *Creativity as an educational objective for disadvantaged students.* Storrs, CT: National Research Center on the Gifted and Talented.

Runco, M. A. (1993). Operant theories of insight, originality, and creativity. *American Behavioral Scientist, 37,* 59–74.

Runco, M. A. (1994a). Cognitive and psychometric issues in creativity research. In S. G. Isaksen, M. C. Murdock, R. L. Firestien, & D. J. Treffinger (Eds.), *Understanding and recognizing creativity* (pp. 331–368). Norwood, NJ: Ablex.

Runco, M. A. (1994b). Conclusions concerning problem finding, problem solving, and creativity. In M. A. Runco (Ed.), *Problem finding, problem solving, and creativity* (pp. 272–290). Norwood, NJ: Ablex.

Runco, M. A. (1994c). Creativity and its discontents. In M. P. Shaw & M. A. Runco (Eds.), *Creativity and affect* (pp. 102–123). Norwood, NJ: Ablex.

Runco, M. A. (1996, Summer). Personal creativity: Definition and developmental issues. *New Directions for Child Development,* no. 72, pp. 3–30.

Runco, M. A., & Albert, R. S. (1985). The reliability and validity of ideational originality in the divergent thinking of academically gifted and nongifted children. *Educational and Psychological Measurement, 45,* 483–501.

Runco, M. A., & Albert, R. S. (in press). *Theories of creativity* (rev. ed.). Cresskill, NJ: Hampton.

Runco, M. A., & Basadur, M. (1993). Assessing ideational and evaluative skills and creative styles and attitudes. *Creativity and Innovation Management, 2,* 166–173.

Runco, M. A., & Chand, I. (1994). Problem finding, evaluative thinking, and creativity. In M. A. Runco (Ed.), *Problem finding, problem solving, and creativity* (pp. 40–76). Norwood, NJ: Ablex.

Runco, M. A., & Charles, R. (1993). Judgments of originality and appropriateness as predictors of creativity. *Personality and Individual Differences, 15,* 537–546.

Runco, M. A., Ebersole, P., & Mraz, W. (1991). Self-actualization and creativity. *Journal of Social Behavior and Personality, 6,* 161–167.

Runco, M. A., Eisenman, R., & Harris, S. (1997). *Explicit instructions for originality and appropriateness.* Unpublished manuscript.

Runco, M. A., Johnson, D., & Gaynor, J. R. (in press). The judgmental bases of creativity and implications for the study of gifted youth. In A. Fishkin, B. Cramond, & P. Olszewski-Kubilius (Eds.), *Creativity in youth: Research and methods.* Cresskill, NJ: Hampton.

Runco, M. A., & Nemiro, J. (1996). *Instructions and creative performance.* Unpublished manuscript.

Runco, M. A., & Okuda, S. M. (1991). The instructional enhancement of the ideational originality and flexibility scores of divergent thinking tests. *Applied Cognitive Psychology, 5,* 435–441.

Runco, M. A., Okuda, S. M., & Thurston, B. J. (1991). Environmental cues and divergent thinking. In M. A. Runco (Ed.), *Divergent thinking* (pp. 79–85). Norwood, NJ: Ablex.

Runco, M. A., & Pezdek, K. (1984). The effect of television and radio on children's creativity. *Human Communications Research, 11,* 109–120.

Runco, M. A., Reiter-Palmon, R., Smith, W., Seino, S. (1997). *Procedural and conceptual explicit instructions and creative thinking.* Unpublished manuscript.

Runco, M. A., & Richards, R. (Eds.). (1998). *Eminent creativity, everyday creativity, and health.* Norwood, NJ: Ablex.

Runco, M. A., & Sakamoto, S. O. (1996). Optimization as a guiding principle in research on creative problem solving. In T. Helstrup, G. Kaufmann, & K. H. Teigen (Eds.), *Problem solving and cognitive processes: Essays in honor of Kjell Raaheim* (pp. 119–144). Bergen, Norway: Fagbokforlaget Vigmostad & Bjorke.

Saracho, O. (1992). Preschool children's cognitive style and play and implications for creativity. *Creativity Research Journal, 5,* 35–47.

Schaffner, K. (1994). Discovery in biomedical science: Logic or intuitive genius? *Creativity Research Journal, 4,* 351–363.

Shapiro, R. J. (1970). The criterion problem. In P. E. Vernon (Ed.), *Creativity* (pp. 257–269). New York: Penguin.

Sheldon, K. (1995). Creativity and goal conflict. *Creativity Research Journal, 8,* 299–306.

Simon, H. A., & Chase, W. (1973). Skill in chess. *American Scientist, 61,* 394–403.

Simonton, D. K. (in press). Historiometric studies of creative genius. In M. A. Runco (Ed.), *Creativity research handbook* (Vol. 2). Cresskill, NJ: Hampton.

Singer, J., & Singer, D. (in press). Imagining possible worlds to confront and create realities. In M. A. Runco (Ed.), *Creativity research handbook* (Vol. 2). Cresskill, NJ: Hampton.

Skinner, B. F. (1975). *About behaviorism*. New York: Knopf.

Smith, G. J. W. (1990). Creativity in old age. *Creativity Research Journal, 3,* 249–264.

Smith, G. J. W., & Van der Meer, G. (1994). Creativity through psychosomatics. *Creativity Research Journal, 7,* 159–170.

Smith, G. J. W., & Van der Meer, G. (1997). Perception and creativity. In M. A. Runco (Ed.), *Creativity research handbook* (Vol. 1). Cresskill, NJ: Hampton.

Smith, K. L. R., Michael, W. B., & Hocevar, D. (1990). Performance on creativity measures with examination-taking intended to induce high or low levels of test anxiety. *Creativity Research Journal, 3,* 265–280.

Sneed, C., & Runco, M. A. (1992). The beliefs adults and children hold about television and video games. *Journal of Psychology, 126,* 273–284.

Stohs, J. H. (1992). Intrinsic motivation and sustained art activity among male fine and applied artists. *Creativity Research Journal, 5,* 245–252.

Stokes, T. F., & Baer, D. M. (1977). An implicit technology of generalization. *Journal of Applied Behavior Analysis, 10,* 349–367.

Tobias, S. (1985). Test anxiety: Interference, defective skills, and cognitive capacity. *Educational Psychologist, 20,* 135–142.

Toplyn, G., & Maguire, W. (1991). The differential effect of noise on creative task performance. *Creativity Research Journal, 4,* 337–347.

Torrance, E. P. (1974). *The Torrance Tests of Creative Thinking*. Bensenville, IL: Scholastic Testing Services.

Tweney, R. D. (1996). Presymbolic processes in scientific creativity. *Creativity Research Journal, 9,* 163–172.

Vosburg, S. (in press). Mood and unconstrained idea production. *Creativity Research Journal.*

Voss, H. G. (1977). The effect of experimentally induced activation on creativity. *Journal of Psychology, 96,* 3–9.

Wallace, E. (1991). The genesis and microgenesis of sudden insight. *Creativity Research Journal, 4,* 41–50.

Wallace, D., & Gruber, H. E. (1989). *Creative people at work: Twelve cognitive case studies*. New York: Oxford University Press.

Wallach, M. A. (1970). Creativity. In P. A. Mussen (Ed.), *Manual of child psychology* (Vol. 1, pp. 1211–1271). New York: Wiley.

Wallach, M. A., & Kogan, N. (1965). *Modes of thinking in young children*. New York: Holt, Rinehart, & Winston.

Wallas, G. (1926). *The art of thought*. New York: Harcourt, Brace, Jovanovich.

Ward, W. C. (1969). Creativity and environmental cues in nursery school children. *Developmental Psychology, 1,* 543–547.

Ward, W. C., Kogan, N., & Pankove, E. (1972). Incentive effects in children's creativity. *Child Development, 43,* 669–676.

Weber, R. (1996). Toward a language of invention and synthetic thinking. *Creativity Research Journal, 9,* 353–367.

Weisberg, R. W. (1992). Metacognition and insight during problem-solving: Comment on Metcalfe. *Journal of Experimental Psychology: Learning, Memory, and Cognition, 18,* 426–431.

Weisberg, R. W., & Alba, J. W. (1981). An examination of the alleged role of fixation in the solution of several insight problems. *Journal of Experimental Psychology: General, 110,* 169–192.

Wikstrom, B.-M., Ekvall, G., & Sandstrom, S. (1994). Stimulating the creativity of elderly women through works of art. *Creativity Research Journal, 7,* 171–182.

Zajonc, R. B. (1980). Feeling and thinking: Preferences need no inferences. *American Psychologist, 35,* 151–175.

5 The Case Study Method and Evolving Systems Approach for Understanding Unique Creative People at Work

HOWARD E. GRUBER AND DORIS B. WALLACE

INTRODUCTION

In the evolving systems approach to the case study method, there are three guiding ideas: The creative person is unique, developmental change is multidirectional, and the creative person is an evolving system. The necessary uniqueness of the creative person argues against efforts to reduce psychological description to a fixed set of dimensions. The creative person is not conveniently "far out" along some well-charted path: She or he is unique in unexpected ways. Indeed, it may never be possible to make more than a few obvious generalizations about ways in which all creative people are alike.

The prevailing image of psychological change in developmental theory unfortunately is one of unilinear, cumulative, predictable, and irreversible growth in accordance with a species-general standard sequence. For those using the evolving systems approach, however, development is not restricted to a unilinear pathway since an evolving system does not operate as a linear sequence of cause–effect relationships but displays, at every point in its history, multicausal and reciprocally interactive relationships both among the internal elements of the system and between the organism and its external milieu. Whether change is cumulative and whether it is structurally developmental or not must be worked out in each instance by investigators.

Thus, the evolving system of the creative person is multicausal and unpredictable – that is, unique. It is unpredictable in the sense that one cannot know exactly what will be the next work that an artist will create, nor can one forecast the next revolutionary theory in art or science. Predictability may be a false god. Nontrivial novelty cannot be predicted. Biologists could never have known how to predict the evolution of the camel; but once faced with the camel and informed about its systematic place in an evolving biosphere, they could hope to understand its evolutionary significance. With well-educated hindsight, we may be able to understand the various solutions that come about in response to some eco-pressure for change. With enough foresight, we may also be able to make contingent "predictions," such as

A certain organism will become extinct unless it migrates to a cooler climate;

or

Unless a radical creative approach is found for dealing with automotive pollution, industrial societies will asphyxiate themselves.

In the study of creativity, as an alternative to the methodological battle cry of prediction and control, we propose a two-part approach: detailed analytic and sometimes narrative description of each case and efforts to understand each case as a unique functioning system.

Methodological issues are never purely and simply methodological. Overtly or not, they always call into play deeply held convictions about the nature of knowledge and truth. Just

93

as form and content are inseparable, epistemic passions lurk everywhere. Nevertheless, it is our task to disentangle these issues where we can. There are various useful strategies for organizing the investigation of a creative case. The main path we follow in this essay is intended to show some lines that an investigator might actually pursue. It should be said, however, that we are not looking for some magic that makes creativity happen; we do not search for the origins of creativity or for a single model of the creative personality. On the contrary, we ask how creative work works. What do people do when they are being creative? How does the creative person deploy available resources to do what has never been done before?

What is a creative case? What do we mean by creative work? Like most definitions of creativity, ours includes novelty and value: The creative product must be new and must be given value according to some external criteria. But we add a third criterion, purpose – creative products are the result of purposeful behavior – and a fourth, duration – creative people take on hard projects lasting a long time. (Indeed, their aspirations and purposes often outlive them.) Creative work is a long undertaking to be reckoned in months, years, or decades. Beethoven once made the following statement:

I carry my thoughts about with me for a long time, often for a very long time before writing them down. I can . . . be sure that . . . I shall not forget [a theme] even years later. I change many things, discard others and try again and again until I am satisfied; then, in my head, I begin to elaborate the work . . . the underlying idea never deserts me. It rises, it grows. I hear and see the image in front of me from every angle. (Hamburger, 1952, p. 194)

The criterion of duration gives special meaning to the criterion of purpose, extending creative work over time and capturing the notion of a creative life. To live a creative life is one of the intentions of the creative person.

Implicit in our criteria of purpose and duration – each of which assumes that creative work is inherently a temporal process – is the idea of difficulty. If a particular creative work was easy and obvious, we would not think of it as especially creative since many people would be doing it. If there were no constraints, novelty might not be so difficult to produce. Part of the difficulty of achieving a creative outcome arises from the need to make it compatible with human purposes and with the society and culture in which the work takes place. The creative person may well start with a wild idea. Soon it becomes familiar and, within a private universe, no longer wild. But to be effective the creator must be in touch with the norms and beliefs of some others so that the product will be one that they can accommodate and relish. Even the person who is far ahead of the times must have some community, however limited, with which to engage and connect. For example, during his most secretive years, Darwin isolated himself from the scientific community, but only with regard to the work he was doing on evolutionary theory. In other respects he was, in that period of his life, well ensconced in the world of science, holding office in professional societies, giving papers at meetings, and collaborating with various experts in different branches of biology (see Gruber, 1974/1981).

Einstein provides another example. During the years when he was working out the special theory of relativity, he met regularly in an informal group of three men who dubbed themselves the "Olympia Academy." They usually met in Einstein's apartment and discussed everything under the sun – and probably the sun itself – but especially Einstein's theories.

Of more recent vintage is the story that the physicist-mathematician, Freeman Dyson relates. When he saw that the physics community, including its most brilliant members, could not understand Richard Feynman's unorthodox methods for solving problems in quantum electrodynamics, he undertook to serve as the bridge: He worked steadily with

Feynman over a period of months, until he had mastered Feynman's diagrammatic-visual approach and could transmit it to others of more algebraic bent (Dyson, 1979; Schweber, 1994).

When the gap between the creator and others is too great, two primary strategies are possible: to modify the work to make it more acceptable or to educate the potential audience to greater acceptance. Both of these strategies show others the way from the present to the future.

HISTORY, THEORY, AND METHOD

To see where our methodological approach is situated in the spectrum of possible approaches, a brief survey is in order. One exclusion should be mentioned, works known as *psychobiography*. We have omitted this area because it deals primarily with the personality and social relations of the person. We intend this remark not as a criticism, but as a logical consequence of our commitment to the study of the creative process, to the study of the creative person at work. In some of our writing we have referred to our work as "cognitive case studies," not to exclude aesthetic, affective, and moral issues, but to avoid the appearance of taking on the tasks of the psychobiographer.

The year 1950 is often hailed as the moment of rejuvenation of creativity research after psychology's long sojourn in the desert of behaviorism. That was the year of Guilford's (1950) Presidential Address to the American Psychological Association, in which he advanced the goal of psychometric and factor-analytical approaches to the abilities and other characteristics of the creative person. The factors were to be discovered by the construction of tests of creativity that could be administered to large enough samples to make factor analysis possible. Thus, Guilford's approach was centered on component abilities, and correlational studies of them, in which it was assumed that the more the subject had of a certain ability the more it contributed to that person's overall creativity. The main ability that was distilled out of a vast research effort was "divergent thinking." Without going far into this subject, we can say at least three things. First, decades later, there is remarkably little evidence concerning divergent thinking in highly creative people (Barron & Harrington, 1981). Second, it is not self-evident how the ability to produce many ideas is related to the ability to produce a few superb ones. Third, the question remains open: Just how does the creative person at work go about making use of the ability to produce ideas? For further discussion see Ochse (1990) and Weisberg (1993).

The difference between our approach and factor analysis is that our "factors" are derived from the doings and sayings of actual creators. Can a description be both analytic and holistic? Yes, as in Wertheimer's formulation of the laws of perceptual organization, such as proximity, similarity, and common fate. For a description to be holistic without being vacuous, it must make use of some tools of analysis.

Five years before Guilford's presidential address, Max Wertheimer, one of the founders of Gestalt psychology, brought out his book, long in the making, *Productive Thinking* (1945). This work dealt with seven cases, each at chapter length. Three of the cases – Gauss, Galileo, Einstein – were creative thinkers of the highest order. Wertheimer's treatment of problem solving emphasizes its analogy with perception, using structural concepts such as transformation, recentering, gap filling, and figure–ground reversal. Non-Gestaltists borrowing from the theory often put the emphasis on sudden insight, the so-called Gestalt switch. As a characterization of Gestalt theory this is a little misleading. For example, Wertheimer's treatment of Einstein (whom he knew and interviewed) described 10 phases in a nine-year process eventuating in the special theory of relativity, with many questions left unanswered.

Wertheimer's approach emphasizing structural transformations spread out over time resembles our constructionist approach. A. I. Miller (1984) gives this a fuller and more historical account, which is, nevertheless, in tune with major aspects of Gestalt theory.

In spite of their profound differences, Guilford and Wertheimer have one thing in common, a preoccupation with problem solving. There was an earlier tradition, represented by Titchener's *Lectures on the Experimental Psychology of the Thought Processes* (1909), in which the emphasis was on the experiential aspects of thinking, such as visual imagery or feelings of a problem state. With the rise of behaviorism, such experiential, phenomenological studies went out of favor. In more recent years there has been an upsurge of interest in inner experience as such, with special emphasis on visual imagery. However, there is not yet a solid body of knowledge about the role of such processes in creative work. From all this it can be seen that there is a close relation between theory and method in the study of creativity. Indeed, it might almost be said that the method is the theory in the sense that it specifies what is considered important and worthy of study.

Each major theoretical approach has its own methodological commitments and attitudes toward measurement. In the factorial approach, measurement is the key requirement. The guideline is that everything that exists exists in some quantity and can therefore be measured. But the actual position taken is even stronger: Everything important *should* be measured.

In the Gestalt approach, measurement hardly appears. The key concern is to understand the structure of the situation that the subject confronts and to understand how the creator transforms the situation by a series of moves analogous to perceptual phenomena, as mentioned earlier. In spite of the Gestaltists' emphasis on structure, they are not usually grouped with the "structuralists." The latter are concerned with structures exhibited in varying situations, as though they were carried from one to another in the mind of the thinking subject, thus providing trans-situational norms. The Gestaltists, on the other hand, emphasize structures to be found *within* situations, to be found by getting inside rather than standing outside and above, moving "straight from the heart of the thinker to the heart of his object, of his problem" (Wertheimer, 1945, p. 236).

The structuralists – who might also be called constructionists, epigeneticists, or developmentalists – are closely related to the Gestaltists, with one major difference noted earlier. Indeed, Piaget liked to say that he had almost become a Gestaltist, before he discovered the problems of development. Perhaps it could be said that Wertheimer tended to go more deeply into fewer tasks or problems, while the structuralists, more concerned with discovering universal norms, necessarily had to look at many problems of a given class (i.e., dealing with space, time, causality, chance). Of course, the major difference is that Piaget was deeply concerned with the problem of development, whereas the Gestaltists, with their root metaphor founded in the perceptual situation of the moment, tended to ignore problems of development.

Methodologically, the most striking characteristic of Piaget's work is his use of the "clinical method." This means, in the first place, deeply probing interviews centered around some cognitive task selected by the investigator. The child is asked to solve some problem and is both observed and queried as to his or her thought processes while solving it. This much is not so different from other investigators of problem solving, except that there is less interest in finding "the" solution and more in probing for process. This is well expressed in the title of Ginsburg's (1997) book: *Entering the Child's Mind: The Clinical Interview in Psychological Research and Practice.*

But there is another characteristic of the clinical method that goes beyond the single interview. Typically, in Piaget's realm, a group of investigators is working on a set of 10 to 20 related problems or experiments. This is necessary for the structuralist approach, since the aim is not so much to find out how the child solves this or that problem, but to understand the epistemic structure that regulates a whole class of tasks, for that is the structure developing. We consider this work to be germane to our work on creative thinking; indeed, some people would argue that the child discovering some concept, like conservation of matter under transformations of shape, is being just as creative as Archimedes when he took his famous bath. Piaget himself said now and then that childhood is the most creative time of life.

What distinguishes Piaget's version of developmentalism from our use of the case study method to elaborate the evolving systems approach is our interest in the *individual.* Piaget would argue that his goal was to get beyond the psychological individual in order to attain the "epistemic subject," or the set of regulatory norms that any knowing system must develop. In an interview in 1975 Piaget put it this way:

> Generally speaking – and I'm ashamed to say it – I'm not really interested in individuals, in the individual. I'm interested in what is general in the development of intelligence and knowledge, whereas psychoanalysis is essentially an analysis of individual situations, individual problems." (Bringuier, 1977/1980, p. 86)

This lack of interest in the individual showed itself throughout his work, not least in the simple fact that each child who participated in the Piagetian experiments did so only once. There was no effort to characterize enduring characteristics or concerns of the individual or to map out the developmental pathway actually taken by an individual. And this, of course, is exactly the focus and preoccupation leading to our use of the case study method and the evolving systems approach.

Our interest in the creative process requires that we look searchingly at each case we take up. Whereas Piaget and similar structuralists may have neglected the wider context in which the person develops, we have found it necessary and fascinating to pay careful attention to it – but without losing sight of our central concern with the question, How does each creative person do it? And it must be added that one set of contexts for our work has been all that we could learn from other approaches to creativity. An excellent contribution exhibiting this kind of prolonged attention to the creative individual – prolonged over years, so that one can see and grasp the developmental pathways taken – is the work of Franklin (1994) on seven women artists. Contrary to the notion of a single set of stages to which all developmental processes must conform, Franklin found "three modes of change: *generative problem solving, focused exploration, and converging streams*" (p. 172). The point here is not to commit oneself to a new orthodoxy hailing just these three types of developmental pathway; rather, the point is to encourage a wider search for varieties of pathways and to take note of the heterogeneity to be found even within a group of women artists who have much in common with each other.

Similar in their theoretical intent and methodological approach are Gruber's (1974/1981) work on Darwin, Wallace and Gruber's collection of 12 cognitive case studies (1989), a further collection published as a special issue of the *Journal of Adult Development* (see Gruber, 1996b, for details), and a special issue of the *Creativity Research Journal* constituting a collection of 10 studies of scientists (see A. I. Miller, 1996, for details). This volume is also a good starting point for tracking Holmes's fine studies of Bernard, Lavoisier, and Krebs. Of particular interest is a special issue of the *Creativity Research Journal* carrying autobiographical accounts by five Nobel laureates and some others, all in the biomedical field (see O'Reilly and Holmes, 1994, for details). As one of the participants in the symposium on which these accounts are based, Gruber has the impression that the process of discovery in the biomedical field is quite different from that in the physical sciences.

In general, the studies just listed share the common feature of giving a modicum of background information and then focusing intensely on the detailed structure of the individual creative process as exhibited in each study. *A Passion for Science,* a collection produced by Wolpert and Richards (1988), demonstrates effectively that it is possible to maintain the same perspective of the developmental process in relatively brief studies. There is a steady accumulation of biographies and a few autobiographies of scientists, many of which do maintain a balance between the purely personal and cognitive-creative issues. Of these we cite only one, chosen in part because its title alone says so much that is relevant to our project: *A Feeling for the Organism: The Life and Work of Barbara McClintock* (Keller, 1983). Taking our "organism" to be the creative person at work, it does seem that we are moving toward capturing the feeling.

$N = 1$ OR $N = $ MANY?

For the most part the rubric *case study method* has been used to refer to studies in which there is one central figure, $N = 1$. This has had two purposes. First, to make the task more feasible. If the study is to be about the creator's work, it seems obviously easier to know one creator and describe his or her work thoroughly than to grapple with many. Second, we are frankly interested in celebrating individuals and the idea of individuality, rescuing them from the conceptual pigeonholes of "species-specific behavior," the "bell curve," and the "epistemic subject." As we show later, we believe this respect for the individual can be achieved without losing sight of the many ways in which creators are embedded in their social contexts. Indeed, it behooves the investigator of the single case to search assiduously for the right movement between these two poles. The decision to do so is not itself a solution to the problem, it is only a methodological proposal. There will be at least as many solutions as there are cases.

The central point is not really the size of N, but rather the shaping of the case study so that it maintains a primary focus on the creative work. Moreover, the investigator must choose the case or cases with some sense of his or her own intellectual assets, in other words, some confidence of an adequate level of understanding the work itself.

In some instances, of course, dealing with more than one case at a time becomes essential for understanding the work. The Curies, the Wright brothers, Marx and Engels, the Marx brothers, Inhelder and Piaget, Braque and Picasso, Gilbert and Sullivan – all are examples of close collaborations. Then there are cases of convergence of efforts initially independent, such as the work of Feynman, Dyson, Schwinger, and Tomonaga mentioned earlier; this case has aspects both of collaboration (Feynman and Dyson) and of convergence of independent streams (Feynman, Schwinger, and Tomonaga).

Gardner's work (1993) represents yet another rationale for multiple case studies. He selected seven individuals using two main criteria: First, there was to be one from each of the seven types of "intelligence" that he had singled out earlier (Gardner, 1983); second, all of the individuals lived within a relatively narrow historical period – their life spans run from 1856 (Freud the earliest born) to 1973 (Picasso the last to die). The others are Einstein, Stravinsky, Eliot, Graham, and Gandhi. These seven did not know each other and did not work together. But, Gardner argues, they can be taken as makers of the modern era. Of course, Gardner does not go into the details of their actual creative work at the same level as might be expected of a scholar choosing a narrower range of subjects. Nevertheless, he achieves a decent balance between concern for the work itself, for its historical context, and for the creative person doing it. For a more detailed examination of this work see Gruber (1996c).

CASE AS SYSTEM: PERSON AND MILIEU

Csikszentmihalyi (1988) has criticized Gruber (1988) for focusing attention on the evolving person while neglecting its ever-present and inseparable partner, the evolving milieu. There is some justice in this criticism, at least as far as it pertains to the 1988 article. But in Gruber's key work, *Darwin on Man: A Psychological Study of Scientific Creativity* (1974/1981), that requirement has been rather fully met by an institutional approach. In the section on "the intellectual setting," there is a chapter on general ideological conditions prevailing in Darwin's world, a chapter on the role of the family in shaping his *Weltanschauung,* and a chapter on Darwin's teachers. There is also a chapter on the relationships between public and private knowledge, so important in Darwin's case and in other cases where dangerous ideas are at stake. This public–private relationship is expanded in an appendix added to the 1981 edition, which was omitted from the original work (Gruber, 1974/1981) and which is further expanded in a later publication (Gruber, 1994). The latter also goes more deeply into the relation between Darwin and Wallace, especially with regard to the issue of public and private knowledge.

There is, then, more than one way to treat the person as a system within systems. The tripartite division – field, domain, person – that permeates the work of Feldman, Csikszentmihalyi, and Gardner (1994) is a very useful approach. Gruber's approach has been to situate the individual within a set of milieus that corresponds to the institutional framework within which the person develops. To be sure, no list of institutions is as yet cast in stainless steel. Nevertheless, the institutional approach has the merit that, for the most part, institutions are relatively easy to define and identify: Family, school, workplace, and community make a good beginning. Then there are subtler and sometimes more transitory institutions, like the European students' *Wanderjahr* and the "invisible colleges" that are described by some sociologists of science.

This approach is amplified later under the heading of "Contextual Frames." For the moment, the point we wish to stress is that there are various ways of parceling out a creative life into the societal arrangements within which it unfolds. Karl Marx may be out of fashion now, but not so long ago a discussion of this subject, creativity and society, would probably include some reference to social class. In the Darwin case, social class seems particularly relevant (see, e.g., Moore, 1985); in Einstein's case, not. Or, as Marx's collaborator Friedrich Engels (1894) wrote of "social history":

Anyone therefore who sets out in this field to hunt down final and ultimate truths, truths which are pure or absolutely immutable, will bring home but little, apart from platitudes and commonplaces of the sorriest kind. (p. 104)

Of course, one person's platitudes are another's beatitudes, so Engels's admonition may not be always germane. Still, the key point remains: The student of the creative case must not use the task of examining context as substituting for the task of penetrating the case in all its inwardness.

SCALE

There is yet another distinction to observe in shaping a case study – the issue of scale. Some case studies focus on the single opus, as in Arnheim's (1962) work on Picasso's *Guernica.* This choice of focus probably requires both the deepest technical knowledge and the greatest understanding, for the investigator must try to penetrate the creator's moves down to the last brush stroke. At the other extreme is a broad focus on the oeuvre, which requires that the investigator perceive the broad movements of the creator's thinking, intuit his or her *Weltanschauung,* understanding the life task that animates the oeuvre. This distinction between opus and oeuvre has hardly been noticed, much less used as a guide in shaping case studies. Tentatively we recommend that each investigator at least try out several such foci as part of the process of choosing the most fruitful orientation for a particular study.

MULTIPLE FACETS

Creative work is always a many-faceted undertaking. Whether a given facet is a description to be attributed to the creator or to the investigator may vary. But we bear in mind the need for a certain humility: Any facet of which we may become aware owes its origin to something the creator said or did, and was therefore something of which the creator was most probably aware as well.

It will be seen that facets sometimes lie within other facets. Since any further hierarchical organization of the system may be quite labile, we simply number the upcoming facets successively as they occur in this account. Any description of these facets is bound to be incomplete, and every case study must involve careful choices of the facets to be dwelt on. These choices will take into account the scientific aims of the investigator, the particulars of the case, and the availability of material for study. The facets we take up here are quite similar to the ones we suggest to our students. Experience has shaped our plan and shows that it is a workable guide for the study of a wide assortment of creative cases.

Treating the study of the creative case as comprising a large number of distinct facets does risk losing sight of the individual as a whole person. That would resemble the surgeon's verdict: "The operation was a success but the patient died." Our approach, however, is holistic in several senses. First, in our treatment of each facet, we aim at completeness. For example, in dealing with the creator's purposes we use the network of enterprise as a way of considering all of his or her enterprises. Second, we try to deal with several main facets together, in their interaction – for it is in these interactions that we recapture the whole quality of the creator. Third, our conception of the creative person at work as comprising three great subsystems – knowledge, purpose, and affect – obligates the investigator to deal with the way they come together in the person as a whole. The concept of loose coupling contributes to this holism: The components are joined together but not in the same way for any two cases. We must therefore study them in their particulars and in their concrete detail to understand how this creator differs from that one. Fourth, our own interest in development and our insistence on the idea that creative work is extended in time requires that the investigator examine the case at more than one moment in time. This in turn leads to the construction of narrative as a natural component of any case study.

The level of analysis we aim at resembles the physiologist's. First, study some organ of the body, then study how that organ contributes to and is affected by its manifold connections with other organs, that is, the system as a whole.

As we move along in this discussion we will encounter certain facets, each of which is large enough to deserve at least a whole chapter, something akin to organ systems such as the central nervous system, the skeletal system, the endocrine system, and so on. Some of these facets will be dealt with at length, others only mentioned. Some lie comfortably within one or another of the three great subsystems mentioned earlier – knowledge, purpose, and affect. Others cut across them. For example, metaphors are often both cognitive and affective expressions, such as Blake's line, "The tygers of wrath are wiser than the horses of instruction" (1790/1946, p. 254).

Facet 1: Uniqueness

Murray and Kluckhohn (1950) maintained that every person is like all others in some respects, like some others in some respects, and like no others in some respects, referred to by Wallace (1989a) as Alpha, Beta, and Gamma, respectively. But it is the *distribution* and *configuration* of Alpha, Beta, and Gamma – how they are represented and entangled so to speak – that makes up the whole person and the person's individuality and uniqueness,

Omega. So when we study the creative person, we are studying aspects of Omega, not merely Gamma (like no others). Most psychometric studies of creativity try to identify attributes that creative people have in common. In terms of our theoretical framework, their focus is on Beta (like some others). Unfortunately, this blurs important issues. Attributes such as high aspiration level, obsession with work, and good problem-solving skills can be observed not only among world-class creators, but also among many a corporate person in a gray flannel suit.

Facet 2: The Epitome

The narrative in the case study method will include an epitome, a succinct account of what the creator achieved and how this compares with contemporaries working in the same vineyard. The point is not to decide who is "the greatest." Rather, the aim is to understand the obstacles that our case faced and how he or she dealt with them. In a more extended account the question will be posed, What led up to and what followed from the work in question? This would at least touch on precursors and descendants of the case. Perhaps even more important would be an account of the general situation in which these historical movements occurred.

Facet 3: Systems of Belief

From the narrative that can be constructed of Darwin's evolving system of beliefs during the voyage, a schematization can be drawn. As shown in Figure 5.1, Darwin's belief system evolved through some four or five major stages from 1831 to 1836. In 1838, Darwin himself constructed a different schematization of his thinking at an early stage in his search for a workable theory of evolution. In the B Notebook, his first notebook on evolution, at the top of page 36 he wrote "I think" followed by the celebrated schematization of the irregularly branching tree of nature evolving (Figure 5.2).

Darwin's case is among those few where we have a *sequential* record of the individual's thinking. Fortunately for us, although he did not date every entry, he recorded his ideas and observations in bound notebooks, often numbering the pages himself. This makes it possible to see each of Darwin's tree diagrams in sequence (at least six are known), and to make some sense of what was troubling his thinking, leading to each new version of the diagram. Thus, he recorded his thinking in two modalities, verbal and visual graphics. While the Darwin manuscripts are unusually rich, we believe that most creators leave a trail rich enough to tax all our hindsight, wit, and wisdom as we struggle to explore and make sense of it all. The student of the case must be bold enough to *interpret* the material available.

Darwin worked in an intellectual climate that revered the seemingly definitive, all-inclusive, and successful determinism of Newton. This attitude provided a philosophy of science that relied on general laws and an embodiment of scientific knowledge in a form that Darwin hoped to extend from physical to biological science. This intent is expressed in the famous last paragraph of the *Origin of Species*, where Darwin wrote:

There is grandeur in this view of life, with its several powers, having been originally breathed into a few forms or into one; and that whilst this planet has gone cycling on according to the fixed law of gravity, from so simple a beginning endless forms most beautiful and most wonderful have been, and are being, evolved. (1859, p. 490)

At one level, Darwin was an exponent of this determinism. And yet at another level he was the chief originator of an alternative approach to nature, both probabilistic and nondeterminist. Or, in an alternative formulation suggested by Schweber, Newtonian thought is

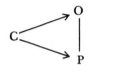

A. 1832 and before: The Creator has made an organic world (*O*) and a physical world (*P*) ; *O* is perfectly adapted to *P*.

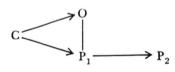

B. 1832–1834: The physical world undergoes continuous change, governed by natural laws as summarized in Lyell's *Principles of Geology.* In other respects, *B* resembles *A*.

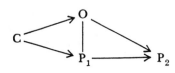

C. 1835: The activities of living organisms contribute to the evolution of the physical world, as exemplified by the action of the coral organism in making coral reefs. In other respects, *C* resembles *B*.

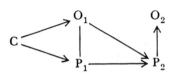

D. 1836–1837: Changes in the physical world imply changes in the organic world, if adaptation is to be maintained; the direct action of the physical milieu induces the appropriate biological adaptations. In other respects, *D* resembles *C*.

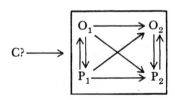

E. 1838 and after: The physical and organic worlds are both continuously evolving and interacting with each other. The Creator, if one exists, may have set the natural system in being, but He does not interfere with its operation, standing *outside* the system.

Figure 5.1. Darwin's changing worldview, 1832–1838. During the years of the *Beagle* voyage and immediately following, Darwin's general worldview evolved through five major phases. From Gruber (1974/1981, p. 127).

based on a conservation principle, whereas Darwinian thought is based on a principle of maximization – life fills up the available niches and creates new ones unpredictably. Life becomes as complex and perfect as possible (Schweber, 1985, pp. 47–55), and each new becoming opens the way to new possibilities (Piaget, 1981/1987).

Evidently then, in his historical situation, Darwin was poised between an old and highly successful way of thought and a new way just coming into focus. The reader will no doubt have noticed that the dilemmas which Darwin faced in this regard resemble those faced by students of creative thinking who may have been raised in quite deterministic ways of thinking still prevalent in psychology. Thus, students of creative work may profit by being sensitive to what they can learn from their cases. In the case study method the narrative is a jumping-off point for reflective thought. The case study method is not the royal road to the best way of thinking; it is only an approach that may help us to enrich our repertoires for understanding the many ways of creative work.

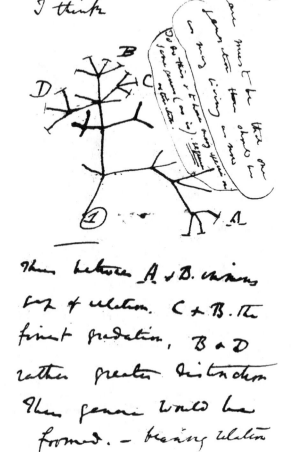

Figure 5.2. Darwin's third diagram of the tree of life. Darwin began his first notebook on evolution in July 1837. The first and second tree diagrams appear on p. 26. The third, shown here, appears on p. 36. In a much more elaborate and formal version, it is the only diagram in *On the Origin of Species*, written 21 years later. From Cambridge University Library. Reproduced in Gruber (1974/1981), p. 143.

Facet 4: Modalities of Thought

In discussions of creative work one hardy, perennial group of questions concerns the modality in which the creator thinks. Is all really creative thinking visual? What about musical composition? Did Wordsworth really think in iambic pentameter? Do mathematicians think in equations? If the real work of thinking is unconscious, does it have to take place in some specifiable modality or is there "amodal" thought analogous to Michotte, Thinès, and Crabbé's (1964) amodal perception? Did Aristotle really say that "metaphor is the essence of real thought"? And, urgently, how can this investigator work out this case's modalities of thought?

Since we are delving into the realm of private experience, we cannot expect all the questions to be answerable, or all the answers to be firm. But we can at least approach some of the issues. For example, A. I. Miller (1996) argues that at a certain point in the history of theoretical physics, in 1923, "Bohr's planetary atom was abandoned" and replaced by a model using simple harmonic oscillators. "This is a non visual metaphor because each atomic electron is represented by an infinity of harmonic oscillators" (p. 115). What can we learn from this? First, metaphors have histories. Second, a transformation can occur from one modal-

ity to another (visual to nonvisual, in this instance). Third, metaphors and their transformations are consequential: In this instance, the developments in question led to the formulation of modern quantum mechanics. Finally, it may take a considerable degree of expert
knowledge to penetrate some niches in the tangled bank of the mind. See Gruber (1996a)
for a fuller treatment of the modality question.

In the study of metaphor there has been a strong tendency to take one or another
metaphor and work it to death, using it as the command center of a given creator's thinking.
When Gruber did his work on Darwin's use of metaphor, he began with the image of the
irregularly branching tree of nature. But he soon discovered that Darwin made use of four
or five families of metaphors just to clarify the idea of evolution through natural selection.
Moreover, each variant within a family made sense, that is, had a function in the web of Darwin's argument. A similar argument, made by Osowski (1989), applies to William James's
chapter "The Stream of Thought" in his *Principles of Psychology* (1890/1950).

These findings led us to the concept of an "ensemble of metaphors" (Gruber, 1978). This
has now become the recommendation that the investigator examine all the metaphors in a
given text and try to express how, taken together, they represent a field of meaning. Although
this is a useful approach it does lead to one major complication. When the creator is not making a metaphor, what is he or she doing? Associating ideas? Constructing a causal chain?
Describing a scene? Recounting or constructing a narrative? Classifying objects or people
or events? Without some such taxonomy it may not be possible to answer the question,
Under what circumstances does a given creator resort to metaphor (not forgetting that one
possible answer is "always")?

Nevertheless, with all its complications the examination of ensembles of metaphor is a
promising way to delineate the main lines of a developing thought process. It was put to
good use by Osowski (1989) in his analysis of the family of metaphors in which James's most
famous metaphor, the stream of consciousness, is embedded (James, 1890/1950).

Facet 5: Multiple Timescales

It would be difficult if not impossible to construct the narrative of a case study using only
one timescale. Short-term activities and experiences are embedded within longer episodes,
and so on. Arnheim (1962) gives a penetrating account of one month in Picasso's life, the
month in which he created *Guernica*, the mural depicting the horror of the Nazi raid on a
holy city in Spain. The mural is widely acclaimed as one of Picasso's most important works.
But to understand it and the processes that produced it, one needs to look at Spanish political history, the community of artists in Paris in the 1930s, Picasso's own development as an
artist, and the moment-by-moment flow of work. These events each have their appropriate
timescales, ranging from a few minutes to many decades.

Wallace's study (1989b) of the British novelist Dorothy Richardson is an interesting example of the discovery of the interrelating timescales within which the creator worked. In
Richardson's case there were the decades of an actual life as depicted in her autobiographical novel; there was the much longer period in which the writer composed the novel; and
there were other timescales of events in both domains.

Facet 6: Purposeful Work and Networks of Enterprise

As we have already emphasized, an overall purpose is central to creative work and is part of
the motivation to go on working for long periods or for a lifetime. As this process is set in
motion, ideas and projects proliferate and the means for achieving the overall purpose
become more numerous and more complex. Organization is needed to order this work, to

set subsidiary goals, and to benefit the person's working economy as a whole. The work entails mundane activities or tasks, and it requires identifying and solving problems that arise out of a given project. Thus, the course of a single project is hierarchically organized: projects, problems, tasks. But there is another level of the organization of work, *enterprises*. An enterprise is an enduring group of related activities aimed at producing a series of kindred products. An enterprise embraces a number of projects. Most typically, as one project is completed new possibilities come to the fore, to be undertaken next or later. Finishing a project rarely leads to a state of rest; rather it triggers further work, as if completion furnishes the momentum to go on. Thus, each enterprise is self-replenishing. Einstein formulated the special theory of relativity in 1905, then took 11 years more for the general theory of relativity, then went on to struggle and search for a unified field theory (see, e.g., Pais, 1982). In spite of his commitment to a unitary theory, for purposes of analysis – that is, to understand how he organized his work – we can arrange his works under different categorical headings or enterprises.

To construct a network of enterprise it may be advisable to begin with a simple scheme, such as the dichotomy that Gruber noted in his examination of Darwin's activities during the *Beagle* voyage: Most of Darwin's work during the voyage could be classified as either geological or zoological, and it was revealing to plot the changing outputs of work in these domains over the five years of the voyage. What this revealed is that Darwin's work in geology far outweighed his zoological work.

But work at the frontier typically reveals other challenges, and the network grows more complex. An early stage in Darwin's development, the "notebook years" immediately following the *Beagle* voyage, can be schematized as a branching structure producing a trichotomy – roughly, geology, general evolutionary theory, human evolution. This trichotomy is embodied in the notebooks that Darwin kept during the years 1835–1839 (Figure 5.3). Of course, it is a great simplification, as each notebook contains a wide variety of topics.

In Piaget's case, his 60 books and longer monographs provided the database and produced a network composed of 10 enterprises – each with its own starting date and many cross-connections. The 10 strands are natural history, religion, epistemology and synthesis, sociology, logic, ontology, biology, representation, perception, education. Doubtless, when the process for Piaget's whole oeuvre (over 1,000 items) is completed new categories will emerge, and new connections among them.

With a refined enough eye and enough time for reflection, one can always produce more categories. There are "lumpers" and "splitters" here just as in any taxonomic effort. But our goal is not to discover the one true network of enterprise or taxonomy, but to get an overall view of the creative person at work and to discover interesting lines for further study. Sometimes simplification is appropriate. For example, in his late twenties and early thirties van Gogh moved away from his early religious preoccupations and toward full commitment to a life in art. This movement and the vacillations of a long transitional period are well revealed by plotting the occurrences of remarks on these two subjects in his letters to his brother Theo (Wimpenny, 1994). Once we have established the reciprocal waxing and waning of the two preoccupations of religion and art, further reflection is called for, to examine the sense in which van Gogh remained a deeply spiritual person. So we must learn and relearn for each case how to navigate between simplicity and complexity and between countable objectivity and a sensitive, literate reading of the creator's products.

Some of our colleagues have interpreted the idea of networks of enterprise as meaning that the more enterprises there are, the more creative the person. This parallels and closely resembles the fallacy that high scores on tests of divergent thinking are tokens of great creativity. As Gruber (1982) has noted:

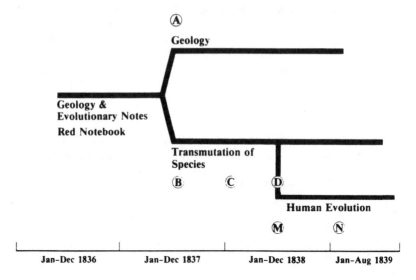

Figure 5.3. Darwin's evolving network of enterprise, 1836–1839. The organization of Darwin's notebooks reveals the main branches of his emerging network of enterprise. Adapted from Herbert (1980).

Baldwin, in his 1898 presidential address to the American Psychological Association, "On Selective Thinking," ridiculed this scattershot image of thought ("scatterbrained" he called it) and spoke of human creativity as the product of purposeful, reflective thought." (p. 4)

DYNAMIC FEATURES OF THE ORGANIZATION OF PURPOSE. From the investigator's point of view, the purposes of a network of enterprise are, first, to provide an overview of the patterns of continuity and relationships among enterprises by showing the course of the work as a whole over the years or decades of working life in a simplified form and, second, to serve as a counterpoint to the detailed and hermeneutic narrative derived from examining texts such as the person's notebooks, critical comments, autobiographical accounts, correspondence, and creative products.

Mapping a network of enterprise is a task performed standing "outside" the case (see the later section "Investigator Roles"). It enables one to see the development of the creative person's work enterprises over a lifetime as an aerial map. For example, midway in the *Beagle* voyage Darwin was thinking about the way in which billions of coral organisms made the coral islands of the Pacific. Soon after the voyage he gave two papers, both on the ways in which organismic action remakes the Earth. The first was his paper explaining his theory of the formation of coral reefs (Darwin, 1837a). The second was his paper explaining how the action of the digestive systems of billions of earthworms is constantly transforming vegetable matter into topsoil (Darwin, 1837b). Without knowing about the coral reef paper, the worm paper would seem to come out of nowhere. Darwin's study of earthworms continued until 1882, the year of his death and also the year of publication of his book about worms (Darwin, 1882). This is a wonderful example of the pursuit of different enterprises in parallel, that is, during the same time period – since the worm work was done in parallel with everything else that Darwin did during those 45 years.

A common pattern in creative work is this simultaneity of enterprises. The creative person is often engaged in more than one enterprise at a time. For example, as noted, during the *Beagle* voyage Darwin wrote copiously on zoology, geology, and other topics. After the voyage, beginning in 1836, the development of Darwin's enterprises is represented in the various notebooks he kept (Gruber 1974/1981). As is clear in Figure 5.3, Darwin began the Red Notebook in 1836. This book mostly contains his geological notes, but it also includes some of his earliest notes on evolution. By mid-1837, Darwin began a separate notebook (the A Notebook) entirely devoted to geology. *The very same day* he started the B Notebook containing his first notes on the transmutation of species. When the B Notebook was full, Darwin began the C Notebook in which he continued his transmutation notes and began to write about the evolution of mind. When this notebook was full, Darwin continued the transmutation notes in the D Notebook and the same day began the M and N Notebooks, which dealt with aspects of human evolution, such as the expression of emotion in and the continuity between *Homo sapiens* and other animals. Figure 5.3 shows this branching and simultaneity in Darwin's enterprises. The development of differentiation and specialization is striking and occurred when an enterprise had proliferated to the point where it demanded separate status.

A second feature that a network of enterprise reveals is continuity. By organizing the work into distinct enterprises, it becomes possible to put tasks aside and resume them without always starting from scratch. The paraphernalia of writing, labeling, and filing and the separate social and professional networks corresponding to the various tasks and projects support this twin need for differentiation and stabilization.

The simultaneity and duration of enterprises (which we have found in cases we and our colleagues have studied) have other advantages. Resuming work on an enterprise after a lapse means that the fruits of work gained from other enterprises can be applied to the work at hand; techniques learned or refined or knowledge acquired in one enterprise can be put to use in another. Another way of looking at patterns of interrelationships of this kind is to see them as a web of interruption and resumption, such that a task or project undertaken in one enterprise becomes an interruption in another. Seen in this way, the interruption itself eventually moves the creator to resume work in the interrupted enterprise. Interruptions of this kind have well-known dynamic effects in short-term laboratory situations (Lewin, 1935). The concept of the network of enterprise permits the application of the same line of thought on the scale of one's life history. It evokes a picture of the creative mind as a system, in Newton's words, "never at rest" (Westfall, 1980, p. ii).

As described earlier, the network of enterprise is a phenomenon drawn up by the investigator as seen from his or her point of view. But from the point of view of the creative person, there are other things to be said. At any temporal point in the network, the creative person probably sees the future of his or her work differently – perhaps less distinctly in the long-term for example – than is depicted in the network drawn over a life by the investigator. But looked at cross-sectionally rather than longitudinally, the network represents, at any point in time, the creative person's self-conscious understanding of the history, present state, and future concept of his or her work.

In addition to the sense in which we say that several enterprises may be active at the same time, there are some enterprises that have gone dormant. The evidence justifying the word *dormant* rather than discontinued is the fact that when the person resumes an interrupted activity, he or she does not begin at the beginning but takes cognizance of the work done earlier. Indeed, the creator is likely to have a number of means available to accomplish this purpose, such as notebooks and early studies or drafts, old colleagues who can be looked up when appropriate, and the unfinished work itself. More generally, both the dormant and the active sectors of the network of enterprise contribute to the creator's maintenance of his or her self-concept, and this is necessary for creative work.

In a fully worked out network of enterprise one would want to consider its relation to the paradigms within which the creator functions. This is a neglected question in several ways. First, we do not know what proportion of a person's work is paradigmatic versus what proportion is consciously outside and – as in Darwin's case and Piaget's – undermines the paradigm. Second, suppose that two or more creators each worked wholly within an identical set of paradigms. They would not do so in the same sequences or with the same emphases, or, most important, with the same extraparadigmatic intent regarding the whole. For example, in the post-*Beagle* years Darwin worked in very conventional ways with a number of colleagues expert in diverse domains. At the same time, his work on evolutionary theory was revolutionary and secret. In the long run it may have been less important that it was secret than that it was extraparadigmatic. Third, it is not clear how the dichotomy, paradigmatic and revolutionary, applies to creative work outside the sciences.

The network of enterprise is a system of goals. One of the important ways in which goals are maintained and managed is by making *initial sketches.* These provisional productions can take many forms, such as project proposals to potential patrons, actual sketches, or even dreams. When Picasso set out to paint *Guernica,* he made a small rough sketch of what he was aiming at. In seeming self-contradiction, Picasso said, "The first 'vision' remains almost intact in spite of appearances," but a moment later he said, "A picture is not thought out and settled beforehand. While it is being done it changes as one's thoughts change" (Arnheim, 1962, p. 30). We can understand the conjunction of these two remarks if we think of the initial sketch as having both exploratory and regulatory functions. How the creator manages to balance these different functions must be discerned anew in each case. Most homeostatic systems are negative feedback systems: The controls are set to make corrections that eliminate deviations from some desired value (such as blood temperature equals 98.6°F). But creative systems require some positive feedback: When an interesting deviation from a norm occurs, the system responds by noticing, labeling, and amplifying it (Maruyama, 1963). This central problem in the study of creative cases – how novelties are seized upon and elaborated – has hardly been identified, much less carefully examined and applied to specific cases.

Facet 7: Problem Solving

As discussed earlier, when the modern impulse to study creativity gathered momentum in the years following World War II, there was a focus on problem solving as the facet of greatest interest. Laboratory studies of problem solving are fascinating in their own right but do not necessarily address the topic in ways that are very revealing for the study of creativity. This led to a rather wide search for other important aspects of the creative process, such as the facets we have taken up in this chapter. The pendulum of interest swung away from problem solving. With the case study method, however, the investigator is responsible for taking up what is important to the creator, not only what is fashionable. We believe we are now in a good position to return to problem solving as an important facet of the creative process.

Ochse (1990) and Weisberg (1993) each give good accounts of research in this area. Problem finding, heuristics and computer modeling, and incubation are prominent elements of this research. Wallas's (1926) four-stage theory (preparation, incubation, illumination, and verification) is often reiterated.

In conducting a case study, all of these topics are of potential importance. At the same time, if we pay adequate attention to the issue of timescale, all of them are transformed. Generally speaking, people think in order to solve problems. The excellent problem solver may have gotten beyond that point: Problem solving comes relatively easily. It may be more apt to say that the creator sets him- or herself problems in order to think. The creator is not necessarily a better problem solver. The main point is to develop a new point of view, a perspective from which new problems are seen and old ones are seen in a new light. Charles Darwin was probably not as versatile, eloquent, or brilliant as Thomas Huxley. All Darwin did was to develop a new point of view and the determination to reexamine every problem from that perspective. Our task as investigators of the case is to discover how this came about.

Facet 8: Contextual Frames

In addition to its central focus on some aspects of the development of the creator's work, the case study should take into account a series of contexts or contextual systems (Csikszentmihalyi, 1988) within which the creative work proceeds. The first of these is the set of enterprises most directly relevant to those being studied. The second is the person's oeuvre and overall purposes, revealed in the network of enterprise. The third context is the person's professional milieu – teachers, colleagues, collaborators, critics, and so on.

The fourth context concerns the subject's families – the family of origin and the current family – and their role in the development and support of the subject's creative life and work. Wordsworth had as a collaborator his sister Dorothy, who also took charge of his domestic needs. Many women who want to do independent creative work have had and still have great difficulty in constructing a life that supports their work and fulfills their other needs. Woolf argued the case in her *A Room of One's Own* (1929/1957), and more recently Hanscombe and Smyers (1987) have done so. The cost to women has been either to forgo other roles – those of wife or mother, for example – or to do it all with inadequate support.

It is not often enough noted that family members may play a role not only in shaping the child but in the creative process itself. Consider these well-known examples:

> Darwin and his grandfather Erasmus
> Van Gogh and his brother Theo
> Einstein and his uncle Jakob
> Wordsworth and his sister Dorothy
> Anna Freud and her father Sigmund
> The Wright brothers
> The Brontë siblings

Finally, the fifth context is the sociohistorical milieu, which may have an important influence on the subject's work. Gruber (1974/1981) argued that Darwin's long delay in publishing *On the Origin of Species* was in large part due to his fear of a hostile reception. But this did not constrain his creative work; nor was he miserable because of it. Freud and many others left Hitler's Third Reich to work productively elsewhere. James Joyce left Ireland and Catholicism for Trieste in order to free himself from a constricting environment. Creative people may feel themselves to be marginal: They are breaking new ground, forging a new point of view that is, as they progress in their work, more and more at odds with their contemporaries and their rulers. This was the case for Galileo, Locke, and Descartes. Persecution is a recurrent feature of the history of creative work. But there have been creators who presented their work to the world and found it accepted without great travail, Poincaré, Henry Moore, Edison, and Picasso, among many. The person's position in the sociohistorical period depends on the nature of the work, whether it is being made public, how loudly it speaks beyond a specialized audience to the general public, and the degree of religious and political tolerance that impinges on the creator.

These five contexts form a series of frames in the case study method. The subject, of course, both produces these contexts and is shaped by them. But the investigator, too, must be familiar with them as frames of reference for the study. Ideally, they are integrated into the case study as part of the creator's system of thought and meaning that accompanies and affects the work. In a case study of reasonable length, not all of these contexts can be dealt with exhaustively. The investigator must make choices.

Facet 9: Values

Under the heading of values we group affect, aesthetic experience, and morality. We think it reasonable to characterize our approach as cognitive and developmental. For better or worse, this has meant that certain aspects of creative work have been neglected – by us and by like-minded colleagues. In some respects we have been constrained by decades of exalting the notion of "value-free science," of embracing cultural and ethical relativism, of questioning the meaning of truth unless it is put between quotation marks. The relation between creativity and morality has been neglected as a subject of investigation. Cases like that of Gandhi are immensely instructive, but there are very few who combine the advancing of truly innovative ideas (such as Gandhi's spiritual doctrine of nonviolence) with determined political struggle (such as Gandhi's leadership of the Indian liberation movement). Consequently, we must think both about the great moralists and about those creators for whom moral concerns are something of an avocation. Even supposing it is true that by the age of 40 or 50 most creators have done their best work, the remaining years will leave almost half a lifetime for something else. What will that something be? The dilemma facing creators in today's world is well expressed by Lewis Hyde:

How is the artist to nourish himself, spiritually as well as materially, in an age whose values are market values and whose commerce consists almost exclusively in the purchase and sale of commodities? (quoted in Gablik, 1984, p. v)

A similar set of concerns runs through the special issue of the *Creativity Research Journal* entitled "Creativity in the Moral Domain" (Gruber & Wallace, 1993). For the moment, we simply take note of a need that is already upon us and that will in all likelihood intensify. It follows that students of creativity should look for new ways of incorporating such concerns in their work.

CONCLUSION

The deliberate choice of the case study method, especially as contrasted with other methods, raises difficult epistemological questions. Here we will take up three issues: the locus of creativity, the investigator's roles, and the problem of reliability and validity.

The Locus of Creativity

Granting fully that creative work takes place within a complex social manifold, can we take a further step and withdraw from our emphasis on the unique creative individual as the creator, that is as the locus of creative work? Csikszentmihalyi (1994) has argued that we must do so. First, he proposes a $4 \times 3 \times 4$ matrix for characterizing types of creative work, that is, 48 cells in the matrix. Then he points out that "there are already thousands of psychological studies concentrating in just one of these cells – the quantitative, empirical approach to individual traits" (p. 154). He concludes that this means that "creativity is not something that takes place inside the head of a person but is the product of a far larger and more mysterious process" (p. 155).

This approach is certainly one option. It has the merit of forcing us to reexamine the excessive individualism of much creativity research. But it is tantamount to arguing that because an organ exists within an organism, the special functions of that organ do not really take place within the organ. Our approach is somewhat different. We avoid as much as possible the reification of a quantity called "creativity" in the belief that it is more fruitful to ask what creators *do*. We agree that there are something like the 4 levels (culture, instititution, working group, person) specified in the 48-cell matrix. But the "person," who is relegated to 4 of the 48 cells, can be located both in geographical and conceptual space and is no less real for that. As for mystery, as much as we strive to demystify creative work, it remains mysterious enough.

Investigator Roles

The issue of objectivity is critical. In the case study method, the investigator has two central roles, a phenomenological one and a critical one or, to put it another way, an inside and an outside role (Table 5.1). In the phenomenological role, the investigator strives to enter the mind of the subject of the case and to reconstruct the meaning of the subject's experience from the latter's point of view. This is an attempt to achieve objectivity by putting aside one's own biases. In this role, the investigator comes as close as possible to the case.

The equally essential critical role is one in which the investigator stands outside the case to appraise the data and to explain and interpret them. Here objectivity is achieved by putting aside the *subject's* biases, by distancing oneself from the subject, and by evaluating "from a height." Thus, both phenomenological and critical roles aim at objectivity and both entail interpretation. The investigator is continually moving between these two roles.

Reliability and Validity

Coming from a cognitive and experimental background, it might well be said that we are foolhardy to give up the blessings of precision and verifiability for the vagaries of the case study method, especially with our focus on studies in which $N = 1$. As long as we restrict ourselves to one case, how do we know we are right? Even if we are right about the case, what good is it if we cannot generalize to other cases? A decade or two ago there were very few such cognitive case studies. Now that there are many more, don't we face the problem of bringing them to bear on each other in a synthesis both wider and more penetrating? How do we approach the problem of objectivity – especially when we insist that the student of the case must immerse him- or herself in the world of the creator chosen for study? We have several replies.

First, it could be suggested that immersion in a single case, with the combination of scope and density needed to do it justice, represents a world well lost, as compared with the narrowness and aridity of other approaches. We emphatically do not take this position. Instead, we retain the hope of arriving at the kind of documented synthesis that might be attained by bringing different methods to bear on the same problem. To do that, of course, would require reforming many questions. Although we have insisted on the uniqueness of each case, that does leave room for a few interesting generalizations.

For example, a number of case studies have led to the so-called 10-year rule, the finding that it takes about 10 years for an individual or small group to effect significant revision in their own ways of thought. This is not the sort of finding that one could achieve without going about it one case at a time. On the surface, what with telescoping and forgetting, it is easy for the creator to experience the rush of delight when a great insight finally comes and to omit in the telling the years of work that were necessary to reach that moment. Without the accumulation of some 20 or more pertinent and striking cases, we could never have reached this conclusion; without attacking these cases one at a time we could never have

Table 5.1. *Investigator Roles*

Phenomenological Role	Critical Role
Inside the subject	Outside the subject
Objectivity achieved by setting aside one's own bias	Objectivity achieved by setting aside the subject's bias
Close to subject	Distant from subject
Interpretive	Interpretive

accumulated them in this fashion. For more on this see Gruber (1974/1981, 1995) and Sternberg and Davidson (1995).

For another example, consider the idea of networks of enterprise. As a potential factual finding, such networks were staring us in the face for decades, even centuries. But to focus attention on them, to name them and to show how they function in particular cases, required the assiduous application of the case study method, first in one case, then in a number of others, as discussed in this chapter.

Finding commonalties among different cases resembles Francis Galton's (1883) method of composite portraiture: Photographs of faces are adjusted to the same size and then super-imposed by multiple exposures. The resulting composite is "the portrait of a type and not of an individual" (p. 222). Galton applied this method to such "types" as Englishmen, criminals, army officers, family members, and racial groups. Galton argued that these "generic" images are "much more than averages. . . . They are real generalizations, because they include the whole of the material under consideration" (p. 233). In other words, they are like large statistical tables for considering together all the traits that go into making a particular type. Accidental traits are washed out. And Galton adds that reducing the size of the eventual print eliminates even more idiosyncratic detail, and so much the better!

Another photographic innovation dating from the same period came from the work of Eadweard Muybridge, beginning in the 1870s. He was interested in the analysis of bodily motion. He arranged batteries of cameras so that he could take a series of photographs of a creature in motion – a rabbit or a horse running, or a man walking – so closely spaced that the viewer could see the actual sequence of each movement (de Vries, 1971).

Thus, each of these methods has its advantages, one for eliminating detail and representing a static version of a type, the other for capturing very fine detail and representing the precise dynamic sequences in which activity unfolds.

To complete the visual metaphor of the different aspects of a case study, we would have to add something like the medical drawings of a ball and socket joint or other structures in which part is closely fitted to part. This articulation of parts, both in structure and function, is the most important thing the case study method allows and is completely absent from the most sophisticated techniques of measurement and statistical inference known to psychologists.

The evolution of such structural articulation is what Darwin (1859) had in mind when he wrote of "correlation of growth":

> The whole organization is so tied together during its growth and development, that when slight variations in any one part occur, and are accumulated through natural selection, other parts become modified. (p. 143)

It is this kind of almost perfect fitting that we would like to accomplish through the case study method. This is a far cry from the modern concept of correlation as used in research on creativity, in which a value of $r = .25$ to $.50$ may be hailed as statistically significant.

It is the scope and density of the creator's thought that permits the student of the case to search for ideas analogous to the beautiful mechanisms of adaptation that so amazed Darwin and his contemporaries. Darwin's notebooks about evolution (Barrett, Gautrey, Herbert, Kohn, & Smith, 1987; see also Gruber 1974/1981) reveal him as a person also thinking about thinking and provide some useful guides for the study of other cases. In this essay we have made much use of the Darwin case. The interplay among his organizations of purpose, affect, and knowledge, as well as his manifold relations with other scientists, are richly brought out in his early notebooks (Gruber, 1974/1981; Keegan & Gruber, 1983).

Throughout this essay we have made assumptions that may be seen as contradictory. On the one hand, the creator sets a high level of aspiration and expects or at least hopes to be efficacious, to make a difference. Yet the yield for a lifetime of effort may be small. At one point in his early notebooks Darwin wrote acceptingly of this dilemma:

Mention persecution of early Astronomers. – then add chief good of individual scientific men is to push their science a few years in advance only of their age. (C Notebook, p. 123, written about June 1838; in Barrett et al., 1987, p. 276)

A little earlier he had remarked that this slowness of thought was painful to undergo:

This multiplication of little means & bringing the mind to grapple with great effect produced [in long periods of time], is a most laborious, & painful effort of the mind." (C Notebook, p. 75, written about May 1838; in Barrett et al., 1987, p. 263)

Easy or hard, the interconnectedness of all life-forms puts constraints on rate of change. In our era we have our spotted owl struggle to teach us how difficult it is for people to accept this constraint. Darwin had already remarked on a similar situation: "Even one species of hawk decreasing in number must effect instantaneously all the rest" (D Notebook, p. 135, written Sept. 28, 1838, as part of the celebrated moment of Malthusian insight; in Barrett et al., 1987, p. 375).

Our emphasis on the role of the individual in the creative process should not be taken to mean that only lives that make a big difference are creative and worthwhile. Making small differences and even innovations that counteract change may be the most important forms of creative work in the years of the upcoming century that is almost upon us. If creative work is to be organismic, to express this feeling for the organism, perhaps it must be for the most part modest.

In a striking passage, Wittgenstein expressed this feeling:

When we first begin to *believe* anything, what we believe is not a single proposition, it is a whole system of propositions. (Light dawns gradually over the whole.) (1969, p. 21)

NOTE

We would like to thank the colleagues whose doctoral dissertations form part of the support structure for this essay: Richard Brower, Camille Burns, Chantal Bruchez-Hall, Anne Coddington, Ruth Daniels, Sara Davis, Nancy Ferrara, Donald Hovey, Linda Jeffrey, Robert Keegan, Roberta Mitchell, Martha Moore-Russell, Jeffrey Osowski, Alan Schwartz, Laura Tahir, Fernando Vidal, Doris Wallace, Crystal Woodward, and Marta Zahaykevich.

REFERENCES

Arnheim, R. (1962). *The genesis of a painting: Picasso's "Guernica."* Berkeley: University of California Press.
Barrett, P. H., Gautrey, J., Herbert, S., Kohn, D., & Smith, S. (Eds.). (1987). *Charles Darwin's Notebooks, 1836–1844.* Ithaca, NY: Cornell University Press.

Barron, F., & Harrington, D. M. (1981). Creativity, intelligence, and personality. *Annual Review of Psychology, 32,* 439–476.

Blake, W. (1790/1946). The marriage of heaven and hell. In A. Kazin (Ed.), *The portable Blake* (pp. 249–266). New York: Viking.

Bringuier, J-C. (1980). *Conversations with Jean Piaget.* Chicago: University of Chicago Press. (Original work published 1977)

Csikszentmihalyi, M. (1988). Where is the evolving milieu? A response to Gruber (1981). *Creativity Research Journal, 1,* 60–67.

Csikszentmilhalyi, M. (1994). The domain of creativity. In D. H. Feldman, M. Csikszentmihalyi, & H. Gardner (Eds.), *Changing the world, a framework for the study of creativity* (pp. 154–155). London: Praeger.

Darwin, C. (1837a). On certain areas of elevation and subsidence in the Pacific and Indian oceans, as deduced from the study of coral formations. *Proceedings of the Geological Society of London, 21,* 552–554. (Presented May 31, 1837)

Darwin, C. (1837b). On the formation of mould. *Transactions of the Geological Society of London, 1840,* 505–509. (Read November 1, 1837)

Darwin, C. (1859). *On the origin of species.* London: Murray.

Darwin, C. (1882). *The formation of vegetable mould through the action of worms, with observations on their habits.* London: Murray.

de Vries, L. (1971). *Victorian inventions.* New York: McGraw-Hill.

Dyson, F. (1979). *Disturbing the universe.* New York: Harper.

Engels, F. (1894). *Herr Eugen Duehring's revolution in science.* New York: International Publishers.

Feldman D. H., Csikszentmihalyi, M., & Gardner, H. (1994). *Changing the world: A framework for the study of creativity.* London: Praeger.

Franklin, M. B. (1994). Narratives of change and continuity: Women artists reflect on their work. In M. B. Franklin & B. Kaplan (Eds.), *Development and the arts: Critical perspectives* (pp. 165–191). Hillsdale, NJ: Erlbaum.

Gablik, S. (1984). *Has modernism failed?* New York: Thames & Hudson.

Galton, F. (1883). *Inquiries into human faculty and its development.* London: Dent.

Gardner, H. (1993). *Creating minds: An anatomy of creativity seen through the lives of Freud, Einstein, Picasso, Stravinsky, Eliot, Graham, Gandhi.* New York: Basic.

Ginsburg, H. P. (1997). *Entering the child's mind: The clinical interview in psychological research and practice.* New York: Oxford.

Gruber, H. E. (1978). Darwin's 'Tree of Nature' and other images of wide scope. In J. Wechsler (Ed.), *On aesthetics in science,* 121–142. Cambridge, MA: MIT Press.

Gruber, H. E. (1981). *Darwin on man: A psychological study of scientific creativity* (rev. ed.). Chicago: University of Chicago Press. (Original work published 1974)

Gruber, H. E. (1982). Foreword. In J. M. Broughton & D. J. Freeman-Moir (Eds.), *The cognitive-development psychology of James Mark Baldwin* (pp. xv–xx). Norwood, NJ: Ablex.

Gruber, H. E. (1988). The evolving systems approach to creative work. *Creativity Research Journal, 1,* 27–51,

Gruber, H. E. (1994). On reliving the *Wanderjahr:* The many voyages of the *Beagle. Journal of Adult Development, 1,* 47–69.

Gruber, H. E. (1995). Insight and affect in the history of science. In R. J. Sternberg & J. E. Davidson (Eds.), *The nature of insight* (pp. 397–431). Cambridge, MA: MIT Press.

Gruber, H. E. (1996a). The life space of a scientist: The visionary function and other aspects of Jean Piaget's thinking. *Creativity Research Journal, 9,* 251–266.

Gruber, H. E. (1996b). Starting out: The early phases of four creative careers – Darwin, van Gogh, Freud, and Shaw. *Journal of Adult Development, 3,* 1–6.

Gruber, H. E. (1996c). Book review of Howard Gardner's: *Creating minds: An anatomy of creativity seen through the lives of Freud, Einstein, Picasso, Stravinsky, Eliot, Graham and Gandhi. Journal of Creative Behavior, 30,* 213–227.

Gruber, H. E., & Wallace, D. B. (1993). Special issue: Creativity in the moral domain. *Creativity Research Journal, 6*(1&2), 1–200.

Guilford, J. P. (1950). Creativity. *American Psychologist, 5,* 444–454.

Hamburger, M. (Ed. and Trans.). (1952). *Beethoven: Letters and journals and conversations.* New York: Pantheon.

Hanscombe, G., & Smyers, V. L. (1987). *Writing for their lives: The modernist women, 1910–1940.* London: Women's Press.

Hyde, L. (1983). *The gift: Imagination and the erotic life of property.* New York: Dover.

James, W. (1950). *The principles of psychology* (2 vols.). New York: Dover. (Original work published 1890)

Keegan, R. T., & Gruber, H. E. (1983). Love, death and continuity in Darwin's thinking. *Journal of the History of the Behavioral Sciences, 19,* 15–30.

Keller, E. F. (1983). *A feeling for the organism: The life and work of Barbara McClintock.* San Francisco: Freeman.

Lewin, K. (1935). *A dynamic theory of personality: Selected papers.* New York: McGraw-Hill.

Maruyama, M. (1963). The second cybernetics: Deviation-amplifying mutual causal processes. *American Scientist, 51,* 164–179.

Michotte, A., Thinès, G., & Crabbé, G. (1964). Les compléments amodaux des structures perceptives (Amodal complements of perceptual structures). *Studia Psychologica.* Louvain: University of Louvain.

Miller, A. I. (1984). *Imagery in scientific thought creating twentieth-century physics.* Boston: Birkhäuser.

Miller, A. I. (1996). Metaphors in creative scientific thought. *Creativity Research Journal, 9,* 113–130.

Moore, J. R. (1985). Darwin of Downe: The evolutionist as squarson-naturalist. In D. Kohn, *The Darwinian heritage* (pp. 435–482). Princeton, NJ: Princeton University Press.

Murray, H. A., & Kluckhohn, C. (Eds.). (1950). *Personality in nature, society, and culture.* New York: Knopf.

Ochse, R. (1990). *Before the gates of excellence: The determinants of creative genius.* Cambridge University Press.

O'Reilly, W. G., & Holmes, F. L. (1994). Creativity and discovery. An introduction to the special issue. *Creativity Research Journal 7*(3 & 4), 221–223. [Special issue of *Creativity Research Journal,* sponsored by the Royal Society of Medicine, London, October 1989]

Osowski, J. V. (1989). Ensembles of metaphor in the psychology of William James. In D. B. Wallace & H. E. Gruber (Eds.), *Creative People at Work* (pp. 127–145). New York: Oxford.

Pais, R. S. (1982). *"Subtle is the Lord . . ." the science and the life of Albert Einstein.* New York: Oxford University Press.

Piaget, J. (1987). *Possibility and necessity* (2 vols.). Minneapolis: University of Minnesota Press. (Original work published 1981)

Schweber, S. S. (1985). The wider British context in Darwin's theorizing. In D. Kohn (Ed.), *The Darwinian heritage* (pp. 35–70). Princeton, NJ: Princeton University Press.

Schweber, S. S. (1994). *QED and the men who made it. Dyson, Feynman, Schwinger and Tomonaga.* Princeton, NJ: Princeton University Press.

Sternberg, R. J., and Davidson, J. E. (1995). *The nature of insight* Cambridge, MA: MIT Press.

Titchener, E. B. (1909). *Lectures on the experimental psychology of the thought processes.* New York: Macmillan.

Wallace, D. B. (1989a). Studying the individual: The case study method and other genres. In D. B. Wallace & H. E. Gruber (Eds.), *Creative people at work: Twelve cognitive case studies* (pp. 25–43). New York: Oxford University Press.

Wallace, D. B. (1989b). Stream of consciousness and reconstruction of self in Dorothy Richardson's *Pilgrimage.* In D. B. Wallace & H. E. Gruber (Eds.), *Creative people at work: Twelve cognitive case studies* (pp. 147–169). New York: Oxford University Press.

Wallace, D. B., Gruber, H. E. (Eds.). (1989). *Creative people at work: Twelve cognitive case studies.* New York: Oxford University Press.

Wallas, G. (1926). *The art of thought.* New York: Harcourt Brace.

Weisberg, R. W. (1993). *Creativity: Beyond the myth of genius.* New York: Freeman

Wertheimer, M. (1945). *Productive thinking.* New York: Harper.

Westfall, R. S. (1980). *Never at rest: A biography of Isaac Newton.* Cambridge University Press.

Wimpenny, N. (1994). The development of Vincent van Gogh's creative belief systems preceding his commitment to art. Unpublished student paper, Teachers College, Columbia University.

Wittgenstein, L. (1969). *On certainty.* New York: Harper & Row.

Wolpert, L., & Richards, A. (1988). *A passion for science.* New York: Oxford University Press.

Woolf, V. (1957). *A room of one's own.* New York: Harcourt, Brace, Jovanovich. (Original work published 1929)

6 Creativity from a Historiometric Perspective

DEAN KEITH SIMONTON

What is creativity? How can creativity be measured? What factors predict the appearance or demonstration of creativity? How can the psychologist even begin to tackle these questions? Let us begin with the last issue, for on that response depends the answer to the more fundamental issues. For some time psychologists have had three major methods at their disposal.

First, psychologists can design and execute laboratory experiments. Here creativity is usually defined as the successful solution of problems that require some degree of insight (see, e.g., Sternberg & Davidson, 1995). Less commonly the production of original ideas is required, the creativity then being assessed by some panel of judges or other means (see, e.g., Amabile, 1996; Martindale, 1973; Sternberg & Lubart, 1995). By carefully manipulating the situation in which this behavior takes place, psychologists can learn the conditions that most favor creativity. The "subjects" (or participants) in these experiments are most often college students who need to earn extra credit in an introductory psychology course, although occasionally the subjects are individuals who might actually call themselves "creative" without too much immodesty.

Second, psychologists can conduct psychometric studies of individuals. Most often, these inquiries examine individuals according to their performance on so-called creativity tests (Barron & Harrington, 1981). Less frequent, but probably more valuable, are those psychometric investigations that examine persons whose credentials as creators is far less in doubt. The classic illustration is the series of investigations carried out at the Institute of Personality Assessment and Research at the University of California, Berkeley (e.g., Barron, 1969; MacKinnon, 1978). Here accomplished writers, architects, and other creative individuals were invited to undergo extensive assessment via cognitive tests, personality scales, biographical inventories, one-on-one interviews, and other assessment techniques. Their test scores are then contrasted with those obtained from subjects in a control group who could be matched with respect to age, training, and other pertinent factors. The ultimate aim is to isolate those individual difference variables that predict creative performance in the real world.

Third, psychologists can examine those creative individuals whose status as creators is unquestionable, because they are persons who have secured a lasting reputation for their original contributions to human civilization (Simonton, 1984d). In other words, the subjects in these inquiries have names that have "gone down in history" – names like Newton, Descartes, Tolstoy, Leonardo da Vinci, and Beethoven. The biographical and historical record concerning these luminaries is quantified and their creative output often subjected to content analysis – all directed at teasing out those personal traits and social circumstances that contribute to sociocultural success. Creativity in these inquiries is most often measured in terms of differential eminence, an artist like Michelangelo being judged as more creative than a painter like, say, Hendrick Bloemaert (e.g., Simonton, 1984a).

116

This third methodological approach is called *historiometry* and constitutes the subject of the current chapter. After first defining exactly what this method entails, I will provide a brief history of its historical development, and then outline some of the central topics addressed by this distinctive type of research.

DEFINING THE METHODOLOGY

Stated most formally, historiometry is that "scientific discipline in which nomothetic hypotheses about human behavior are tested by applying quantitative analyses to data concerning historical individuals" (Simonton, 1990c, p. 3). This definition becomes less formidable if we break it down into its three components.

1. Historiometry seeks to test nomothetic hypotheses concerning human behavior. The goal is thus the discovery of general laws or statistical relationships that transcend the particulars of the historical record – that go beyond the "names, dates, and places." Hence, when the method is applied to the study of creativity, historiometric inquiries might test conjectures or predictions about which developmental experiences, personality traits, or environmental factors contribute to exceptional creative achievement. This nomothetic orientation diverges significantly from the idiographic approach, which assigns great stress on the more idiosyncratic principles that govern the actions of specific individuals, without concern for whether these regularities might be generalized to whole groups of persons (Runyan, 1982).

2. Quantitative analyses are the sine qua non of historiometric investigations. This quantification manifests itself at two distinct levels. To start with, the investigator must transform the rich, ambiguous, and usually qualitative facts of history into the more precise and clear numerical measurements on well-defined variables relevant to the nomothetic hypotheses at hand. For instance, the investigator might assess intelligence, motivations, or traumatic childhood experiences along some kind of dimension, the outcome being a series of numbers along some scale that represents the magnitude of the characteristic or the intensity of the experience. When these quantitative measures are obtained, the historiometician can then advance to the next step, subjecting these variables to statistical analyses that allow the investigator to confirm or reject the substantive hypotheses. The statistical techniques most frequently used in historiometric work include multiple regression, factor analysis, structural equation and latent-variable models, and time-series analysis.

3. Historical individuals, not college students or survey respondents, are the subjects of historiometric inquiries. Historiometric samples contain personalities who have "made history" in an important domain of human achievement. In the particular case of creativity, historiometric researchers will study those individuals who have some claim to the epithet "creative genius." Often this will mean that the participants in a historiometric study will be deceased, but this is not an absolute requirement. Someone who has earned a Nobel Prize for literary or scientific accomplishment would certainly qualify for inclusion in an investigation even if that individual were still alive.

The plural form of the phrase "historical individuals" must be noted. Almost without exception, historiometric studies entail multiple cases, the N at times even approaching thousands of eminent creators (e.g., Simonton, 1976f, 1988b, 1992c). The sample size must be respectably large if we wish to apply the full arsenal of sophisticated statistical techniques. After all, in multivariate analyses the number of cases must exceed by a comfortable margin the number of variables under investigation. More important, the number of cases must be large enough to ensure that the empirical results truly have some claim to nomothetic status. We wish to isolate those findings that hold for famous creators in general, without respect to the idiosyncrasies of any one creative personality. To be sure, historiometric inquiries will occasionally focus on a single prototypical creator, such as Beethoven or Shakespeare, who exemplify a specific type of creative activity (e.g., Derks, 1989, 1994; Ohlsson, 1992; Sears, Lapidus, Cozzens, 1978; Simonton, 1986e, 1987a, 1989b, 1990b). Nonetheless, even in these studies, the number of statistical units will be large enough to perform complex statistical analyses. Some trick will be used, such as changing the unit of analysis from the creative individual to the creative product (compositions, plays, poems, etc.).

The definition just presented helps us distinguish historiometry from other methods with which it is sometimes confused. First of all, historiometric inquiries are distinct from psychohistory and psychobiography. Although these scholarly activities also begin with historical data, psychohistorians and psychobiographers apply qualitative analyses to confirm idiographic questions about particular individuals or events (Elms, 1994). In many respects, these practitioners are more focused on historical issues and techniques than on scientific problems and methods (Simonton, 1983d). This stark contrast in emphasis is well illustrated by Freud's (1910/1964) classic psychobiography of Leonardo da Vinci, in which he tried to ground the artist's sexual orientation and work habits in some early childhood experiences.

An enterprise more intimately related to historiometrics is cliometrics. Like the historiometrician, the cliometrician applies quantitative methods to historical data with the aim of arriving at conclusions with the maximum scientific rigor. Nonetheless, cliometrics is more like psychohistory in the sense that it is more interested in idiographic than nomothetic questions. A good illustration is the work of Robert Fogel, who won the 1993 Nobel Prize for his application of cliometrics to economic history. Fogel's pioneer investigations addressed such issues as the economic profitability of slavery in the antebellum American South (Fogel & Engerman, 1974) and the contributions of the railroads to the economic development of the American West (Fogel, 1964).

Therefore, historiometry is the only method that exploits historical data in a simultaneously quantitative and nomothetic fashion. In a loose way, we can say it integrates features drawn from psychometrics, psychohistory, and cliometrics. As in psychometrics and cliometrics, historiometry is dedicated to quantitative analysis; but like psychohistory and cliometrics, historiometry concentrates on historically important people and events. Finally, historiometrics shares with psychometrics the quest for nomothetic statements that are not constrained by a singular time and place.

A BRIEF HISTORY OF THE METHOD

As might befit a method devoted to a special form of historical analysis, historiometry has a long history. Indeed, it actually represents the oldest approach to the scientific study of creativity! The first published historiometric inquiry is found in *Sur l'homme* (Treatise on man) by Adolphe Quetelet (1835/1968), the Belgian astronomer, meteorologist, mathematician, sociologist, and poet. This 1835 monograph contains the first quantitative study of how creative productivity fluctuates across the life span. In particular, by counting the number of plays produced by English and French dramatists during the course of their careers, Quetelet established that output was a curvilinear, single-peaked function of age and that quality of output was strongly associated with quantity. Not only are these conclusions still valid today (Simonton, 1997b), but this same substantive question was addressed by George M. Beard (1874) just a few decades later. Thus, this is easily the oldest topic scrutinized by historiometric methods.

Unfortunately, almost another century had to elapse before this subject was again taken up by historiometric researchers (Simonton, 1988a). Accordingly, the technique might have receded into obscurity were it not for Francis Galton, who we may consider to be the genuine "father of historiometry." This English scientist, explorer, and anthropologist was a notable methodological innovator, and among his first innovations in the behavioral sciences were the historiometric analyses published in his 1869 volume *Hereditary Genius.* The central argument of this book was that outstanding accomplishments tend to run in family lineages owing to the genetic transmission of intellectual and motivational capacity. To make his case, Galton gathered many examples of extensive pedigrees among eminent individuals, and then showed how the kinship frequencies far exceeded reasonable expectation. Even if many of Galton's arguments have had to undergo subsequent qualifications and refinements (Bramwell, 1948; Kroeber, 1944; Simonton, 1983c, 1988b, 1991c, 1996), *Hereditary Genius* eventually became not only a classic in psychology, but additionally the first truly influential historiometric study of exceptional creativity.

Many investigators pursued the pathways first opened by Galton's pioneer work. Just a handful of years later, Alphonse de Candolle (1873), the Swiss botanist, published a historiometric inquiry into the environmental conditions that most favor the creative activities of notable scientists. Shortly after the turn of the century, the English psychologist Havelock Ellis published *A Study of British Genius,* which discerned the biographical and sociocultural factors that underlie the emergence of eminent personalities, including famous creators (see Ellis, 1926). About the same time, historiometry made inroads across the Atlantic when it found an advocate in James McKeen Cattell (1903, 1910), the illustrious U.S. psychologist. The dissemination of the technique was greatly enhanced when Cattell acquired the journal *Science* in 1894, which he edited for a half century, making it a major vehicle for the publication of historiometric investigations (e.g., Dennis, 1956; Lehman, 1958).

Among the numerous items that were published in *Science* in the first half of this century were two papers by Frederick Woods (1909, 1911). These two papers formally christened the approach. The 1909 paper was entitled "A New Name for a New Science," the new name being "historiometry." Woods defined this as a scientific study in which "the facts of history of a more personal nature have been subjected to statistical analysis by some more or less objective method" (p. 703), adding that "historiometry bears the same relation to history that biometry does to biology" (p. 703). Woods then closed this paper by listing a dozen studies that he thought represented good examples of this novel methodology. The 1911 paper explicitly advertised the approach with the title "Historiometry as an Exact Science." Here Woods noted that the technique was ideally suited for research on the "psychology of genius."

Unfortunately, *genius* can refer to eminent leaders as much as to famous creators, and Woods himself chose to apply historiometric methods to the study of historic leadership (Woods, 1906, 1913). Even though this research did indeed inspire many subsequent investigations, including a study by a psychologist no less than Edward L. Thorndike (1936, see also Simonton, 1984f), this research tradition deserves no discussion here. More germane are the later studies of creative geniuses that identified themselves quite explicitly as historiometric inquiries. Among these diverse studies, the most important by far is a monumental investigation conducted by Catharine Cox (1926). To appreciate this work's importance, we must put it in proper context, which requires that we begin with Lewis M. Terman.

Terman was fascinated with intelligence, including its relation with achievement. Early in his career he adapted the original Binet-Simon intelligence test into English, producing what eventually became known as the Stanford-Binet test. To validate his notions about the consequences of having a high IQ, Terman initiated a famous longitudinal study of children whom he had identified as intellectually gifted (Terman, 1925). Terman wanted to demonstrate that children with high IQs would become extremely accomplished adults. The consequences was the series of books collectively entitled *Genetic Studies of Genius*, the last volume of which appeared posthumously (Terman & Oden, 1959). Yet Terman's methodological toolbox was not confined to psychometrics. Inspired by Woods, Terman thought it might be feasible to estimate IQ scores for eminent individuals. Significantly, he chose as his test case one of the pioneers in historiometric methodology, using historiometric methods to assess that individual's IQ. In 1917, Terman published the paper entitled "The Intelligence Quotient of Francis Galton in Childhood." By taking the then-current definition of IQ as a literal quotient – as a ratio of mental to chronological age – the author of *Hereditary Genius* received a genius-level score just shy of 200.

When Terman began his longitudinal study, this pilot historiometric analysis could be taken a step further. Cox was a graduate student of his in search of a dissertation topic. And what she decided to do was to take the same technique that Terman applied to the biography of Galton to obtain comparable IQ scores for 301 eminent individuals, about 200 of whom were world-famous creators. Her aim was essentially the inverse of what her mentor was trying to do in the longitudinal investigation. Cox hoped to show that those who attain distinction as adults would have been selected as intellectually gifted children if they had been given the Stanford-Binet test. Because this goal seemed to be achieved, Cox's study became the second volume of the *Genetic Studies of Genius* series (Cox, 1926). Yet it is also essential to recognize that Cox went beyond the mere calculation of 301 IQ scores. She also set aside a group of 100 eminent subjects for a special analysis in which she could assess their scores on 67 character traits. Cox also related the cognitive and personality scores with a measure of achieved eminence that she derived from Cattell (1903). The upshot is a product that, for its time, embodied the state of the art in historiometric methods.

After earning her Ph.D. Cox moved on to other substantive topics that demanded more mainstream methodologies. Even so, many psychologists published follow-up inquiries using historiometric methods (e.g., Albert, 1971; Raskin, 1936; Simonton, 1976a; Walberg, Rasher, & Parkerson, 1980), and some notable psychologists even introduced new questions and techniques that greatly widened the scope of empirical inquiry (e.g., Dennis, 1955; Farnsworth, 1969; Lehman, 1953; Martindale, 1990; McClelland, 1961; Suedfeld, 1985; Thorndike, 1950). Moreover, researchers in neighboring behavioral sciences made significant contributions to other facets of historiometric inquiry (e.g., Brannigan & Wanner, 1983a, 1983b; Cerulo, 1988, 1989; Gray, 1958, 1961, 1966; Naroll et al., 1971; Richardson & Kroeber, 1940). Historiometry has thereby become a highly successful approach to the study of exceptional creativity. This success will become manifest when we survey the range of issues treated in the historiometric literature.

CENTRAL TOPICS

Creativity is an extremely complex phenomenon, and outstanding creativity is probably even more so (Eysenck, 1995). As a consequence, there exists more than one perspective from which historiometricians have studied the phenomenon. Three perspectives have dominated the research, however. These concern the developmental, differential, and social foundations of historic creativity (see also Simonton, 1994b, for more extensive discussion, and Simonton, 1997d, for an anthology of the author's historiometric studies).

The Developmental Psychology of Exceptional Creativity

One distinctive feature of historiometric inquiries into creativity is their truly life-span scope (Simonton, 1987b, 1988a). Illustrious creators can be examined from the moment of conception to the very instant of death, plus everything that takes place within this long interval. For convenience, however, we can divide the life span into phases: the early period in which an individual acquires creative potential and the mature period in which the individual realizes that accumulated potential (Simonton, 1984a).

THE FOUNDATIONS OF CREATIVITY. It was not a loose claim to say that historiometricians have studied creative genius from the moment of conception. After all, several researchers have followed up Galton's (1869) pioneer scrutiny of family pedigrees in order to tease out the possible genetic basis of creativity (Bramwell, 1948; Cox, 1926; Simonton, 1983c; Woods, 1906). Other researchers have studied how the placement of a creator's birth in the seasonal cycle may shape the type and degree of distinction achieved (Huntington, 1938; Kaulins, 1979). Particularly provocative is the inclination of eminent individuals to be born in the early months of the year, a disposition that might even reflect prenatal influences.

However, the vast majority of historiometric inquiries have focused on the following six developmental variables:

1. *Birth order.* Galton (1874) was the first behavioral scientist to suggest that creative achievement may be related to being the firstborn child (Schachter, 1963), and many other studies have pursued this hypothesis using biographical data (Albert, 1980; Bullough, Bullough, Voight, & Kluckhohn, 1971; Goertzel, Goertzel, & Goertzel, 1978). Interestingly, the relationship of ordinal position to success depends on the domain of creativity. Where status quo scientists and classical composers are more likely to be firstborns (Clark & Rice, 1982; Schubert, Wagner, & Schubert, 1977; Terry, 1989), revolutionary scientists and creative writers are more likely to be later borns (Bliss, 1970; Sulloway, 1996). This parallels a similar contrast between establishment versus revolutionary political leaders (L. H. Stewart, 1977).

2. *Intellectual precocity.* Several historiometricians have examined the relationship between the precocious appearance of domain-relevant cognitive skills and later adulthood creative achievement (Cox, 1926; Simonton, 1991d; Walberg et al., 1980). Also germane to this question is the research on how certain "crystallizing experiences" are sometimes necessary to launch a future creator on the proper developmental path (Walters & Gardner, 1986). These experiences may include a chance encounter with a book of poetry, a mathematical text, or a painting that evokes intellectual excitement in the youthful talent.

3. *Childhood trauma.* Yet another collection of inquiries have concentrated on how traumatic events, such as parental loss or orphanhood, may contribute to the development of creative potential (Albert, 1971; Eisenstadt, 1978; Eisenstadt, Haynal, Rentchnick, & De Senarclens, 1989; Martindale, 1972; Silverman, 1974; Woodward, 1974). Especially interesting is how the frequency and intensity of these experiences may help determine the domain in which creative achievement is attained, for artistic creators tend to come from far less auspicious settings than do scientific creators (Berry, 1981; Goertzel et al., 1978; Simonton, 1986a).

4. *Family background.* Still other early developmental factors include socioeconomic class, religious affiliation or heritage, immigrant status, and familial relationships (Arieti, 1976; Berry, 1981; Goertzel et al., 1978; Lehman & Witty, 1931; Moulin, 1955; Raskin, 1936; Simonton, 1976a, 1986b; Veblen, 1919; Walberg et al., 1980). Of particular interest is the tendency for creative individuals to come from somewhat marginalized home environments.

5. *Education and special training.* Historiometric studies have also examined the impact of formal education, such as the importance of the level of formal education attained or the degree of scholastic excellence displayed (Goertzel et al., 1978; Hudson, 1958; Pressey & Combs, 1943; Simonton, 1983b, 1986b). A closely related question is the contribution of specialized professional training to creative development (Gieryn & Hirsh, 1983; Hayes, 1989; Simonton, 1984e, 1986b, 1991b, 1992b). Just as future creative geniuses often originate in marginal family backgrounds, so is there a tendency for the most notable creators to

have emerged from something less than mainstream educational and professional environments.

6. *Role models and mentors.* A great many studies have scrutinized the repercussions of exposure to role models, mentors, and masters in the emergence of creative talent (Sheldon, 1979, 1980; Simonton, 1975d, 1976f, 1977b, 1978b, 1984a, 1988b, 1992c; Walberg et al., 1980). These influences can operate in complex ways, sometimes encouraging creative development, other times discouraging such growth (especially when it results in excessive imitation of the work of others). The positive benefits are most likely to accrue when the creative talent is exposed to a large number of quite diverse models and mentors (see, e.g., Simonton, 1984a).

THE MANIFESTATIONS OF CREATIVITY. Once the creative career begins, historiometricians can study how the probability of making a creative contribution changes with age. We already noted that this constitutes the oldest research topic in the field (Beard, 1874; Quetelet, 1835/1968). Even so, Harvey C. Lehman was the first historiometrician who devoted an entire research program to this question (e.g., Lehman, 1953, 1958, 1962, 1963, 1966a, 1966b). This work provided the basis for numerous follow-up investigations (e.g., Bullough, Bullough, & Mauro, 1978; Dennis, 1966; Diemer, 1974; Han, 1989; Simonton, 1977a, 1984b, 1989a; Zhao & Jiang, 1985, 1986). Some of these inquiries focus on the connection between quantity and quality of productive output over the career (R. A. Davis, 1987; Lehman, 1953; Over, 1988, 1989; Quetelet, 1835/1968; Simonton, 1977a, 1985; Weisberg, 1994), others examine shifts in the impact or content of creative output (Inhaber & Przednowek, 1976; Root-Bernstein, 1989; Root-Bernstein, Bernstein, & Garnier, 1993; Simonton, 1992b), whereas yet other investigations concentrate on the ages at which individuals create their landmark works (Abt, 1983; Adams, 1946; Hermann, 1988; Lyons, 1968; Manniche & Falk, 1957; Pressey & Combs, 1943; Raskin, 1936; Simonton, 1975a, 1977b, 1991a, 1991b, 1992c, 1997b; Visher, 1947; Zhao, 1984; Zhao & Jiang, 1986; Zusne, 1976). In addition, a number of investigators have assessed the correlations among creative precocity, longevity, and output rate (Dennis, 1954b; Simonton, 1977b, 1991a, 1991b, 1992b; Zhao & Jiang, 1986; Zusne, 1976).

As a result of this historiometric work, we can now conclude with great confidence that: (a) creative output tends to be a curvilinear, inverted backwards-J function of age; (b) age must be defined in terms of length of time actively engaged in a creative domain, or career age, rather than in terms of strict chronological age; (c) quality of output is closely connected to sheer quantity, so that the single best creative product tends to appear at that point in the career when the creator is the most prolific overall; (d) the overall age functions, including the placement of the first, best, and last creative contributions, are contingent upon the specific domain of creative activity; and (e) individuals differences in creative productivity account for more variance in output in a given career period than does age, so that truly prolific creators in their final years may be much more productive than less notable contributors who are at their career peaks (Simonton, 1988a, 1997b).

Apropos of the creative longevity issue, a handful of investigations have probed the changes in creativity that appear in the very last years of a creator's life (Haefele, 1962; Lindauer, 1992, 1993a, 1993b; Simonton, 1989c). Most provocative is the evidence that artists may exhibit a distinctive "late-life style" and that composers may display the "swan-song phenomenon" – both representing a dramatic shift in the type of creativity shown in their final years. Finally, I must note the numerous studies regarding the onset of death. These address such questions as the specific timing of the final day (Harrison & Kroll, 1985–1986, 1989–1990; Harrison & Moore, 1982–1983; Zusne, 1986–1989), the characteristic life span of creators in different domains (Cox, 1926; Ellis, 1926; Kaun, 1991; Raskin, 1936; Simonton, 1975a, 1991a, 1997a). and the effect of longevity on both productivity and posthumous reputation (Lehman, 1943; Mills, 1942; Simonton, 1976a, 1977b, 1984d).

Over the course of a creator's life, more can be anticipated than mere changes in creative productivity. A creator's fundamental interests, values, and obsessions may undergo profound transformations as well. This has been indicated by several historiometric studies (Mackavey, Malley, & Stewart, 1991; Sears et al., 1978; Simonton, 1977a, 1980b, 1983a, 1986e). For instance, the complexity of information processing may shift across the life span, particularly in the last couple years of a creator's life (Porter & Suedfeld, 1981; Suedfeld, 1985; Suedfeld & Bluck, 1993; Suedfeld & Piedrahita, 1984). Even more provocative is the historiometric work that provides support for "Planck's hypothesis," namely the conjecture that older scientists are less receptive to scientific innovations than are their younger colleagues (Hull, Tessner, & Diamond, 1978; Messerli, 1988; Oromaner, 1977; J.A. Stewart, 1986; Sulloway, 1996; see also Diamond, 1980; Whaples, 1991).

The Differential Psychology of Extraordinary Creativity

The psychologists who founded historiometric methods – such as Quetelet, Galton, J. M. Cattell, Thorndike, and Cox – were all extremely interested in individual differences. They often wondered whether cross-sectional variation on certain predictor variables correlated with significant criterion variables, such as creative achievement. The historiometric examination of the world's most illustrious creators permitted the study of the most extreme scores on the criterion. In any case, this fascination with the differential psychology of outstanding creativity persists to the present day. Some investigators examine intellectual skills, others personality traits, and still others look at intelligence and character combined (Cox, 1926; Knapp, 1962; Simonton, 1976a, 1991d; Thorndike, 1950; Walberg et al., 1980; White, 1931). Probably the most daring among these various inquiries are those that apply established psychometric instruments to historical data. To illustrate, R. B. Cattell (1963) adapted his Sixteen Personality Factor Questionnaire to biographical data with the aim of discerning the typical profile of eminent scientists. Likewise, several researchers have exploited the Thematic Apperception Test in order to assess motives from literary and artistic creations (Bradburn & Berlew, 1961; Cortés, 1960; Davies, 1969; McClelland, 1961, 1975; Winter, 1973). One important consequence of these diverse studies is the realization that the portrait of the creative genius that arises from historiometric research seems to parallel closely the picture that has emerged from the psychometric examination of contemporary creators (Eysenck, 1995; Simonton, 1994b).

Of course, researchers cannot identify the predictors of creative accomplishment without having a suitable criterion measure. Accordingly, many investigators have devoted attention to discovering the psychometric properties of the two main criteria variables favored in historiometric research. In the first place, some historiometricians have examined lifetime creative productivity. In addition to proving that this behavioral indicator enjoys both considerable face validity and extremely respectable reliability (Simonton, 1984h, 1991a, 1991b, 1992b), researchers have isolated some theoretically provocative distributional characteristics (Dennis, 1954a, 1954c; Lotka, 1926; Price, 1963; Simonton, 1988c; cf. Martindale, 1995; Zusne, 1985; Zusne & Dailey, 1982). In particular, the distribution of creative output is by no means normal, but extremely skewed right, with a rather long upper tail.

Other researchers have analyzed the psychological implications of eminence or posthumous reputation, establishing along the way the cross-cultural and transhistorical stability of the received consensus (Helmreich, Spence, & Thorbecke, 1981; Martindale, 1995; Over, 1982; Rosengren, 1985; Simonton, 1984h, 1991c; Zusne, 1987; Zusne & Dailey, 1982; cf. J. M. Cattell, 1903; Galton, 1869). Furthermore, these two criteria of creative achievement

have been shown to be strongly and positively correlated, thereby providing mutual validation (R. A. Davis, 1987; Dennis, 1954a, 1954c; Ludwig, 1992b; Price, 1963; Rushton, 1984;
Simonton, 1977b, 1991a, 1991b, 1992b). In fact, a very small proportion of creators in any
creative activity will typically dominate both the productive output and the received acco-
lades (see, e.g., Cole & Cole, 1972; Green, 1981; Oromaner, 1985).

Finally, I should note that two important topics have received attention in recent historiometric research. First, some researchers have begun to focus on creative achievement in
women (Hayes, 1989; Over, 1990; Sicoli, 1995; Simonton, 1992a; Stariha & Walberg, 1995).
Second, several investigators have tackled the ancient issue of the relationship between creative genius and psychopathology (W. M. Davis, 1986; Karlson, 1970; Lester, 1991; Ludwig,
1990, 1992a, 1995; Martindale, 1972; Post, 1994; Weisberg, 1994). For the most part, this
historiometric work concurs with the psychometric studies that suggest that an important
truth may dwell behind the proverbial image of the "mad genius" (Eysenck, 1995).

The Social Psychology of Phenomenal Creativity

Creativity is by no means an autistic activity. Even the most prominent creative genius operates within a social context (Csikszentmihály, 1990). At the rudimentary level, creators must
effectively communicate their ideas to other individuals, whether they be colleagues, disciples, audiences, or appreciators. It is this successful act of communication, indeed, that cer-
tifies mere originality as bona fide creativity. Not surprisingly, many historiometric inquiries
have attempted to tease out the attributes of creative products that allow them to exert the
necessary influence over others. Almost all of this research concentrates on aesthetic products, much of it applying objective content analysis to literature (Derks, 1989, 1994; Simonton, 1989b, 1990b, 1997e) and music (Simonton, 1984g, 1986a, 1987a, 1994a, 1995b). There
has even been some preliminary surveys of such art forms as film (Boor, 1990, 1992). In
recent years, some investigators have tried to determine whether scientific contributions
might also be open to historiometric analyses (Donovan, Laudan, & Laudan, 1988; Faust &
Meehl, 1992; Meehl, 1992; Simonton, 1992b, 1995a). Remarkably, computer programs have
already been written that can discern the roots of creative impact among genre as varied as
poetry, music, and psychological journal articles (Simonton, 1980b, 1980c, 1984f, 1989b,
1990b, 1992b, 1995b).

Historiometricians have elevated analyses to yet higher levels as well. For example, several investigations have studied how an individual's creativity is helped or hindered by different kinds of social interactions, such as collaborations and rivalries (Jackson & Padgett,
1982; Price, 1965; Simonton, 1984a, 1992b, 1992c). At an even more grand level than these,
interactions are the societal forces that determine the content and degree of creativity exhibited by whole generations of creators (Simonton, 1984c). These massive and impersonal
influences from the *Zeitgeist* or *Ortgeist* fall roughly into four categories:

1. *Cultural factors,* such as the prevailing disciplinary or aesthetic milieu (Hasenfus, Martindale, & Birnbaum, 1983; Martindale, 1975; Schneider, 1937; Simonton, 1975b, 1975c,
1976d, 1976f, 1992a, 1992b, 1996). A particular topic in this group that has received considerable empirical scrutiny is multiple discovery and invention (Brannigan & Wanner,
1983a, 1983b; Merton, 1961; Price, 1963; Schmookler, 1966; Simonton, 1978a, 1979, 1986c,
1986d, 1986f). This is the intriguing phenomenon in which two or more scientists independently arrive at the same creative idea. Although the traditional explanation evokes the concept of the *Zeitgeist,* the historiometric research reveals a much more complex process
(Simonton, 1988c).

2. *Societal factors,* including such variables as population growth, social structure, and
position of minority groups (Hayes, 1989; Kuo, 1986, 1988; Lehman, 1947; Matossian &

Schafer, 1977; McGuire, 1976; Simonton, 1997c; Yuasa, 1974). For example, there is evidence that the stylistic features in the visual arts may largely reflect the degree to which the social system is more hierarchical than egalitarian (Dressler & Robbins, 1975).

3. *Economic factors,* especially general prosperity and direct investment (Inhaber, 1977; Kuo, 1988; Padgett & Jorgenson, 1982; Rainoff, 1929; Schmookler, 1996; Simon & Sullivan, 1989). There is some truth to the ancient idea that economic growth may stimulate a renaissance in creative activity (see, e.g., H. T. Davis, 1941), albeit material wealth alone cannot guarantee that creativity will be maintained (see also Kavolis, 1964).

4. *Political factors* (Kuo, 1986, 1988; Price, 1978; Simonton, 1976b, 1976e, 1976g, 1980a, 1986a, 1986e, 1987a; Winter, 1973). Of these, the impact of war on creative activity has probably drawn the most attention (Cerulo, 1984; Price, 1978; Simonton, 1976b, 1976e, 1976g, 1980a, 1986a, 1986e, 1987a). Such systematic violence not only exerts a transient depressing influence on the magnitude and nature of concurrent creative output, but additionally can have effects on creativity decades later.

Cutting across these four categories is the historiometric literature on cyclical theories of cultural creativity (Gray, 1958, 1961, 1966; Klingemann, Mohler & Weber, 1982; Kroeber, 1944; Lowe & Lowe, 1982; Marchetti, 1980; Peterson & Berger, 1975; Rainoff, 1929; Sheldon, 1979, 1980; Simonton, 1976c; Sorokin, 1937–1941; Sorokin & Merton, 1935). Perhaps the most innovative of these diverse inquiries is the extensive work that Martindale (1975, 1990) has published on stylistic change in the arts. After first providing an evolutionary theory of stylistic creativity (Martindale, 1984b, 1986a), Martindale then tested the theory's central predictions by applying sophisticated content-analytical methods to actual creative products (e.g., Martindale, 1984a, 1986b; Martindale & Uemura, 1983). He has made a convincing case that the constant pressure on the artist to create ever more original products may underlie the emergence and exhaustion of successive aesthetic styles.

I should end by noting that many sociocultural variables operate as developmental factors that determine the emergence of exceptional creativity (Simonton, 1984c). In other words, these factors define the milieu in which a talented youth grows so as to shape both the nature and the level of creative accomplishments of the future adult.

CONCLUSION

This overview of the historiometric literature should have provided a good notion of the impressive contributions this approach has made to the scientific study of creativity. Sometimes these contributions consist in the corroboration of empirical findings obtained by more mainstream methods. A good example is the convergence between historiometric and psychometric inquiries into the relation between psychopathology and creative genius. At the same time, many of the empirical results in the historiometric literature could not have been divulged by any alternative technique, whether laboratory experiments or psychometric investigations. Thus, the historiometric literature is far from redundant or superfluous. In addition, although historiometry suffers from certain methodological drawbacks, it enjoys several crucial advantages that more than compensate for any liabilities (see Simonton, 1990a, 1990b). The most obvious of these assets, of course, is the ability to engage in the scientific study of creativity in its most stellar form. The subjects of historiometric inquiries are undoubted exemplars of creative genius. For that reason alone, historiometry will continue to make unique contributions to our understanding of this important phenomenon.

REFERENCES

Abt, H. A. (1983). At what ages did outstanding American astronomers publish their most cited papers. *Publications of the Astronomical Society of the Pacific, 95,* 113–116.

Adams, C. W. (1946). The age at which scientists do their best work. *Isis, 36,* 166–169.

Albert, R. S. (1971). Cognitive development and parental loss among the gifted, the exceptionally gifted and the creative. *Psychological Reports, 29,* 19–26.

Albert, R. S. (1980). Family positions and the attainment of eminence: A study of special family positions and special family experiences. *Gifted Child Quarterly, 24,* 87–95.

Amabile, T. M. (1996). *Creativity in context.* Boulder, CO: Westview.

Arieti, S. (1976). *Creativity: The magic synthesis.* New York: Basic.

Barron, F. X. (1969). *Creative person and creative process.* New York: Holt, Rinehart, & Winston.

Barron, F. X., & Harrington, D. M. (1981). Creativity, intelligence, and personality. *Annual Review of Psychology, 32,* 439–476.

Beard, G. M. (1874). *Legal responsibility in old age.* New York: Russell.

Berry, C. (1981). The Nobel scientists and the origins of scientific achievement. *British Journal of Sociology, 32,* 381–391.

Bliss, W. D. (1970). Birth order of creative writers. *Journal of Individual Psychology, 26,* 200–202.

Boor, M. (1990). Reliability of ratings of movies by professional movie critics. *Psychological Reports, 67,* 243–257.

Boor, M. (1992). Relationships among ratings of motion pictures by viewers and six professional movie critics. *Psychological Reports, 70,* 1011–1021.

Bradburn, N. M., & Berlew, D. E. (1961). Need for achievement and English economic growth. *Economic Development and Cultural Change, 10,* 8–20.

Bramwell, B. S. (1948). Galton's *Hereditary Genius* and the three following generations since 1869. *Eugenics Review, 39,* 146–153.

Brannigan, A., & Wanner, R. A. (1983a). Historical distributions of multiple discoveries and theories of scientific change. *Social Studies of Science, 13,* 417–435.

Brannigan, A., & Wanner, R. A. (1983b). Multiple discoveries in science: A test of the communication theory. *Canadian Journal of Sociology, 8,* 135–151.

Bullough, V., Bullough, B., & Mauro, M. (1978). Age and achievement: A dissenting view. *Gerontologist, 18,* 584–587.

Bullough, V. L., Bullough, B., Voight, M., & Kluckhohn, L. (1971). Birth order and achievement in eighteenth century Scotland. *Journal of Individual Psychology, 27,* 80.

Candolle, A. de (1873). *Histoire des sciences et des savants depuis deux siecles.* Geneva: Georg.

Cattell, J. M. (1903). A statistical study of eminent men. *Popular Science Monthly, 62,* 359–377.

Cattell, J. M. (1910). A further study of American men of science. *Science, 32,* 633–648.

Cattell, R. B. (1963). The personality and motivation of the researcher from measurements of contemporaries and from biography. In C. W. Taylor & F. Barron (Eds.), *Scientific creativity: Its recognition and development* (pp. 119–131). New York: Wiley.

Cerulo, K. A. (1984). Social disruption and its effects on music: An empirical analysis. *Social Forces, 62,* 885–904.

Cerulo, K. A. (1988). Analyzing cultural products: A new method of measurement. *Social Science Research, 17,* 317–352.

Cerulo, K. A. (1989). Variations in musical syntax: Patterns of measurement. *Communication Research, 16,* 204–235.

Clark, R. D., & Rice, G. A. (1982). Family constellations and eminence: The birth orders of Nobel Prize winners. *Journal of Psychology, 110,* 281–287.

Cole, J. R., & Cole, S. (1972). The Ortega hypothesis. *Science, 178,* 368–375.

Cortés, J. B. (1960). The achievement motive in the Spanish economy between the 13th and 18th centuries. *Economic Development and Cultural Change, 9,* 144–163.

Cox, C. (1926). *The early mental traits of three hundred geniuses.* Stanford, CA: Stanford University Press.

Csikszentmihaly, M. (1990). The domain of creativity. In M. A. Runco & R. S. Albert (Eds.), *Theories of creativity* (pp. 190–212). Newbury Park, CA: Sage.

Davies, E. (1969, November). This is the way Crete went – Not with a bang but a simper. *Psychology Today,* pp. 43–47.

Davis, H. T. (1941). *The analysis of economic time series.* Bloomington, IN: Principia.

Davis, R. A. (1987). Creativity in neurological publications. *Neurosurgery, 20,* 652–663.

Davis, W. M. (1986). Premature mortality among prominent American authors noted for alcohol abuse. *Drug and Alcohol Dependence, 18,* 133–138.

Dennis, W. (1954a). Bibliographies of eminent scientists. *Scientific Monthly, 79,* 180–183.

Dennis, W. (1954b). Predicting scientific productivity in later maturity from records of earlier decades. *Journal of Gerontology, 9,* 465–467.

Dennis, W. (1954c). Productivity among American psychologists. *American Psychologist, 9,* 191–194.

Dennis, W. (1955). Variations in productivity among creative workers. *Scientific Monthly, 80,* 277–278.

Dennis, W. (1956). Age and productivity among scientists. *Science, 123,* 724–725.

Dennis, W. (1966). Creative productivity between the ages of 20 and 80 years. *Journal of Gerontology, 21,* 1–8.

Derks, P. L. (1989). Pun frequency and popularity of Shakespeare's plays. *Empirical Studies of the Arts, 7,* 23–31.

Derks, P. L. (1994). Clockwork Shakespeare: The Bard meets the Regressive Imagery Dictionary. *Empirical Studies of the Arts, 12,* 131–139.

Diamond, A. M., Jr. (1980). Age and the acceptance of cliometrics. *Journal of Economic History, 40,* 838–841.

Diemer, G. (1974). Creativity versus age. *Physics Today, 27,* 9.

Donovan, A., Laudan, L., & Laudan, R. (Eds.). (1988). *Scrutinizing science: Empirical studies of scientific change.* Dordrecht: Kluwer.

Dressler, W. W., & Robbins, M. C. (1975). Art styles, social stratification, and cognition: An analysis of Greek vase painting. *American Ethnologist, 2,* 427–434.

Eisenstadt, J. M. (1978). Parental loss and genius. *American Psychologist, 33,* 211–223.

Eisenstadt, J. M., Haynal, A., Rentchnick, P., & De Senarclens, P. (1989). *Parental loss and achievement.* Madison, CT: International Universities Press.

Ellis, H. (1926). *A study of British genius* (rev. ed.). Boston: Houghton Mifflin.

Elms, A. C. (1994). *Uncovering lives: The uneasy alliance of biography and psychology.* New York: Oxford University Press.

Eysenck, H. J. (1995). *Genius: The natural history of creativity.* Cambridge University Press.

Farnsworth, P. R. (1969). *The social psychology of music* (2nd ed.). Ames: Iowa State University Press.

Faust, D., & Meehl, P. E. (1992). Using scientific methods to resolve questions in the history and philosophy of science: Some illustrations. *Behavior Therapy, 23,* 195–211.

Fogel, R. W. (1964). *Railroads and American economic growth.* Baltimore: Johns Hopkins University Press.

Fogel, R. W., & Engerman, S. L. (1974). *Time on the cross.* Boston: Little, Brown.

Freud, S. (1964). *Leonardo da Vinci and a memory of his childhood* (A. Tyson, Trans.). New York: Norton. (Original work published 1910).

Galton, F. (1869). *Hereditary genius: An inquiry into its laws and consequences.* London: Macmillan.

Galton, F. (1874). *English men of science: Their nature and nurture.* London: Macmillan.

Gieryn, T. F., & Hirsh, R. F. (1983). Marginality and innovation in science. *Social Studies of Science, 13,* 87–106.

Goertzel, M. G., Goertzel, V., & Goertzel, T. G. (1978). *Three hundred eminent personalities: A psychosocial analysis of the famous.* San Francisco: Jossey-Bass.

Gray, C. E. (1958). An analysis of Graeco-Roman development: The epicyclical evolution of Graeco-Roman civilization. *American Anthropologist, 60,* 13–31.

Gray, C. E. (1961). An epicyclical model for Western civilization. *American Anthropologist, 63,* 1014–1037.

Gray, C. E. (1966). A measurement of creativity in Western civilization. *American Anthropologist, 68,* 1384–1417.

Green, G. S. (1981). A test of the Ortega hypothesis in criminology. *Criminology, 19,* 45–52.

Haefele, J. W. (1962). *Creativity and innovation.* New York: Reinhold.

Han, H. (1989). Linear increase law of optimum age of scientific creativity. *Scientometrics, 15,* 309–312.

Harrison, A. A., & Kroll, N. E. A. (1985–1986). Variations in death rates in the proximity of Christmas: An opponent process interpretation. *Omega: Journal of Death and Dying, 16,* 181–192.

Harrison, A. A., & Kroll, N. E. A. (1989–1990). Birth dates and death dates: An examination of two baseline procedures and age at time of death. *Omega: Journal of Death and Dying, 20,* 127–137.

Harrison, A. A., & Moore, M. (1982–1983). Birth dates and death dates: A closer look. *Omega: Journal of Death and Dying, 13,* 117–125.

Hasenfus, N., Martindale, C., & Birnbaum, D. (1983). Psychological reality of cross-media artistic styles. *Journal of Experimental Psychology: Human Perception and Performance, 9,* 841–863.

Hayes, J. R. (1989). *The complete problem solver* (2nd ed.): Hillsdale, NJ: Erlbaum.

Helmreich, R. L., Spence, J. T., & Thorbecke, W. L. (1981). On the stability of productivity and recognition. *Personality and Social Psychology Bulletin, 7,* 516–522.

Hermann, D. B. (1988). How old were the authors of significant research in twentieth century astronomy at the time of their greatest achievements? *Scientometrics, 13,* 135–138.

Hudson, L. (1958). Undergraduate academic record of Fellows of the Royal Society. *Nature, 182,* 1326.

Hull, D. L., Tessner, P. D., & Diamond, A. M. (1978). Planck's principle: Do younger scientists accept new scientific ideas with greater alacrity than older scientists? *Science, 202,* 717–723.

Huntington, E. (1938). *Season of birth: Its relation to human abilities.* New York: Wiley.

Inhaber, H. (1977). Scientists and economic growth. *Social Studies of Science, 7,* 514–526.

Inhaber, H., & Przednowek, K. (1976). Quality of research and the Nobel prizes. *Social Studies of Science, 6,* 33–50.

Jackson, J. M., & Padgett, V. R. (1982). With a little help from my friend: Social loafing and the Lennon-McCartney songs. *Personality and Social Psychology Bulletin, 8,* 672–677.

Karlson, J. I. (1970). Genetic association of giftedness and creativity with schizophrenia. *Hereditas, 66,* 177–182.

Kaulins, A. (1979). Cycles in the birth of eminent humans. *Cycles, 30,* 9–15.

Kaun, D. E. (1991). Writers die young: The impact of work and leisure on longevity. *Journal of Economic Psychology, 12,* 381–399.

Kavolis, V. (1964). Economic correlates of artistic creativity. *American Journal of Sociology, 70,* 332–341.

Klingemann, H.-D., Mohler, P. P., & Weber, R. P. (1982). Cultural indicators based on content analysis: A secondary analysis of Sorokin's data on fluctuations of systems of truth. *Quality and Quantity, 16,* 1–8.

Knapp, R. H. (1962). A factor analysis of Thorndike's ratings of eminent men. *Journal of Social Psychology, 56,* 67–71.

Kroeber, A. L. (1944). *Configurations of culture growth.* Berkeley: University of California Press.

Kuo, Y. (1986). The growth and decline of Chinese philosophical genius. *Chinese Journal of Psychology, 28,* 81–91.

Kuo, Y. (1988). The social psychology of Chinese philosophical creativity: A critical synthesis. *Social Epistemology, 2,* 283–295.

Lehman, H. C. (1943). The longevity of the eminent. *Science, 98,* 270–273.

Lehman, H. C. (1947). The exponential increase of man's cultural output. *Social Forces, 25,* 281–290.

Lehman, H. C. (1953). *Age and achievement.* Princeton, NJ: Princeton University Press.

Lehman, H. C. (1958). The chemist's most creative years. *Science, 127,* 1213–1222.

Lehman, H. C. (1962). More about age and achievement. *Gerontologist, 2,* 141–148.

Lehman, H. C. (1963). Chronological age versus present-day contributions to medical progress. *Gerontologist, 3,* 71–75.

Lehman, H. C. (1966a). The most creative years of engineers and other technologists. *Journal of Genetic Psychology, 108,* 263–270.

Lehman, H. C. (1966b). The psychologist's most creative years. *American Psychologist, 21,* 363–369.

Lehman, H. C., & Witty, P. A. (1931). Scientific eminence and church membership. *Scientific Monthly, 33,* 544–549.

Lester, D. (1991). Premature mortality associated with alcoholism and suicide in American writers. *Perceptual and Motor Skills, 73,* 162.

Lindauer, M. S. (1992). Creativity in aging artists: Contributions from the humanities to the psychology of old age. *Creativity Research Journal, 5,* 211–231.

Lindauer, M. S. (1993a). The old-age style and its artists. *Empirical Studies and the Arts, 11,* 135–146.

Lindauer, M. S. (1993b). The span of creativity among long-lived historical artists. *Creativity Research Journal, 6,* 231–239.

Lotka, A. J. (1926). The frequency distribution of scientific productivity. *Journal of the Washington Academy of Sciences, 16,* 317–323.

Lowe, J. W. G., & Lowe, E. D. (1982). Cultural pattern and process: A study of stylistic change in women's dress. *American Anthropologist, 84,* 521–544.

Ludwig, A. M. (1990). Alcohol input and creative output. *British Journal of Addiction, 85,* 953–963.

Ludwig, A. M. (1992a). Creative achievement and psychopathology: Comparison among professions. *American Journal of Psychotherapy, 46,* 330–356.

Ludwig, A. M. (1992b). The Creative Achievement Scale. *Creativity Research Journal, 5,* 109–124.

Ludwig, A. M. (1995). *The price of greatness: Resolving the creativity and madness controversy.* New York: Guilford.

Lyons, J. (1968). Chronological age, professional age, and eminence in psychology. *American Psychologist, 23,* 371–374.

Mackavey, W. R., Malley, J. E., & Stewart, A. J. (1991). Remembering autobiographically consequential experiences: Content analysis of psychologists' accounts of their lives. *Psychology and Aging, 6,* 50–59.

MacKinnon, D. W. (1978). *In search of human effectiveness.* Buffalo, NJ: Creative Education Foundation.

Manniche, E., & Falk, G. (1957). Age and the Nobel Prize. *Behavioral Science, 2,* 301–307.

Marchetti, C. (1980). Society as a learning system: Discovery, invention, and innovation cycles. *Techno-logical Forecasting and Social Change, 18*, 267–282.

Martindale, C. (1972). Father absence, psychopathology, and poetic eminence. *Psychological Reports, 31*, 843–847.

Martindale, C. (1973). An experimental simulation of literary change. *Journal of Personality and Social Psychology, 25*, 319–326.

Martindale, C. (1975). *Romantic progression: The psychology of literary history.* Washington, DC: Hemisphere.

Martindale, C. (1984a). Evolutionary trends in poetic style: The case of English metaphysical poetry. *Computers and the Humanities, 18*, 3–21.

Martindale, C. (1984b). The evolution of aesthetic taste. In K. J. Gergen & M. M. Gergen (Eds.), *Historical social psychology* (pp. 347–370). Hillsdale, NJ: Erlbaum.

Martindale, C. (1986a). Aesthetic evolution. *Poetics, 15*, 439–473.

Martindale, C. (1986b). The evolution of Italian painting: A quantitative investigation of trends in style and content from the late Gothic to the Rococo period. *Leonardo, 19*, 217–222.

Martindale, C. (1990). *The clockwork muse: The predictability of artistic styles.* New York: Basic.

Martindale, C. (1995). Fame more fickle than fortune: On the distribution of literary eminence. *Poetics, 23*, 219–234.

Martindale, C., & Uemura, A. (1983). Stylistic evolution in European music. *Leonardo, 16*, 225–228.

Matossian, M. K., & Schafer, W. D. (1977). Family, fertility, and political violence, 1700–1900. *Journal of Social History, 11*, 137–178.

McClelland, D. C. (1961). *The achieving society.* New York: Van Nostrand.

McClelland, D. C. (1975). *Power: The inner experience.* New York: Irvington.

McGuire, W. J. (1976). Historical comparisons: Testing psychological hypotheses with cross-era data. *International Journal of Psychology, 11*, 161–183.

Meehl, P. E. (1992). Cliometric metatheory: The actuarial approach to empirical, history-based philosophy of science. *Psychological Reports: Monograph Supplement, 71*, 339–467.

Merton, R. K. (1961). Singletons and multiples in scientific discovery: A chapter in the sociology of science. *Proceedings of the American Philosophical Society, 105*, 470–486.

Messerli, P. (1988). Age differences in the reception of new scientific theories: The case of plate tectonics theory. *Social Studies of Science, 18*, 91–112.

Mills, C. A. (1942). What price glory? *Science, 96*, 380–387.

Moulin, L. (1955). The Nobel Prizes for the sciences from 1901–1950: An essay in sociological analysis. *British Journal of Sociology, 6*, 246–263.

Naroll, R., Benjamin, E. C., Fohl, F. K., Fried, M. J., Hildreth, R. E., & Schaefer, J. M. (1971). Creativity: A cross-historical pilot survey. *Journal of Cross-Cultural Psychology, 2*, 181–188.

Ohlsson, S. (1992). The learning curve for writing books: Evidence from Professor Asimov. *Psychological Science, 3*, 380–382.

Oromaner, M. (1977). Professional age and the reception of sociological publications: A test of the Zuckerman-Merton hypothesis. *Social Studies of Science, 7*, 381–388.

Oromaner, M. (1985). The Ortega hypothesis and influential articles in American sociology. *Scientometrics, 7*, 3–10.

Over, R. (1982). The durability of scientific reputation. *Journal of the History of the Behavioral Sciences, 18*, 53–61.

Over, R. (1988). Does scholarly impact decline with age? *Scientometrics, 13*, 215–223.

Over, R. (1989). Age and scholarly impact. *Psychology and Aging, 4*, 222–225.

Over, R. (1990). The scholarly impact of articles published by men and women in psychology journals. *Scientometrics, 18*, 71–80.

Padgett, V., & Jorgenson, D. O. (1982). Superstition and economic threat: Germany, 1918–1940. *Personality and Social Psychology Bulletin, 8*, 736–741.

Peterson, R. A., & Berger, D. G. (1975). Cycles in symbol production: The case of popular music. *American Sociological Review, 40*, 158–173.

Porter, C. A., & Suedfeld, P. (1981). Integrative complexity in the correspondence of literary figures: Effects of personal and societal stress. *Journal of Personality and Social Psychology, 40*, 321–330.

Post, F. (1994). Creativity and psychopathology: A study of 291 world-famous men. *British Journal of Psychiatry, 165*, 22–34.

Pressey, S. L., & Combs, A. (1943). Acceleration and age of productivity. *Educational Research Bulletin, 22*, 191–196.

Price, D. (1963). *Little science, big science.* New York: Columbia University Press.

Price, D. (1965). Networks of scientific papers. *Science, 149*, 510–515.

Price, D. (1978). Ups and downs in the pulse of science and technology. In J. Gaston (Ed.), *The sociology of science* (pp. 162–171). San Francisco: Jossey-Bass.

Quetelet, A. (1968). *A treatise on man and the development of his faculties.* New York: Franklin. (Reprint of 1842 Edinburgh translation of 1835 French original).

Rainoff, T. J. (1929). Wave-like fluctuations of creative productivity in the development of West-European physics in the eighteenth and nineteenth centuries. *Isis, 12,* 287–319.

Raskin, E. A. (1936). Comparison of scientific and literary ability: A biographical study of eminent scientists and men of letters of the nineteenth century. *Journal of Abnormal and Social Psychology, 31,* 20–35.

Richardson, J., & Kroeber, A. L. (1940). Three centuries of women's dress fashions: A quantitative analysis. *Anthropological Records, 5,* 111–150.

Root-Bernstein, R. S. (1989). *Discovering.* Cambridge, MA: Harvard University Press.

Root-Bernstein, R. S., Bernstein, M., & Garnier, H. (1993). Identification of scientists making long-term, high-impact contributions, with notes on their methods of working. *Creativity Research Journal, 6,* 329–343.

Rosengren, K. E. (1985). Time and literary fame. *Poetics, 14,* 157–172.

Runyan, W. M. (1982). *Life histories and psychobiography.* New York: Oxford University Press.

Rushton, J. P. (1984). Evaluating research eminence in psychology: The construct validity of citation counts. *Bulletin of the British Psychological Society, 37,* 33–36.

Schachter, S. (1963). Birth order, eminence, and higher education. *American Sociological Review, 28,* 757–768.

Schmookler, J. (1966). *Invention and economic growth.* Cambridge, MA: Harvard University Press.

Schneider, J. (1937). The cultural situation as a condition for the achievement of fame. *American Sociological Review, 2,* 480–491.

Schubert, D. S. P., Wagner, M. E., & Schubert, H. J. P. (1977). Family constellation and creativity: First-born predominance among classical music composers. *Journal of Psychology, 95,* 147–149.

Sears, R. R., Lapidus, D., & Cozzens, C. (1978). Content analysis of Mark Twain's novels and letters as a biographical method. *Poetics, 7,* 155–175.

Sheldon, J. C. (1979). Hierarchical cybernets: A model for the dynamics of high level learning and cultural change. *Cybernetica, 22,* 179–202.

Sheldon, J. C. (1980). A cybernetic theory of physical science professions: The causes of periodic normal and revolutionary science between 1000 and 1870 A.D. *Scientometrics, 2,* 147–167.

Sicoli, C. M. L. (1995). Life factors common to women who write popular songs. *Creativity Research Journal, 8,* 265–276.

Silverman, S. M. (1974). Parental loss and scientists. *Science Studies, 4,* 259–264.

Simon, J. L., & Sullivan, R. J. (1989). Population size, knowledge stock, and other determinants of agricultural publication and patenting: England, 1541–1850. *Explorations in Economic History, 26,* 21–44.

Simonton, D. K. (1975a). Age and literary creativity: A cross-cultural and transhistorical survey. *Journal of Cross-Cultural Psychology, 6,* 259–277.

Simonton, D. K. (1975b). Interdisciplinary creativity over historical time: A correlational analysis of generational fluctuations. *Social Behavior and Personality, 3,* 181–188.

Simonton, D. K. (1975c). Invention and discovery among the sciences: A p-technique factor analysis. *Journal of Vocational Behavior, 7,* 275–281.

Simonton, D. K. (1975d). Sociocultural context of individual creativity: A transhistorical time-series analysis. *Journal of Personality and Social Psychology, 32,* 1119–1133.

Simonton, D. K. (1976a). Biographical determinants of achieved eminence: A multivariate approach to the Cox data. *Journal of Personality and Social Psychology, 33,* 218–226.

Simonton, D. K. (1976b). The causal relation between war and scientific discovery: An exploratory cross-national analysis. *Journal of Cross-Cultural Psychology, 7,* 133–144.

Simonton, D. K. (1976c). Do Sorokin's data support his theory?: A study of generational fluctuations in philosophical beliefs. *Journal for the Scientific Study of Religion, 15,* 187–198.

Simonton, D. K. (1976d). Ideological diversity and creativity: A re-evaluation of a hypothesis. *Social Behavior and Personality, 4,* 203–207.

Simonton, D. K. (1976e). Interdisciplinary and military determinants of scientific productivity: A cross-lagged correlation analysis. *Journal of Vocational Behavior, 9,* 53–62.

Simonton, D. K. (1976f). Philosophical eminence, beliefs, and zeitgeist: An individual-generational analysis. *Journal of Personality and Social Psychology, 34,* 630–640.

Simonton, D. K. (1976g). The sociopolitical context of philosophical beliefs: A transhistorical causal analysis. *Social Forces, 54,* 513–523.

Simonton, D. K. (1977a). Creative productivity, age, and stress: A biographical time-series analysis of 10 classical composers. *Journal of Personality and Social Psychology, 35,* 791–804.

Simonton, D. K. (1977b). Eminence, creativity, and geographic marginality: A recursive structural equation model. *Journal of Personality and Social Psychology, 35,* 805–816.

Simonton, D. K. (1978a). Independent discovery in science and technology: A closer look at the Poisson distribution. *Social Studies of Science, 8,* 521–532.

Simonton, D. K. (1978b). Intergenerational stimulation, reaction, and polarization: A causal analysis of intellectual history. *Social Behavior and Personality, 6,* 247–251.

Simonton, D. K. (1979). Multiple discovery and invention: Zeitgeist, genius, or chance? *Journal of Personality and Social Psychology, 37,* 1603–1616.

Simonton, D. K. (1980a). Techno-scientific activity and war: A yearly time-series analysis, 1500–1903 A. D. *Scientometrics, 2,* 251–255.

Simonton, D. K. (1980b). Thematic fame and melodic originality in classical music: A multivariate computer-content analysis. *Journal of Personality, 48,* 206–219.

Simonton, D. K. (1980c). Thematic fame, melodic originality, and musical zeitgeist: A biographical and transhistorical content analysis. *Journal of Personality and Social Psychology, 38,* 972–983.

Simonton, D. K. (1983a). Dramatic greatness and content: A quantitative study of eighty-one Athenian and Shakespearean plays. *Empirical Studies of the Arts, 1,* 109–123.

Simonton, D. K. (1983b). Formal education, eminence, and dogmatism: The curvilinear relationship. *Journal of Creative Behavior, 17,* 149–162.

Simonton, D. K. (1983c). Intergenerational transfer of individual differences in hereditary monarchs: Genes, role-modeling, cohort, or sociocultural effects? *Journal of Personality and Social Psychology, 44,* 354–364.

Simonton, D. K. (1983d). Psychohistory. In R. Harré & R. Lamb (Eds.), *The encyclopedic dictionary of psychology* (pp. 499–500). Oxford: Blackwell.

Simonton, D. K. (1984a). Artistic creativity and interpersonal relationships across and within generations. *Journal of Personality and Social Psychology, 46,* 1273–1286.

Simonton, D. K. (1984b). Creative productivity and age: A mathematical model based on a two-step cognitive process. *Developmental Review, 4,* 77–111.

Simonton, D. K. (1984c). Generational time-series analysis: A paradigm for studying sociocultural influences. In K. Gergen & M. Gergen (Eds.), *Historical social psychology* (pp. 141–155). Hillsdale, NJ: Erlbaum.

Simonton, D. K. (1984d). *Genius, creativity, and leadership: Historiometric inquiries.* Cambridge, MA.: Harvard University Press.

Simonton, D. K. (1984e). Is the marginality effect all that marginal? *Social Studies of Science, 14,* 621–622.

Simonton, D. K. (1984f). Leaders as eponyms: Individual and situational determinants of monarchal eminence. *Journal of Personality, 52,* 1–21.

Simonton, D. K. (1984g). Melodic structure and note transition probabilities: A content analysis of 15, 618 classical themes. *Psychology of Music, 12,* 3–16.

Simonton, D. K. (1984h). Scientific eminence historical and contemporary: A measurement assessment. *Scientometrics, 6,* 169–182.

Simonton, D. K. (1985). Quality, quantity, and age: The careers of 10 distinguished psychologists. *International Journal of Aging and Human Development, 21,* 241–254.

Simonton, D. K. (1986a). Aesthetic success in classical music: A computer analysis of 1935 compositions. *Empirical Studies of the Arts, 4,* 1–17.

Simonton, D. K. (1986b). Biographical typicality, eminence, and achievement style. *Journal of Creative Behavior, 20,* 14–22.

Simonton, D. K. (1986c). Multiple discovery: Some Monte Carlo simulations and Gedanken experiments. *Scientometrics, 9,* 269–280.

Simonton, D. K. (1986d). Multiples, Poisson distributions, and chance: An analysis of the Brannigan-Wanner model. *Scientometrics, 9,* 127–137.

Simonton, D. K. (1986e). Popularity, content, and context in 37 Shakespeare plays. *Poetics, 15,* 493–510.

Simonton, D. K. (1986f). Stochastic models of multiple discovery. *Czechoslovak Journal of Physics, B 36,* 138–141.

Simonton, D. K. (1987a). Musical aesthetics and creativity in Beethoven: A computer analysis of 105 compositions. *Empirical Studies of the Arts, 5,* 87–104.

Simonton, D. K. (1987b). Developmental antecedents of achieved eminence. *Annals of Child Development, 5,* 131–169.

Simonton, D. K. (1988a). Age and outstanding achievement: What do we know after a century of research? *Psychological Bulletin, 104,* 251–267.

Simonton, D. K. (1988b). Galtonian genius, Kroeberian configurations, and emulation: A generational time-series analysis of Chinese civilization. *Journal of Personality and Social Psychology, 55,* 230–238.

Simonton, D. K. (1988c). *Scientific genius: A psychology of science.* Cambridge University Press.

Simonton, D. K. (1989a). Age and creative productivity: Nonlinear estimation of an information-processing model. *International Journal of Aging and Human Development, 29,* 23–37.

Simonton, D. K. (1989b). Shakespeare's sonnets: A case of and for single-case historiometry. *Journal of Personality, 57,* 695–721.

Simonton, D. K. (1989c). The swan-song phenomenon: Last-works effects for 172 classical composers. *Psychology and Aging, 4,* 42–47.

Simonton, D. K. (1990a). History, chemistry, psychology, and genius: An intellectual autobiography of historiometry. In M. Runco & R. Albert (Eds.), *Theories of creativity* (pp. 92–115). Newbury Park, CA: Sage.

Simonton, D. K. (1990b). Lexical choices and aesthetic success: A computer content analysis of 154 Shakespeare sonnets. *Computers and the Humanities, 24,* 251–264.

Simonton, D. K. (1990c). *Psychology, science, and history: An introduction to historiometry.* New Haven, CT: Yale University Press.

Simonton, D. K. (1991a). Career landmarks in science: Individual differences and interdisciplinary contrasts. *Developmental Psychology, 27,* 119–130.

Simonton, D. K. (1991b). Emergence and realization of genius: The lives and works of 120 classical composers. *Journal of Personality and Social Psychology, 61,* 829–840.

Simonton, D. K. (1991c). Latent-variable models of posthumous reputation: A quest for Galton's G. *Journal of Personality and Social Psychology, 60,* 607–619.

Simonton, D. K. (1991d). Personality correlates of exceptional personal influence: A note on Thorndike's (1950) creators and leaders. *Creativity Research Journal, 4,* 67–78.

Simonton, D. K. (1992a). Gender and genius in Japan: Feminine eminence in masculine culture. *Sex Roles, 27,* 101–119.

Simonton, D. K. (1992b). Leaders of American psychology, 1879–1967: Career development, creative output, and professional achievement. *Journal of Personality and Social Psychology, 62,* 5–17.

Simonton, D. K. (1992c). The social context of career success and course for 2,026 scientists and inventors. *Personality and Social Psychology Bulletin, 18,* 452–463.

Simonton, D. K. (1994a). Computer content analysis of melodic structure: Classical composers and their compositions. *Psychology of Music, 22,* 31–43.

Simonton, D. K. (1994b). *Greatness: Who makes history and why.* New York: Guilford.

Simonton, D. K. (1995a). Behavioral laws in histories of psychology: Psychological science, metascience, and the psychology of science. *Psychological Inquiries, 6,* 89–114.

Simonton, D. K. (1995b). Drawing inferences from symphonic programs: Musical attributes versus listener attributions. *Music Perception, 12,* 307–322.

Simonton, D. K. (1996). Individual genius and cultural configurations: The case of Japanese civilization. *Journal of Cross-Cultural Psychology, 27,* 354–375.

Simonton, D. K. (1997a). Achievement domain and life expectancies in Japanese civilization. *International Journal of Aging and Human Development, 44,* 103–114.

Simonton, D. K. (1997b). Creative productivity: A predictive and explanatory model of career trajectories and landmarks. *Psychological Review, 104,* 66–89.

Simonton, D. K. (1997c). Foreign influence and national achievement: The impact of open milieus on Japanese civilization. *Journal of Personality and Social Psychology, 72,* 86–94.

Simonton, D. K. (1997d). *Genius and creativity: Selected papers.* Greenwich, CT: Ablex.

Simonton, D. K. (1997e). Imagery, style, and content in 37 Shakespeare plays. *Empirical Studies of the Arts, 15,* 15–20.

Sorokin, P. A. (1937–1941). *Social and cultural dynamics* (4 vols.). New York: American Book.

Sorokin, P. A., & Merton, R. K. (1935). The course of Arabian intellectual development, 700–1300 A.D. *Isis, 22,* 516–524.

Stariha, W. E., & Walberg, H. J. (1995). Childhood precursors of women's artistic eminence. *Journal of Creative Behavior, 29,* 269–282.

Sternberg, R. J., & Davidson, J. E. (Eds.). (1995). *The nature of insight.* Cambridge, MA: MIT Press.

Sternberg, R. J., & Lubart, T. I. (1995). *Defying the crowd.* New York: Free Press.

Stewart, J. A. (1986). Drifting continents and colliding interests: A quantitative application of the interests perspective. *Social Studies of Science, 16,* 261–279.

Stewart, L. H. (1977). Birth order and political leadership. In M. G. Hermann (Ed.), *The psychological examination of political leaders* (pp. 205–236). New York: Free Press.

Suedfeld, P. (1985). APA presidential addresses: The relation of integrative complexity to historical, professional, and personal factors. *Journal of Personality and Social Psychology, 47,* 848–852.

Suedfeld, P., & Bluck, S. (1993). Changes in integrative complexity accompanying significant life events: Historical evidence. *Journal of Personality and Social Psychology, 64,* 124–130.

Suedfeld, P., & Piedrahita, L. E. (1984). Intimations of mortality: Integrative simplification as a predictor of death. *Journal of Personality and Social Psychology, 47,* 848–852.

Sulloway, F. J. (1996). *Born to rebell: Birth order, family dynamics, and creative lives.* New York: Pantheon.

Terman, L. M. (1917). The intelligence quotient of Francis Galton in childhood. *American Journal of Psychology, 28,* 209–215.

Terman, L. M. (1925). *Mental and physical traits of a thousand gifted children.* Stanford, CA: Stanford University Press.

Terman, L. M., & Oden, M. H. (1959). *The gifted group at mid-life.* Stanford, CA: Stanford University Press.

Terry, W. S. (1989). Birth order and prominence in the history of psychology. *Psychological Record, 39,* 333–337.

Thorndike, E. L. (1936). The relation between intellect and morality in rulers. *American Journal of Sociology, 42,* 321–334.

Thorndike, E. L. (1950). Traits of personality and their intercorrelations as shown in biography. *Journal of Educational Psychology, 41,* 193–216.

Veblen, T. (1919). The intellectual preeminence of Jews in modern Europe. *Political Science Quarterly, 34,* 33–42.

Visher, S. S. (1947). Starred scientists: A study of their ages. *American Scientist, 35,* 543, 570, 572, 574, 576, 578, 580.

Walberg, H. J., Rasher, S. P., & Parkerson, J. (1980). Childhood and eminence. *Journal of Creative Behavior, 13,* 225–231.

Walters, J., & Gardner, H. (1986). The crystallizing experience: Discovering an intellectual gift. In R. J. Sternberg & J. E. Davidson (Eds.), *Conceptions of giftedness* (pp. 306–331). Cambridge University Press.

Weisberg, R. W. (1994). Genius and madness? A quasi-experimental test of the hypothesis that manic-depression increases creativity. *Psychological Science, 5,* 361–367.

Whaples, R. (1991). A quantitative history of the *Journal of Economic History* and the cliometric revolution. *Journal of Economic History, 51,* 289–301.

White, R. K. (1931). The versatility of genius. *Journal of Social Psychology, 2,* 460–489.

Winter, D. G. (1973). *The power motive.* New York: Free Press.

Woods, F. A. (1906). *Mental and moral heredity in royalty.* New York: Holt.

Woods, F. A. (1909). A new name for a new science. *Science, 30,* 703–704.

Woods, F. A. (1911). Historiometry as an exact science. *Science, 33,* 568–574.

Woods, F. A. (1913). *The influence of monarchs.* New York: Macmillan.

Woodward, W. R. (1974). Scientific genius and loss of a parent. *Science Studies, 4,* 265–277.

Yuasa, M. (1974). The shifting center of scientific activity in the West: From the sixteenth to the twentieth century. In N. Shigeru, D. L. Swain, & Y. Eri (Eds.), *Science and society in modern Japan* (pp. 81–103). Tokyo: University of Tokyo Press.

Zhao, H. (1984). An intelligence constant of scientific work. *Scientometrics, 6,* 9–17.

Zhao, H., & Jiang, G. (1985). Shifting of world's scientific center and scientists' social ages. *Scientometrics, 8,* 59–80.

Zhao, H., & Jiang, G. (1986). Life-span and precocity of scientists. *Scientometrics, 9,* 27–36.

Zusne, L. (1976). Age and achievement in psychology: The harmonic mean as a model. *American Psychologist, 31,* 805–807.

Zusne, L. (1985). Contributions to the history of psychology: No. 38. The hyperbolic structure of eminence. *Psychological Reports, 57,* 1213–1214.

Zusne, L. (1986–1989). Some factors affecting the birthday–deathday phenomenon. *Omega: Journal of Death and Dying, 17,* 9–26.

Zusne, L. (1987). Contributions to the history of psychology: No. 45. Coverage of contributors in histories of psychology. *Psychological Reports, 61,* 343–350.

Zusne, L., & Dailey, D. P. (1982). History of psychology texts as measuring instruments of eminence in psychology. *Revista de Historia de la Psicologia, 3,* 7–42.

PART III

Origins of Creativity

7   *Biological Bases of Creativity*

COLIN MARTINDALE

Creativity is a rare trait. This is presumably because it requires the simultaneous presence of a number of traits (e.g., intelligence, perseverance, unconventionality, the ability to think in a particular manner). None of these traits is especially rare. What is quite uncommon is to find them all present in the same person. One imagines that all of these traits have biological bases. In this chapter, I shall focus upon the type of thought involved in creative insight. First, I describe the nature of this type of thought; then I present arguments as to why it must be based upon specific physiological states; finally, I review evidence that it is in fact so based.

A creative idea is one that is both original and appropriate for the situation in which it occurs. It would seem that creative productions always consist of novel combinations of pre-existing mental elements. As Poincaré (1913) noted, "To create consists of making new combinations of associative elements which are useful" (p. 286). Creative ideas, he further remarked, "reveal to us unsuspected kinships between other facts well known but wrongly believed to be strangers to one another" (p. 115).

To create, then, involves the realization of an analogy between previously unassociated mental elements. On the verbal level, creativity involves production of novel statements of the form "A is like B" or statements involving novel modifiers for A. Hugo's image, "I climbed the bitter stairs" is more creative than, say, "I climbed the steep stairs." The only real difference at this level between poetry and science or technology concerns what – if anything – is concluded from such analogies. The poet writes a poem. The technologist builds a machine. The inspiration for McCormack's reaper was the idea that grain is like hair. Not being a poet, McCormack went on to reason that clippers cut hair and that, therefore, something like clippers could cut grain.

The formal similarity between scientific and artistic inspiration is mirrored in the similarity in self-reports concerning creative inspiration. For neither scientists nor artists do novel ideas seem to arise from intellectual deduction. Ghiselin (1952) concluded after a study of such reports that "production by a process of purely conscious calculation seems never to occur" (p. 14). Besides being nonintellectual, creation is reported as being automatic and effortless. For example, composition was quite easy for Mozart, because he just copied down the melodies he "heard" in his mind. Something similar occurs in the creation of literature. A large number of great authors have remarked that they created by copying down auditory mental images or by describing visual mental images. Blake's (1803/1906) comment is not especially unusual: "I have written this poem from immediate dictation, 12 or sometimes 20 or 30 lines at a time without premeditation, and even against my will." Though scientists deal with abstract concepts, their creative ideas very often arise as spontaneous mental images. An example would be Kekulé's discovery of the benzene ring by having a reverie about a snake biting its own tail (Ghiselin, 1952).

We may divide the creative process into several stages originally suggested by Helmholtz

(1896) and Wallas (1926). The stages are preparation, incubation, illumination or inspiration, and verification or elaboration. Preparation involves thinking about or learning the mental elements thought to be relevant to the problem at hand. Helmholtz noted that a solution was often not found at this time unless the problem was a trivial one. His practice was to set the problem aside. This is the period of incubation. After some time, the solution simply occurred to him. This is the stage of illumination or inspiration. Finally, during the stage of elaboration, the new idea is subjected to logical scrutiny and put into its final form.

THEORIES OF CREATIVITY

Unless we know how more and less creative people differ on the psychological level, we will not know what sorts of biological differences to look for. Accordingly, I begin with a brief review of some major theories of creativity. As we shall see, the theories suggest certain physiological differences between more and less creative people.

Primary Process Cognition

Kris (1952) proposed that creative individuals are better able to alternate between primary process and secondary process modes of thought than are uncreative people. The primary process–secondary process continuum is the main dimension along which cognition varies (Fromm, 1978). Primary process thought is found in normal states such as dreaming and reverie, as well as in abnormal states such as psychosis and hypnosis. It is autistic, free-associative, analogical, and characterized by concrete images as opposed to abstract concepts. Secondary process cognition is the abstract, logical, reality-oriented thought of waking consciousness. According to Kris, creative inspiration involves a "regression" to a primary process state of consciousness. Because primary process cognition is associative, it facilitates the discovery of new combinations of mental elements. On the other hand, creative elaboration involves a return to a secondary process state. Because uncreative people are more or less "stuck" at one point on the primary process–secondary process continuum, they are unable to think of creative ideas. Kris's hypothesis reminds us of Schopenhauer's remark that "a great poet . . . is a man who, in his waking state, is able to do what the rest of us do in our dreams" (quoted by Weber, 1969, p. 94).

Several lines of evidence are supportive of Kris's theory that creative people have easier access to primary process modes of thought. They report more fantasy activity (Lynn & Rhue, 1986), remember their dreams better (Hudson, 1975), and are more easily hypnotized than uncreative people (Lynn & Rhue, 1986). Wild (1965) showed directly that they are better able to shift between use of primary process and secondary process cognition. Martindale and Dailey (1996) found that the more creative a person is, the more primary process content his or her fantasy stories contains. Suler (1980) gives a review of the lines of evidence directly or indirectly linking creativity and primary process thinking.

Schizophrenia – a primary process state according to psychoanalytic theory – and creativity are related in a number of ways. Because highly creative individuals are overrepresented among the relatives of schizophrenics (Heston, 1966; Karlsson, 1968; McNeil, 1971), there may be a direct genetic link (Jarvik & Chadwick, 1973). Creative people obtain quite high scores on tests of psychoticism (Eysenck, 1995). Furthermore, schizophrenics and highly creative subjects do not differ in the unusualness of their performance on object-sorting tasks (Dykes & McGhie, 1976). They are also similar in the remoteness of their responses on word association tasks (Eysenck, 1995).

Defocused Attention

Mendelsohn (1976) proposed that individual differences in focus of attention are the cause of differences in creativity: "The greater the attentional capacity, the more likely the combinatorial leap which is generally described as the hallmark of creativity" (p. 366). In order to become aware of a creative idea, one must obviously have the elements to be combined in the focus of attention at the same time. If one can attend to only two things at the same time, only one possible analogy can be discovered at that time; if one could attend to four things at once, six possible analogies could be discovered; and so on. There is evidence that uncreative individuals do seem to have more narrowly focused attention than do creative ones (Dewing & Battye, 1971; Dykes & McGhie, 1976).

Associative Hierarchies

Mental elements are associated with one another to various degrees. For example, on a word association task, if the stimulus word is *table*, the most likely response is *chair*. *Food* is a somewhat less probable response, but *airplane* is much less probable. Because people are consistent in the probabilities of the responses they make to any given stimulus, we may plot an associative hierarchy for the stimulus. People differ in the steepness of their associative hierarchies. A person with a steep hierarchy has just a few responses to make to a stimulus. Hypothetically, the mental representation of the stimulus is strongly bonded to just a few other mental representations. On the other hand, a person with a flat associative hierarchy has more associations to the stimulus. In this case, the close associates are less strongly connected to the stimulus and the remote associates are more strongly connected to the stimulus than is the case for the person with steep associative hierarchies. Mednick (1962) proposed that creative individuals have relatively flat associative hierarchies, whereas uncreative individuals have relatively steep associative hierarchies. This, he argues, accounts for ability of the creative person to make the remote associations that are the basis of creative ideas.

According to Mednick's theory, the relative ordering of elements on associative hierarchies is similar for creative and uncreative people. What differs is the relative strength of the responses. Research with continuous word association supports this contention. At first, creative and uncreative people give similar responses in a similar order. However, creative people continue to respond at a fairly steady rate, whereas uncreative people run out of responses.

Summary

Kris's, Mednick's, and Mendelsohn's theories are more or less identical but expressed in very different vocabularies. Defocused attention is a property of primary process cognition (Martindale, 1981). Defocused attention and flat associative hierarchies are cognitive and behavioristic ways of describing exactly the same phenomenon (Mendelsohn, 1976).

CREATIVITY AND CORTICAL ACTIVATION

There are theoretical reasons to expect that creativity is related to general level of cortical arousal. A number of theorists have dealt with the construct of general level of activation or arousal (e.g., Duffy, 1962; Hebb, 1955). Arousal is viewed as a continuum, ranging from sleep through alert wakefulness to states of emotional tension. It is related to learning and performance in an inverted-U-shaped manner, with optimal performance at medium levels of arousal (Hebb, 1955; Yerkes & Dodson, 1908). As task complexity increases, the optimal level of arousal decreases. Simple tasks are performed most efficiently at relatively high levels of arousal, whereas more complex tasks require lower levels of arousal. Lindsley (1960) draws a parallel between cortical activation as measured by the EEG and state of consciousness: As one moves from alert wakefulness through fantasy, and reverie to sleep, cortical activation measured directly by EEG frequency and inversely by EEG amplitude decreases. This suggests a parallel with the secondary process–primary process continuum. Hypothetically, medium levels of activation are optimal for secondary process states of consciousness, whereas both high and low levels of arousal should co-occur with primary process states.

The proposed relationship allows us to translate Kris's hypothesis into a physiological hypothesis: If creative subjects are more variable on the primary–secondary process continuum, then they should also be more variable on the arousal continuum. The curvilinear relationship does not permit us to determine on purely theoretical grounds whether creativity should go along with high-arousal or low-arousal states. However, self-reports of creative geniuses suggest that creative inspiration is most likely in low-arousal, reverie-like states.

Induced Cortical Activation

Though he did not state it explicitly, Hull (1943) was probably the first to imply that there is a relationship between creativity and arousal. His Behavioral Law is that increases in *drive* (what we today call general level of arousal) make the dominant response to a stimulus even more dominant: That is, increases in arousal make behavior more stereotypical and decreases in arousal make behavior more variable. Of course, Hull himself produced experimental evidence for this law with studies of lower animals. Increases in arousal steepen associative gradients, whereas decreases in arousal flatten them. We recall Mednick's hypothesis that more creative people have flatter associative gradients than do less creative people. Osgood (1960) and Meisels (1967) showed that written language becomes more stereotyped under conditions of increased arousal. A number of studies of word association tasks (e.g., Coren & Shulman, 1971; Horton, Marlowe, & Crowne, 1963) and creativity tests (e.g., Dentler & Mackler, 1964; Krop, Alegre, & Williams, 1969) have demonstrated that stress reliably produces decreases in originality. Brainstorming techniques were originally proposed as methods of facilitating creative ideas. In fact, they decrease creativity (e.g., Lindgren & Lindgren, 1965). This makes sense in light of Zajonc's (1965) hypothesis that the mere presence of others increases arousal. Intense white noise – which increases cortical arousal – has been shown to produce decrements on tests of creativity (Martindale & Greenough, 1973). Even the arousal caused by rewards seems to decrease creativity (Amabile, 1983). It is safe to conclude that induced increases in arousal cause decreases in creativity, originality, and variability of behavior.

Resting Level of Arousal

We have no special reason to expect creativity to be related to basal, or resting, level of arousal. In fact, there is not a very strong relationship. There is evidence that highly creative people exhibit somewhat higher basal levels of arousal than do less creative people. Subjects who are more original in their word associations (Trapp & Kausler, 1960; Worrell & Worrell, 1965) or on paper-and-pencil tests of creativity (e.g., Maddi & Andrews, 1966) score higher on tests of anxiety than their low-scoring counterparts. Martindale (1977) found positive correlations between basal skin conductance and two tests of creativity. Florek (1973) found that creative painters have a very fast basal heart rate, but a control group was not included in the study. On the other hand, Cropley, Cassell, and Maslany (1970) and Kennett and Cropley (1973) report that creative people have low levels of serum uric acid. This implies low basal arousal. However, serum uric acid is positively correlated with physical activity, and there is evidence that creative people are less physically active than uncreative people (Maddi, 1965). Of course, inactivity could itself be interpreted as a behavioral sign of low arousal.

Wyspianski, Barry, and Dayhaw (1963) found that highly creative people have lower basal EEG alpha-wave amplitude (alpha-wave amplitude is an inverse measure of cortical activation) than do less creative subjects. Martindale (1990) summarized a series of seven studies concerning creativity and EEG measures. In only two of these studies were significant differences between high- and low-creative subjects on basal EEG measures of cortical arousal detected. However, in almost all of the studies, more creative people exhibited slightly higher basal levels of cortical arousal. It is probably the case that creativity is associated with a high resting level of arousal. However, we must look elsewhere to find a strong linkage between creativity and neural activity.

Variability in Level of Arousal

Given our analogy with Kris's theory, we should expect creativity to be related to variability in level of arousal, rather than with basal level of arousal. If creativity is related to psychoticism, as Eysenck (1995) hypothesizes, we should also expect to find more variability of physiological arousal in highly creative people. There is evidence supportive of this hypothesis. In laboratory studies, more creative subjects show more spontaneous galvanic skin response fluctuations (Martindale, 1977), greater heart rate variability (Bowers & Keeling, 1971), and – at least in some cases – more variability in EEG alpha amplitude (Martindale & Hasenfus, 1978). There is also evidence that they show the greatest amount of variability in arousal during creative inspiration, as opposed to baseline conditions (Florek, 1973; Martindale & Hasenfus, 1978). Given the relation between creativity and bipolar disorders (Goodwin & Jamison, 1990), it seems likely that creative people might also show long-term swings in level of arousal.

Creative Cognition and Cortical Arousal

If creativity is not strongly related to one's average level of cortical arousal, then perhaps it is related to arousal while one is engaged in the act of creation. This does, in fact, seem to be the case. Martindale and Hines (1975) measured amount of EEG alpha-wave activity – an inverse measure of cortical arousal – while subjects took the Alternate Uses Test (a fairly pure measure of creativity), the Remote Associates Test (an index of both creativity and intelligence), and an intelligence test. High-creative subjects showed differential amounts of cortical activation across the three tasks, whereas the medium- and low-creative subjects did not. The high-creative group showed lowest arousal while taking the Alternate Uses Test, somewhat higher arousal while taking the Remote Associates Test, and even higher arousal while taking the intelligence test. The medium- and low-creative groups exhibited high arousal while taking all three tests. The pattern is the one we would expect if creative activity requires the defocused attention produced by low levels of cortical activation. Virtually any task involving mental effort produces an increase in cortical activation. Thus, it is noteworthy that the highly creative group in this experiment was actually less aroused while taking the Alternate Uses Test than during baseline recording.

These findings lead to the hypothesis that, when asked to be original, as they are on the Alternate Uses Test, creative people exhibit defocused attention accompanied by low levels of cortical activation. On the other hand, uncreative people focus their attention too much, and this prevents them from thinking of original ideas. These differences should be most apparent during the inspirational phase of the creative process, because this is the stage where defocused attention is useful. Elaboration requires focused attention. Thus, there should be no differences in arousal during this stage. Martindale and Hasenfus (1978) tested this hypothesis. EEG activity was measured while people thought about a story they would write (the analogue of the inspirational phase) and while they wrote the story (the analogue of the elaboration phase). All of the subjects were asked to be as creative as possible in making up their stories. As predicted, highly creative people exhibited lower levels of cortical activation during the inspirational phase than did less creative people, and no differences in activation were present during the elaboration phase. In a second study, half of the subjects were urged to be as creative as possible, whereas nothing was mentioned about creativity or originality to the other half of the subjects. Creative subjects showed lower levels of cortical activation during the analogue of the inspirational stage if they were told to be creative. However, no differences were found when subjects were not asked to be creative.

These studies lead to the conclusion that creative and uncreative people differ in cortical activation only under quite specific circumstances: during the inspirational phase of the creative process. Furthermore, this difference is found only when people are trying to be creative. Thus, when creative people were asked to make up a story but the importance of making it creative was not mentioned, they did not differ from uncreative people in their level of cortical activation.

Self-control of Cortical Arousal

How can we explain the preceding results? A possible (but incorrect) explanation would be that creative people are more capable of controlling their own level of arousal. When asked to be creative, they use this ability to induce the low level of arousal that is necessary for creative inspiration. Kamiya (1969) was the first to show that people can control their level of cortical arousal. In his biofeedback paradigm, subjects are asked to keep a light on or off. The light is controlled by the person's own brain waves. For example, the only way to turn the light on may be to produce alpha waves. Kamiya showed that subjects can keep the light on or off at above-chance levels and that they get better with practice.

If creative people were adept at self-control of cortical arousal, they should perform well on biofeedback tasks. Two experiments (Martindale & Armstrong, 1974; Martindale & Hines, 1975) designed to test this hypothesis yielded consistent results: Creative people are not very good at biofeedback tasks. Initially, their performance is better than that of less creative people. However, this advantage is lost after only several minutes. After that, uncreative people become better and better at controlling the amount of alpha that they produce. On the other hand, the performance of highly creative people actually deteriorates. Specifically, the amount of alpha drifts upwards across trials regardless of whether they are trying to produce or suppress alpha waves. The low levels of arousal that creative people show during creative inspiration are evidently not due to self control.

Creativity, Disinhibition, and Reactivity

At least in retrospect, the poor performance of creative people on biofeedback tasks should not be surprising. When creative people are asked to describe themselves, they use words that stress disinhibition and lack of control (Martindale, 1972, 1989). Martindale (1989) and Eysenck (1995) have argued that creativity is a disinhibition syndrome. That is, creative people are characterized by a lack of both cognitive and behavioral inhibition. Eysenck (1995) links creativity with the personality dimension of psychoticism. Both theories are close to the degeneration theories of genius proposed by Lombroso (1895) and Nordau (1895). The gist of degeneration theories is that degeneration (a construct similar to psychoticism) predisposes one to criminality, psychoses of all types, and genius. The concept of degeneration was formulated by Morel (1857) and gained wide acceptance across the course of the nineteenth century. On the mental level, degeneration was seen as involving a weakening of higher, inhibitory brain centers. This weakening allows lower, more primitive functions to emerge in an uncontrolled fashion (Talbot, 1898, p. 316). In other words, degeneration is a disinhibition syndrome (Martindale, 1971). Morel (1857) and later theorists hypothesized that degeneration is initially caused by environmental factors such as diet, climate, and toxins. It is then passed genetically – and somehow exacerbated – from generation to generation. Of course, the notion that an environmentally acquired disorder can be transmitted genetically collapsed with the demise of Lamarckian theories of evolution.

It would seem that the entirety of degeneration theory was rejected because Morel (1857) and his followers were wrong about the genetic transmission of what they called degeneration. However, that they were wrong about this does not mean that they were wrong about the unitary nature of the construct of what they called degeneration. As I have pointed out elsewhere (Martindale, 1971), the track record of degeneration theorists is actually quite good. They were well aware of crucial facts about creativity and psychosis that were not rediscovered for about 60 years.

Lombroso (1895) listed the following traits of degeneration:

Apathy, loss of moral sense, frequent tendencies to impulsiveness or doubt, psychical inequalities owing to the excess of some faculty (memory, aesthetic taste, etc.) or defect of other qualities (calculation, for example), exaggerated mutism or verbosity, morbid vanity, excessive originality, and excessive preoccupation with self, the tendency to put mystical interpretations on the simplest facts, the abuse of symbolism and of special words which are used as an almost exclusive mode of expression. (pp. 5–6)

In describing geniuses, Lombroso (1895) mentioned several other degenerative stigmata: vagabondage, composition in a "somnambulistic state," poor integration of personality traits, oversensitivity, overemotionality, extreme forgetfulness, perseveration, and alternation between excessive energy and excessive fatigue.

Nordau (1895, pp. 15–33) provided a slightly different group of traits of degeneration:

1. Abulia
2. Inability to focus attention and consequent inability to differentiate relevant from irrelevant
3. Tendency to "inane reverie": free-associative thinking with inability to suppress "irrelevant" associates
4. Vague and incoherent thought
5. Overemotionality
6. "Moral insanity"
7. Rebellious inability to adapt to the environment
8. Pessimism
9. "Ego-mania"

These traits overlap considerably with traits of those who test high on psychoticism (Eysenck, 1995): aggressive, cold, egocentric, impersonal, creative, impulsive, antisocial, unempathic, tough-minded, and characterized by overinclusive thinking or "wide associative horizons."

Self-reports of highly creative people almost all stress the effortlessness of creative inspiration. Creativity seems not to be based upon self-control or willpower. Just the opposite seems to be the case. Creative people have used a variety of often bizarre methods that they believed helped them to be more creative. These methods do not include self-control; rather, they involve automatic reaction to a stimulus (Martindale, 1981). For example, some creators have used drugs and alcohol in the probably mistaken belief that they facilitate creativity. Clearly, no self-control is involved here, because such substances automatically induce changes in cortical arousal. Other methods that would seem to be nothing more than odd eccentricities in fact produce physiological effects. To take perhaps the most extreme example, the German poet Schiller's practice of writing while his feet were plunged in ice water was in fact an efficient method of increasing blood flow to his brain (Ribot, 1906). Perhaps the most common method used by creators is withdrawal so extreme that it verges on sensory deprivation, a condition that lowers cortical arousal (Schultz, 1965). The image of the withdrawn artist is ubiquitous: Vigny advocating withdrawal into a "tower of ivory," Hölderlin imprisoned in his tower at Tübingen, Proust isolating himself in his cork-lined rooms.

Creativity, Oversensitivity, and Habituation

Why do creators withdraw in the first place? Generally, it is not because they know that such a procedure may facilitate creativity. Rather, it is because of oversensitivity. Proust's withdrawal was forced upon him because normal levels of light and noise were painfully intense for him. Creative people quite often say that they are sensitive or oversensitive. While such claims are often dismissed as mere posing, it would seem that such people are reporting accurate self-assessments.

There is evidence that creative people are in fact physiologically overreactive. Martindale and Armstrong (1974) found more alpha blocking in response to onset of a tone in more creative subjects than in less creative ones. Martindale (1977) delivered a series of electric shocks to people. The more creative a person was, the more intense he or she rated any given shock. Martindale (1977) also found a correlation between creativity and augmentation on a kinaesthetic aftereffect task. Augmentation on this task is conventionally interpreted as meaning that an individual "amplifies" the intensity of stimuli. Martindale, Anderson, Moore, and West (1996) measured skin potential responses to a series of moderately intense tones. (Skin potential is believed to covary directly with cortical activation.) Two findings were of interest. More creative subjects showed much larger skin potential response to the tones than did less creative people. Further, they took twice as long to habituate to the tones as did uncreative subjects. The slow habituation of creative people may be related to their tendency to stick with a problem until they have solved it, rather than tiring of it and moving on to something else.

Creativity and Need for Novelty and Stimulation

Creative people show a trait that seems to be at odds with their oversensitivity and slow rate of habituation: They love novelty, which is known to increase cortical arousal (Berlyne, 1971). The French poet Charles Baudelaire expressed the attitude of many creative people when he remarked that "the beautiful is always bizarre." Going along with this preference is an active dislike for things that are not novel. As the English writer George Moore (1886/1959) remarked, "The commonplace, the natural, is constitutionally abhorrent" (p. 61). Koestler (1964) notes that scientific geniuses tend to have "on the one hand skepticism, often carried to the point of iconoclasm, in their attitude toward traditional ideas and dogmas" as contrasted with "an open-mindedness that verges on naive credulity towards new concepts" (p. 518). There is also experimental evidence that creativity is correlated with preference for novelty (Houston & Mednick, 1963) as well as with need for stimulation in general (Farley, 1985).

How can creative people crave stimulation if they are oversensitive? The probable cause is that withdrawal – because of oversensitivity – leads to a lowering of the level of arousal. This, in turn, leads to a craving for novelty. Note that creative people usually seek mental stimulation rather than the strong stimuli of, say, real-world adventure.

Creativity and Brain Scans

Several exciting new techniques allow us to image mental activity by measuring regional bloodflow or regional glucose uptake in the brain. Unfortunately, these techniques have not yet been used to study creative thinking. This is a gap in our knowledge that I hope will soon be filled. One can use positron emission tomography (PET) to measure brain glucose metabolic rate (GMR). GMR is an index of how activated a region of the brain is. The general finding has been that GMR is negatively related to intelligence and to the degree to which one has learned a problem (Haier, Siegel, Tang, Abel, & Buchsbaum, 1992). That is, the more intelligent one is or the better one has learned to solve a problem, the less activated one's brain is. There is also a negative correlation between verbal fluency – which may be an aspect of creativity – and GMR (Parks et al., 1988).

It is generally thought that this negative relationship is due to synaptic pruning (Huttenlocher, 1979). The number of synaptic connections per neuron rises from birth until around the age of 5. After the age of 5, synaptic connectivity falls to a much lower level. Thus, GMR falls as well. Synaptic pruning hypothetically has to do with removal of irrelevant or redundant neuronal connections.

Haier (1993) offers the hypothesis that insufficient neural pruning (as evidenced by excessive GMR) can cause mental retardation. On the other hand, excessive neural pruning, as evidenced by very low GMR, results in psychiatric disorders. Most interestingly, he hypothesizes that neural pruning intermediate between the normal level and the psychopathological level may result in creativity. This is a testable hypothesis that certainly should be tested.

CREATIVITY AND HEMISPHERIC ASYMMETRY

Theoretical Rationale

There are reasons to believe that creativity should be related to differential activation of the right and left hemispheres of the brain, as well as to general level of cortical arousal. Galin (1974) and Hoppe (1977) have argued that the right hemisphere operates in a primary process manner, whereas the left hemisphere operates in a secondary process fashion. Their arguments are based upon findings that verbal, sequential, and analytical processes tend to be carried out in the left hemisphere, whereas global, parallel, and holistic processes are carried out in the right hemisphere. If this is the case, then we can again "neurologize" Kris's theory of creativity: Because creative people have more access to primary process cognition, they should show more right hemisphere – as compared with left hemisphere – activation than less creative people, at least during periods of creative activity. There is no reason to expect differences during baseline recording or performance of noncreative tasks.

A number of theorists have proposed similar hypotheses. Others (e.g., Britain, 1985) however, have proposed that hemispheric balance may be crucial for creativity. The difference in opinion may be a mere semantic one. In a resting state, the left hemisphere is usually more activated than the right. A task that induces right-hemisphere activation and left-hemisphere deactivation may in absolute terms produce balance – that is, both hemispheres are equally activated. However, in reference to baseline levels, the task could be interpreted as having activated the right hemisphere more than the left.

There are other reasons for suspecting that the right hemisphere should be connected with creativity. A good deal of evidence shows that most brain centers involved in the perception and production of music are located in the right hemisphere (see Martindale, 1981, for a review). Similarly, a number of centers necessary for creating visual art are segregated in the right hemisphere. There is evidence that the right hemisphere is more involved in the production of mental images than is the left (e.g., Seamon & Gazzaniga, 1973). Based on research on split-brain patients (e.g., Gazzaniga & Hillyard, 1971), it would seem that the right hemisphere possesses a rather comprehensive lexicon but that it is chaotically arranged. That is, it understands words but not how they go together in a grammatical or propositional manner. Access to such an "alternative" lexicon could certainly be of use to a poet.

Penfield and Roberts (1958) performed experiments in which exposed cortex was mildly stimulated. When certain areas of the right temporal cortex were stimulated, their patients reported extremely vivid auditory and visual images. Recall that many literary creators have argued that their work was essentially "dictated." Jaynes (1976) has argued that such quasi-hallucinatory experience is a product of intense right-hemisphere activity.

Induced Right-Hemisphere Activation

There is some evidence that procedures known to increase right-hemisphere activation can facilitate creativity. At least in highly hypnotizable subjects, hypnosis increases right-hemisphere activation. Gur and Raynor (1976) found that such subjects performed better on tests of creativity when hypnotized than when not hypnotized. Marijuana also increases right-hemisphere activation. At least in low doses, it facilitates performance on tests of creativity; however, higher doses produce decrements in performance (Weckowicz et al., 1975). Music also has been shown to facilitate performance on creativity tests (Kaltsounis, 1972). Harkins and Macrosson (1990) examined the effect upon creativity of a 10-week course purported to develop right-hemisphere functions. The course led to significant improvements on two tests of creativity, but had no effect on five other tests of creativity.

A word displayed in the left visual field is processed first by the right hemisphere, whereas a word displayed in the right visual field is processed first by the left hemisphere. Words presented in the left visual field elicit more unusual word associations than do words presented in the right visual field (Dimond & Beaumont, 1974). Right-hemisphere activation is accompanied by leftward eye movements, whereas left-hemisphere activation is accompanied by rightward eye movements. Subjects perform slightly better on creativity tests if they are forced by specially constructed goggles to look leftward as opposed to rightward while taking the tests (Hines & Martindale, 1974).

Individual Differences on Noncreative Tasks

Several studies have found positive correlations between creativity and a tendency to make leftward eye movements (indicative of right-hemisphere activation) when answering questions (Harnad, 1972; Katz, 1983). Katz (1986) compared the performance of more and less creative architects, scientists, and mathematicians on paper-and-pencil tests hypothetically tapping right- and left-hemisphere dominance. More creative architects tended to be left dominant and more creative mathematicians and scientists tended to be right dominant. Katz interpreted his findings as implying that more creative individuals have sufficient capabilities in the hemisphere needed for their profession (right hemisphere for architects and left hemisphere for scientists and mathematicians) and that their creativity arises from their extra abilities in the contralateral hemisphere.

Katz (1983) and Uemura (1980) carried out a series of studies examining the performance of more and less creative subjects on dichotic listening and split-visual-field tachistoscopic tasks. In a dichotic-listening task, a stimulus is presented to either the right or left ear. Stimuli presented to the right ear are first processed by the left hemisphere and vice versa. With such tasks there is generally a left-hemisphere advantage for verbal material and a right-hemisphere advantage for recognition of musical melodies. In a split-visual-field tachistoscopic task, a stimulus is briefly presented in either the right or the left visual field. As mentioned earlier, stimuli presented in the left visual field are processed first by the right hemisphere and vice versa. The general finding is one of a left-hemisphere advantage for linguistic stimuli and a right-hemisphere advantage for complex spatial stimuli.

In both studies, creativity was positively correlated with a left-hemisphere advantage for verbal stimuli when presented either verbally or visually. That is, the more creative a person was, the better he or she did when the stimuli were processed by the left hemisphere. Uemura found a negative correlation between creativity and right-hemisphere advantage on a split-visual-field spatial task. Katz found that more creative people did not show the usual right-hemisphere advantage on a dichotic-listening melody recognition task. It would seem that on all of the tasks, more creative subjects used the left hemisphere more than would be expected on the basis of previous findings with the general population. None of Katz's or Uemura's tasks involved creative performance. As was the case with general arousal, it seems to be that the predicted differences are found only during creative activity.

Hemispheric Asymmetry During Creative Activity

Hudspith (1985) measured right- and left-hemisphere activity during a baseline condition and while subjects tried to think of a word associatively related to two presented words. This task is analogous to Mednick's (1962) Remote Associates Test of creativity. No differences between more and less creative people were found during baseline recording. During the word association task, more creative people showed greater right-hemisphere activation than did less creative people, but the difference was not statistically significant. However, only 10 subjects were used in each group, so statistical power was low.

Martindale, Hines, Mitchell, and Covello (1984) reported on three experiments concerning the relationship between creativity and hemispheric asymmetry as measured by EEG activity. In none of the experiments were there significant differences in resting, or basal, asymmetry between more and less creative subjects. In two of the experiments, creativity was assessed with paper-and-pencil tests. In these experiments, the creative task was to either write down or speak aloud a fantasy story. Hemispheric activity during creative activity showed the same pattern in both experiments: Highly creative subjects exhibited more right- than left-hemisphere activation; those of medium creativity showed strong asymmetry in the opposite direction; and very uncreative subjects showed about equal activation in both hemispheres.

In the third experiment, student artists were compared with artistically untrained subjects. EEG was recorded while subjects made a drawing of a cow vertebra and while they read an article on economics. As expected, the student artists showed much greater right- than left-hemisphere activity during the drawing task than did the control group. The reading task was included in order to measure asymmetry during a noncreative task. On this task, the artists also showed more asymmetry than did the control group, but in the opposite direction from that found during the drawing task. Left-hemisphere activation was greater than right-hemisphere activation, and this was more the case for the artists than for the nonartists. Thus, it would seem that creative people rely more on the right hemisphere than on the left only during the creative process and not in general.

CREATIVITY AND FRONTAL-LOBE ACTIVATION

Eysenck (1995) and Martindale (1989) argue that highly creative people tend to be deficient in cognitive inhibition. The frontal lobes are involved in such inhibition (Bjorklund & Kipp, 1996; West, 1996). If Eysenck and Martindale are correct, then we would expect to find lower levels of frontal-lobe activation in creative as compared with uncreative people.

Hudspith (1985) measured EEG activity in frontal and posterior locations in 10 more and 10 less creative people. Measurements were taken during a baseline condition, during verbal association (thinking of a word associated with two other words), and during an imagery task (imagining what an object would look like if folded). No differences were found during baseline recording. However, during both tasks, more creative people showed higher-amplitude frontal theta-wave activity. This indicates less frontal-lobe activation. During the imagery task, more creative people also showed higher-amplitude frontal alpha-wave activity. This also indicates less frontal-lobe activation. However, these differences were only marginally significant, probably because of the small number of subjects.

BASIS FOR PHYSIOLOGICAL DIFFERENCES

The question arises as to whether the physiological differences described earlier are causes or effects of different modes of thought in more and less creative individuals. Nineteenth-century investigators such as Flechsig (1896) claimed to find reliable differences in cranial capacity and anatomical differences in the brains of geniuses as compared with normal subjects. Such studies have been criticized on methodological grounds, but have not been redone with modern methods. We know that some EEG patterns are heritable, but there is no evidence concerning the more specific patterns I have discussed.

Recent studies of the heritability of creative test performance have yielded contradictory results. Nichols (1978) reviewed 10 twin studies of divergent thinking. On average, they indicated a heritability of .21 for tests of divergent thinking. On the other hand, contrary to Galton (1869/1902), there is no evidence that creativity runs in families (Bullough, Bullough, & Mauro, 1981). Waller, Bouchard, Lykken, Tellegen, and Blacker (1993) have recently suggested a solution to this contradiction. They argue that creativity is characterized by what Lykken (1981) calls emergenesis. The latter refers to a higher-order trait (e.g., creativity) emerging only if all of a number of other traits (e.g., intelligence, psychoticism, perseverance) are present. Emergenic traits can be highly heritable, but do not run in families, because family members are unlikely to have *all* of the required traits. Waller et al. (1993) report on the heritability of an adjective checklist measure of creativity that was given to participants in the Minnesota Study of Twins Reared Apart. Their findings indicate that scores even on this test seem to be emergenic. For monozygotic twins, they obtained a heritability estimate of .54, whereas the heritability estimate for dizygotic twins was not significantly different from zero.

SUMMARY

We have seen that the creative act involves the discovery of an analogy between two or more ideas or images previously thought to be unrelated. This discovery does not arise from logical reasoning but, rather, emerges as a sudden insight. All of the theories of creativity reviewed say essentially the same thing – that creative inspiration occurs in a mental state where attention is defocused, thought is associative, and a large number of mental representations are simultaneously activated. Such a state can arise in three ways: low levels of cortical activation, comparatively more right- than left-hemisphere activation, and low levels of frontal-lobe activation. Creative people do not exhibit all of these traits in general but only while engaged in creative activity.

REFERENCES

Amabile, T. (1983). *The social psychology of creativity.* New York: Springer-Verlag.

Berlyne, D. E. (1971). *Aesthetics and psychobiology.* New York: Appleton-Century-Crofts.

Bjorklund, D. P., & Kipp, K. (1996). Parental investment theory and gender differences in the evolution of inhibition mechanisms. *Psychological Bulletin, 120,* 163–188.

Blake, W. (1906). Letter to Thomas Butts. In A. G. B. Russell (Ed.), *The letters of William Blake.* London: Methuen. (Original work published 1803).

Bowers, K. S., & Keeling, K. R. (1971). Heart-rate variability in creative functioning. *Psychological Reports, 29,* 160–162.

Britain, A. W. (1985). Creativity and hemisphere functioning: A second look at Katz's data. *Empirical Studies of the Arts, 3,* 105–107.

Bullough, V., Bullough, B., & Mauro, M. (1981). History and creativity: Research problems and some possible solutions. *Journal of Creative Behavior, 15,* 102–116.

Coren, S., & Schulman, M. (1971). Effects of an external stress on commonality of verbal associates. *Psychological Reports, 28,* 328–330.

Cropley, A. J., Cassell, W. A., & Maslany, G. W. (1970). A biochemical correlate of divergent thinking. *Canadian Journal of Behavioral Science, 2,* 174–180.

Dentler, R. A., & Mackler, B. (1964). Originality: Some social and personal determinants. *Behavioral Science, 9,* 1–7.

Dewing, K., & Battye, G. (1971). Attention deployment and non-verbal fluency. *Journal of Personality and Social Psychology, 17,* 214–218.

Dimond, S., & Beaumont, J. G. (1974). Experimental studies of the hemisphere function in the human brain. In S. Dimond & J. G. Beaumont (Eds.), *Hemisphere function in the human brain* (pp. 48–88). New York: Halsted.

Duffy, E. (1962). *Activation and behavior.* New York: Wiley.

Dykes, M., & McGhie, A. (1976). A comparative study of attentional strategies in schizophrenics and highly creative normal subjects. *British Journal of Psychiatry, 128,* 50–56.

Eysenck, H. (1995). *Genius: The natural history of creativity.* Cambridge University Press.

Farley, F. (1985). Psychobiology and cognition: An individual differences model. In J. Strelau, F. Farley, & A. Gale (Eds.), *The biological bases of personality and behavior* (Vol. 1, pp. 1–36). Washington, DC: Hemisphere.

Flechsig, P. E. (1896). *Gehirn und Seele.* Leipzig: Veit.

Florek, H. (1973). Heart rate during creative ability. *Studia Psychologia, 15,* 158–161.

Fromm, E. (1978). Primary and secondary process in waking and in altered states of consciousness. *Journal of Altered States of Consciousness, 4,* 115–128.

Galin, D. (1974). Implications for psychiatry of left and right cerebral specializations: A neurophysiological context for unconscious processes. *Archives of General Psychiatry, 31,* 572–583.

Galton, F. (1962). *Hereditary genius: An inquiry into its laws and consequences.* Cleveland: World Publishing. (Original work published 1869).

Gazzaniga, M. S., & Hillyard, S. A. (1971). Language and speech capacity of the right hemisphere. *Neuropsychologia, 9,* 273–280.

Ghiselin, B. (Ed.). (1952). *The creative process.* Berkeley: University of California Press.

Goodwin, F. K., & Jamison, K. R. (1990). *Manic-depressive illness.* New York: Oxford University Press.

Gur, R. C., & Raynor, J. (1976). Enhancement of creativity via free-imagery and hypnosis. *American Journal of Clinical Hypnosis, 18,* 237–249.

Haier, R. J. (1993). Cerebral glucose metabolism and intelligence. In P. A. Vernon (Ed.), *Biological approaches to the study of human intelligence* (pp. 317–332). Norwood, NJ: Ablex.

Haier, R. J., Siegel, B., Tang, C., Abel, L., & Buchsbaum, M. S. (1992). Intelligence and changes in regional cerebral glucose metabolic rate following learning. *Intelligence, 16,* 415–426.

Harkins, J. D., & Macrosson, W. K. (1990). Creativity training: An assessment of a novel approach. *Journal of Business and Psychology, 5,* 143–148.

Harnad, S. (1972). Lateral saccades and the nondominant hemisphere. *Perceptual and Motor Skills, 34,* 653–654.

Hebb, D. O. (1955). Drives and the C.N.S. (conceptual nervous system). *Psychological Review, 62,* 243–253.

Helmholtz, H. von (1896). *Vorträge und Reden.* Brunswick, Germany: Friedrich Vieweg.

Heston, L. L. (1966). Psychiatric disorders in foster home reared children of schizophrenic mothers. *British Journal of Psychiatry, 112,* 819–825.

Hines, D., & Martindale, C. (1974). Induced lateral eye movements and creative and intellectual performance. *Perceptual and Motor Skills, 39,* 153–154.

Hoppe, K. (1977). Brains and psychoanalysis. *Psychoanalytic Quarterly, 46,* 220–224.

Horton, D. L., Marlowe, D., & Crowne, D. (1963). The effect of instructional set and need for social approval on commonality of word association responses. *Journal of Abnormal and Social Psychology, 66,* 67–72.

Houston, J. P., & Mednick, S. A. (1963). Creativity and the need for novelty. *Journal of Abnormal and Social Psychology, 66,* 137–141.

Hudson, L. (1975). *Human beings: The psychology of human experience.* New York: Anchor.

Hudspith, S. (1985). *The neurological correlates of creative thought.* Unpublished Ph.D. dissertation, University of Southern California, Los Angeles, California.

Hull, C. L. (1943). *Principles of behavior.* New York: Appleton-Century-Crofts.

Huttenlocher, P. R. (1979). Synaptic density in human frontal cortex: Developmental changes and effects of aging. *Brain Research, 163,* 195–205.

Jarvik, I. F., & Chadwick, S. B. (1973). Schizophrenia and survival. In M. Hammer, K. Salzinger, & S. Sutton (Eds.), *Psychopathology,* (pp. 138–150). New York: Wiley.

Jaynes, J. (1976). *The origin of consciousness in the breakdown of the bicameral mind.* New York: Houghton Mifflin.

Kaltsounis, B. (1972). Effect of sound on creative performance. *Psychological Reports, 34,* 653–654.

Kamiya, J. (1969). Operant control of EEG alpha rhythm and some of its reported effects on consciousness. In C. Tart (Ed.), *Altered states of consciousness* (pp. 507–517). New York: Wiley.

Karlsson, J. L. (1968). Genealogical studies of schizophrenia. In D. Rosenthal & S. S. Kety (Eds.), *The transmission of schizophrenia* (pp. 201–236). Oxford: Pergamon.

Katz, A. N. (1983). Creativity and individual differences in asymmetrical cerebral hemispheric functioning. *Empirical Studies of the Arts, 1,* 3–16.

Katz, A. N. (1986). The relationship between creativity and cerebral hemisphericity for creative architects, scientists, and mathematicians. *Empirical Studies of the Arts, 4,* 97–108.

Kennett, K. F., & Cropley, A. J. (1973). Serum uric acid: A biochemical correlate of divergent thinking. Paper presented at the annual conference of the British Psychological Society, London.

Koestler, A. (1964). *The act of creation.* New York: Macmillan.

Kris, E. (1952). *Psychoanalytic explorations in art.* New York: International Universities Press.

Krop, H. D., Alegre, C. E., & Williams, C. D. (1969). Effects of induced stress on convergent and divergent thinking. *Psychological Reports, 24,* 895–898.

Lindgren, H. C., & Lindgren, F. (1965). Brainstorming and orneriness as facilitators of creativity. *Psychological Reports, 16,* 577–583.

Lindsley, D. B. (1960). Attention, consciousness, sleep and wakefulness. In J. Field (Ed.), *Handbook of Physiology: Section 1. Neurophysiology* (pp. 156–183). Washington, DC: American Physiological Society.

Lombroso, C. (1895). *The man of genius.* London: Walter Scott.

Lykken, D. T. (1981). Research with twins: The concept of emergenesis. *Society for Psychophysical Research, 19,* 361–372.

Lynn, S. J., & Rhue, J. W. (1986). The fantasy-prone person: Hypnosis, imagination, and creativity. *Journal of Personality and Social Psychology, 51,* 404–408.

Maddi, S. R. (1965). Motivational aspects of creativity. *Journal of Personality, 33,* 330–347.

Maddi, S. R., & Andrews, S. (1966). The need for variety in fantasy and self description. *Journal of Personality, 34,* 610–625.

Martindale, C. (1971). Degeneration, disinhibition, and genius. *Journal of the History of the Behavioral Sciences, 7,* 177–182.

Martindale, C. (1972). Femininity, alienation, and arousal in the creative personality. *Psychology, 9,* 3–15.

Martindale, C. (1977). Creativity, consciousness, and cortical arousal. *Journal of Altered States of Consciousness, 3,* 69–87.

Martindale, C. (1981). *Cognition and consciousness.* Homewood, IL: Dorsey.

Martindale, C. (1989). Personality, situation, and creativity. In J. A. Glover, R. R. Ronning, & C. R. Reynolds (Eds.), *Handbook of creativity* (pp. 211–228). New York: Plenum.

Martindale, C. (1990). Creative imagination and neural activity. In R. Kunzendorf & A. Sheikh (Eds.), *Psychophysiology of mental imagery: Theory, research, and application* (pp. 89–108). Amityville, NY: Baywood.

Martindale, C., Anderson, K., Moore, K., & West, A. N. (1996). Creativity, oversensitivity, and rate of habituation. *Personality and Individual Differences, 20,* 423–427.

Martindale, C., & Armstrong, J. (1974). The relationship of creativity to cortical activation and its operant control. *Journal of Genetic Psychology, 124,* 311–320.

Martindale, C., & Dailey, A. (1996). Creativity, primary process cognition, and personality. *Personality and Individual Differences, 20,* 409–414.

Martindale, C., & Greenough, J. (1973). The differential effects of increased arousal on creative and intellectual performance. *Journal of Genetic Psychology, 123,* 329–335.

Martindale, C., & Hasenfus, N. (1978). EEG differences as a function of creativity, stage of the creative process, and effort to be original. *Biological Psychology, 6,* 157–167.

Martindale, C., & Hines, D. (1975). Creativity and cortical activation during creative, intellectual, and EEG feedback tasks. *Biological Psychology, 3,* 71–80.

Martindale, C., Hines, D., Mitchell, L., & Covello, E. (1984). EEG alpha asymmetry and creativity. *Personality and Individual Differences, 5,* 77–86.

McNeil, T. F. (1971). Prebirth and postbirth influence on the relationship between creative ability and recorded mental illness. *Journal of Personality, 39,* 391–406.

Mednick, S. A. (1962). The associative basis of the creative process. *Psychological Review, 69,* 220–232.

Meisels, M. (1967). Test anxiety, stress, and verbal behavior. *Journal of Consulting Psychology, 31,* 577–582.

Mendelsohn, G. A. (1976). Associative and attentional processes in creative performance. *Journal of Personality, 44,* 341–369.

Moore, G. (1959). *Confessions of a young man.* New York: Capricorn. (Original work published 1886)

Morel, B. A. (1857). *Traité des dégénérescences physiques, intellectuelles et morales de l'espèce humaine.* Paris: Baillière.

Nichols, R. C. (1978). Twin studies of ability, personality, and interests. *Homo, 29,* 158–173.

Nordau, M. (1895). *Degeneration.* London: Heinemann.

Osgood, C. E. (1960). Some effects of motivation on style on encoding. In T. A. Sebeok (Ed.), *Style in language* (pp. 293–306). Cambridge, MA: MIT Press.

Parks, R. W., Loewenstein, D. A., Dodrill, K. L., Barker, W. W., Yoshii, F., Chang, J. Y., Emran, A., Apicella, A., Sheramata, W., & Duara, R. (1988). Cerebral metabolic effects of a verbal fluency test: A PET scan study. *Journal of Clinical and Experimental Neuropsychology, 10,* 565–575.

Penfield, W., & Roberts, L. (1958). *Speech and brain mechanisms.* Princeton, NJ: Princeton University Press.

Poincaré, H. (1913). *The foundations of science.* Lancaster, PA: Science Press.

Ribot, T. (1906). *Essay on the creative imagination.* London: Kegan Paul.

Schultz, D. P. (1965). *Sensory restriction: Effects on behavior.* New York: Academic.

Seamon, J. G., & Gazzaniga, M. S. (1973). Coding strategies and cerebral laterality effect. *Cognitive Psychology, 5,* 249–256.

Suler, J. (1980). Primary process thinking and creativity. *Psychological Bulletin, 88,* 155–165.

Talbot, E. S. (1898). *Degeneracy: Its causes, signs, and results.* New York: Scribner's.

Trapp, E., & Kausler, D. (1960). Relationship between MAS scores and association values of nonsense syllables. *Journal of Experimental Psychology, 59,* 233–238.

Uemura, A. K. (1980). *Individual differences in hemispheric lateralization.* Unpublished Ph.D. dissertation, University of Maine, Orono.

Wallas, G. (1926). *The art of thought.* New York: Harcourt, Brace, & World.

Waller, N. G., Bouchard, T. J., Lykken, D. T., Tellegen, A., & Blacker, D. M. (1993). Creativity, heritability, familiality: Which word does not belong? *Psychological Inquiry, 4,* 235–237.

Weber, J. P. (1969). *The psychology of art.* New York: Delacorte.

Weckowicz, T., Fedora, O., Mason, J., Radstaak, D., Bay, K., & Yonge, K. (1975). Effect of marijuana on divergent and convergent production cognitive tests. *Journal of Abnormal Psychology, 84,* 386–398.

West, R. L. (1996). An application of prefrontal cortex function theory to cognitive aging. *Psychological Bulletin, 120,* 272–292.

Wild, C. (1965). Creativity and adaptive regression. *Journal of Personality and Social Psychology, 2,* 161–169.

Worrell, J., & Worrell, L. (1965). Personality conflict, originality of response and recall. *Journal of Consulting Psychology, 29,* 55–62.

Wyspianski, J. O., Barry, W. F., & Dayhaw, L. T. (1963). Brain wave amplitude and creative thinking. *Revue de l'Université d'Ottawa,* pp. 260–276.

Yerkes, R. M., & Dodson, J. D. (1908). The relation of strength of stimulus to rapidity of habit formation. *Journal of Comparative and Neurological Psychology, 18,* 459–482.

Zajonc, R. (1965). Social facilitation. *Science, 149,* 269–274.

8   Evolving Creative Minds: Stories and Mechanisms

CHARLES J. LUMSDEN

Does a passion to create drive the human species, making us utterly different from all other living things with which we share the planet? Or do our capacities for novelty, great and small, link smoothly to those in other species, so that human creativity is really a variant on a theme repeated countless times in the history of life? Are we to understand ourselves as expressing a "regional dialect" for innovation – unique and special in its own way to be sure, but nonetheless a restyling of universal evolutionary stratagems?

Stressing descent with modification, Darwinism seems to say that we are both special *and* mundane. Is this a fact of human evolution or a fact of evolution's inability to explain humanity? Just partially humbled by our place in the Earth's teeming pattern of life Darwinians reach, Prometheus-like, past psychology and even past philosophy to explain our behaviors, minds, and social forms in a language once reserved for debates about hybrid corn or fungus growing among ants. What is going on?

Blame it on the cognitive revolution. In the breezy days of behaviorist populism, evolution, following Darwin's lead, was content largely with speculations about the origins of instinct and drives. This was the thin end of the wedge that evolutionists have driven into the mind as behaviorism has thawed into cognitive science and the mysteries of consciousness, intention, self-awareness, and human genius returned from the fringes of scientific respectability to crowd the center of human science. The linchpin, of course, has been the aggressive détente set up between the brain scientists and the mind scientists. The wall is down. Increasingly, claims to a proper study of humankind are taken as the common, if controversial, property of both parties (Churchland, 1995, is a good example – one of many recently – of epistemic détente in action). As we will see, biological evolution withers without organic matter, filled with heritable variations, on which to work its seeming magic. But once the mind–brain connection gains a toehold, evolutionary exegesis follows swiftly, and it has, buoyed by a remarkable volume of anthropological, ethological, paleontologic and genetic fieldwork among human and animal populations.

Resembling evolved organisms to an uncanny degree, the "definitions" of creativity I have seen in the literature (e.g., Amabile, 1983; Boden, 1991, 1994; Hofstadter, 1995; Sternberg, 1988; Sternberg & Davidson, 1995) carry the unique imprint of their progenitors while suggesting some mild degree of consensus: creativity as a kind of capacity to think up something new that people find significant. It is possible to be more precise than this, of course, and in order to maintain consistency with my earlier usage (starting with Findlay & Lumsden, 1988) I shall by *creative process* have in mind those mental events by which an organism intentionally (Dennett, 1996) goes beyond its prior experience to a novel and appropriate outcome. *Creativity* will refer to that tantalizing constellation of personality and intellectual traits shown by people who, when given a measure of free rein, spend significant amounts of time engaged in the creative process. Outcomes achievable in principle by creative organisms can vary hugely in their novelty and significance. The Wright brothers, for instance,

153

could have stayed home and made better bicycles instead of undertaking their momentous journeys to Kitty Hawk (Bradshaw, 1996; Freedman, 1991), with all the difficulties and deprivations those entailed.

An *outcome* is a product of the creative process. Bach fugues and Gödel numbers and our kids' Web pages are all outcomes of the creative process in this sense. The creative process need not have an outcome consistent with the organism's originating intentions. But it can, as the invented world that is home to our species demonstrates. In science, outcomes often teach us something about the world that predates our intentions and are called discoveries. "Discovery" seems less apt a moniker for outcomes like paintings and rock concerts; "works" is more common.

An *innovation*, finally, refers to an outcome that attains some level of adoption in the society under consideration. Outcomes can fail to turn into innovations or be lethargic in making the transition through a lack of attributed value (so only lately has van Gogh found fiscally astronomic value in the eyes of the marketplace) or because the discoverer "sits" on the breakthrough, or through sheer happenstance ("market share"; remember VHS vs. Beta?). Can evolutionary science offer any insights into what is happening in such diverse circumstances, over and above that already possible through psychology and the neurosciences?

I think the answer is a guarded yes because evolutionary science treats questions of special relevance to creativity research. These are the "why" questions. As in the behavioral sciences, much of biology is concerned with "how" questions: how cells divide, how long-term memories are stored in the brain, how parents socialize offspring. These are familiar questions dealing with process and mechanism. Evolutionists, however, want answers to the whys rather than the hows of anatomy, physiology, and behavior: why cells divide in a certain way or why parents sometimes behave altruistically toward their offspring.

The question why? demands the study of history – the history of individuals (development, socialization, learning, choice), the history of their culture and society, and ultimately the history of their population. The history of biological process (recall the thin end of the wedge, the biology of the brain driven by evolutionists into the study of the mind) is by definition evolution. Let us consider this latter point more carefully, because above all it is important to know why human creativity is *as it is*, rather than some other way it might have been (why aren't we all Blakes or Bachs?) had the past been different.

DICE AND SPLICE

The modern or neo-Darwinian theory of evolution (NDT hereafter) is a synthesis of Darwin's natural selection (Darwin, 1859) with Mendelian genetics and population biology. Codified in a series of masterworks by Dobzhansky (1937), Fisher (1930), Haldane (1932), Mayr (1970), and Wright (1968), NDT by 1950 rested on a broad base of empirical and mathematical discoveries that continues to be deepened and elaborated. Although space does not allow me to review NDT at length (exciting surveys with some emphasis on behavior are Brandon & Burian, 1984; Dawkins, 1986; Dennett, 1995; Maynard Smith, 1982; Raff, 1996; Williams, 1966, 1992; D. S. Wilson, 1980; E. O. Wilson, 1975, 1978), its core idea can be immediately grasped.

For neo-Darwinists, evolution is a dramatically creative, albeit nonintentional natural process pivoted on a tension between the genesis and the shaping of raw diversity. Even though the chemical reasons were not grasped until the advent of molecular genetics in this century, it was well known in Darwin's time that many traits (such as the color of your eyes or your ability to roll your tongue into a tube, to cite current examples) passed in a seemingly deterministic fashion between parents and their offspring. Individuals differed from one another, and some of these differences were heritable.

In retrospect and filtered through 140 years of refinement and exegesis, Darwin's key insight today seems the model of obvious simplicity: If a heritable trait varies among individuals and if a change from one "version" of that trait to another also changes (increases or decreases) the organism's reproductive ability, then over time we can expect to see those versions of the trait associated with greater reproductive ability become more common in the population. This is because the individuals with these versions will have the greater number of offspring, which inherit the version and in their turn leave the greater number of (grand)offspring, and so on. If, moreover, individuals must compete for scarce resources, such as nourishment or shelter or mates, then over time many of the other versions may vanish altogether. This is natural selection in action.

For example, suppose that in a hypothetical species individuals vary in their ability to taste a particular poison, owing to differences in genes at one or more places on the chromosomes. The gene codes, say, for a cell-surface receptor protein able to bind molecules of the poison and trigger neuronal signaling, conferring the ability to taste the poison. The opposing gene variant provides no such ability because the receptor site of the protein it encodes does not bind the poison at all. The poison is present in the food or water. Individuals with the "taster" variant of the gene detect the substance, avoid it, and survive. Those possessing "nontaster" versions consume the poison and die. As a result, the frequency of the taster variant increases in the population, and a larger percentage of the population has the hereditary ability to avoid the poison. This change from one generation to the next is evolution by natural selection. In the vernacular of population biology, the individuals able to taste the poison are said to have "increased genetic fitness," and the taster trait is spoken of as "adaptive" relative to the population's specific circumstances.

Many factors can change or disrupt the otherwise systematic shift over time in the relative abundance of these versions. Environmental change can reverse the reproductive impact of specific traits. Traits adaptive in themselves may interlock in unexpectedly deleterious configurations. For example, the taster gene variant might also confer a drastically reduced sensitivity to sexual pheromones, so that even though fewer tasters die from the poison than do nontasters, they reproduce far less, so that over time it is the nontaster rather than the taster version that increases in frequency. And so on.

Natural selection culls diversity. No heritable diversity, no natural selection. But where does the organic diversity, the evolutionary raw material, come from? At least four processes are known to sustain the continued appearance of new gene variants or new patterns of gene organization in biological populations:

- mutation – physical events that change one or more "letters" of an organism's nucleotide "text"
- recombination – physical events that mix and match gene variants among parental chromosomes during sex cell formation
- migration – the arrival in a population of individuals carrying novel variants of genes
- sex itself

For NDT the primary role of sex is more subtle than straightforward reproduction or behavioral frolic. It is the creation of genetic diversity among offspring. An organism that reproduces without sex, say by hatching unfertilized eggs, can replicate its genome exactly, gene by gene, without wasting time on the rituals of courtship. But if all offspring are identical (mutation helps asexual organisms ensure that they are not, but pales in comparison with the creative powers of sex), they may be less likely to withstand important changes in the environment. Sex mixes the genes of at least two sometimes-consenting participants and endows offspring with more than one copy of each gene, which may differ from each other and therefore hedge against hard times. Sex can be slower than nonsex in terms of the rate at which natural selection can change gene frequencies within the population, but it provides a more diverse array of genetic combinations to present to the world.

Sex also underlies recombination, a chemical dance among parental chromosomes in which whole chunks of deoxyribonucleic acid (DNA) from one parent get swapped with those from the other as the chromosomes are sorted, lined up, copied, and finally shunted into place in the sex cells. A very potent recombinant event is gene duplication, where two or more copies of the same gene get inserted into a chromosome in this molecular version of cut and paste. Freed from their normal role in cell physiology, the "backup copies" of the gene may diverge from their ancestral structure with fewer or no immediate harmful consequences for the organism, allowing new gene products to form and enter the cellular matrix. Many of the proteins that control cell activity in your body are thought to trace their origins to duplication events among genes or parts of genes.

The master architects of NDT knew mutation and recombination as diversity-creating processes indifferent to natural selection: The physics by which genes splice or one nucleotide base becomes another (or is mistaken for another during gene replication) goes forward unruffled by the adaptive struggles of the organism. Of course, mutation and recombination are not necessarily arbitrary in the sense that any conceivable variation in an organism's structure and function can be produced by just one mutative or recombinative step. The biochemical control net of development may damp out a change or shunt its effects toward specific outcomes. NDT requires only that the effects be arbitrary relative to the "direction" in which natural selection is acting. Then, over time, the cumulative change in the population as more and more mutative and recombinant events occur and are passed into succeeding generations might be very great indeed. (Sex, as usual, is even more interesting; what sex cells get together is very much tied to natural selection and has given rise to "sexual selection," a major evolutionary subject in its own right starting with Darwin, 1871.)

Would it not be handy then, for an organism to get physics working more directly in its adaptive needs, in the sense that it could more often mutate those genes whose change would improve the relevant traits? Why waste time changing eye color when there's a poison to be detected or successes to be had by being more creative? Such closet Lamarkism is anathema to NDT. In the autumn of 1988 John Cairns, Julie Overbaugh, and Stephan Miller rocked the neo-Darwininan applecart when they reported, in *Nature,* experiments on the humble bacterium *Escherichia coli* purporting to show mutation influenced by adaptive "need." If *E. coli* with an inoperative version of the gene segment *Lac,* the working version of which gives the cell an ability to digest the sugar lactose, were put in a broth containing lactose as their only carbon source, the cells seemed to crank up *Lac's* rate of mutation preferentially. As Cairns, Overbaugh, and Miller (1988) interpreted the situation, the bacteria detected the presence of lactose and channeled their dwindling resources into producing mutations most likely to help them out of their adaptive jam.

The response to the work of Cairns et al., along with later experiments alleging evidence for directed mutation (also for the most part in bacteria), has been swift, sharp, and on the whole decidedly negative, focusing on potential flaws in the experimental designs as well as alternative, traditional interpretations for the data. Cochrane (1996), Keller (1992), and Sniegowski and Lenski (1995) survey this lively topic. Big epistemic stakes obviously ride on directed mutation, and it is clear that the null hypothesis of random mutation will be stoutly defended. For the moment, the nature and evolutionary prominence of directed, or adaptive, mutation is, despite its fascination, best regarded as highly provisional and little understood.

WILL IT BE MICRO OR MACRO?

It was Darwin's view that environments could be sufficiently stable to allow natural selection to operate over long times, producing gradual but cumulative differences among biological populations. The creation of small amounts of difference by natural selection over relatively short periods of time is no longer a terribly controversial issue. This is *micro*evolution.

Microevolution sometimes proceeds by means other than natural selection. Mutations can occur at such a high frequency as to elevate the percentage of mutants in the population without the effect of natural selection. Immigrants can bring new genes into the population at a high enough rate to change its overall genetic composition. In small sexual populations, the statistics of assortment among recombinant genomes can itself become an important determinant of the relative abundances of the gene variants. These phenomena occur and are at times significant, but current evidence indicates that they are much less potent than natural selection in directing evolution over longer periods of time. In other words, natural selection is the dominant mode of directed change in microevolution.

Natural selection ultimately must work on gene changes trickling through the cell biology of organ development, and through any limitations that the physical laws of chemical reaction place on the form and interactions of cells, tissues, and organs (e.g., Goodwin, 1994; Kauffman, 1993). The nonlinear properties of the biochemistry and the structural physics of the materials and forces holding an organism together are of special importance in this regard. In nonlinear systems, what you get out is not necessarily proportional to what you put in; it can be wildly different, organized into specific ranges of exotic pattern and behavior (an excellent introduction to nonlinearity is Kaplan & Glass, 1995). Thus, otherwise small changes in genes, acting through the nonlinear "constraints" of developmental biophysics (Goodwin, 1994) and molecular biology (Raff, 1996), might be of large effect in organismic development or be damped out by the nonlinear cushioning even more than we might expect.

Far more controversial than microevolution is NDT's capacity to explain *macro*evolution and the origin of species: its proposal that, properly extended, continued gradual accumulation of small differences under natural selection ultimately could create new species (populations of organisms isolated reproductively from each other), and beyond that the higher-order taxonomic clusters of body plans and behaviors recognized to order the diversity of all living things. The evolution of creativity has strong macroevolutionary overtones. Play and innovation behaviors are not unique to us but occur in many species, especially those with larger brains, warm blood, and complex social structures (Fagen, 1981, is the classic synthesis). The evolution of humankind also is a macroevolutionary process in itself, a succession of bipedal species within the genus *Homo* that fades gradually into the bones of long-vanished primate ancestors.

The wrangles over macroevolution have been heard as announcing the death of Darwinism. NDT, like history and God, is allegedly at an end (e.g., Goodwin, 1995; King, 1996). Not so. Modern work has placed NDT, and with it gradualism and the concept of natural selection, alongside alternative hypotheses about the large-scale evolutionary mechanisms at work behind the fossil record and ecological diversity. It would be premature to claim that data currently are sufficient to allow any of these hypotheses to be rigorously posed, tested, and refuted. There are hints of a whole spectrum of temporal patterns across which evolutionary change may be arrayed, from smooth gradual progressions in some cases to intricate patterns interweaving long periods of little or no change (so-called stasis) with shorter bursts of evolutionary innovation (Raff, 1996). The play of developmental constraints against environmental shifts and genetic variation may figure in the transitions between stasis and change in such modes of "punctuated equilibrium" (Eldredge, 1989; Gould & Eldredge, 1977). As we will see later, this includes our own fossil record of human creativity.

As the debates over macroevolution continue, it is important to keep in mind the difference between change per se and *directed* change – genomically ad hoc leaps into the unknown versus the systematic remodeling of populations over time. Mutative and recombinative mechanisms, for example, excel in ad hoc leaps, possibly scrambling the biochemistry of organic development to produce really novel forms. They may figure in circumscribed intervals in the history of life linked to sudden bursts of diversity.

Apart from the barely understood mechanism of directed mutation, the usual suspect for systematic change is natural selection. The integrative nature of development makes it possible, however, that some trait we deem adaptively important actually is "going along for the ride" because ontogeny constrains it to change when the trait on which natural selection really is acting changes. Evolutionary biologists sometimes call these "free riders" *preadaptations,* and they are interesting because they can reshape evolution by suddenly opening adaptive opportunities uncorrelated with previous adaptive trends.

ANY GENES WITH THAT?

Just as Darwin worked without a proper theory of inheritance, the master synthesizers of NDT and its subsequent applications to behavior and population dynamics (Dawkins, 1976; Maynard Smith, 1982; Williams, 1962; D. S. Wilson, 1980; E. O. Wilson, 1975; Wynne-Edwards, 1962) were forced to work without a proper theory of organismic development. The link between gene activity and the "finished" organism had to be fudged through an almost hieroglyphic shorthand, a statistical algebra that skipped over ontogeny.

The direct link, if there is one in a mathematical sense, is between a change in a gene and a change in the organism (and thus in its pattern of development). There is no such link between a gene and a "trait" per se: Genes code for gene products (other molecules that regulate the genome, or proteins active in the structure and physiology of the cell). Nothing else. The unfolding of the organism in development passes the information of the genes into the matrix of interaction with the cellular material of the preexisting egg, where the conditions of the environment and laws of chemical physics enter the picture, governing the flow of material and chemical reactions. The molecular language that genes speak to each other is now partially understood by developmental biologists, allowing them to trace with increasing precision the action of individual gene products in shaping the organism.

Thus, there are no genes "for" sexual preference or enjoyment of clean environments or musical precocity, although there may be genes in which a change in turn changes such traits, perhaps significantly. The information-rich stretches of nucleotide "text" in DNA translate into ribonucleic acid (RNA), which may in turn be read off into strings of amino acids that fold to make proteins in the cell, or into sites through which the transcriptive activity of yet other DNA locations in the genome can be regulated (turned off or on, or increased or decreased in their likelihood of entering an active or an inactive state). Regulator sites on the genome can regulate yet other regulators and so on, making complex chains of control and a strong capacity for self-organizing activity of the genome in its interactions with the rest of the cell (Kauffman, 1993) and within cell populations during development.

While it is tempting to simplify such a picture of distributed nonlinear genetic interaction and integrated genomic activity by a conceptual elision, replacing *genetic change* → *trait change* with *gene → trait*, this genetic reductionism is incorrect and rashly misleading. Talk about genes of major effect means that within a target population differences in a trait among individuals can be traced in significant part to differences among their genomes, not to differences in the environment (or in the laws of physics that sustain their ontogeny and physiology). Such a claim is not equivalent to asserting that the specific trait is determined or blueprinted in the gene itself, or that the environment or chemical physics of development is irrelevant. The rhetoric of molecular biology at times equates the information content of a genome to a sort of "blueprint" (Goodwin, 1994, 1995; King, 1996), a polynucleotide ribbon holding little snapshots of the organism and its parts just like your undeveloped film holds still-invisible images when you drop it off for processing. To build an organism all we need, apparently, is the DNA sequence and some developer. But even in fast-paced fantasies like Jurassic Park, you'll recall that the carnosaurs did not spring phoenix-like out of heaps of coiled DNA: The nucleic acid had to go back into the chemical soup of the embryonic environment, joining with other biochemicals to form a cell that grew into hungry predators and big profits. The DNA is not a blueprint except in the clubhouse stretch of a tired metaphor, but it is a principal subsystem of development's tempos and modes, the one to which we look in most organisms to explain the origins of heritable variation. Changes in genes can change ontogenetic tempos and modes, and with them physiology and behavior.

SHORT CIRCUITS

Seen through the peephole of statistical correlation across generations, heritable variation among humans has another source: culture. We live in a world of invented meaning, a devised world that our species has created for itself, surrounded by social things of our own making. Crisscrossing the lines of genetic inheritance by which humans reproduce their bodies is the flux of culture; deprived of it we have human bodies but not human minds. This is our niche. Whereas most animal evolution arises from the differential replication of genetic information, human evolution is tied up with the differential transmission of both genetic and cultural information. I readily admit that it does culture no full justice to force it into partnership with a desiccated term like *information*. I shall do so here only because I see no other that works quite as well within the space constraints at hand. Cultural information refers very loosely to the stories, ideas, and behavioral stratagems shared among people in every society on the planet – and without which we are unable to be in the world in a manner that is meaningful to each other, and perhaps to ourselves (Randall, 1995). "Information" in our digital age makes it sound as though culture is particulate in the way our genome, that twisted ribbon of discrete DNA base pairs, ultimately is. But culture, and the action of human creativity on it, are replete with information that is continuous and irreducible, whose potential meaning and significance cannot be exhausted – paintings, texts, symphonies, and so on. This gives culture a density of packed meaning unknown in the genetic world (Lumsden, 1989). Changes in the abundance of a variant of a story or invention over time is cultural evolution in its simplest, currently tractable form.

Anthropologists and evolutionists need to know how independent genetic biological evolution and cultural evolution have been (and are) as they have run forward from our primate beginnings 5–7 million years ago. My study of data drawn from developmental psychology, cognitive science, and the comparative ethology of animal societies that show some rudiments of cultural transmission (Bonner, 1980) offers tentative support for the hypothesis that human culture and the human genome are not evolving independently on their own, isolated tracks. The neurobiology of culture learning makes them codependent, resulting in the process of gene–culture coevolution (Lumsden & Wilson, 1981).

Gene–culture coevolution in human beings appears to be organized around a mechanism of information inheritance termed gene–culture transmission. In gene–culture transmission, genome activity picks a special mode of organismic development. The neuronal learning rules of gene–culture transmission influence the likelihood of some rather than other variants of cultural information, causing large changes in the child's pattern of enculturation. The reductive nature of the term *information* makes it sound as though this statement deals with patently absurd alternatives such as a preference for blue jeans rather than black jeans being carried in the learning rules, but this is not the meaning at all. The core issue is the species-specific nature of our minds: our culture-dependent self-awareness, the grammatical foundations of our uniquely human language, our cross-cultural bias for avoiding brother–sister incest in courtship and mating ceremonies – systems of meaning and understanding acquired by children quickly, effectively, and without intensive teaching.

In gene–culture coevolution a circuit of reciprocity operates in which genome subsystems affecting neurogenesis and culture learning shift in response to culture changes that effect the differential transmission of the underlying gene variants. While the analysis of mathematical models of gene–culture coevolution indicates that natural selection can strongly affect the rate and direction of coevolution, the results of natural selection can be markedly different from those expected on the basis of genetic reasoning alone. Developmental processes for culture learning, for example, can create nonlinear couplings between genomic and cultural change, with surprising results (e.g., Findlay, 1991; Findlay & Lumsden, 1988; Lumsden, 1984, 1985; Lumsden & Wilson, 1981). The diversity of evolutionary outcomes can increase, as can the rates at which they are approached. Altruistic and cooperative behavior can spread through a population without the aid of kin selection, reciprocal altruism, or any of the mechanisms traditionally brought to bear on the evolution of human social behavior. Higher-order evolutionary processes such as group selection can be more important than if evolution is purely by genetic means.

Human creativity is the fire that drives gene–culture coevolution. From creativity flow innovations, the raw material of cultural diversity. Cultural evolution, whether considered alone or in the context of gene–culture coevolution, stalls flat if diversity is zero. The action of gene–culture coevolution on this created diversity, starting with culture's modest beginnings in prehominid times, has made us human. The physical record of gene–culture coevolution's track through time – the fossils and the artifacts – offers surprising insights into our species' quirky, obsessive penchant for innovating with culture.

SAY IT'S NOT JUST SO

Just-so stories, unfortunately, comprise the bulk of what passes for explanatory discourse in evolutionary psychology, including its applications to human creativity. Often interesting in their own right, they are best understood as elements of a prescientific method of coming to terms with complex historical data. Such stories begin by adopting the "adaptationist program" (Gould & Lewontin, 1979): The traits we observe in organisms are there because they help spread copies of the genes associated with them; in other words, the traits are adaptive. Natural selection, the prime mover of evolutionary change, winnowed them from among the competing options. To understand specific structures, functions, or behaviors, we accept that they are adaptations and try to guess what it is about them that could help genes spread.

But must they be adaptations? Of course not. Our look at micro- and macroevolution and the physics of ontogeny has made it plain that any number of "forces" are continuously at work in shaping biological diversity and organismic design. Natural selection is one among these. Its primacy needs to be carefully evaluated for each case, with data illuminating the comparative roles of all elements of the evolutionary mechanism. To do otherwise risks falling into fallacies of unwarranted extrapolation. That, plus two other traits of just-so stories to be considered next, is why adaptationist discourse can spark such debate, even among evolutionists.

A common adjunct of just-so storytelling is the extreme genetic reductionism based on the erroneous formula *gene → trait* (cf. *change in gene → change in trait [maybe]*, discussed earlier). Individuals do not duplicate themselves during the process of reproduction. They replicate their genes and then scatter them into the future. If a gene blueprints a trait, then it is easy to portray individuals as passive, gene-programmed vessels for polynucleotide replicators. All traits of an organism become nothing more than enabling devices for the expansive replication of hereditary material. As we saw earlier, the differential replication of gene variants is a universal property of biological evolution, but not because one gene equals one trait or because all the genes taken together make up a blueprint in which the organism resides homunculus-like.

Like New Testament parables, just-so stories instruct and entertain. We will meet some of them later. As scientific objects they are best regarded, I would like to suggest, as the work (not the best work) of a young science on its way to discovering how to make testable predictions about biological history. In the hands of contemporary masters of the genre (scholars such as Dawkins, 1976, and E. O. Wilson, 1978, for example), they rivet attention on key adaptive issues while stimulating debate. They are, however, no substitute for refutable hypotheses, that is, conjectures that not only rationalize what is known but stick their necks out to predict, and then be beneficially smashed apart in consequence.

WHAT WE KNOW

We are a young species, and our species "family," its genus, is also a new kid on the block – barely 5–7 million years old, a moment in macroevolutionary time. A few hours in a tenure hearing or a faculty promotions committee will remind even the staunchest *sapiens*-phile that we remain fully primate in the major parameters of our social behaviors, as well as in our anatomy and physiology. Seen against the macroevolutionary backdrop afforded by all the social species currently known (E. O. Wilson, 1975, is still the incomparable reference here; see also Trivers, 1985, and Tudge, 1996), we are not pushing the primate envelope all that hard.

Genetically we are very close to our nearest living relatives, the chimpanzees, given what superficially seems to be our physical and cognitive differences from them. In fact, so close are humans and *Pan* in details of anatomy, physiology, chromosome structure, biochemistry, and gene sequence that they resemble many pairs of animal species, such as fruitflies and birds, known to have split from each other only during the past million years! In his recent overviews of human evolution, to which the interested reader can turn for much more background than will be needed here (see also Tattersall, 1993, and references therein), Jared Diamond (1992, 1995) notes that recent studies put the fraction of our genome in which we actually differ from the common and the pygmy chimpanzees at about 1.6%, a number that falls to under 0.2% when allowance is made for the portion of this minute difference that is likely to be so-called junk DNA (free-rider polynucleotide text with no known function).

Such small numbers are remarkable, but they need be surprising only in view of an extreme genetic reductionism that seeks to draw a straight line from genes to the "finished" organism. You will recall from the discussion of nonlinear dynamics in development that even minute inputs (changes to the system) can cause big results by nudging it across a threshold, triggering a big change – a burst in brain size or voice box redesign, for example.

In the nonlinear world, 0.2% or less can go a long way if conditions are right. No empirical evidence I know of currently supports a conjecture that such a nonlinear bifurcation separates us from our primate and hominid cousins. The idea is interesting though.

The pattern of physical evolution expressed by the exquisite array of prehuman fossils and artifacts suggests that creativity's fingerprint on our history will need careful interpretation. In a word, things seem to have been very slow for creativity for a very long time in the ancestral paleoworld. Hominids were upright and bipedal by around 4 million years ago. Some 2 million years later *Homo habilis* was abroad in East Africa and hominid brain size was increasing (650 cm^3 in round figures; compared with about 400 in the chimp, 450 in *Australopithecus africanus,* and 1,200–1,400 in modern humans; Tobias, 1971, 1979). A burst in cranial capacity lasted from the follow-on *Homo erectus* at 1.5–1.7 million years (900–1,000 cm^3, roughly) through to around 100 millennia ago, when it leveled off with the appearance of the first anatomically modern *Homo sapiens* in southern Africa.

So 5–7 million years ago we were, so to speak, still sitting in the trees; 3 million years later we were standing upright and using simple but effective stone tools; almost 2 million years after that we were still using stone tools, albeit of greater diversity and impressive refinement. Along the way fire got harnessed and some of us eventually began burying our dead, accompanied perhaps by rituals of pre-interment bodily adornment. But judged purely on the basis of the physical evidence, a quarter-million generations of hominid creativity had changed our invented world about as much as the handicrafts made by a modern child change the content of their closets in the dozen or so years between kindergarten and college.

Then, about 40–50 millennia ago, in western Europe, 50 millennia years after the appearance of people with brains as big as ours and skeletons hooked together just like the ones we have, material creativity took off: specialized and compound tools, fabricated dwellings, long-distance trade, the masterpieces of cave art.

The minds of *Homo habilis, Homo erectus,* and the earliest *Homo sapiens* have vanished along with all but the most obvious and enduring traces of their creative activity. So the data available are biased (one is perhaps justified in saying almost hopelessly biased) toward the least ephemeral signs of their minds' best work. Methods are now needed for sensing the traces that innovative ephemera leave on such fossil and paleocultural assemblages. It is important not to underestimate the role in our evolution of innovated social ephemeral like the earliest chants and narratives (Kreindler & Lumsden, 1994). Our childhood encounters with them build our minds. There can be no serious evolutionary theses about creativity until this paleoarcheology of ephemera has been developed to its limits and integrated fully with the data on "endurables," and the fieldwork on play and innovation in animals integrated with human data.

Suppose, however, that such future work produces a story of creativity's evolution in the genus *Homo* more or less consistent with what we now know, so that the small groups of *habilis* and *erectus* were as short on sharable ideas, tales, ceremonies, and chants as they were on types of implements as they huddled against the Pleistocene night. We then return to face the troubling discord between a fossil record that shows a rush toward big brains, agile hands, and bipedal locomotion but a long, slow climb in the press of creativity out into the world – a crawl that ended with a burst of material innovation about 400 centuries ago.

FALLING LARYNXES AND NOISY NEIGHBORS

There are some good stories told by evolutionists to reconcile the phylogeny of artifact diversity with the notion of Darwinian adaptation. These synthetic tales are worth looking at because they show alternative patterns in which the evidence, briefly introduced earlier, can be marshaled in support of specific functional interpretations. Properly developed, these interpretations might someday reach a point at which they will give novel, refutable predictions. Let us consider a few examples.

Jared Diamond (1992, 1995), whose recent considerations of human paleobiology I have referred to, has suggested that we can understand the mismatch between the run of brain size and inventive diversity in the following way: hold back about 0.01% of our genome and suppose that changes in it put spoken language into its modern form, about 40 millennia ago. Creativity, boosted by the recombinant powers of language and linguistic cognition in their modern forms, blasted off. Using primate and anthropological examples, Diamond infers that before the hominid mind took hold of modern language, we were basically somewhat smarter chimps, getting by on utterances akin to human pidgins and creoles. Changes in that bit of our genome renovated our vocal tract and hooked it properly into our already enlarged brains, with its ready-and-waiting processing power. We could now communicate more effectively about novel ideas and, perhaps, equipped Fodor-like with a more powerful "language of thought," dice and splice ideas in our heads, the better to come up with fresh ideas in the first place. The 60-millennium stretch between early *sapiens* and the creative explosion tuned up our ability to utter vowels and consonants and the way our brains did complex grammar, allowing us to leave *erectus* and *neanderthalensis* in the dust.

Perhaps. But what held back that critical 0.01% for so long – one small step, after all? And can we be confident that the complexity of modern human grammatical capacity was a necessary condition for Upper Paleolithic artifact diversity? Is language really a sine qua non for creativity in general? What about adaptive opportunities provided by more creative approaches to social interactions (Cheney & Seyfarth, 1990; Cosmides & Tooby, 1992) of courtship, mate competition, and matters of sexual selection (Trivers, 1985)? Language only, or something more? Was there really an inventive stasis prior to the Upper Paleolithic, so that a burstlike, punctuated-equilibrium metaphor is appropriate to the data? Perhaps diversity was increasing in the usual way all along (e.g., Tobias, 1979, fig. 14). Many evolutionary trends in innovation follow exponential curves, for example, or logistic curves whose initial behavior is essentially exponential (Hamblin, Jacobsen, & Miller, 1973, is a nice compendium of examples from the time period in which the neo-Darwinian synthesis was being created). The early part of an exponential curve can look very flat, particularly if sampled at coarse resolution. Once the slope of the exponential (which is always increasing) and the magnitude of the curve (which is also always increasing) rise above our method's level of resolution, we get a signal, like a blip suddenly appearing on a radar screen. Coarse sampling can make a gradual pattern look like a jump

John Pfeiffer (1982) ties the Upper Paleolithic's cognitive and creative upswing to broader patterns of change involving population growth and steadily increasing pressures on the people and the land. Put crudely, for perhaps the first time in human history necessity became the true parent of invention and creative outcomes found increasingly receptive audiences: more people, more hungry and harassed people with a need, more people to spread the news, more places to spread the news to. Creativity made innovations that allowed people to make more people faster, further increasing the pressure for innovation. (Perhaps the creative potential had always been there, dormant, awaiting necessity's cold bite.) The gene – culture connection locked in and the "modern" period of rapidly intensifying creativity in human history erupted. The load of cultural information pressing down on ever more complicated networks of band societies, where people could not yet read or write, opened new opportunities for people adept at drawing; the underground sanctuaries at places like Lascaux became "socialization machines" in whose bowels rhythmic ceremony, sensory deprivation, and exposure to "virtual worlds" compellingly rendered on the cavern walls helped ingrain band norms and wisdom.

Perhaps. It helps to have an audience, though even a Leonard Bernstein or a Garth Brooks needs to press CDs if they are playing to a future specialized in tracking endurables rather than the murmurs of ephemera. Or, perhaps, creativity was not stalled at some uninspired pseudochimp level or triggered by noisy neighbors, but moved steadily from pattern to pattern as hominids moved down out of the trees and steadily toward skyscrapers. Merlin Donald (1993) has suggested that our records of both *Homo erectus* and the early *Homo sapiens* bear the signs of major changes in cognition and culture linked to creativity. The breakthrough for *erectus*, supporting its (eventual) transcontinental journeys and harnessed fire, was vastly improved voluntary motor control involving the whole body, not just the vocal tract, serving mimesis and allowing it to reenact, share, and plan – to create what Donald calls a "gestural prototheater of everyday life." The second breakthrough is similar to the changes suggested by Diamond, involving reorganization of the vocal tract and attendant neuroanatomy, higher-speed speech skills, and the breakthrough to one of the more potent channels of ephemera creation: lexical invention and the proliferation of vocabularies supporting planning and narrative-based enculturation (Kreindler & Lumsden, 1994).

Perhaps. But do we know that kinematic aping was any more important than creolic vocalization in coming to terms with the challenges faced by *erectus*? Human creativity is intentional and the activity of a self-aware mind. Where is consciousness and how is its evolution tied to the story of creativity? Perhaps the earlier adaptive need was for self-awareness first and foremost, the better to outwit game and rival suitors. Perhaps this transformation of consciousness was well along by the Upper Paleolithic and completed its journey as an unexpected spin-off of, say, vocal tract redesign. Creativity is a flirtation with complexity, the risks of change bearing against imagined triumphs. Neural processes serving such a capacity must, at the very least, be able to pack and shuffle a lot of information in the tight space of a hominid cranium already occupied with other duties. Perhaps human creativity does hang suspended in history by a thread spun from less than 0.2% of our DNA, but maybe the critical change was not voice or language, but a delicate elaboration in the pattern of cortical wiring, to which burst the Paleolithic bandwidth for splicing ideas and testing their merits. Maybe it was a need for better sleep to ward off the stresses of band life that favored neural rewiring for subtly altered REM, with a burst in dreaming and creativity (e.g., Feldman, 1988). Evolution can be like that, one thing triggering another in unexpected, even preadaptive cascades. Perhaps.

Wonderful speculations like those offered by Diamond, Pfeiffer, and Donald can be multiplied indefinitely. They are part of the circum-scientific mythology by which we try to make sense of ourselves. Even the best ones, such as the examples visited here, ingenious in their formulation and valuable in the unity they bring to diverse data, are guesses cast in the adaptationist mode. Too soft to refute as they stand, they induce more than they deduce. But that, I believe, must hardly be considered the point. Evolution is a young science of nature's most complex creations; if we are to write an evolution of creativity that merits the label scientific, future work must understand how to test the validity of the adaptationist stance itself, as well as deductive models placed within it, deconstructing both relentlessly when needed to unearth creativity's true phylogeny.

SOME QUESTIONS

The evolutionary science of creativity does not exist. One day it may, but the subtle nature of the mental phenomena at issue and the spotty nature of the historical makes the task formidable, perhaps impossible – in other words, irresistible. In broad summary, I would like to suggest that the following need to be kept in mind if we are to move evolution and creativity closer together:

1. It is clear that something happened in the Upper Paleolithic. Not so clear is whether this is the first poke of a long-preexisting signal above some background, or an evolutionary breakthrough, or something else yet again. How do we find out?

2. Quantitative modeling may be increasingly helpful in tying numerical counts of artifact categories to creativity. Good evolutionary hypotheses should be able to predict the mathematical form of the diversity curve in times like the Upper Paleolithic "explosion." Can they?

3. Creativity might not compute. Roger Penrose (1994) has argued at length that human creative thinking is noncomputable. This is not a statement on bounds caused by finite resources like the number of nerve calls or the amount of memory. It is about the limits achievable by following algorithms, however large or complex. Algorithms or their equivalent are the basis of all mathematical approaches to the mind, including the ones used so far in computer models of creative work. If Penrose is on target (Dennett, 1995, states the reasons why most people think he's not, as does Penrose himself), all of these efforts are wrong because creativity is not computation, and somewhere in evolution, most likely on the branch leading to us, there appeared noncomputable minds with our creative phenotype. Can this debate be opened to empirical testing?

4. Computability might create. In total contrast to Penrose's position is the hypothesis that creativity can be understood precisely because it *is* an algorithm (Dasgupta, 1994; Langley, Simon, Bradshaw, & Zytkow, 1987). It can be written out and put in a computer. Since at least the time of Campbell's (1960) seminal paper on variation and retention, evolutionary metaphors have stimulated psychologists' reasoning about human creativity (Gruber & Davis, 1988; Perkins, 1994, 1995; Simonton, 1993; Sternberg & Lubart, 1995). Computer models like BACON (Langley et al., 1987) and AARON (McCorduck, 1991) take the next step. By following algorithms they do seemingly creative work in complex domains such as physics (BACON) and artistic drawing (AARON). Is our vaunted creativity a lot simpler than we'd like to suppose?

5. Great minds matter, but how much and for whom? Creativity research has plumbed the achievements of a few dead minds (Bloom, 1994; Boorstin, 1994; Gardner, 1993; Kearney, 1988; Perkins, 1981; Petroski, 1994; Simonton, 1988). Our myths laud the Homers, the Newtons, the Michelangelos – geniuses and heroes all. But we know too little about the influence such individuals exert on social history (Csikszentmihalyi, 1988), let alone on evolutionary history (Findlay & Lumsden, 1988). In the play of contingency and catastrophe, what (or who) matters (Shermer, 1993)? Chaos theory has made the "butterfly effect" into a modern parable. Nonlinear systems like societies and ecosystems can get into "chaotic states" in which they are exquisitely sensitive to small effects (Lansdown, 1991). The weather is a popular example: The butterfly flapping it wings in an Amazonian rain forest sets off the hurricane that trashes the Gulf coast of Texas. Not always of course; the conditions must be poised just so. Would our creative great ones have dominated culture regardless of timing, or did they happen to be flapping their wings at the right moment in history? Is this the butterfly effect in action?

6. Playing for descent? Sitting with us on our branch of the evolutionary tree are many other species for which play is a key mechanism of learning and skill rehearsal in the young. A glib spin on human creativity would trace its origins to an evolved delay that keeps play and the desire for novelty, exploration, and experimentation – in many species the prerogative of the young – open through adulthood. How are human creativity and animal play in fact related?

7. Is there one engine or many? Evolutionary biologists are beginning to follow the lead of psychologists (Gardner, 1992; Sternberg, 1985) in recognizing intelligence specialized for specific domains such as language, visual expression, or social interactions (Cheney & Seyfarth, 1990). But creativity is still too often treated as a monolithic penchant for variation and

selection. Did creativity actually take off because hominids had an adaptive opportunity for one domain, like language?

A principal question asks what can keep future thinking about puzzles such as these from being just a lot of adaptationist tales under the subject heading "How We Got Inventive." I see no alternative to demanding of evolution what we demand of any science, historical or otherwise, namely conjectures that can be tested in the hard light of new data. There is no reason at present to suppose that such tests will cast natural selection from its place as a key shaper of biodiversity and organic form. But better methods will give us a more precise understanding of just when and where adaptation has been important and how it has worked in concert with the other processes of evolution to shape the creative mind.

REFERENCES

Amabile, T. (1983). *The social psychology of creativity.* New York: Springer-Verlag.
Bloom, H. (1994). *The Western canon: The books and school of the ages.* New York: Riverhead.
Boden, M. A. (1991). *The creative mind: Myths and mechanisms.* New York: Basic.
Boden, M. A. (1994). What is creativity? In M. A. Boden (Ed.), *Dimensions of creativity* (pp. 75–117). Cambridge, MA: MIT Press.
Bonner, J. T. (1980). *The evolution of culture in animals.* Princeton, NJ: Princeton University Press.
Boorstin, D. J. (1994). *The creators: A history of heroes of the imagination.* New York: Vintage.
Bradshaw, G. (1996). "To Fly Is Everything": A virtual museum of the invention of the airplane. http://hawaii.cogsci.uiuc.edu/invent/airmuseum.html
Brandon, R. N., & Burian, R. M. (Eds.). (1984). *Genes, organisms, populations: Controversies over the units of selection.* Cambridge, MA: MIT Press.
Cairns, J., Overbaugh, J., & Miller, S. (1988). The origin of mutants. *Nature, 335,* 142–145.
Campbell, D. (1960). Blind variation and selective retention in creative thought as in other knowledge processes. *Psychological Review, 67,* 380–400.
Cheney, D. L., & Seyfarth, R. M. (1990). *How monkeys see the world.* Chicago: University of Chicago Press.
Churchland, P. M. (1995). *The engine of reason, the seat of the soul: A philosophical journey into the brain.* Cambridge, MA: MIT Press.
Cochrane, E. (1996). Viva Lamark: A brief history of the inheritance of acquired characteristics. Aeon, 2: http://www.ames.net/aeon/article/vivalam.htm
Cosmides, L., & Tooby, J. (1992). Cognitive adaptations for social exchange. In J. H. Barkow, L. Cosmides, & J. Tooby (Eds.), *The adapted mind: Evolutionary psychology and the generation of culture* (pp. 162–228). New York: Oxford University Press.
Csikszentmihalyi, M. (1988). Society, culture, and person: A systems view of creativity. In R. J. Sternberg (Ed.), *The nature of creativity: Contemporary psychological perspectives* (pp. 325–339). Cambridge University Press.
Darwin, C. (1859). *On the origin of species.* London: John Murray. Harvard University Press issued a facsimile of the 1st edition, with an Introduction by Ernst Mayr, starting in 1964.
Darwin, C. (1871). *The descent of man, and selection in relation to sex.* London: John Murray. Princeton University Press issued a facsimile of the 1st edition, with an Introduction by John Tyler Bonner and Robert M. May, starting in 1981.
Dasgupta, S. (1994). *Creativity in invention and design: Computational and cognitive explorations of technological originality.* Cambridge University Press.
Dawkins, R. (1976). *The selfish gene.* Oxford: Oxford University Press. A revised edition appeared in 1989.
Dawkins, R. (1986). *The blind watchmaker.* New York: Norton.
Dennett, D. C. (1995). *Darwin's dangerous idea: Evolution and the meanings of life.* New York: Simon & Schuster.
Dennett, D. C. (1996). *Kinds of minds: Toward an understanding of consciousness.* New York: Basic.
Diamond, J. (1992). *The rise and fall of the third chimpanzee: The evolution and future of the human animal.* London: Vintage.
Diamond, J. (1995). The evolution of human inventiveness. In M. P. Murphy & L. A. J. O'Neill (Eds.), *What is life? The next fifty years: Speculations on the future of biology* (pp. 41–55). Cambridge University Press.

Dobzhansky, T. (1937). *Genetics and the origin of species.* New York: Columbia University Press.

Donald, M. (1993). Human cognitive evolution: What we were, what we are becoming. *Social Research, 60,* 143–70.

Eldredge, N. (1989). *Time frames: The evolution of punctuated equilibria.* Princeton, NJ: Princeton University Press.

Fagen, R. (1981). *Animal play behavior.* New York: Oxford University Press.

Feldman, D. H. (1988). Creativity: Dreams, insights, and transformations. In R. J. Sternberg (Ed.), *The nature of creativity: Contemporary psychological perspectives* (pp. 271–297). Cambridge University Press.

Findlay, C. S. (1991). Fundamental theorem of natural selection under gene-culture transmission. *Proceedings of the National Academy of Sciences of the United States of America, 88,* 4874–4876.

Findlay, C. S., & Lumsden, C. J. (1988). The creative mind: Toward an evolutionary theory of discovery and innovation. *Journal of Social and Biological Structures, 11,* 3–55.

Fisher, R. A. (1930). *The genetical theory of natural selection.* Oxford: Clarendon.

Freedman, R. (1991). *The Wright brothers: How they invented the airplane.* New York: Scholastic.

Gardner, H. (1992). *Multiple intelligences: The theory in practice.* New York: Basic.

Gardner, H. (1993). *The creators of the modern era.* New York: Basic.

Goodwin, B. C. (1994). *How the leopard changed its spots: The evolution of complexity.* New York: Scribner's.

Goodwin, B. C. (1995, May 19). Neo-Darwinism has failed as an evolutionary theory. The THES, http://thesis.newsint.co.uk/SPECIAL/goodwin.html

Gould, S. J., & Eldredge, N. (1977). Punctuated equilibria: The tempo and mode of evolution reconsidered. *Paleobiology, 3,* 115–151.

Gould, S. J., & Lewontin, R. C. (1979). The spandrels of San Marco and the panglossian paradigm: A critique of the adaptationist programme. *Proceedings of the Royal Society of London, B 205,* 581–598.

Gruber, H. E., & Davis, S. N. (1988). Inching our way up Mount Olympus: The evolving-systems approach to creative thinking. In R. J. Sternberg (Ed.), *The nature of creativity: Contemporary psychological perspectives* (pp. 243–70). Cambridge University Press.

Haldane, J. B. S. (1932). *The causes of evolution.* London: Longmans, Green.

Hamblin, R. L., Jacobsen, R. B., & Miller, J. L. L. (1973). *A mathematical theory of social change.* New York: Wiley-Interscience.

Hofstadter, D. (1995). *Fluid concepts and creative analogies: Computer models of the fundamental mechanisms of thought.* New York: Basic.

Kaplan, D., & Glass, L. (1995). *Understanding nonlinear dynamics.* New York: Springer-Verlag.

Kauffman, S. A. (1993). *The origins of order: Self-organization and selection in evolution.* New York: Oxford University Press.

Kearney, R. (1988). *The wake of the imagination.* Minneapolis, MN: Minneapolis University Press.

Keller, E. F. (1992). Between language and science: The question of directed mutation in molecular genetics. *Perspectives in Biology and Medicine, 35,* 292–306.

King, D. (1996). An interview with Professor Brian Goodwin. *GenEthics News, 11,* 6–8. Also at http://www.peak.org/~armstroj/goodwin.html

Kreindler, D. M., & Lumsden, C. J. (1994). Extracting a narrative's causal gist. *Journal of Experimental Child Psychology, 58,* 227–251.

Langley, P., Simon, H., Bradshaw, G. L., & Zytkow, J. M. (1987). *Scientific discovery: Computational explorations of the creative process.* Cambridge, MA: MIT Press.

Lansdown, J. (1991). Chaos, design and creativity. In A. J. Crilly, R. A. Earnshaw, & H. Jones (Eds.), *Fractals and chaos* (pp. 212–224). New York: Springer-Verlag.

Lumsden, C. J. (1984). Parent – offspring conflict over the transmission of culture. *Ethology and Sociobiology, 5,* 111–129.

Lumsden, C. J. (1985). Color categorization: A possible concordance between genes and culture. *Proceedings of the National Academy of Sciences of the United States of America, 82,* 5805–5808.

Lumsden, C. J. (1989). The gene's tale. *Biology and Philosophy, 4,* 495–502.

Lumsden, C. J., & Wilson, E. O. (1981). *Genes, mind, and culture: The coevolutionary process.* Cambridge, MA: Harvard University Press.

Maynard Smith, J. (1982). *Evolution and the theory of games.* Cambridge University Press.

Mayr, E. (1970). *Populations, species, and evolution.* Cambridge, MA: Belknap Press of Harvard University Press.

McCorduck, P. (1991). *Aaron's code: Meta-art, artificial intelligence, and the work of Harold Cohen.* New York: Freeman.

Minksy, M. (1986). *The society of mind.* New York: Simon & Schuster.

Penrose, R. (1994). *Shadows of the mind: A search for the missing science of consciousness.* New York: Oxford University Press.

Perkins, D. (1981). *The mind's best work.* Cambridge, MA: Harvard University Press.

Perkins, D. (1994). Creativity: Beyond the Darwinian paradigm. In M. A. Boden (Ed.), *Dimensions of creativity* (pp. 119–142). Cambridge, MA: MIT Press.

Perkins, D. (1995). Insight in minds and genes. In R. J. Sternberg & J. E. Davidson, (Eds.), *The nature of insight* (pp. 495–533). Cambridge, MA: MIT Press.

Petroski, H. (1994). *The evolution of useful things.* New York: Vintage.

Pfeiffer, J. E. (1982). *The creative explosion: An inquiry into the origins of art and religion.* New York: Harper & Row.

Raff, R. A. (1996). *The shape of life: Genes, development, and the evolution of animal form.* Chicago: University of Chicago Press.

Randall, W. L. (1995). *The stories we are: An essay on self-creation.* Toronto: University of Toronto Press.

Shermer, M. (1993). The chaos of history: On a chaotic model that represents the role of contingency and necessity in historical sequences. *Nonlinear Science Today, 2*(1) 3–13.

Simonton, D. K. (1988). *Scientific genius: A psychology of science.* Cambridge University Press.

Simonton, D. K. (1993). Blind variations, chance configurations, and creative genius. *Psychological Inquiries, 4,* 225–228.

Sniegowski, P. D., & Lenski, R. E. (1995). Mutation and adaptation: The directed mutation controversy in evolutionary perspective. *Annual Review of Ecology and Systematics, 26,* 553–578.

Sternberg, R. J. (1985). *Beyond IQ: A triarchic theory of human intelligence.* Cambridge University Press.

Sternberg, R. J. (Ed.). (1988). *The nature of creativity: Contemporary psychological perspectives.* Cambridge University Press.

Sternberg, R. J., & Davidson, J. E. (Eds.). (1995). *The nature of insight.* Cambridge, MA: MIT Press.

Sternberg, R. J., & Lubart, T. I. (1995). An investment perspective on creative insight. In R. J. Sternberg & J. E. Davidson (Eds.), *The nature of insight* (pp. 535–558). Cambridge, MA: MIT Press.

Tattersall, I. (1993). *The human odyssey: Four million years of human evolution.* New York: Prentice-Hall.

Tobias, P. V. (1971). *The brain in hominid evolution.* New York: Columbia University Press.

Tobias, P. V. (1979). *Evolution of human brain, intellect and spirit.* First Abbie memorial lecture., University of Adelaide, South Australia, October 12. Adelaide: Information Office of the University of Adelaide.

Trivers, R. L. (1985). *Social evolution.* Reading, MA: Benjamin-Cummings.

Tudge, C. (1996). *The time before history: 5 million years of human impact.* New York: Scribners.

Williams, G. C. (1966). *Adaptation and natural selection.* Princeton, NJ: Princeton University Press.

Williams, G. C. (1992). *Natural selection: Domains, levels, and challenges.* New York: Oxford University Press.

Wilson, D. S. (1980). *The natural selection of populations and communities.* Menlo Park, CA: Benjamin.

Wilson, E. O. (1975). *Sociobiology: The new synthesis.* Cambridge, MA: Belknap Press of Harvard University Press.

Wilson, E. O. (1978). *On human nature.* Cambridge, Mass.: Harvard University Press.

Wright, S. (1968). *Evolution and the genetics of populations* (Vols. 1–4). Chicago: University of Chicago Press.

Wynne-Edwards, V. C. (1962). *Animal dispersion in relation to social behavior.* Edinburgh: Oliver & Boyd.

9 *The Development of Creativity*

DAVID HENRY FELDMAN

INTRODUCTION

In a recent review of research on creativity, Sternberg and Lubart (1996) found that most approaches to the topic have been unidimensional, choosing to focus on one or another aspect of creativity to the neglect of others. This tendency to isolate a single dimension of the topic has had the effect of distorting the findings of research; a single feature (say, cognitive processes) is taken to be the whole of creativity, while other equally important features (say, motivation or cultural context) are ignored (Sternberg & Lubart, 1996). Along with a number of others (e.g., Csikszentmihalyi, 1988a, 1988b; Feldhusen & Goh, 1995; Feldman, 1990; Gardner, 1993; Simonton, 1988), Sternberg and Lubart (1996) recommend a multidimensional approach to the study of creativity:

> We believe that confluence theories offer a relatively newer and more promising approach to the study of creativity. They . . . are based in psychological theory and are susceptible to experimental test; they use concepts from the mainstream of psychological theory and research; they do not attempt to view creativity as a special case of ordinary representation and process; and, perhaps most important, they are multidisciplinary, calling upon the various aspects of psychology. (p. 686)

This chapter will follow the recent trend toward conceptualizing creativity as a multidimensional construct, and creative accomplishment as representing the interaction or confluence among these dimensions (Gardner, 1983/1993, 1988, 1989; Sternberg & Lubart, 1996).

We are concerned here primarily with the more rare and profound manifestations of creativity, although work done at more modest levels of creative accomplishment is also touched upon. The most important shift in the field has been from the measurement and development of presumably general underlying traits of creative ability toward analysis and explanation of remarkable instances of real-world creative accomplishment.

Another conclusion of the Sternberg and Lubart review is that, compared with other topics like reading acquisition or metacognition, relatively little research has been done on creativity regardless of approach. A preoccupation with testing for creativity as if it were a trait analogous to intelligence led the field into a narrow and limited conception of creativity. In the effort to operationalize variables and gain experimental control over them, extreme simplification of what is meant by creativity was tolerated. One of the consequences of the tendency to restrict creativity to a set of abilities like fluency, flexibility, and originality (see Guilford 1950, 1970; Torrance, 1962) was an impoverished conception of development. Development in the psychometric context meant strengthening existing abilities or teaching abilities to those lacking in them (Wallach, 1971, 1985).

In recent years there have been efforts to broaden the concept of creativity pursued in research, which has led to increased interest in the field. According to Sternberg and Lubart, the amount of research on creativity has increased during the past two decades but still lags far behind most mainstream topics in psychology. It is an assumption of the present chapter that a broader and richer notion of *development* will also need to be a central feature of the emerging multidimensional paradigm for the field of creativity studies (Feldman, 1974, 1980, 1982, 1989a; Feldman, Csikszentmihalyi, & Gardner, 1994; Sternberg & Lubart, 1996).

And so, to Sternberg and Lubart's (1996) recommendation that confluence theories should guide the field, we add the proviso that such theories must also be developmental if they are to achieve their purposes fully. Creative accomplishemnt, after all, is nothing if not a developmental shift, a significant reorganization of knowledge and understanding, which can lead to changes in products, ideas, beliefs, and technologies (Feldman, 1974, 1988, 1989a). Creativity is quintessentially a developmental matter.

We will first describe some of the major dimensions of creativity, then discuss some of the ways in which these dimensions develop to increase or decrease the probability that creative outcomes will result from their interaction. Finally, we will try to describe how the trajectories and sequences of change within and across dimensions may lead to a glimpse of creativity that does justice to the complexity and importance of the construct (Csikszentmihalyi, 1989a, 1989b, 1990; Gardner, 1988, 1989, 1993).

UNIVERSAL AND NONUNIVERSAL DEVELOPMENT

If a broader and richer conception of development is to be an important part of the study of creativity, as has been argued, it is necessary to say what notion of development should be used. Recent advances in developmental science have provided the basis for accounts of developmental change that help frame the study of creativity (Case & Okamoto, 1996; Cole, 1992; Feldman, 1986, 1989a, 1989b, 1994a, 1994b; Fischer, Knight, & Van Parys, 1993; Karmiloff-Smith, 1992; Keil, 1984, 1989; Sternberg, 1996; Vygotsky, 1934/1962, 1978).

Historically, within the field of developmental psychology the study of development has tended to be concerned with natural progressions that occur in the physical, mental, social, linguistic, and emotional realms. The field has tended to be normative in its focus, aiming to characterize the common milestones and turning points that each of us encounters as we approach succeeding periods of life. This preoccupation with common or universal sequences of change has meant that the study of development has tended to be far removed from the topic of creativity.

One exception to this tendency was Freud's theory of psychosexual development (Jones, 1961), which interpreted creative products as manifestations of sexual or aggressive fantasies put into socially acceptable forms (Abra, 1988). Even with Freud's theory, though, the intent of the theory was universal, that is, to show the common conflicts and experiences that give rise to the need to find sources of expression, some of which are labeled creative. There was little in Freud's theory to help understand or explain the quality of a particular creative product or the features that distinguish a particularly creative person from many others who were less creative and working in the same field (Abra, 1988; Ochse, 1990).

At the same time as the study of creativity has moved away from a global construct and into studies of the specific fields in which creative activity takes place, the study of development moved away from universal sequences and toward more domain-specific sequences of change (Case & Okamoto, 1996; Feldman, 1980, 1986, 1994a, 1995; Gardner, 1983/1993; Karmiloff-Smith, 1992; Rogoff, 1990; Vygotsky, 1934/1962, 1978).

Within both fields it is increasingly seen as necessary to plot the course of change within domains, variously defined in different frameworks. Some developmental frameworks have chosen to focus on relatively broad domains that are presumed to be universal at least in human populations, such as language, space, number, music, physics, mathematics (see

Karmiloff-Smith, 1992), while others have moved beyond such areas into domains that are less commonly achieved, such as chess, pottery making, poetry, computer programming, tailoring, and surgery (Campbell, Brown, & DiBello, 1992; Feldman, 1994; Lave, 1991; Simon & Chase, 1973; Sternberg, 1984).

In one instance, a developmental framework has been constructed specifically to find relationships between creative and more common processes of developmental change (Feldman, 1974, 1980, 1986, 1994a, 1994b, 1995). An assumption of this "nonuniversal" theory is that there are many instances of developmental change that are not of the universal or near universal sort, but that nonetheless meet appropriate criteria for developmental or large-scale qualitative change.

Criteria for labeling something a developmental change in nonuniversal theory include a tendency to transcend the constraints of current cognitive structures, relatively rapid change, relatively large-scale reorganization of structures, a tendency to be irreversible, placement within a sequence or set of sequences of progressive shifts, distinctive "transition mechanisms" that account for movement from one step in a sequence to the next, and certain emotional markers such as appreciation of a new perspective, confidence in a particular interpretation, or changed aesthetic and critical judgments (Feldman, 1980, 1986, 1989b, 1994a, 1995; Keil, 1984, 1989; Perkins, 1988). Creative reorganizations are therefore among the more powerful developmental advances identified within nonuniversal theory (Feldman, 1989b).

Having identified creative advances as among the many developmental shifts of nonuniversal theory, we must also point out that creative reorganizations of knowledge are not all the same; they can range from clever, innovative, refreshing new interpretations of well-known entities (flower arrangements, mousetraps, musical scores, commercial messages) to establishing an entirely new set of principles from which to explain and explore a major realm of human experience (relativity, evolution, genetic transmission, consciousness). Creative contributions also vary in terms of the kinds of hurdles that are overcome: solving a well-defined problem, establishing a new paradigm or conceptual framework, a tour de force of a performance, an exemplary act that galvanizes a major shift in society and culture, or creating a new technology or product (Gardner, 1983/1993).

Each of the several varieties of creative achievements deserves to be studied in its own right, as well as in the context of a framework that interprets all such efforts as multifaceted, interactive, and developmental. A first order of business is a description of some of the key dimensions of creativity.

DIMENSIONS OF CREATIVE DEVELOPMENT

As we have seen, a vision of creativity has been called for that includes not only the cognitive processes that are involved in problem solving, insight, and the like, but also personal qualities like social and emotional characteristics, family and educational matters that might be relevant, critical features of various fields, domains, the social/cultural contextual issues and historical events that may bear on the process, and possibly other aspects not yet identified (see Feldman, 1990; Gardner, 1989, 1983/1993; Gruber, 1981/1991; Sternberg & Lubart, 1996).

If we are to conceptualize creativity as involving several dimensions, it is useful to summarize what these dimensions include:

1. Cognitive processes
2. Social/emotional processes
3. Family aspects: growing up and current
4. Education and preparation: formal and informal

    5. Characteristics of the domain and field
    6. Social/cultural contextual aspects
    7. Historical forces, events, trends

An adequate analysis of creativity involves (at least) these seven dimensions or aspects; clearly, no single investigator can do more than a fraction of the work necessary to produce an adequate account of all seven dimensions. The scope of creativity research is therefore exceptionally broad and the need for ways to integrate the findings of disparate researchers' work into an overall framework exceptionally important (see Medawar, 1969). Toward that end, we can now place each promising source of developmental data beside each of the identified aspects of the process.

Holding constant only one of the seven dimensions (the broad historical moment or epoch during which development took place), Howard Gardner (1983/1993) examined the lives and works of seven creative individuals in seven different fields: Albert Einstein, Pablo Picasso, Igor Stravinsky, T. S. Eliot, Martha Graham, and Mohandas Gandhi. These individuals were arguably among the most remarkable creators of their era and may stand among the more important figures of history. We will use this and other recent studies to illustrate the kinds of results that are accumulating along the seven dimensions of creativity and the interactions among them that increase the likelihood that creative achievements will result.

Cognitive Processes

Gardner and others have found that it is not necessarily cognitive *precocity* that characterizes children who will later produce creative works of the first rank (cf. Bloom, 1985; Gruber, 1981/1991). Other than Picasso, none of the seven subjects in Gardner's sample was a classic child prodigy (cf. Feldman, with Goldsmith, 1991; Feldman, 1994b). Each, however, did display striking cognitive strengths that were specific to the relevant domain, and each also worked around equally profound intellectual weaknesses. Picassso, for example, possessed remarkable drawing abilities even as a young child, but was a very poor student academically (Gardner, 1983/1993).

What was striking in every instance was how rapidly the individuals moved through the levels of their chosen domain once they became committed to it. They ranged from toddlers to young adults when they became engaged and then committed, but once engaged, their trajectory was steep and rapid toward the heights of the domain.

In a number of instances Gardner was able to identify a turning point or "crystallizing experience" that set the course of development for the youngster (Feldman, 1971; Simonton, 1992; Walters & Gardner, 1986). This notion of a critical moment when the young mind is focused and organized toward a known purpose was first used by Feldman (1971, 1974) to refer to an integration of basic cognitive structures; it has since become broadened to include sudden attachment to a domain, along with the motivation and sense of purpose that comes from knowing what one wants to do in life. The formative power of a crystallizing experience is illustrated by a contemporary example:

Like many scientists, Geerat "Gary" Vermeij, 49, remembers the precise moment when he decided to pursue his career; "I was in the fourth grade. I had this teacher who brought back shells from Florida. They were beautiful – glossy on the inside, sculptured in the outside. I was overwhelmed. I knew from then on that I would be a biologist." (Ryan, 1996, p. 10)

How someone enters a field as a novice and moves toward higher and higher levels of mastery is an issue of great interest in the study of the development of creativity (Feldman, 1994a, 1994b). Chess player Bobby Fischer became a grandmaster at age 15 after starting to play at 5, setting a standard that has rarely been approached since he achieved that rating in 1958, although Hungarian prodigy Judit Polgar did so in 1991. Ms. Polgar also began play-

Table 9.1. *Dimensions of Creativity and Their Developmental Sources*

Dimension	Developmental Source
Cognitive processes	Cognitive development
Social/emotional processes	Social/emotional development
Family	Family dynamics, genetics
Education/preparation	Education, socialization
Domain and field	History of subject matter
Societal/cultural influences	Anthropology, sociology
Historical influences	History, evolution

ing at 5 and has reached Master status a few months younger than Fischer did. Using Fischer's achievements as a benchmark to gauge future prospects has become commonplace in the chess world (McFadden, 1992).

A pattern found among Gardner's seven cases is what is now called the "10-year rule," the finding that it takes a minimum of 10 years to move from novice to master in any of the domains so far studied. Herbert Simon and William Chase (1973) first proposed the 10-year rule on the basis of their studies of chess players. In each of the seven cases in Gardner's study, a decade of concentrated, sustained effort seems to be required to reach the point when it becomes possible to produce a great work or achieve world-renowned success.

A number of cognitive scientists have attempted to describe differences between novices and experts in various fields and to offer explanations about how one might move from one toward the other (see Chi, Glaser, & Farr, 1988; Ericsson, 1996). Possible explanations for increasing expertise range from simple functions of the number of hours of serious practice (see Ericsson & Charness, 1994; Sloboda, 1996) to more talent-based interpretations (see Sternberg, 1996; Winner, 1996).

In attempting to shed light on the development of creativity in its more powerful forms, the critical period of preparation is the decade or so that is spent in mastering the domain. It is not simply a matter of learning the facts and principles involved in carrying out activities within the domain that must be understood. The relationship between the individual novice and a unique domain during a particular era may help unravel the mystery as to why some very few people feel the need to transform a domain, while most others are content to work within its existing boundaries and possibilities (Feldman, 1988, 1994b; Feldman, Csikszentmihalyi & Gardner, 1994; Gardner, 1983/1993; Simonton, 1992, 1996).

One difference between those who soar to the heights of a domain and those who lose their loft along the way is in how well matched the two – person and domain – are during the critical period of mastery development. In the case of most prodigies (although perhaps not Mozart or Picasso), the fit between child and domain is near perfect, almost as if one were made for the other. The prodigy tends to be someone for whom the domain as it exists provides an almost endless source of challenge, satisfaction, expression, and exploration, a *coincidence* of relevant qualities (Feldman with Goldsmith, 1991).

For the person who will transform a domain, there must also develop a significant *asynchrony* between mind and domain such that the mind encounters significant dissatisfaction with what the domain currently offers. Gardner found in his seven cases that there were early signs of restlessness and dissatisfaction with aspects of their chosen domains (Gardner, 1988, 1983/1993). The asynchronies, Gardner found, were of just the sort that made significant change in the domain most likely; these asynchonies were labeled fruitful, being neither too minor to provoke much of a reaction nor too profound so as to engender disgust and disaffection for the domain itself. This "optimal discrepancy" between creator and domain extends a principle in the study of developmental change that has been well established for several decades (see Hunt, 1961; Piaget, 1970; Vygotsky, 1978).

Social/Emotional Processes

It has been shown in psychometric studies of creativity that certain personal qualities and experiences tend to be characteristic of people rated as creative. The psychometrically based work of Barron (1953), MacKinnon (1962), and colleagues in the 1950s and 1960s produced an attractive personal profile that has stood up well to further empirical test. More creative individuals tended to reflect a "high level of effective intelligence, . . . openness to experience, . . . freedom from petty restraints . . . , . . . esthetic sensitivity, . . . cognitive flexibility, . . . independence, . . . high level of energy . . . , unquestioning commitment" (Mackinnon, 1962, p. 310).

Based on recent studies of more extreme cases, that profile has been clarified and found to be less of an ideal type than thought in the earlier literature. Among others, Jeanne Bamberger (1991), Howard Gruber (1989/1991), and Howard Gardner (1993) have shown that, as might be expected, the qualities of the individuals in these extreme cases do not emerge as altogether positive.

In Gardner's (1983/1993) study, all seven individuals had difficulty forming close friendships or deep emotional relationships. Friends, lovers, wives, and husbands were important, to be sure, but more for what they contributed to the creator's purposes than for their intrinsic value. All seven individuals also worked hard at getting their work known and recognized, and formed and maintained relationships as part of that process. Since they felt marginal in certain respects, it was part of their struggle to make a name for themselves at the center of their field. Finally, each of the creators seemed to benefit from an intense, supportive relationship during the period during which a major breakthrough in the work was underway, after which the relationship became less intense or disappeared altogether.

Family

A number of features of family history and dynamics emerged in Gardner's seven cases. The families tended to be neither wealthy nor poor, to live in places away from the major cities but not removed from the influence of the fields in which the creators would practice. The family atmosphere was not especially warm, but the children's needs were well attended to. They were taught moral values and expected to adhere to them. When their interests and strengths emerged in the family context, they were supported and encouraged. Where resources were limited, the creators as children received a disproportional share.

Although a pattern of involvement in the target domain was not explored in Gardner's cases, it has shown up in other studies. Bloom (1985) found that performers at the highest levels in several different fields (piano, neurosurgery, swimming, and mathematics) typically had a family history in which at least two generations participated in the same field or a closely related one. Being raised in an environment where there is natural access to the domain and encouragement to participate in it seems to be very important. Not having these advantages lowers the likelihood that a child will become involved in that field. It also raises the likelihood of conflict between parents and child if there is a mismatch between family practice and tradition and the child's natural inclinations (Feldman & Piirto, 1994). The field of family systems theory has been developed to help unravel the strands of mutual influence between parents and children, with matches and mismatches in talents and valuings of various fields being one aspect of the overall process (Fine & Carlson, 1992; Jenkins-Friedman, 1992; Minuchin, 1985).

Among the many aspects of families that may make a difference in identification, encouragement, training, and direction of talent are their genetic history, the age of parents when children are born, birth order of the children, their gender and gender mix, the kinds of jobs or positions that parents hold, amount and kinds of family resources, and religious beliefs and commitments (Feldman & Piirto, 1994). As Simonton (1984, 1988, 1992, 1996) has noted, birth order often emerges as a factor in the achievement of eminence, as does parental loss. In a study of genius cited by Simonton (Eisenstadt, 1978), more than one-quarter of the subjects had lost a parent by age 10, more than two-thirds by 15, almost half by 21. Some studies have tried to speculate on the reasons why factors like birth order, loss of parent, and others have been associated with exceptional achievement, but few clear-cut explanations have emerged thus far (Simonton, 1984, 1992, 1996).

Finally, a number of investigators have found that some sort of trauma other than parental loss during childhood has been present in the lives of those who have produced great works (see Albert, 1990; Miller, 1981, 1989). These traumas typically have taken place as part of family life itself, although not always. Picasso, for example, was traumatized by an earthquake when he was 3 (Gardner, 1983/1993). There has been ample evidence to support the belief that early trauma is often present in the lives of great creators; on the other hand, there are notable cases in which there is little evidence of such trauma. Charles Darwin apparently lived in a warm and stable family (Gruber, 1981/1991).

What may be reasonable to assume given the current state of knowledge is that it takes enormous energy, commitment, focus, and perseverance to produce great work. The source of this motivation may vary from person to person, but it must come from somewhere. For some individuals there is a natural passion for a field, for others it may be sought as a refuge from difficult circumstances. For many creators the satisfaction of doing the work is sufficient motivation for a lifetime. For others there is a need to prove that one is worthy of respect and admiration, or to prove that parents or siblings underestimated one's value, or to provide refuge from trauma: one or all of these may function to keep the process going.

Trauma per se, then, is not the issue; it is the *effect* of trauma on the child's motivation that is crucial. If it does not serve the purposes of talent development and creative expression, trauma would more likely distort or intrude into the efforts of the child to pursue mastery in the chosen domain.

Education/Preparation

It is taken for granted that teachers, mentors, schools, and other sources of preparation for later creative work are critical to its success, although in extreme cases it is often believed that creative genius emerges full blown from childhood without the need for systematic preparation in the field; the opposite is closer to the truth (Feldman, with Goldsmith, 1991; Gardner, 1993; Wallace & Gruber, 1989). With extreme cases especially, the need for appropriate teachers, educational arrangements, and mentors is striking. For child prodigies (not all of whom turn out to be great creators, of course), the role of teachers, mentors, and guides has been well documented (Feldman, with Goldsmith, 1991; Goldsmith, 1990).

Contrary to popular belief, the more extreme the case of the prodigy, the more important the optimal preparation in the field turns out to be. This is particularly true at transition points, when wise counsel and support can make the difference between a process that continues on course and one that is distorted or aborted altogether (Bamberger, 1991; Gardner, 1993).

The importance of formal schooling in the lives of great creators has been controversial. There are those who (like Einstein and Piaget) have claimed that formal schooling was anathema to their development, while others (like Darwin) found positive things to say about academic environments, but not about specific classes or requirements. Still others credit going to school, particularly during the adolescent years and later, as having changed their lives and directed them toward their creative destinies (see Cox, Daniel, & Boston, 1985).

Being a stellar student is clearly not a prerequisite to the production of great creative work. The importance of doing well in school varies with the field and the individual. Freud was an outstanding student, for example, but Einstein was not. For artistic fields and those where personal, social, and/or spiritual qualities are central, a person's performance in school tends to be of less importance than in the sciences (Gardner, 1993; Simonton, 1984, 1988).

If specific preparation within the domain or discipline is distinguished from schooling, then a generalization can be made that proper preparation is crucial. What form this preparation must take varies from field to field and person to person; indeed, the challenge of providing just the right sort of preparation is one of the greatest ones facing those who hold this responsibility. How talented should a student be to justify a commitment of resources for his or her training? How much should training be formal, how much done through apprenticeships? What sequence of experiences is optimal, how strict should discipline be, and when should work be subject to critical appraisal? These and many other issues need to be visited and revisited regularly along the way.

At what point has a person reached the limits that guided preparation can confer? How does one sustain the trajectory of talent development through the transition from student to professional performer? Questions such as these must be asked and answered wisely as the student reaches the highest levels of mastery within a challenging domain (Albert, 1990; Feldman, with Goldsmith, 1991; Goldsmith, 1990).

Mentorship is an aspect of preparation that often plays a crucial role in the development of great creativity. Particularly in the sciences, the guidance and support from a more experienced senior person has proved to be of great importance in the lives of some of our most significant contributors (Cox, Daniel, & Boston, 1985; Piirto, 1992). The apprenticeship tradition in the visual arts has also been an enduring one, almost always critical to the development of a great artist's skills (Csikszentmihalyi, 1988a, 1988b, 1990; Getzels & Csikszentmihalyi, 1976).

After most of the formal training for work in a field is done, it is common to find that the unique form of a creator's work is forged within a small group of peers, particularly when a new style, approach, theory, or paradigm is in the wind. All seven of Gardner's subjects seemed to benefit from forming a set of personal and professional relationships with peers who could help them with their work and their careers (Gardner, 1983/1993). The group is catalytic to the transformation of style and content, and sometimes to the domain as a whole. Picasso, Braque, and others created cubism as a group, although in time Picasso (and to a lesser degree Braque) emerged as first among equals (Gardner, 1983/1993).

The enduring belief that great creativity is developed largely alone, without assistance from teachers, mentors, peers, and intimate groups is largely a myth. Although in varying degrees from individual to individual, from domain to domain, and from era to era, as Simonton (1984, 1988, 1990, 1992, 1996) has shown, it would be a distorted view of the development of great creativity to focus on individuals alone (Feldman, 1990; Kasof, 1995a, 1995b).

Recognizing that there are important aspects of the development of great creativity that transcend the individual's talent, family, and personal motivation to succeed in no way diminishes the importance of the individual; it simply shows that there are interpersonal, social, and educational relationships that are almost always critical to the story (see Amabile, 1983, 1985, 1990; Kasof, 1995a, 1995b):

Clearly, the reigning illusion of the independence of creativity from context is absurd, and the source-centered, dispositionist agenda that has dominated creativity research since the field's inception can explain only a small fraction of the important determinants of creativity. (Kasof, 1995b, p. 459)

Domain

As social psychologists, sociologists, and others have become more interested in the development of creativity, an increasing body of knowledge about the transpersonal aspects of the process has become available (see Amabile, 1983, 1985, 1990; Kasof, 1995a, 1995b; Simonton, 1984, 1988, 1990, 1992, 1996). The same cannot be said, however, for domain specialists, at least not to the same degree. There has, however, been increased interest in the relationship between the history of a domain and the development of expertise within the domain (Piaget & Garcia, 1983; Strauss, 1988).

Piaget had a long-standing and deep interest in the possible correspondences between the history of mathematics and physics and the natural sequence of transformations in children's understanding of them (Bringuier, 1980; Garcia, 1987; Piaget & Garcia, 1983). Piaget found that the content and structure of a domain change over time, including the domain's underlying principles, range of topics, unsolved problems or unresolved issues, and technologies and techniques for acquiring and extending its borders (Feldman, 1994a, 1994b; Perkins, 1988). This work has been useful in showing where historical shifts in the knowledge structure of a domain tend to correspond to developmental natural shifts in children's understanding of that domain.

The talents, skills, and sensibilities that are necessary for great advance in a field change with time. The study of economics in the 1920s and 1930s was dominated by broad historical analyses, but by the 1960s its leading edge required mathematical modeling and statistical expertise of the most sophisticated sort. During the same era, a shift in the field of physics occurred; a preoccupation with field theory during Einstein's early professional years gave way to work that emphasized quantum-mechanical accounts of matter (Gardner, 1983/1993). As a result, Einstein found himself increasingly isolated and outside the mainstream of the rapidly developing science that he had himself revolutionized. The broad, general level at which relativity theory worked did not explain atomic and subatomic activity. More than a mere technical issue, Einstein's aesthetic and spiritual sensibilities required that there be an overall order and design to the universe. Quantum theory proposed that no such order exists or, in principle, could exist.

The argument is not that Einstein's towering contributions should be seen as any less important than they were; the argument is that those contributions were made by a mind with strengths and weaknesses matching superbly the challenges faced by the physics of the early part of the twentieth century. They were in turn less well matched to the physics of the mid-twentieth century. Had Einstein's youth occurred 30, 40, or 50 years later, it is therefore much less likely that we would be writing about him here.

Howard Gardner (1983/1993) makes this point well in *Creating Minds:*

Einstein's longtime secretary Helen Dukas once declared: "If Einstein had been born among the polar bears, he still would have been Einstein." I do not believe for a moment that Einstein's genius would have been equally realized across domains; theoretical physics as it had evolved at the beginning of this century was clearly the optimal area for a man of his gifts (and limitations) to tackle. (p. 129)

With all of this said, of the several facets of the development of creativity that we have identified, the role of the domain in the process is probably the least well understood, perhaps because it has received the least attention thus far (Feldman, Csikszentmihalyi, &

Gardner, 1994). We know that domains change because they are transformed by great creative effort. We also know that a close examination of major shifts in domains will very likely reveal how great creative work is accomplished. The focus of research has begun to shift from the more common or universal changes revealed through comparison of historical shifts within an individual's progress to studies of the unique interplay between a remarkable individual's mind and a domain's most challenging problems (Feldman, 1994a, 1994b; Gruber, 1982, 1981/1991).

Field

How creativity develops (or even *if* it develops) can be greatly affected by the state of a field of knowledge during the critical period for a given individual. Fields are sometimes healthy, vigorous, expansive, and lucrative, while in other periods the reverse is true. There are moments when a field is excessively rigid in its practices and other moments when it allows great diversity, locations where conformity to rigid practice is required and others where experimentation is the rule. At some points the barriers (e.g., class, race, religion, gender requirements) to entry into a field may be formidable and/or arbitrary and other points when entry is more open or where diversity is explicitly sought (e.g., under affirmative action programs or laws). Each variation in a field's characteristics will affect how creativity develops within its confines or how the confines are changed to accommodate new visions of the domain.

The field is the source of acceptance or rejection of potentially creative contributions and the source of judgment about a work's long-term importance. The mechanisms through which these processes take place vary widely, ranging from highly formal gatekeeping and review processes built on carefully conceptualized hierarchies of accepted quality (e.g., in ballet) to highly informal, market-driven indicators of quality as judged by untrained evaluators (e.g., in popular music). Although no systematic study of these variables among fields has been done, informal observations have produced rich descriptions (see Ericsson, 1966; Feldman, 1994b).

For example, Getzels and Csikszentmihalyi (1976) began a decades-long study of artists and their professional development (see Csikszentmihalyi, 1988a, 1988b; Csikszentmihalyi & Robinson, 1986). As part of that study, Getzels and Csikszentmihalyi and their collaborators carefully documented the processes by which aspiring artists made contacts in the field, sought locations for display and sale of their works, courted critics and collectors, found venues for influencing others and recruiting disciples for their artistic programs, and adapted to changing tastes, styles, and prejudices within the art world (Csikszentmihalyi, 1990).

To take an example from Csikszentmihalyi's (1990) analysis of both historical and contemporary artists:

> Rembrandt's contemporaries did not believe he was that creative and preferred the work of several painters less well known to us. . . . Rembrandt's "creativity" was constructed after his death by art historians who placed his work in the full context of the development of European painting. . . . The point is that without the comparative evaluation of art historians, Rembrandt's creativity would not exist. (pp. 198–199)

Csikszentmihalyi extends the argument to the sciences as well, noting that Mendel's experiments on peas were invested with great theoretical significance only much later, after Darwin's work was accepted (and after Mendel's death), in the context of an evolutionary paradigm in need of evidence to support it (see Brannigan, 1981).

Societal/Cultural Influences

Feldman's (1994a, 1994b) construct of a "cultural organism" – the process of organizing resources for the purposes of developing creativity of the most extreme sort – is related to but not quite the same as the field. A cultural organism exists to set and sustain the conditions that allow for such creativity. A cultural organism includes all those who lend support to the enterprise of producing great work, whether or not they are formally trained in the field or are formally identified with it.

A highly refined (if largely informal) cultural organism has evolved around classical music (see Feldman, 1994a, 1994b): from control of the most prized and valuable instruments (who gets to play a Stradivarius violin), to the many festivals and competitions that winnow and sift talent, selecting and encouraging some and relegating others to the provinces, to the most humble establishments designed to make access and initial engagement as easy as possible (the neighborhood piano teacher, the music store that stocks and services instruments and equipment), to the volunteers who keep many of the bottom levels of the "organism" replenished and well nourished.

Cultural organisms involve more than the selection of promising innovations and the establishment of criteria for excellence within the field. The cultural organism that provides an informal context for the field may include some functions and people who are not, formally speaking, part of the field. For example, ticket agents, concessionaires, sponsors, and vendors are part of the support system for professional sports. Similarly, agents, attorneys, architects, and other professionals may have specialized roles to play in the cultural organism, but not be directly involved in the practice of the field itself or in its selection, preparation, or evaluation functions.

Cultural organisms vary in the extent to which they exhibit hierarchical levels, degrees of overall coherence, consensus, singleness of purpose, and effectiveness in carrying out their mission. Again, no systematic comparative study has been done that describes variation between cultural organisms (or even what the main vectors of variation might be), but it is clear that something like cultural organisms exist to husband resources, recruit support, fend off threats, celebrate achievement, and guarantee the continued existence of the field. While a set of interrelated functions such as has just been described is utterly essential to the development of creativity at the highest levels, relatively little systematic knowledge of the nature of such entities is yet available (Feldman, 1994a, 1994b).

Beyond the activities that are directly or indirectly associated with a specified domain, there are important qualities about the society within which the activities take place and the culture in which that society is embedded. Here the rich descriptive and conceptual work done in the fields of sociology and anthropology are potentially very useful. Societies of course vary widely in how their activities are organized and run, and these variations no doubt play major roles in the development and expression of creativity at all levels, particularly the highest. There are even those (e.g., Skinner, 1972) who claim that creativity is *determined* by the social and cultural context within which it grows and develops.

There are indeed certain instances in which social/cultural realities largely determine the possibility or lack of possibility for developing creativity in a given field. If the society's religious commitments preclude certain members of a domain from participation, there is little likelihood that such a member will develop the ability to express creative potential in that domain. Some religions (e.g., certain fundamentalist Christian groups) proscribe girls from being involved in professional musical careers. Some societies (e.g., South Africa for most of its history) restrict whole groups of its members to certain defined roles in society; a person would have to leave his or her country to pursue mastery of a forbidden domain, or risk severe, even fatal, sanctions.

Cultures also raise or lower the probability of developing great creativity in certain fields by virtue of the value and importance placed on them. In Iceland, for example, chess is a highly valued, even revered form of creative expression. It is unlikely that a potential chess player (of either gender) is overlooked. Something similar might be said of the United States and basketball: The culture is tuned to detect potential in this sport, to develop the talent to its fullest, and to richly reward excellence at the highest levels.

Other cultures have invested in the arts and produced amazing works as a consequence. The first 25 years of the fifteenth century in Florence, Italy, is an example of almost singular quality and quantity of creative expression in sculpture, painting, and architecture (Csikszentmihalyi, 1988a, 1988b). The period marks the high point of the Renaissance in Western cvilization. As Csikszentmihalyi (1988b) notes: "It was [the] tremendous involvement of the entire community in the creative process that made the Renaissance possible. And it was not a random event, but a calculated, conscious policy on the part of those who had wealth and power" (p. 336). The motives for developing creativity clearly need not be uplifting to be successful in producing works of the highest quality.

While a great deal is known about societies and the cultures within which they exist, less is known about the ways in which creative potential is selected, channeled, developed, and rewarded within and between social contexts. Historiometric studies have begun to sort out how different forms of social life interact with different forms of creative expression. Simonton (1984, 1988, 1990) has examined the tendency of inventiveness to surge up and down during periods of less and more restrictive governments. Combining quantitative efforts such as Simonton's with rich qualitative descriptions of particular cases and their contexts, such as Gruber's (1981/1991) study of English life during Darwin's day should lead to a much better understanding of the interplay between social/cultural context and the development of great creativity.

Historical Influences

Unless one is a reincarnationist of a particular sort, little can be done to select the time or place where one's life begins. The moment of conception is what it is, and the period of prenatal development is largely the running out of a biological clock with little room for adjustment. And yet if one could pick the time and place of one's birth (not to mention the family one is born into; see earlier sections), it could profoundly affect every aspect of life: the climate, safety, and security of life, as well as the availability of food, water, shelter, and crucial resources requisite to engagement in a domain. Fantasies about time travel play on the wish to be able to move forward and backward through time, to experience a place that no longer exists or might only exist if history proceeds along a certain path. Although we may like to believe that talent is talent and drive to achieve is drive to achieve, the evidence suggests that the situation is far more complex, with a great deal of what is necessary for creativity beyond the control of the individual (Feldman, with Goldsmith, 1991; Goldsmith, 1990; but see Mackenzie, 1988).

Among the "chance" events in the development of creativity would have to be the many determinants of the process that are a straightforward function of the time, place, and circumstances of one's birth (Csikszentmihalyi, 1994; Perkins, 1988; Simonton, 1988, 1992, 1996). A child who has all the natural talents, inclinations, and sensibilities to become a great queen is unlikely to do so if she is born in a democratic country with no tradition of royalty, to a family of minority status during a period of extreme isolation from other countries. (The U.S. movie star Grace Kelly may be a partial exception; she became the queen of Monaco by marrying its king. Lisa Halaby, an American of Arab descent who graduated from Princeton University, is the queen of Jordan, another partial exception.) The point is that the kinds of opportunities for developing one's talents are constrained and channeled by the time and place of birth, which is perhaps a reason why astrology enjoys considerable credibility in some cultures in spite of having no scientific basis for its predictions and interpretations (Feldman, 1990).

Beyond the matter of the moment of birth are the many historical events that, once born, will potentially make a difference in the developmental process. War is certainly one of the most exreme of these, as is a natural disaster (e.g., earthquake, volcano eruption, monsoon) that can change (or even take) a life; Picasso was deeply affected by an earthquake when he was a 3-year-old child (Gardner, 1993).

In studing historical events, trends, and patterns and their effects on creative expression, Dean Simonton (1984) has found a number of interesting relationships:

Political fragmentation emerged as the single best predictor of creativity. Further, I found some reason to suspect that political fragmentation operates as a developmental influence. . . . Aristotle was the teacher of Alexander the Great, but tiny Athens and not the Macedonian Empire must take credit for Aristotle's intellectual development. . . . It appears that creative development depends on exposure to diversity. (pp. 144–145)

Because of historiometric work such as that done by Simonton, a great deal is known about the interaction between patterns of history, the structure of society, and the development of creativity. Yet it is safe to say that the field has only recently begun to uncover key relationships and to assess their impact on the many forms that creative expression may take (see Simonton, 1992).

SUMMARY AND CONCLUSION

We have seen that the study of creativity has shifted away from relatively modest abilities that give rise to many clever or innovative ideas and toward the achievement of exceptional contributions to respected fields of human endeavor. Along with this shift has come an interest in the developmental course of such achievements, ranging from the biological background and physical underpinnings of the creative person to the broad historical patterns of events that constrain and select among the many possible contributions those who will be encouraged.

Between the biology of the individual and the history of a civilization lie several intermediate realms of influence on the developmental process; among these are the intellectual, personal, social, and emotional qualities of the individual; birth order and gender within the family, as well as the family's traditions across generations, including commitments to a particular field of activity; the selection of a specific domain, each of which has a developmental history of its own; a professional field that surrounds the domain with support systems, selection mechanisms, and other influences each of which also has a unique history; the particular social and cultural contexts within which the developmental process will take place, as well as the history of the relevant society and culture; and, finally, natural events and circumstances that influence the lives of future creative individuals, sometimes in profound ways (Cole, 1992; Gardner, 1989, 1993). As Peter Medawar (1969) has written:

We have come to recognize, then, that the study of creativity and its development is one of the broadest and largest topics for research: The analysis of creativity in all its forms is beyond the competence of any one accepted discipline. It requires a consortium of talents: Psychologists, biologists, philosophers, computer scientists, artists, and poets would all expect to have their say. (p. 46)

To this list we could easily add intellectual historians and historians of the disciplines ("domains" in the present context), developmental scientists from all disciplines, sociologists, anthropologists, and ecologists.

A few studies have explicitly embraced a multidimensional, interactive, and developmental perspective. Howard Gruber's (1981/1991) masterful study of Darwin was an early example of how to approach one of the great creative contributions of Western civilization using a concatenation of relevant aspects of the process, focusing on the "insight" that gave Darwin the solution to the problem of evolution. Gruber has called his framework an "evolving systems approach" because it explicitly labeled the changing systems that needed to interact fruitfully over time for Darwin to produce his great work (Wallace & Gruber, 1989). Gruber showed how Darwin's achievement, with the publication of *The Origin of the Species* in 1859 as the focal event, involved the interaction of many related facets, revealing the complexity as well as the coherence of a profoundly influential creative process (Gruber & Davis, 1988; Gruber 1981/1991). Case studies based on Gruber's framework have since been conducted on a number of other exceptional individuals (Wallace & Gruber, 1989).

Mihalyi Csikszentmihalyi and Howard Gardner have proposed the most explicit multidimensioned models of the creative process (Csikszentmihalyi, 1988a, 1988b, 1990; Gardner, 1988, 1993). Csikszentmihalyi (1988a, 1988b, 1990) has proposed that at least three dimensions must be conceptualized as interacting if an adequate view of the creative process is to be achieved. The dimensions that Csikszentmihalyi proposed include the *individual,* the *domain,* and the *field.* When creative work is done, it is done by individuals, but individuals work with other individuals and groups within an organized body of knowledge, with its own concepts, vocabulary, technologies, and techniques for practice. Domains, in turn, exist in the context of broader fields that organize their activity. The field is the place where decisions are made about entry or acceptance, requirements for various levels of recognition of expertise, vehicles for display, curatorial functions, commercial activities, and institutional and organizational matters.

Gardner's framework is among the most explicit about being developmental; for example, he chooses the "relation between the child and the adult creator" as his central theme in the study of seven "creators of the modern era" that we have discussed (Gardner, 1993, p. 29). Csikszentmihalyi's approach is actually more interactive than developmental in the sense that he emphasizes the need to consider individual, domain, and field as a dynamic set of mutual influences (Csikszentmihalyi, 1988a, 1988b, 1990). Development is implicit in Csikszentmihalyi's theory, but is not described in much detail. Feldman's nonuniversal theory is explicitly developmental, but has not been used to analyze individual cases of creativity, so its viability for this purpose is not known (Feldman, 1994a, 1994b, 1995).

We have seen that a great piece of work always occurs in the context of a set of social and cultural contexts and constraints, including the domain that it transforms and the field that judges its significance, and of course these would also have to be part of an overall representation were it to approach a complete story (Cole, 1992). Clearly we are far from being able to represent more than a fraction of the information about a given individual's development through time.

Even if we were, there is still the question of where in the midst of the many strands of development the novel idea comes from and how it is produced; about this deep question we still have relatively little to say. There is productive work going on within the cognitive sciences to better describe how processes like insight may work (Sternberg & Davidson, 1995), and impressive efforts at simulating great discoveries so as to better comprehend how they were originally made (see Simon, 1986; Langley, Simon, Bradshaw, & Zytkow, 1987). Perhaps when these studies are better integrated with the developmental dimensions of creativity, we will be closer to a plausible explanation of how and by whom remarkable creative works are achieved.

After all, Piaget (1971) thought that explaining novelty was the highest goal for his theory of cognitive development:

For me, the real problem is how to explain novelties. I think that novelties, i.e., creations, constantly intervene in development . . . the crux of my problem . . . *is to try and explain how novelties are possible and how they are formed.* (pp. 192–194)

Piaget labored mightily to find an adequate answer to the fundamental question of how novel thoughts can be constructed from a system that, prior to the novelty, did not have the capacity for thought at the new level. But Piaget did not succeed in finding a satisfactory solution to the "mystery of the stages," as he called it (see Feldman, 1989b; Piaget, 1971, 1975, 1982; Piattelli-Palmerini, 1980), or "the miraculous transition," as it has been called more recently (Siegler & Munakata, 1993).

Ironically, we may find that if current trends in research continue, we will know more about everything that leads up to and follows the great breakthroughs in understanding before we know much more about the breakthroughs themselves. Also ironically, it may be that the study of developmental shifts *other* than the great creative ones will tell us more about how creative works are achieved. It should be clear, though, that whatever direction research goes, the study of creativity and the study of development are inextricably entwined.

Knowing full well that fundamental questions remain to be answered about how we have come to be the only creative creature on the planet – creative in the sense that we are capable of transcending the constraints of our current modes of thought and devising dramatically new ones – we must nonetheless pursue research and theory as best we can, following the most promising leads wherever they take us. The field of creativity studies is itself a developmental entity, and it is in a state of intense transition (see Csikszentmihalyi, 1990; Feldman, 1988).

Although we are a long way from an adequate explanation for creative advance, we have as a field of inquiry productively begun the long, hard process of learning about how great works come to be produced, by whom, and through what developmental process. A better understanding of the development of creativity is therefore one of the more challenging, long-term, and worthwhile goals that humanity might, in all its creative arrogance, aspire to achieve in the decades to come.

REFERENCES

Abra, J. (1988). *Assaulting Parnassus: Theoretical views of creativity.* Lanham, NY: University Press of America.
Albert, R. (1990). Identity, experiences, and career choice among the exceptionally gifted and eminent. In M. Runco & R. Albert (Eds.), *Theories of creativity* (pp. 13–34). Newbury Park, CA: Sage.
Amabile, T. (1983). *The social psychology of creativity.* New York: Springer-Verlag.
Amabile, T. (1985). Motivation and creativity: Effects of motivational orientation on creative writers. *Journal of Personality and Social Psychology, 48,* 393–399.
Amabile, T. (1990). Within you, without you: The social psychology of creativity, and beyond. In M. Runco & R. Albert (Eds.), *Theories of creativity* (pp. 61–91). Newbury Park, CA: Sage.
Bamberger, J. (1991). *The mind behind the musical ear: How children develop musical intelligence.* Cambridge, MA: Harvard University Press.
Barron, F. (1953). Complexity–simplicity as a personality dimension. *Journal of Abnormal and Social Psychology, 48,* 393–399.
Bloom, B. (Ed.). (1985). *Developing talent in young people.* New York: Ballantine.
Brannigan, A. (1981). *The social basis of scientific discoveries.* Cambridge University Press.
Campbell, R., Brown, N., & DiBello, A. (1992). The programmer's burden: Developing expertise in computer programming. In J. Hoffman (Ed.), *The psychology of expertise* (pp. 269–294). New York: Springer-Verlag.
Case, R., & Okamoto, Y. (1996). The role of central conceptual structures in the development of children's thought. *Monographs of the Society for Research in Child Development, 61,* nos. 1–2.
Chi, M., Glaser, R., & Farr, M. (Eds.). (1988). *The nature of expertise.* Mahway, NJ: Erlbaum.
Cole, M. (1992). Context, modularity, and the cultural constitution of development. In L. Winegar &

J. Valsiner (Eds.), *Children's development within social context* (Vol. 2, pp. 5–31). Hillsdale, NJ: Erlbaum.

Cox, J., Daniel, N., & Boston, B. (1985). *Educating able learners: Programs and practices.* Austin: University of Texas Press.

Csikszentmihalyi, M. (1988a). Motivation and creativity: Toward a synthesis of structural and energistic approaches to cognition. *New Ideas in Psychology, 6,* 159–176.

Csikszentmihalyi, M. (1988b). Society, culture, and person: A systems view of creativity. In R. Sternberg (Ed.), *The nature of creativity* (pp. 325–339). Cambridge University Press.

Csikszentmihalyi, M. (1990). The domain of creativity. In M. A. Runco & R. S. Albert (Eds.), *Theories of creativity* (pp. 190–212). Newbury Park, CA: Sage.

Csikszentmihalyi, M. (1994). Memes versus genes: Notes from the culture wars. In D. Feldman, M. Csikszentmihalyi, & H. Gardner (Eds.), *Changing the world: A framework for the study of creativity* (pp. 159–172). Westport, CT: Greenwood.

Csikszentmihalyi, M., & Robinson, R. (1986). Culture, time and the development of talent. In R. Sternberg & J. Davidson (Eds.), *Conceptions of giftedness* (pp. 264–284). Cambridge University Press.

Eisenstadt, J. M. (1978). Parental loss and genius. *American Psychologist, 33,* 211–223.

Ericsson, K. A. (Ed.). (1996). *The road to excellence: The acquisition of expert performance in the arts and sciences, sports and games.* Mahwah, NJ: Erlbaum.

Ericsson, K. A., & Charness, N. (1994). Expert performance: Its structure and acquisition. *American Psychologist, 49,* 725–747.

Feldhusen, J. F. & Goh, B. E. (1995). Assessing and accessing creativity: An interpretive review of theory, research, and development. *Creativity Research Journal, 8,* 231–247.

Feldman, D. H. (1971). Map understanding as a possible crystallizer of cognitive structures. *American Educational Research Journal, 8,* 485–501.

Feldman, D. H. (1974). Universal to unique: A developmental view of creativity and education. In S. Rosner & L. Abt (Eds.), *Essays in creativity* (pp. 45–85). Croton-on-Hudson, NY: North River Press.

Feldman, D. H. (1980). *Beyond universals in cognitive development.* Norwood, NJ: Ablex.

Feldman, D. H. (Ed.). (1982). *Developmental approaches to to giftedness and creativity.* San Francisco: Jossey-Bass.

Feldman, D. H. (1986). How development works. In I. Levin (Ed.), *Stage and structure: Reopening the debate* (pp. 284–306). Norwood, NJ: Ablex.

Feldman, D. H. (1988). Creativity: Dreams, insights, and transformations. In R. Sternberg (Ed.), *The nature of creativity* (pp. 271–297): Cambridge University Press.

Feldman, D. H. (1989a). Creativity: Proof that development occurs. In W. Damon (Ed.), *Child development today and tomorrow* (pp. 240–260). San Francisco: Jossey-Bass.

Feldman, D. H. (1989b). Universal to unique: Toward a cultural-genetic epistemology. *Archive de Psychologie, 56,* 271–279.

Feldman, D. H. (1990). Four frames for the study of creativity. *Creativity Research Journal, 2,* 104–111.

Feldman, D. H., with Goldsmith, L. T. (1991). *Nature's gambit: Child prodigies and the development of human potential.* New York: Teachers College Press.

Feldman, D. H. (1992). Has there been a paradigm shift in gifted education? In N. Colangelo, S. Assouline, & D. Ambroson (Eds.), *Talent development: Proceedings from the 1991 Henry B. and Jocelyn Wallace National Research Symposium on Talent Development* (pp. 89–94). Unionville, NY: Trillium.

Feldman, D. H. (1994a). *Beyond universals in cognitive development* (2nd ed.). Norwood, NJ: Ablex.

Feldman, D. H. (1994b). Child prodigies: A distinctive form of giftedness. *Gifted Child Quarterly, 37,* 188–193.

Feldman, D. H. (1995). Learning and development in nonuniversal theory. *Human Development, 38,* 315–321.

Feldman, D. H., Csikszentmihalyi, M., & Gardner, H. (1994). *Changing the world: A framework for the study of creativity.* Westport, CT: Greenwood.

Feldman, D. H., & Piirto, J. (1994). Parenting talented children. In M. Bornstein (Ed.), *Handbook of parenting* (pp. 285–304). Mahwah, NJ: Erlbaum.

Fine, M. J., & Carlson, C. (Eds.). (1992). *The handbook of family-school intervention: A systems perspective.* Needham Heights, MA: Allyn & Bacon.

Fischer, K. W., Knight, C. C., & Van Parys, M. (1993). Analyzing diversity in developmental pathways. In R. Case & W. Edelstein (Eds.), *The new structuralism in cognitive development: Theory and research on individual pathways* (pp. 33–56). Basil: Karger.

Garcia, R. (1987). Sociology of science and sociogenesis of knowledge. In B. Inhelder, D. deCaprona, & A. Cornu-Wells (Eds.), *Piaget today* (pp. 125–140). Mahway, NJ: Erlbaum.

Gardner, H. (1983/1993). *Frames of mind.* New York: Basic.

Gardner, H. (1988). Creative lives and creative works: A synthetic scientific approach. In R. Sternberg (Ed.), *The nature of creativity* (pp. 298–324). Cambridge University Press.

Gardner, H. (1989). Creativity: An interdisciplinary perspective. *Creativity Research Journal, 1,* 8–26.

Gardner, H. (1993). *Creating minds: An anatomy of creativity seen through the lives of Freud, Einstein, Picasso, Stravinsky, Eliot, Graham, and Gandhi.* New York: Basic.

Geertz, C. (1973). *The interpretation of cultures.* New York: Basic.

Getzels, J. W., & Csikszentmihalyi, M. (1976). *The creative vision: A longitudinal study of problem finding in art.* New York: Wiley.

Goldsmith, L. T. (1990). The timing of talent: The facilitation of early prodigious achievement. In M. Howe (Ed.), *Encouraging the development of exceptional skills and talents* (pp. 17–31). Leicester: British Psychological Society.

Gruber, H., & Davis, S. (1988). Inching our way up Mount Olympus: The evolving systems approach to creative thinking. In R. Sternberg (Ed.), *The nature of creativity* (pp. 243–270). Cambridge University Press.

Guilford, J. P. (1950). Creativity. *American Psychologist, 5,* 444–454.

Guilford, J. P. (1970). Creativity: Retrospect and prospect. *Journal of Creative Behavior, 4,* 149–163.

Hunt, J. McV. (1961). *Intelligence and experience.* New York: Ronald.

Jeffrey, L. R. (1989). Writing and rewriting poetry: William Wordsworth. In D. Wallace & H. Gruber (Eds.), *Creative people at work* (pp. 69–89). New York: Oxford University Press.

Jenkins-Friedman, R. (1992). Families of gifted children and youth. In M. Fine & C. Carolson (Eds.), *The handbook of family-school intervention: A systems perspective* (pp. 175–186). Needham Heights, MA: Allyn & Bacon.

Jones. E. (1961). *The life and works of Sigmund Freud.* New York: Basic.

Karmiloff-Smith, A. (1992). *Beyond modularity: A developmental perspective on cognitive science.* Cambridge, MA: MIT Press.

Kasof, J. (1995a). Explaining creativity: The attributional perspective. *Creativity Research Journal, 8,* 311–366.

Kasof, J. (1995b). Social determinants of creativity: Status expectations and the evaluation of original products. *Advances in Group Processes, 12,* 167–220.

Keil, F. (1984). Mechanisms in cognitive development and the structure of knowledge. In R. Sternberg (Ed.), *Mechanisms of cognitive development* (pp. 81–99). San Francisco: Freeman.

Keil, F. (1989). *Semantic and conceptual development.* Cambridge, MA: Harvard University Press.

Langley, P., Simon, H., Bradshaw, G. L., & Zytkow, J. M. (1987). *Scientific discovery.* Cambridge, MA: MIT Press.

Lave, J. (1991). Situated learning in communities of practice. In L. Resnick, J. Levine, & D. Teasly (Eds.), *Perspectives in socially shared cognition* (pp. 63–82). Washington, DC: American Psychological Association.

Mackenzie, V. (1988). *The boy lama.* New York: Harper & Row.

Mackinnon, D. (1962). The personality correlates of creativity: A study of American architects. *Proceedings of the Fourteenth Congress of Applied Psychology, 2,* 11–39.

McFadden, R. D. (1992, February 4). Youngest grandmaster ever is 15, ferocious (and female). *New York Times,* pp. 14–15.

Medawar, P. (1969). *Induction and intuition.* Philadelphia: American Philosophical Society.

Miller, A. (1981). *Drama of the gifted child.* New York: Doubleday.

Miller, A. (1989). *The untouched key: Tracing childhood trauma in creativity and destructiveness.* New York: Doubleday.

Minuchin, P. (1985). Families and individual development: Provocations from the field of family therapy. *Child Development, 56,* 289–302.

Nisbet, R. A. (1969). *Social change and history.* New York: Oxford University Press.

Nisbet, R. A. (1979). *History of the ideas of progress.* New York: Oxford University Press.

Ochse, R. (1990). *Before the gates of excellence: The determinants of creative genius.* Cambridge University Press.

Perkins, D. (1988). The possibility of invention. In R. Sternberg (Ed.), *The nature of creativity* (pp. 362–385). Cambridge University Press.

Piaget, J. (1970). Piaget's theory. In P. Mussen (Ed.), *Carmichael's manual of child psychology* (Vol 1, pp. 703–732). New York: Wiley.

Piaget, J. (1971). The theory of stages in cognitive development. In D. Freen, M. Ford, & G. Flamer (Eds.), *Measurement and Piaget* (pp. 1–11). New York: McGraw-Hill.

Piaget, J. (1975). *The development of thought: The equilibration of cognitive structures.* New York: Viking.

Piaget, J. (1982). Creativity. In J. M. Gallagher & D. K. Reid (Eds.), *The learning theory of Piaget and Inhelder* (pp. 221–229). Monterey, CA: Brooks-Cole.

Piaget, J., & Garcia, R. (1983). *Psychogenese et histoire des sciences.* Paris: Flammarion.

Piattelli-Palmerini, M. (1980). *Language and learning: The debate between Jean Piaget and Noam Chomsky.* Cambridge, MA: Harvard University Press.

Piirto, J. (1992). *Understanding those who create.* Dayton: Ohio Psychology Press.

Rogoff, B. (1990). *Apprenticeship in thinking: Cognitive development in social context.* New York: Oxford University Press.

Ryan, F. (1996, July). He feels the shape of the past, *Parade Magazine,* pp. 13–15.

Shweder, R. A., & LeVine, R. A. (Eds.). (1984). *Culture theory: Essays on mind, self, and emotion.* Cambridge University Press.

Siegler, R. S., & Munakata, Y. (1993, Winter). Beyond the immaculate transition: Advances in the understanding of change. *Newsletter of the Society for Research in Child Development,* pp. 3–13.

Simon, H. A. (1986). What we know about the creative process. In R. Kuhn (Ed.), *Frontiers in creativity and innovative management* (pp. 3–20). Cambridge, MA: Ballinger.

Simon, H. A., & Chase, W. (1973). Skill in chess. *American Scientist, 61,* 364–403.

Simonton, D. K. (1984). *Genius, creativity, and leadership.* Cambridge, MA: Harvard University Press.

Simonton, D. K. (1988). Creativity, leadership, and chance. In R. Sternberg (Ed.), *The nature of creativity* (pp. 386–426). Cambridge University Press.

Simonton, D. K. (1990). History, chemistry, psychology, and genius: An intellectual autobiography of historiometry. In M. Runco & R. Albert (Eds.), *Theories of creativity* (pp. 92–115). Newbury Park, CA: Sage.

Simonton, D. K. (1992). The child parents the adult: On getting genius from giftedness. In N. Colangelo, S. Assouline, & D. Ambroson (Eds.), *Talent development: Proceedings from the 1991 Henry B. and Jocelyn Wallace National Research Symposium on Talent Development* (pp. 278–297). Unionville, NY: Trillium.

Simonton, D. K. (1996). Creative expertise: A life-span developmental perspective. In K. Ericcson (Ed.), *The road to excellence: The acquisition of expert performance in the arts and sciences, games and sports* (pp. 227–253). Mahwah, NJ: Erlbaum.

Skinner, B. F. (1972). A behavioral model of creation. In B. F. Skinner (Ed.), *Cumulative record: A selection of Papers* (pp. 345, 350–355). Englewood Cliffs, NJ: Prentice-Hall.

Sloboda, J. A. (1996). The acquisition of musical performance expertise: Deconstructing the "talent" account of individual differences in musical expressivity. In K. Ericcson (Ed.), *The road to excellence: The acquisition of expert performance in the arts and sciences, sports and games* (pp. 107–126). Mahwah, NJ: Lawrence.

Sternberg, R. (1996). Costs of expertise. In K. Ericcson (Ed.), *The road to excellence: The acquisition of expert performance in the arts and sciences, sports and games* (pp. 347–354). Mahwah, NJ: Lawrence.

Sternberg, R., & Lubart, T. (1995). *Defying the crowd: Cultivating creativity in a culture of conformity.* Glencoe, IL: Free Press.

Sternberg, R., & Lubart, T. (1996). Investing in creativity. *American Psychologist, 51,* 677–688.

Strauss, S. (Ed.). (1988). *Ontogeny, phylogeny, and historical development.* Norwood, NJ: Ablex.

Torrance, E. P. (1962). *Guiding creative talent.* Englewood Cliffs, NJ: Prentice-Hall.

Torrance, E. P. (1988). The nature of creativity as manifest in its testing. In R. J. Sternberg (Ed.), *The nature of creativity* (pp. 43–75). Cambridge University Press.

Vygotsky, L. (1934/1962). *Thought and language.* Cambridge, MA: MIT Press.

Vygotsky, L. (1978). *Mind in society.* Cambridge, MA: Harvard University Press.

Wallace, D., & Gruber, H. (Eds.). (1989). *Creative people at work.* New York: Oxford University Press.

Wallach, M. (1971). *The creativity–intelligence distinction.* New York: General Learning Press.

Wallach, M. (1985). Creativity testing and giftedness. In F. Horowitz & M. O'Brien (Eds.), *The gifted and the talented: Developmental perspectives* (pp. 99–132). Washington, DC: American Psychological Association.

Wallach, M., & Wing, C. (1969). *The talented student: A validation of the creativity–intelligence distinction.* New York: Holt, Rinehart, & Winston.

Walters, J., & Gardner, H. (1986). The crystallizing experience: Discovering an intellectual gift. In R. Sternberg & J. Davidson (Eds.), *Conceptions of giftedness* (pp. 306–331). Cambridge University Press.

Winner, E. (1996). The rage to master: The decisive role of talent in the visual arts. In K. Ericcson (Ed.), *The road to excellence: The acquisition of expert performance in the arts and sciences, sports and games* (pp. 255–301). Mahwah, NJ: Erlbaum.

PART IV

Creativity, the Self, and the Environment

10   *Creative Cognition*

THOMAS B. WARD, STEVEN M. SMITH, AND
RONALD A. FINKE

It will come as no surprise to readers of this volume that humans are an enormously creative species. In a relatively short span of time, geologically speaking, we have gone from fashioning rocks into our first primitive tools to building spacecraft that allow us to retrieve rocks from other planets. Many other species use implements, and some even modify found objects to improve their utility, but as far as we can determine, none other than humans have built upon those tool-making skills to reach beyond the grip of Earth's gravity. There really is something uniquely generative about human cognition.

A question that naturally arises in considering human accomplishment is the extent to which it springs from the singular efforts of a few individuals whose minds work in special and mysterious ways versus the more distributed efforts of the vast bulk of humanity whose minds all work in roughly the same, plainly generative ways. Is cumulative creative progress the province of a small set of geniuses or should the glory be spread more broadly?

We do not pretend to have the answer to this question in its grandest sense, but we do have the perspective that the capacity for creative thought is the rule rather than the exception in human cognitive functioning. We claim that (a) the hallmark of *normative* human cognition is its generative capacity to move beyond discrete stored experiences, (b) the processes that underlie this generativity are open to rigorous experimental investigation, and (c) creative accomplishments, from the most mundane to the most extraordinary, are based on those ordinary mental processes that, at least in principle, are observable. These assumptions form the cornerstone of the *creative cognition* approach to understanding human creativity (Finke, Ward, & Smith, 1992; Smith, Ward, & Finke, 1995), which is the focus of the present chapter.

Creative cognition is a natural extension of its parent discipline, cognitive psychology, and it has two major goals. The first is to advance the scientific understanding of creativity by adapting the concepts, theories, methods, and frameworks of mainstream cognitive psychology to the rigorous study and precise characterization of the fundamental cognitive operations that produce creative and noncreative thought. Given the striking generativity of the human mind, there is an equally striking dearth of exactly these sorts of research efforts. Creative cognition seeks to fill the void.

The second goal is to extend the scientific understanding of cognition in general by conducting experimental observations of the cognitive processes that operate when people are engaged in plainly generative tasks. Most research in cognition has examined performance in largely receptive tasks rather than explicitly generative situations, and since generative activities comprise a major portion of human mental functioning, we are missing crucial pieces of the cognitive puzzle.

In the sections that follow we highlight the striking generativity of ordinary human cognition, elaborate on the creative cognition approach, and give representative examples of research that further the goals of creative cognition. We conclude with some observations about how creative cognition can help to resolve some long-standing controversies concerning creativity.

THE NORMATIVE NATURE OF HUMAN CREATIVITY

A commonly held belief about creativity is that it is limited to a certain class of gifted or specially talented people. By this view, only a minority are capable of genuine creative thinking (i.e., "creative geniuses"), and thus creativity has little bearing on the everyday cognitive activities of the general population. A corollary of this argument is that geniuses use cognitive processes that are radically different from those employed by most individuals and that may not be accessible to the methods of cognitive science (e.g., Hershman & Lieb, 1988).

In contrast, creative cognition emphasizes the idea that creative capacity is an essential property of normative human cognition and that the relevant processes are open to investigation. Though they are not always recognized as such, examples of the fundamental nature of human generativity abound. Beyond the obvious examples of artistic, scientific, and technological advancement that are usually listed as instances of creativity, there is the subtler, but equally compelling generativity associated with everyday thought. One of the most widely noted examples of the latter is our undeniably flexible use of language through which we craft an infinite variety of novel constructions using a relatively small set of rules (Chomsky, 1972; Pinker, 1984), but there are many other examples as well. For instance, the mere fact that we readily construct a vast array of concrete and abstract concepts from an ongoing stream of otherwise discrete experiences implies a striking generative ability; concepts are creations. Further, our concepts need not be built up gradually from multiple exposures. We seem able to create goal-derived categories as we need them to satisfy the requirements of the immediate situation (Barsalou, 1983, 1991), and we can readily modify the ordinary typicality structure of concepts by adopting different perspectives (Barsalou, 1987). We also have the capacity to combine concepts to generate more complex ones, to map properties analogically across domains, to comprehend and produce figurative language, and to perform many other functions that go well beyond the information as directly and literally given.

Far from being unusual, these generative cognitive processes are commonplace and normative. They are part of the normative operating characteristics of ordinary minds. Further, because the novel outcomes produced by these generative processes serve important purposes, they satisfy the twin criteria of creative products: novelty and utility. More significantly, it is not just that these processes are, in themselves, creative; by the creative cognition view these processes also underlie creativity in all its forms, from the most prosaic to the most exalted, from the young child who refers to cold symptoms as a "soggy nose" to the development of the theory of relativity. Hence, to understand creativity fully, we must understand these processes fully.

To be sure, all is not flexibility. People, even those who achieve notable creative accomplishments, seem to have an equally pervasive tendency to be trapped by prior experiences and to carry over knowledge that would be better left behind (Ward, Finke, & Smith, 1995). Thus, an important goal of creative cognition is to specify the factors and processes that determine how much and which portions of existing knowledge will be applied to new situations, and the precise ways in which such information can either facilitate or inhibit creative functioning.

By noting that generativity is a salient aspect of normative cognitive functioning, we are not arguing against the existence of individual differences in creativity. There is no doubt that some individuals produce more creative outcomes than others, and a limited few achieve extreme levels of accomplishment (see, e.g., Eysenck, 1995; Simonton, 1994). However, a central tenet of creative cognition is that those differences are understandable in terms of variations in the use of specifiable processes or combinations of processes, the intensity of application of such processes, the richness or flexibility of stored cognitive structures to which the processes are applied, the capacity of memory systems (such as working memory), and other known and observable fundamental cognitive principles (see Simonton, 1997; and Ward, Smith, & Vaid, 1997, for a counterpoint). Creative cognition explicitly rejects the notion that extraordinary forms of creativity are the products of minds that operate according to principles that are fundamentally different than those associated with normative cognition, and that are largely mysterious and unobservable. Creative cognition, being rooted in experimental cognitive psychology, makes heavy use of basic laboratory studies of "normative creativity" (see Ward et al., 1997), but with the firm belief in the continuity of cognitive functioning between mundane and extraordinary creative performance.

Creative cognition also acknowledges that a range of factors other than cognitive processes contribute to the likelihood of any individual generating a tangible product that would be judged to be "creative." These would include factors such as intrinsic motivation, situational contingencies, the timeliness of an idea, the value that different cultures place on innovation, and so on (see, e.g., Amabile, 1983; Basala, 1988; Lubart & Sternberg, 1995; Runco & Chand, 1995; Sternberg & Lubart, 1991). Nevertheless, we concentrate on mental operations largely because we assume that many noncognitive factors achieve their impacts by way of their influence on cognitive functioning. For instance, an individual who is intrinsically motivated to solve some difficult problem might be more likely than a less motivated individual to craft an ingenious solution, but the solution itself would emerge from the cognitive processes applied. Increased motivation would influence the tendency to engage in the rigorous application of analogical reasoning, mental model simulation, conceptual combination, or other basic processes, but it would be the variations in the processes themselves that would be the proximal cause of the difference in the quality of ideas that different thinkers would produce.

A HEURISTIC MODEL

An early general framework for the creative cognition approach was the Geneplore model of creative functioning (Finke et al., 1992), which was intended as a broadly descriptive, heuristic model rather than an explanatory theory of creativity. The central proposal was that many creative activities can be described in terms of an initial generation of candidate ideas or solutions followed by extensive exploration of those ideas. The initial ideas are sometimes described as "preinventive" in the sense that they are not complete plans for some new product, tested solutions to vexing problems, or accurate answers to difficult puzzles. Rather they may be an untested proposal or even a mere germ of an idea, but they hold some promise of yielding outcomes bearing the crucial birthmarks of creativity: originality and appropriateness. The Geneplore model assumes that, in most cases, one would alternate between generative and exploratory processes, refining the structures according to the demands or constraints of the particular task.

Processes, Structures, and Constraints

Examples of some common types of generative processes include the retrieval of existing structures from memory (Perkins, 1981; Smith, 1995; Ward, 1994, 1995), the formation of simple associations among those structures (Mednick, 1962) or combinations of them (Baughman & Mumford, 1995; Hampton, 1987; Murphy, 1988), the mental synthesis of new structures (Thompson & Klatzky, 1978), the mental transformation of existing structures into new forms (Shepard & Feng, 1972), analogical transfer of information from one domain to another (Gentner, 1989; Holyoak & Thagard, 1995; Novick, 1988), and categorical reduction, in which existing structures are conceptually reduced to more primitive constituents (Finke et al., 1992).

Exploratory processes can include the search for novel or desired attributes in the mental structures (Finke & Slayton, 1988), the search for metaphorical implications of the structures (Ortony, 1979), the search for potential functions of the structures (Finke, 1990), the evaluation of structures from different perspectives or within different contexts (Barsalou, 1987; Smith, 1979), the interpretation of structures as representing possible solutions to problems (Shepard, 1978), and the search for various practical or conceptual limitations that are suggested by the structures (Finke et al., 1992).

Creative thinking can thus be characterized in terms of how these various processes are employed or combined. For example, a writer might generate the beginnings of a new plot line by mentally combining familiar and exotic concepts, and then explore the ramifications of their combination in fleshing out the details of the story (see, e.g., Donaldson, 1992; Ward et al., 1995). Similarly, a scientist might generate candidate analogies designed to understand one domain in terms of another, and then rigorously scrutinize those analogies to test their descriptive or explanatory utility (e.g., Gentner et al., 1997). An inventor might mentally synthesize the parts of different objects, and then explore how the structure might be interpreted as representing a new invention or concept (Finke, 1990). Thus, by considering various types of generative and exploratory processes and their interactions, one can study diverse aspects of creativity within a broad, cognitive framework.

The Geneplore model also makes a distinction between the cognitive processes that are used in creative cognition and the types of mental structures on which they operate. For instance, Finke et al. (1992) proposed that a particular class of mental structures, called *preinventive structures,* play an important role in creative exploration and discovery. These structures can be thought of as internal precursors to the final, externalized products of a creative act. They can be generated with a particular goal in mind or simply as a vehicle for open-ended discovery. They can be complex and conceptually focused or simple and relatively ambiguous, depending on the situation or the requirements of the task.

Examples of preinventive structures include symbolic visual patterns and diagrams (Finke & Slayton, 1988), representations of three-dimensional objects and forms (Finke, 1990), mental blends of basic concepts (Hampton, 1987; Murphy, 1988), exemplars of novel or hypothetical categories (Ward, 1994, 1995), mental models representing physical or conceptual systems (Johnson-Laird, 1983), and verbal combinations that give rise to new associations and insights (Mednick, 1962). Which type of preinventive structure is most appropriate would depend on the nature of the task or problem.

The Geneplore model also assumes that constraints on the final product can be imposed on either the generative or exploratory phases at any time. This allows the model to be applied to many different types of situations and restrictions. For example, constraints on resources might limit the types of structures that could be generated, whereas constraints on practicality might limit the types of interpretations that are allowable. The ideal time for imposing these constraints is an empirical question that can be addressed in creative cognition research.

The relationship among generative processes, exploratory processes, preinventive structures, and constraints is presented in Figure 10.1. As depicted, the model assumes that the two distinct processing stages, generation and exploration, are used in most instances of creative cognition. In the generative stage, processes such as mental synthesis, mental transformation, and exemplar retrieval give rise to preinventive structures, which are then used or interpreted in the exploratory stage by examining their emergent properties and consid-

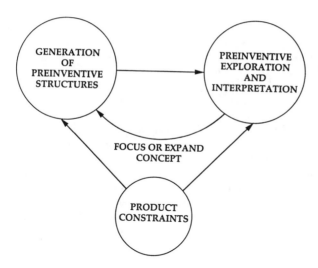

Figure 10.1. The basic structure of the Geneplore model. Preinventive structures are constructed during an initial, generative phase, and are interpreted during an exploratory phase. The resulting creative insights can then be focused on specific issues or problems, or expanded conceptually, by modifying the preinventive structures and repeating the cycle. Constraints on the final product can be imposed at any time during the generative or exploratory phase. From Finke, Ward, and Smith (1992).

ering their implications. As discussed, these preinventive structures might consist of imagined three-dimensional forms, mental models and designs, and exemplars for novel or hypothetical categories. After the exploratory stage is completed, the preinventive structures can then be refined or regenerated in light of the discoveries and insights that might have occurred. The process can then be repeated, until the preinventive structures result in a final, creative idea or product.

Family Resemblance in Creative Cognition

In our approach to creative cognition, we avoid trying to define creativity in any absolute way or by using a single set of cognitive processes or properties. Instead, we prefer to adopt a "family resemblance" view of creative cognition, similar to that used to characterize category membership (e.g., Rosch & Mervis, 1975). That is, we regard creative thinking as involving various subsets of generative and exploratory processes, and types of preinventive structures, where no one particular process or structure must necessarily be present. Accordingly, most instances of creative cognition will display at least some of these processes and structures, and there are no sharp boundaries between creative and noncreative thinking.

One advantage of this characterization is that, in addition to recognizing that everyday and extraordinary forms of creativity are linked by a common set of processes, creative and noncreative thinking can also be seen as lying along a continuum. The extent to which generative processes, exploratory processes, and preinventive structures are involved and give rise to emergent features merely increases the likelihood that a creative idea or product will result. There is thus considerable overlap between creative and noncreative cognition. This is another reason why we prefer to base the study of creative cognition on traditional concepts in cognitive science, rather than trying to propose a distinct class of processes and structures specifically tailored to creative thinking.

The creative cognition approach is relatively new, but it has already made enormous strides. Here we focus on some examples of the types of investigations that have been carried out under the general framework of creative cognition. We will consider creative cognition approaches to the traditional creativity topics of insight and incubation, as well as the issues of conceptual expansion, recently encountered information, conceptual combination, and creative imagery.

Although it may be the case that some of the cognitive processes we examine tend to be more prevalent during initial generation of proto-ideas, whereas others are more evident during exploration, the Geneplore model also explicitly describes creative functioning as a continual iteration of generative and exploratory steps, as novel ideas are brought to fruition. Thus, it is not always certain whether a particular process should be thought of as being exclusively involved in generation as opposed to exploration. In the sections that follow, we describe a wide range of processes that are crucial to creativity without necessarily attempting to classify them as primarily generative or exploratory.

Insight

A telling example of the creative cognition approach is Schooler and Melcher's (1995) investigation of insight, a topic of long-standing interest in creativity circles, but one that until recently has received little experimental attention from cognitive psychologists. Schooler and Melcher point out that mainstream cognitive psychology may have ignored insight as a topic of investigation, at least in part because anecdotal accounts of dramatic insights and nonexperimental observations of such phenomena tend to highlight the unconscious aspects of insightful solutions. For example, the chemist Kekule supposedly had his key insight into the molecular structure of benzene after having dreamed of coiled snakes that represented ring-shaped structures. The mathematician Poincaré reported having made his sudden discovery of a new expression for Fuchsian functions while stepping onto a bus. Indeed, Koestler (1964) suggested that conscious thought, especially in the form of language, might actually inhibit the unconscious forming of connections that underlies insightful leaps. If creative insights occur in sudden, unpredictable ways and if conscious thought might inhibit insights, how could they ever be studied under controlled laboratory conditions?

It is understandable that experimental cognitive psychologists might shy away from such notions, because on the surface they seem to imply a type of process that may not yield to experimental observation. However, Schooler and Melcher went on to describe an ingenious set of studies that shed light on the phenomenon. They reasoned that, if conscious verbalization inhibits the unconscious processes needed for achieving insights, then requiring subjects to engage in concurrent verbalization should disrupt performance on insight problems, and this is exactly the pattern observed. They also noted that performance on analytic, noninsight problems was not disrupted by concurrent verbalization, which indicates that the effect is not a generalized decline in problem-solving ability. Rather it seems to be a specific deficit in insight problem solving associated with engaging in conscious verbalization.

Schooler and Melcher also went on to summarize other findings that related various individual differences – such as perceptual-restructuring ability and field dependence – to performance on insight problems, thereby providing suggestive evidence for various proposed unconscious elements of insight. Overall then, Schooler and Melcher's work demonstrates clearly that the approaches of cognitive psychology can be applied to study even the most mysterious-seeming of creativity topics, such as insightful leaps.

Other recent work on insight has also begun to relate basic cognitive processing issues to creative thinking. For instance, studies have examined whether new insights occur rapidly and without much warning, in a manner similar to perceptual restructuring (e.g., Metcalfe, 1986; Metcalfe & Weibe, 1987) or whether they occur in predictable increments based on identifiable properties of prior knowledge (e.g., Weisberg, 1995; Weisberg & Alba, 1981). One approach to this issue has used an on-line metacognitive-monitoring technique for investigating insight problem solving (Metcalfe, 1986; Metcalfe & Weibe, 1987). While working on problems, subjects tell, every 10 seconds, how "warm" or "cold" they feel, that is, how near to a solution they feel from moment to moment. Metcalfe's studies show that when people solve noninsight problems, their feelings of warmth increase incrementally until the solution is reached, but when they solve insight problems their sense of finding an impending solution is very sudden, coming on with little warning. These experiments provide empirical evidence of insight, as opposed to naturalistic cases that retrospectively examine historically important insight experiences, such as Poincaré's mathematical insights, or Mullis's unintentional discovery of the polymerase chain reaction (see Ward et al., 1995). Although the rarity of historical insights may seem to place such phenomena beyond the reach of empirical science, these studies demonstrate creative ways of evoking and studying the remarkable phenomenon of insight.

Extending Concepts

As noted, the mere fact that we build extensive and elaborate conceptual structures is an indicator of the essential generative power of the human mind. Further, the fact that those structures serve important functions such as classification, understanding, and prediction indicates that they possess utility, an important criterion for creative products. Hence, at its core, human conceptual functioning is a creative phenomenon. Nevertheless, even within this realm of generativity certain aspects of conceptualization are particularly central to creative cognition and we highlight some of them here.

One of the most common creative uses of concepts is to extend them in the service of developing new ideas, an activity that Ward et al. (1997) referred to as conceptual expansion. Consider for instance, what a fiction writer, an architect, and a chef might have in common. Each might begin with a familiar concept, such as "unlikely hero," "single-family dwelling," or "fish stew," and create something new from that base. In so doing, each would extend the boundaries of the existing concept, and each would craft a product bearing critical resemblances to prior instances of the concept.

Anecdotal and historical accounts from real-world settings highlight the fact that new ideas, even highly creative ones, often develop as minor extensions of familiar concepts. Sometimes this mapping of old to new can facilitate progress, as in the case of many well-known inventions (see Basala, 1988), and sometimes it can inhibit, as in the case of lost productivity due to reliance on outmoded organizational structures (e.g., Hammer & Champy, 1993). Because the properties of existing concepts can have positive and negative effects on the form of new ideas, it is important to understand the processes involved in conceptual expansion in all its forms.

By way of its ties to the extensive cognitive literature on the nature and structure of concepts, creative cognition provides a framework for understanding these important varieties of human creativity. A number of recent studies, for example, have attempted to characterize how the central properties of known concepts or recent experiences influence the development of new ideas (e.g., Cacciari, Levorato, & Cicogna, 1997; Jansson & Smith, 1991; Marsh, Landau, & Hicks, 1996; Smith, Ward, & Schumacher, 1993; Ward, 1994).

As an example of this approach to conceptual expansion, Ward (1994) gave subjects the task of imagining an animal that lived on another planet. The subjects provided drawings depicting what the imaginary animal might look like, and raters assessed the presence of familiar properties such as bilateral symmetry, sensory organs, arms, and legs, which are characteristic attributes of most Earth animals (e.g., Ashcraft, 1987; Tversky & Hemenway, 1984).

The vast majority of these novel creatures displayed many features in common with those of typical Earth animals. In particular, most of the exemplars were bilaterally symmetric and possessed two eyes, two ears, and two or four legs (see Figure 10.2 for examples of creatures). This was true even though the planet was described as being very different from Earth. Further, the same pattern obtains even when people are encouraged to develop aliens that are "wildly different" from Earth animals and when they are released from the expectation that what they imagine must be something that can be drawn (Ward & Sifonis, 1997). Such findings suggest that people's knowledge about the typical features of familiar categories structures their imaginative creations, even for unfamiliar or unusual categories. Knowing the categories that are being drawn upon can allow one to predict many of the properties of imaginative creations.

Significantly, these structuring effects generalize to different conceptual domains and to different age and ability groups. Sifonis (1995), for example, asked subjects to design restaurants for a novel birdlike species of aliens. She asked some subjects to design locales where the creatures might get a quick bite to eat and others to design establishments where they might acquire a leisurely meal, and she found that their creations embodied many of the central properties of fast-food and fine dining restaurants, respectively.

Sifonis's work is also important in that it highlights a distinction between the initial generation of an idea and extended exploration of that idea. In one sense, the task of designing a restaurant for birdlike aliens is one of conceptual combination. That is, one must find a way to combine or integrate the concept of restaurant with that of bird.

Much research on conceptual combination examines the initial interpretations that people generate for novel pairings of concepts (see later). For instance, given the combination "bird restaurant" out of context, people might use generative processes to produce candidate interpretations such as "a restaurant for birds," "a restaurant where one can only eat chicken or other bird-based dishes," or even "a restaurant shaped like a bird."

In contrast, Sifonis supplied subjects with the initial interpretation of a "restaurant for birds," thereby eliminating the need for them to use comprehension processes to generate preinventive candidate interpretations. Thus, she primarily examined the exploratory processing by which people fleshed out the mapping of known restaurant properties to their novel creations.

Cacciari et al. (1997) extended the observation of structuring effects to younger age groups. They had 5- and 10-year-old children draw animals and houses that did not exist and found at least as much conceptual structuring in the younger age group as in the older one. As in the case of the college students tested by Ward (1994), children in both age groups produced symmetric imaginary creatures that were highly likely to possess standard sense organs and appendages. Interestingly, the younger children were less likely than the older ones to cross conceptual boundaries (e.g., to put animate features, such as eyes, on their imaginary houses), a finding consistent with an earlier report by Karmiloff-Smith (1990).

Even professional science fiction writers tend to develop suspiciously Earth-like extraterrestrials, as a cursory viewing of the bulk of contemporary science fiction movies and TV shows will reveal. Content analyses of science fiction collections confirm that structuring that uses symmetry, eyes, and legs is the norm rather than the exception (Ward, 1994).

The structuring exhibited by science fiction writers also helps to illustrate the role of constraints in the Geneplore model. Although a writer might be able to envision a creature bear-

Figure 10.2. Examples of what a creature on another planet might look like, generated in experiments on structured imagination. Adapted from Ward (1994).

ing no resemblance whatever to Earth animals, he or she would also be constrained by the need to communicate with a potential audience and to relate any novel ideas to what is already familiar (see, e.g., Ward et al., 1995). Thus, the very practical goals of selling books or attracting moviegoers might constrain a writer from deviating too far from existing Earth animal properties.

Subsequent studies have also revealed the impact of several different aspects of conceptual structures. For example, Ward (1994) explored the influence of correlated attributes as a structuring principle in creative imagination. Traditional studies on categorization have shown that certain groups of features tend to occur together in natural, real-world categories (e.g., Rosch, Mervis, Gray, Johnson, & Boyes-Braem, 1976). For instance, in animal categories, the feature "wings" tends to occur more often with "feathers" than with "fur." To determine whether similar types of feature correlations would occur in the generation of creative exemplars, Ward had subjects imagine and draw animals from a planet described as being completely different from Earth, and different groups were either told that the creatures had feathers, scales, or fur or were given no information about their attributes.

The subjects in the "feather" condition were significantly more likely to include wings and beaks as additional features, whereas those in the "scales" condition were significantly more likely to include fins and gills, relative to those in the "fur" or control conditions. Self-reports collected after subjects created their animals indicated that they tended to base them on particular instances of known birds, fish, or mammals, in the feather, scales, and fur conditions, respectively. Thus, the different instructions led to the retrieval of different instances of Earth animals, whose properties were then projected onto the novel entities. Figure 10.3 presents examples of creatures generated in these conditions.

We are not suggesting that existing knowledge will always reduce the creative potential of new ideas. In fact, it is the human capacity to accumulate knowledge and to build new ideas on what has come before that underlies our enormous generativity and makes creativity possible. However, there may be times when certain central properties of existing concepts are better left behind, and the creative cognition approach provides a way of considering how this might be accomplished.

Ward (1994) proposed that structuring effects can be attributed to creators being led down a path of least resistance. When instantiating the problem of developing a new idea, they are drawn to retrieve typical, specific instances of a known concept and then to project the properties of those instances to the empty frame of the novel idea. Because properties at more abstract levels of representation will necessarily be less specific and constraining than those tied to specific instances, an important implication of this view is that encouraging people to move to more abstract problem characterizations will lead to more innovation.

Additional exemplar generation studies have in fact revealed that accessing knowledge at very abstract levels does lead to a greater potential for innovation. For example, Ward (1993) found that when subjects were instructed to consider the environment of the imagined planet and what attributes the creature would have to have in order to survive there, they developed more innovative creatures, in terms of deviations from the characteristic features of Earth animals. In a more applied domain, Condoor, Brock, and Burger (1993) have suggested that mechanical engineers are more likely to develop innovative products if they begin by considering a highly abstract characterization of the problem than if they begin by considering specific solutions to earlier problems.

At the same time, research on creative cognition is nicely convergent with evidence from more traditional approaches to creativity, such as case studies. For instance, anecdotal observations about real-world invention have also stressed the role of abstraction in leading to important innovations (e.g., Rossman, 1964). These case studies can provide a check on the ecological validity of the general principles, whereas the laboratory findings of creative cognition can provide empirical confirmation of the role those principles supposedly play.

Recently Activated Knowledge

The studies described thus far were largely concerned with the impact of long-term existing knowledge structures. However, the mainstream cognitive psychological focus of the creative cognition approach leads naturally to a distinction between such effects and those due to priming or activation of knowledge by recent experiences. Thus, a related topic that has been addressed in recent studies is the extent to which creative products can be influenced by features that are depicted in previously seen examples. Smith et al. (1993) devised a task in which subjects were to generate new designs for toys. Smith et al. varied whether or not the subjects were shown examples of possible designs, which contained certain key features. As shown in Figure 10.4, each example toy included a ball as part of the design, involved a high level of physical activity, and used electronic devices. This example depicts a game called "tether tennis," in which a person bounces a ball between two rackets, with an electronic counter that automatically records the number of successful hits.

Although subjects in the two conditions generated the same average number of new

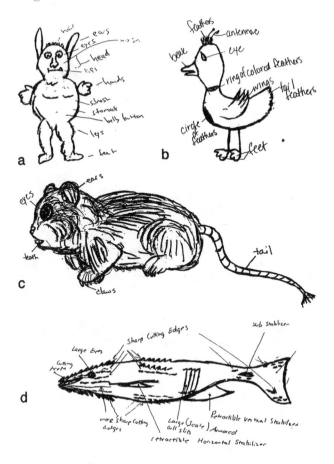

Figure 10.3. Examples of imaginary creatures generated in experiments on structured imagination, under either (a) control instructions or the the constraints that it had to possess: (b) feathers, (c) fur, and (d) scales. From Ward (1994).

designs, the group that had seen the examples were much more likely to include the kinds of features that were depicted in those examples in their own designs. This was true even when the subjects were explicitly told to make their designs as different as possible from the examples. Subsequent work by Marsh et al. (1996) has confirmed and extended these findings.

Figure 10.5 presents the design of one subject who had viewed the example shown in Figure 10.4. This subject had conceived of an "auto pitcher," in which a person can practice hitting a baseball that is electronically guided along a particular path. All three of the key features that had been depicted in the previous example were incorporated into this design. In contrast, a typical design from a subject who had not seen that example is shown in Figure 10.6. This was a design for "water jets," a toy that is attached to a faucet and launches small airplanes at regular intervals. The design shows little resemblance to those in the preceding figures. In related work, Jansson and Smith (1991) have demonstrated a similar influence of design fixation among professional engineers, implying that previous exemplars can influence the content of imaginative creations even in the case of design experts.

These findings point to the need for special care when relying on examples to solve prob-

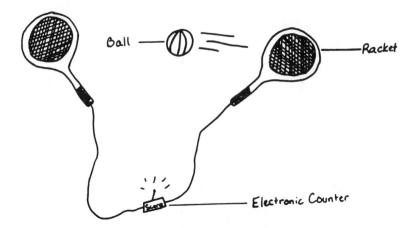

Figure 10.4. Example of a novel toy shown to subjects in studies on fixation in creative idea generation. All example toys contained electronic devices, used a ball, and involved a high degree of physical activity. In this particular toy, called "tether tennis," a person bounces the ball between the rackets, and the number of successful hits is automatically recorded by an electronic counter. From Smith, Ward, and Schumacher (1993).

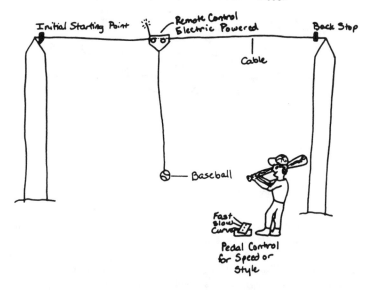

Figure 10.5. Example of a toy generated by a subject after having viewed the example shown in Figure 10.4. This toy, called an "auto pitcher," allows one to practice hitting a baseball, which is guided electronically along a cable. Note that the design contains all three of the major features depicted in the previous example. From Smith, Ward, and Schumacher (1993).

lems. Ordinarily, examples are regarded as beneficial aids in performing a given task. However, it is clear that they can also hinder innovation. Accordingly, further work in creative cognition can help to identify when such examples would help and when they would hurt.

Studies of memory blocking have also begun to provide new insights into the nature of creative thinking. For example, studies on interference and inhibition suggest ways in which

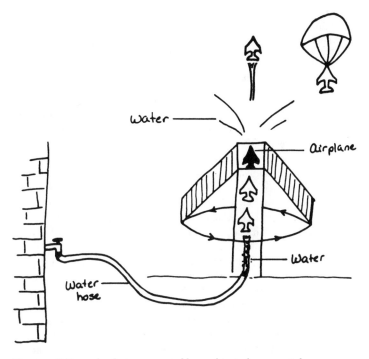

Figure 10.6. Example of a toy generated by a subject who was not shown any example toys. In using this toy, called "water jets," one hooks the hose to a faucet, and toy airplanes are launched at regular intervals. Note that this design bears little resemblance to that shown in Figure 10.4. From Smith, Ward, and Schumacher (1993).

creative thinking might be facilitated (Smith, 1995; Smith & Blankenship, 1991; Smith et al., 1993). Such studies have also begun to reveal the cognitive processes that underlie incubation (Smith & Vela, 1991), intuition (Bowers, Regehr, Balthazard, & Parker, 1990), and other phenomena that have traditionally been regarded as unresearchable.

One phenomenon that has been studied is the involuntary or unavoidable nature of certain mental blocks that can impede or constrain creative thinking. Can people avoid or escape traps in problem solving and creative idea generation? In some cases researchers have found that a simple warning is enough to avoid a mental set. Luchins and Luchins (1959), for example, described how a mental set (aka, *Einstellung*) brought about by repeated use of a single solution could be avoided if subjects were given warnings in advance. Other studies, however, give a different picture. An extensive set of experiments by Smith and Tindell (1997) studied involuntary mental blocks caused by negative priming in a word fragment completion task. After seeing the negative prime ANALOGY, subjects have great difficulty solving the word fragment A_L_ _GY. This block occurs even if subjects are warned in advance that thinking about the negative primes will obstruct their ability to solve word fragments. Involuntary blocking has also been demonstrated by Smith et al. (1993), Marsh et al. (1996), and Ward and Sifonis (1997), all of whom have shown that conformity effects in creative idea generation are not diminished when subjects are urged to give ideas very different from the examples they view. Likewise, Jansson and Smith (1991) found that engineering design students who were instructed to avoid certain negative features of an example they had seen nonetheless incorporated those negative features in their creative designs. Future studies in this area must delimit the circumstances in which mental blocks are likely to be unavoidable, as well as investigate methods for recognizing and overcoming involuntary blocks to problem solving and creative thinking.

Conceptual Combination

Several keen observers of the creative process have identified the synthesis or merging of previously separate concepts as being crucial to human creativity (e.g., Baughman & Mumford, 1995; Koestler, 1964; Mobley, Doares, & Mumford, 1992; Rothenberg, 1979), and creators themselves regularly comment on the generative power inherent in considering novel combinations of concepts (see, e.g., Donaldson, 1992, Freeman, 1993). Donaldson, for instance, developed the underpinnings of his fantasy series on Thomas Covenant, The Unbeliever, by merging the concept of "an unwillingness to accept the possibility of fantasy worlds" with that of "leprosy." He crafted a character who was unwilling to believe in the apparent reality of an otherwise pleasant fantasy world for fear of abandoning the rigorous self-inspection procedures that had helped him avoid serious health problems as a leprosy sufferer in the real world.

On a more mundane level, a plethora of everyday examples suggests that producing and comprehending even simple combinations could be appropriately labeled as creative, if only in the sense that new mental structures are brought into being or elaborated. Where before there were just the separate, well-known concepts of "soccer" and "mom," the 1996 presidential election saw the birth of "soccer moms," whose votes were vigorously courted by the major contenders. It is reasonable to suppose that, prior to encountering the term, most people did not have a coherent mental representation for such a subset of the voting population, but developed it in the service of understanding the phrase. The ease with which such novel mental representations are formed gives evidence of the generative power of conceptual combination. As it turns out, soccer moms also resulted in the emergent property of "political clout," which is not generally attributed to soccer or moms separately. Again it appears that mundane and extraordinary forms of creativity may be endpoints on a continuum, with conceptual combination being one of the important underlying causal processes they share.

Somewhat separate from these historical and anecdotal accounts, experimentally oriented psycholinguists and cognitive psychologists have intensely scrutinized the basic processes involved in comprehending combinations of concepts (see Wisniewski, 1996, 1997). Although such studies have been motivated largely by issues relevant to language comprehension, rather than creativity itself, a clearly established finding from these investigations is that properties often emerge in a combination that were not evident in any of its constituents (e.g., Hampton, 1987; Murphy, 1988; Wilkenfeld, 1995). Because these emergent properties are a source of novelty, they confirm the speculation that conceptual combination can contribute to creative functioning, and they highlight the fact that well-controlled laboratory studies can examine such functioning.

A variety of models have been developed to account for how people comprehend combinations of concepts (e.g., Cohen & Murphy, 1984; Gagne & Shoben, 1997; Hampton, 1987; Murphy, 1988; Rips, 1995; Smith & Osherson, 1984; Thagard, 1997), and a growing body of empirical studies attests to the continued interest in this topic. Here we simply highlight some of this work that, consistent with the creative cognition approach, provides a rigorous look at the fundamental nature of a process that is crucial to creativity.

Hampton (1997) has provided an analysis of the circumstances under which emergent properties are most likely to be observed in a combination, and he has highlighted different processes that might produce emergence. He notes that emergent attributes are relatively uncommon for reasonably familiar conjunctions, such as "birds that are also pets," and that those that are found tend to result from retrieving knowledge about specific known instances of the conjunction. For example, "talking" is not generally true of most pets or most birds, but may be regarded as an important attribute of their conjunction, pet birds. Presumably "talking" emerges from the combination because people retrieve familiar instances of pet birds that do talk (e.g., parrots). Hampton thus concludes that there is little evidence for creative emergence for these types of familiar combinations.

In contrast, emergent attributes occur much more commonly for combinations that result in imaginary objects, and those that do occur tend to be based on elaborate problem solving or on scenario construction. For example, when faced with the task of imagining fruit that was also furniture, subjects introduced properties such as "regenerates itself." Presumably the property emerged as a solution to the basic incompatibility between the durability of furniture and the perishable nature of fruit.

Hampton's (1987) attribute inheritance model provides a way of conceptualizing the need for such elaborate processing. The model states that any attribute that is necessary for either constituent of a conjunction will be inherited by the conjunction and that any attribute that is impossible for either constituent will not be inherited. Because furniture ought to be durable and fruit is perishable, these principles of inheritance drive a conflict that forces the comprehender to reason from aspects of world knowledge that go well beyond the boundaries of the individual concepts, and hence result in emergence. What this illustrates is that models designed to account for basic cognitive functioning can have important implications for our understanding of when and how creative outcomes will be observed.

Wilkenfeld (1995) has also provided evidence from laboratory studies of conceptual combination that can enhance our understanding of creative functioning. She attempted to test the proposition that concepts which are more discrepant will result in more creative outcomes than those that are more compatible (see, e.g., Rothenberg, 1979, 1995). Wilkenfeld asked subjects to provide two different definitions for combinations of similar (e.g., guitar harp) and dissimilar concepts (e.g., motorcycle carpet) and to list attributes of the separate and combined concepts. She found that dissimilar pairs resulted in more emergence, but only on the first definition.

Wilkenfeld interpreted the result using Markman and Gentner's (1993) model of structural alignment. Similar pairs have compatible structures that allow the comprehender to merge them easily, and consequently they evoke little emergence from information outside the parent concepts. Dissimilar pairs are less readily aligned and foster a search beyond the parent concepts to resolve the conflicts in their structures. Once the easy initial alignment for similar pairs is exhausted in the service of producing the first definition, they behave more like dissimilar pairs, requiring a search outside the ordinary bounds of the component concepts to conceive a new definition. As in the case of Hampton's analysis then, Wilkenfeld's work reveals how laboratory studies based on theories about fundamental cognitive processes can shed light on issues of long-standing interest in the world of creativity.

Other recent studies also highlight how the similarity of the concepts in a combination can influence processing. Wisniewski (1996, 1997) has identified three strategies by which people interpret combinations: finding some relation to link them, constructing a property of one in the other, and forming a hybrid or blend of the two. For instance, a skunk bird might be a bird that eats skunks, a bird that smells bad, or some novel creature that might result if a skunk and bird could breed. Wisniewski has shown that relation linking is more common with dissimilar pairs, whereas property construction and hybridization are more common with similar pairs.

Wisniewski is also quite explicit that property interpretations are not simply the copying of an attribute from one concept to another. A zebra clam might well be striped, but the stripes are not a mere copy of a zebra's stripes. They are modified in whatever way is needed to make them compatible with what we know about clams. Thus, even a conceptual combination strategy that does not seem, on the surface, to be very creative, nevertheless reveals important generative properties.

Finally, Thagard (1997) presented a coherence-based account of the role of conceptual combination in creativity. This model makes use of the notion of multiple constraint satisfaction; each of the components places constraints on the possible interpretations of the combination. The cognitive system searches for the interpretation that provides the most coherent account given all of the constraints. If the most coherent interpretation available is still not deemed to be sufficiently coherent, other processes can come into play that open the possibility for more creative outcomes. Thagard's focus on assessing the coherence of initial candidate interpretations is thus consistent with the Geneplore model's suggestion of a split between generative processes that produce preinventive structures, and exploratory processes that test their viability and modify them as needed.

Creative Imagery

There is little doubt from historical and anecdotal accounts that imagery plays a central role in creative functioning, and research in creative cognition has provided experimental evidence on this important phenomenon. Finke (1990) developed a novel procedure for exploring the discovery of creative inventions under laboratory conditions. Subjects were asked to imagine forms that could be obtained by merging a randomly determined set of three parts selected from the larger set depicted in Figure 10.7. Their basic task was then to interpret the forms as representing a practical object or design.

In one condition, the subjects were free to choose the interpretive category in advance. The allowable categories consisted of furniture, personal items, vehicles, scientific instruments, appliances, tools and utensils, weapons, and toys and games. In a second condition, the category was specified in advance by the experimenter and was chosen at random. In a third condition, the interpretive category was also chosen randomly, but was specified only after the subjects had constructed their imagined forms. The resulting inventions were rated for originality and practicality and were classified into creative and noncreative categories using consensual agreement among judges.

The greatest number of creative inventions were obtained when the interpretive categories were specified only after the subjects had completed their forms, whereas the fewest number of creative inventions were obtained when the subjects were free to choose the interpretive categories at any time. These findings suggest that delaying the search for creative interpretations until after the preinventive structures are initially completed may enhance creative discovery.

Apparently, innovation can be fostered by developing preinventive structures that are relatively uncontaminated by knowledge of the specific goal or task. This suggests that in addition to the clearly valuable approach of letting the form of an idea be derived from the function it must satisfy, another valuable approach may be to let the form itself suggest new and potentially useful functions (Getzels & Csikszentmihalyi, 1976; Perkins, 1981).

Examples of objects that were classified as creative inventions in these experiments are shown in the next two figures. The preinventive structure shown in Figure 10.8 was inter-

Figure 10.7. Set of parts from which three were chosen at random for creative imagery task.

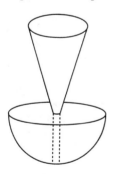

Figure 10.8. The "contact lens remover," an example of a creative invention obtained in studies on creative mental synthesis, constructed using a half sphere, cone, and tube. One places the rubber cone against the contact lens, covers the back of the tube with a finger, lifts the contact off the eye, and then removes the contact from the cone by releasing the finger from the tube. From Finke (1990).

preted as a "contact lens remover," which works by placing the rubber cone against the contact lens, covering the hole at the back, and then moving the device away from the eye. Figure 10.9 shows an invention called the "universal reacher," which can be used to retrieve keys and other items that fall into hard-to-reach places. The wire is drawn out of the spherical housing and can be bent as needed to reach the lost item.

It is important to note, however, that these ideas should not be viewed as representing

Figure 10.9. The "universal reacher," another example of a creative invention, constructed using a hook, sphere, and wire. The wire is drawn out of the sphere and can be shaped and bent to retrieve things that fall into hard-to-reach places, while the hook allows the device to be secured so that both hands can be used to guide the wire. From Finke (1990).

final, workable inventions, but rather as invention prototypes. In most cases, these designs would require further refinement or modification in order to actually work as conceived.

These methods for generating creative inventions have been extended to examine more abstract types of interpretations of preinventive structures (Finke, 1990). The subjects were instructed to interpret their forms as representing an abstract idea or concept within a particular subject category, rather than as a concrete object or invention. The allowable categories consisted of architecture, physics and astronomy, biology, medicine, psychology, literature, music, and political science. After the subjects had generated their forms, they were either given one of the categories, selected at random, or were allowed to choose the category themselves. The resulting concepts were then rated according to their originality and sensibility and were again classified into creative and noncreative categories.

As with creative inventions, subjects were more likely to discover a creative concept when the interpretive categories were specified randomly than when they were freely chosen. The use of unexpected categories evidently encourages the exploration of interpretive possibilities that were not considered when the preinventive structures were initially generated, which thereby enhances creative discovery.

An example of a creative concept obtained in these experiments is presented in Figure 10.10. This is the concept of "viral cancellation," which was discovered by one subject after having generated a preinventive form and having been given the category "medicine." The basic idea represented by the structure is that two viruses attempting to invade the same cell might possibly cancel one another, curing or preventing the disease. Many of the conceptual discoveries obtained in this study resembled those reported in some of the earlier, anecdotal accounts of creative insight, except that they had now been elicited in the context of a controlled experiment.

Of course, experts are normally much better than novices at developing interpretations of a given structure that would be judged by others in the field as being both novel and sensible. For example, Kekule's famous image of a snake would not have meant the same thing to someone who knew nothing about chemistry. Thus, although expert knowledge may be profitably suspended during the generation of preinventive structures, it is certainly useful when those structures are subsequently explored.

The studies already described represent only a small sample of the kinds of studies that have been and could be conducted in creative cognition. A number of other recent studies highlight other aspects of creative cognitive processes, such as the types of emergent properties and categories that can result from metaphor comprehension (Becker, in press; Glucksberg & Keysar, 1990; Tourangeau & Rips, 1991), the role of diagrams in scientific discovery and creativity (Cheng & Simon, 1995), and the importance of both distant and near analogies in historical and contemporary scientific reasoning (Dunbar, 1997; Gentner et al., 1997). These and other recent efforts show how it is possible to study creative thinking using the general methods of cognitive science. In particular, they show that people can often make

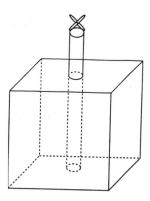

Figure 10.10. The concept of "viral cancellation," an example of conceptual interpretations of preinventive structures, represented using a tube, cross, and cube. The idea is that two viruses attempting to invade a cell may cancel one another, curing or preventing the disease. From Finke (1990).

genuine creative discoveries, under laboratory conditions, using processes and structures that have been studied in more traditional areas of cognitive science. They also suggest how traditional theories in cognitive science can be applied to creativity and how findings obtained in these more creative contexts can then raise new issues about basic cognitive processes.

RESOLVING CONTROVERSIES REGARDING THE NATURE OF CREATIVITY

Studies on creative cognition can also help to resolve some classic controversies surrounding the nature of creativity. In this section, we consider three of these controversies and how they might be addressed in creative cognition research.

Goal-Oriented Versus Exploratory Creativity

Is it better to have clear goals or problems in mind when trying to come up with creative ideas, or is it better to generate creative ideas first, and then consider their implications? On the one hand, there is evidence that creative insights normally arise when people are focused on particular problems (e.g., Bowers et al., 1990; Kaplan & Simon, 1990). On the other hand, there is evidence that creativity is enhanced when one adopts the more general, "problem-finding" attitude of trying to discover interesting issues and possibilities (e.g., Bransford & Stein, 1984; Getzels & Csikszentmihalyi, 1976).

In creative cognition, it becomes evident that this is not an either/or question. The relative merits of keeping particular goals in mind may depend on many factors, including whether or not a person has already generated a preinventive structure, whether the problem is close to being solved or is not yet fully formulated, and whether the knowledge that would be accessed in meeting the goals is abstract or specific. Studies in creative cognition can therefore help to identify those situations where goal-oriented approaches would be more successful and those where more open, exploratory approaches would be more successful.

Domain-Specific Versus Universal Creativity Skills

Are there general creativity skills that one can master, or does creativity tend to be restricted to particular tasks or domains? As mentioned previously, there is considerable evidence that creative performance is tied to expertise in a particular field, which enables the person to retrieve relevant information and to recognize when a new idea is likely to be valid or significant (e.g., Clement, 1989; Langley, Simon, Bradshaw, & Zytkow, 1987; Perkins, 1981; Weisberg, 1986). However, others have proposed that there are broad, creativity skills that can be acquired and applied across many types of problems and situations (Finke, 1990, 1995; Guilford, 1968; Koestler, 1964).

Studies of creative cognition suggest that both positions are partly right. Knowing how to efficiently explore and interpret a preinventive structure clearly depends on experience and expertise. However, as suggested by studies on creative concepts and inventions, certain broad, creativity skills very likely exist. For example, the same, general methods can be used to discover a new type of appliance, a new form of transportation, or a new concept in medicine. Expert knowledge may be most useful when applied in conjunction with general principles for generating and exploring preinventive structures.

Structured Versus Unstructured Creativity

Are creative insights normally derived from existing cognitive structures and representations, or are they chanced upon arbitrarily? Again, the field of creativity has been divided on this issue. According to one position, randomness plays an important role in creativity, leading to novel variations in thinking and allowing one to depart from conventional patterns (e.g., Bateson, 1979; Findlay & Lumsden, 1988; Johnson-Laird, 1988). According to another position, creative discovery is systematic and organized and is based on highly structured processes (e.g., Perkins, 1981; Ward, 1994; Weisberg, 1986).

Again, the creative cognition approach makes it clear that this is not an either/or question. Rather, the methods of creative cognition permit one to determine the relative roles that randomness and structure play in creative discovery. Studies on exemplar generation and design fixation show that creative imagination is a highly structured activity, and is thus not an arbitrary process or one that results simply from random associations among ideas. Random selection of components or interpretive categories can, however, enhance creativity by forcing one to abandon conventional ways of exploring and interpreting preinventive structures.

CONCLUSIONS

We have proposed that creative cognition represents a natural extension of contemporary work in cognitive science to the domain of creative thinking. The generative and exploratory processes that play key roles in creative cognition have already been investigated in many noncreative contexts, and by studying them in more creative contexts they can provide new insights into the nature of creativity, its underlying mechanisms, and how creativity can be enhanced.

In addition to helping clarify the nature of creative thinking, creative cognition also raises new, empirical questions for traditional areas of cognitive science. For instance, studies on creative imagination suggest new issues that could be explored in mental imagery and problem solving, such as the role that preinventive structures might play in representing graphic information or solving geometric problems. Findings from studies on creative exemplar generation have implications for current research on how people form new conceptual categories. Findings from studies on design fixation suggest new issues that could be explored in traditional work on information retrieval and interference. Research on creative cognition can thus make useful contributions to current studies in cognitive science and vice versa.

In conclusion, our main purpose has been to demonstrate how creativity can be studied using the methods of cognitive science and to propose that it is now time to accept creativity as a legitimate part of this field. Just as behaviorism helped to legitimize the study of behavior, and cognitive psychology helped to legitimize the study of the mind, our hope is that creative cognition will help to legitimize the study of the creative mind.

REFERENCES

Amabile, T. M. (1983). *The social psychology of creativity.* New York: Springer-Verlag.

Ashcraft, M. H. (1978). Property norms for typical and atypical items from 17 categories: A description and discussion. *Memory & Cognition, 6,* 227–232.

Barsalou, L. W. (1983). Ad hoc categories. *Memory & Cognition, 11,* 211–227.

Barsalou, L. W. (1987). The instability of graded structure: Implications for the nature of concepts. In U. Neisser (Ed.), *Concepts and conceptual development: Ecological and intellectual factors in categorization* (pp. 101–140). Cambridge University Press.

Barsalou, L. W. (1991). Deriving categories to achieve goals. In G. H. Bower (Ed.), *The psychology of learning and motivation: Advances in research and theory* (Vol. 27, 1–64). New York: Academic.

Basala, G. (1988). *The evolution of technology.* Cambridge University Press.

Bateson, G. (1979). *Mind and nature.* London: Wildwood House.

Baughman, W. A., & Mumford, M. D. (1995). Process-analytic models of creative capacities: Operations influencing the combination and reorganization processes. *Creativity Research Journal, 8,* 37–62.

Becker, A. H. (in press). Emergent and common features influence metaphor interpretation. *Metaphor and Symbolic Activity.*

Bowers, K. S., Regehr, G., Balthazard, C., & Parker, K. (1990). Intuition in the context of discovery. *Cognitive Psychology, 22,* 72–109.

Bransford, J. D., & Stein, B. S. (1984). *The ideal problem solver.* New York: Freeman.

Cacciari, C., Levorato, M. C., & Cicogna, P. (1997). Imagination at work: Conceptual and linguistic creativity in children. In T. B. Ward, S. M. Smith, & J. Vaid (Eds.), *Creative thought: An investigation of conceptual structures and processes* (pp. 145–177). Washington, DC: American Psychological Association.

Cheng, P. C.-H, & Simon, H. A. (1995). Scientific discovery and creative reasoning with diagrams. In S. M. Smith, T. B. Ward, & R. A. Finke (Eds.), *The creative cognition-approach* (pp. 205–228). Cambridge, MA: MIT Press.

Chomsky, N. (1972). *Language and mind.* New York: Harcourt, Brace, Jovanovich.

Clement, J. (1989). Learning via model construction and criticism: Protocol evidence on sources of creativity in science. In G. Glover, R. Ronning, and C. Reynolds (Eds.), *Handbook of creativity: Assessment, theory and research* (pp. 341–381). New York: Plenum.

Cohen, B., & Murphy, G. L. (1994). Models of enoncents. *Cognitive Science, 8,* 27–58.

Condoor, S. S., Brock, H. R., & Burger, C. P. (1993, June). *Innovation through early recognition of critical design parameters.* Paper presented at the meeting of the American Society for Engineering Education, Urbana, IL.

Donaldson, S. R. (1992). *The real story.* New York: Bantam.

Dunbar, K. (1997). How scientists think: On-line creativity and conceptual change in science. In T. B. Ward, S. M. Smith, & J. Vaid (Eds.), *Creative thought: An investigation of conceptual structures and processes* (pp. 461–494). Washington, DC: American Psychological Association.

Eysenck, H. J. (1995). *Genius: The natural history of creativity.* Cambridge University Press.

Findlay, C. S., & Lumsden, C. J. (1988). The creative mind: Toward an evolutionary theory of discovery and invention. *Journal of Social and Biological Structures, 11,* 3–55.

Finke, R. A. (1990). *Creative imagery: Discoveries and inventions in visualization.* Hillsdale, NJ: Erlbaum.

Finke, R. A. (1995). Creative realism. In S. M. Smith, T. B. Ward, & R. A. Finke (Eds.), *The creative cognition approach* (pp. 301–326). Cambridge, MA: MIT Press.

Finke, R. A., & Slayton, K. (1988). Explorations of creative visual synthesis in mental imagery. *Memory & Cognition, 16,* 252–257.

Finke, R. A., Ward, T. B., & Smith, S. M. (1992). *Creative cognition: Theory, research, and applications.* Cambridge, MA: MIT Press.

Freeman, J. (1993). *Mark Tansey.* San Francisco: Chronicle Books.

Gagne, C. L., & Shoben, E. J. (1997). The influence of thematic relations on the comprehension of non-predicating combinations. *Journal of Experimental Psychology: Learning, Memory, and Cognition, 23,* 71–87.

Gentner, D. (1989). The mechanisms of analogical learning. In S. Vosniadou & A. Ortony (Eds.), *Similarity and analogical reasoning* (pp. 199–241). Cambridge University Press.

Gentner, D., Brem, S., Ferguson, R., Wolff, P., Markman, A. B., & Forbus, K. (1997). Analogy and creativity in the works of Johannes Keplar. In T. B. Ward, S. M. Smith, & J. Vaid (Eds.), *Creative thought: An investigation of conceptual structures and processes* (pp. 403–459). Washington, DC: American Psychological Association.

Getzels, J. W., & Csikszentmihalyi, M. (1976). *The creative vision: A longitudinal study of problem finding in art.* New York: Wiley.

Glucksberg, S., & Keysar, B. (1990). Understanding metaphorical comparisons: Beyond similarity. *Psychological Review, 97,* 3–18.

Guilford, J. P. (1968). *Intelligence, creativity, and their educational implications.* San Diego: Knapp.

Hammer, M., & Champy, J. (1993). *Reengineering the corporation.* New York: HarperBusiness.

Hampton, J. A. (1987). Inheritance of attributes in natural concept conjunctions. *Memory & Cognition, 15,* 55–71.

Hampton, J. A. (1997). Emergent attributes in combined concepts. In T. B. Ward, S. M. Smith, & J. Vaid (Eds.), *Creative thought: An investigation of conceptual structures and processes* (pp. 83–110). Washington, DC: American Psychological Association.

Hershman, D. J., & Lieb, J. (1988). *The key to genius.* Buffalo, NY: Prometheus.

Holyoak, K. J., & Thagard, P. R. (1995). *Mental leaps.* Cambridge, MA: MIT Press.

Jansson, D. G., and Smith, S. M. (1991). Design fixation. *Design Studies, 12,* 3–11.

Johnson-Laird, P. N. (1983). *Mental models: Towards a cognitive science of language, inference, and consciousness.* Cambridge, MA: Harvard University Press.

Johnson-Laird, P. N. (1988). *The computer and the mind: An introduction to cognitive science.* Cambridge, MA: Harvard University Press.

Kaplan, C. A., & Simon, H. A. (1990). In search of insight. *Cognitive Psychology, 22,* 374–419.

Karmiloff-Smith, A. (1990). Constraints on representational change: Evidence from children's drawing. *Cognition, 34,* 57–83.

Koestler, A. (1964). *The act of creation.* New York: Macmillan.

Lubart, T. I., & Sternberg, R. J. (1995). An investment approach to creativity. In S. M. Smith, T. B. Ward, & R. A. Finke (Eds.), *The creative cognition approach* (pp. 269–302). Cambridge, MA: MIT Press.

Luchins, A. S., & Luchins, E. H. (1959). *Rigidity of behavior.* Eugene: University of Oregon Press.

Markman, A. B., & Gentner, D. (1993). Splitting the differences: A structural alignment view of similarity. *Journal of Memory and Language, 32,* 517–535.

Marsh, R. L., Landau, J. D., & Hicks, J. L. (1996). How examples may (and may not) constrain creativity. *Memory & Cognition, 24,* 669–680.

Mednick, S. A. (1962). The associative basis of the creative process. *Psychological Review, 69,* 220–232.

Metcalfe, J. (1986). Feelings of knowing in memory and problem solving. *Journal of Experimental Psychology: Learning, Memory, and Cognition, 12,* 288–294.

Metcalfe, J., & Wiebe, D. (1987). Intuition in insight and non-insight problem solving. *Memory & Cognition, 15,* 238–246.

Mobley, M. I., Doares, L. M., & Mumford, M. D. (1992). Process analytic models of creative capacities: Evidence for the combination and reorganization process. *Creativity Research Journal, 5,* 125–155.

Murphy, G. L. (1988). Comprehending complex concepts. *Cognitive Science, 12,* 529–562.

Novick, L. (1988). Analogical transfer, problem similarity, and expertise. *Journal of Experimental Psychology: Learning, Memory, and Cognition, 14,* 510–520.

Ortony, A. (1979). Beyond literal similarity. *Psychological Review, 86,* 161–180.

Perkins, D. N. (1981). *The mind's best work.* Cambridge, MA: Harvard University Press.

Pinker, S. (1984). *Language learnability and language development.* Cambridge, MA: Harvard University Press.

Rips, L. J. (1995). The current status of research on concept combination. *Mind and Language, 10,* 72–104.

Rosch, E., & Mervis, C. B. (1975). Family resemblances: Studies in the internal structure of categories. *Cognitive Psychology, 7,* 573–605.

Rosch, E., Mervis, C. B., Gray, W. D., Johnson, D. M., & Boyes-Braem, P. (1976). Basic objects in natural categories. *Cognitive Psychology, 8,* 382–439.

Rossman, J. (1964). *Industrial creativity: The psychology of the inventor.* New Hyde Park, NY: University Books.

Rothenberg, A. (1979). *The emerging goddess.* Chicago: University of Chicago Press.

Rothenberg, A. (1995). Creative cognitive processes in Kekule's discovery of the structure of the benzene molecule. *American Journal of Psychology, 108,* 419–438.

Runco, M. A., & Chand, I. (1995). Cognition and creativity. *Educational Psychology Review, 7,* 243–267.

Schooler, J. W., & Melcher, J. (1995). The ineffibility of insight. In S. M. Smith, T. B. Ward, & R. A. Finke (Eds.), *The creative cognition approach* (pp. 97–133). Cambridge, MA: MIT Press.

Shepard, R. N. (1978). Externalization of mental images and the act of creation. In B. S. Randhawa and W. E. Coffman (Eds.), *Visual learning, thinking, and communication* (pp. 133–189). New York: Academic.

Shepard, R. N., & Feng, C. (1972). A chronometric study of mental paper folding. *Cognitive Psychology, 3,* 228–243.

Sifonis, C. M. (1995). Scene schemas and creativity: Examining the influence of schema based knowledge on the creative process. Unpublished master's thesis, Texas A&M University, College Station, TX.

Simonton, D. K. (1994). *Greatness: Who makes history and why.* New York: Guilford.

Simonton, D. K. (1997). Creativity in personality, developmental, and social psychology: Any links with cognitive psychology. In T. B. Ward, S. M. Smith, & J. Vaid (Eds.), *Creative thought: An investigation of conceptual structures and processes* (pp. 309–324). Washington, DC: American Psychological Association.

Smith, E. E., & Osherson, D. N. (1984). Conceptual combination with prototype concepts. *Cognitive Science, 8,* 337–361.

Smith, S. M. (1979). Remembering in and out of context. *Journal of Experimental Psychology: Human Learning and Memory, 5,* 460–471.

Smith, S. M. (1995). Fixation, incubation, and insight in memory and creative thinking. In S. M. Smith, T. B. Ward, & R. A. Finke (Eds.), *The creative cognition approach* (pp. 135–156). Cambridge, MA: MIT Press.

Smith, S. M., & Blankenship, S. E. (1991). Incubation and the persistence of fixation in problem solving. *American Journal of Psychology, 104,* 61–87.

Smith, S. M., & Tindell, D. R. (1997). Memory blocks in word fragment completion caused by involuntary retrieval of orthographically similar primes. *Journal of Experimental Psychology: Learning, Memory and Cognition, 23,* 355–370.

Smith, S. M., & Vela, E. (1991). Incubated reminiscence effects. *Memory & Cognition, 19,* 168–176.

Smith, S. M., Ward, T. B., & Finke, R. A. (Eds.), (1995). *The creative cognition approach.* Cambridge, MA: MIT Press.

Smith, S. M., Ward, T. B., & Schumacher, J. S. (1993). Constraining effects of examples in a creative generation task. *Memory & Cognition, 21,* 837–845.

Sternberg, R. J., & Lubart, T. I. (1991). An investment theory of creativity and its development. *Human Development, 34,* 1–31.

Thagard, P. (1997). Coherent and creative conceptual combinations. In T. B. Ward, S. M. Smith, & J. Vaid (Eds.), *Creative thought: An investigation of conceptual structures and processes* (pp. 129–141). Washington, DC: American Psychological Association.

Thompson, A. L., & Klatzky, R. L. (1978). Studies of visual synthesis: Integration of fragments into forms. *Journal of Experimental Psychology: Human Perception and Performance, 4,* 244–263.

Tourangeau, R., & Rips, L. (1991). Interpreting and evaluating metaphors. *Journal of Memory and Language, 30,* 452–472.

Tversky, B., & Hemenway, K. (1984). Objects, parts, and categories. *Journal of Experimental Psychology: General, 113,* 169–193.

Ward, T. B. (1993, November). *The effect of processing approach on category exemplar generation.* Paper presented at the meeting of the Psychonomic Society, Washington, DC.

Ward, T. B. (1994). Structured imagination: The role of conceptual structure in exemplar generation. *Cognitive Psychology, 27,* 1–40.

Ward, T. B. (1995). What's old about new ideas? In S. M. Smith, T. B. Ward, & R. A. Finke (Eds.), *The creative cognition approach* (pp. 157–178). Cambridge, MA: MIT Press.

Ward, T. B., Finke, R. A., & Smith, S. M. (1995). *Creativity and the mind: Discovering the genius within.* New York: Plenum.

Ward, T. B., & Sifonis, C. M. (1997). Task demands and generative thinking: What changes and what remains the same? *Journal of Creative Behavior, 31,* 245–259.

Ward, T. B., Smith, S. M., & Vaid, J. (1997). Conceptual structures and processes in creative thought. In T. B. Ward, S. M. Smith, & J. Vaid (Eds.), *Creative thought: An investigation of conceptual structures and processes* (pp. 1–27). Washington, DC: American Psychological Association.

Weisberg, R. W. (1995). Case studies of creative thinking: Reproduction versus restructuring in the real world. In S. M. Smith, T. B. Ward, & R. A. Finke (Eds.), *The creative cognition approach* (pp. 53–72). Cambridge, MA: MIT Press.

Weisberg, R. W. (1986). *Creativity, genius and other myths.* New York: Freeman.

Weisberg, R. W., & Alba, J. W. (1981). An examination of the alleged role of "fixation" in the solution of several "insight" problems. *Journal of Experimental Psychology: General, 110,* 169–192.

Wilkenfeld, M. J. (1995). Conceptual combination: Does similarity predict emergence? Unpublished master's thesis, Texas A&M University, College Station, TX.

Wisniewski, E. J. (1996). Construal and similarity in conceptual combination. *Journal of Memory and Language, 35,* 434–453.

Wisniewski, E. J. (1997). Conceptual combination: Possibilities and aesthetics. In T. B. Ward, S. M. Smith, & J. Vaid (Eds.), *Creative thought: An investigation of conceptual structures and processes* (pp. 51–81). Washington, DC: American Psychological Association.

11 From Case Studies to Robust Generalizations: An Approach to the Study of Creativity

EMMA POLICASTRO AND HOWARD GARDNER

TWO APPROACHES TO SOCIAL SCIENCE

There are two distinct bases on which contributions in the social sciences can be constructed. The first can be termed the "cumulative" approach. Here, one takes as a point of departure the most closely related scientific work done by previous theoreticians and researchers and attempts to build upon it. The contrasting approach can be called the "phenomenon" approach. Here one begins with the clearest instance of the phenomenon in general and attempts to construct a social-scientific explanation, and program of research, based upon a thorough understanding of the phenomenon.

The study of intelligence provides a ready example of these two approaches. In the cumulative approach, researchers begin with earlier attempts to operationalize intelligence – typically through standardized tests – and then they either correlate psychometric intelligence with some other variable of interest (say, creativity or success at work) or vary the actual tests in some way. In the phenomenon approach, the investigator begins with an unambiguous example of intelligent behavior and then tries to derive social-scientific principles therefrom. Such otherwise diverse instances as Wertheimer's (1945) Gestalt examination of Einstein's thinking process and de Groot's (1965) cognitive approach to chess players reflect the latter approach.

These two approaches have also been manifest in studies of creativity. While there have been earlier efforts to look at creative thought and production (Freud, 1958; Ghiselin, 1952; H.A. Murray, 1938), sustained psychological work began only with the postwar studies of Getzels and Jackson (1962), Guilford (1950), Torrance (1962), and their colleagues. This work was strongly influenced by the psychometric tradition of intelligence testing. The essential idea of this approach is that creative thought involves divergent thinking; the individual who is able to produce many relevant but noncanonical associations to a stimulus (e.g., geometrical form, houehold object, story title) in a short period of time is judged to be creative, and this capacity is thought to be at least partially independent of psychometric intelligence. Workers in this tradition accepted the basic operationalization and attempted to construct a research domain on that foundation.

While the psychometric approach to intelligence is generally considered to be one of psychology's greatest success stories (Brown & Herrnstein, 1976), the same cannot be said about this cumulative approach to the study of creativity. While these measures are sufficiently reliable, their validity has never been adequately accepted, particularly once one transcends the "cocktail party" variety of creative production. Indeed, not only do high scorers fail to distinguish themselves in creations that society prizes, but the very "core" abilities that have been captured in the tests seem remote from the lengthy development of skills, and the risk-taking stance, that emerges from the study of lives of highly creative individuals.

As a result, a growing number of researchers have adopted one or another version of the phenomenon approach. John-Steiner (1985) has examined the records kept by individuals who are highly creative; Gruber (1981, 1982) has studied the scientific notebook of Darwin and the scientific trajectory of Piaget; Arnheim (1962) has elucidated the efforts of Picasso as he undertook one ambitious painting; Csikszentmihalyi (1996) has examined the later lives of nearly a hundred individuals who have been highly creative. Taking a more quantitative tack, Simonton (1994) has conducted dozens of historiometric studies: He has sought to answer long-standing questions about creativity through the judicious collection of historical data about the lives of unambiguously creative workers.

Our own work has been situated in between the phenomenon and the cumulative traditions. Like Gruber and Arnheim, we have begun with careful studies of the lives and works of highly creative individuals. These ranks have included artists (Pablo Picasso, T. S. Eliot, Igor Stravinsky, Virginia Woolf) and scientists (Freud, Einstein, Norman Geschwind, Carleton Gajdusek), as well as individuals from other domains (Gandhi). But in the course of carrying out these studies, we have been searching for principles, norms, and regularities, which move us in the direction of the historiometric laws pursued more directly by Simonton and by other researchers like Kroeber (1944) and Martindale (1990). In this way, we see ourselves as moving toward a cumulative stance (Gardner 1993a, 1997a, 1997b).

In what follows, we describe four of the principal characteristics of an approach that – in explicit contrast to the psychometric approach – begins with the phenomena of unambiguous creativity. We define a *creative individual* as a person whose works exert a significant effect upon the domain(s) in which that person works; correlatively, *creative works* are those that significantly influence future work in that domain. As will be apparent, we have been significantly affected by the "systems approach" of Csikszentmihalyi (1996; Chapter 16, this volume); creativity is seen not solely as the product of an individual mind, but rather as the result of a dynamic interaction among the creative *individual,* the *domain* in which he or she works, and the set of judges (or *field*) that assesses the quality of work(s) that have been executed. Following the description of our general approach, we conclude by citing some of the principal regularities – and contrasts – that have emerged from our phenomenon-based studies.

CHARACTERISTICS OF A PHENOMENON-BASED APPROACH

Holistic Involvement in Work

By stressing the term *holistic,* we challenge the notion of a "trivial pursuit" version of creativity. Creative talent entails a holistic involvement in a process that is highly complex, deeply meaningful to the person, usually prolonged, and demanding. Research into the lives of highly creative individuals shows that creators put enormous amounts of time and energy into their work, and that they tend to be totally involved in and obsessed about their métier (Gardner, 1993a; Gruber, 1981). Such individuals are well known for – consciously or unconsciously – taking their work with them all the time and wherever they go.

Consider Einstein, who could work on the same problem without interruption for hours and even days. Some of the topics that interested him remained on his mind for decades. For relaxation he turned to music and sailing, but often his work would continue during these moments as well; he usually had a notebook in his pocket so that he could jot down any idea that came to him. Once, after the theory of relativity had been put forth, he confessed to his colleague Wolfgang Pauli, "For the rest of my life I want to reflect on what light is" (quoted in Gardner, 1993a, p. 103).

Talented individuals generate creative work in the context of prolonged, meaningful, and intrinsically motivating pursuits, which demand total immersion. The other side of the coin is that they must leave many of the delights of personal and avocational pursuits aside for the sake of their mission. Einstein, for instance, conceded that much had to be given up to become the kind of scientist he wished to be. Only monomaniacs, he confessed to his friend Besso, made scientific discoveries.

Storr (1988) goes as far as to hold that major creativity is incompatible with normal family life. Analyzing the cases of Kant, Wittgenstein, and Newton, he observes that they showed "a lack of close involvement with other human beings" (p. 166). Storr contends that if these creators had had wives and families, "their achievements would have been impossible. For the higher reaches of abstraction demand long periods of solitude and intense concentration which are hard to find if a man is subject to the emotional demands of a spouse and children" (p. 166). The same case might be made for creative women like Martha Graham: According to a friend, "Martha felt that she must cut from her life all deep emotional involvements, all attachments, all comforts, even moments of leisure, and beyond that, love involving family and children. She gave everything to her work, withheld nothing, kept nothing apart. She was obsessed" (Gardner, 1993a, p. 300).

To be sure, creative masters such as Einstein, Freud, Gandhi, and Picasso did have wives and children. Their relationships to their families, however, entailed problems. Einstein, for instance, was quite happy to be on his own from earliest life and did not crave companionship. This lack of craving for another person may well explain why neither of his marriages was a success and why his relations to his two sons were also unsatisfactory. In working out problems, Einstein once recalled, "I lived in solitude in the country and noticed how the monotony of quiet life stimulates the creative mind" (Gardner, 1993a, p. 103). It is well known that Gandhi had poor relations with his wife and children; and we know that Freud went through some periods of sharp loneliness, especially preceding his major breakthroughs. Both Gandhi and Freud unilaterally decided to relinquish any kind of sexual relationships when they were still young – apparently for the sake of their broader missions.

Some extroverted creators, such as Picasso, have many social and romantic relationships. But if one takes a closer look into their private lives, such individuals tend not to get deeply involved with anyone, even in the midst of extensive social interactions. Picasso, for instance, had many friends and lovers throughout his life, but he always showed an egocentric behavioral pattern: He could be perfectly charming, gracious, and generous when he wanted to, but at the same time he stood prepared to sacrifice anyone and everyone who stood in the way of his work, all too often showing an arrogant disregard for others.

Gardner (1993a) observed that the major creators he studied became so caught up in the pursuit of their work mission that they sacrificed the possibility of a rounded personal existence. In Gardner's view, they forged a bargain, or Faustian arrangement: In exchange for the preservation of their unusual gifts, they would sacrifice both others and their own non-work-related activities.

It is too early to tell whether such a Faustian bargain holds as a general pattern beyond the sample of recent creators studied by Gardner. We can confidently assert that creative masters take their work very seriously: Such individuals are continually engaged in facing major challenges, which they cannot solve superficially and which demand profound concentration and total immersion in the problem at hand. They do not seem to have much energy left for getting deeply involved with other people or other activities.

Serious creativity is not a pursuit that one works on from nine to five on weekdays or something that one turns on and off at will. The question remains whether and to what extent some aspects of the holistic pattern hold for individuals who are also creative, but in a more limited sense, such as the successful entrepreneur, the original strategist, and the R&D inventor.

In all likelihood, the magnitude of the involvement should be proportional to the magnitude of the task at hand, and limited forms of creativity probably do not entail the extreme absorption – at the expense of normal social interactions – that major creativity entails.

Links to Specific Domains

We know that creative responses of wide and enduring impact are linked or infused into specific domains, involving different kinds of skills, distinct types of knowledge, and a significant period of specialized training (Gardner, 1993b). The term *domain* here refers to "bodies of disciplined knowledge, which have been structured culturally, and which can be acquired, practiced, and advanced through the act of creating" (Li & Gardner, 1993, p. 4). This definition includes the arts, crafts, sciences, and other professions.

A domain-centered analysis challenges the psychometric notion that creativity is an abstract property that some individuals have regardless of their previous experience or the domain that is under consideration. Research shows that even creative masters need a significant period of specialized training and practice in a particular cultural domain before they can make any significant breakthrough (Bloom, 1985). Mozart, for example, who was a child prodigy from an early age, had been composing for at least a decade before he could regularly produce works that are considered worthy of inclusion in the repertory.

The relationship between creative talent and domain expertise has been consistently reported (Amabile, 1996). In a general sense, this connection has to hold true. Making a valuable contribution to any domain necessarily implies discerning what is important from what is not within that same domain (knowing *that*). It also implies a skillful use of the tools and techniques that are available and permissible in particular disciplines (knowing *how*).

On the other hand, some scholars conceive of creativity as a set of general traits that can be applied to various domains regardless of expertise (Torrance, 1962). There is some truth to this argument: Traits such as fluency, flexibility, and originality tend to be associated with innovative behavior in various domains. But creative responses of wide scope and scale do not arise "out of the blue." Individuals who generate these responses also tend to have high levels of expertise in the same domain or in related areas.

To be sure, creativity entails significant periods of specialized training: It takes approximately a decade for an individual to master a domain and to come to the level of technical expertise that is expected of an adult professional. And it can take up to a decade of experience, after this initial mastery, before anyone can make an extraordinary creative achievement (Gardner, 1993a). As instances of such achievements, we have in mind such works as Einstein's theory of relativity, Gandhi's beliefs and practices of *satyagraha,* and the breakthroughs captured in Picasso's *Les desmoiselles d'Avignon,* Stravinsky's *Le sacre du printemps,* Eliot's *The Waste Land,* and Graham's *Frontier.*

The following question remains: Why do domain-specific constraints lead some experts to generate creative responses, while the "same" domain-specific constraints may lead other experts to generate performances that are competent, but not creative?

Possibly there are individual differences in cognitive style, which influence the way we encode, organize, and retrieve information. Thus, even if two subjects are experts in the same domain, they might each be responding to a different set of subjectively constructed constraints. It may also be that potential creators are energized by the experience of challenging the accepted norms, while experts are content to pursue accepted practices (Csik-szentmihalyi, 1990; Gardner, 1997a; Sternberg & Lubart, 1991).

Generative Cognitive Style

Psychometricians hold that divergent thinking and ideational fluency are the essential features that distinguish creative from noncreative people. Nevertheless, the psychometric notions of divergent thinking and ideational fluency fall short of distinguishing imagination from fantasy, relevant from irrelevant material, and contextually valid from rambling associations.

In our view, creative talent involves a *generative cognitive style,* which entails the following three components: (a) imagination, (b) sense of domain relevance, and (c) intrapersonal intelligence. Imagination leads to originality; sense of domain relevance leads to high quality; and intrapersonal intelligence checks illusory and/or emotional interferences in the process of constructing a novel but appropriate representation.

IMAGINATION. Imagination is a form of playful analogical thinking that draws on previous experiences, but combines them in unusual ways, generating new patterns of meaning. Considerable evidence demonstrates that a playful approach to the task at hand increases the likelihood of producing creative results (Amabile, 1983; Bruner, Jolly, & Sylva, 1976). Obviously, logical thinking with its rigorous rules does not leave room for free play, while imaginative thinking does allow for playful associations to occur within contextual constraints, leading to the generation of contextually valid patterns of meaning.

The relevance of imagination has been noted by many. In Einstein's words, for instance, "to raise new questions, new possibilities, to regard old problems from a new angle, requires imagination and makes real advance in science" (Jay, 1989, p. 40). Paradoxically, however, in the history of Western thought, "meaning, respectable meaning, was identified with the logical thinking of humankind, while human imaginative thought was identified with the animistic, the irrational, the illogical, the instinctual, the repressible, and ultimately the dangerous" (E. L. Murray, 1986, p. 235).

In our view, one problem lies in the fact that many scholars use the word *imagination* as synonymous with *fantasy,* generating unwarranted confusion. We suggest the following distinction: Imagination should denote the generation of patterns of meaning that are contextually valid and that serve an adaptive function towards reality;[1] fantasy should denote subjective expression of needs, conflicts, and wishes. Fantasy also serves an adaptive function in that it contributes to the subject's intrapsychic equilibrium, in the Freudian sense. Here we stress that imagination generates potentially creative ideas, while fantasy generates illusions.

SENSE OF DOMAIN RELEVANCE. The second component of a generative cognitive style is an accurate sense of domain relevance; individuals who produce creative ideas also seem to have a flair for distinguishing what is important from what is not.

According to Boden (1990), major creators seem to "have a better sense of domain relevance than the rest of us." In other words, they appear to be "guided by powerful domain-relevant principles on to promising pathways which we cannot even see" (p. 254). Similarly, the major scientists studied by Davidson and Sternberg (1984) outperformed their less able peers at sifting out relevant information, among other things.

Autobiographical testimonies also support this claim. Mathematician Henri Poincaré, for instance, reported that "sterile combinations do not even present themselves to the mind of the inventor" (1952, p. 36). Einstein is quoted as saying, "In physics I soon learned to scent out that which was able to lead to fundamentals and to turn aside from everything else, from the multitude of things that clutter up the mind and divert it from the essential" (quoted in Gardner, 1993a, p. 104).

INTRAPERSONAL INTELLIGENCE. The third component of a generative cognitive style is intrapersonal intelligence (Gardner, 1993a, 1993b); this capacity helps in making subtle distinctions among cognitive and emotional processes, as one means of understanding and guiding one's own creative behavior.

The inception of new ideas involves a great deal of implicit cognitive processing, which the creative person must be able to understand and manage in subtle ways. In fact, distinguishing the tacit inception of new ideas from other associative patterns – which may be implicit, but misleading – entails a finely honed introspective capacity. Only this introspection allows a person to make subtle distinctions between productive imagination and mere fantasy, intuitive tendencies and emotional reactions, creative intuitions and intuitive misconceptions.

A subject may assert confidently, "This will work out fine." Nevertheless, this person may be in fact expressing an illusion, a wish, and/or a feeling, rather than a creative intuition; without intrapersonal intelligence, he or she may be unable to tell the difference. In other words, intrapersonal intelligence may help us to distinguish among "the lunatic, the lover, and the poet" inside ourselves, since they may appear to be "of imagination all compact," as Shakespeare pointed out (*Midsummer Night's Dream*, Act V, sc. 1).

In sum, the kind of knowledge associated with high levels of expertise is necessary but not sufficient for explaining creative responses. Talented individuals also appear to have a generative cognitive style, entailing a powerful imagination, an accurate sense of domain relevance, and a fine intrapersonal intelligence. Imagination leads to originality; sense of domain relevance leads to high quality; and intrapersonal intelligence checks illusory and/or emotional interferences in the process of constructing a novel representation.

Developmental Emphases: Macroscopic and Microscopic

Two kinds of development are significant for understanding major creative achievements: *macrodevelopment,* the life-long development of a "network of enterprises" (Gruber, 1981), and *microdevelopment,* the developmental sequence of representational changes that takes place in making a particular innovative work "from private intuitions to public symbol systems" (Gardner & Nemirovsky, 1991).

MACRODEVELOPMENT. The formulation of major works can take decades and requires explanatory concepts that can encompass a wide time course. Gruber and his colleagues (Wallace & Gruber, 1989) have conducted significant research in this area, paying careful attention to the way in which generative ideas and sets of ideas evolve and deepen over significant periods of time.

On the basis of such studies, Wallace and Gruber (1990) maintain that all creative work of a high order presupposes three "evolving systems": those of knowledge, purpose, and affect. While these systems are only "loosely coupled," their interaction over time helps one understand the ebb and flow of creative activity over the course of a productive human life. To describe the pattern of work in the life of a creative individual, Gruber and his colleagues adopt the organizing concept of a "network of enterprise." As Gruber (1989) expresses it:

The network of enterprise provides a structure that organizes a complex life. In the course of a single day or week, the activities of the person may appear, from the outside, as a bewildering miscellany. But the person is not disoriented or dazzled. He or she can readily map each activity onto one or another enterprise. (p. 13)

In an extensive study of Darwin, and in smaller-scale studies of other scientists and artists, Gruber and his colleagues have documented the evolution of ideas over long periods of time. Considering the long-term development of Darwin's ideas, Gruber notes the following five features: (a) the preoccupation with and return to certain major themes, such as man, mind, materialism, variation, and transformation; (b) the intricate and extensive network of enterprises in which Darwin engages, reflected in his decades-long interest in such diverse topics as barnacles, earthworms, geological strata, and emotional expression; (c) certain images of wide scope that permeate Darwin's work, such as that of nature as a tangled bank, or the diversity of species as a branching tree; (d) the broad goals that energize and guide the choice of daily activities and larger-scale projects; and (e) Darwin's keen affective tie to his projects, which is traced to his early love for all natural things (Gruber, 1981).

MICRODEVELOPMENT. In addition to the macrodevelopmental nature of such "evolving systems," researchers have identified a microdevelopmental sequence that major creators follow in making specific works. Talented individuals seem to have an intuitive sense, as they commence their creative work in earnest, about what their final product will be like (Arnheim, 1962; Gardner & Nemirovsky, 1991; Gruber 1981; Holmes, 1985); it usually takes them much time and effort to develop these initial intuitions into fully articulated final products. Such creative intuitions can be viewed as early steps in a developmental sequence of representational changes from vague, syncretic, and implicit forms of knowledge toward more differentiated, integrated, and explicit ones.

Relevant examples of such a developmental sequence are Picasso's creation of *Guernica,* Darwin's formulation of the principle of natural selection, and Cantor's vision of the completed infinite. In what follows we discuss the cases of Darwin and Cantor.

Gruber (1981) conducted detailed analyses of Darwin's notebooks, finding that Darwin appeared to have implicitly prefigured some of his most relevant ideas in his early writings. For example, Darwin claimed that his insight into the principle of natural selection came from reading Malthus's *Essay on Population.* But according to Gruber, "This idea occurs in various forms in his notebooks before he read Malthus" (p. 118). Although Darwin might not have integrated these hunches into a coherent representation before he read Malthus, they nevertheless were related to the development of his thinking, as can be gathered from observing the sequence of his notes (Gruber, 1981).

Piaget puzzled over the fact that, "even in a creator of the greatness of Darwin" (quoted in Gruber, 1981, p. viii), the passage from the implicit to the explicit is extremely slow. According to Piaget, this delay implies that "making things explicit leads to the construction of a structure which is partially new, even though it is virtually contained in those structures which preceded it" (p. viii). In a general sense, some of Darwin's most relevant ideas were intuitively present in his thought and represented in his early writings; in a more specific sense, however, it also took him much time and effort to develop this tacit knowledge into a fully differentiated and integrated theoretical structure.

Gardner and Nemirovsky (1991) conducted detailed analyses of the creative processes of Sigmund Freud (as psychologist) and Georg Cantor (as mathematician). The authors discerned analogous processes for both creators, who started off with early private intuitions about the realms they sought to explain and ended up with clear symbolic (and public) articulations. As an example, the complex process that Cantor followed in order to articulate his intuitive vision of the completed infinite was described by Gardner and Nemirovsky (1991) as follows:

> The construction of the new intuition was far from linear; he set forth in many directions, some of which shed light, others of which were quickly abandoned. Successive articulations (in the form of definitions, symbols, statements, etc.) of this intuition allowed him to envision new areas to explore, and also to transcend the private sphere towards more publicly enunciated views. We can sense the tension which Cantor felt between intuition and rigorous proof as we consider three phases of his creative process: construction of local coherences, devising and revising symbols, and formulating a new thema. (p. 6)

In sum, creative masters seem to have an intuitive sense, as they begin their creative work, about what their final product will be like. But intuition is not the whole story. The cognitive sequence followed by major creators like Picasso, Darwin, Freud, and Cantor proves extremely complex. Early intuitions require the support of other cognitive processes and long periods of persistent work before they can be successfully articulated into valuable final products.

Creative masters are continually engaged in complex developmental processes that evolve in the midst of open-ended endeavors. Such individuals define new problems, devise original products or responses, and discover unknown (or neglected) sets of issues that call for fresh exploration. Much must unfold before the field can behold a final work and deem it creative.

PATTERNS OF CREATIVITY

If any area of human psychology cautions against premature generalization, it is the area of creativity research. Creative individuals and creative products are defined by their unusual nature; and so the very generalization that emerges from the study of one group of creativity individuals, or creative contexts, is at risk of being undermined by the next set of phenomenally based studies.

Our own studies have brought out some unsuspected differences in types of creativity, even as they have pointed out some apparent regularities. We review each of these tentative findings.

Kinds of Creative Behaviors

When we first began our studies, we expected – in line with much earlier work – that all creative behavior might be thought of as some kind of problem solving (Newell & Simon, 1972). We noted Getzel's and Csikszentmihalyi's (1976) important demonstration that creators can be distinguished as much by their ability to find and pose new problems as by the capacity to solve problems posed by someone else. We have found, however, that it is useful to conceptualize at least five different forms of creative behavior.

First, some creators tend to engage in the *solution of problems,* a task that can be highly creative when the problem is important and has not yet been solved. One modern example is the discovery of the structure of the double helix by James Watson and Francis Crick; another is the recent proof of Fermat's last theorem.

Second, some creators prefer to engage in *theory building.* This activity can be highly creative when the creator constructs a set of concepts that account for existing data and organizes them in a way that sheds new light on – and points to new directions in – the domain in which he or she works. Einstein's, Freud's, and Darwin's principal scientific activities entailed theory building.

Third, many artists and inventors engage in the creation of some kind of a permanent work in a symbolic system. That work can then be examined, performed, exhibited, and evaluated by others who are knowledgeable in the domain. There is typically a distance between the occasion of creation and the times when the work is encountered and evaluated. Noted examples include Eliot's *The Waste Land,* Picasso's *Guernica,* or Beethoven's *Eroica* symphony.

A fourth kind of creative activity is the *performance of a ritualized work.* Some works can only be apprehended in performance, and the creativity inheres chiefly in the particular characteristics of the specific performance. The prototypical example is the performance of a dance by Martha Graham. While the dance can in principle be notated and performed by someone else, in fact Graham's creativity adhered significantly in her unique capacity to perform in a distinctive and valued way. In art forms where notations do not exist, or where the notations fail to capture important aspects of the performance, the performance *is* the work.

The fifth kind of creative activity involves *high-stake performances.* Typically, an individual actually carries out a series of actions in public in order to bring about some kind of social or political change. Our prototypical instance here is the set of protests, fasts, and nonviolent confrontations engaged in by Gandhi and his followers. In contrast to ritualized artistic performances, where the steps can be worked out in advance, this performance is determinedly "high stake." It is not possible to work out the details of the performance in advance because much of it depends upon the reactions of the audience or the combatants. Other examples would include military engagements, athletic contests, and presidential debates.

Each of these creative forms has particularly strong (although not exclusive) associations with specific domains and disciplines. One expects more often to find scientists engaged in problem solving and theory building; writers, painters, composers, and inventors engaged in creating permanent works; dancers and actors involved in stylistic performances; and political leaders engaged in high-stake performances.

What attracts certain creators to certain forms? This is a complex question, which involves factors of temperament, ability, and personality. High-energy individuals, for example, may be attracted to creative performances. If someone shows creative behavior of one kind, it does not necessarily follow that he or she may be equally capable of showing creative behavior in other kinds of activities.

Kinds of Creators

Even as creative behaviors can be usefully distinguished from one another, creators also demonstrate several different accents in their work. Two dimensions stand out: the extent to which the creator accepts the current domains as given (as compared with challenging the delineation of domains), and the extent to which the creator is concerned with a world of objects and symbols that denote objects and object relations (as compared with a focus on the world of persons). These two axes yield four distinct kinds of creators.

The master is an individual who accepts the current domain as delineated and seeks to realize the genres of that domain to the most superlative degree. The prototypical example here is Mozart. Mozart so thoroughly exploited the forms of the classical musical era that he stimulated (or perhaps necessitated) a Romantic reaction, as exemplified in the music of Beethoven, Schumann, Chopin, and other creators of the next generation. Other masters would include artists like Shakespeare, Henry James, and Rembrandt.

The maker is an individual who, whatever his or her mastery of the current domains, is driven by a compulsion to challenge current domain practices and, ultimately, to create new domains or subdomains. Scientists like Einstein, Darwin, and Freud are individuals who are best thought of as makers. Within the arts, iconoclastic figures like Stravinsky or Schoenberg, T. S. Eliot or James Joyce, challenge the accepted practices of the domain in which they have been working.

The introspector is a person whose creativity is devoted to the exploration of his or her own psyche. Among twentieth-century literary artists, Proust and Woolf are exemplary introspectors. A figure from the social sciences noted for his introspective creativity is Freud.

The influencer also explores the personal world, but directs his or her creative capacities toward affecting other individuals. Political leaders are prototypical exemplars. Among the creative influencers of our time are Gandhi, Eleanor Roosevelt, and Nelson Mandela.

Of course, these four kinds of creators are ideal types. Many creative individuals exemplify more than one of these stances. And the four dimensions may also nest in one another: Thus, Freud was a maker, whose innovation occurred in the personal realm, while Mozart was a master, whose innovations centered on the manipulation of musical symbol systems.

Life Course

Our studies of creative lives have indicated some intriguing and unexpected parallels in the biographies of creative individuals – at least those drawn from the past century. We have summarized these regularities in a portrait of the EC (Exemplary Creator; Gardner, 1993a, chap. 10). Among the intriguing features are birth in an area at some remove from a center of culture; a regular bourgeois childhood, with a strict disciplinary regime at home; moving during or after adolescence to a major cultural center; discovering other young individuals with similar talents and ambition; selection of a domain from a limited range of options; willingness to challenge authority, either directly or through the creation of works that run counter to current orthodoxy; up to a decade invested in mastering a domain; a slow realization that current work in the domain is fundamentally flawed; exploration of areas that are considered dangerous or remote; a feeling of isolation; and the importance of cognitive and affective support at the time of a breakthrough.

Even following the breakthrough achieved by the creator, one can observe certain predicable patterns. These include subsequent breakthroughs at approximate 10-year intervals; later breakthroughs tend to be more integrative and synthetic, less abrupt and iconoclastic. Creators observe uses of their work that are alien to their initial intent, and must determine whether to try to influence these illegitimate uses. Associates of the individual are often at great risk of personal trauma, as the creator rarely cares much for others. Indeed, as the creator ages, he or she is more and more identified with the work itself. As we noted, a Faustian bargain has been struck where little else but the work counts.

Fruitful Asynchrony: A Key to Continued Creative Lives

All of us are deviants from a hypothetical norm. And many of us are, frankly, marginal to the mainstream of society – because of the patterns of our minds, our personalities, the accidents of our birth, the events that happened to us, our families, and our communities during the course of our lives.

It is difficult to conclude that creative individuals are more deviant or more marginal than the rest of us, because we do not have consensual measures of amount or type of deviance. We do know that many highly creative individuals lost one or both parents when young (Goertzel & Goertzel, 1962) and that there are intriguing correlations between certain disorders, like manic-depressive disease, and certain creative behaviors, such as the writing of

fiction (Jamison, 1993). But since most orphans and mentally disturbed individuals do not stand out in terms of creativity, the most that we can say is that such conditions may under certain circumstances be contributory.

What emerges from studies of highly creative individuals is a different but related phenomenon. Creative individuals stand out not on account of their "asynchrony" from the society per se, but rather in light of the ways in which they deal with these deviations. Rather than becoming despondent or shifting to another line of work, creative individuals are characterized by their disposition to convert differences into advantages. Gardner and Wolf (1988) have referred to the capacity of certain individuals to exploit their differences from the norm as *fruitful asynchrony.*

A few examples from our own case studies can convey a flavor of this phenomenon. Freud, an ambitious Jew from a relatively impoverished family, decided to pursue a career in science. When he failed to achieve status as a world-class researcher, he exploited his particular strengths in the linguistic and interpersonal areas to create a new quasi-scientific domain called psychoanalysis. Einstein, an indifferent student in several respects, stood out from other scientists in his combination of mathematical and spatial gifts; these became the foundation of his most important discoveries about relativity. Virginia Woolf was marginal in terms of her status as a woman in a male-dominated society and, in addition, because of her bisexual inclinations. She placed her own introspections, and her extreme sensitivity to personal relations, at the center of her artistry.

Indeed, highly creative individuals are distinguished from peers in at least three respects. First of all, they tend to *reflect* a great deal on their goals, their success in achieving them, and the lessons learned from efforts that did not go well. Second, they can analyze their strengths and weaknesses, and then *leverage* their own strengths to the optimum; they do not wallow obsessively about areas where they may be less gifted. Finally, they have a special capacity to *frame* apparent defeats or failures, not as occasions to give up, but rather as prods to greater achievement and as situations where they can learn new lessons. The French economist Jean Monnet, father of the European Economic Community, once declared, "I regard every defeat as an opportunity." Similar phrases are found in the speeches and the writings of nearly every creative individual that we have studied in depth.

CONCLUSION

After many years of neglect, and a relatively short and (in our view) unproductive romance with the psychometric tradition, the study of creativity has been energized in recent years. As the offerings to this *Handbook* indicate, there is far from any consensus on how best to approach this topic; and the consequent flowering of methods and approaches is probably a benevolent development at this early point in the history of the domain and the life of the field.

We have taken a straightforward phenomenal approach. We begin with individuals who stand out as uncontroversial exemplars of one or another form of creative achievement. We study their lives and their works and attempt to discover patterns that emerge – patterns that refer to the individual, to other similar individuals, to individuals from the same domain, and, in rare circumstances, to the full gamut of creative individuals. In this vein, we hope ultimately to construct a bridge from the idiographic approaches of Gruber and Arnheim to the nomothetic stance of Simonton and Martindale: Perhaps ultimately we and others working in this tradition will lay the groundwork for a new cumulative approach to creativity.

No doubt many of the tentative generalizations that we have put forth will need to be modified or even scuttled. Even the generalizations that Simonton has tendered, on the basis of a much larger database, are scarcely immune to challenge. Far from being discouraged by such challenges, however, we draw inspiration from our creative masters; we find them energizing in two respects. First, our own understanding can only be enriched if we have to reconstrue the generalizations in order to account for systematic deviations from our findings. Second, a science of creativity should be able to account not only for patterns but also for exceptions – for individuals who are exceptional (such as Newton in his isolation from others, or Marie Curie, who overcame an unprecedented number of obstacles). A better understanding of these anomalous cases may harbor special implications for science, as well as important lessons for ordinary human beings.

NOTE

1 In this context, reality is defined by the set of contextual constraints imposed by individual talent, domain, and audience. Such definition is extensive to various kinds of reality, be they scientific, artistic, political, or otherwise.

REFERENCES

Amabile, T. (1983). *The social psychology of creativity.* New York: Springer-Verlag.
Amabile, T. (1996). *Creativity in context.* Boulder, CO: Westview.
Arnheim, R. (1962). Picasso's *Guernica.* Berkeley: University of California Press.
Bloom, B. S. (1985). *Developing talent in young people.* New York: Ballantine.
Boden, M. (1990). *The creative mind.* New York: Basic.
Brown, R., and Herrnstein, R. (1976). *Psychology.* Boston: Little, Brown.
Bruner, J. S., Jolly, A., and Sylva, K. (Eds.). (1976). *Play.* London: Penguin.
Csikszentmihalyi, M. (1990). *Flow.* New York: HarperCollins.
Csikszentmihalyi, M. (1996). *Creativity.* New York: HarperCollins
Davidson, J., and Sternberg, R. (1984). The role of insight in intellectual giftedness. *Gifted Child Quarterly, 28,* 58–64.
de Groot, A. (1965). *Thought and choice in chess.* The Hague: Mouton.
Freud, S. (1958). *Creativity and the unconscious* (B. Nelson, Ed.). New York: Harper & Row.
Gardner, H. (1993a). *Creating minds.* New York: Basic.
Gardner, H. (1993b). *Frames of mind: The theory of multiple intelligences.* New York: Basic.
Gardner, H. (1993c). Five forms of creativity: A developmental perspective. Paper prepared for the Wallace National Symposium on Talent Development, University of Iowa, May 20. Published in N. Colangelo et al. (Eds.), *Proceedings* (317). Dayton: Ohio Psychology Press.
Gardner, H. (1993d). *Multiple intelligences: The theory in practice.* New York: Basic.
Gardner, H. (1997-a). *Extraordinary minds.* New York: Basic.
Gardner, H. (1997-b). Norman Geschwind as a creative scientist. In O. Devinsky and S. Schachter (Eds.), *Behavioral neurology and the legacy of Norman Geschwind* (pp. 47–52). New York: Raven.
Gardner, H., and Nemirovsky, R. (1991). From private intuitions to public symbol systems: An examination of creative process in Georg Cantor and Sigmund Freud. *Creativity Research Journal, 4,* 1–21.
Gardner, H., and Wolf, C. (1988). The fruits of asynchrony: Creativity from a psychological point of view. *Adolescent Psychiatry, 15,* 105–123.
Getzels, J., and Csikszentmihalyi, M. (1976). *The creative vision.* New York: Wiley.
Getzels, J., and Jackson, P. (1962). *Creativity and intelligence.* New York: Wiley.
Ghiselin, B. (1952). *The creative process.* New York: Mentor.
Goertzel, V., and Goertzel, M. G. (1962). *Cradles of eminence.* Boston: Little, Brown.
Gruber, H. (1981). *Darwin on man* (2nd ed.). Chicago: University of Chicago Press.
Gruber, H. (1982). Piaget's mission. *Social Research, 49,* 239–264.
Guilford, J. P. (1950). Creativity. *American Psychologist, 5,* 445–454.
Holmes, F. (1985). *Lavoisier and the chemistry of life.* Madison: University of Wisconsin Press.
Jamison, K. (1993). *Touched with fire: Manic depressive illness and the artistic temperament.* New York: Free Press.
Jay, E. (1989). *Problem finding: Understanding its nature and mechanism.* Qualifying paper, Harvard Graduate School of Education, Cambridge, MA.
John-Steiner, V. (1985). *Notebooks of the mind.* Albuquerque: University of New Mexico Press.

Kroeber, A. (1944). *Configurations of cultural growth.* Berkeley: University of California Press.

Li, J., and Gardner, H. (1993). How domains constrain creativity: The case of traditional Chinese and Western painting. *American Behavioral Scientist, 37*(11), 94–101.

Martindale, C. (1990). *The clockwork muse.* New York: Basic.

Murray, E. L. (1986). *Imaginative thinking and human existence.* Pittsburgh, PA: Duquesne University Press.

Murray, H. A. (1938). *Explorations in personality.* New York: Oxford University Press.

Newell, A., and Simon, H. (1972). *Human problem-solving.* Englewood Cliffs, NJ: Prentice-Hall.

Poincaré, H. (1952). Mathematical creation. In B. Ghiselin (Ed.), *The creative process.* New York: New American Library.

Simonton, D. K. (1994). *Greatness.* New York: Guilford.

Sternberg, R., and Lubart, T. (1991). An investment theory of creativity and its development. *Human Development, 34,* 1–31.

Storr, A. (1988). *Solitude.* New York: Free Press.

Torrance, E. P. (1962). *Guiding creative talent.* Englewood Cliffs, NJ: Prentice-Hall.

Wallace, D., and Gruber, H. (1990). *Creative people at work.* New York: Oxford University Press.

12 Creativity and Knowledge: A Challenge to Theories

ROBERT W. WEISBERG

An important component of research in creativity has been the development of theories concerning the mechanisms underlying creative thinking. Modern theories of creative thinking have been advanced from many different viewpoints, ranging from Guilford's pioneering psychometric theory (e.g., 1950; see also Runco, 1991) to those developing out of clinical interests, broadly conceived (e.g., Eysenck, 1993). Other theories have developed out of Gestalt psychology (e.g., Wertheimer, 1982), traditional associationistic experimental psychology (e.g., Mednick, 1962), Darwinian theory (e.g., Campbell, 1960; Simonton, 1988, 1995); social-psychological perspectives (e.g., Amabile, 1983), investment perspectives (e.g., Sternberg & Lubart, 1995), and modern cognitive science (e.g., Martindale, 1995). In this chapter, I examine one critical issue confronting all such theories: the role of knowledge in creativity.

Although the various theoretical views proposed by psychologists appear on the surface to be very different, there is among many of them, including all those just cited, one critical assumption concerning the relationship between knowledge and creativity. Since creative thinking by definition goes beyond knowledge, there is implicitly or explicitly assumed to be a tension between knowledge and creativity. Knowledge may provide the basic elements, the building blocks out of which are constructed new ideas, but in order for these building blocks to be available, the mortar holding the old ideas together must not be too strong. Thus, while it is universally acknowledged that one must have knowledge of a field if one hopes to produce something novel within it, it is also widely assumed that too much experience can leave one in ruts, so that one cannot go beyond stereotyped responding. The relationship between knowledge and creativity is assumed, therefore, to be shaped like an inverted U, with maximal creativity occurring with some middle range of knowledge.

The notion that the relationship between knowledge and creativity is one of tension has a long history in psychology. Indeed, that general idea has been presented so often, in such a broad range of contexts, that it can be looked upon as a cliché (Frensch & Sternberg, 1989). However, although the "tension" view is the dominant one in modern theory, there has been proposed another view of the relationship between knowledge and creativity. A number of researchers have argued the opposite of the tension view, that is, that knowledge is positively related to creativity. Rather than breaking out of the old to produce the new, creative thinking builds on knowledge (Bailin, 1988; Gruber, 1981; Hayes, 1989; Kulkarni & Simon, 1988; Weisberg, 1986, 1988, 1993, 1995b). This view can be called the "foundation" view.

The purpose of the present chapter is to discuss these contradictory approaches to the relationship between creativity and knowledge. The chapter will first briefly summarize the tension view of the role of knowledge in creativity and briefly examine research that has been taken to support it. I will then review research that has examined the relation between knowledge and creativity. Research relevant to this question comes from several related areas. A set of quantitative studies investigating this issue centers on the "10-year rule" in development of master-level work in creative fields (e.g., Hayes, 1989). It has been found consistently that creative individuals have required an extensive amount of time between their initial exposure to the field and production of their first significant work. Such results indicate, indirectly at least, that the ability to do creative work depends on deep knowledge of one's chosen field. There also has been a number of qualitative case studies that have examined the career development of eminent individuals in a number of creative fields (e.g., Csikszentmihalyi, 1996; Gardner, 1993; Gruber, 1981). These studies have all found evidence that deep immersion in one's chosen field is necessary before innovation is produced.

The next question concerns what occurs during those years of development. Research has demonstrated the role of extensive amounts of deliberate practice, entailing thousands of hours spread over many years, in the acquisition of master levels of complex skills (e.g., Bloom, 1985; Ericsson, Krampe, & Clemens, 1993). Furthermore, there is evidence that developing masters practice at close to the maximal level.

The basic conclusion from this review is that extensive domain-specific knowledge is a prerequisite for creative functioning. Accommodating these findings will require a change in the way in which we conceptualize the relationship between creativity and knowledge. In the final section of the chapter, I discuss an alternative conception of the role of knowledge in creative thinking.

THE TENSION BETWEEN KNOWLEDGE AND CREATIVITY

In an early discussion of the relationship between knowledge and creativity, James (1880), described the thinking patterns of "the highest order of minds" as having the following characteristics:

Instead of thoughts of concrete things patiently following one another in a beaten track of habitual suggestion, we have the most rarefied abstractions and discriminations, the most unheard of combination of elements, the subtlest associations of analogy; in a word, we seem suddenly introduced into a seething cauldron of ideas, where everything is fizzling and bobbling about in a state of bewildering activity, where partnerships can be joined or loosened in an instant, treadmill routine is unknown, and the unexpected seems only law. (p. 456)

James here makes several important claims. First, "partnerships" of ideas can be joined or loosened in an instant, which indicates that any given combination of ideas is as probable as any other. This leads to the conclusion that specific past experience is not influencing the combinations that occur. A similar inference follows from James's statement that the thought processes of these "highest order of minds" bring about the "most unheard of" combinations, presumably unheard of to thinker as well as to the audience. This again is a claim for the independence of creative thought from knowledge. Similarly, James's observation that "treadmill routine is unknown" points to the independence of this thought from ordinary knowledge. In a later writing, James (1908) carried this reasoning further and explicitly emphasizes the negative influence of habit on thinking:

The force of habit, the grip of convention, hold us down on the Trivial Plane; we are unaware of our bondage because the bonds are invisible, their restraints acting below the level of awareness. They are the collective standards of value, codes of behavior, matrices with built in axioms which determine the rules of the game, and make most of us run, most of the time, in the grooves of habit – reducing us to the status of skilled automata which Behaviorism proclaims to be the only condition of man. (p. 64)

James's view could be looked upon as a relatively radical claim concerning the role of knowledge in creative thinking. He is saying that knowledge is only in the very loosest sense related to true creativity, and may be detrimental to it.

A similar position was advocated by the Gestalt psychologists (e.g., Scheerer, 1963; Wertheimer, 1982; for further discussion, see Weisberg, 1995a), who proposed the well-known distinction between reproductive and productive thought. The former, which depended on reproduction of previously successful behaviors, involved staying in old thought habits and would fail when something truly novel was demanded. Productive thought was the basis for insight and true novelty of thinking. The crucial issue for the productive or insightful thinker was to be able to use past experience on a general level, while still being able to deal with each new problem situation on its own terms. In this way, one does not become fixated, that is, trapped by attempting to apply specific knowledge to situations in which it turns out not to be relevant (Scheerer, 1963; Wertheimer, 1982). Such behavior would be a reduction to James's (1908) "skilled automata."

Guilford (1950), in his pioneering analysis of creative thinking emphasized the role of "divergent" thinking in the development of new ideas. This mode of thought enables the thinker to produce new ideas by breaking away, or diverging, from previously established ideas. DeBono (1968), perhaps the most well-known industrial consultant on creativity training, voices the same opinion. "Too much experience within a field may restrict creativity because you know so well how things *should be done* that you are unable to escape to come up with new ideas" (p. 228).

Koestler's (1964) often-cited discussion of creativity also emphasizes the necessity for creative thinking to break out of the boundaries set by knowledge, in the form of habit:

Habit is thus second nature . . . at any rate as regards its importance in adult life; for the acquired habits of our training have by that time inhibited or strangled most of the natural impulsive tendencies which were originally there. Ninety-nine hundredths or, possibly, nine hundred and ninety-nine thousandths of our activity is purely automatic and habitual. (p. 363)

Amabile (1989, pp. 48–49) summarizes her views on creativity in the context of a discussion of how to increase the chances of raising children who can think creatively. She presents the following as some of the thinking styles that are often observed in creative adults and children: (1) Breaking set, that is, breaking out of your old patterns of thinking about something; (2) breaking out of scripts, which is much the same thing; and (3) perceiving freshly, that is, changing one's old ways.

A number of researchers have stated explicitly the belief that situations which demand creative thinking are so novel that one's past experience cannot be applied to them without large-scale modification. Another way of saying the same thing is to propose that "true" creative thinking produces results of such novelty that they are unrelated to what came before. For example, Hausman (1984) claims that there is a break between the creative product and the past: The novelty inherent in creativity means that the creative product is not comprehensible or analyzable in terms of what was known before. Concomitantly, he also assumes that the creative product must have developed independently of the creator's knowledge or past experience:

[A] created object exhibits a complex structure that is new and is unprecedented and un-predicted. It appears to be unaccounted for by its antecedents and available knowledge, and it is thus disconnected with its past. In this sense, it occurs in the midst of discontinuity. (p. 9)

Campbell (1960) makes a similar point in an influential paper that proposed a Darwinian perspective on creative thinking. Such a perspective assumes that creative ideas, like the mutations that provide the raw material on which natural selection operates, are the results of a "blind" process. This is necessary, according to Campbell, to bring about true advances in knowledge:

Between a modern experimental physicist and some virus-type ancestor there has been a tremendous gain in knowledge about the environment. . . . It has represented repeated "breakouts" from the limits of available wisdom, for if such expansions had represented only wise anticipations, they would have been exploiting full or partial knowledge already achieved. Instead, real gains must have been the products of explorations going beyond the limits of foresight and prescience, and in this sense blind. In the instances of such real gains, the successful explorations were in origin as blind as those which failed. (pp. 380–381)

A similar point is made by Simonton (1995), who has taken Campbell's basic view and elaborated it into a wide-ranging theory of creative development and creative process:

For the kinds of problems on which historical creators stake their reputations, the possibilities seem endless, and the odds of attaining the solution appear nearly hopeless. At this point, problem solving becomes more nearly a random process, in the sense that the free-associative procedure must come into play. Only by falling back on this less disciplined resource can the creator arrive at insights that are genuinely profound. (pp. 472–473)

We see here a consistency of opinion concerning the need for creative thinking to go beyond the bounds of knowledge in order to produce true advances. This is seen as necessary for true creativity because it is assumed that changes in the environment demand it. I will now very briefly examine selected research that provides support for the tension view, which will demonstrate how researchers have approached the relevant issues. It has been shown that the relation between education and creative achievement is curvilinear, as the tension view assumes; and it has been shown that past experience can interfere with effective adjustment to novel situations. That is, using one's past experience results in negative transfer in new situations.

The U-Shaped Relation Between Education and Creativity

Simonton (1984, chap. 4) has analyzed the relationship between outstanding creative accomplishment and level of formal education. He examined the lives of more than 300 eminent individuals, born between 1450 and 1850, who had been included in an earlier study of the roots of genius. Some of the individuals included in the study were Leonardo, Galileo, Mozart, Rembrandt, and Beethoven. Simonton determined the level of formal education that each individual had achieved, and also scored the level of eminence the person had attained, based on an archival measure: the amount of space devoted to the individual in several standard reference works.

When eminence was plotted as a function of level of education, it was found that the relationship was curvilinear, an inverted U, with the peak of eminence occurring at about midway through undergraduate training. Fewer or more years of training (including postgraduate training) were associated with lower levels of eminence. Thus, one could argue that higher levels of knowledge (presumably brought about by graduate training) had a negative effect on creativity.

Past Experience and Negative Transfer

Well-known studies by Luchins and Luchins on problem-solving set (e.g., 1959) have shown that individuals can easily be induced to perform inefficiently in problem-solving situations, as a result of success with one specific solution. Experimental participants were sometimes so fixated on "blindly" applying that previously successful solution to new problems that simpler solutions would be overlooked. The new problem might not even be solved by the experienced problem solvers, although naive participants solved it with no difficulty. Thus, past success had trapped the knowledgeable participants into habitual modes of thought, and when the world changed, so that the previously successful solution did not work, they were incapable of adapting.

This perspective has recently been carried forth by Frensch and Sternberg (e.g., 1989), who showed that experts in bridge were less able than were novices to adjust to changes in the rules of the game. Two sorts of changes were made by Frensch and Sternberg. Surface changes involved changes in the names and order of suits; deep or conceptual change involved having the player who lost the last trick, rather than the winner, lead the next one. Both novices and experts were tested on the two types of changes. Experts were particularly affected by the deep changes and had a harder time adjusting to them than did the novices. Once again, knowledge made for less flexible thinking in adjusting to changes in the world. In this study, as in those by Luchins and Luchins (1959), the experts would have been better off knowing nothing.

Conclusions

This brief discussion has served to introduce the tension view and research presented in its support. The next section investigates more directly the question of the relation between knowledge and creativity. Two related sets of studies will be examined. The first is research that has examined career development of acknowledged masters in several domains and which has found that a large amount of time in the discipline is required before one makes a significant contribution (the 10-year rule). Second, there is evidence that much of this time is spent internalizing what has already been done in the discipline; master-level performance only comes after years of extensive deliberate practice. Further, there is evidence that individuals who achieve master-level ability may practice at close to the human maximum, rather than at some intermediate level, as the tension view would lead one to expect.

DEVELOPMENT OF MASTER-LEVEL PERFORMANCE IN CREATIVE FIELDS: THE 10-YEAR RULE

Hayes (1989) carried out a study of the role of what he called preparation in creative production. The basic question that Hayes investigated was the time needed to reach master-level performance. He examined career development in several fields requiring creative thinking, such as musical composition, painting, and poetry. The results, which were consistent across fields, showed that even the most noteworthy and "talented" individuals required many years of preparation before they began to produce the work on which their reputations were built.

Composers

To examine the development of skill in musical composition, Hayes examined the biographies of 76 composers, listed in a standard reference work (Schoenberg, 1970), for whom enough information was available to determine when they began the study of music. Hayes calculated the length of time between the beginning of each composer's career, as defined by introduction to musical instruction, and production of the individual's first "notable" work or "masterwork." In defining such a work, Hayes used an "archival" measure: the number of recordings of the work available.

Based on this criterion, Hayes identified over 500 notable works produced by his sample of composers throughout their careers. Of these works, only 3 were composed before year

10 of the composer's career, and those 3 works were composed in years 8 and 9. Hayes described the average pattern of career productivity for composers as beginning with what he called "10 years of silence," which led to the first masterwork. Following the initial masterwork, there was then a rapid increase in notable works, through career years 10–25. This was followed by stable productivity through years 25–49, and finally a gradual decline.

As an example of the widespread generality of this career profile, we can consider the career of Mozart, perhaps the most precocious and undoubtedly one of the most prolific of all composers. Mozart's first masterwork was the Piano Concerto no. 9 (K. 271), actually his 12th work in that genre, produced in 1777, which was more than 10 years into Mozart's career. Thus, although Mozart began his career very early, he still required a significant amount of time before he made his mark.

Painters

A similar analysis was carried out by Hayes (1989) of career development in painters. Biographies of 131 painters were examined, in order to determine time of initiation of the individual's painting career. Time to production of the first notable work was then determined. In this study, notable works were defined as those reproduced in at least one of several standard histories of painting. The career development of painters showed the same pattern as musicians. There was an initial 6-year period of what Hayes calls noncreativity, culminating in the first masterwork. This period of development was followed by a rapid increase over the next 6 years in the production of masterworks. The level of production remained stable for about 25 years, followed by a gradual decline.

Here again, the careers of even the most precocious and productive painters, such as Pablo Picasso, can be described by this function. Picasso began to paint under the tutelage of his father, also a painter, at about age 9. His first notable works were produced at about age 15. Picasso proclaimed that he painted like Raphael from the very beginning, but this does not seem to be true (Pariser, 1987; Richardson, 1991). Pariser examined the juvenile drawings of Picasso, Paul Klee, and Toulouse-Lautrec and concluded that all three artists went through a developmental sequence, in which they learned to draw and paint. They had to grapple with and overcome problems of representation that all children must go through before they can accurately represent objects on canvas or paper. These artists showed evidence of dealing with these issues in the same way as do less gifted children, although perhaps at a faster pace.

Poets

Wishbow (1988, as cited by Hayes, 1989) carried out a biographical study of 66 eminent poets. A notable poem was defined as one included in a major anthology of poetry. We once again find the same pattern of career development: no notable poem was written earlier than 5 years into the poet's career. Furthermore, of the 66 poets examined, 55 required 10 years until production of their first notable work.

Conclusions

Hayes (1989), following Chase and Simon (1973), proposed that preparation, in the sense of immersion in a discipline, is required for creative achievement. Composers, painters, and poets, like the chess masters studied by Chase and Simon, require significant periods of time to acquire sufficient knowledge and skills to perform in their fields at world-class levels. It should be noted that at this point little of specificity can be said concerning the amount of time needed for development of the ability to produce notable creative work in a given domain. All that can be said is that a significant amount of time is involved, much more than would be involved in simply learning the rudiments of the domain. The label "10-year rule" is thus a bit misleading, since we have seen differences among domains in Hayes's studies.

In addition, little can be said concerning why there might be differences between domains in the average amount of time required, and why different individuals require different amounts of time to produce their first masterwork. Individual differences might be based in part on talent, that is, the ability to function within a given domain (Gardner, 1993). Also, Bloom (1985) and Feldman (e.g., 1986) discuss some of the social factors, including familial factors, that play a role in determining whether or not an individual will achieve high levels of accomplishment in various domains (see also Csikszentmihalyi, 1996). At this point, the only conclusion to be drawn is that a long period of time in a domain seems to be a necessary, although not sufficient, condition for notable contribution.

These caveats notwithstanding, the results of Hayes's study are impressive in several ways. First, the uniformity of findings within and across disciplines is remarkable. Within each field, the analysis included individuals from very different historical epochs, and yet the same pattern of long-term development was seen. Furthermore, the same pattern also held across such different fields as painting and poetry. Similar findings have been reported by other investigators. In a seminal case study of creative achievement, Gruber (1981) examined Darwin's development of the theory of evolution through natural selection. Although we cannot do justice here to Gruber's painstaking and deep analysis, the overall pattern of Darwin's development supports the necessity of deep immersion in a field.

Interview studies by Bloom and co-workers (Bloom, 1985) of individuals who achieved world-class levels of performance in a variety of domains (e.g., sculpture, mathematics, and tennis) also supported the 10-year rule. As well, Gardner (1993) presented studies of eminent individuals in a variety of areas, one in each of his seven postulated domains of intelligence: Albert Einstein (logical-mathematical); Picasso (visual-spatial); Igor Stravinsky (music); Martha Graham (bodily-kinesthetic); Mahatma Gandhi (interpersonal); Sigmund Freud (intrapersonal); and T. S. Eliot (language). One of the main conclusions from his studies was the long period of development in each person's career before he or she produced the first work of significance. That is, the careers of these renowned individuals exemplified the 10-year rule. In addition, these individuals produced more than one major work (e.g., Picasso's *Les demoiselles d'Avignon* [1907] and *Guernica* [1937]), and Gardner concluded that the 10-year rule held for each of those works. That is, a significant period of time intervened between major works.

THE YEARS OF "SILENCE": PRACTICE, PRACTICE, PRACTICE

An important question left unanswered by research on the 10-year rule involves what is happening during the years of development. As we have seen, Hayes (1989) called the time before individual's production of significant work the "silent" or "uncreative" period, but it must be noted that much is occurring during those years. The activities during the silent period do not have direct positive consequences as far as the individual's reputation is concerned, since no masterworks are produced. These activities must be of crucial importance, however, because they lay the foundation for the individual's subsequent production of masterworks.

One might speculate that the individual is becoming fully immersed in the discipline during the silent period, but the results of Hayes's studies provide no direct evidence for this. The biographical studies of Gardner (1993) and Gruber (1981) provide qualitative evidence for such an immersion. The interview studies of Bloom and co-workers (Bloom, 1985), to be discussed further shortly, also support this conclusion. Quantitative information on what occurs during this period comes from recent work by Ericsson and his colleagues (e.g., Ericsson & Charness, 1994; Ericsson, Krampe, & Clemens, 1993), who have examined the role of what they call deliberate practice in the development of master-level skills.

Deliberate Practice and the Development of Expert Performance

Deliberate practice consists of a set of activities specifically designed to improve performance in some skill (Ericsson et al., 1993). Among these are: application of structured methods, rather than haphazard working; involvement of a tutor or coach, although not usually in every practice session; feedback to the student; and repeated chance for the student to attend to the critical aspects of the situation and his or her performance. That is, the individual is able to go over again and again, under the eye of the coach, the specific parts of the skill that require improvement, and then work further alone.

Deliberate practice is contrasted with two other forms of activity: play and work. Play is, of course, carrying out some activity for its own sake. Many individuals report that as children they began some activity as play, but they then changed to practice as they became more serious about a possible career in that discipline. Play does not have the structure of deliberate practice, and so cannot bring about systematic improvement. Work involves performance or competition, for external reward, and the performer is expected to be at his or her best. Work therefore usually would not provide the opportunity for deliberate practice, since problematic aspects of the skill cannot be isolated and repeated. Indeed, problematic aspects of the skill would probably be actively avoided at such times.

In Ericsson's view, there is essentially no limit to the level of performance an individual can reach in any skill (Ericsson et al., 1993; see also Bloom, 1985). Some broad limits are set by genetic factors, but if the person is capable of carrying out the activity, then, with sufficient deliberate practice, he or she can reach the highest level of performance. However, this practice must extend over years, and it requires extensive resources on the part of the would-be performer and his or her support group (usually the family; see Bloom, 1985, and Feldman, 1986). Resources involve time and energy, as well as access to teachers. Deliberate practice demands a high degree of effort on the part of the learner, because he or she must commit full attention for the entire session for the practice to be effective. This limits the length of sessions; deliberate practice therefore can only be carried out for a limited amount of time per day. In order to maintain a practice schedule, the learner must be able to recover from one session before the next is scheduled. Studies that have varied the length of practice sessions from 1 to 8 hours have found that maximal improvement occurred with sessions of 2 to 4 hours in length (Ericsson et al., 1993, p. 370), and teachers of music recommend shorter sessions, separated by breaks.

In order to examine the role of deliberate practice in the development of master-level skills, Ericsson et al. (1993) studied musicians of different levels of skill and assessed the amount of practice and other activities they engaged in. The sample consisted of a group of elite professional violinists, and three groups of student violinists at a prestigious music school. The elite violinists were members of one of two world-class symphony orchestras. In order to obtain student violinists of different levels of skill, indirect criteria were used. The professors at the school were asked to identify the students who had the best chance of achieving careers as international soloists; the professors also nominated "good" violinists from the same department. Finally, a group of violin students were identified who planned careers in music education. These students were presumably at a level of skill lower than the others.

These four groups of violinists were interviewed concerning their activities, musical and otherwise, and the groups of students were asked to keep diaries of their activities over a week. The interviews involved rating various activities as to their career relevance, the effort they entailed, and how enjoyable they were. In their ratings, the violinists differentiated among musical activities, with deliberate practice being rated as most relevant, but also highly effortful, and not enjoyable. Playing with others was rated more enjoyable and less effortful than deliberate practice, but also less relevant. These results supported the framework of Ericsson et al. which assumed that deliberate practice is most important for the development of skill, but at a cost of much effort. It was also found that the more elite violinists spent more time practicing, and also more time sleeping. This supported the idea that practice was effortful and necessitated sleep for recovery from the effort expended.

Based on the interviews, Ericsson et al. determined that the better violinists had begun study of the violin earlier in life and had practiced more throughout their careers. The interviews plus the diaries allowed an estimate of the amount of practice the groups of violinists had engaged in, from the time they had begun study until the age of 20. The groups were reliably different in this regard: the best violinists were each estimated as having accumulated more than 10,000 hours of practice, compared with approximately 8,000 hours for the good violinists and 4,000 hours for the music teachers.

In addition, based on information concerning the length of typical practice sessions and the extra time spent in sleep by the best violinists, Ericsson et al. concluded that the best violinists were practicing close to the maximum that they could sustain. A second study, of high-level pianists, supported the conclusions from the study of violinists. Furthermore, studies cited by Ericsson et al. (e.g., of writers) also indicate that the capacity to sustain deliberate effortful work is limited and that individuals at the highest levels of accomplishment work at close to their limit.

These results are an indication that "too much practice" does not seem to stifle accomplishment. In the domains studied by Ericsson et al., the relationship between practice and achievement seems to be a positive and monotonic function of practice, not the inverted U postulated by the tension view. The contradiction between this conclusion and Simonton's (1984) study of the relationship between education and creative accomplishment will be examined later.

The same conclusion can be drawn from the interview studies conducted by Bloom and co-workers (Bloom, 1985). These researchers interviewed more than 20 individuals in each of several fields who had achieved high levels of success, including athletics (tennis players ranked in the top ten worldwide and Olympic swimmers), music (award-winning piano soloists), artists (award-winning sculptors), and scientists (neurologists and mathematicians who had been recognized for excellence in early career development). In all these fields, attainment of excellence was foreshadowed by years of immersion in the activity, accompanied by strong support by a network of individuals, including parents and coaches. Furthermore, although some of the fields investigated might more obviously require creativity (e.g., sculpture, neurology, and mathematics versus tennis, swimming, and playing the piano), the pattern of years of preparation was found in the former as well as the latter.

The Question of Creativity

One might object that the research on deliberate practice is not relevant to the study of creativity, because such fields as musical performance or athletics may require minimal creativity. However, as just indicated, several of the fields investigated by Bloom and co-workers (1985), albeit on only a qualitative level, undoubtedly involve creativity (sculpture, neurology, mathematics). Furthermore, it can be argued that musical performance and athletics can involve creativity. The highest level of instrumentalists, those who have achieved careers as soloists, are selected presumably because of the personal interpretations that they apply to the pieces they play. That is, they are capable of communicating emotion to their listeners.

This communication of emotion presumably indicates that the player learns something more than a well-rehearsed series of unchanging movements, since not all performers are able to communicate emotion to the same high degree. The pianists interviewed by Bloom and his colleagues (Bloom, 1985) reported that the final stage of their training entailed study with what could be called a "master teacher," an individual who in most cases had achieved international acclaim as a soloist. Such teachers accepted as students only those young people who demonstrated high levels of potential in auditions and who were recommended by highly respected lower-level teachers. The students reported that the master teachers were not interested in perfecting piano technique. Rather, they were concerned with the student's developing a personal style of communicating the emotion in the music. Thus, each developing soloist must "create" his or her own style of playing, and performing music can be looked upon as a creative activity.

Athletic skills at the highest level also have creative components. In such sports as tennis, basketball, and hockey, to name a few, the basic activity is unstructured, and therefore requires constant improvisation. The outstanding athlete in such domains has therefore learned more than how to repeat a set of moves in the same way each time. Thus, the results from studies of musical performers and athletes have relevance to the understanding of creative thinking. In addition, as noted earlier, studies of the development of artists and scientists by Bloom and his co-workers present results concerning practice and immersion in the discipline that parallel the findings with musicians and athletes (Bloom, 1985).

The potential importance of the findings of Bloom and co-workers and of Ericsson et al. points to the necessity of examining the careers of individuals in other fields that unquestionably entail creative thinking. The next section presents evidence concerning the importance of practice and development of knowledge in musical composition (including composition "on-line," i.e., jazz improvisation), unquestionably a creative skill. No relatively direct assessment of patterns of practice and other activities is possible in the case of such individuals as Mozart. However, indirect evidence supports the findings from the studies of Bloom and co-workers (Bloom, 1985) and of Ericsson et al. (1993); that is, immersion in the discipline is a prerequisite for creative accomplishment.

PRACTICE AND CREATIVITY IN MUSICAL COMPOSITION

Who Wrote Mozart's First Seven Piano Concertos?

Evidence that deliberate practice is important in the development of musical composition comes from a consideration of Mozart's production of concertos for piano and orchestra. As mentioned earlier, Mozart's first masterwork as identified by Hayes (1989) was the Piano Concerto no. 9, K. 271. This piece was composed more than 10 years into Mozart's career, when he was 21 years old. Mozart's first four piano concertos (K. 37, 39, 40, 41) were produced in June–July, 1767; Mozart's age was 11. However, calling these works piano concertos by Mozart is misleading, since they contain no original music by him: They were constructed out of works of five other composers.

The next three works of this type (K. 107, nos. 1–3) were written in 1772, when Mozart was 16. These works too contain no original music by Mozart: They were works of Johann Christian Bach (the youngest son of J. S. Bach), who had become an important composer in his own right; they were merely arranged by Mozart for a new combination of instruments.

These works are not numbered as piano concertos. The first piano concerto containing orig-inal music by Mozart was no. 5 (K. 175); this was produced in 1773, when Mozart was 17. This piece did not meet Hayes's (1989) criterion for a masterwork, however.

This pattern of development indicates that Mozart's earliest musical experiences involved immersion in the works of others, and probably involved use of the earlier composers' works as models for how certain compositional problems could be handled. This activity could be considered deliberate practice, under the direction of Mozart's father, an established musi-cian of some renown, who could be considered a master teacher. In addition, since the young Mozart was also a performer, he probably played these works in his performances, producing still deeper immersion.

A similar pattern is seen in Mozart's production of symphonies. Mozart's first symphony (K. 16) was produced in London in 1764, when he was 8. Several others were produced in the next year. When one contemplates that fact, one is overwhelmed by such an accom-plishment by one so young. However, as with the piano concertos, Mozart went through a significant period of development as a symphonist. Those early symphonies were very dif-ferent from the later ones, which are the ones with which listeners are most familiar. Mozart's final three symphonies, usually acknowledged as his greatest (e.g., Zaslaw, 1989), are large-scale works: They are comprised of four large-scale movements and require approximately 30–40 minutes to perform. In addition, each contains innovative elements that places it on a high plane of artistic achievement in the history of music.

The early symphonies, on the other hand, are very different from the later ones in struc-ture, emotional scale, and innovation. They were composed when Mozart and his father were visiting London, where the young composer was taken under the wing of Johann Chris-tian Bach, who had established himself in England as a composer and musical entrepreneur. Bach had composed a number of symphonies for use in concerts that he promoted in Lon-don in partnership with C. F. Abel, another German composer who had found favor there. (Abel had also written symphonies for their concerts.) These "preclassical" symphonies were very different than those produced by the next generation of composers, including Haydn, the mature Mozart, and the young Beethoven. They almost always consist of three short movements, usually in tempos of fast, slow, fast, and a simple harmonic structure.

Mozart's first symphonies are closely modeled after those of Bach (and Abel), in structure and substance. They too are made up of three short movements, in tempos of fast, slow, fast, and a simple harmonic structure. A similar pattern can be seen in the development of Mozart as a composer of chamber music, for example, in his string quartets: His early works are closely modeled on those of earlier composers, and innovation occurs only later. The involvement of a young composer-to-be in the works of his predecessors, while perhaps no surprise, is contrary to the assumption of a tension between knowledge and creativity. If Mozart learned by copying the works of others, then why was he not doomed to repeat them? Similar questions arise from the study of the development of jazz musicians.

Development of Improvisation Skills in Jazz Musicians

Jazz is perhaps the most "open" and "free" of all the Western arts. Learning to improvise would seem to be a case in which relying on what has been done before (even on what *you* have done before), would doom one from the start. However, in this domain also, creative skill comes about only after deep immersion into the past, again in the form of deliberate practice. Jazz musicians, even those of the highest degree of skill and reputation, report that they learn to play from records, by learning solos of the masters from previous generations, note by note (Berliner, 1994; Kernfeld, 1995; Owens, 1995). They learn others' solos until they can play them back effortlessly (often a whole repertoire of solos and "licks"), and this forms the basis for the development of the ability to go beyond what they have learned and to create new music. The new music may be related to the models that they have "internalized," in the sense that often one can tell who has influenced a given player, but the new music will go beyond the music of the model, sometimes in relatively radical ways. Here again, one might have expected that these aspiring jazz players were dooming themselves to a lifetime of repetition of the works of others, but that is not what necessarily happens.

Analysis of performances of jazz musicians of the highest rank has provided some specifics concerning the way in which improvisational skills depend on knowledge. Owens (1995) has analyzed the recorded solos of Charlie Parker (1920–1955), who is recognized as the greatest improviser in modern jazz. Parker is the individual most responsible, along with Dizzy Gillespie, for the transition from the swing of the 1930s to the bebop and modern jazz of the 1940s and early 1950s. Parker was legendary for playing fluently at incredible speed, with some of his solos recorded at tempos of 400+ beats per minute. (It is difficult for a listener to even beat one's foot in time with such tempos.) He was also recognized for never repeating himself.

Perhaps surprisingly, given Parker's reputation, Owens (1995) has reported that Parker can be characterized as a "formulaic" improviser. Over his career, Parker acquired a large repertoire of formulas – patterns of notes, ranging from two- or three-note clusters to strings encompassing perhaps a dozen notes – which he used in his solos. A significant proportion of even Parker's greatest solos were constructed from these formulas, some of which might be repeated every eight or nine measures.

Parker's formulas were developed in several ways. Some can be traced to specific musicians in the previous swing generation, about whom Parker was very knowledgeable. He was, at least once, heard in his nightclub dressing room, between shows, playing from memory a solo of Lester Young, a swing musician of great renown. Excerpts from the recorded solos of Young and other swing musicians (e.g., Coleman Hawkins) can be heard in Parker's recorded solos. Other formulas were what could be called "common currency" among Parker's peers, in that the same formulas were used by many of them. Finally, other formulas were developed by Parker himself, during his practice and playing sessions.

Thus, Parker's ability to play fluently and without repetition is attributed by analysts to his large and well-learned repertoire of formulas (Kernfeld, 1995; Owens, 1995). At the speeds at which Parker played, so it is argued, it would have been impossible to compose new music truly from scratch; one must have precomposed pieces to use. The more of these formulas one has mastery over, the less chance of repeating oneself.

Johnson-Laird (e.g., 1988) has recently developed a computer model of jazz improvisation, based on heuristics, that is, a set of rules of thumb that can be used to produce improvisations. Johnson-Laird begins with the fact that jazz musicians begin by imitating the work of others. In Johnson-Laird's analysis, a crucial aspect of the development of the jazz musician is that on the basis of this imitation, the jazz musician must develop a skill of improvisation that can run efficiently in real time, since there is no revision possible in jazz. In Johnson-Laird's view, these skills involve the musician's abstraction of principles of improvisation from the internalized models. The principles are used to choose notes to be played at a given point in the performance, based in part on the harmonic structure of the piece being played and in part on what the performer has just played.

Johnson-Laird (1988) assumes that an improviser chooses notes to meet two criteria. (1) Based on knowledge of harmony, the player chooses notes that fit the present chord or that can be used to link one chord with another. (2) The player also tries to vary the structure of the solo, so that, for example, if he or she has played a series of small steps in a scale, a larger step will then be played, to add interest to the developing melody. In Johnson-Laird's view, this sort of scheme is plausible as a model of human improvisation, because it places minimal demands on memory. He has developed this model as a computer program, which is given a sequence of chords as input and produces as output an improvised series of notes.

One question that arises in response to Johnson-Laird's analysis of improvisation involves the recurring formulas in solos of even the greatest improvisers. Johnson-Laird's model would seemingly not produce such patterns, because it simply runs through its heuristics. Also, and related, is the question of *style* of improvisation. That is, knowledgeable listeners can identify players on the basis of hearing them play, which is related to the patterns of improvisation already discussed. It is not clear that Johnson-Laird's model would have a recognizable style, in the way that Parker had a style. These sorts of results indicate that improvisation may be more directly based on memory than Johnson-Laird assumes. This leaves us with the question of how memory functions "on-line" during improvisation, about which nothing is known at present.

Learning to Write Hits: The Beatles

As a further example of the role of practice in creative development, we can consider the career of the Beatles. The first hit single written by John Lennon and Paul McCartney was "Love Me Do," which was recorded in 1962 and reached the no. 17 slot in the British hit parade in December of that year. It was followed in 1963 by "Please Please Me" (released January 17, reached no. 1 February 22; this was their first no. 1 hit); "From Me to You" (released April 11, reached no. 1 after two weeks); "She Loves You" (released August 23, no. 1 for four months); and "I Want to Hold Your Hand" (released November 29, no. 1 in a week, displacing "She Loves You"). What had preceded this outburst of creative activity? The answer is the same as we have seen for Mozart and jazz musicians: practice, practice, practice (Davies, 1968; Lewisohn, 1992).

The Beatles developed out of the Quarry Men, a musical group formed by Lennon in March 1957 at age 17, soon after he received his first guitar. Lennon had earlier been taught the rudiments of music by his mother. In July, McCartney saw them perform at a dance. McCartney's father was a musician, and Paul had some experience with the trumpet and guitar. After the dance, he met the group and played for them. He also showed them how to tune a guitar, something that the Quarry Men had not yet mastered. Later in July, McCartney was asked to join the group. In March 1958, George Harrison (just turned 15) joined the group. Ringo Starr was the last to join, in 1962, although he had played with the group in public a number of times before that. By that time, the group had gone through several name changes, and their musical style had changed from "skiffle," a British-bred variation of U.S. folk music, to U.S. popular music – rhythm and blues, country and western, rockabilly, and rock and roll. The Beatles, like Mozart and many jazz musicians, were both performers and composers. At the time Lennon and McCartney began writing songs, however, relatively few pop musicians wrote their own songs. Elvis Presley, one of their early idols, did not, although Buddy Holly, Chuck Berry, and Little Richard, also favorites of theirs, did.

No detailed information is available on the Beatles' actual practice regimen, but one can get a feeling for the activities they engaged in by considering their public performances. Although Ericsson et al. (1993) distinguish between performance (as work) and deliberate practice, this distinction may not be particularly sharp in the case of the Beatles. They seemed to have used their early performances as opportunities to hone their craft, in addition to whatever deliberate practice and rehearsal they carried out at other times (Lewisohn, 1992, p. 23). They played the same songs repeatedly over these performances, which gave them chances to work out problems in playing as a group, as well as to improve their indi-

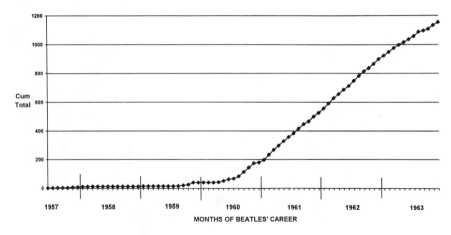

Figure 12.1. The Beatles' cumulative performances until the advent of Beatlemania (1964).

vidual skills. The cumulative frequency of Beatles' performances over the group's performing career until the advent of Beatlemania is displayed in Figure 12.1. Beginning in mid-
1960, they were performing approximately 400 times per year – on average, more than once
per day.

The frequency data in Figure 12.1 are simply numbers of performances and do not consider the amount of time involved in each performance, which in some cases was considerable. As an example, we can consider their five engagements in Hamburg, Germany. The
first of these, from August 17 to November 30, 1960, consisted of a total of 106 nights, during which they were on stage for 5+ hours each night. Their second booking in Hamburg,
April 1 to July 1, 1961, encompassed 92 nights and 503 hours on stage. The third engagement, April 13 to May 31, 1962, added another 48 nights and 172 hours on stage. The last
two Hamburg engagements, in November and December 1962, added approximately 90
hours of performing. Thus, these engagements alone provided more than 270 nights and
approximately 1,250 hours on stage.

The Hamburg engagements were the most work-intensive of the Beatles' performing
career, but they also had approximately 400 other engagements between 1957 and the end
of 1962. Even if these latter engagements encompassed only one on-stage hour each, which
surely is an underestimate, one is still approaching cumulative performance times of 2,000
hours, without taking into account *any* off-stage rehearsal and practice at all. It should be
noted that this cumulative time is less than the cumulative times estimated for young violinists and pianists by Ericsson et al. (1993). In pursuing a career in popular music, the Beatles were engaged in a less skill-demanding activity than playing and composing classical
music, so that less cumulative practice was needed to reach the highest level of accomplishment. However, the Beatles still worked very hard before they hit the big time.

We now have seen that the early career of the Beatles can be looked upon as a time of
much practice. The next question is: What were they practicing? As with the other artists
already discussed, the initial intensive efforts by the Beatles involved immersion in the works
of others. Figure 12.2 presents a summary, over the Beatles' performance career, of the proportion of Lennon–McCartney songs entering their performance repertoire. For the first six
years (1957–1962), of more than 250 different songs in their repertoire, approximately 90%
were "cover" versions of songs written and recorded by others. The Beatles' early performing years were centered on the works of others. Furthermore, the early Beatles' cover ver-

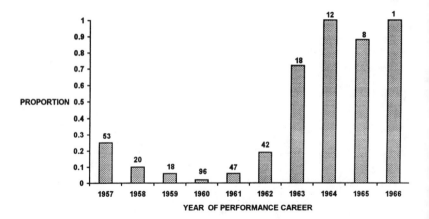

Figure 12.2. Proportion of Beatles' songs entering the Beatles' performance repertoire in each year of their career. The numeral at the top of each bar indicates the number of songs added to the performance repertoire each year.

sions are very close imitations of the originals. Any novelty that occurs is almost exclusively the result of them forgetting or misinterpreting the words.

In contrast, from 1963 to 1966, over 80% of the 39 songs entering the Beatles' performance repertoire were their own. During these later years, they produced a large number of their own songs and used them in their performances; almost everything new that they sang had been written by them. Thus, Lennon and McCartney learned very well the works of others before they produced a significant number of works.

In one respect, the results in Figure 12.2 are not particularly impressive. Of course the Beatles sang the songs of others before producing many of their own: What else would one expect? Early in their career they simply had not had enough time to write many songs, so that is why they sang songs by others. From this skeptical view, the only difference between the early and late Beatles' songs is their quantity. The years of practice might have had no effect other than giving Lennon and McCartney time to write more songs.

However, there is evidence that in addition to being relatively few in number, early Lennon–McCartney songs were judged to be of lower quality than later ones, which supports the claim that over the years of immersion, Lennon and McCartney were learning their craft. One can adopt Hayes's (1989) method to investigate this and can examine the release of Beatles' songs on records. Whether or not a song is released on record is presumably the result of judgments concerning its quality.

First, let us limit the analysis to songs that were actually performed at some point during the Beatles' 10-year performing career. Some songs that they wrote, especially early songs, never were performed in public, which could be taken as an early elimination of weaker songs. Thus, the relatively few Lennon-McCartney songs performed in the early years had already undergone a selection process for quality. However, even if we restrict the analysis to songs that were performed, we still find that many were not released on recordings. Figure 12.3 shows the proportion of Beatles' songs composed in each half of their performance career that were released on records at any time during their recording career, which extended until 1970. There was a much higher proportion of late songs released, providing support for the claim that the Beatles had to learn their trade as songwriters. The difference in recording frequencies shown in the figure is significant ($\chi^2(1) = 26.43$, $p < .0001$).

One might argue that the reason the early songs were not recorded was because the deci-

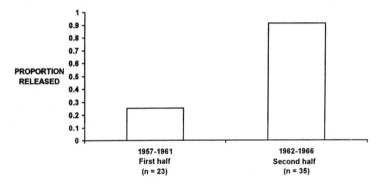

Figure 12.3. Beatles' songs released on records, as a function of when they were written.

sion makers at their recording company did not want to take a chance on them. Once the Beatles established themselves, on the other hand, then anything they produced was probably considered worth recording. Thus, the quality of the songs might not have changed; rather, the criteria were less strict once the Beatles were established. However, many of the early songs were ignored even after the group was established, when early work must have been given new scrutiny. Even this new scrutiny was not enough to produce strong interest in many early songs. It is only in recent years, with the production of exhaustive anthologies of Beatles' material, that a significant number of these early songs has been released.

In addition, one can also examine the amount of innovation involved in various Beatles' songs, in this case by considering critics' and historians' assessments of various works. Based on this criterion, there is little doubt that the Beatles' unique contribution to popular music occurred in the period 1965–1967, beginning with the production of the albums *Rubber Soul* and *Revolver*, and reaching a high point with *Sergeant Pepper's Lonely Hearts Club Band* (e.g., Lewisohn, 1992). Thus, the Beatles' innovations occurred in what one could designate as the third stage of their career, the three being (1) cover versions of others' works, (2) production of their own works, but within the existing styles, and (3) significant innovation.

In conclusion, development of the Beatles parallels that of Mozart and the jazz musicians just discussed, as well as that of the groups studied by Bloom and co-workers (Bloom, 1985) and Ericsson et al. (1993) and the individuals studied by Gardner (1993). All these cases have indicated that years of immersion in a discipline is a precursor for the capacity to produce novel work.

The Question of the Control Group

A question can be raised concerning the interpretation of data on cumulative practice and their relation to creativity. One could argue that the Beatles' data by themselves tell us nothing about the development of creative skills. If one wishes to conclude that the years of practice were causally related to the Beatles' creative output, then, so it could be argued, it is necessary to compare the Beatles with unsuccessful rock groups, to show that the Beatles worked harder than the latter did.

However, the hypothesis under consideration is that a large amount of domain-specific practice is *necessary* for the development of the skills that underlie creative accomplishment, not that practice is sufficient for creative accomplishment. Production of masterworks requires not only a large amount of practice, but also the coming together of a number of different sorts of external factors, many of which are independent of the amount of study and practice put in by a given individual. One's works must be accepted by the professional decision makers and the audience before they become masterworks, that is, before they are put into books that survey the history of a field, where they will be found by cognitive psychologists looking for evidence of creative accomplishment. If, for example, George Martin at Parlophone records had not responded positively to the Beatles' demonstration recordings that their manager played for him, then all their practice would have been wasted. These issues are discussed in more detail in Weisberg (1986, 1993; see also Csikszentmihalyi, 1988, 1996).

Thus, the strongest version of the hypothesis being examined here is that one will never find an individual who has made a significant contribution to a creative discipline without first having deep initial immersion in that discipline. If one can show that the Beatles spent close to the maximum amount of available time honing their skills, then one does not need to examine unsuccessful groups, because the relevant data come from successful individuals. Furthermore, although there may still be a question of whether playing the violin is a creative activity, Ericsson et al. (1993) did carry out an analysis that included control groups, in the sense that they assessed the amount of practice engaged in by violinists of different levels of accomplishment, and found that the higher-achieving violinists had practiced more.

REEXAMINATION OF EMPIRICAL SUPPORT FOR TENSION VIEW

Earlier in the chapter I briefly reviewed two pieces of evidence that seem to provide strong support for the tension view: the inverted-U-shaped relationship between formal education and creative accomplishment (Simonton, 1984), and laboratory studies of problem-solving set, that is, negative transfer when previously successful methods must be modified in response to changes in the situation (Frensch & Sternberg, 1989; Luchins & Luchins, 1959). Since those results are in conflict with the conclusion that, in creative work, practice makes perfect, it would be of value to consider them once again. These studies are only a small sample of evidence supporting the tension view. However, since they are obviously contradictory of the present conclusions, they are worth examining here, if only to demonstrate that support of the tension view is not as solid as it might seem.

Formal Education and Creative Accomplishment

Simonton's (1984) study on its face provides strong support for the tension view, but a question remains. Simonton examined the relation between *formal education* and creative accomplishment over a lifetime, but that does not directly examine the relationship between *knowledge* and creativity. We do not know what the relationship is in creative individuals between formal education and knowledge in their fields. Formal education and knowledge might not be directly related, which would mean that Simonton's results might not in actuality be contradictory to the present view.

It is informative to consider some of the cases included in the sample studied by Simonton. Darwin, for example, did not go beyond a bachelor's degree. However, by the time he returned from the voyage of the *Beagle,* he probably had more first-hand knowledge about the development of species than anyone else in the world (Gruber, 1981). So although his formal education might have ended with the baccalaureate, his acquisition of knowledge did not. By the time he had created the theory of evolution through natural selection, he had been working on the problem for years. As another example, Faraday left school at age 14 to begin an apprenticeship to a bookbinder (Tweney, 1989). However, he had an interest in reading the books that he was binding, and over the next several years carried out a program of self-education. At the age of 23, he was able to obtain the post of assistant to Humphrey Davy, a scientist, who served as his mentor in the development of his career, although Faraday soon went beyond Davy in accomplishment. However, Faraday's accomplishment was based on deep knowledge of the scientific work of the day. Similarly, although Mozart had little in the way of formal education, his musical training began at a very early age and extended over a significant period of time before he made his mark.

One significant aspect of Simonton's study is that he used a sample of eminent individuals born between 1450 and 1850. Knowledge changed significantly over that long stretch of time, and it is difficult to extrapolate to modern education based on conclusions drawn from educational levels of past centuries. For example, since scientific fields especially changed drastically over that time, it is not clear that someone obtaining a bachelor's degree at the end of the nineteenth century had "the same amount" of education in his or her chosen field as did an individual who received a bachelor's degree 300 years ago. That is, the earlier bachelor's degree may have been closer to a modern-day Ph.D. as concerns knowledge about one's field. It should also be noted that in the investigations of present-day neurologists and mathematicians by Bloom and co-workers (Bloom, 1985), all the participants had obtained the Ph.D.

Thus, although the relationship between formal education and creative accomplishment may be an inverted U, that does not necessarily contradict the view that the relation between knowledge and creativity is positive. Formal education and knowledge in one's field can be independent.

Knowledge, Rigidity, and Creativity: Positive Transfer in Creative Thinking

There is no doubt that negative transfer in problem solving can be demonstrated in laboratory situations (Frensch & Sternberg, 1989; Luchins & Luchins, 1959). Participants experience difficulty when "deep" changes in a problem-solving situation demand that the thinker modify previously successful responses in a significant way. Furthermore, the degree of negative transfer seems to be a function of the amount of past experience in the situation; in such modified situations, expertise turns out to be a disadvantage.

There is, however, an important assumption that must be considered before we conclude that those laboratory demonstrations support the general claim that expertise is detrimental to creative thinking. Laboratory demonstrations of negative transfer are of interest because they are assumed to be microcosms of real-world situations. We are thus led to ask if creative thinking in the real world is in fact demanded by situations in which there have been "deep" changes, which would make one's past experience detrimental. Or, when creative thinking occurs in the real world, are the situations only different on the surface from past situations, in which case past experience would be an asset? Or might some mixed circumstance hold?

If there are connections between present and past situations (i.e., if past and present situations differ only in surface attributes), then it would be useful for the thinker to use the past as the basis for responding to the present. Even if one's knowledge is not totally applicable to the present situation, because the present is indeed different than the past, one's knowledge would still be a reasonable place to begin. Furthermore, modifying one's past experience to make it fit the unique aspects of the present situation would also be reasonable. Recent analyses indicate that, contrary to the assumption of "deep" change which underlies the tension view, many situations in which significant creative advances occurred were similar enough to old situations that knowledge from the old situation was usable (Weisberg, 1993, 1995b).

We can consider first the development of two of Picasso's most important paintings, *Les demoiselles d'Avignon* and *Guernica*. In both cases, Picasso's initial sketches for the new work were based closely on earlier work, his own and that of other artists. The ideas in the sketches were then elaborated and extended, in one case radically, as Picasso worked further on the paintings. The radical change was in response to the work of other artists. However, in the present context, the important point is that the creation of these new works of art did not begin with a rejection of what had come before. Rather, the new work could be looked upon as an elaboration of what had come before. As well, Calder's development of mobiles (nonrepresentational moving sculpture, driven by the wind) was based on work he had done earlier, again elaborated as the result of his exposure to work by others.

Similar processes are seen in Edison's development of the electrical lighting system, to make his lightbulb practical as an in-home device. He used an extant system, that for natural gas lighting, as the basis for his new system. The Wright brothers' flying machine was also based on extant work, although in this case, that work was much less useful. The Wrights were therefore forced to rely on themselves to a large degree and to work out many problems, large and small, that plagued their work. However, in this case too one does not find examples of free-associative thinking and the whole-hearted rejection of the past. The development of the steam engine and the cotton gin follow the same sort of path.

These examples are but a few of many that could be cited to support the conclusion that creative thinking is firmly rooted in the past. Positive transfer of past experience can occur because many real-world situations that require creative thinking are not like a bridge game in which the low card from the last trick now leads (Frensch & Sternberg, 1989). However, some situations do involve deep changes, and are particularly informative in the present context.

A situation in which there turned out to be deep changes was the development by Watson and Crick of the double-helix model of DNA (Olby, 1974; Watson, 1968). Watson and Crick decided first of all that the structure of DNA might be a helix of some sort, based on earlier work by Linus Pauling, who not long before had proposed that the structure of the protein alpha-keratin was helical. This decision served to focus Watson and Crick's investigation on specific questions of the structure, but the initial direction of their work came about through the adoption of Pauling's orientation. A straightforward extension of past work provided the basis for the creation of something new.

However, this discovery also involved negative transfer, which provides a case study of what happens in the real world when there has been a deep change in the situation. The double helix of DNA is formed by two phosphate–sugar "backbones" linked together in a structure similar to a spiral staircase, with the rungs constructed out of pairs of nitrogen-rich bases (adenine, thymine, cytosine, and guanine). Before ultimately determining the correct base pairings (adenine with thymine; cytosine with guanine), Watson spent time considering the possibility of "like-with-like" pairings – adenine with adenine, thymine with thymine, and so on. One reason for Watson's interest in this possibility may have been his past experience with such structures in graduate school (Olby, 1974). Watson spent time attempting to work with the like-with-like scheme before it was rejected and the correct pairings were worked out, essentially by trial and error (Watson, 1968).

Several important points come from this example. First, there was negative transfer at the specific level of base pairings, but there was undoubtedly positive transfer overall. That is, without Watson and Crick's initial assumption that the molecule was a helix, which was positive transfer from Pauling's work, little or no progress would have been made. It is not possible in such a case to quantify the amount of positive versus negative transfer, but some relevant information can be gleaned from the behavior at the same time of Rosalind Franklin, another investigator who was studying the structure of DNA. According to several sources (e.g., Olby, 1974; Watson, 1968), Franklin claimed that she was attempting to determine the structure with the fewest assumptions possible. That is, she may have been attempting to analyze the structure from the bottom up, without assuming anything about it as a working hypothesis. It may be significant that Franklin was not able to determine the structure of DNA before Watson and Crick. So, although this is obviously not an experimental study with a true control group, the results are consistent with the conclusion that positive transfer from similar situations involving analysis of organic macromolecules was on the whole helpful to Watson and Crick.

In addition, although there may have been negative transfer at one point in Watson and Crick's formulation of the double helix, it must be emphasized that the correct model was ultimately worked out. That is, any negative transfer was overcome. Watson did not respond like the participants in a water-jar-set experiment, who, through previous success with problems with a complex solution, become incapable of solving a simple problem. When Watson was repeatedly unsuccessful in constructing a model with like-with-like pairings that could account for the relevant data, he (with input from Crick and others) rejected the like-with-like structure. Thus, the "blindness" of participants in water jar studies is not analogous to what happened in this case of creative accomplishment: Any set that might have existed was overcome.

It would be interesting to examine other cases from this perspective, to determine the frequency of positive versus negative transfer and to see where success and/or failure occurred. The fact that negative transfer was overcome in the case of the double helix, does not, of course, preclude cases in which negative transfer was strong enough to interfere with the ultimate discovery. No data are available at present to address this issue. The important conclusion for the present discussion, however, is that laboratory studies of negative transfer in problem solving may have only limited relevance to the broader study of creative thinking (see also Weisberg, 1995b).

KNOWLEDGE AND HEURISTICS IN SCIENTIFIC DISCOVERY. Simon and co-workers (e.g., Kulkarni & Simon, 1988; Langley, Simon, Bradshaw, & Zytkow, 1987) have proposed that scientific discoveries can be analyzed in terms of heuristics, some of which may develop out of immersion in the discipline. As one example, Kulkarni and Simon modeled Krebs's discovery of the ornithine cycle and concluded that half the heuristics in the model were based on past experience within the relevant domain. Furthermore, the particular advantage that Krebs possessed was his facility with a technique learned during his training.

Langley et al. (1987) have also argued that some scientific discoveries are the result of very general heuristics, which are not based on deep immersion in a domain of expertise. For example, in an analysis of Kepler's discovery of the three laws of planetary motion that bear his name, Langley et al. assume that all that was required were several heuristics concerned with patterns in sets of *numbers*. That is, knowledge concerning planetary motion was not at all relevant to the discovery of the laws. The computer model that was developed to simulate Kepler's discovery had no information about astronomy in its database.

Similarly, Dunbar (e.g., 1995) has carried out laboratory simulations of scientific creativity, in which naive undergraduates have been able to make scientific discoveries under controlled laboratory conditions. The students are given information corresponding to the results from experiments and are able to use a computer simulation to design and carry out further experiments of their own. Dunbar reports that participants in his studies are able to replicate the Nobel Prize–winning discovery by Monod and Jacob of regulator genes, which control the activity of other genes. The students are successful even though they are chosen because they lack anything but the most superficial knowledge in the domain of genetics.

The computer simulations of Kepler's discoveries (Langley et al., 1987) and the student simulations of the work of Jacob and Monod (Dunbar, 1995) raise interesting issues concerning how knowledge is used in creative thinking. First of all, these findings raise the question of whether it is always necessary to have immersion in the domain. If Kepler's discovery can be simulated with a computer model or by undergraduates with no knowledge of astronomy, then did Kepler need his knowledge? Similarly, if naive undergraduates can simulate Jacob and Monod's discovery, then why did Monod and Jacob need advanced training? One possibility is that Jacob and Monod needed their knowledge to understand the problem in the first place, as it existed in the world. That is, the undergraduates in Dunbar's (1995) study were given the very end of the whole enterprise. By that time, much work had already been done in analyzing the problem and setting up the relevant experiments, which could then be used in the simulation exercise.

It is also of interest to consider whether such simulations would be possible with other scientific problems. For example, could naive undergraduates discover the double helix? The discovery of the double helix involved several different components, among which were the number and position of the backbones, the structure of the backbones, the pitch of the helix, the positions of the bases, and the pairings of the bases. For all of these except the last, undergraduates would not know even where to begin. For example, in order to determine number and position of the backbones, one would have to know how to read x-ray diffraction patterns, and one would also have to know how they are obtained. None of this would be possible without expertise. Determining the base pairings, on the other hand, is little more than working out a simple jigsaw puzzle, once the problem has been narrowed down. Thus, different scientific problems may require different types of knowledge, which is an issue worth investigating further.

RETHINKING THE RELATIONSHIP BETWEEN CREATIVITY AND KNOWLEDGE: HOW IS KNOWLEDGE USED IN CREATIVE THINKING?

If it is concluded for the present that creativity and knowledge are positively related, we are still left with the question of specifying how knowledge is actually used in creative thinking. Since most recent theorizing concerning creative thinking has been based on the tension view, the main concern has been with understanding how the thinker can break away from knowledge. Accordingly, little has been said about how knowledge is extended to new situations. Therefore, little in the way of specific proposals can be offered here, although some speculations are possible.

Knowing the Territory

Bailin (1988) has argued that, rather than being independent of the past, as James (1880), Hausman (1984), and others have claimed, even the most radically new creative products must be tied to the past. In Bailin's view, there can be no creativity if a product is not strongly rooted in the past, because in order for the audience to even understand the product, we must have some frame of reference, and this can only be supplied by the past. Without some sort of reference to the past, there would be no coherence: The product would make no sense to us.

Bailin's argument is framed from the perspective of the audience viewing the product, but we can easily extend it to the creative person as well. When a person makes some innovation, no matter how radical, in order for that product to make sense to the creator, he or she must be able to link it to what has been done before. Therefore, in order to have produced it in the first place, the thinker must have started with something from the past. And any changes introduced, which may serve to turn the product into something radically new, were probably also based on knowledge. How else could one know how to modify something?

A related view is that if one does not know the discipline, one cannot go beyond it. It is reasonable to assume that all individuals engaged in creative fields are motivated to produce something new. Therefore, if they did not know what had been done, they could not move significantly beyond it. However, this does not provide a complete understanding for why years of immersion seem to be necessary for creative accomplishment. Would not simple familiarity do as well? If one were reasonably familiar with a domain, then one would be able to tell whether or not something were familiar. So we are still left with the question of why deep immersion is necessary.

Immersion Results in Automatic Processing

A different sort of possibility is that deep immersion provides extensive opportunities for practicing any skills, such as playing the piano, required to create within the domain, which makes them automatic. Automaticity of skills may be necessary for the production of novelty, for example, improvisation of new melodies. However, this speculation does not specify *how* automaticity leads to novelty. Perhaps when a skill becomes automatic, one can then allocate capacity to production of novelty. One does not have to think about how to express one's ideas, one can just do it as the ideas become available. This view proposes that the value of immersion is to perfect a skill, so that carrying it out does not drain capacity.

Deep immersion might also lead to development of heuristics. It might be that understanding the methods in some domains, such as the sciences, requires time because of their complexity. In order to understand x-ray diffraction, for example, one needs to know many different things, several of which are built on others, and so forth. As indicated earlier, at this point, little more than speculation can be offered concerning how knowledge is used during creative thinking.

WHAT ARE THE DIFFERENCES BETWEEN CREATIVE AND NONCREATIVE THINKERS?

The conclusion that knowledge plays a positive role in creative thinking leads to a different perspective concerning the question of individual differences in creative thinking. Perhaps the basic difference between a creative and noncreative thinker, assuming equivalent levels of motivation, etc., is the knowledge that they bring to the situation. A related idea is that, if one takes the perspective of the creative thinker, we should be able to understand relatively directly where any creative idea came from. That is, if we knew what the creative thinker knew, we would be able to understand how the new idea came about. As an example, consider the following situation, discussed by DeBono (1968):

For many years physiologists could not understand the purpose of the long loops in the kidney tubules: it was assumed that the loops had no special function and were a relic of the way the kidney had evolved. Then one day an engineer looked at the loops and at once recognized that they could be part of a counter-current multiplier, a well-known engineering device for increasing the concentration of liquids. In this instance, a fresh look from outside provided an answer to something that had been a puzzle for a long time. (pp. 148–149)

On the basis of this sort of example, DeBono recommends that in order to solve a recalcitrant problem, one should adopt a fresh perspective, in this case that of the engineer. That is, in a classic statement of the tension view, one is urged to break away from one's knowledge. However, *from the perspective of the engineer,* there was nothing new involved: He was able to apply his knowledge relatively directly to the new situation he was presented with, because of a straightforward relationship between what he saw and what he knew. For the engineer, this response was just another example of recognizing something familiar. The engineer's behavior can be explained by theories of pattern recognition; we do not need a theory of creativity to understand what he was able to do. It is only from the perspective of the perplexed physiologist that there is anything requiring explanation in terms of creative thinking.

Thus, if we can get into the database of the creative thinker, we may be able to understand creative thinking as a process based on the direct application of knowledge. It is only when we examine the situation from outside, as an ignorant observer, that we feel the necessity to postulate basic differences between creative and noncreative individuals. That is, it may not be necessary to assume that creative individuals differ from the noncreative in any significant way, except for the knowledge they possess.

As a specific example of how we can understand creative thinking without postulating anything in the way of exotic processes, we can consider again Watson and Crick's development of the double-helix model of DNA. A number of other well-regarded researchers, including Pauling, Maurice Wilkins, and Franklin, were also working on the structure of DNA. Why was it that Watson and Crick produced the structure, and these others did not? Based on the tension view, one might be led to speculate that something about Watson and Crick's mode of thinking or personalities allowed them to break away from previous knowledge and to develop the new. However, we have already seen that a cornerstone of Watson and Crick's work was available knowledge. There may be a direct answer to the question of why Watson and Crick were successful while the others were not: If one considers various components of the ultimate model of DNA, all of them were available to only Watson and Crick (Weisberg, 1993). Therefore, they were able to construct the model while the others were not. Nothing further is required as far as explanation is concerned; one does not have to assume that Watson and Crick were different (or better) thinkers than the others. They simply had available what was needed to develop the correct model of DNA, and the others did not. Although this explanation of the achievement of Watson and Crick may leave one unsatisfied ("Surely there is more to it than that!"), if on the right track, it allows us to understand how at least one creative advance came about without postulating anything in the way of extraordinary aspects of the creative individual.

A related objection to this conclusion is the hypothetical example of the deeply knowledgeable person who does not produce significant creative work. An example is the individual who writes textbooks (thereby presumably demonstrating encyclopedic knowledge), but who does not produce innovation. However, the level of expertise needed to write a textbook is not the same as that developed through deep immersion in a discipline. People who write texts are not, under the present conception of knowledge (loose though it is), deeply knowledgeable. Of course, it is still possible that a deeply knowledgeable person might never produce innovation within his or her domain or expertise. As discussed earlier, knowledge is necessary, not sufficient, for creative achievement.

CONCLUSIONS

The present chapter argues that the relation between creativity and knowledge is much more straightforward than theories of creativity typically assume: One may be able to understand creative thinking by determining the knowledge that the creative thinker brings to the situation he or she is facing. The reason that one person produced some innovation, while another person did not, may be due to nothing more than the fact that the former knew something that the latter did not. Furthermore, this knowledge may not have been of an extraordinary sort. This view, if correct, means that we do not need special theories to explain creative thinking. Rather, we simply need a complete theory of thinking. Theories of creative thinking may be theories in search of phenomena to explain.

NOTE

Thanks are due to Robert Sternberg and Lynn Hasher for comments on an earlier version of this chapter.

REFERENCES

Amabile, T. (1983). *The social psychology of creativity.* New York: Springer-Verlag.
Amabile, T. (1989). *Growing up creative: Nurturing a lifetime of creativity.* New York: Crown.
Bailin, S. (1988). *Achieving extraordinary ends: An essay on creativity.* Dordrecht: Kluwer Academic.
Berliner, P. F. (1994). *Thinking in jazz: The infinite art of improvisation.* Chicago: University of Chicago Press.
Bloom, B. S. (Ed.). (1985). *Developing talent in young people.* New York: Ballantine.
Campbell, D. T. (1960). Blind variation and selective retention in creative thought as in other knowledge processes. *Psychological Review, 67,* 380–400.
Chase, W. G., & Simon, H. A. (1973). Perception in chess. *Cognitive Psychology, 4,* 55–81.
Csikszentmihalyi, M. (1988). Society, culture, person: A systems view of creativity. In R. J. Sternberg (Ed.), *The nature of creativity* (pp. 325–339). Cambridge University Press.
Csikszentmihalyi, M. (1996). *Creativity: Flow and the psychology of discovery and invention.* New York: HarperCollins.
Davies, H. (1968). *The Beatles: An authorized biography.* New York: Random House.
DeBono, E. (1968). *New think: The use of lateral thinking in the generation of new ideas.* New York: Basic.
Dunbar, K. (1995). How scientists really reason: Scientific reasoning in real-world laboratories. In R. J. Sternberg & J. E. Davidson (Eds.), *The nature of insight* (pp. 365–396). Cambridge, MA: MIT Press.
Ericsson, K. A., & Charness, N. (1994). Expert performance: Its structure and acquisition. *American Psychologist, 49,* 725–747.
Ericsson, K. A., Krampe, R. Th., & Clemens, T.-R. (1993). The role of deliberate practice in expert performance. *Psychological Review, 103,* 363–406.
Eysenck, H. J. (1993). Creativity and personality: Suggestions for a theory. *Psychological Inquiry, 4,* 147–178.
Feldman, D. H. (1986). *Nature's gambit: Child prodigies and the development of human potential.* New York: Basic.
Frensch, P. A., & Sternberg, R. J. (1989). Expertise and intelligent thinking: When is it worse to know better? In R. J. Sternberg (Ed.), *Advances in the psychology of human intelligence* (Vol. 5, pp. 157–188). Hillsdale, NJ: Erlbaum.
Gardner, H. (1993). *Creating minds: An anatomy of creativity seen through the lives of Freud, Einstein, Picasso, Stravinsky, Eliot, Graham, and Gandhi.* New York: Basic.
Gruber, H. E. (1981). *Darwin on man: A psychological study of scientific creativity* (2nd ed.). Chicago: University of Chicago Press.
Guilford J. P. (1950). Creativity. *American Psychologist, 5,* 444–454.
Hausman, C. (1984). *Discourse on novelty and creation.* Albany: State University of New York Press.
Hayes, J. R. (1989). Cognitive processes in creativity. In J. A. Glover, R. R. Ronning, & C. R. Reynolds (Eds.), *Handbook of creativity* (pp. 135–145). New York: Plenum.
James, W. (1880). Great men, great thoughts, and the environment. *Atlantic Monthly, 46,* 441–459.
James, W. (1908). *Talks to teachers on psychology.* New York: Henry Holt.
Johnson-Laird, P. N. (1988). Freedom and constraint in creativity. In R. J. Sternberg (Ed.), *The nature of creativity: Current psychological perspectives* (pp. 202–219). Cambridge University Press.
Kernfeld, B. (1995). *What to listen for in jazz.* New Haven, CT: Yale University Press.
Koestler, A. (1964). *The act of creation.* New York: Macmillan.
Kulkarni, D., & Simon, H. A. (1988). The processes of scientific discovery: The strategy of experimentation. *Cognitive Science, 12,* 139–175.

Langley, P., Simon, H. A., Bradshaw, G. L., & Zytkow, J. M. (1987). *Scientific discovery: Computational explorations of the creative process.* Cambridge, MA: MIT Press.

Lewisohn, M. (1992). *The complete Beatles chronicle.* New York: Harmony.

Luchins, A. S., & Luchins, E. H. (1959). *Rigidity of behavior.* Eugene: University of Oregon Press.

Martindale, C. (1995). Creativity and connectionism. In S. M. Smith, T. B. Ward, & R. A. Finke (Eds.), *The creative cognition approach* (pp. 249–268). Cambridge, MA: MIT Press.

Mednick, S. A. (1962). The associative basis of the creative process. *Psychological Review, 69,* 220–232.

Olby, R. (1974). *The path to the double helix: The discovery of DNA.* Seattle: University of Washington Press.

Owens, T. (1995). *Bebop: The music and its players.* New York: Oxford University Press.

Pariser, D. (1987). The juvenile drawings of Klee, Toulouse-Lautrec, and Picasso. *Visual Arts Research, 13,* 53–67.

Richardson, J. (1991). *A life of Picasso: Vol. 1. 1881–1906.* New York: Random House.

Runco, M. A. (1991). *Divergent thinking.* Norwood, NJ: Ablex.

Scheerer, M. (1963). Problem-solving. *Scientific American, 208,* 118–128.

Schoenberg, H. (1970). *The lives of the great composers.* New York: Norton.

Simonton, D. K. (1984). *Genius, creativity, and leadership.* Cambridge University Press.

Simonton, D. K. (1988). Creativity, leadership, and chance. In R. J. Sternberg & J. E. Davidson (Eds.), *The nature of creativity: Current psychological perspectives* (pp. 386–426). Cambridge, MA: MIT Press.

Simonton, D. K. (1995). Foresight in insight? A Darwinian answer. In R. J. Sternberg & J. E. Davidson (Eds.), *The nature of insight* (pp. 465–494), Cambridge, MA: MIT Press.

Sternberg, R. J., & Lubart, T. I. (1995). An investment perspective on creative insight. In R. J. Sternberg & J. E. Davidson, (Eds.), *The nature of insight* (pp. 535–558). Cambridge, MA: MIT Press.

Tweney, R. D. (1989). Fields of enterprise: On Michael Faraday's thought. In D. B. Wallace & H. E. Gruber (Eds.), *Creative people at work: Twelve cognitive case studies* (pp. 91–106). New York: Oxford University Press.

Watson, J. D. (1968). *The double helix,* New York: Signet.

Weisberg, R. W. (1986). *Creativity: Genius and other myths.* New York: Freeman.

Weisberg, R. W. (1988). Problem solving and creativity. In R. J. Sternberg (Ed.), *The nature of creativity: Contemporary psychological perspectives* (pp. 148–176). Cambridge, MA: MIT Press.

Weisberg, R. W. (1993). *Creativity: Beyond the myth of genius.* New York: Freeman.

Weisberg, R. W. (1995a). Prolegomena to theories of insight in problem solving: A taxonomy of problems. In R. J. Sternberg & J. E. Davidson (Eds.), *The nature of insight* (pp. 157–196). Cambridge, MA: MIT Press.

Weisberg, R. W. (1995b). Case studies of creative thinking: Reproduction versus restructuring in the real world. In S. M. Smith, T. B. Ward, & R. A. Finke (Eds.), *The creative cognition approach* (pp. 53–72). Cambridge, MA: MIT Press.

Wertheimer, M. (1982). *Productive thinking* (enlarged edition). Chicago: University of Chicago Press.

Zaslaw, N. (1989). *Mozart's symphonies: Context, performance practice, reception.* New York: Oxford.

13 *Creativity and Intelligence*

ROBERT J. STERNBERG AND LINDA A. O'HARA

What is the relationship between creativity and intelligence? Creativity has often been defined as the process of bringing into being something novel and useful. Intelligence may be defined as the ability to purposively adapt to, shape, and select environments (Sternberg, 1985a). Although there are many other definitions of both intelligence (see "Intelligence and Its Measurement," 1921; Sternberg & Detterman, 1986) and creativity (see Glover, Ronning, & Reynolds, 1989; Policastro & Gardner, Chapter 11, this volume; Rothenberg & Hausman, 1976; Sternberg, 1988), these definitions tend to share at least some elements with these consensual definitions.

What about the relationship between the two? R. Ochse (1990) said, "If intelligence means selecting and shaping environments, it *is* creativity" (p. 104). In order to select or shape the environment to suit oneself, one requires the imagination to create a vision of what the environment should be and of how this idealized environment can become a reality. On the other hand, the ability to adapt to the environment – to change oneself to suit the environment – typically involves little or no creativity, and may even require one to suppress creativity, as when one realizes that adaptation to a school or job environment means keeping one's creative ideas to oneself, or else risking a low grade or job evaluation. According to Getzels and Csikszentmihalyi (1972), creativity and intelligence may represent different processes and intelligence may be required in widely varying degrees in different fields of creative endeavor. For example, a great amount of intelligence may not be needed to be a creative artist but certainly would be expected in a Nobel Prize–winning physicist. One could also say that creativity is required in widely different degrees in different fields of intelligent behavior.

Are creativity and intelligence the same or not? If not, how are they related, if at all? In this chapter, we will review work that covers the five possible answers to that question: (1) Creativity is a subset of intelligence; (2) intelligence is a subset of creativity; (3) creativity and intelligence are overlapping sets; (4) creativity and intelligence are essentially the same thing (coincident sets); and (5) creativity and intelligence bear no relation at all to each other (disjoint sets). All of these relations have been proposed. The most conventional view is probably that of overlapping sets, that intelligence and creativity overlap in some respects, but not in others. But the other views deserve serious attention as well.

We shall consider each of the relations in turn, realizing that these set relations are idealizations that cannot possibly do justice to the complexity and richness of extant theories of either intelligence or creativity. We shall limit our consideration primarily to theories and research on human intelligence, although, of course, artificial intelligence also can provide key insights into the nature of creativity (see, e.g., Boden, 1991, 1994; Johnson-Laird, 1988; Langley, Simon, Bradshaw, & Zytkow, 1987).

CREATIVITY AS A SUBSET OF INTELLIGENCE

In his original test of intelligence, Binet (1896, as cited in Brown, 1989) included an inkblot for children to describe in order to measure imagination, but Binet later dropped it because he could not develop a reliable scoring system for it. Later, in the 1905 scale, Binet and Simon included open-ended items such as giving rhyming words, completing sentences, and constructing sentences that contain three given words in order to tap creativity; but again, he dropped the items measuring creativity in a later version of the test (Brown, 1989). It appears that Binet's troubles with creativity tests foreshadowed the frustrations that future researchers would have for over a century. J. P. Guilford is one researcher who persisted with creativity tests despite the frustrations.

Guilford's Structure-of-Intellect Model

Guilford (1950, 1967, 1970, 1975) had an enormous impact on the field of creativity when he pointed out (Guilford, 1950) that creativity was a relatively neglected field of study, a claim that has been made recently as well (Sternberg & Lubart, 1996). Guilford almost single-handedly created psychometric interest in the study of creativity.

In this Structure of the Intellect (SI) model, Guilford (1967) suggested three basic dimensions of intelligence, which form a cube: (1) operations – cognition, memory, divergent production, convergent production, evaluation; (2) content – figural, symbolic, semantic, behavioral; and (3) products – units, classes, relations, systems, transformations, implications. By crossing the 5 operations, 4 contents, and 6 products, one gets 120 factors (a number that Guilford increased in his later life). Most relevant for creativity is Divergent Production, which involves a broad search for information and the generation of numerous novel answers to problems, as opposed to one single correct answer, which represents convergent production. As Divergent Production is just one of the 5 operations of the intellect, creativity can be seen as a subset of intelligence. Guilford also pointed out that the facets of his model of intelligence that involved creativity were typically not measured by conventional tests of intelligence (and, half a century later, still aren't). Conventional tests of intelligence most often require convergent operations to produce a single correct answer to multiple-choice questions.

Guilford (1975) identified a number of factors involved in creative problem solving (see also Ochse, 1990, for a review), including (a) Sensitivity to Problems – the ability to recognize problems, (b) Fluency – number of ideas, (c) Flexibility – shifts in approaches, and (d) Originality – unusualness. These abilities could be further broken down. For example, Guilford distinguished among Ideational Fluency (the ability to produce various ideas rapidly in response to certain preset requirements), Associational Fluency (the ability to list words associated with a given word), and Expressional Fluency (the ability to organize words into phrases or sentences). Similarly, Flexibility could be broken down into Spontaneous Flexibility (the ability to be flexible, even when it is not necessary to be so) and Adaptive Flexibility (the ability to be flexible when it is necessary, as in certain types of problem solving).

Guilford devised a number of tests of creativity, which were then adapted and expanded upon in the battery of Paul Torrance (1974). For example, a test of divergent production of semantic units is, "Name all the things you can think of that are white and edible" (Guilford, 1975, p. 42). A test of production of alternative relations is, "In what different ways are a father and daughter related?" (p. 42). A test of production of systems is, "Write as many sentences as you can using the words *desert food,* and *army,*" (p. 42). Other tests include producing clever titles for short stories, listing unusual uses for common objects such as bricks or coat hangers, and listing the consequences of a given event, for example, that people didn't need to sleep.

Guilford and Hoepfner (1966) gave 204 ninth-graders 45 different divergent production tests and found a mean correlation of .37 between the California Test of Mental Maturity (CCTM, an IQ measure) and the semantic divergent production tests, and a mean correlation of .22 between the CCTM and the visual-figural divergent production tests. They also noted that the scatter plots of the IQ and divergent production data points were triangular shaped as opposed to the customary elliptical distribution seen in correlations. The triangular plots indicated that students low in IQ were also low in divergent production tests but that students high in IQ were scattered over much of the whole range in divergent production tests (Guilford & Christensen, 1973). This finding was replicated by Daniel Schubert (1973) with an army sample.

Guilford's approach to testing has been enormously influential in the field of creativity, but today has lost some of its appeal, in part because the tests seem only weakly to relate to other kinds of ratings of creativity and to measure somewhat trivial aspects of the phenomenon (Amabile, 1996; Beittel, 1964; Merrifield, Gardner, & Cox, 1964; Piers, Daniels, & Quackenbush, 1960; Skager, Schultz, & Klein, 1967; Wallach & Kogan, 1965; Yamamoto, 1964).

Cattell's Model

Although Raymond Cattell (1971) is more well known for his theory of crystallized and fluid intelligence, he also posited a list of primary abilities that are similar to, but less complex than, Guilford's model of 120 factors. Cattell's list of primary abilities includes: Verbal, Numerical, Spatial, Perceptual Speed (Figural Identification), Speed of Closure (Visual Cognition, Gestalt Perception), Inductive Reasoning, Deductive Reasoning, Rote Memory, Mechanical Knowledge and Skill, Word Fluency, Ideational Fluency, Restructuring Closure (Flexibility of Closure), Flexibility versus Firmness (Originality), General Motor Coordination, Manual Dexterity, Musical Pitch and Tonal Sensitivity, Representational Drawing Skill, Expressional Fluency, Motor Speed, Musical Rhythm and Timing, and Judgment. Cattell, then, saw the creativity-relevant abilities of Originality and Ideational Fluency as a subset of the primary abilities.

Cattell (1971) criticized Guilford for his factor analytic rotational procedures, which, according to Cattell, led to Guilford's overrating the role of divergent thinking in creativity. (See a similar criticism in Horn & Knapp, 1973.) And, like the other critics of Guilford's tests, Cattell (1971) argued that

the verdict that a test measures creativity is only a projection of the test constructor's personal view about what creativity is. Thus, in the intellectual tests designed by Guilford's students and many others who have worked on creativity in this decade, creativity has finished up by being evaluated simply as oddity or bizarreness of response relative to the population mean or as output of words per minute, etc. This indeed comes close to mistaking the shadow for the substance. (p. 409)

Cattell believed real-life creative performance was determined by one's general intelligence first, particularly fluid intelligence (reasoning ability) as opposed to crystallized intelligence (knowledge or learned material), and then by personality factors.

Gardner's Theory of Multiple Intelligences

Similar to but less extensive than Cattell's proposed set of abilities is the proposed set of intelligences in Howard Gardner's (1983, 1993, 1995) theory of multiple intelligences (MI). According to Gardner, intelligence is not a unitary entity but rather a collection of eight distinct intelligences. According to this view, people can be intelligent in a variety of ways. For example, a poet is intelligent in a way that is different from the way that an architect is, who is intelligent in a way that is different from the way a dancer is. Moreover, these intelligences can be used in a variety of ways, including but not limited to creative ways. Thus, creative functioning is one aspect (a subset) of the multiple intelligences. The eight intelligences are (a) linguistic (as in writing a poem or a short story), (b) logical mathematical (as in solving a logical or mathematical proof), (c) spatial (as in getting the "lay of the land" in a new city), (d) bodily-kinesthetic (as in athletics or dancing), (e) musical (as in composing a sonata or playing the cello), (f) interpersonal (as in finding an effective way to understand or interrelate to others), (g) intrapersonal (as in achieving a high level of self-understanding), and (h) naturalist (as in seeing complex patterns in the natural environment).

Gardner (1993) has analyzed the lives of seven individuals who made highly creative contributions in the twentieth century, with each specializing in one of seven multiple intelligences: Sigmund Freud (intrapersonal), Albert Einstein (logical-mathematical), Pablo Picasso (spatial), Igor Stravinsky (musical), T. S. Eliot (linguistic), Martha Graham (bodily-kinesthetic),and Mohandas Gandhi (interpersonal). Charles Darwin would be an example of someone with extremely high naturalist intelligence. Gardner points out, however, that most of these individuals actually had strengths in more than one intelligence and that they had notable weaknesses as well in others (e.g., Freud's weaknesses may have been in spatial and musical intelligences).

Although creativity can be understood in terms of uses of the multiple intelligences to generate new and even revolutionary ideas, Gardner's (1993) analysis goes well beyond the intellectual. For example, Gardner points out two major themes in the behavior of these creative giants: They tended to have a matrix of support at the time of their creative breakthroughs, and they tended to drive a "Faustian bargain" whereby they gave up many of the pleasures that people typically enjoy in life in order to attain extraordinary success in their careers.

Gardner further follows Csikszentmihalyi (1988, 1996) in distinguishing between the importance of the domain (the body of knowledge about a particular subject area) and the field (the context in which this body of knowledge is studied and elaborated, including the persons working with the domain, such as critics, publishers, and other "gatekeepers"). Both are important to the development and, ultimately, the recognition of creativity.

INTELLIGENCE AS A SUBSET OF CREATIVITY

According to a second model, intelligence can be viewed as a subset of creativity. Creativity comprises intelligence plus other things, whatever these other things may be.

Sternberg and Lubart's Investment Theory

A representative theory of this kind is Sternberg and Lubart's (1991, 1995, 1996) investment theory of creativity (see also Rubenson & Runco, 1992, for a related approach wherein the theorists postulate the existence of creative potential for each individual as the product of initial endowments and active investments in creative ability). According to Sternberg and Lubart's theory, creative people, like good investors, buy low and sell high. But their buying and selling is in the world of ideas. In particular, they generate ideas that – like stocks with low price-to-earnings ratios – are relatively unpopular or even openly disrespected. They attempt to convince other people of the worth of these ideas. Then they sell high, meaning that they let other people pursue their extant ideas while they move on to their next unpopular idea.

Sternberg and Lubart (1995) argue that there are six main elements that converge to form creativity: intelligence, knowledge, thinking styles, personality, motivation, and the environment. Intelligence is thus just one of six forces that, in confluence, generate creative thought and behavior.

According to the theory, three aspects of intelligence are key for creativity: synthetic, analytical, and practical abilities. These three aspects are drawn from Sternberg's (1985a, 1988, 1996) triarchic theory of human intelligence. They are viewed as interactive and as working together in creative functioning.

Synthetic ability is the ability to generate ideas that are novel, high in quality, and task appropriate. Because creativity is viewed as an interaction between a person, a task, and an environment, what is novel, high in quality, or task appropriate may vary from one person, task, or environment to another.

The first key element of synthetic ability is what Sternberg (1985a) refers to as a meta-component, which is a higher-order executive process used in planning, monitoring, and evaluating task performance. This metacomponent is one of redefining problems. In other words, creative people may take problems that other people see, or they themselves have previously seen, in one way, and redefine them in a totally different way. In this sense, they "defy the crowd." For example, they may decide that the fact that many of their friends are buying houses in a certain community indicates not good value, but bad value, because houses in that community have already been bid up in price by high demand. Or they may take a problem that they have seen in one way and redefine it. For example, they may decide that, rather than trying to make more money to meet expenses, they should instead lower their expenses. Sternberg and Lubart point out that redefining problems involves both an ability and an attitude – the ability to do it effectively, but also the attitude whereby one decides to do it in the first place.

Sternberg devised several convergent tests of the ability to see problems in new ways. In one kind of problem (Sternberg, 1982; Tetewsky & Sternberg, 1986), based on Nelson Goodman's so-called new riddle of induction (see Goodman, 1955), participants were taught about novel concepts, such as *grue* (green until the year 2000 and blue thereafter) and *bleen* (blue until the year 2000 and green thereafter). The participants were then tested in their ability to solve induction problems using conventional concepts as well as novel concepts. Scores on these tests were moderately related to scores on conventional tests of fluid intelligence (i.e., tests of the ability to think flexibly and in novel ways, such as geometric matrix problems). Most significantly, the information-processing component that seemed best to identify the creative thinkers was one that involved flexibly switching back and forth between conceptual systems (*green-blue*, on the one hand, and *grue-bleen*, on the other).

Another type of item (Sternberg & Gastel, 1989a, 1989b) required participants to solve analogies and other kinds of induction problems, but with either factual premises (e.g., "Birds can fly") or counterfactual premises (e.g., "Sparrows can play hopscotch"). Scores on the counterfactual items were moderately related to scores on conventional fluid-intelligence tests, and the counterfactual items seemed to be the better measure of the ability to redefine conventional ways of thinking.

The synthetic part of intelligence as applied to creativity also involves three knowledge acquisition components, or processes used in learning. These three processes, in the context of creativity, are bases of insightful thinking. They are called selective encoding, which involves distinguishing relevant from irrelevant information; selective combination, which involves combining bits of relevant information in novel ways; and selective comparison, which involves relating new information to old information in novel ways. For example, Bohr's model of the atom as a miniature "solar system" was based on a selective-comparison insight, relating the atom to the solar system. Freud's hydraulic model of the mind was also based on a selective-comparison insight.

Sternberg and Davidson (1982; see also Davidson, 1986, 1995; Davidson & Sternberg, 1984) tested this theory of insight in a variety of studies, including one using mathematical insight problems (e.g., "If you have blue socks and brown socks in a drawer mixed in a ratio of 4 to 5, how many socks do you have to take out of the drawer in order to be assured of having a pair of the same color?"). They found that the three kinds of insights could be separated via different kinds of problems, and that correlations between the insight problems and conventional tests of fluid intelligence were moderate. They also found that it was possible to teach elementary school students to improve their insightful thinking.

According to this theory, the analytical part of intelligence – that which is measured in part by conventional tests of intelligence – is also involved in creativity. This ability is required to judge the value of one's own ideas and to decide which of one's ideas are worth pursuing. Then, if a given idea is worth pursuing, analytical ability can further be used to evaluate the strengths and weaknesses of the idea and thereby to suggest ways in which the idea can be improved. People with high synthetic but low analytical abilities will probably need others to fulfill this judgmental role, lest they pursue their less rather than more valuable ideas.

The third intellectual ability involved in creativity is practical ability – the ability to apply one's intellectual skills in everyday contexts. Because creative ideas often tend to be rejected, it is very important for people who wish to have a creative impact to learn how to communicate their ideas effectively and how to persuade others of the value of their ideas. In essence, practical ability is involved in the "selling" of the idea, whether the idea is in the domain of art (where selling may be to a gallery, potential purchasers, or critics), literature (where selling may be to a publisher or a public), science (where selling may be to relatively conservative scientific peers), or entrepreneurship (where selling may be to venture capitalists who are willing to fund only the most promising business innovations). Because creativity is in the interaction of the person, task, and environment, the failure to sell the idea properly may result in its never being dubbed creative, or in its being recognized as creative only after the creator's death.

Sternberg, Ferrari, Clinkenbeard, and Grigorenko (1996; see also Sternberg, 1997; Sternberg & Clinkenbeard, 1995) suggested that because the analytical, synthetic, and practical aspects of abilities are only weakly related, students who are adept in one of these abilities might not benefit particularly from instruction aimed at another of the abilities, and in particular, creative students might not benefit particularly well from instruction as it is given in the schools, which typically emphasizes memory and analytical abilities. In an experiment, they found that high school students who were taught in a way that better matched their own pattern of abilities (e.g., analytic or synthetic) tended to achieve at higher levels than students who were taught in a way that more poorly matched their pattern of abilities.

It is important to say something of the role of knowledge in the investment theory, because knowledge is itself the basis of an important aspect of intelligence, sometimes called crystallized intelligence (e.g., Cattell, 1971; Horn & Cattell, 1966). According to the investment theory, knowledge is a double-edged sword. On the one hand, in order to advance a field beyond where it is, one needs the knowledge to know where the field is. Even reactions in opposition to existing ideas require knowledge of what those existing ideas are. On the other hand, knowledge can impede creativity by leading an individual to become entrenched. The individual can become so used to seeing things in a certain way that he or she starts to have trouble seeing them, or even imagining them, in any other way. The expert therefore may sacrifice flexibility for knowledge. There is actually evidence that experts in a field may have more difficulty than novices adjusting to changes in the fundamental structure of the domain in which they are working (Frensch & Sternberg, 1989).

According to Sternberg and Lubart's (1995) investment theory, creativity also demands the investment of thinking style, personality, motivation, and the environment. Thinking style refers to a preference for thinking in novel ways of one's own choosing rather than following the crowd. To prefer this thinking style, one needs a certain personality that is capable of defying the crowd and the motivation to be persistent and determined to overcome the many obstacles encountered in any creative endeavor. The environment most conducive to creativity is one that reduces some of these obstacles, that reduces the risks inherent in any new idea or activity, and that rewards the people who take those risks.

Sternberg and Lubart (1995) tested the investment theory by asking people to generate creative products in four domains, choosing two from among a variety of topics they were given: writing (e.g., "the keyhole," "2983"), are (e.g., "earth from an insect's point of view," "beginning of time"), advertising (e.g., "brussels sprouts," "cufflinks"), and science (e.g., "How could we know if there were extraterrestrial aliens hidden among us?"). They found only moderate correlations across the four domains, as well as moderate correlations of averaged ratings of creativity of products with tests of fluid intelligence, although the generality of creativity may depend in part upon the population being tested (see Runco, 1987).

Smith's Hierarchy

Another interesting view of intelligence as a subset of creativity is one based on Bloom's *Taxonomy of Educational Objectives* and tested by Leon Smith (1970, 1971). The basic assumption of the taxonomy is that cognitive processes can be placed along a cumulative and hierarchical continuum, beginning with the major class of knowledge and proceeding through the classes of comprehension, application, analysis, synthesis, and evaluation. Intellectual ability is required in the first four processes and creative ability is required for the last two: synthesis and evaluation. Because the categories are cumulative and hierarchical, synthesis and evaluation demand the skills underlying the preceding levels (i.e., intelligence) in addition to the new behavior – creativity. Hence, in Smith's view, intelligence is a subset of creativity.

Smith (1970) gave 141 eleventh graders an intelligence test, two creativity tests, and taxonomic tests. He used the intelligence and creativity tests to predict performance in the taxonomic tests via a multiple regression analysis. He found that the percentage of variance that intelligence accounted for was significant for each of the first four classes (knowledge – 34%, comprehension – 53%, application – 50%, and analysis – 28%). Creativity did not significantly explain any further variance for these four classes, consistent with the theory. Again, in accordance with the theory, both intelligence (contributing 49% and 31%, respectively) and creativity (contributing 20% and 14%, respectively) made significant, independent, and overall contributions to individual-differences variation on the synthesis and evaluation subtests.

CREATIVITY AND INTELLIGENCE AS OVERLAPPING SETS

The view of creativity and intelligence as overlapping sets implies that in some ways creativity and intelligence are similar, but in other ways they are different. Discussing the similarities, Barron (1963) proposed:

If one defines originality as the ability to respond to stimulus situations both adaptively and unusually, and if one defines intelligence simply as the ability to solve problems, then at the upper levels of problem-solving ability the manifestation of intelligence will be also a manifestation of originality. That is to say, the very difficult and rarely solved problem requires by definition a solution that is original. (p. 219)

Highlighting the differences between intelligence and creativity, Roe (1963/1976) suggested:

> The creative process is probably closest to problem solving, but it differs from it in a number of ways. In problem solving, the immediate goal is a specific one, and logical and orderly modes of approach are appropriate – if not always used. In the creative process there is no such clear goal as a rule, and illogical modes of thought are common. Newell, Shaw, and Simon (1958) consider that "creative activity appears simply to be a special class of problem-solving activity characterized by novelty, unconventionality, persistence, and difficulty in problem formulation." A major differentiation is the extent of the involvement of the whole person; in the creative process this is very great, and noncognitive and emotional elements loom large, but they are a barrier to effective problem solving. (p. 172)

Another way of distinguishing creativity from intelligence has been proposed by George Shouksmith (1973), who said that judging the correctness or "rightness" of a response is an attempt to measure logical reasoning or intelligence, whereas judging the "goodness" of a response, that is, the extent to which an answer or problem solution is fitting or appropriate to the problem or situation, is a creativity measure. The overlap would represent responses that are both right and good.

One reason that the view of creativity and intelligence as overlapping sets may be the most conventional view is that it is the most well known due to the impressive amount of work done by its proponents. Examples are Catherine Cox and Lewis Terman's investigations of historical geniuses (Cox, 1926) and all of the studies done with the various professional occupations conducted by researchers connected with the Institute of Personality Assessment and Research (IPAR) at the University of California at Berkeley, such as Donald MacKinnon (1962, 1967, 1975), Frank Barron (1963, 1969), Ravenna Helson (1971/1976), and Harrison Gough (1957).

Cox's 301 Geniuses

Catherine Cox (1926), working with Lewis Terman, published IQ estimates for 301 of the most eminent persons who lived between 1450 and 1850. They selected their list from a list of 1,000 prepared by James McKeen Cattell, who determined eminence by the amount of space allotted in biographical dictionaries. From Cattell's list, they deleted hereditary aristocracy and nobility unless those individuals distinguished themselves beyond status due to their birth, those born before 1450, those with a rank over 510 on the original list, and eleven names for whom no records were available. These deletions left 282 persons whose IQs were summarized as Group A. In addition, they discussed a Group B, which consisted of 19 miscellaneous cases from those over 510 on the original list, bringing the grand total to 301.

To estimate IQ, Cox, Terman, and Maud Merrill (Cox, 1926) examined biographies, letters, and other writings and records for evidence of the earliest period of instruction; the nature of the earliest learning; the earliest productions; age of first reading and of first mathematical performance; typical precocious activities; unusually intelligent applications of knowledge; the recognition of similarities or differences; the amount and character of the reading; the range of interests; school standing and progress; early maturity of attitude or judgment; the tendency to discriminate, to generalize, or to theorize; and family standing. Their IQ estimates are, of course, necessarily subjective. In a sense, though, the estimates have an ecological validity with regard to real-life intelligence that is not seen in standard IQ tests. The reported IQs were the average of the three expert raters mentioned above, namely, Cox, Terman, and Merrill. Interrater reliability was .90 for the childhood estimate and .89 for the young adulthood estimate (calculated from intercorrelations in Cox, 1926, pp. 67–68).

An example of some of the factors that contributed to their estimates can be seen in a description of Francis Galton (not in the list; he was born in 1822 and published *Hereditary*

Genius in 1869), whose IQ Terman estimated to be 200. "Francis knew his capital letters by twelve months and both his alphabets by eighteen months; . . . he could read a little book, *Cobwebs to Catch Flies,* when 2½ years old, and could sign his name before 3 years" (Cox 1926, pp. 41–42). By 4 years of age, he could say all the Latin substantives and adjectives and active verbs, could add and multiply, read a little French, and knew the clock. At 5, he was quoting from Walter Scott. By 6, he was familiar with the *Iliad* and the *Odyssey:* At 7, he was reading Shakespeare for fun and could memorize a page by reading it twice. Clearly, Galton's record is one of an exceptional child.

Cox concluded that the average IQs of the group, 135 for childhood and 145 for young adulthood, were probably too low because of instructions to regress toward the mean of 100 for unselected populations (whereas this group's means were 135 and 145) whenever data were unavailable. Also, unreliability of the data may have caused regression to the mean. One of the problems that Cox noted in the data was a strong correlation, .77, between IQ and the reliability of the available data: The more reliable the data, the higher the IQ, and the higher the IQ, the more reliable the data upon which it was based. She concluded that if more reliable data had been available, all of the IQs would have been estimated to be higher. She therefore corrected the original estimates, bringing the group average up to 155 for childhood and 165 for young adulthood. The corrected young adulthood IQ estimates by occupation group are shown in Table 13.1.

Table 13.2 provides a sampling of the participant pool in Cox's data set. As Cox is careful to point out, the IQs are not estimates of the actual person's IQ, but rather estimates of the record of that person. "The IQ of Newton or of Lincoln recorded in these pages is the IQ of the Newton or of the Lincoln of whom we have record. But the records are admittedly incomplete" (Cox, 1926, p. 8).

Cox (1926, p. 55) found the correlation between IQ and rank order of eminence to be .16, plus or minus .039, after correcting for unreliability of the data. Dean Simonton (1976) reexamined the Cox data using multiple regression techniques and showed that the correlation between intelligence and ranked eminence that Cox found was an artifact of unreliability of data and, especially, of a time-wise sampling bias – those more recently born had both lower estimated IQs and lower ranks of estimated eminence. In Simonton's analysis, the relationship between intelligence and ranked eminence was zero if birth year was controlled for (Simonton, 1976, pp. 223–224). In any case, Cox (1926) recognized the role of factors other than IQ in eminence and concluded that "high but not the highest intelligence, combined with the greatest degree of persistence, will achieve greater eminence than the highest degree of intelligence with somewhat less persistence" (p. 187).

Institute of Personality Assessment and Research

The Institute of Personality Assessment and Research (IPAR) was established at the University of California at Berkeley in 1949. Its objective was the development and use of psychological assessment techniques in the study of effectively functioning persons as opposed to persons with some pathology. The stimulus for this center had been the experience of several psychologists in the assessment program during World War II of the Office of Strategic Services, whose mission it was to select men to be spies, counterespionage agents, leaders of resistance groups behind enemy lines, creators of propaganda designed to destroy the enemy's morale, and leaders of other irregular warfare assignments (Barron, 1963; MacKinnon, 1967, 1975). The group's first study, as could be predicted, was with graduate students at Berkeley. But over the years, MacKinnon studied architects and the members of the U.S. Mt. Everest expedition; Barron studied U.S. Air Force officers, business administrators, artists, and writers; Helson studied male and female mathematicians; and Gough studied

Table 13.1. *Cox's (1926) Estimated IQs by Occupation*

Group	Number	Percentage	Corrected IQ Estimate
Philosophers	22	8	180
Scientists	39	14	175
Nonfiction writers	43	15	170
Religious leaders	23	8	170
Fiction writers	52	18	165
Revolutionary statesmen	9	3	165
Statesmen and politicians	43	15	165
Artists	13	5	160
Musicians	11	4	160
Soldiers	27	10	140
Average	282	100	165

Table 13.2. *Selected Individuals in Cox's (1926) Data Set*

Name	Cattell's Rank Order of Eminence	Corrected IQ Estimate
Napoleon Bonaparte	1	145
Arouet de Voltaire	2	190
Francis Bacon	3	180
J. W. Goethe	4	210 (the highest)
Martin Luther	5	170
Isaac Newton	7	190
George Washington	10	140
Michelangelo	15	180
Abraham Lincoln	23	150
Thomas Jefferson	49	160
W. A. Mozart	56	165
Charles Darwin	68	165
Ludwig van Beethoven	121	165

research scientists and validated the Adjective Check List and the California Psychological Inventory in the course of many studies.

A typical study would involve a nomination and ranking of the most creative people in a field by some experts in that field, such as professors, superiors, journal editors, and critics, and the administration of a battery of tests, including many of Guilford's divergent-thinking tests, some intelligence measure and various personality self-descriptions and projective tests, such as the Thematic Apperception Test or the Rorschach Inkblot Test, to those who agreed to attend a three-day weekend assessment workshop in Berkeley. The weekend provided numerous occasions for several staff members to interview and observe the participants in informal social interaction, situational tests, group discussions, charades, and other exercises. Typically, 10 participants would be assessed in a weekend by six or seven staff members. Ratings from the weekend assessments would be compared to ratings of the less creative professionals in a field who were matched for age and geographic location of their practice and assessed through a battery of procedures sent to them through the mail.

Describing the relationship between creativity and intelligence ratings was just one part of the IPAR studies. Much more emphasis was placed on the personality variables identified in creative persons, which are not covered at length in this chapter. One study of 343 military officers sheds light on some personality variables that distinguish creative persons from intelligent persons. Barron (1963) found that those who scored high in originality but low in intelligence (measured by the Concept Mastery Test, which includes synonyms – antonyms and verbal analogies) described themselves as "affected, aggressive, demanding, dependent, dominant, forceful, impatient, initiative, outspoken, sarcastic, strong, suggestible" (p. 222). Those who scored high in intelligence but low in originality described themselves as "mild, optimistic, pleasant, quiet, unselfish" (p. 222). Barron said:

When one compares these self-descriptions with the staff descriptions of subjects who are *both* original and intelligent, it appears that intelligence represents the operation of the reality principle in behavior, and is responsible for such characteristics as the appropriate delay of impulse-expression and the effective organization of instinctual energy for the attainment of goals in the world as it is. (p. 223)

Barron (1963) summarized the many IPAR studies by saying:

Over the total range of intelligence and creativity a low positive correlation, probably in the neighborhood of .40, obtains; beyond an I.Q. of about 120, however, measured intelligence is a negligible factor in creativity, and the motivational and stylistic variables upon which our own research has laid such stress are the major determiners of creativity. (p. 242)

The relative importance of intelligence and personality or motivation variables can be demonstrated in this anecdote about Edison. Once Cyrus Eaton, who was hard of hearing, asked Thomas Edison, who also was hard of hearing, to perfect the hearing aid. Edison refused, saying, "I don't want to hear that much" (Crovitz, 1970, p. 56).

Three basic findings concerning conventional conceptions of intelligence as measured by IQ and creativity are generally agreed upon (see, e.g., Barron & Harrington, 1981; Lubart, 1994). First, creative people tend to show above-average IQs, often above 120 (see Renzulli, 1986). This figure is not a cutoff, but rather an expression of the fact that people with low or even average IQs do not seem to be well represented among the ranks of highly creative individuals. Cox's (1926) geniuses had an estimated average IQ of 165. Barron estimated the mean IQ of his creative writers to be 140 or higher, based on their scores on the Terman Concept Mastery Test (Barron, 1963, p. 242). The other groups in the IPAR studies, that is, mathematicians and research scientists, were also above average in intelligence. Anne Roe (1952, 1972), who did similarly thorough assessments of eminent scientists before the IPAR group was set up, estimated IQs for her participants to be between 121 and 194, with medians between 137 and 166, depending on whether the IQ test was verbal, spatial, or mathematical.

Second, above an IQ of 120, IQ does not seem to matter as much to creativity as it does below 120. In other words, creativity may be more highly correlated with IQ below an IQ of 120, but only weakly or not at all correlated with it above an IQ of 120. (This relationship is often called the threshold theory. See the contrast with Hayes's, 1989, certification theory discussed below.) In the architects study, in which the average IQ was 130 (significantly above average), the correlation between intelligence and creativity was –.08, not significantly different from zero (Barron, 1969, p. 42). But in the military officer study, in which participants were of average intelligence, the correlation was .33 (Barron, 1963, p. 219). These results suggest that extremely highly creative people often have high IQs, but not necessarily that people with high IQs tend to be extremely creative.

Some investigators (e.g., Simonton, 1994; Sternberg, 1996) have suggested that very high IQ may actually interfere with creativity. Those who have very high IQs may be so highly rewarded for their IQ-like (analytical) skills that they fail to develop the creative potential within them, which may then remain latent. In a reexamination of the Cox (1926) data,

Simonton (1976) found that the eminent leaders showed a significant negative correlation, –.29, between their IQs and eminence. Simonton (1976) explained that

leaders must be understood by a large mass of people before they can achieve eminence, unlike the creators, who need only appeal to an intellectual elite. . . . Scientific, philosophical, literary, artistic, and musical creators do not have to achieve eminence in their own lifetime to earn posterity's recognition, whereas military, political, or religious leaders must have contemporary followers to attain eminence. (pp. 220, 222)

Third, the correlation between IQ and creativity is variable, usually ranging from weak to moderate (Flescher, 1963; Getzels & Jackson, 1962; Guilford, 1967; Herr, Moore, & Hasen, 1965; Torrance, 1962; Wallach & Kogan, 1965; Yamamoto, 1964). The correlation depends in part upon what aspects of creativity and intelligence are being measured and how they are being measured, as well as in what field the creativity is manifested. The role of intelligence is different in art and music, for instance, than it is in mathematics and science (McNemar, 1964).

The Three-Ring Model

These facts suggest another conceptualization of the relation between creativity and intelligence whereby the two overlap (e.g., creative people need a certain IQ level) but are non-identical. Renzulli (1986), for example, has proposed a "three-ring" model, whereby giftedness is at the intersection among above-average ability (as measured in the conventional ways), creativity, and task commitment. The circles for ability and creativity thus overlap.

Renzulli distinguishes between "schoolhouse" and "creative-productive" giftedness, noting that to be gifted in the one way does not necessarily imply giftedness in the other. Schoolhouse giftedness is conventional giftedness in taking tests and learning lessons, whereas creative-productive giftedness is giftedness in the generation of creative ideas. The people gifted in the two ways are often different. We therefore need to be very careful in using conventional IQ tests to identify the gifted, because we are likely to miss the creatively productive gifted. This point is further elaborated below in the section on creativity and intelligence as disjoint sets.

Mednick and the Remote Associates Test

An obvious drawback to the tests used and assessments done by the researchers at IPAR, as well as by Anne Roe and Guilford, is the time and expense involved in administering them as well as the subjective scoring of them. In contrast, Mednick (1962) produced a 30-item, objectively scored, 40-minute test of creative ability called the Remote Associates Test (RAT). The test is based on his theory that the creative thinking process is the formation of associative elements into new combinations that either meet specified requirements or are in some way useful (Mednick, 1962). Because the ability to make these combinations and arrive at a creative solution necessarily depends on the existence of the stuff of the combinations (i.e., the associative elements) in a person's knowledge base and because the probability and speed of attainment of a creative solution are influenced by the organization of the person's associations, Mednick's theory suggests that creativity and intelligence are very related; they are overlapping sets.

The RAT consists of the test taker's supplying a fourth word that is remotely associated with three given words. Samples (not actual test items) of given words are (Mednick, 1962, p. 227):

1. rat	blue	cottage
2. railroad	girl	class
3. surprise	line	birthday
4. wheel	electric	high
5. out	dog	cat

We give the answers later (see note 1) so readers can have the fun of trying the examples first.

Correlations of .55, .43, and .41 have been shown between the RAT and the WISC (Wechsler Intelligence Scale for Children), the SAT verbal, and the Lorge-Thorndike Verbal intelligence measures, respectively (Mednick & Andrews, 1967). Correlations with quantitative intelligence measures were lower (r = .20 to .34). Correlations with other measures of creative performance were more variable (Andrews, 1975).

Implicit Theories

Another approach that has suggested an overlapping-circles model for creativity and intelligence makes use of people's implicit theories, or folk conceptions, of intelligence and creativity. Sternberg (1985b) asked laypeople as well as specialists in four fields (physics, philosophy, art, and business) to give information that, through a data-analytic technique called nonmetric multidimensional scaling, could yield their implicit theories of creativity and intelligence (as well as of wisdom).

Sternberg found that people's implicit theories of creativity seemed to involve eight main components: (a) nonentrenchment (seeing things in novel ways), (b) integration and intellectuality, (c) aesthetic taste and imagination, (d) decisional skill and flexibility, (e) perspicacity (intuition, acuteness of perception, discernment, or understanding), (f) drive for accomplishment and recognition, (g) inquisitiveness, and (h) intuition. Their implicit theories of intelligence involved six components: (a) practical problem-solving ability, (b) verbal ability, (c) intellectual balance and integration, (d) goal orientation and attainment, (e) contextual intelligence (i.e., intelligence in their everyday environments), and (f) fluid thought. The two constructs are thus seen to have some overlap, for example, in the importance of setting and reaching goals and of thinking in flexible (fluid) and nonentrenched ways. When people were asked to rate hypothetically described individuals in terms of their creativity and intelligence, Sternberg (1985b) found a correlation of .69 between their ratings of creativity and intelligence.

CREATIVITY AND INTELLIGENCE AS COINCIDENT SETS

Haensly and Reynolds (1989) argue that creativity and intelligence should be viewed as a "unitary phenomenon," that is, as a conjoint set. They propose that creativity is an expression of intelligence.

Some researchers, such as Weisberg (1986, 1988, 1993) and Langley et al. (1987), have argued that the mechanisms underlying creativity are no different from those underlying normal problem solving of the kind involved in problems that do not seem, on their surface, to involve any need for creative thinking. According to these investigators, work is adjudged as creative when ordinary processes yield extraordinary results. Perkins (1981) refers to this view as the "nothing special" view. According to this view, if we want to understand creativity, we need look no further than to studies of ordinary problem solving.

For example, Weisberg and Alba (1981) had people solve the notorious nine-dot problem, in which people are asked to connect all of the dots, which are arranged in the shape of a square with three rows of three dots each, using no more than four straight lines, never arriving at a given dot twice, and never lifting their pencil from the page. The problem can be solved only if people allow their line segments to go outside the periphery of the dots (see note 2). Typically, solution of this task had been viewed as hinging upon the insight that one had to go "outside the box." Weisberg and Alba showed that even when people were given the insight, they still had difficulty in solving the problem. In other words, whatever is required to solve the nine-dot problem, it is not just some kind of extraordinary insight.

CREATIVITY AND INTELLIGENCE AS DISJOINT SETS

A number of investigators have taken great pains to show that creativity is different from intelligence, that is, that they are disjoint sets (e.g., Getzels & Jackson, 1962; Torrance, 1975; Wallach & Kogan, 1965). Although none of these investigators suggest and many explicitly deny that creativity and intelligence are completely unrelated, their emphasis is clearly in that direction. Their goal seems to have been to focus attention on a problem with relying on traditional IQ tests to identify gifted children. A story told by Donald MacKinnon (1962; which he believed was first told by Mark Twain) illustrates the issue and the importance of recognizing potential talent in order to provide the kind of environment that will facilitate its development and expression. The story

is about a man who sought the greatest general who had ever lived. Upon inquiring as to where this individual might be found, he was told that the person he sought had died and gone to Heaven. At the Pearly Gates he informed St. Peter of the purpose of his quest, whereupon St. Peter pointed to a soul nearby. "But that," protested the inquirer, "isn't the greatest of all generals. I knew that person when he lived on earth, and he was only a cobbler." "I know that," replied St. Peter, "but if he had been a general he would have been the greatest of them all." (p. 484)

The risks of failing to identify talent are also evident in Hayes's (1989) proposed alternative to the 120 IQ threshold theory discussed in the overlapping sets section. According to Hayes's certification theory, creativity and IQ are not intrinsically related. However, in order to display creativity in one's work, one must have attained a position with a certain degree of freedom of expression. For instance, a college professor has more freedom to display creativity in her work than does an assembly line worker. Positions with this kind of freedom typically require a college degree, sometimes also a graduate degree. Academic performance is correlated with IQ. Therefore, it may be that one's opportunity to be creative depends on an IQ high enough to get the degree that is a certification for the types of jobs in which one can display creativity.

Getzels and Jackson

Getzels and Jackson (1962) gave five creativity measures to 245 boys and 204 girls in 6th through 12th grade and compared the results to scores from IQ tests (either a Binet, a Henmon-Nelson, or a WISC), which the school had already administered. The focus of their work was to identify two groups of students (one high in intelligence but not in creativity and one high in creativity but not in intelligence) and study the nature of their behavior in school, their value orientations, fantasies and imaginative productions, and their family environment.

Their five creativity measures were word association, uses for things, hidden shapes, fables, and make-up problems. These tests are typical examples of creativity tests used by other researchers.

In word association, children were asked to give as many definitions as possible to fairly common words (e.g., *bolt, bark, sack*). The score depended on the absolute number of definitions and number of different categories into which these definitions could be placed. For example, a high score for the word *bolt* would be given to "to fasten down, to run away quickly, to eat food rapidly, a bolt of cloth, a horse bolts, a bolt of lightning." (Getzels & Jackson, 1962, p. 17).

In uses for things, children were asked to give as many uses as they could for objects that customarily have a stereotyped function attached to them. This test is similar to Guilford's test items, such as uses for a brick, paper clip, or toothpick. The score depended on the number of uses and their originality. A high score for *brick* would be given to "bricks can be used for building. You can also use a brick as a paperweight. Use it as a doorstop. You can heat a brick and use it as a bed warmer. You can throw a brick as a weapon. You can hollow out the center of a brick and make an ashtray" (Getzels & Jackson, 1962, p. 18).

In hidden shapes, which is part of Cattell's objective-analytical test battery, children were presented with 18 simple geometric figures, each of which was followed by four complex figures. The children were asked to find the geometric figures hidden in the more complex form.

In fables, children were presented with four fables in which the last lines were missing. The children were then asked to compose three different endings for each fable: a moralistic, a humorous, and a sad ending. The "Mischievous Dog" is an example:

A rascally dog used to run quietly to the heels of every passerby and bite them without warning. So his master was obliged to tie a bell around the cur's neck that he might give notice wherever he went. This the dog thought was very fine indeed, and he went about tinkling it in pride all over town. But an old hound said . . . (Getzels & Jackson, 1962, p. 18)

The score again depended on the number, appropriateness, and originality of the endings.

In make-up problems, children were presented with four complex paragraphs, each containing many numerical statements, and were required to make up as many mathematical problems as they could with the information given. One example describes a man who buys a house for so much money, puts so much down, and makes monthly payments for the mortgage and other expenses. The question, "How long will it be before Mr. Smith had saved enough on heating costs to make up for what he had paid for insulating the house?" received more credit than did the question, "How much did Mr. Smith still owe after his down payment?" Getzels & Jackson, 1962, p. 19

Intercorrelations among the creativity measures ranged from .153 between fables and hidden shapes to .488 between make-up problems and word association. The average of the correlations between IQ and the creativity measures were .26. The lowest correlation was between IQ and fables, .12 for girls and .13 for boys; the highest was .39 between IQ and make-up problems for girls and .38 between IQ and word association for boys. It should be noted that the average IQ in the school was 132, beyond the point where there is much expected relationship between creativity and IQ. The correlations, then, may support Burt's (1962/1970) criticism that tests for creativity could form a part of any ordinary battery for testing the general factor of intelligence. McNemar (1964) estimated the correlation of the combined creativity scores and IQ for the total sample, which Getzels and Jackson failed to provide, to be .40. This correlation of .40, McNemar said, was greatly attenuated because of the usual measurement errors, the restricted range of IQ (mean of 132), and the fact that the IQs are a mixture from the Stanford-Binet, Henmon-Nelson, and Wechsler tests. A correlation corrected for these attenuating factors would lend even more support to Burt's and McNemar's points that the creativity tests used here are very much like intelligence tests.

The high-creativity group in Getzels and Jackson's (1962) study (15 boys and 11 girls) consisted of those students who scored in the top 20% of the summed creativity measures but below the top 20% in IQ. The high-intelligence group (17 boys and 11 girls) scored in the top 20% in IQ but below the top 20% in creativity. Wallach and Kogan (1965) criticized Getzels and Jackson for summing the creativity measures when the tests were no more correlated with each other than they were with IQ.

Getzels and Jackson (1962) made a major point of the fact that despite a 23-point difference in mean IQ between the high-creativity group (127) and the high-IQ group (150), surprisingly, the school achievement scores of the two groups were equally superior to the achievement scores of the school population as a whole. McNemar (1964), in a scathing criticism, said that if the authors had bothered to give the correlations among IQ, creativity, and total school achievement for the entire group, one could deduce "that creative ability is not as important as IQ for school achievement – just the opposite of their position" (p. 879).

Getzels and Jackson (1962) found that the students in the high-IQ group were more desirable to their teachers than were the students in the high-creativity group. The high-IQ students desired the same qualities for themselves that they believed were important for success and that they believed teachers approved of more so than did students in the high-creativity group. For high-IQ students, the relationship between the qualities they valued for themselves and those they believed lead to success as adults was quite close, $r = .81$. That is, these students appeared to be highly success oriented. For the high-creativity students, there was practically no relationship ($r = .10$) between the qualities *they* valued and those they believed led to success as adults. These students appeared not to buy into the conventional standards of adult success and, indeed, reported much more unusual career aspirations, such as adventurer, inventor, and writer, than did the high-IQ students, who more often aspired to be doctors, lawyers, and professors.

Sense of humor stood out as a high-ranking ideal quality for the high-creativity group over the high-IQ group. The high-creativity students ranked sense of humor 3rd out of 13 qualities, after getting along with others and emotional stability, as a quality they aspired to have in their ideal selves, whereas the high-IQ students ranked it 9th. High marks, high IQ, and goal directedness were all higher in the ideal selves of the high-IQ students.

In the various open-ended tests and drawings, high-creativity students were significantly higher than the high-IQ students in stimulus-free themes, unexpected endings, humor, incongruities, and playfulness, as well as violence. The high-creativity students seemed to use the stimulus largely as a point of departure for self-expression, versus the high-IQ students, who focused on the stimulus as the point to be communicated or the task to be accomplished. Some noteworthy examples are presented next.

In response to the picture stimulus perceived most often as a man sitting in an airplane reclining his seat on his return from a business trip or professional conference, one high-IQ student gave this response:

Mr. Smith is on his way home from a successful business trip. He is very happy and he is thinking about his wonderful family and how glad he will be to see them again. He can picture it, about an hour from now, his plane landing at the airport and Mrs. Smith and their three children all there welcoming him again. (Getzels & Jackson, 1962, p. 39)

One high-creativity student gave this response to the same picture:

This man is flying back from Reno where he has just won a divorce from his wife. He couldn't stand to live with her anymore, he told the judge, because she wore so much cold cream on her face at night that her head would skid across the pillow and hit him in the head. He is now contemplating skid-proof face cream. (Getzels & Jackson, 1962, p. 39)

When asked to draw a picture entitled "Playing Tag in the School Yard," high-IQ students were much more likely than high-creativity students to draw details and label parts of their drawing, such as drawing a building and labeling it a school, and to concentrate on communicating and being understood, whereas high-creativity students were much less bound by the specific details of the instructions and less worried about being misunderstood. For instance, for the playing tag drawing, one high-creativity student returned the blank sheet of paper with the title changed to "Playing Tag in the School Yard – During a Blizzard" (Getzels & Jackson, 1962, p. 43).

Wallach and Kogan

Wallach and Kogan (1965) argued that a serious flaw in the work of Getzels and Jackson (1962) was that creativity is not measured well in the testlike situations they used. To correct this flaw, Wallach and Kogan devised a series of gamelike, untimed tests for 151 fifth graders. Their five creativity measures were rated as to uniqueness and number and included:

1. Instances – Name all the round things, things that make a noise, square things, things that move on wheels that you can think of. For round things, life savers, mouse hole, and drops of water were unique responses; buttons, plate, and door knob were not.
2. Alternative uses – Name all the different ways you could use a newspaper, automobile tire, shoe, button, knife, cork, key, chair. For newspaper, "rip it up if angry" was a unique response; "make paper hats" was not (Wallach & Kogan, 1965, p. 32).
3. Similarities – Tell all the ways in which a _____ and a _____ are alike: cat and mouse, milk and meat, curtain and rug, potato and carrot, train and tractor, grocery store and restaurant, violin and piano, radio and telephone, watch and typewriter, desk and table. For milk and meat, "They are government inspected" was a unique response; "They come from animals" was not (p. 33).
4. Pattern meanings – Tell me all the things you think this could be? Student was presented with eight drawings of various combinations of geometric shapes. For a picture of a triangle surrounded by three circles, "three mice eating a piece of cheese" was a unique response; "three people sitting around a table" was not (p. 35).
5. Line meanings – Similar to pattern meanings, except with drawings of lines. For a simple straight horizontal line, "stream of ants" was a unique response; "stick" was not (p. 35).

Wallach and Kogan (1965) also had 10 general intelligence measures, which included subtests from the WISC, School and College Ability Tests (SCAT), and Sequential Tests of Educational Progress (STEP). They noted correlations of .41 among the creativity measures, .51 among the intelligence measures, and .09 between the creativity and intelligence measures.

Wallach and Kogan (1965, 1972) divided their students into four groups based on their scores on the various tests: high creativity and high intelligence (HC-HI), low creativity and high intelligence (LC-HI), high creativity and low intelligence (HC-LI), and low creativity and low intelligence (LC-LI).

In the HC-HI group, students had the highest level of self-confidence, self-control, and freedom of expression, were outgoing and popular with their peers, had the highest levels of attention span and concentration and interest in academic work, and were the most sensitive to physiognomic stimuli; that is, they were able to discuss affective and expressive connotations of stimuli, beyond just physical or geometric descriptions. They also demonstrated highly disruptive, attention-seeking behavior, which suggested enthusiasm and overeagerness. They had a tendency to admit to some feelings of anxiety, which seemed to serve as an energizing factor for them.

In the LC-HI group, students were more reserved and addicted to school achievement to the extent that they believed academic failure would be a catastrophe. They were also less likely to seek attention in disruptive ways and less likely to express unconventional ideas, but were still popular with peers. They were the least anxious of all the groups. They performed best in the presence of evaluation pressures. They appeared to have an excessive fear of making a mistake. Having a clear understanding of the expectations of others allowed them to know the "right" way of behaving.

In the HC-LI group, students were at the greatest disadvantage in the classroom. They were the most cautious and hesitant, the least self-confident, the least sought after by peers, the most deprecatory of their own work, and the least able to concentrate. They displaced highly disruptive, attention-seeking behavior, which suggested an incoherent protest against their plight. They were more likely to cope with academic failure by social withdrawal and performed best when evaluation pressures were absent. They seemed to have an excessive fear of being evaluated, in contrast to the LC-HI group. Like the HC-HI group, they were more willing to postulate relationships between somewhat dissimilar events.

In the LC-LI group, students appeared to compensate for poor academic performance by social activity. They were more extroverted, less hesitant, and more self-confident than the HC-LI group.

Torrance

Torrance (1963) replicated the Getzels and Jackson (1962) study and found similar results to theirs. He also followed up on their sample and noted that 55% of the high-creativity group ended up in unconventional occupations, compared with only 9% of the high-intelligence group, lending some support to the ecological validity of the creativity tests (Torrance, 1975). In a separate long-range predictive validity study of 236 high school students tested with the Torrance Tests of Creative Thinking (TTCT) in 1959 and followed up in 1971, Torrance (1975) found a canonical correlation of .51 for the combined scores on the creativity test battery and later creative achievement.

In developing the TTCT, Torrance (1975) experimented with variations in time limits as well as with unlimited time and various instructions and found that in thousands of administrations of the TTCT, none of the stress due to a testing environment that Wallach and Kogan (1965) tried to eliminate by using their gamelike exercises was evident.

In a summary of a total of 388 correlations from a variety of dissertation studies and published studies, Torrance (1975) observed that "all along the data have seemed to support the conclusion that these two variables [intelligence and creativity] are related only moderately" (Torrance, 1975, p. 287). "The median of 114 coefficients of correlation involving figural measures was .06; for the 88 correlations involving verbal measures, the median was .21; and for the 178 correlations involving both verbal and figural measures combined, the median was .20" (1975, p. 287). He emphasized the finding that "no matter what measure of IQ is chosen, we would exclude about 70% of our most creative children if IQ alone were used in identifying giftedness" (1963, p. 182).

Practice Effects

Recently, some investigators have suggested that creativity and intelligence may be disjoint because of practice effects (Ericsson, 1996; Ericsson & Faivre, 1988; Ericsson, Krampe, & Tesch-Römer, 1993). According to this view, expertise of any kind, including creative expertise, develops as a result of deliberate practice, whereby an individual practices with a mind to improve his or her performance. Creative expertise thus is not really an ability at all, but rather a result of deliberate practice in a domain and, particularly, in doing creative work in a domain. Indeed, many researchers have spoken of the 10-year rule (e.g., Gardner, 1993;

Simonton, 1994), whereby significant creative production seems to require 10 years of active work in a field.

Ericsson and his colleagues have done a number of studies, showing that expertise of various kinds does indeed seem to correlate with deliberate practice. In a variety of fields, deliberate practice is correlated with eminence. Roe (1952) concluded, after her investigation of eminent scientists, that more than your capacity for a particular field, how well you do is "a function of how hard you work at it" (p. 170). At the present time, however, the evidence is largely correlational, meaning that it is difficult to assess the causal chain. It may be, for example, that people with creative or other talent are more motivated to engage in deliberate practice than are those without such talent. Nevertheless, the deliberate-practice view of creativity cannot be ruled out, and clearly, deliberate practice facilitates creative work and may even be necessary for it, whether or not it is also sufficient.

CONCLUSION

At the very least, creativity seems to involve synthetic, analytical, and practical aspects of intelligence: synthetic to come up with ideas, analytical to evaluate the quality of those ideas, and practical to formulate a way of effectively communicating those ideas and of persuading people of their value. But beyond the basics, it is difficult to find substantial agreement among those working in the field.

Despite a substantial body of research, psychologists still have not reached a consensus on the nature of the relation between creativity and intelligence, nor even of exactly what these constructs are. All possible set relations between creativity and intelligence have been proposed, and there is at least some evidence to support each of them. The negative side of this state of affairs is that we can say little with certainty about the relation between creativity and intelligence, and creativity's fate as a legitimate area of research is still debated between "hard" and "soft" scientists. The debate is old. In 1879, Francis Galton said, "Until the phenomenon of any branch of knowledge have been subjected to measurement and number, it cannot assume the status and dignity of a science" (Crovitz, 1970, p. 24). The positive side is that for those seeking an important, open research question, that of the relation between creativity and intelligence is worth considering. The question is theoretically important, and its answer probably affects the lives of countless children and adults. We therefore need elucidation of good answers as soon as possible.

NOTES

The work reported herein was supported under the Javits Act program (Grant R206R50001) as administered by the Office of Educational Research and Improvement, U.S. Department of Education. The findings and opinions expressed in this report do not reflect the positions or policies of the Office of Educational Research and Improvement or the U.S. Department of Education.

1 Answers to the sample RAT items: (1) cheese, (2) working, (3) party, (4) chair or wire, (5) house.
2 The solution to the nine-dot problem is as follows:

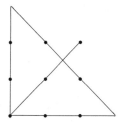

REFERENCES

Amabile, T. M. (1996). *Creativity in context*. Boulder, CO: Westview.

Andrews, F. M. (1975). Social and psychological factors which influence the creative process. In I. A. Taylor & J. W. Getzels (Eds.), *Perspectives in creativity* (pp. 117–145). Chicago: Aldine.

Barron, F. (1963). *Creativity and psychological health*. Princeton, NJ: Van Nostrand.

Barron, F. (1969). *Creative person and creative process*. New York: Holt, Rinehart, & Winston.

Barron, F., & Harrington, D. M. (1981). Creativity, intelligence, and personality. *Annual Review of Psychology, 32,* 439–476.

Beittel K. R. (1964). Creativity in the visual arts in higher education: Criteria, predictors, experimentation and their interactions. In C. W. Taylor (Ed.), *Widening horizons in creativity*. New York: Wiley.

Boden, M. (1991). *The creative mind: Myths and mechanisms*. New York: Basic.

Boden, M. (Ed.). (1994). *Dimensions of creativity*. Cambridge, MA: MIT Press.

Brown, R. T. (1989). Creativity: What are we to measure. In J. A. Glover, R. R. Ronning, & C. R. Reynolds (Eds.), *Handbook of creativity* (pp. 3–32). New York: Plenum.

Burt, C. L. (1970). Critical notice, In P. E. Vernon (Ed.), *Creativity: Selected readings* (pp. 203–216). Baltimore: Penguin. (Reprinted from *British Journal of Educational Psychology, 32,* 1962, 292–298)

Cattell, R. B. (1971). *Abilities: Their structure, growth and action*. Boston: Houghton Mifflin.

Cox, C. M. (1926). *The early mental traits of three hundred geniuses*. Stanford, CA: Stanford University Press.

Crovitz, H. F. (1970). *Galton's walk: Methods for the analysis of thinking, intelligence, and creativity*. New York: Harper & Row.

Csikszentmihalyi, M. (1988). Society, culture, and person: A systems view of creativity. In R. J. Sternberg (Ed.), *The nature of creativity* (pp. 325–339). Cambridge University Press.

Csikszentmihalyi, M. (1996). *Creativity*. New York: HarperCollins.

Davidson, J. E. (1986). The role of insight in giftedness. In R. J. Sternberg & J. E. Davidson (Eds.), *Conceptions of giftedness* (pp. 201–222). Cambridge University Press.

Davidson, J. E. (1995). The suddenness of insight. In R. J. Sternberg & J. E. Davidson (Eds.), *The nature of insight* (pp. 125–155). Cambridge, MA: MIT Press.

Davidson, J. E., & Sternberg, R. J. (1984). The role of insight in intellectual giftedness. *Gifted Child Quarterly, 28,* 58–64.

Ericsson, K. A. (Ed.). (1996). *The road to excellence*. Mahwah, NJ: Erlbaum.

Ericsson, K. A., & Faivre, I. A. (1988). What's exceptional about exceptional abilities? In I. K. Obler & D. Fein (Eds.), *The exceptional brain: Neuropsychology of talent and special abilities* (pp. 436–473). New York: Guilford.

Ericsson, K. A., Krampe, R. T., & Tesch-Römer, C. (1993). The role of deliberate practice in the acquisition of expert performance. *Psychological Review, 100,* 363–406.

Flescher, I. (1963). Anxiety and achievement of intellectually gifted and creatively gifted children. *Journal of Psychology, 56,* 251–268.

Frensch, P. A., & Sternberg, R. J. (1989). Expertise and intelligent thinking: When is it worse to know better? In R. J. Sternberg (Ed.), *Advances in the psychology of human intelligence* (Vol. 5, pp. 157–158). Hillsdale, NJ: Erlbaum.

Gardner, H. (1983). *Frames of mind: The theory of multiple intelligences*. New York: Basic.

Gardner, H. (1993). *Creating minds*. New York: Basic.

Gardner, H. (1995). *Leading minds*. New York: Basic.

Getzels, J. W., & Csikszentmihalyi, M. (1972). The creative artist as an explorer. In J. McVicker Hunt (Ed.), *Human intelligence* (pp. 182–192). New Brunswick, NJ: Transaction Books.

Getzels, J. W., & Jackson, P. W. (1962). *Creativity and intelligence: Explorations with gifted students*. New York: Wiley.

Glover, J. A., Ronning, R. R., & Reynolds, C. R. (Eds.). (1989). *Handbook of creativity* New York: Plenum.

Goodman, N. (1955). *Fact, fiction, and forecast*. Cambridge, MA: Harvard University Press.

Gough, H. G. (1957). *California psychological inventory manual*. Palo Alto, CA: Consulting Psychologists Press.

Guilford, J. P. (1950). Creativity. *American Psychologist, 5,* 444–454.

Guilford, J. P. (1967). *The nature of human intelligence*. New York: McGraw-Hill.

Guilford, J. P. (1970). Creativity: Retrospect and prospect. *Journal of Creative Behavior, 4,* 149–168.

Guilford, J. P. (1975). Creativity: A quarter century of progress. In I. A. Taylor & J. W. Getzels (Eds.), *Perspectives in creativity* (pp. 37–59). Chicago: Aldine.

Guilford, J. P., & Christensen, P. W. (1973). The one-way relation between creative potential and IQ. *Journal of Creative Behavior, 7,* 247–252.

Guilford, J. P., & Hoepfner, R. (1966). Creative potential as related to measures of IQ and verbal comprehension. *Indian Journal of Psychology, 41,* 7–16.

Haensly, P. A., & Reynolds, C. R. (1989). Creativity and intelligence. In J. A. Glover, R. R. Ronning, & C. R. Reynolds (Eds.), *Handbook of creativity* (pp. 111–132). New York: Plenum.

Hayes, J. R. (1989). Cognitive processes in creativity. In J. A. Glover, R. R. Ronning, & C. R. Reynolds (Eds.), *Handbook of creativity* (pp. 135–145). New York: Plenum.

Helson, R. (1976). Women and creativity. In A. Rothenberg & C. R. Hausman (Eds.), *The creativity question* (pp. 242–250). Durham, NC: Duke University Press. (Reprinted from Women mathematicians and the creative personality, *Journal of Consulting and Clinical Psychology, 36,* 1971, 210–211, 217–220)

Herr, E. L., Moore, G. D., & Hasen, J. S. (1965). Creativity, intelligence, and values: A study of relationships. *Exceptional Children, 32,* 114–115.

Horn, J. L., & Cattell, R. B. (1966). Refinement and test of the theory of fluid and crystallized intelligence. *Journal of Educational Psychology, 57,* 253–270.

Horn, J. L., & Knapp, J. R. (1973). On the subjective character of the empirical base of Guilford's Structure-of-Intellect model. *Psychological Bulletin, 80,* 33–43.

Intelligence and Its Measurement: A Symposium (1921). *Journal of Educational Psychology, 12,* 123–147, 195–216, 271–275.

Johnson-Laird, P. N. (1988). Freedom and constraint in creativity. In R. J. Sternberg (Ed.), *The nature of creativity* (pp. 202–219). Cambridge University Press.

Langley, P., Simon, H. A., Bradshaw, G. L., & Zytkow, J. M. (1987). *Scientific discovery: Computational explorations of the creative processes.* Cambridge, MA: MIT Press.

Lubart, T. I. (1994). Creativity. In R. J. Sternberg (Ed.), *Thinking and problem solving* (pp. 290–332). San Diego: Academic.

MacKinnon, D. (1962). The nature and nurture of creative talent. *American Psychologist, 17,* 484–495.

MacKinnon, D. (1967). The highly effective individual. In R. L. Mooney & T. A. Razik (Eds.), *Explorations in creativity* (pp. 55–68). New York: Harper & Row.

MacKinnon, D. (1975). IPAR's contribution to the conceptualization and study of creativity. In I. A. Taylor & J. W. Getzels (Eds.), *Perspectives in creativity* (pp. 60–89). Chicago: Aldine.

McNemar, Q. (1964). Lost: Our intelligence? Why? *American Psychologist, 19,* 871–882.

Mednick, M. T., & Andrews, F. M. (1967). Creative thinking and level of intelligence. *Journal of Creative Behavior, 1,* 428–431.

Mednick, S. A. (1962). The associative basis of the creative process. *Psychological Review, 69,* 220–232.

Merrifield, P. R., Gardner, S. F., & Cox, A. B. (1964). *Aptitudes and personality measures related to creativity in seventh-grade children.* Reports of the Psychological Laboratories of the University of Southern California; No. 28.

Ochse, R. (1990). *Before the gates of excellence.* Cambridge University Press.

Perkins, D. N. (1981). *The mind's best work.* Cambridge, MA: Harvard University Press.

Piers, E. V., Daniels, J. M., & Quackenbush, J. F. (1960). The identification of creativity in adolescents. *Journal of Educational Psychology, 51,* 346–351.

Renzulli, J. S. (1986). The three-ring conception of giftedness: A developmental model for creative productivity. In R. J. Sternberg & J. E. Davidson (Eds.), *Conceptions of giftedness* (pp. 53–92). Cambridge University Press.

Roe, A. (1952). *The making of a scientist.* New York: Dodd, Mead.

Roe, A. (1972). Patterns of productivity of scientists. *Science, 176,* 940–941.

Roe, A. (1976). Psychological approaches to creativity in science. In A. Rothenberg & C. R. Hausman (Eds.), *The creativity question* (pp. 165–175). Durham, NC: Duke University Press. (Reprinted from M. A. Coler & H. K. Hughes, Eds. [1963] *Essays on creativity in the sciences* [pp. 153–154, 166–172, 177–182]. New York: New York University Press)

Rothenberg, A., & Hausman, C. R. (Eds.). (1976). *The creativity question.* Durham, NC: Duke University Press.

Rubenson, D. L., & Runco, M. A. (1992). The psychoeconomic approach to creativity. *New Ideas in Psychology, 10,* 131–147.

Runco, M. A. (1987). The generality of creative performance in gifted and nongifted children. *Gifted Child Quarterly, 31*(3), 121–125.

Schubert, D. S. (1973). Intelligence as necessary but not sufficient for creativity. *Journal of Genetic Psychology, 122,* 45–47.

Shouksmith, G. (1973). *Intelligence, creativity and cognitive style.* London: Angus & Robertson.

Simonton, D. K. (1976). Biographical determinants of achieved eminence: A multivariate approach to the Cox data. *Journal of Personality and Social Psychology, 33*, 218–226.

Simonton, D. K. (1994). *Greatness: Who makes history and why?* New York: Guilford.

Skager, R. W., Schultz, C. B., & Klein, S. P. (1967). Quality and quantity of accomplishments as measures of creativity. *Journal of Educational Psychology, 56*, 31–39.

Smith, I. L. (1970). IQ, creativity, and the taxonomy of educational objectives: Cognitive domain. *Journal of Experimental Education, 38*(4), 58–60.

Smith, I. L. (1971). IQ, creativity, and achievement: Interaction and threshold. *Multivariate Behavioral Research, 6*(1), 51–62.

Sternberg, R. J. (1982). Natural, unnatural, and supernatural concepts. *Cognitive Psychology, 14*, 451–488.

Sternberg, R. J. (1985a). *Beyond IQ: A triarchic theory of human intelligence.* Cambridge University Press.

Sternberg, R. J. (1985b). Implicit theories of intelligence, creativity, and wisdom. *Journal of Personality and Social Psychology, 49*, 607–627.

Sternberg, R. J. (1988). *The triarchic mind: A theory of human intelligence.* New York: Viking.

Sternberg, R. J. (1996). *Successful intelligence.* New York: Simon & Schuster.

Sternberg, R. J. (1997). What does it mean to be smart? *Educational Leadership, 54*, 20–24.

Sternberg, R. J., & Clinkenbeard, P. (1995). A triarchic view of identifying, teaching, and assessing gifted children. *Roeper Review, 17*(4), 255–260.

Sternberg, R. J., & Davidson, J. E. (1982, June). The mind of the puzzler. *Psychology Today.* pp. 37–44.

Sternberg, R. J., & Detterman, D. K. (Eds.). (1986). *What is intelligence? Contemporary viewpoints on its nature and definition.* Norwood, NJ: Ablex.

Sternberg, R. J., Ferrari, M., Clinkenbeard, P., & Grigorenko, E. L. (1996). Identification, instruction, and assessment of gifted children: A construct validation of a triarchic model. *Gifted Child Quarterly, 40*, 129–137.

Sternberg, R. J., & Gastel, J. (1989a). Coping with novelty in human intelligence: An empirical investigation. *Intelligence, 13*, 187–197.

Sternberg, R. J., & Gastel, J. (1989b). If dancers ate their shoes: Inductive reasoning with factual and counterfactual premises. *Memory and Cognition, 17*, 1–10.

Sternberg, R. J., & Lubart, T. I. (1991). An investment theory of creativity and its development. *Human Development, 34*(1), 1–32.

Sternberg, R. J., & Lubart, T. I. (1995). *Defying the crowd: Cultivating creativity in a culture of conformity.* New York: Free Press.

Sternberg, R. J., & Lubart, T. I. (1996). Investing in creativity. *American Psychologist, 51*(7), 677–688.

Tetewsky, S. J., & Sternberg, R. J. (1986). Conceptual and lexical determinants of nonentrenched thinking. *Journal of Memory and Language, 25*, 202–225.

Torrance, E. P. (1962). *Guiding creative talent.* Englewood Cliffs, NJ: Prentice-Hall.

Torrance, E. P. (1963). Explorations in creative thinking in the early school years: A progress report. In C. W. Taylor & F. Barron (Eds.), *Scientific creativity: Its recognition and development* (pp. 173–183). New York: Wiley.

Torrance, E. P. (1974). *The Torrance Tests of Creative Thinking: Technical-norms manual.* Bensenville, IL: Scholastic Testing Service.

Torrance, E. P. (1975). Creativity research in education: Still alive. In I. A. Taylor & J. W. Getzels (Eds.), *Perspectives in creativity* (pp. 278–296). Chicago: Aldine.

Wallach, M., & Kogan, N. (1965). *Modes of thinking in young children.* New York: Holt, Rinehart, & Winston.

Wallach, M., & Kogan, N. (1972). Creativity and intelligence in children. In J. McVicker Hunt (Ed.), *Human intelligence* (pp. 165–181). New Brunswick, NJ: Transaction Books.

Weisberg, R. (1986). *Creativity, genius and other myths.* New York: Freeman.

Weisberg, R. (1988). Problem solving and creativity. In R. J. Sternberg (Ed.), *The nature of creativity* (pp. 148–176). Cambridge University Press.

Weisberg, R. W. (1993). *Creativity: Beyond the myth of genius.* New York: Freeman.

Weisberg, R. W., & Alba, J. W. (1981). An examination of the alleged role of "fixation" in the solution of several "insight" problems. *Journal of Experimental Psychology: General, 110*, 169–192.

Yamamoto, K. (1964). Creativity and sociometric choice among adolescents. *Journal of Social Psychology, 64*, 249–261.

14   The Influence of Personality on Artistic and Scientific Creativity

GREGORY J. FEIST

Imagine for a moment, the following conversation between a 4-year-old and her mother:

"Mommy, where did I come from?"
"From your father and me."
"Where did you and Daddy come from?"

At this point, the mother heaves a sigh of relief because no more detailed explanation of the process is required, and answers, "From your grandparents." The conversation goes on to a few more generations before the little girl becomes more interested in her toys and leaves this line of questioning.

Wondering about the nature of creativity is in essence one form of the "Where did I come from" question, namely "Where did it come from?" The above conversation is an important one, for two reasons. First, it reminds us that humans are inherently curious about how things come into being and, second, our answers tend to be reductive. We all wonder were we come from, and so it is only natural that when we see something we have never seen before we wonder, "Where did that came from?" The most obvious and superficial answer is, "from its creator." For some – like the 4-year-old girl – this answer suffices. For most people, however, it does not. We want to know more specifically about the processes and conditions that allow one person to create what others never imagined. How one person differs from others is exactly what is meant by individual differences, and with this emphasis on individual differences we move close to a personality explanation, the topic of this chapter. Indeed, one purpose of this chapter is to demonstrate that personality is an important answer to the questions, "Where did that come from and why was she or he able to create it?"

Before doing so, however, let me say a few words about how personality and creativity are defined. When I tell people I am a personality psychologist, they often wonder what a personality psychologist is. As I frequently tell my students, there is something specific to what psychologists mean by the word *personality*. Psychologists most often define it in terms of individual differences and behavioral consistency, with the latter coming in two forms: situational and temporal. Situational consistency focuses on whether people behave consistently in different situations, whereas temporal consistency focuses on whether they behave consistently over time. Let's take the trait of friendliness, for example. We would only label a person as "friendly" if we observe him or her behaving in a friendly manner over time and in many different situations, and in situations in which other people did not behave as friendly.

Moreover, if I tell people that my primary interest is creativity, they sometimes argue, as many academic psychologists have, that creativity by definition is mysterious and beyond the pale of empirical scrutiny. That may be true concerning the process of creativity, but it fails to distinguish two other important and observable aspects to creativity, namely the person and the product. The inner workings of the creative mind may forever be outside of direct observation, but the behavioral dispositions of the person creating are not. The question, however, of what is creative behavior and creative work is still unanswered. Psychologists and philosophers who study the creative process, person, and product are in consensus about what is "creative": novel and adaptive solutions to problems (Amabile, 1996; Feist, 1993; MacKinnon, 1970; Rothenberg & Hausman, 1976; Simonton, 1988; Sternberg, 1988). The adaptive criterion is necessary to distinguish truly creative thinking from merely different and/or pathological thinking.

Now we can return to the question of how some people are consistently able to come up with novel and adaptive solutions when most others are not. The most intriguing issue raised with regard to personality and creativity is the potential causal link between the two domains. The more general form of the question of whether traits cause behavior, attitudes, or talents (see McCrae & Costa, 1995) can be framed more specifically: Does personality cause or influence creative achievement? The primary purpose of this chapter is to demonstrate that personality has an influence on creative achievement in art and science, by reviewing the literature on personality and creativity and organizing it around two criteria of causality: covariance and temporal precedence.

Much contention and acrimony accompanying a term such as *cause* can be avoided if we clarify its meaning. Rosenthal and Rosnow (1991) have argued that three criteria must be met before one can consider a causal relationship between two variables: (a) covariation, (b) temporal precedence, and (c) ruling out extraneous explanations. Simply put, covariation concerns the degree to which X covaries with Y. If X and Y do not covary, then they cannot possibly be causally related. Temporal precedence is the idea that X must precede Y in time if it is to have a causal influence on it. Finally, if we are to conclude that X has a causal influence on Y we must be able to rule out alternative explanations – X and only X must cause Y. By defining cause in these operational terms, we can address the extent to which personality "causes" creative achievement. In this sense, "cause" and "influence" can be used interchangeably.

Indeed, the first two criteria (covariation and temporal precedence) map nicely onto the two main components of personality, individual differences and temporal consistency. The covariation criterion can be examined by studying how individual differences relate to artistic and scientific creative ability. Assuming, however, that the connection between creative personality and achievement can be demonstrated, is it fair to talk about the "creative personality" monolithically? The individual difference traits that distinguish creative artists may not be the same as those that distinguish creative scientists. Therefore, in the individual difference section of this chapter I will review the literatures for artistic and scientific creativity separately and then discuss whether the distinguishing traits of the artists generalize to scientists.

In similar fashion, the temporal consistency of creative personality can shed light on the temporal precedence criterion. Do the distinguishing traits of creative people measured at an earlier time in life continue to distinguish them from their peers later in life? If traits do not distinguish young creative people from their less creative peers, but do so later in life, then these traits clearly cannot precede creativity. The temporal consistency section, therefore, will review longitudinal studies that have examined the consistency of creative personality. Yet a second form of consistency can be explored – that of creative achievement. Are young gifted people likely to maintain and realize their creative potential by becoming true creative geniuses in adulthood? In this section I will therefore review longitudinal studies that have examined whether early creative potential is actualized, with emphasis being placed on the Terman studies of genius.

In a third section of the chapter I will integrate the first two sections by reviewing theories that provide underlying mechanisms connecting personality to creative achievement. In other words, if there is a connection between personality and creativity, what plausible biological and/or psychological mechanisms could be responsible for their association? The recent theories of Eysenck, Russ, Busse and Mansfield, as well as the five-factor model will be highlighted. In the final section of the chapter I will summarize what we know and do not yet know after 45 years of empirical research and make suggestions for further exploration.

INDIVIDUAL DIFFERENCES IN CREATIVE PERSONALITY: EVIDENCE OF COVARIATION

Personality and Artistic Creativity

Before delving into the literature on personality differences in artistic creativity, I need to say a few words about how artist was defined and to whom artists were compared. For operational purposes, I defined *artist* most broadly to include not only visual artists (painters, sculptors, cinematographers, photographers, architects), but also literary (writers, poets) and performing artists (musicians, singers, dancers, actors). Students as young as high school were included if they showed artistic interest and/or promise. Furthermore, in order to demonstrate that personality meaningfully covaries with artistic creativity, I included studies in the review only if they compared the personality characteristics of artists versus nonartists.

NONSOCIAL TRAITS: OPENNESS TO EXPERIENCE, FANTASY, AND IMAGINATION. Although such a finding may appear self-evident, it is important to document the empirical support (or lack thereof) for the idea that artists are more open to experience and open to fantasy and imagination than are nonartists (see Table 14.1). For example, Domino (1974) studied a group of cinematographers and found that they were quite willing and interested in seeking out new experiences. More recently, Pufal-Struzik (1992) examined personality differences between 177 creative artists (painters, poets, writers, and film directors) and their less creative peers. Using Cattell's Sixteen Personality Factor Questionnaire (16 PF), she found that creative artists were more aesthetically oriented, imaginative, and intuitive.

NONSOCIAL TRAITS: IMPULSIVITY AND LACK OF CONSCIENTIOUSNESS. Closely related to their rebellious nonconforming dispositions (see later), artists appear to be rather impulsive and rate low on conscientiousness (see Table 14.1). One illustrative study in this regard was conducted by Dudek, Bernèche Bérubé, and Royer (1991). Using self-reports on the Adjective Check List, they examined the personality characteristics of art students and nonart controls and found that art students were significantly lower on the self-control (impulsivity) and need for order (conscientiousness) scales. Another example was a study conducted by Walker, Koestner, and Hum (1995), who investigated the personalities of highly eminent artists and compared them with eminent controls (political, judicial, and military leaders). Personality was assessed by raters reading the last 50 pages of autobiographies (to focus on adulthood) and rating the subject using the California Q-set (CQS). The CQS ratings revealed that the artists were significantly more impulsive and less conscientious than their noncreative peers.

NONSOCIAL TRAITS: ANXIETY, AFFECTIVE ILLNESS, AND EMOTIONAL SENSITIVITY. Another common stereotype of the artist is that of an emotionally labile, manic, expressive, and sensitive person (see Feist, 1991; Rossman & Horn, 1972; Rothenberg, 1990; Runco & Bahleda, 1986). The real question, however, concerns whether empirical

Table 14.1. *Consistent Personality Findings from the Literature Comparing Artists and Nonartists*

Trait Category	Trait	Citation
Nonsocial	Openness to experience Fantasy-oriented Imagination	Alter (1989) Bachtold & Werner (1973) Barron (1972) Barton & Cattell (1972) Cross et al. (1967) Csikszentmihalyi & Getzels (1973) Domino (1974) Eiduson (1958) Feist (1989) Getzels & Csikszentmihalyi (1976) Hall & MacKinnon (1969) Holland & Baird (1968) Kemp (1981) MacKinnon (1962) Martindale (1975) Pufal-Struzik (1992) Rossman & Horn (1972) Schaefer (1969, 1973) Shelton & Harris (1979) Walker et al. (1995) Zeldow (1973)
	Impulsivity Lack of conscientiousness	Bachtold & Werner (1973) Bakker (1991) Barron (1972) Barton & Cattell (1972) Cross et al. (1967) Drevdahl & Cattell (1958) Dudek et al. (1991) Getzels & Csikszentmihalyi (1976) Götz & Götz (1979) Hall & MacKinnon (1969) Hammond & Edelmann (1991) Helson (1977) Mohan & Tiwana (1987) Pufal-Struzik (1992) Schaefer (1969, 1973) Walker et al. (1995) Zeldow (1973)
	Anxiety Affective illness Emotional sensitivity	Andreasen & Glick (1988) Bakker (1991) Barron (1972) Cross et al. (1967) Csikszentmihalyi & Getzels (1973) Dudek (1968) Drevdahl & Cattell (1958) Eiduson (1958) Getzels & Csikszentmihalyi (1976) Götz & Götz (1979) Hall & MacKinnon (1969) Hammer (1966) Hammond & Edelmann (1991) Helson (1977) Jamison (1993) Kemp (1981) Ludwig (1995) Marchant-Haycox & Wilson (1992)

Table 14.1 (*cont.*)

Trait Category	Trait	Citation
		Martindale (1975)
		Mohan & Tiwana (1986)
		Richards (1994)
		Richards & Kinney (1990)
		Schaefer (1969, 1973)
		Shelton & Harris (1979)
		Walker et al. (1995)
		Wills (1983)
		Wilson (1984)
	Drive	Alter (1989)
	Ambition	Bakker (1988, 1991)
		Cross et al. (1967)
		Csikszentmihalyi & Getzels (1973)
		Domino (1974)
		Drevdahl & Cattell (1958)
		Dudek et al. (1991)
		Eiduson (1958)
		Getzels & Csikszentmihalyi (1976)
		Hammer (1966)
		Helson (1977)
		Kemp (1981)
		Marchant-Haycox & Wilson (1992)
		Schaefer (1969, 1973)
		Wilson (1984)
Social	Norm doubting	Amos (1978)
	Nonconformity	Bachtold & Werner (1973)
	Independence	Barron (1972)
		Barton & Cattell (1972)
		Cross et al. (1967)
		Csikszentmihalyi & Getzels (1973)
		Domino (1974)
		Drevdahl & Cattell (1958)
		Dudek et al. (1991)
		Getzels & Csikszentmihalyi (1976)
		Hall & MacKinnon (1969)
		Helson (1977)
		Holland & Baird (1968)
		Kemp (1981)
		MacKinnon (1962)
		Pufal-Struzik (1992)
		Rossman & Horn (1972)
		Schaefer (1969, 1973)
		Shelton & Harris (1979)
		Zeldow (1973)
	Hostility	Barton & Cattell (1972)
	Aloofness	Cross et al. (1967)
	Unfriendliness	Drevdahl & Cattell (1958)
	Lack of warmth	Dudek et al. (1991)
		Eysenck (1995)
		Getzels & Csikszentmihalyi (1976)
		Götz & Götz (1979)
		Hall & MacKinnon (1969)
		Hammond & Edelmann (1991)
		Marchant-Haycox & Wilson (1992)
		Mohan & Tiwana (1987)
		Schaefer (1969, 1973)
		Wilson (1984)

research supports or fail to supports this stereotype. In this case, it does. Research suggests that artists are indeed more emotional and sensitive than nonartists (see Table 14.1). For instance, Marchant-Haycox and Wilson (1992) administered the Eysenck Personality Profile to 162 performing artists (actors, dancers, musicians, and singers) and found that they scored significantly higher than control subjects on anxiety, guilt, and hypochondriasis. Similarly, Hammond and Edelmann (1991), using the Eysenck Personality Questionnaire, found that professional actors scored significantly higher on the neuroticism scale than did nonactor comparison subjects.

A related and rather consistent finding has been the association between artistic creativity and the disposition toward affective illness. In the most impressive study of its kind, Ludwig (1995) examined the relative rates of mental and affective illness in 1,005 eminent people in 18 professions. Ludwig's main finding was that all forms of psychopathology (alcohol and drug abuse, psychosis, anxiety disorders, somatic problems, and suicide, among others) were more common in the artistic professions than in all other professions. Other research, however, suggests that bipolar affective disorder is more closely linked with artistic creativity than is unipolar affective disorder (Andreasen & Glick, 1988; Feist, in press; Jamison, 1993; Richards, 1994; Richards & Kinney, 1990; Russ, 1993). Andreasen and Glick's (1988) work on a sample of 30 gifted writers and 30 control subjects is illustrative. They found that writers were more likely to suffer from affective disorder than were control subjects (80% to 30%) and, more specifically, were more likely to suffer from bipolar disorder (43% to 10%). However, the two groups did not differ on their rates of unipolar depression.

Not all studies have found high levels of anxiety among creative artists (Barton & Cattell, 1972; Buttsworth & Smith, 1994; Feist, 1989; Walker et al., 1995). Buttsworth and Smith (1994) administered the 16 PF to 255 undergraduate music students and compared them with 296 undergraduate psychology students. Results revealed that the music students had more stability (Factor C) and less Anxiety (Factor II) than the psychology students. Similarly, Walker et al. (1995) found that eminent artists were more depressed but not more anxious than their noncreative eminent peers.

NONSOCIAL TRAITS: DRIVE AND AMBITION. One last nonsocial personality characteristic that tends to distinguish artists from nonartists is drive and ambition (see Table 14.1). For example, Dudek et al. (1991) reported significantly higher levels of need for achievement in a sample of professional artists compared with almost 400 nonartist adults. Similarly, Bakker (1988, 1991) found that adolescent dancers were more achievement oriented and driven than were an adolescent comparison group.

SOCIAL TRAITS: NORM DOUBTING, NONCONFORMITY, AND INDEPENDENCE. There are also a set of interpersonal and socially oriented personality traits that are relevant to artistic creativity, one of which is rebellion, or nonconformity. Artists, perhaps more than almost any other members of society, tend to question and rebel against established norms. Some may even argue that questioning, challenging, and pushing the limits of what is acceptable may be the defining traits of being an artist in modern society. The empirical literature on personality and artistic creativity supports the nonconforming, rebellious nature of artists (see Table 14.1). For instance, Hall and MacKinnon (1969) found that the most creative architects scored low on the "communality," "good impression," and "achievement via conformance" scales of the California Psychological Inventory (CPI) and scored low on the "affiliation" scale of the Adjective Check List, but high on its autonomy scale. This pattern of results depicts personalities that are conflicted, impulsive, nonconformist, rule doubting, skeptical, independent, and not concerned with obligations or duties. Similarly, research using the 16 PF suggests that artists are low on Conformity (Factor G), and high on Radicalism (Factor Q_1) and Self-Sufficiency (Factor Q_2). For instance, Barton and Cattell (1972) and Bachtold and Werner (1973) reported the preceding pattern of results on female samples of artists. Only one study has reported a negative relationship between being an artist and radicalism (Buttsworth & Smith, 1994), and it was a study of performance-oriented music students.

SOCIAL TRAITS: HOSTILITY, ALOOFNESS, UNFRIENDLINESS, AND LACK OF WARMTH. Research has also pointed toward a cluster of asocial and even antisocial personality dispositions associated with artistic creativity (see Table 14.1). In one of the earliest studies of its kind, Drevdahl and Cattell (1958) examined the relationship between artistic creativity and personality in three samples of artists (writers, visual artists, and science fiction writers). All three groups scored much lower than norms on the 16 PF Factor A (Warmth). Similarly, Getzels and Csikszentmihalyi (1976) investigated a sample of successful art students and found very low levels of Warmth (Factor A) on the 16 PF. Furthermore, Eysenck's notion of psychoticism, which consists of traits such as aggression, aloofness, antisocial and egocentric behavior, and tough-mindedness, tends to be higher in artists than nonartists (Götz & Götz, 1979; Hammond & Edelmann, 1991; Mohan & Tiwana, 1987). The only null result on psychoticism was reported by Wills (1983); the only null result on warmth was reported by MacKinnon (1962); and the only positive relationship on agreeableness was reported by Walker et al. (1995).

SOCIAL TRAITS: INTROVERSION. One of the more consistent findings from the personality literature of artists is that they tend to be rather introverted (see Table 14.1). Indeed, Storr (1988) has argued that the ability to be alone and away from others is a necessary prerequisite for creative activity. Only those who make time to be by themselves can spend the necessary amount of time thinking and creating.

A few studies, however, have reported high levels of extraversion among creative artists, but these have been with performing artists such as actors or opera singers (Hammond & Edelmann 1991; Wilson, 1984). For instance, using the Eysenck Personality Questionnaire and a shyness and sociability scale, Hammond and Edelmann (1991) reported elevated Extraversion and Sociability scores and depressed Shyness scores in a sample of 51 professional actors when compared with a sample of 52 nonactors.

In sum, the personality of the creative artist suggests a person who is imaginative, open to new ideas, drives, neurotic, affectively labile, but for the most part asocial and at times even antisocial.

Personality and Scientific Creativity

One could argue that science has more latitude of creative expression than art. That is, scientific investigations can range from the very routine, rote, and prescribed to the revolutionary and highly creative breakthrough. In fact, as Kuhn (1970) argued, much of the time science is relatively mundane and "normal," whereas only rarely does some individual produce truly "revolutionary science." Granted, some art can be very derivative and merely technical, yet anyone who makes a living at art must be rather creative. Scientists, on the other hand, can make a living being little more than technicians. Therefore, the appropriate comparison group for the creative scientist is the less creative scientist rather than the nonscientist. Furthermore, I classified a sample in the "science" category if it consisted of either professionals or students in natural science, biological science, social science, engineering, invention, or math.

NONSOCIAL TRAITS: OPENNESS TO EXPERIENCE AND FLEXIBILITY OF THOUGHT. A consistent finding in the personality and creativity in science literature has been that creative and eminent scientists tend to be more open to experience and more flexible in thought than are less creative and eminent scientists (see Table 14.2). Many of these findings stem from data on the flexibility scale (Fe) of the CPI (Feist & Barron, 1996; Garwood, 1964; Gough, 1961; Helson, 1971; Helson & Crutchfield, 1970; Parloff & Datta, 1965). The Fe scale taps into flexibility and adaptability of thought and behavior, as well as the preference for change and novelty (Gough, 1987). The few studies that have reported either no effect or a negative effect of flexibility in scientific creativity have been with student samples (Davids, 1968; Smithers & Batcock, 1970).

NONSOCIAL TRAITS: DRIVE, AMBITION, AND ACHIEVEMENT. The most eminent and creative scientists also tend to be more driven, ambitious, and achievement oriented than their less eminent peers (see Table 14.2). Busse and Mansfield (1984), for instance, studied the personality characteristics of 196 biologists, 201 chemists, and 171 physicists, and commitment to work (i.e., "need to concentrate intensively over long periods of time on one's work") was the strongest predictor of productivity (i.e., publication quantity), even when holding age and professional age constant. Of course, drive and ambition are predictive of success in other fields as well, but it is nevertheless important to demonstrate its effect in science as well. Helmreich, Spence, Beane, Lucker, and Matthews (1980) studied a group of 196 academic psychologists and found that different components of achievement and drive had different relationships with objective measures of attainment (i.e., publications and citations). With a self-report measure, they assessed three different aspects of achievement: mastery (preferring challenging and difficult tasks), work (enjoying working hard), and competitiveness (liking interpersonal competition and bettering others). According to Amabile's (1996) well-known typology, the first two measures could be classified as "intrinsic motives" and the last measure could be an "extrinsic motive." Helmreich and his colleagues found that mastery and work were positively related to both publication and citation totals, whereas competitiveness was positively related to publications but negatively related to citations. Being intrinsically motivated (mastery and work) appears to increase one's productivity and positive evaluation by peers (citations), whereas wanting to be superior to peers leads to increased productivity, and yet a lower positive evaluation by peers. The inference here is that being driven by the need for superiority may backfire in terms of having a negative impact on the field. Indeed, in a further analysis their 1980 data set of the male psychologists, Helmreich and colleagues (Helmreich, Spence, & Pred, 1988) factor-analyzed the Jenkins Activity Survey and extracted an Achievement Striving factor and an Impatience/Irritability factor. Achievement Striving was positively related to both citation and publication counts, whereas Impatience/Irritability was related to neither publications nor citations.

SOCIAL TRAITS: DOMINANCE, ARROGANCE, HOSTILITY, AND SELF-CONFIDENCE. In the highly competitive world of science, especially big science, where the most productive and influential continue to be rewarded with more and more of the resources, success is more likely for those who thrive in competitive environments, that is, for the dominant, arrogant, hostile, and self-confident (see Table 14.2). For example, Van Zelst and Kerr (1954) collected personality self-descriptions on 514 technical and scientific personnel from a research foundation and a university. Holding age constant, they reported significant partial correlations between productivity and describing oneself as "argumentative," "assertive," and "self-confident." In one of the few studies to examine female scientists, Bachtold and Werner (1972) administered Cattell's 16 PF to 146 women scientists and

Table 14.2. *Consistent Personality Findings from the Literature Comparing Creative and Less Creative Scientists*

Trait Category	Trait	Citation
Nonsocial	Openness to experience Flexibility of thought	Feist & Barron, 1996 Garwood, 1964 Gough, 1961 Helson, 1971 Helson & Crutchfield, 1970 Parloff & Datta, 1965 Parloff, Datta, Kleman, & Handlon, 1968 Roco, 1993 Rossman & Horn, 1972 Schaefer, 1969 Shapiro, 1968 Van Zelst & Kerr, 1954 Wispe, 1963
	Drive Ambition Achievement	Albert & Runco, 1987 Bloom, 1956 Busse & Mansfield, 1984 Chambers, 1964 Davids, 1968 Erickson et al., 1970 Feist, 1993 Gantz, Erickson, & Stephenson, 1972 Gough, 1961 Helmreich et al., 1980 Helmreich et al., 1988 Holland, 1960 Ikpaahindi, 1987 Lacey & Erickson, 1974 Rushton et al., 1983 Schaefer, 1969 Shapiro, 1968 Simon, 1974 Van Zelst & Kerr, 1954 Wispe, 1963
Social	Dominance Arrogance Hostility Self-confidence	Bachtold & Werner, 1972 Chambers, 1964 Davids, 1968 Erickson et al., 1970 Feist, 1993 Gantz et al., 1972 Garwood, 1964 Gough, 1961 Ham & Shaughnessy, 1992 Helmreich et al., 1988 Helson & Crutchfield, 1970 Lacey & Erickson, 1974 McDermid, 1965 Parloff & Datta, 1965 Parloff, et al., 1968 Rossman & Horn, 1972 Rushton et al., 1983 Schaefer, 1969 Shapiro, 1968 Van Zelst & Kerr, 1954 Wispe, 1963

Table 14.2 (cont.)

Trait Category	Trait	Citation
	Autonomy	Albert & Runco, 1987
	Introversion	Bachtold & Werner, 1972
	Independence	Bloom, 1956
		Busse & Mansfield, 1984
		Chambers, 1964
		Davids, 1968
		Erickson et al., 1970
		Garwood, 1964
		Helson, 1971
		Helson & Crutchfield, 1970
		Holland, 1960
		Lacey & Erickson, 1974
		Parloff & Datta, 1965
		Roco, 1993
		Roe, 1952
		Rossman & Horn, 1972
		Rushton et al., 1987
		Schaefer, 1969
		Smithers & Batcock, 1970
		Terman, 1955
		Van Zelst & Kerr, 1954

found that they were significantly different from women in general on 9 of the 16 scales, including Dominance (Factor E) and Self-confidence (Factor O). Similarly, Feist (1993) recently reported a structural equation model of scientific eminence in which the path between observer-rated hostility and eminence was direct and the path between arrogant working style and eminence was indirect but significant.

SOCIAL TRAITS: AUTONOMY, INTROVERSION, AND INDEPENDENCE. The scientific elite also tend to be more aloof, asocial, and introverted than their less creative peers (see Table 14.2). In a classic study concerning the creative person in science, Roe (1952, 1953) found that creative scientists were more achievement oriented and less affiliative than were less creative scientists. In another seminal study of the scientific personality, Eiduson (1962) found that scientists were independent, curious, sensitive, intelligent, emotionally invested in intellectual work, and relatively happy. Similarly, Chambers (1964) reported that creative psychologists and chemists were markedly more dominant, ambitious, and self-sufficient, and had more initiative as compared with less creative peers. Helson (1971) compared creative female mathematicians with less creative female mathematicians, matched on IQ. Observers blindly rated the former as having more "unconventional thought processes," as being more "rebellious and non-conforming," and as being less likely to judge "self and others in conventional terms." More recently, Rushton, Murray, and Paunonen (1987) conducted factor analyses of the personality traits most strongly loading on the Research factor (in contrast to a Teaching factor) in two separate samples of academic psychologists. Among other results, they found that "independence" tended to load on the Research factor, whereas "extraversion" tended to load on the Teaching factor.

To summarize the distinguishing traits of creative scientists: They are generally more open and flexible, driven and ambitious, and although they tend to be relatively asocial, when they do interact with others, they tend to be somewhat prone to arrogance, self-confidence, and hostility.

Generalizability of Personality Traits of Creative People

Historically most reviews of the creativity and personality literature have either failed to distinguish between artistic and scientific creativity or have not explicated the unique characteristics of each domain (Barron & Harrington, 1981; Dellas & Gaier, 1970; Mumford & Gustafson, 1988; Stein, 1968). Given the accumulation of findings on personality and creativity, however, we are now in a position to be more systematic and discriminating with the trends and patterns that have developed. One way of doing so is by making explicit the similarities and differences between the different creative domains, in particular, art and science.

Personality Characteristics Unique to Creative Artists and Scientists

Compared with creative scientists, artists appear to be more anxious, emotionally labile, and impulsive. More generally, therefore, the artistically creative person appears to have a disposition toward intense affective experience (Andreasen & Glick, 1988; Bamber, Bill, Boyd, & Corbett, 1983; Csikszentmihalyi & Getzels, 1973; Gardner, 1973; Getzels & Csikszentmihalyi, 1976; Jamison, 1993; Ludwig, 1995; Richards, 1994; Russ, 1993; Simonton, 1988). To quote Russ (1993), "One of the main differences between artistic and scientific creativity may be the importance of getting more deeply into affect states and thematic material in artistic creativity" (p. 67). To the extent that art is more often an introspective journey and science more of an externally focused one (see Gardner, 1973), it is not surprising that artists would be more sensitive to and expressive of internal emotional states than are scientists. This is not to say that the creative process in art is exclusively emotional and in science exclusively nonemotional. Research suggests that that is not the case (Feist, 1991). The discovery stages of scientific creativity are often very intuitive and emotional, just as the elaboration stages of artistic creativity can be very technical and tedious. Yet dispositionally, artists and scientists generally do tend to differ on the degree to which they are sensitive to their own and other people's emotional states.

The second core set of unique characteristics of the artistic personality can be classified as low socialization and low conscientiousness. Although it is true that low socialization and nonconformity are traits of both creative artists and scientists (Barron, 1963, 1972; Cattell & Drevdahl, 1955; Csikszentmihalyi & Getzels, 1973; Hall & MacKinnon, 1969; Helson, 1971; Kemp, 1981; Ochse, 1990), the form that nonconformity takes may be different in the two professions. Artists and not scientists, for instance, tend to be much lower than the norm on the "socialization," "communality," "tolerance," and "responsibility" scales of the CPI (e.g., Barron, 1972; Domino, 1974; Zeldow, 1973) and the Q_1 (Radical) scale of the 16 PF (Csikszentmihalyi & Getzels, 1973; Drevdahl & Cattell, 1958; Kemp, 1981). The low socialization and responsibility scores are indicative of people who very much question, doubt, and struggle with social norms. Perhaps artists are more actively nonconformist or asocialized than are scientists, who may be less overt in their nonconformity. Consistent with the idea that scientists are less actively nonconforming than are artists, scientists in general tend to be more conscientious and orderly than are nonscientists (Kline & Lapham, 1992; Rossman & Horn, 1972; Schaefer, 1969; Wilson & Jackson, 1994). When one considers that traits such as being "organized," "planful," "not careless," and "not slipshod" make up the conscientiousness dimension (John, 1990), it is not surprising that scientists would score higher on the dimension than could artists.

Personality Commonalities Between Creative Artists and Scientists

If emotional lability, impulsivity, nonconformity, and rebelliousness tend to distinguish artists from scientists, then what personality characteristics do creative artists and scientists tend to have in common?

The evidence suggests that the creative person (artist or scientist) in general is distinguished by relatively high levels of asocial characteristics, namely introversion, independence, hostility, and arrogance (Bachtold & Werner, 1972; Csikszentmihalyi & Getzels, 1973; Dudek et al., 1991; Feist, 1993, 1994; Garwood, 1964; Guastello & Shissler, 1994; Kline & Lapham, 1992; Ochse, 1990; Rushton et al., 1987; Storr, 1988; Zeldow, 1973). Many have argued that isolation, withdrawal, and independence are necessary conditions of creative achievement (Barron, 1963, 1972; Csikszentmihalyi & Getzels, 1973; Ochse, 1990; Storr, 1988). For instance, Storr (1988) argued that present-day Western society overemphasizes interpersonal relationships as the source of happiness and well-being and underemphasizes the solitude of creative achievement. In addition, Feist (1993, 1994) has demonstrated the prevalence of hostility among highly creative scientists. In his model of scientific eminence, observer ratings of hostility and arrogance each had direct and indirect effects on eminence (Feist, 1993). Furthermore, the personality constellations of scientists who think complexly about research were quite distinct from those who think complexly about teaching (Feist, 1994). Specifically, the former were seen by others as more hostile and exploitative, whereas the latter were viewed as more gregarious and warm.

A second cluster of distinguishing traits revolve around the need for power and for diversity of experience: drive, ambition, self-confidence, openness to experience, flexibility of thought, and active imagination. In order to achieve and to go against the norms, one must have a rather high energy level and be driven (see Amabile, 1996; Barron, 1963, 1972; Sheldon, 1995; Sternberg & Lubart, 1995). Belief in what one is doing and the ambition to do it originally are probably related to the high degree of self-confidence often seen in creative individuals. It is then only a short step from drive and self-confidence to arrogance and hostility. If one is intrinsically driven by a task and has a need to be alone, unbothered by others, as is often true of creative people, then social approval and social niceties are not likely to be high on one's list of priorities. Hostility and arrogance may, therefore, be a result of complete dedication and devotion to work, and anything that detracts from that work would be the object of scorn and hostility.

TEMPORAL CONSISTENCY IN CREATIVE PERSONALITY: EVIDENCE OF TEMPORAL PRECEDENCE

Consistency of Creative Personality

The only methodology that provides a possible answer to the temporal precedence (which comes first) question is longitudinal research. Only longitudinal studies can speak to whether the distinguishing traits of creative people measured at an earlier time in life continue to distinguish them from their peers later in life. Showing that traits such as independence, introversion, openness, hostility, and dominance exist in high levels early in life may not mean that they precede creativity, but such a pattern of results would be consistent with precedence of personality. On the other hand, if these are not the traits that distinguish young creative people from their less creative peers, but do so later, then they clearly cannot precede creativity. Are there any longitudinal studies that find a set of personality traits that distinguish young creative people from their less creative peers but do not later in life?

No, the literature overwhelmingly points toward the consistency of creative personality (Camp, 1994; Dudek et al., 1991; Dudek & Hall, 1991; Feist, 1995; Getzels & Csikszentmihalyi, 1976; Helson, 1987; Helson, Roberts, & Agronick, 1995; Schaefer, 1973; Stohs, 1990; Terman, 1954). For example, Schaefer (1973) conducted a five-year follow-up investigation of creative young adults who were originally tested in adolescence. The adolescent sample consisted of 100 participants in each of the following four criterion groups: creative art/writing males, creative science males, creative art females, and creative writing females. There were also 100 participants in four matched control groups. Roughly half of each sample participated in a replication five years later. Many of the same scales (i.e., autonomy, self-control, and nurturance) that distinguished creative adolescents from their peers continued to distinguish the two groups in early adulthood. In other research on the consistency of creative personality, Dudek and Hall (1991) studied three groups of architects and concluded that "it is evident that Group III [the less creative architects] retained its social conformity and Group I [the creative architects] its spontaneity and independence over the 25 years" (p. 218). Finally, Helson, Roberts, and Agronick (1995) found that creative women at age 52 were consistently rated by observers at age 21 and age 43 as being aesthetically oriented, interesting, driven, rebellious, independent, and not conventional, conservative, or submissive.

Consistency of Creative Achievement

We have now seen that the distinguishing personality traits of creative people tend to be rather stable from adolescence or early adulthood on. It is also possible that possessing certain personality characteristics may play a vital role in determining which gifted and talented children go on to actualize their potential and which do not. Indeed, although there is a mounting body of evidence that intellectual precocity and giftedness foreshadow educational attainment and career success, they do not appear to systematically foreshadow adult creative achievement. Let me be more specific. Gifted children (i.e., those with high IQs) are more likely to be more successful in school, obtain higher degrees, and are more likely to go into professional and/or business professions than are less gifted students (Benbow & Minor, 1986; Benbow & Stanley, 1982; Cox, 1926; Holahan & Sears, 1995; Lubinski & Benbow, 1994; Pyryt, 1992; Tomlinson-Keasey & Keasey, 1993; Wise, Steel, & McDonald, 1979). A surprisingly high proportion of gifted students, however, do not continue in careers in which they exhibited precocious talents or do not make significant creative contributions to their field as adults (Arnold, 1992; Barron & Harrington, 1981; Cramond, 1994; Farmer, 1988; Gough, 1976; Guilford, 1959; Helson, 1987; Hudson, 1958; MacKinnon, 1960; Marland, 1972; Milgram & Hong, 1994; Simonton, 1988; Sternberg, 1988; Subotnik, Duschl, & Selmon, 1993; Subotnik & Steiner, 1992; Tannenbaum, 1983; Taylor, 1963; Winner & Martino, 1993). The study by Milgram and Hong (1994) is a good example. They studied a group of high school students over an 18-year period and found that while grades were related to academic success, they were not related to any adult accomplishment measures, including a creative outcome measure. Creative thinking at age 18, however, did predict work accomplishment at age 36. As Farmer (1988) also pointed out, only 42% of the male and 22% of the female extremely precocious students went on to choose science or math graduate programs (cf. Benbow, 1988; Benbow & Lubinski, 1993). In addition, Subotnik and Steiner (1992) reported in a group of high school Westinghouse Science winners that only five years after being so designated, almost 20% of the gifted young males and nearly 40% of the gifted young female scientists were not pursuing scientific careers. Finally, in one of the few longitudinal studies of musical precocity, Winner and Martino (1993) found that early musical talent often did not translate into adult creative achievement in music.

If giftedness is a poor predictor of creative achievement, then are there any consistent psychological processes that suggest who will continue on or who will make creative contributions? There is some evidence that gender (females being more likely to drop out) and motivation (Subotnik, Duschl, & Selmon, 1993) predict creative achievement, but certain personality traits also play a role (Albert, 1991; Butler-Por, 1993; Helson, 1987; Lindsay, 1978; Tomlinson-Keasey & Keasey, 1993; Tomlinson-Keasey & Little, 1990; Trost, 1993). For instance, Helson (1987) divided into two groups subjects who in college were nominated by faculty members to have the highest potential for creative achievement. The two groups were composed of those who were and were not in creative and successful careers (writers, dancers, artists, psychotherapists, etc.) at age 43. The former were labeled "successful careerists," whereas the latter were labeled "other nominees." Personality data were collected on both groups at ages 21, 27, and 43, so prospective and contemporary personality comparisons could be made between the successful careerists and the other nominees. Helson found that, at age 21, the successful careerists were more dominant, independent, achievement-oriented, self-accepting, and psychologically minded but were less sociable than the other nominees. At age 27 they were still more achievement-oriented and psychologically minded and less sociable. And finally, at age 43 the successful careerists were more independent, empathic, status-oriented, self-accepting, responsible, and achievement-oriented, and still less sociable than other nominees.

Without a doubt the most ambitious and extensive longitudinal study of giftedness has been the one begun by Lewis Terman in the 1920s. More than 1,500 children with IQs greater than 135 were followed over the course of their entire lives (in fact, the study is still being conducted). Extensive follow-ups were conducted on average every 10 years. One relevant finding from the Terman study has been that adolescent personality predicts later educational attainment (Tomlinson-Keasey & Keasey, 1993; Tomlinson-Keasey & Little, 1990). Using factor analysis and structural equations models, and taking advantage of the multiple measures and very large sample size of the study, Tomlinson-Keasey and Little (1990) found that adolescent sociability and social responsibility (empathy) had direct influences on educational attainment. Moreover, intellectual determination (i.e., drive or achievement motivation) had a direct impact on maintaining intellectual skill. Tomlinson-Keasey and Keasey (1993) also reported that for gifted women (i.e., holding IQ constant at a mean of 148), observer personality ratings made during adolescence were predictive of educational attainment. Adolescent girls who were rated by teachers and parents as being highest on intellectual determination and social responsibility (i.e., empathy conscientiousness) were most likely to obtain college and postgraduate degrees.

In sum, to the question of whether adolescent talent translates into adult success, the answer is a rather clear yes. There is little doubt that highly intelligent children are more likely than their classmates to obtain higher grades in school, obtain higher educational degrees, and in general go into well-paying professional careers. But are they more likely to be truly creative? The answer appears to be no. Surprisingly often, the most talented children and adolescents go on to lead relatively uncreative lives. Indeed, precocious intellectual talent may be neither necessary nor sufficient for true creative achievement in adulthood.

Such a lack of predictive validity of intellectual aptitude tests can be explained by the small relationship between intelligence and creativity (Barron & Harrington, 1981; Getzels, 1987; MacKinnon, 1978; Magnusson & Backteman, 1978; Milgram & Hong, 1994; Rossman & Horn, 1972; Sternberg, 1986; Sternberg & Lubart, 1995; Wallach, 1970; Winner & Martino, 1993). To quickly solve multiple choice problems that have known solutions involves conver-

gent or analytical thinking skills, whereas to creatively solve open-ended problems that have no known solutions involves divergent or intuitive thinking skills (Guilford, 1950, 1959, 1987; Simonton, 1988, 1989; Sternberg, 1986). Creativity is fluency, flexibility, usefulness, and originality of association, not speed at solving verbal and/or mathematical multiple-choice problems. It should come as no surprise, therefore, that creative potential and creative ability are better predictors of later creative achievement than is intellectual ability (Barron & Harrington, 1981; Milgram & Hong, 1994; Rossman & Horn, 1972; Sternberg & Lubart, 1995).

INTEGRATIVE THEORY LINKING PERSONALITY AND CREATIVITY

If personality does covary with creative achievement and there is temporal stability of creative personality, then do we have theoretical models connecting personality and creativity? Furthermore, are there plausible and testable biological and/or psychological mechanisms linking the two? Recently, a number of theoretical models have begun to propose plausible and testable explanations for the connection. Recall that the most consistent correlates of creativity in both art and science are introversion, drive, ambition, openness, flexibility, autonomy or introversion, and hostility and arrogance. A few theories have attempted to connect each of them to creative achievement.

Perhaps the most ambitious and inclusive recent theory of personality and creativity is the one offered by Eysenck (1993, 1995). Eysenck has proposed a causal theory of creativity that begins with genetic determinants, hippocampal formation (of dopamine and serotonin), cognitive inhibition, and psychoticism, which in turn leads to trait creativity and ultimately creative achievement. The most appealing aspect of this model, although speculative in parts, is that it is testable. What is of particular interest in Eysenck's model are the relationships between genetic and neurochemical processes and trait creativity (i.e., personality), which is the direct precursor to creative achievement. For instance, a key component implicated in Eysenck's biologically based model is cortical arousal. High arousal is associated with a narrowing of attention, whereas low arousal is associated with a widening of attention. Furthermore, Eysenck and other researchers have found that creativity depends on a wide attentional focus and an expansion of cognitive searching to the point of overinclusion, a defining characteristic of psychoticism (Eysenck, 1995; Isen, Daubman, & Nowicki, 1987; Jamison, 1993; Mendelsohn, 1976). Therefore, one would predict that creative thinking might be related to low cortical arousal. Colin Martindale has established a research program that has tested this idea systematically and has consistently found support for it (Martindale, 1981; Martindale & Armstrong, 1974; Martindale & Greenough, 1973; Martindale & Hasenfus, 1978; Martindale, Hines, Mitchell, & Covello, 1984). For example, as measured by stress, high arousal reduces creative solutions to problems (Martindale & Greenough, 1973), and, as measured by EEG (percent time spent in alpha states), low arousal was related to more creative problem solving (Martindale & Armstrong, 1974). However, low cortical arousal is evident only during the inspiration stage and not throughout creative insight or during baseline measures. In fact, creative individuals tend to have higher resting arousal levels (Martindale & Armstrong, 1974), which is consistent with the high cortical arousal of introversion and its relation to creativity (Eysenck, 1990, 1995).

More generally, trying to explain the connection between creativity and psychoticism, Woody and Claridge (1977) wrote: "Both [psychoticism and creativity] may tap a common factor associated with the willingness to be unconventional or engage in mildly antisocial behaviour" (p. 247). As mentioned earlier, radical, unconventional, asocial, or even antisocial behaviors are probably more common among artists than scientists, but these traits are nonetheless elevated in creative scientists relative to norms (Bachtold, 1976; Barton & Cattell, 1972; Getzels & Csikszentmihalyi, 1976; Helson, 1971; Rushton, 1990; Rushton, Murray, & Paunonen, 1983; Wilson & Jackson, 1994). Whether unconventionality is antecedent to or consequent of creativity is of course open to question.

However, it is not unbridled psychoticism that is most strongly associated with creativity, but psychoticism tempered by high ego strength or ego control. Paradoxically, creative people appear to be simultaneously very labile and unstable and yet can be rather controlled and stable (Barron, 1963; Eysenck, 1995; Feist, in press; Fodor, 1995; Richards, Kinney, Lunde, Benet, & Merzel, 1988; Russ, 1993). As Barron (1963) argued over 30 years ago: "Thus the creative genius may be at once naïve and knowledgeable, being at home equally to primitive symbolism and to rigorous logic. He is both more primitive and more cultured, more destructive and more constructive, occasionally crazier and yet adamantly saner, than the average person" (p. 224).

In addition, Russ (1993) elaborated on the facilitative effect that affective traits play in the creative process and developed a model that conceptually integrates much of the known empirical findings concerning the relationship between creativity and affective dispositions. For instance, she hypothesized that access to affect-laden thoughts (primary process thought and affective fantasy) and openness to affective states leads to the divergent-thinking abilities of free association, breadth of attention, and fluidity of thought, as well as to the transformation abilities of shifting sets and cognitive flexibility. These paths are essentially the same as those Eysenck proposed connecting affective states, overinclusive thinking, and creativity. Furthermore, Russ suggested that taking affective pleasure in challenge and being intrinsically motivated results in an increased sensitivity to problems and problem finding. Being sensitive, open, and flexible in thought are in turn important personality dispositions related to creativity. In sum, there are theoretical and empirical reasons for recognizing the connection between affective states, affective traits, and creative ability and achievement.

Although coming from the context of scientific creativity, Mansfield and Busse (1981) also developed an integrated model of personality and creativity (cf. Helmreich et al., 1980). Their model includes not only paths between personality and creativity, but also developmental antecedents as precursors of personality. Based on empirical findings, they suggested that particular developmental antecedents precede personality characteristics, which in turn precede the creative process. The developmental antecedents associated with creative people are low emotional intensity of the parent–child relationship, parental fostering of autonomy, parental intellectual stimulation, and apprenticeship. These are antecedent to the personality traits of autonomy, flexibility and openness, need to be original, commitment to work, need for professional recognition, and, finally, aesthetic sensitivity. Finally, Mansfield and Busse proposed that these traits facilitate the crucial stages involved in creative achievement: selection of the problem, extended effort working on the problem, setting constraints, changing constraints, and, finally, verification and elaboration. One interesting yet difficult to support assumption of their model is that personality precedes the development of creativity.

The field of personality psychology has recently witnessed the widespread adoption of the five-factor model (FFM; Digman, 1990; McCrae & John, 1992), which argues that there are five fundamental bipolar dimensions to personality: openness, neuroticism, extraversion, agreeableness, and conscientiousness. Although few researchers have directly examined the relationship between creativity and the FFM (Dollinger & Clancy, 1993; McCrae, 1987; Mumford, Costanza, Threlfall, Baughman, & Reiter-Palmon 1993), enough work has accumulated on separate FFM dimensions and creativity that I can summarize the consistent trends. The strongest relationship exists between creativity and openness, but relationships also have been reported between each of the other four dimensions and creativity: neuroticism (Andreason & Glick, 1988; Bakker, 1991; Hammond & Edelmann, 1991; Kemp, 1981;

Marchant-Haycox & Wilson, 1992), lack of conscientiousness (Drevdahl & Cattell, 1958; Getzels & Csikszentmihalyi, 1976; Kemp, 1981; Shelton & Harris, 1979; Walker et al., 1995), introversion (Bachtold & Werner, 1973; Busse & Mansfield, 1984; Chambers, 1964; Cross, Cattell, & Butcher, 1967; Helson, 1971, 1977; Pufal-Struzik, 1992; Roco, 1993; Rossman & Horn, 1972; Rushton et al., 1987; Zeldow, 1973), and lack of agreeableness (Barton & Cattell, 1972; Dudek et al., 1991; Eysenck, 1995; Feist, 1993, 1994; Getzels & Csikszentmihalyi, 1976; Hall & MacKinnon, 1969; Helmreich et al., 1988; Helson & Crutchfield, 1970; Lacey & Erickson, 1974; McDermid, 1965). This is not to say that all who have explored the relationship between the FFM and creativity have found each personality dimension to relate to creativity (Dollinger & Clancy, 1993; Feist, 1989; McCrae, 1987; Woody & Claridge, 1977). However, many of these null or negative results were conducted on general population samples and not on creative artists or scientists. Although not yet established empirically, it may be that the five factors are more consistently related to artistic and scientific creativity than to everyday creativity. Future research must be conducted, however, before such a conclusion can be made. At the very least, however, openness to experience is related to creativity, so how do we account for this association? McCrae (1987) suggests there were three possible reasons for the link. First, open people may be more fascinated with the open-ended, creative, problem-solving tasks and they may simply score higher on such tasks. Second, open people may have developed cognitive skills associated with creative, divergent thinking, namely flexibility and fluidity of thought. And third, open people may have an interest in seeking sensation and more varied experiences, and this experiential base may serve as the foundation for flexibility and fluency of thinking. Again, more research is needed to determine the validity of these speculations.

CONCLUSIONS

Fascination with creative genius has compelled many of greatest minds of Western culture to put pen to paper, including but not limited to Socrates, Plato, Aristotle, Kant, Wordsworth, Coleridge, Poe, Galton, Russell, Poincare, Freud, Bergson, Einstein, Maslow, Rogers, and Skinner (see Ghiselin, 1952; Rothenberg & Hausman, 1976; Vernon, 1970). As Sternberg and Lubart (1995, 1996) have recently pointed out, few topics are of greater importance to psychology than creativity. Universities, businesses, the arts, entertainment, and politics – in other words, all of the major institutions of modern society – are each driven by their ability to create and solve problems originally and adaptively, that is, creatively. Therefore, the ultimate success and survival of these institutions depend on their ability to attract, select, and maintain creative individuals. So what do we know about the creative personality after 45+ years of systematic empirical work? Table 14.3 summarizes what we know and what this chapter has presented. Certain personality traits consistently covary with creativity, yet there are some domain specificities; the temporal stability of creative personality is consistent with the idea that the distinguishing personality traits may precede creative achievement; finally, giftedness as measured by IQ tests tends not to be a very valid predictor of adult creative achievement. Some of these conclusions may appear to be deceptively simple, but they go far in demonstrating that personality as a construct and its study as a discipline offer a unique and important perspective on creativity and the creative process.

Gaps in the Literature and Work for the Future

There is still a long way to go before consensus can be reached on some of the more difficult and pressing problems of the creative personality. If we have begun to establish covariation between personality and creativity, we have only begun to address temporal prece-

Table 14.3. *Summary of Major Conclusions*

Creative people in art and science tend to be open to new experiences, less conventional and less conscientious, more self-confident, self-accepting, driven, ambitious, dominant, hostile, and impulsive.

Creative people in art and science do not share the same unique personality profiles: Artists are more affective, emotionally unstable, as well as less socialized and accepting of group norms, whereas scientists are more conscientious.

The traits that distinguish creative children and adolescents tend to be the ones that distinguish creative adults. The creative personality tends to be rather stable.

Childhood academic intelligence (giftedness) is a relatively poor predictor of adult creative achievement.

dence and have all but ignored ruling out extraneous variables as explanations. For instance, no one has begun systematic investigation of creative potential and ability in young children and followed them through adolescence and adulthood. Such research has been conducted on intelligence and giftedness (see, e.g., Subotnik & Arnold, 1994), but not creativity. How stable is creativity from early childhood to adulthood? Are creativity and intelligence always distinct or do they diverge only after a certain age? How do the dispositions toward originality interact with the other psychological processes important to creative achievement, namely development, cognition, and social influence? Finally, do other psychological processes account for the correlations between personality and creativity? Only once these questions are examined systematically and empirically can the theoretical models of the creative person be evaluated, tested, and modified (Eysenck, 1993, 1995; Feist & Gorman, 1998; Helmreich et al., 1980; Mansfield & Busse, 1981).

Empirical research over the past 45 years makes a rather convincing case that creative people behave consistently over time and situation and in ways that distinguish them from others. The creative personality does exist and personality dispositions regularly and predictably relate to creative achievement in art and science. How the two develop, however, and their influence on one another for the most part are little understood. Perhaps in the next 45 years someone with the requisite constellation of personality characteristics and creative ability will focus his or her energies on the topic and come up with a creative solution.

NOTE

I am grateful to Erika Rosenberg and John Nezlek for their comments on an earlier draft of this chapter. Preparation of this chapter was supported in part by a grant from the Committee on Faculty Research at the College of William and Mary.

REFERENCES

Albert, R. S. (1991). People, processes, and developmental paths to eminence: A developmental-interactional model. In R. M. Milgram (Ed.), *Counseling gifted and talented children: A guide for teachers, counselors, and parents* (pp. 75–93). Norwood, NJ: Ablex.

Albert, R. S., & Runco, M. (1987). The possible different personality dispositions of scientists and non-scientists. In D. N. Jackson and J P Rushton (Eds.), *Scientific excellence* (pp. 67–97). Beverly Hills, CA: Sage.

Alter, J. B. (1989). Creativity profile of university and conservatory music students. *Creativity Research Journal, 2*, 184–195.

Amabile, T. (1996). *Creativity in context.* New York: Westview.

Amos, S. P. (1978). Personality differences between established and less-established male and female creative artists. *Journal of Personality Assessment, 42*, 374–377.

Andreasen, N. C., & Glick, L. D. (1988). Bipolar affective disorder and creativity: Implications and clinical management. *Comprehensive Psychiatry, 29*, 207–216.

Arnold, K. D. (1992). Undergraduate aspirations of career outcomes of academically talented women: A discriminant analysis. *Roeper Review, 15,* 169–175.

Bachtold, L. M. (1976). Personality characteristics of women of distinction. *Psychology of Women Quarterly, 1,* 70–78.

Bachtold, L. M., & Werner, E. E. (1972). Personality characteristics of women scientists. *Psychological Reports, 31,* 391–396.

Bachtold, L. M., & Werner, E. E. (1973). Personality characteristics of creative women. *Perceptual and Motor Skills, 36,* 311–319.

Bakker, F. C. (1988). Personality differences between young dancers and non-dancers. *Personality and Individual Differences, 9,* 121–131.

Bakker, F. C. (1991). Development of personality in dancers: A longitudinal study. *Personality and Individual Differences, 12,* 671–681.

Bamber, J. H., Bill, J. M., Boyd, F. E., & Corbett, W. D. (1983). In two minds: Arts and science differences at sixth-form level. *British Journal of Educational Psychology, 53,* 222–233.

Barron, F. (1963). *Creativity and psychological health.* New York: Van Nostrand.

Barron, F. (1972). *Artists in the making.* New York: Seminar Press.

Barron, F., & Harrington, D. (1981). Creativity, intelligence, and personality. *Annual Review of Psychology, 32,* 439–476.

Barton, K., & Cattell, H. (1972). Personality characteristics of female psychology, science and art majors. *Psychological Reports, 31,* 807–813.

Benbow, C. P. (1988). Sex differences in mathematical reasoning ability in intellectually talented preadolescents: Their nature, effects, and possible causes. *Behavioral and Brain Sciences, 11,* 169–183.

Benbow, C. P., & Lubinski, D. (1993). Psychological profiles of the mathematically talented. Some sex differences and evidence supporting their biological basis. In G. R. Bock and K. Ackrill (Eds.), *The origins and development of high ability* (pp. 44–66). Chichester: Wiley.

Benbow, C. P., & Minor, L. L. (1986). Mathematically talented students and achievement in the high school sciences. *American Educational Research Journal, 23,* 425–436.

Benbow, C. P., & Stanley, J. C. (1982). Consequences in high school and college of sex differences in mathematical reasoning ability: A longitudinal perspective. *American Educational Research Journal, 19,* 598–622.

Bloom, B. S. (1956). Report on creativity research at the University of Chicago. In C. W. Taylor (Ed.), *The 1955 University of Utah Research Conference on the Identification of Creative Scientific Talent.* Salt Lake City: University of Utah Press.

Busse, T. V., & Mansfield, R. S. (1984). Selected personality traits and achievement in male scientists. *Journal of Psychology, 116,* 117–131.

Butler-Por, N. (1993). Underachieving gifted students. In K. A. Heller, F. J. Monks, & A. H. Passow (Eds.), *International handbook of research and development of giftedness and talent* (pp. 649–688). Oxford: Pergamon.

Buttsworth, L. M., & Smith, G. A. (1994). Personality of Australian performing musicians by gender and by instrument. *Personality and Individual Differences, 5,* 595–603.

Camp, G. C. (1994). A longitudinal study of correlates of creativity. *Creativity Research Journal, 7,* 125–144.

Cattell, R. B., & Drevdahl, J. E. (1955). A comparison of the personality profile (16 PF) of eminent researchers with that of eminent teachers and administrators, and the general population. *British Journal of Psychology, 46,* 248–261.

Chambers, J. A. (1964). Relating personality and biographical factors to scientific creativity. *Psychological Monographs: General and Applied, 78,* 1–20.

Cox, C. (1926). *Genetic studies of genius: Vol. 2. The early mental traits of three hundred geniuses.* Stanford, CA: Stanford University Press.

Cramond, B. (1994). The Torrance Tests of Creative Thinking: From design through establishment of predictive validity. In R. F. Subotnik & K. D. Arnold (Eds.), *Beyond Terman: Contemporary longitudinal studies of giftedness and talent* (pp. 229–254). Norwood, NJ: Ablex.

Cross, P. G., Cattell, R. B., & Butcher, H. J. (1967). The personality pattern of creative artists. *British Journal of Educational Psychology, 37,* 292–299.

Csikszentmihalyi, M., & Getzels, J. W. (1973). The personality of young artists: An empirical and theoretical exploration. *British Journal of Psychology, 64,* 91–104.

Davids, A. (1968). Psychological characteristics of high school male and female potential scientists in comparison with academic underachievers. *Psychology in the Schools, 3,* 79–87.

Dellas, M., & Gaier, E. L. (1970). Identification of creativity: The individual. *Psychological Bulletin, 73,* 55–73.

Digman, J. M. (1990). Personality structure: Emergence of the five-factor model. *Annual Review of Psychology, 41,* 417–440.

Dollinger, S. J., & Clancy, S. M. (1993). Identity, self, and personality. Part 2, Glimpses through the autophotographic eye. *Journal of Personality and Social Psychology, 64,* 1064–1071.

Domino, G. (1974). Assessment of cinematographic creativity. *Journal of Personality and Social Psychology, 30,* 150–154.

Drevdahl, J. E., & Cattell, R. B. (1958). Personality and creativity in artists and writers. *Journal of Clinical Psychology, 14,* 107–111.

Dudek, S. (1968). Regression and creativity. *Journal of Nervous and Mental Disease, 147,* 535–546.

Dudek, S. Z., Bernèche, R., Bérubé, H., & Royer, S. (1991). Personality determinants of the commitment to the profession of art. *Creativity Research Journal, 4,* 367–389.

Dudek, S. Z., & Hall, W. B. (1991). Personality consistency: Eminent architects 25 years later. *Creativity Research Journal, 4,* 1213–231.

Eiduson, B. T. (1958). Artist and non-artist: A comparative study. *Journal of Personality, 26,* 13–28.

Eiduson, B. T. (1962). *Scientists: Their psychological world.* New York: Basic.

Erickson, C. O., Gantz, B. S., & Stephenson, R. W. (1990). Logical and construct validation of a short-form biographical inventory predictor of scientific creativity. *Proceedings, 78th Annual Convention,* APA, 151–152.

Eysenck, H. J. (1990). Biological dimensions of personality. In L. A. Pervin (Ed.), *Handbook of personality theory and research* (pp. 244–276). New York: Guilford.

Eysenck, H. J. (1993). Creativity and personality: Suggestions for a theory. *Psychological Inquiry, 4,* 147–178.

Eysenck, H. J. (1994). Creativity and personality: Word association, origence, and psychoticism. *Creativity Research Journal, 7,* 209–216.

Eysenck, H. J. (1995). *Genius: The natural history of creativity.* Cambridge University Press.

Farmer, H. S. (1988). Predicting who our future scientists and mathematicians will be. *Behavioral and Brain Sciences, 11,* 190–191.

Feist, G. J. (1989). [Creativity in art and science students]. Unpublished raw data.

Feist, G. J. (1991). Synthetic and analytic thought: Similarities and differences among art and science students. *Creativity Research Journal, 4,* 145–155.

Feist, G. J. (1993). A structural model of scientific eminence. *Psychological Science, 4,* 366–371.

Feist, G. J. (1994). Personality and working style predictors of integrative complexity: A study of scientists' thinking about research and teaching. *Journal of Personality and Social Psychology, 67,* 474–484.

Feist, G. J. (1995, October). *Do hostile and arrogant scientists become eminent or are eminent scientists likely to become hostile and arrogant.* Paper presented at the annual conference of the Society for Social Studies of Science, Charlottesville, VA.

Feist, G. J. (in press). Affective states and traits in creativity: Evidence for non-linear relationships. In M. A. Runco (Ed.), *Creativity Research Handbook* (Vol. 2.). Cresskill, NJ: Hampton.

Feist, G. J., & Barron, F. (1996). [Longitudinal study of 1950 graduate students]. Unpublished raw data.

Feist, G. J., & Gorman, M. E. (1998). The psychology of science: Review and integration of a nascent discipline. *Review of General Psychology, 2,* 3–47.

Fodor, E. M. (1995). Subclinical manifestations of psychosis-proneness, ego-strength, and creativity. *Personality and Individual Differences, 18,* 635–642.

Gantz, B. S, Erickson, C. O., & Stephenson, R. W. (1972). Some determinants of promotion in a research and development population. *Conference proceedings for the 72nd Annual Convention of the American Psychological Association.* Washington, DC: American Psychological Association.

Gardner, H. (1973). *The arts and human development: A psychological study of the artistic process.* New York: Wiley.

Garwood, D. S. (1964). Personality factors related to creativity in young scientists. *Journal of Abnormal and Social Psychology, 68,* 413–419.

Getzels, J. W. (1987). Creativity, intelligence, and problem finding: Retrospect and prospect. In S. G. Isaksen (Ed.), *Frontiers of creativity research* (pp. 88–102). Buffalo, NY: Bearly.

Getzels, J. W., & Csikszentmihalyi, M. (1976). *The creative vision.* New York: Wiley.

Ghiselin, B. (Ed.). (1952). *The creative process.* New York: Mentor.

Götz, K. O., & Götz, K. (1979). Personality characteristics of professional artists. *Perceptual and Motor Skills, 49,* 327–334.

Gough, H. G. (1961, February). *A personality sketch of the creative research scientist.* Paper presented at the Fifth Annual Conference on Personnel and Industrial Relations Research, UCLA, Los Angeles, CA.

Gough, H. G. (1976). What happens to creative medical students? *Journal of Medical Education, 51*, 461–467.

Gough, H. G. (1987). *California Psychological Inventory: Administrators guide.* Palo Alto, CA: Consulting Psychologists Press.

Guastello, S., & Shissler, J. (1994). A two-factor taxonomy of creative behavior. *Journal of Creative Behavior, 28*, 211–221.

Guilford, J. P. (1950). Creativity. *American Psychologist, 5*, 444–454.

Guilford, J. P. (1959). Traits of creativity. In H. H. Anderson (Ed.), *Creativity and its cultivation* (pp. 142–161). New York: Harper.

Guilford, J. P. (1987). A review of a quarter century of progress. In S. G. Isaksen (Ed.), *Frontiers of creativity research* (pp. 45–61). Buffalo, NY: Bearly.

Hall, W. B., & MacKinnon, D. W. (1969). Personality inventory correlates of creativity among architects. *Journal of Applied Psychology, 53*, 322–326.

Ham, S., & Shaughnessy, M. F. (1992). Personality and scientific promise. *Psychological Reports, 70*, 971–975.

Hammer, E. F. (1966). Personality patterns in young creative artists. *Adolescence, 1*, 327–350.

Hammond, J., & Edelmann, R. J. (1991). The act of being: Personality characteristics of professional actors, amateur actors and non-actors. In G. Wilson (Ed.), *Psychology and performing arts* (pp. 123–131). Amsterdam: Swets & Zeitlinger.

Helmreich, R. L., Spence, J. T., Beane, W. E., Lucker, G. W., & Matthews, K. A. (1980). Making it in academic psychology: Demographic and personality correlates of attainment. *Journal of Personality and Social Psychology, 39*, 896–908.

Helmreich, R. L., Spence, J. T., & Pred, R. S. (1988). Making it without losing it: Type A, achievement motivation and scientific attainment revisited. *Personality and Social Psychology Bulletin, 14*, 495–504.

Helson, R. (1971). Women mathematicians and the creative personality. *Journal of Consulting and Clinical Psychology, 36*, 210–220.

Helson, R. (1977). The creative spectrum of authors of fantasy. *Journal of Personality, 45*, 310–326.

Helson, R. (1987). Which of those young women with creative potential became productive? Part 2, From college to midlife. In R. Hogan, & W. H. Jones (Eds.), *Perspectives in personality* (Vol. 2, pp. 51–92). Greenwich, CN: JAI.

Helson, R., & Crutchfield, R. S. (1970). Mathematicians: The creative researcher and the average Ph.D. *Journal of Consulting and Clinical Psychology, 34*, 250–257.

Helson, R., Roberts, B., & Agronick, G. (1995). Enduringness and change in creative personality and prediction of occupational creativity. *Journal of Personality and Social Psychology, 69*, 1173–1183.

Holahan, C. K., & Sears, R. R. (1995). *The gifted group in later maturity.* Stanford, CA: Stanford University Press.

Holland, J. (1960). The prediction of college grades from personality and aptitude variables. *Journal of Educational Psychology, 51*, 245–254.

Holland, J. L., & Baird, L. L. (1968). The preconscious activity scale: The development and validation of an originality measure. *Journal of Creative Behavior, 2*, 217–225.

Hudson, L. (1958). Undergraduate academic record of Fellows of the Royal Society. *Nature, 182*, 1326.

Ikpaahindi, L. (1987). The relationship between the needs for achievement, affiliation, power, and scientific productivity among Nigerian veterinary surgeons. *Journal of Social Psychology, 127*, 535–537.

Isen, A., Daubman, K. A., & Nowicki, G. P. (1987). Positive affect facilitates creative problem solving. *Journal of Personality and Social Psychology, 52*, 1122–1131.

Jamison, K. R. (1993). *Touched with fire: Manic-depressive illness and the artistic temperament.* New York: Free Press.

John, O. P. (1990). The "big five" factor taxonomy: Dimensions of personality in the natural language and in questionnaires. In L. A. Pervin (Ed.), *Handbook of personality research and theory* (pp. 66–100). New York: Guilford.

Kemp, A. (1981). The personality structure of the musician. Part I, Identifying a profile of traits for the performer. *Psychology of Music, 9*, 3–14.

Kline, P., & Lapham, S. L. (1992). Personality and faculty in British universities. *Personality and Individual Differences, 13*, 855–857.

Kuhn, T. S. (1970). *The structure of scientific revolutions* (2nd ed.). Chicago: University of Chicago Press.

Lacey, L. A., & Erickson, C. E. (1974). Psychology of the scientist. Part 31, Discriminability of a creativity scale for the Adjective Check List among scientists and engineers. *Psychological Reports, 34*, 755–758.

Lindsay, B. (1978). Leadership giftedness: Developing a profile. *Journal for the Education of the Gifted, 1,* 63–69.

Lubinski, D., & Benbow, C. P. (1994). The study of mathematically precocious youth: The first three decades of a planned 50-year study of intellectual talent. In R. F. Subotnik & K. D. Arnold (Eds.), *Beyond Terman: Contemporary longitudinal studies of giftedness and talent* (pp. 255–281). Norwood, NJ: Ablex.

Ludwig, A. M. (1995). *The price of greatness.* New York: Guilford.

MacKinnon, D. W. (1960). The highly effective individual. *Teachers College Record, 61,* 367–378.

MacKinnon, D. W. (1962). The nature and nurture of creative talent. *American Psychologist, 17,* 484–495.

MacKinnon, D. W. (1970). Creativity: A multi-faceted phenomenon. In J. Roslanksy (Ed.), *Creativity* (pp. 19–32). Amsterdam: North-Holland.

MacKinnon, D. W. (1978). *In search of human effectiveness.* Buffalo, NY: Bearly.

Magnusson, D., & Backteman, G. (1978). Longitudinal stability of person characteristics: Intelligence and creativity. *Applied Psychological Measurement, 2,* 481–490.

Mansfield, R. S., & Busse, T. V. (1981). *The psychology of creativity and discovery: Scientists and their work.* Chicago: Nelson-Hall.

Marchant-Haycox, S. E., & Wilson, G. D. (1992). Personality and stress in performing artists. *Personality and Individual Differences, 13,* 1061–1068.

Marland, S. P., Jr. (1972). *Education of the gifted and talented.* Washington, DC: U.S. Government Printing Office.

Martindale, C. (1975). *Romantic progression: The psychology of literary history.* Washington, DC: Hemisphere.

Martindale, C. (1981). *Cognition and consciousness.* Homewood, IL: Dorsey.

Martindale, C., & Armstrong, J. (1974). The relationship of creativity to cortical activation and its operant control. *Journal of Genetic Psychology, 124,* 311–320.

Martindale, C., & Greenough, J. (1973). The differential effect of increased arousal on creative and intellectual performance. *Journal of Genetic Psychology, 123,* 329–335.

Martindale, C., & Hasenfus, N. (1978). EEG differences as a function of creativity, stage of the creative process and effort to be original. *Biological Psychology, 6,* 157–167.

Martindale, C., Hines, D., Mitchell, L., & Covello, E. (1984). EEG alpha asymmetry and creativity. *Personality and Individual Differences, 5,* 77–86.

McCrae, R. R. (1987). Creativity, divergent thinking, and openness to experience. *Journal of Personality and Social Psychology, 52,* 1258–1265.

McCrae, R. R., & John, O. P. (1992). An introduction to the five-factor model and its applications. *Journal of Personality, 60,* 175–215.

McDermid, C. D. (1965). Some correlates of creativity in engineering personnel. *Journal of Applied Psychology, 49,* 14–19.

Mendelsohn. G. A. (1976). Associative and attentional processes in creative performance. *Journal of Personality, 44,* 341–369.

Milgram, R. M., & Hong, E. (1994). Creative thinking and creative performance in adolescents as predictors of creative attainments in adults: A follow-up study after 18 years. In R. F. Subotnik & K. D. Arnold (Eds.), *Beyond Terman: Contemporary longitudinal studies of giftedness and talent* (pp. 212–228). Norwood, NJ: Ablex.

Mohan, J., & Tiwana, M. (1987). Personality and alienation of creative writers: A brief report. *Personality and Individual Differences, 8,* 449.

Mumford, M. D., Costanza, D. P., Threlfall, K. V., Baughman, W. A., & Reiter-Palmon, R. (1993). Personality variables and problem-construction activities: An exploratory investigation. *Creativity Research Journal, 6,* 365–389.

Mumford, M. D., & Gustafson, S. B. (1988). Creativity syndrome: Integration, application, and innovation. *Psychological Bulletin, 103,* 27–43.

Ochse, R. (1990). *Before the gates of excellence: The determinants of creative genius.* Cambridge University Press.

Parloff, M. B., & Datta, L. (1965). Personality characteristics of the potentially creative scientist. *Science and Psychoanalysis, 8,* 91–105.

Parloff, M. B., Datta, L., Kleman, M., & Handlon, J. H. (1968). Personality characteristics which differentiate creative male adolescents and adults. *Journal of Personality, 36,* 528–552.

Pufal-Struzik, I. (1992). Differences in personality and self-knowledge of creative persons at different ages: A comparative analysis. Special Issue: Geragogics: European research in gerontological education. *Gerontology & Geriatrics Education, 13,* 71–90.

Pyryt, M. C. (1992). The fulfillment of promise revisited: A discriminant analysis of factors predicting success in the Terman study. *Roeper Review, 15,* 178–179.

Richards, R. L. (1994). Creativity and bipolar mood swings: Why the association? In M. P. Shaw & M. A. Runco (Eds.), *Creativity and affect* (pp. 44–72). Norwood, NJ: Ablex.

Richards, R. L., & Kinney, D. K. (1990). Mood swings and creativity. *Creativity Research Journal, 3,* 202–217.

Richards, R. L., Kinney, D. K., Lunde, I., Benet, M., & Merzel, A. (1988). Creativity in manic-depressives, cyclothymes, their normal relatives, and control subjects. *Journal of Abnormal Psychology, 97,* 281–289.

Roco, M. (1993). Creative personalities about creative personality in science. *Revue Roumaine de Psychologie, 37,* 27–36.

Roe, A. (1952). *The making of a scientist.* New York: Dodd, Mead.

Roe, A. (1953). A psychological study of eminent psychologists and anthropologists, and a comparison with biological and physical scientists. *Psychological Monographs: General and Applied, 67,* 1–55.

Rosenthal, R., & Rosnow, R. L. (1991). *Essentials of behavioral research: Methods and data analysis* (2nd ed.). New York: McGraw-Hill.

Rossman, B. B., & Horn, J. L. (1972). Cognitive, motivational and temperamental indicants of creativity and intelligence. *Journal of Educational Measurement, 9,* 265–286.

Rothenberg, A. (1990). *Creativity and madness: New findings and old stereotypes.* Baltimore: Johns Hopkins University Press.

Rothenberg, A., & Hausman, C. R. (Eds.). (1976). *The creativity question.* Durham, NC: Duke University Press.

Runco, M. A., & Bahleda, M. D. (1986). Implicit theories of artistic, scientific, and everyday creativity. *Journal of Creative Behavior, 20,* 93–98.

Rushton, J. P. (1990). Creativity, intelligence, and psychoticism. *Personality and Individual Differences, 12,* 1291–1298.

Rushton, J. P., Murray, H. G., & Paunonen, S. V. (1983). Personality, research creativity, and teaching effectiveness in university professors. *Scientometrics, 5,* 93–116.

Rushton, J. P., Murray, H. G., & Paunonen, S. V. (1987). Personality characteristics associated with high research productivity. In D. Jackson & J. P. Rushton (Eds.), *Scientific excellence* (pp. 129–148). Beverly Hills, CA: Sage.

Russ, S. (1993). *Affect and creativity: The role of affect and play in the creative process.* Hillsdale, NJ: Erlbaum.

Schaefer, C. E. (1969). The self-concept of creative adolescents. *Journal of Psychology, 72,* 233–242.

Schaefer, C. E. (1973). A five-year follow-up study of the self-concept of creative adolescents. *Journal of Genetic Psychology, 123,* 163–170.

Shapiro, R. J. (1968). Creative research scientists. *Psychologia Africana Monograph Supplement, 4*(180).

Sheldon, K. M. (1995). Creativity and self-determination in personality. *Creativity Research Journal, 8,* 23–36.

Shelton, J., & Harris, T. L. (1979). Personality characteristics of art students. *Psychological Reports, 44,* 949–950.

Simon, H. (1974). The work habits of eminent scientists. *Sociology of Work and Occupations, 1,* 327–335.

Simonton, D. K. (1988). *Scientific genius: A psychology of science.* Cambridge University Press.

Simonton, D. K. (1989). Chance-configuration theory of scientific creativity. In B. Gholson, W. R. Shadish, R. A. Neimeyer, & A. C. Houts (Eds.), *Psychology of science.* (pp. 170–213). Cambridge University Press.

Smithers, A. G., & Batcock, A. (1970). Success and failure among social scientists and health scientists at a technological university. *British Journal of Educational Psychology, 40,* 144–153.

Stein, M. (1968). Creativity. In E. F. Borgatta & W. W. Lambert (Eds.), *Handbook of personality theory and research* (pp. 900–942). Chicago: Rand McNally.

Sternberg, R. J. (1986). *The triarchic mind: A new theory of human intelligence.* New York: Viking.

Sternberg, R. J. (1988). A three-facet model of creativity. In R. J. Sternberg (Ed.), *The nature of creativity* (pp. 125–147). Cambridge University Press.

Sternberg, R. J., & Lubart, T. (1995). *Defying the crowd.* New York: Free Press.

Sternberg, R. J., & Lubart, T. (1996). Investing in creativity. *American Psychologist, 51,* 677–688.

Stohs, J. M. (1990). Young adult predictors and midlife outcomes of male fine art careers. *Career Development Quarterly, 38,* 213–229.

Storr, A. (1988). *Solitude: A return to the self.* New York: Free Press.

Subotnik, R. F., & Arnold, K. D. (Eds.). (1994). *Beyond Terman: Contemporary longitudinal studies of giftedness and talent.* Norwood, NJ: Ablex.

Subotnik, R. F., Duschl, R. A., & Selmon, E. H. (1993). Retention and attrition of science talent: A longitudinal study of Westinghouse science talent search winners. *International Journal of Science Education, 15,* 61–72.

Subotnik, R. F., & Steiner, C. L. (1992). Adult manifestations of adolescent talent in science. *Roeper Review, 15,* 164–169.

Terman, L. M. (1954). Scientists and nonscientists in a group of 800 men. *Psychological Monographs, 68,* Whole No. 378.

Terman, L. M. (1955). Are scientists different? *Scientific American, 192,* 25–29.

Tomlinson-Keasey, C., & Keasey, C. B. (1993). Graduating from college in the 1930s: Terman genetic studies of genius. In K. D. Hulbert & S. D. Schuster (Eds.), *Women's lives through time: Educated women of the twentieth century* (pp. 63–92). San Francisco: Jossey-Bass.

Tomlinson-Keasey, C., & Little, T. D. (1990). Predicting educational attainment, occupational achievement, intellectual skill, and personal adjustment among gifted men and women. *Journal of Educational Psychology, 82,* 442–455.

Trost, G. (1993). Prediction of excellence in school, university and work. In K. A. Heller, F. J. Monks, & A. H. Passow (Eds.), *International handbook of research and development of giftedness and talent* (pp. 325–336). Oxford: Pergamon.

Van Zelst, R. H., & Kerr, W. A. (1954). Personality self-assessment of scientific and technical personnel. *Journal of Applied Psychology, 38,* 145–147.

Vernon, P. E. (Ed.). (1970). *Creativity.* Harmondsworth: Penguin.

Walker, A. M., Koestner, R., & Hum, A. (1995). Personality correlates of depressive style in autobiographies of creative achievers. *Journal of Creative Behavior, 29,* 75–94.

Wallach, M. A. (1970). Creativity. In P. H. Mussen (Ed.), *Manual of child psychology* (pp. 1211–1272). New York: Wiley.

Wills, G. I. (1983). A personality study of musicians working in the popular field. *Personality and Individual Differences, 5,* 359–360.

Wilson, G. D. (1984). The personality of opera singers. *Personality and Individual Differences, 5,* 195–201.

Wilson, G. D., & Jackson, C. (1994). The personality of physicists. *Personality and Individual Differences, 16,* 187–189.

Winner, E., & Martino, G. (1993). Giftedness in the visual arts and music. In K. A. Heller, F. J. Monks, & A. H. Passow (Eds.), *International handbook of research and development of giftedness and talent* (pp. 253–281). Oxford: Pergamon.

Wise, L. L., Steel, L., & McDonald, C. (1979). *Origins and career consequences of sex differences in high school mathematics achievement.* Washington D.C: American Institute for Research.

Wispe, L. G. (1963). Traits of eminent American psychologists. *Science, 141,* 1256–1261.

Woody, E., & Claridge, G. (1977). Psychoticism and thinking. *British Journal of Social and Clinical Psychology, 16,* 241–248.

Zeldow, P. B. (1973). Replication and extension of the personality profile of "artists in the making." *Psychological Reports, 33,* 541–542.

15   *Motivation and Creativity*

MARY ANN COLLINS AND TERESA M. AMABILE

A popular stereotype of creative people is that they approach their work with a kind of crazed intensity, often forgoing sleep, food, and other seeming necessities of life in order to advance their creative work. Undoubtedly, this view is one source of the widespread belief that creativity stems from madness. Although the connection between creativity and insanity remains a controversial point, there is considerable anecdotal and empirical evidence that creative production does require a high level of motivation. For example, the novelist John Irving reported spending as many as 12 hours per day, for several consecutive days, while writing his novels. When asked what drove him to work so hard, even years after attaining wide readership, fame, and financial success, he replied: "The unspoken factor is love. The reason I can work so hard at my writing is that it's not work for me" (from an interview reported in Amabile, 1989, p. 56).

What motivation drives creative activity? Is it generally based in the love that Irving describes? Does it derive from the desire to attain ever more wealth and fame, or are there other motivational forces at work? This chapter reviews theory and research on the motivation for creativity, revealing that, although creativity can arise from a complex interplay of motivational forces, motivation that stems from the individual's personal involvement in the work – love, if you will – is crucial for high levels of creativity in any domain.

EARLY VIEWS OF MOTIVATION AND CREATIVITY

For many early creativity theorists, the answer to the question, "What drives creativity?" was considered only in the most basic fashion. There was a general consensus that creative behavior was accompanied by tenacity of purpose (Cox, 1926), passion (Bruner, 1962), devotion (Henle, 1962), driving absorption (Roe, 1952), and persistence (Newell, Shaw, & Simon, 1962). However, there was less attention to what produced this high level of motivation.

The first theories to address the nature of the motivation underlying creativity came primarily from the psychodynamic tradition. Most of these theories explained creative behavior as a way of reducing the tension created by other, unacceptable desires. For example, Freud (1908/1959, 1915/1957) asserted that adults may sublimate or divert excess libidinal energy into more socially acceptable directions, including creative expression. Freud suggested that, similar to the role that play serves for children, creative activity allows adults to work through conflict and provides the opportunity to imbue a fantasy world with emotional content. Other psychodynamic theorists have suggested that creativity may be motivated by the need to atone for unconscious aggressive or destructive impulses (e.g., Fairbain, 1938; Segal, 1957; Sharpe, 1930, 1950; Stokes, 1963). Still others have posited that the reality-oriented ego may utilize the regressive, amoral urges and processes of the unconscious id in

297

order to generate creative ideas via "regression in service of the ego" (Bellak, 1958; Kris, 1952).

Although the belief that creativity provides a means for fulfilling unconscious needs or resolving psychological conflicts has persisted among some theorists (Abra, 1995; Klein, 1976; Ochse, 1990; Storr, 1988), others have described creativity as a means of fulfilling more positive, higher-order needs. For instance, Gedo (1983, in press) argued that creativity may be driven by the healthy desire to master one's environment, a concept labeled "effectance" motivation by White (1959). The motivational force of a need for mastery was also demonstrated in a 25-year study of highly creative women (Cangelosi & Schaefer, 1992). This study identified three underlying psychological needs that seemed to drive these women's creative activities: self-understanding, personal order and control, and emotional regulation.

Although the psychodynamic approach has suggested a number of motives that may lead people to be creative, these ideas have been somewhat tangential to the development of more mainstream perspectives on motivation and creativity. Rather, the predominant line of theoretical and empirical work has arisen from the belief that creativity is motivated by the enjoyment and satisfaction that a person derives from engaging in the creative activity. A corollary proposition is that creativity may be inhibited by external pressures that detract from the person's inherent enjoyment of the activity.

A number of early expressions of these ideas about motivation were made by theorists who argued that creativity could occur only in the absence of external regulation. One of the first of these was Carl Rogers (1954), who believed that creativity was motivated by people's self-actualizing tendencies, the drive to fulfill their potential. Rogers thought that the drive for self-actualization was present in everyone, but in order for it to be fully expressed in creative achievement, certain conditions must hold. In particular, Rogers stressed that creativity must occur in a context of self-evaluation rather than being driven by a concern with being evaluated by others. Thus, creative individuals must value their own internal assessment of their work, a condition that is most likely to emerge in an environment characterized by the absence of external evaluation and the presence of freedom. The importance of freedom from control was also noted by Koestler (1964), who believed such freedom necessary for a person to achieve the unconscious, playful forms of thought that he argued produced creative insights.

Humanistic ideas similar to Rogers's were articulated by Maslow (1943, 1959, 1968). He emphasized that self-actualized creativity was not motivated by a desire for achievement and was also not the result of "working through repressive control of forbidden impulses and wishes" (1968, p. 144), as the psychodynamic tradition argued. Instead, he described self-actualized creativity as the spontaneous expression of the person whose more basic needs have been satisfied. Maslow did acknowledge, however, that not all creativity is self-actualized. He believed that people who possess a special talent may be creative without having achieved self-actualization.

Still other early theorists contended that a crucial part of creativity was a deep love for and enjoyment of the tasks undertaken (Bruner, 1962; Henle, 1962; Torrance, 1962; see also Torrance, 1995). According to Torrance (1962), "The exercise of their [creative individuals'] creative powers is itself a reward, and to them, the most important reward" (p. 120). Similarly, Golann (1962) recognized the importance of deep involvement with the task when he described creativity as motivated by a desire to interact fully with the environment in order to achieve one's "fullest perceptual, cognitive, and expressive potentials" (p. 590).

At a symposium on creativity research held at the University of Colorado in 1962, more formal articulations of these ideas began to emerge. In several writings produced at the close of this meeting, the idea that creativity was supported by a person's involvement with the task and hindered by overconcern with the needs of the ego began to take form. Henle (1962) argued that creativity was accompanied by "detached devotion," in which a person's intense passion, commitment, and interest in the activity were combined with a critical detachment. She went one step beyond this view, however, and proposed conditions that would lead to this "detached devotion":

The condition of intense interest together with detachment can be achieved, in other words, if the ego lends itself to the work rather than dominating the task. The forces responsible for carrying on the work derive to a large extent from the perceived demands of the task itself rather than from the personal needs of the individual. (p. 46)

Crutchfield (1962) further articulated this distinction between ego-involved, or extrinsic, motives for creating, where "the achievement of a creative solution is a means to an ulterior end, rather than the end in itself" (p. 121), and task-involved, or intrinsic, motives, in which the person is driven by "the intrinsic value in the attaining of the creative solution itself" (p. 121). He suggested that, although extrinsic motives may propel a person's initial involvement with or undertaking of the task, they should ideally serve only to provide sufficient contact with the task to engage intrinsic involvement. He believed greater creativity would result when a person was primarily intrinsically motivated to do a task. Crutchfield emphasized that task-involved, or intrinsic, motivation was not characterized by a focus on creativity as an end state or by a need for self-expression. Rather, he described it as evidenced by active engagement with the challenges of the task and total immersion in the activity without regard to the possible rewards awaiting the creator on the achievement of a creative solution. Like Henle, Crutchfield argued that ego involvement prevents detachment from the task and interferes with a person's ability to set aside conventional ideas in favor of less safe but more creative ones. He suggested a basic antipathy between conformity and creative thought, asserting that people who tend to go along with group opinions or beliefs that are contrary to their own will be more motivated by extrinsic, or ego-involved, reasons for creating than will people who remain independent of the group consensus. In several studies, Crutchfield found that people who were inclined to yield to conformity pressures showed lower levels of creativity than did nonconformists.

THE ROLES OF INTRINSIC AND EXTRINSIC MOTIVATION

The identification of two types of motivation – one conducive to creativity and one harmful – was a breakthrough in research on the forces driving creativity. Unfortunately, attention to these two types of motivation was to wane for nearly two decades, while researchers devoted their energies to identifying the personality characteristics (e.g., MacKinnon, 1962; Wallach & Kogan, 1965) and cognitive skills (e.g., Newell et al., 1962) of creative individuals. Then, the concepts of intrinsic and extrinsic motivation reappeared as integral parts of a model that argued for three crucial components involved in the production of creative work: intrinsic task motivation, domain-relevant skills (expertise and talent in the task domain), and creativity-relevant processes (cognitive skills and work styles conducive to the production of novelty) (Amabile, 1983a, 1983b). Building upon the groundwork laid by theorists such as Rogers (1954) and Crutchfield (1962), Amabile (1983a) proposed a two-pronged hypothesis about how motivation affects creativity: "The intrinsically motivated state is conducive to creativity, whereas the extrinsically motivated state is detrimental" (p. 91). Intrinsic motivation is defined as the motivation to engage in an activity primarily for its own sake, because the individual perceives the activity as interesting, involving, satisfying, or personally challenging; it is marked by a focus on the challenge and the enjoyment of the work itself. By contrast, extrinsic motivation is defined as the motivation to engage in an activity primarily in order to meet some goal external to the work itself, such as attaining an expected reward, winning a competition, or meeting some requirement; it is marked by a focus on external reward, external recognition, and external direction of one's work (Crutchfield, 1962; Harlow, 1950; Hunt, 1965; Lepper, Greene, & Nisbett, 1973; Taylor, 1960). Amabile's "intrinsic motivation hypothesis" formed one of the cornerstones of her componential model of creativity (Amabile, 1983a, 1983b), and similar emphases on motivation began to emerge in other theoretical and empirical work on creativity.

Intrinsic Motivation and Creativity

In an extension of Amabile's componential model, Sternberg and Lubart (1991, 1992, 1995, 1996) proposed an investment theory of creativity in which motivation was one of six required resources. They identified *task-focused* motivation as being critical for creativity, and argued that this orientation, while more often produced by intrinsic motivators, may also be produced by some extrinsic motivators that increase an individual's concentration on the task. Woodman and Schoenfeldt's (1989, 1990) interactionist model of creative behavior also acknowledged intrinsic motivation as a component of the individual that is conducive to creative accomplishment. Runco and Chand (1995) also noted the necessity of intrinsic motivation in the creative process, although they described its role as secondary to cognitive processes.

In recent interactive models that consider how an individual's creative abilities develop within a society, Csikszentmihalyi (1990a) and Gardner (1993) included intrinsic motivation as a personal characteristic that contributes to creativity. Extending Crutchfield's work on conformity, Csikszentmihalyi suggested that high levels of intrinsic motivation, accompanied by relatively low levels of extrinsic motivation, may help creative individuals to be more independent of their field because they are less susceptible to pressures to conform.

Csikszentmihalyi's work on problem discovery (Csikszentmihalyi & Robinson, 1986; Getzels & Csikszentmihalyi, 1976) has led him to suggest that the identification of problems that hold the potential for creative solutions is partly driven by an intense interest in and curiosity about a subject matter and by perseverance rooted in the intrinsic rewards experienced by those engaged in processing information. Similarly, Mansfield and Busse (1981) identified commitment to work, which they described as the passionate involvement that characterizes intrinsic motivation, as important for scientific discovery.

Thus, most current theories that have considered the role of motivation in creativity agree that intrinsic motivation is beneficial to creativity; a growing body of empirical work supports this proposition. Studies of the personalities of highly creative people have described them as being totally absorbed in and devoted to their work (Barron, 1963; MacKinnon, 1962). In a set of longitudinal studies following people from elementary school through adulthood, Torrance (1981, 1983, 1987) found that people who were doing what they loved were more creative in their pursuits. A study of talented youth in math and science reported that these creative teens displayed higher levels of intrinsic motivation than their peers (Heinzen, Mills, & Cameron, 1993). Utilizing a case-study approach, Gruber (1986; Gruber & Davis, 1988) also observed that highly creative people possess an intense commitment to their work, manifested as a fascination with a set of problems that sustains their work over a period of years.

Research has also found that creative people are energized by challenging tasks, a sign of high intrinsic motivation. Albert (1990) noted that more eminent creators choose and become passionately involved in challenging, risky problems that provide a powerful sense of pleasure from the opportunity to use their talents. Perkins (1988) has also described how creative people are excited by complex problems and driven by opportunities to solve challenging, boundary-pushing problems. The consequences of seeking challenges that match one's skill have been described extensively by Csikszentmihalyi in his work on "flow" experiences (Csikszentmihalyi, 1990b; Csikszentmihalyi & Csikszentmihalyi, 1988). He proposed that a highly intrinsically motivated state is achieved when people are engaged in an activity where the challenges match their level of skill (Csikszentmihalyi & Csikszentmihalyi, 1988). This flow state has been described as an experience of optimal involvement in an activity – a psychological "high" wherein there are heightened feelings of enjoyment and a centering of concentration, such that even the passage of time may seem to slow. As people become more skilled in a domain, they will search for ever more challenging problems with which to test their skills in order to continue to experience flow. Csikszentmihalyi (1990b) has argued that people involved in creative pursuits actively seek flow experiences and that creativity is more likely to result from such states. Heinzen (1989) also found that moderate levels of challenge were conducive to generating a large number of possible solutions to a problem. Such ideational fluency has been demonstrated to be related to creativity: The more solutions considered, the more likely some will be creative.

The power of intrinsic motivation is so strong that simply thinking about intrinsic reasons for doing a task may be sufficient to boost creativity on that activity (Greer & Levine, 1991; Hennessey & Zbikowski, 1993), especially for those who have an ongoing involvement in the target domain (Amabile, 1996). Indeed, intrinsic motivation may contribute to ongoing involvement. Carney's (1986) longitudinal investigation of art students found that those whose Thematic Apperception Test (TAT) pictures had a good deal of intrinsic imagery – highlighting the joy of creating art – persisted in the field after their schooling and were more likely to achieve eventual success.

Recent work has suggested the existence of relatively stable motivational orientations toward one's work (Amabile, Hill, Hennessey, & Tighe, 1994). Both "trait" intrinsic motivation and "trait" extrinsic motivation have been identified in research employing the Work Preference Inventory (WPI). This personality inventory taps the major components of intrinsic motivation (self-determination, competence, task involvement, curiosity, enjoyment, and interest) and extrinsic motivation (concerns with competence, evaluation, recognition, money, or other tangible incentives, and constraint by others). People who are identified as more intrinsically motivated toward their work on this scale have consistently been found to produce work rated as more highly creative (Amabile et al., 1994). Additionally, people who work in a creative field (e.g., professional artists, research scientists, and student artists) tend to be more intrinsically motivated toward their work than the general population (Amabile et al., 1994; Amabile, Phillips, & Collins, 1996; Pollak, 1992).

Extrinsic Motivation and Creativity

THE UNDERMINING EFFECT. The other side of the intrinsic motivation hypothesis, the proposition that extrinsic motivation undermines creativity, has been the focus of considerably more research, as well as greater controversy. In order to understand the paradigms most frequently employed in this research, it is important to consider how theorists have viewed the relationship between intrinsic and extrinsic motivation. In its original form, the intrinsic motivation hypothesis of creativity reflected the prevailing social-psychological view that intrinsic and extrinsic motivation were inversely related. Thus, high levels of extrinsic motivation were thought to preclude high levels of intrinsic motivation (Calder & Staw, 1975; Lepper et al., 1973). Although Amabile (1983a) acknowledged that consideration of the affective consequences of receiving extrinsic motivators could reveal situations where intrinsic and extrinsic motivation combined in an additive fashion (Porter & Lawler, 1968; Vroom, 1964), most research derived from her original intrinsic motivation hypothesis rested on the assumption that extrinsic constraints should reduce intrinsic interest in a task and lead to lower levels of creativity.

Using a paradigm drawn from research on intrinsic motivation (Lepper et al., 1973), this research has typically had participants engage in an interesting creativity task either in the presence or in the absence of a specific extrinsic constraint or extrinsic motivator. A number of studies in this tradition, as well as some from other paradigms, have revealed the detrimental effects of extrinsic motivators and extrinsic constraints on creativity. One of the first of these studies investigated whether expecting one's work to be evaluated affects creativity. Amabile (1979) asked college women to make a "silly" paper collage either under an extrinsic constraint (expectation of evaluation) or under no constraint. Those in the constraint condition were told that their finished designs would be rated by graduate art students; those in the control condition were told that the experimenter was interested in their mood while doing the task and would not be using their designs as a source of data. Subsequently, a group of artist-judges were asked to rate the collages on creativity, relative to one another. This technique, known as the consensual assessment technique (Amabile, 1982b), asks experts in the field to use their own subjective judgments of creativity and typically yields high interjudge agreement. Results of this study revealed that people who produced their collages under the expectation of evaluation were significantly less creative than those who did not expect their work to be evaluated.

Further studies have confirmed the detrimental effect of expected performance evaluation (an extrinsic constraint) and have also provided evidence that the receipt of positive evaluation prior to performance (an extrinsic motivator) produces negative effects on creativity (Amabile, Goldfarb, & Brackfield, 1990; Bartis, Szymanski, & Harkins, 1988; Berglas, Amabile, & Handel, 1981; Hennessey, 1989; Szymanski & Harkins, 1992). Similarly, people are less creative when simply being watched by others (Amabile, Goldfarb, & Brackfield, 1990). Complementary results emerge in Barron's (1988) work on creative personalities. He reports that creative people distance themselves psychologically from others in order to minimize the negative effects of interpersonal intrusions.

Other extrinsic constraints and extrinsic motivators have been studied. For example, research has also shown that when the way a person does a task is constrained or controlled, resulting in reduced autonomy, creativity is also reduced (Amabile & Gitomer, 1984; Amabile et al., 1996; Greenberg, 1992; Hennessey, 1989; Koestner, Ryan, Bernieri, & Holt, 1984). For example, children who were told they *must* be neat while making a painting because it was a rule produced less creative products than children who were asked to be neat in order to keep the materials in order for other children (Koestner et al., 1984). Even though neatness was stressed to both groups of children, those who were given the instruction in a restrictive, controlling manner produced less creative work than those who were given more informational instructions. On the flip side of this issue of constraint, higher feelings of autonomy or freedom tend to be related to higher levels of intrinsic motivation and creativity (Amabile, Conti, Coon, Lazenby, & Herron, 1996; Amabile & S. Gryskiewicz, 1987; Picariello, 1994; Ryan & Grolnick, 1986).

Competing for prizes to be offered to makers of the "best" products also has been shown to undermine creativity (Amabile, 1982a, 1987). Additionally, contracting for a reward, to be received contingent on task engagement, leads to lower levels of creativity (Hennessey, 1989; Kruglanski, Friedman, & Zeevi, 1971; McGraw & McCullers, 1979). This effect has been observed even when the reward is enjoyed *before* engagement in the creative activity. In one study, children received a reward (playing with a Polaroid camera) prior to engaging in a storytelling activity. Children who had promised to tell a story in return for the opportunity to play with the camera told less creative stories than those who simply engaged in both activities with no contingency attached (Amabile, Hennessey, & Grossman, 1986).

As with intrinsic motivation, simply focusing on extrinsic reasons for doing an activity may be sufficient to affect creativity. For example, creative writers who concentrated on extrinsic reasons for writing subsequently wrote less creative poems than when extrinsic motivation was not a factor (Amabile, 1985). Also, in Carney's (1986) study of art students' TAT imagery, those whose pictures contained more extrinsic imagery were less likely to continue in art after school unless they had achieved immediate success.

The most likely mechanism for the undermining effect of extrinsic motives on creativity is an attentional one. Amabile (1983b) suggested that extrinsic motives could cause people to divide their attention between their extrinsic goals and the task at hand (see also Lepper & Greene, 1978). This decreased focus on the task contrasts with the concentrated attention and task involvement that characterizes high levels of intrinsic motivation (Csikszentmihalyi, 1978; Ruscio, Whitney, & Amabile, in press).

A maze metaphor (Amabile, 1987) illustrates this mechanism. In this metaphor, the creative problem is represented as a maze, with various exits representing successful solutions to the problem. A straightforward, algorithmic, or step-by-step solution is represented by a straight-line path from the entrance to the exit. More unusual or creative solutions can be reached only by taking a more heuristic approach and exploring the maze or problem space. People who are primarily extrinsically motivated to find a solution may rely on more conventional, less creative exits from the maze because they are not involved enough in the task to search for more novel exits. Intrinsically motivated individuals, on the other hand, are more likely to spend time looking for alternative solutions because they enjoy the task. The empirical work of Ruscio et al. (in press) has supported this account.

POSITIVE EFFECTS OF EXTRINSIC MOTIVATION. Although many studies support the notion that extrinsic motives lead people to arrive at less creative solutions, there has been a growing number of studies, particularly those investigating effects of rewards or evaluation, that have suggested that extrinsic motives may not be harmful to creativity in some circumstances. The issue of whether reward helps or hinders creativity has been especially controversial (Eisenberger & Cameron, 1995; Eisenberger & Selbst, 1994). While some of the research showing positive effects of extrinsic motivation on creativity can be explained within the scope of the original intrinsic motivation hypothesis (Amabile, 1983a), other research recently has led to a revised description of the effects of extrinsic motivation (Amabile, 1993, 1996).

A number of studies, designed in the behavior modification tradition have shown positive effects of reward on various aspects of creative performance (e.g., Campbell & Willis, 1978; Eisenberger & Selbst, 1994; Glover, 1980; Halpin & Halpin, 1973; Locurto & Walsh 1976; Milgram & Feingold, 1977; see Amabile, 1983a, 1996 for reviews). In most of these studies, participants were told how to succeed or "be creative" on a particular type of task and were rewarded for increasing these behaviors. Specifically, many studies used some form of creativity test where the behaviors of interest were fluency (number of different responses), flexibility (variety of responses), elaboration (e.g., number of words per response), and originality (statistical infrequency of response). The benefits of reward were most apparent on the behaviors that could be easily modified using an algorithmic, or step-by-step, approach (i.e., elaboration, fluency, and flexibility). When reward was found to enhance originality, subjects had been explicitly instructed to try to generate unusual responses. In contrast, the previous work demonstrating an undermining effect of reward on creativity utilized more heuristic, or open-ended, tasks, such as writing a story or making a collage. When Amabile (1979) took one of these heuristic tasks (creating a collage) and made it algorithmic by telling subjects how to make a collage that would be rated as creative by judges (e.g., tear pieces, use more pieces), she found that external evaluation increased creativity.

However, not all of the findings of positive effects of extrinsic motives on creativity could be explained by this algorithmic/heuristic distinction. A growing body of work has begun to report benefits of extrinsic motives for even heuristic tasks. One of the first of these studies was the aforementioned experiment by Amabile, Hennessey, and Grossman (1986), in which children were rewarded with the opportunity to play with a Polaroid camera prior to telling a story. When children made a deal with the experimenter to tell a story in return for playing with the camera, the typical undermining effect of reward was found. Surprisingly, however, children who told a story after playing with the camera as a *non-contracted-for* reward actually told *more* creative stories than a control group. The children may have perceived the noncontingent reward as a "bonus," which put them in a good mood and heightened their involvement in the storytelling activity.

Another series of studies was specifically designed to determine whether the undermining effects of reward on creativity could be eliminated by "immunizing" participants against the negative effects of reward (Hennessey, Amabile, & Martinage, 1989; Hennessey & Zbikowski, 1993). This immunization was accomplished by having children view and discuss a video in which two attractive children talked about their intrinsic interest and enjoyment in school, as well as strategies they used for distancing themselves from socially imposed extrinsic constraints or motives. Children in a control group viewed a different video. A few days later all the children engaged in a creativity task; as in previously described research on reward, half the children were promised a reward for agreeing to do the task, the other half were given the reward without any contingency established to their task engagement. Results revealed that the undermining effects of reward were not only eliminated for the group of children who received intrinsic motivation training, but these children also seemed to actually be more creative when rewarded.

In the workplace, evaluation or feedback that is informative or constructive or that recognizes creative accomplishment can also be conducive to creativity (Amabile et al., 1996; Amabile & N. Gryskiewicz, 1989; Amabile & S. Gryskiewicz, 1987). Additionally, Gruber's (1986; Gruber & Davis, 1988) case studies of highly creative individuals suggest that while eminent creators such as Darwin and Newton were certainly highly task-involved, they balanced intrinsic reasons for creating with some degree of ego involvement that enabled them to sustain visions of revolutionizing the world's thinking.

REVISED VIEW OF EXTRINSIC MOTIVATION AND CREATIVITY. The work already described, along with theoretical advances in the definition of extrinsic motivation, have led to a revised understanding of how extrinsic motivation affects creativity (Amabile, 1993, 1996). First, the concept of extrinsic motivation has been refined to include two facets: control and information (Deci & Ryan, 1985). Under many conditions, extrinsic motivation will be perceived as externally controlling, but there are times when it may actually be perceived as providing useful, and desired, information. Building upon this distinction, Amabile (1993) identified two types of extrinsic motivators: synergistic extrinsic motivators, which provide information or enable the person to better complete the task and which can act in concert with intrinsic motives; and nonsynergistic, extrinsic motivators, which lead the person to feel controlled and are incompatible with intrinsic motives. Thus, although intrinsic motivation may be inversely related to some types of extrinsic motivation (nonsynergistic), it may combine additively with other, synergistic, extrinsic motivators. This concept of motivational synergy has contributed to a revision of the Intrinsic Motivation Hypothesis (now known as the Intrinsic Motivation Principle): "Intrinsic motivation is conducive to creativity; controlling extrinsic motivation is detrimental to creativity, but informational or enabling extrinsic motivation can be conducive, particularly if initial levels of intrinsic motivation are high" (Amabile, 1996, p. 119).

Other creativity theorists have also suggested that some types of extrinsic motivation may coexist with intrinsic motives in the creative person (Rubenson & Runco, 1992; Sternberg, 1988). In particularly, highly creative individuals, particularly scientists, are thought to have a strong desire for recognition that coexists with their deep intrinsic commitment to their work (Mansfield & Busse, 1981). Csikszentmihalyi (1988) suggested that, while also supported by intrinsic motives, the ability to discover problems was fueled by a sense of dissatisfaction with the current state of knowledge in the domain, which he believed could be driven by extrinsic motives such as the desire for recognition.

Amabile (1993, 1996) describes two mechanisms by which synergistic extrinsic motivators might make positive contributions to creativity. In the first, *extrinsics in the service of intrinsics* – synergistic extrinsic motivators, which support one's sense of competence or increase involvement with the task – may act in concert with high levels of intrinsic motivation to increase creativity. A second possible mechanism for the positive influence of synergistic extrinsic motivators on creativity is the *motivation–work cycle match,* wherein different types of motivation play roles in different parts of the creative process. For instance, Amabile suggests that high levels of intrinsic motivation are particularly important when the emphasis is on novelty. Thus, when individuals are attempting to identify a problem or generate possible solutions, being intrinsically involved in the task and not distracted by extrinsic concerns will help them to produce more original ideas. At other points in the creative process, however, when the greater emphasis is on persistence or evaluation, synergistic extrinsic motivators may play a more important role than will intrinsic interest. Synergistic extrinsic motivators may keep creators involved in a problem through times when they must acquire the skills and information necessary to solve problems within a domain. Also, once a possible solution has been reached, synergistic extrinsic motivators may help creators to appropriately validate and communicate the solution to the field.

Other theorists have also considered the question of where in the creative process motivational forces exert an impact. One of the earliest considerations of this question was Crutchfield's (1962) proposal that extrinsic motives may serve to bring people in contact with a topic that can then engage their interest. This is somewhat compatible with Amabile's identification of the role of extrinsic motives in sustaining energy through the sometimes tedious task of acquiring skills in a domain, although she does suggest that initial problem selection is fueled by intrinsic motives. Mansfield and Busse's (1981) model of scientific creativity also recognized that different motives act on different parts of the creative process. They proposed that problem selection is influenced by the creator's intrinsic need to be original as well as by the extrinsic desire to attain professional recognition. The extended effort required to solve the problem is enabled by a strong commitment to work, which includes a sense of intrinsic involvement with the problem. Finally, the verification and elaboration of the solution is supported both by commitment to work and the need for professional recognition. Taking another perspective, Runco (1994; Runco & Chand, 1995) has argued that intrinsic motivation is often a consequence of discovering a problem, which excites the person's interest and leads to a desire to spend time searching for a solution.

PRACTICAL IMPLICATIONS FOR THE WORKPLACE AND THE CLASSROOM

The best way to help people to maximize their creative potential is to allow them to do something they love (Amabile, 1996; Runco & Chand, 1995; Torrance, 1995). The freedom to choose what to work on allows individuals to seek out questions that they are highly intrinsically motivated to pursue. This high level of intrinsic interest will lay the groundwork for creative achievement. Teachers may incorporate this approach into the classroom by allowing students to choose their own topics for individual or group projects. In the workplace, employees – particularly those in jobs where creativity is highly desirable – should be encouraged to explore ideas that are personally exciting.

Frequently, the issue in both the classroom and the workplace becomes one of maintaining intrinsic motivation. The immunization studies reported earlier (Hennessey et al., 1989; Hennessey & Zbikowski, 1993) suggested that increasing the salience of intrinsic motivation is one way to sustain it. Children's intrinsic motivation and creativity might be enhanced if their parents and teachers engage them in discussions about the intrinsic excitement and joy of learning; adults' intrinsic motivation and creativity at work might be enhanced if their managers establish environments in which people can freely exchange their ideas and explore mutual interests in the work.

Often, we face the task of attempting to sustain intrinsic motivation in the face of controlling extrinsic constraints that have been found to directly undermine intrinsic motivation and creativity: evaluation, surveillance, contracted-for reward, task constraint, and competition. The most straightforward way to preserve intrinsic motivation and enhance creativity is to reduce the emphasis on such extrinsic constraints in the social environment. Although it is impossible to eliminate extrinsic concerns in most academic and employment settings, attempts can be made to reduce their salience or to change their character. For example, teachers might reduce the salience of grade evaluations simply by talking about grades less in the classroom. They might also emphasize the informational nature of these evaluations – as guides to the development of stronger skills – rather than their controlling nature. The effectiveness of this technique of reducing the importance of or reinterpreting extrinsic motivators was demonstrated in the immunization studies (Hennessey et al., 1989; Hennessey & Zbikowski, 1993).

The new theoretical conceptions of motivational synergy also have implications for enhancing the motivational component of creativity (Amabile, 1993). First, any extrinsic factors that support one's sense of competence without undermining one's sense of self-determination should positively contribute to intrinsic motivation. These are the synergistic extrinsic motivators. As suggested by Deci and Ryan (1985), reward, recognition, and feedback that confirm competence, as well as feedback that provides important information on how to improve competence, should have such effects. In addition, extrinsic motivators that serve to directly increase one's involvement in the work itself should also operate in the service of intrinsic motivation. For example, overall project goals that orient a person toward the nature of the task to be accomplished should add to rather than detract from intrinsic motivation and creativity; so should enabling rewards – rewards that involve more time, freedom, or resources to pursue exciting ideas. (The MacArthur Foundation "genius" grants serve as an example of this type of reward.) Similarly, performance feedback should enhance intrinsic motivation and creativity if it is informational – constructive, nonthreatening, and work-focused rather than person-focused.

The concept of motivational synergy leads us to expect that overall creative performance is likely to be optimized if intrinsic motivation is most salient at those stages of the creative process where novel thinking is most crucial – the problem identification stage and the idea generation stage. However, synergistic extrinsic motivators may play a facilitative role at those stages where novelty is less important – the preparation and idea validation stages. For example, some scientists report great excitement during the idea generation and early validation stages of working on particularly complex problems. However, their engagement in the process sometimes flags if difficulties are encountered during the slow and tedious process of working out the fine details to fully develop, validate, and clearly communicate the idea. (Similar effects can be observed with doctoral dissertations!) Some extrinsic motivators, such as clear deadlines or the promise of external reward and recognition, may do little harm at these stages, since flexible, novel thinking is no longer the dominant mode. Indeed, these motivators, as long as they leave the sense of self-determination intact, should serve to keep the individual engaged in the work. Moreover, these extrinsic motivators may actually enhance the appropriateness or value of the work, by attuning the individual to out-come requirements.

In enhancing creativity, it is important to consider not only each of the separate compo-nents of creativity (domain-relevant skills, creativity-relevant processes, and intrinsic task motivation), but also their intersection. Imagine that the components are represented as three partially overlapping circles. The componential model of creativity (Amabile, 1983, 1996) suggests that creativity will be highest in that area where the three components share their greatest overlap – that is, where the individual's domain-relevant skills overlap with the individual's strongest intrinsic interests and creative-thinking processes. In other words, people are most likely to be creative within their "creativity intersection." Identifying this intersection can, in itself, be an important step toward enhancing creativity. This can be par-ticularly important for gifted individuals, who are likely to have strong skills in many differ-ent domains and who may also have high levels of creative-thinking skills. These individuals should strive, and should be helped by their mentors, to discover where their strongest inter-ests lie. It is in those areas of greatest passion that their greatest creativity is likely to emerge.

FUTURE DIRECTIONS

The future of research on motivation and creativity holds many exciting new questions. First, although creativity theorists have begun to consider what influence motivation may exert at different stages of the creative process, to date no research has been conducted to validate these ideas. The concept of a motivation–work cycle match should be tested both in laboratory studies that break apart the creative process and in field studies or interviews with creative individuals. Knowing when particular types of motivation yield the greatest benefits or wreak the greatest harm will help teachers and managers to structure environments more conducive to creative development.

Another area ripe for exploration concerns the identification of specific cognitive processes that mediate the effects of motivation on creativity. One recent study used think-aloud protocols and microcoding of participant behavior to look for differences in how peo-ple who varied in intrinsic involvement processed a set of creativity tasks. The behavior of more intrinsically motivated individuals reflected greater involvement in the activities, and this behavior in turn predicted the creativity of their products (Ruscio et al., in press). Addi-tional cognitive techniques may continue to illuminate the different strategies employed by intrinsically or extrinsically motivated individuals.

Perhaps the most promising area for future investigations of motivation and creativity concerns the consideration of interactions between the motivational context of creative behavior and other factors important to creativity (Amabile, 1996; Runco & Chand, 1995). For example, individual differences in personality or experience may influence the way a person interprets or reacts to extrinsic motives or constraints (Amabile, Phillips, & Collins, 1994). Cheek and Stahl (1986) report that the effects of evaluation on creativity depend on how shy a person is, with shy people being most negatively affected by the expectation of evaluation. Several studies have also found that skill level influences a person's response to evaluation (Conti & Amabile, 1995; Pollak, 1992; Hill, Amabile, Coon, & Whitney, 1994). Less skilled participants were more creative when they expected evaluation, while more skilled participants were more creative under nonevaluation conditions. Perhaps less skilled individuals perceive the evaluation as potentially providing useful information about their competence, and thus interpret it as a synergistic extrinsic motivator. There has also been evidence suggesting that the impact of reward on creativity may differ for advantaged versus disadvantaged children (Johnson, 1974; Torrance, 1995). In addition to the individual differences variables just described, situational or contextual variables may also interact with motivation to influence creativity. The impact of expected evaluation on creativity has been found to vary depending on what type of activity precedes the creativity task (Conti, Amabile, & Pollak, 1995). Participants who engaged in a creative activity prior to the experimental task were more creative when they were not expecting evaluation. No effect of evaluation was found for participants who had not just experienced the opportunity to be creative. The impact of competition on creativity may also be affected by contextual influences. Nonexperimental research on the effects of competition in the workplace has reported that creative performance is higher when competition occurs between groups rather than within groups (Amabile, 1988; Amabile & S. Gryskiewicz, 1987).

In all work on creativity, be it theoretical, empirical, or applied, we believe that there should be a continued push toward more integrated approaches. Our understanding of the relationship between motivation and creativity cannot stand on its own but must be complemented by attention to personality, talent, culture, cognition, and other factors affecting the creative process. One thing we can conclude with confidence is that love for one's work is advantageous for creativity. We can also state with confidence that when factors external to the task distract from or reduce a person's enjoyment, creativity will suffer. Furthermore, we know now that extrinsic factors do not always interfere with a person's love for the task. Although research has begun to identify the conditions under which external concerns harm interest and creativity, a fuller understanding of these complexities requires an integrative approach.

REFERENCES

Abra, J. (1995). Do the muses dwell in Elysium? Death as a motive for creativity. *Creativity Research Journal, 8,* 205–217.

Albert, R. S. (1990). Identity, experiences, and career choice among the exceptionally gifted and eminent. In M. A. Runco & R. S. Albert (Eds.), *Theories of creativity* (pp. 13–34). Newbury Park, CA: Sage.

Amabile, T. M. (1979). Effects of external evaluation on artistic creativity. *Journal of Personality and Social Psychology, 37,* 221–233.

Amabile, T. M. (1982a). Children's artistic creativity: Detrimental effects of competition in a field setting. *Personality and Social Psychology Bulletin, 8,* 573–578.

Amabile, T. M. (1982b). Social psychology of creativity: A consensual assessment technique. *Journal of Personality and Social Psychology, 43,* 997–1013.

Amabile, T. M. (1983a). *The social psychology of creativity.* New York: Springer-Verlag.

Amabile, T. M. (1983b). Social psychology of creativity: A componential conceptualization. *Journal of Personality and Social Psychology, 45,* 357–377.

Amabile, T. M. (1985). Motivation and creativity: Effects of motivational orientation on creative writing. *Journal of Personality and Social Psychology, 48,* 393–399.

Amabile, T. M. (1987). The motivation to be creative. In S. Isaksen (Ed.), *Frontiers in creativity research: Beyond the basics.* Buffalo, NY: Bearly.

Amabile, T. M. (1988). A model of creativity and innovation in organizations, *Research in Organizational Behavior, 10,* 123–167.

Amabile, T. M. (1989). *Growing up creative.* Buffalo, NY: Creative Education Foundation.

Amabile, T. M. (1993). Motivational synergy: Toward new conceptualizations of intrinsic and extrinsic motivation in the workplace. *Human Resource Management Review, 3,* 185–201.

Amabile, T. M. (1996). *Creativity in context: Update to The Social Psychology of Creativity.* Boulder, CO: Westview.

Amabile, T. M., Conti, R., Coon, H., Lazenby, J., & Herron, M. (1996). Assessing the work environment for creativity. *Academy of Management Journal, 39,* 1154–1184.

Amabile, T. M., & Gitomer, J. (1984). Children's artistic creativity: Effects of choice in task materials. *Personality and Social Psychology Bulletin, 10,* 209–215.

Amabile, T. M., Goldfarb, P., & Brackfield, S. (1990). Social influences on creativity: Evaluation, coaction, and surveillance. *Creativity Research Journal, 3,* 6–21.

Amabile, T. M., & Gryskiewicz, N. (1989). The creative environment scales: The work environment inventory. *Creativity Research Journal, 2,* 231–254.

Amabile, T. M., & Gryskiewicz, S. (1987). *Creativity in the R&D laboratory.* Technical report no. 30. Greensboro, NC: Center for Creative Leadership.

Amabile, T. M., Hennessey, B. A., & Grossman, B. S. (1986). Social influences on creativity: The effects of contracted for reward. *Journal of Personality and Social Psychology, 50,* 14–23.

Amabile, T. M., Hill, K. G., Hennessey, B. A., & Tighe, E. (1994). The work preference inventory: Assessing intrinsic and extrinsic motivational orientations. *Journal of Personality and Social Psychology, 66,* 950–967.

Amabile, T. M., Phillips, E. D., & Collins, M. A. (1996). *Creativity by contract: Social influences on the creativity of professional artists.* Unpublished manuscript, Brandeis University, Waltham, MA.

Barron F. (1988). Putting creativity to work. In R. J. Sternberg (Ed.), *The nature of creativity* (pp. 76–98). Cambridge University Press.

Bartis, S., Szymanski, K., & Harkins, S. G. (1988). Evaluation and performance: A two-edged knife. *Personality and Social Psychology Bulletin, 14,* 242–251.

Bellak, L. (1958). Creativity: Some random notes to a systematic consideration. *Journal of Projective Techniques, 22,* 363–380.

Berglas, S., Amabile, T. M., & Handel., M. (1981). *Effects of evaluation on children's artistic creativity.* Unpublished manuscript, Brandeis University, Waltham, MA.

Bruner, J. (1962). The conditions of creativity. In H. Gruber, G. Terrell, & M. Wertheimer (Eds.), *Contemporary approaches to creative thinking* (pp. 1–30). New York: Atherton.

Calder, B., & Staw, B. (1975). Self-perception of intrinsic and extrinsic motivation. *Journal of Personality and Social Psychology, 31,* 599–605.

Campbell, J. A., & Willis, J. (1978). Modifying components of creative behavior in the natural environment. *Behavior Modification, 2,* 549–564.

Cangelosi, D., & Schaefer, C. E. (1992). Psychological needs underlying the creative process. *Psychological Reports, 71,* 321–322.

Carney, S. (1986). *Intrinsic motivation in successful artists from early adulthood to middle age.* Ph.D. dissertation, University of Chicago.

Cheek, J. M., & Stahl, S. (1986). Shyness and verbal creativity. *Journal of Research in Personality, 20,* 51–61.

Conti, R., & Amabile, T. M. (1995, April). *Problem solving among computer science students: The effects of skill, evaluation expectation and personality on solution quality.* Paper presented at the meeting of the Eastern Psychological Association, Boston, MA.

Conti, R., Amabile, T. M., & Pollak, S. (1995). The positive impact of creative activity: Effects of creative task engagement and motivational focus on college students' learning. *Personality and Social Psychology Bulletin, 21,* 1107–1116.

Cox, C. (1926). *Genetic studies of genius: Vol. 2. The early mental traits of three hundred geniuses.* Stanford, CA: Stanford University Press.

Crutchfield, R. (1962). Conformity and creative thinking. In H. Gruber, G. Terrell, & M. Wertheimer (Eds.), *Contemporary approaches to creative thinking* (pp. 120–140). New York: Atherton.

Csikszentmihalyi, M. (1978). Intrinsic rewards and emergent motivation. In M. Lepper & D. Green (Eds.), *The hidden costs of reward* (pp. 205–216). Hillsdale, NJ: Erlbaum.

Csikszentmihalyi, M. (1988). Motivation and creativity: Towards a synthesis of structural and energistic approaches to cognition. *New Ideas in Psychology, 6,* 159–176.

Csikszentmihalyi, M. (1990a). The domain of creativity. In M. A. Runco & R. S. Albert (Eds.), *Theories of creativity* (pp. 190–214). Newbury Park, CA: Sage.

Csikszentmihalyi, M. (1990b). *Flow: The psychology of optimal experience.* New York: Harper & Row.

Csikszentmihalyi, M., & Csikszentmihalyi, I. S. (Eds.). (1988). *Optimal experience: Psychological studies of flow in consciousness.* Cambridge University Press.

Csikszentmihalyi, M., & Robinson, R. (1986). Culture, time, and the development of talent. In R. J. Sternberg & J. E. Davidson (Eds.), *Conceptions of giftedness* (pp. 285–305). Cambridge University Press.

Deci, E. L., & Ryan, R. M. (1985). *Intrinsic motivation and self-determination in human behavior.* New York: Plenum.

Eisenberger, R., & Cameron, J. (1995, September). *Detrimental effects of reward: Reality or myth?* Paper presented at the meeting of the Society for Experimental Social Psychology, Washington, DC.

Eisenberger, R., & Selbst, M. (1994). Does reward increase or decrease creativity? *Journal of Personality and Social Psychology, 66,* 1116–1127.

Fairbain, W. R. D. (1938). Prolegomena to a psychology of art. *British Journal of Psychology, 28*, 288–303.

Freud, S. (1957). The unconscious. In J. Strachey (Ed. and Trans.), *The standard edition of the complete psychological works of Sigmund Freud* (Vol. 14, pp. 166–204). London: Hogarth. (Original work published 1915)

Freud, S. (1959). Creative writers and day-dreaming. In J. Strachey (Ed. and Trans.), *The standard edition of the complete psychological works of Sigmund Freud* (Vol. 9, pp. 142–156). London: Hogarth. (Original work published 1908)

Gardner, H. (1993). *Creating minds: An anatomy of creativity seen through the lives of Freud, Einstein, Picasso, Stravinsky, Eliot, Graham, and Ghandi.* New York: Basic.

Gedo, J. E. (1983). *Portraits of the artist.* New York: Guilford.

Gedo, J. E. (in press). Psychoanalytic theories of creativity. In preparation for M. A. Runco (Ed.), *Handbook of creativity research* (Vol. 1). Cresskill, NJ: Hampton.

Getzels, J. W., & Csikszentmihalyi, M. (1976). *The creative vision: A longitudinal study of problemfinding in art.* New York: Wiley-Interscience.

Glover, J. A. (1980). A creativity-training workshop: Short-term, long-term, and transfer effects. *Journal of Genetic Psychology, 136*, 3–16.

Golann, S. E. (1962). The creativity motive. *Journal of Personality, 30*, 588–600.

Greenberg, E. (1992). Creativity, autonomy, and evaluation of creative work: Artistic workers in organizations. *Journal of Creative Behavior, 26*, 75–80.

Greer, M., & Levine, E. (1991). Enhancing creative performance in college students. *Journal of Creative Behavior, 25*, 250–255.

Gruber, H. E. (1986). The self-construction of the extraordinary. In R. J. Sternberg & J. E. Davidson (Eds.), *Conceptions of giftedness* (pp. 247–263). Cambridge University Press.

Gruber, H. E., & Davis, S. N. (1988). Inching our way up Mount Olympus: The evolving-systems approach to creative thinking. In R. J. Sternberg (Ed.), *The nature of creativity* (pp. 143–169). Cambridge University Press.

Halpin, G., & Halpin, G. (1973). The effect of motivation on creative thinking abilities. *Journal of Creative Behavior, 7*, 51–53.

Harlow, H. F. (1950). Learning and satiation of response in intrinsically motivated complex puzzle performance by monkeys. *Journal of Comparative Physiological Psychology, 43*, 289–294.

Heinzen, T. E. (1989). On moderate challenge increasing ideational creativity. *Creativity Research Journal, 2*, 223–226.

Heinzen, T. E., Mills, C., & Cameron, P. (1993). Scientific innovation potential. *Creativity Research Journal, 6*, 261–269.

Henle, M. (1962). The birth and death of ideas. In H. Gruber, G. Terrell, & M. Wertheimer (Eds.), *Contemporary approaches to creative thinking* (pp. 31–62). New York: Atherton.

Hennessey, B. A. (1989). The effect of extrinsic constraints on children's creativity while using a computer. *Creativity Research Journal, 2*, 151–168.

Hennessey, B. A. (1995). Social, environmental, and developmental issues and creativity. *Educational Psychology Review, 7*, 163–183.

Hennessey, B., Amabile, T., & Martinage, M. (1989). Immunizing children against the negative effects of reward. *Contemporary Educational Psychology, 14*, 212–227.

Hennessey, B. A., & Zbikowski, S. (1993). Immunizing children against the negative effects of reward: A further examination of intrinsic motivation training techniques. *Creativity Research Journal, 6*, 297–308.

Hill, K. G., Amabile, T. M., Coon, H. M., & Whitney, D. (1994). *Testing the componential model of creativity.* Unpublished manuscript, Brandeis University, Waltham, MA.

Hunt, J. McV. (1965). Intrinsic motivation and its role in psychological development. In D. Levine (Ed.), *Nebraska Symposium on Motivation* (Vol. 13). Lincoln: University of Nebraska Press.

Johnson, R. A. (1974). Differential effects of reward versus no-reward instructions on the creative thinking of two economic levels of elementary school children. *Journal of Educational Psychology, 66*, 530–533.

Klein, G. (1976). *Psychoanalytic theory.* New York: International Universities Press.

Koestler, A. (1964). *The act of creation.* New York: Dell.

Koestner, R., Ryan, R. M., Bernieri, F., & Holt, K. (1984). Setting limits on children's behavior: The differential effects of controlling versus informational styles on intrinsic motivation and creativity. *Journal of Personality, 52*, 233–248.

Kris, E. (1952). *Psychoanalytic explorations in art.* New York: International Universities Press.

Kruglanski, A. W., Friedman, I., & Zeevi, G. (1971). The effects of intrinsic incentives on some qualitative aspects of performance. *Journal of Personality, 39*, 606–617.

Lepper, M., & Greene, D. (1978). Overjustification research and beyond: Toward a means–end analysis of intrinsic and extrinsic motivation. In M. Lepper & D. Greene (Eds.), *The hidden costs of reward* (pp. 109–148). Hillsdale, NJ: Erlbaum.

Lepper, M., Greene, D., & Nisbett, R. (1973). Undermining children's intrinsic interest with extrinsic rewards: A test of the "overjustification" hypothesis. *Journal of Personality and Social Psychology, 28,* 129–137.

Locurto, C. M., & Walsh, J. F. (1976). Reinforcement and self-reinforcement: Their effects on originality. *American Journal of Psychology, 89,* 281–291.

MacKinnon, D. W. (1962). The nature and nurture of creative talent. *American Psychologist, 17,* 484–495.

Mansfield, R. S., & Busse, T. V. (1981). *The psychology of creativity and discovery: Scientists and their work.* Chicago: Nelson Hall.

Maslow, A. H. (1943). A theory of human motivation. *Psychological Review, 50,* 370–396.

Maslow, A. H. (1959). Creativity in self-actualizing people. In H. A. Anderson (Ed.), *Creativity and its cultivation* (pp. 83–95). New York: Harper.

Maslow, A. H. (1968). *Toward a psychology of being* (2nd ed.). Princeton, NJ: Van Nostrand Reinhold.

McGraw, K. O., & McCullers, J. C. (1979). Evidence of a detrimental effect of extrinsic incentives on breaking a mental set. *Journal of Experimental Social Psychology, 15,* 285–294.

Milgram, R. M., & Feingold, S. (1977). Concrete and verbal reinforcement in creative thinking of disadvantaged children. *Perceptual and Motor Skills, 45,* 675–678.

Newell, A., Shaw, J. C., & Simon, H. A. (1962). The process of creative thinking. In H. Gruber, G. Terrell, & M. Wertheimer (Eds.), *Contemporary approaches to creative thinking* (pp. 43–62). New York: Atherton.

Ochse, R. (1990). *Before the gates of excellence: The determination of creative genius.* Cambridge University Press.

Perkins, D. N. (1988). The possibility of invention. In R. J. Sternberg (Ed.), *The nature of creativity* (pp. 362–385). Cambridge University Press.

Picariello, M. L. (1994). *Children's perceptions of autonomy in the classroom: Implications for intrinsic motivation, learning, and creativity.* Ph.D. dissertation, Brandeis University, Waltham, MA.

Pollak, S. (1992). *The effects of motivational orientation and constraint on the creativity of the artist.* Unpublished manuscript, Brandeis University, Waltham, MA.

Porter, L., & Lawler, E. E. (1968). *Managerial attitudes and performance.* Homewood, IL: Free Press.

Roe, A. (1952). A scientist examines 64 eminent scientists. *Scientific American, 187,* 21–25.

Rogers, C. (1954). Towards a theory of creativity. *ETC: A Review of General Semantics, 11,* 249–260.

Rubenson, D. L., & Runco, M. A. (1992). The psychoeconomic approach to creativity. *New Ideas in Psychology, 10,* 131–147.

Runco, M. A. (1994). Creativity and its discontents. In M. P. Shaw & M. A. Runco (Eds.), *Creativity and affect* (pp. 53–65). Norwood, NJ: Ablex.

Runco, M. A., & Chand, I. (1995). Cognition and creativity. *Educational Psychology Review, 7,* 243–267.

Ruscio, J., Whitney, D., & Amabile, T. M. (in press). Looking inside the fishbowl of creativity: Verbal and behavioral predictors of creative performance. *Creativity Research Journal.*

Ryan, R. M., & Grolnick, W. S. (1986). Origins and pawns in the classroom: Self-report and projective assessments of individual differences in children's perceptions. *Journal of Personality and Social Psychology, 50,* 550–558.

Segal, H. (1957). A psycho-analytic approach to aesthetics. In M. Klein, P. Heiman, & R. Money-Kyrle (Eds.), *New directions in psychoanalysis* (pp. 384–405). New York: Basic.

Sharpe, E. F. (1930). Certain aspects of sublimation and delusion. *International Journal of Psychoanalysis, 11,* 12–23.

Sharpe, E. F. (1950). Similar and divergent unconscious determinants underlying the sublimations of pure art and pure science. In M. Brierly (Ed.), *Collected papers on psychoanalysis* (pp. 137–154). London: Hogarth.

Sternberg, R. J. (1988). A three-facet model of creativity. In R. J. Sternberg (Ed.), *The nature of creativity* (pp. 125–147). Cambridge University Press.

Sternberg, R. J., & Lubart, T. I. (1991). An investment theory of creativity and its development. *Human Development, 34,* 1–32.

Sternberg, R. J., & Lubart, T. I. (1992). Buy low and sell high: An investment approach to creativity. *Current Directions in Psychological Science, 1,* 1–5.

Sternberg, R. J., & Lubart, T. I. (1995). *Defying the crowd: Cultivating creativity in a culture of conformity.* New York: Free Press.

Sternberg, R. J., & Lubart, T. I. (1996). Investing in creativity. *American Psychologist, 51,* 677–688.

Stokes, A. (1963). *Painting and the inner world.* London: Tavistock.

Storr, A. (1988). *Solitude: A return to the self.* New York: Ballantine.

Szymanski, K,, & Harkins, S. G. (1992). Self-evaluation and creativity. *Personality and Social Psychology Bulletin, 18,* 259–265.

Taylor, D. W. (1960). Toward an information processing theory of motivation. In M. R. Jones (Ed.), *Nebraska Symposium on Motivation, 1960.* Lincoln: University of Nebraska Press.

Torrance, E. P. (1962). *Guiding creative talent.* Englewood Cliffs, NJ: Prentice-Hall.

Torrance, E. P. (1981). Predicting the creativity of elementary school children (1958–1980) – And the teacher who made a difference. *Gifted Child Quarterly, 25,* 55–62.

Torrance, E. P. (1983). The importance of falling in love with "something." *Creative Child and Adult Quarterly, 8,* 72–78.

Torrance, E. P. (1987). Future career image as a predictor of creative achievement in the 22-year longitudinal study. *Psychological Reports, 60,* 574.

Torrance, E. P. (1995). Insights about creativity: Questioned, rejected, ridiculed, ignored. *Educational Psychology Review, 7,* 313–322.

Vroom, V. (1964). *Motivation and work.* New York: Wiley.

Wallach, M. A., & Kogan, N. (1965). *Modes of thinking in young children.* New York: Holt, Rinehart, & Winston.

White, R. (1959). Motivation reconsidered: The concept of competence. *Psychological Review, 66,* 297–323.

Woodman, R. W., & Schoenfeldt, L. F. (1989). Individual differences in creativity: An interactionist perspective. In J. A. Glover, R. R. Ronning, & C. R. Reynolds (Eds.), *Handbook of creativity* (pp. 77–92). New York: Plenum.

Woodman, R. W., & Schoenfeldt, L. F. (1990). An interactionist model of creative behavior. *Journal of Creative Behavior, 24,* 10–20.

16   Implications of a Systems Perspective for the Study of Creativity

MIHALY CSIKSZENTMIHALYI

Psychologists tend to see creativity exclusively as a mental process. In this chapter, I will propose that such an approach cannot do justice to the phenomenon of creativity, which is as much a cultural and social as it is a psychological event. To develop this perspective, I will use a "systems" model of the creative process that takes into account its essential features.

Creativity research in recent years has been increasingly informed by a systems perspective. Starting with the observations of Morris Stein (1953, 1963) and the extensive data presented by Dean Simonton (1988, 1990) showing the influence of economic, political, and social events on the rates of creative production, it has become increasingly clear that variables external to the individual must be taken into account if one wishes to explain why, when, and where new ideas or products arise from and become established in a culture (Gruber, 1988; Harrington, 1990). Magyari-Beck (1988) has gone so far as to suggest that because of its complexity, creativity needs a new discipline of "creatology" in order to be thoroughly understood.

The systems approach developed here has been described before and applied to historical and anecdotal examples, as well as to data collected to answer a variety of different questions (Csikszentmihalyi, 1988b, 1990, 1996; Csikszentmihalyi, Rathunde, & Whalen, 1993; Csikszentmihalyi & Sawyer, 1995; Feldman, Csikszentmihalyi, & Gardner, 1994). In the present context, I will expand the model more rigorously and develop its implications for a better understanding of how the work of genius can be studied.

WHY IS A SYSTEMS APPROACH NECESSARY?

When I started studying creativity more than 30 years ago, like most psychologists I was convinced that it consisted of a purely intrapsychic process. I assumed that one could understand creativity with reference to the thought processes, emotions, and motivations of individuals who produced novelty. But each year the task became more frustrating. In our longitudinal study of artists, for instance, it became increasingly clear that some of the potentially most creative persons stopped doing art and pursued ordinary occupations, while others who seemed to lack creative personal attributes persevered and eventually produced works of art that were hailed as important creative achievements (Csikszentmihalyi, 1990; Csikszentmihalyi & Getzels, 1988; Getzels & Csikszentmihalyi, 1976). To use just a single example, young women in art school showed as much creative potential as their male colleagues, or even more. Yet 20 years later, not one of the cohort of women had achieved outstanding recognition, whereas several in the cohort of men did.

Psychologists have always realized that good new ideas do not automatically translate into accepted creative products. Confronted with this knowledge, one of two strategies can be adopted. The first was articulated by Abraham Maslow (1963) and involves denying the importance of public recognition. In his opinion it is not the outcome of the process that

313

counts, but the process itself. According to this perspective a person who reinvents Einstein's formula for relativity is as creative as Einstein was. A child who sees the world with fresh eyes is creative; it is the quality of the subjective experience that determines whether a person is creative, not the judgment of the world. While I believe that the quality of subjective experience is the most important dimension of personal life, I do not believe that creativity can be assessed with reference to it. If creativity is to retain a useful meaning, it must refer to a process that results in an idea or product that is recognized and adopted by others. Originality, freshness of perceptions, divergent-thinking ability are all well and good in their own right, as desirable personal traits. But without some form of public recognition they do not constitute creativity. In fact, one might argue that such traits are not even necessary for creative accomplishment.

In practice, creativity research has always recognized this fact. Every creativity test, whether it involves responding to divergent-thinking tasks or whether it asks children to produce stories or designs with colored tiles, is assessed by judges or raters who weigh the originality of the responses. The underlying assumption is that an objective quality called "creativity" is revealed in the products, and that judges and raters can recognize it. But we know that expert judges do not possess an external, objective standard by which to evaluate "creative" responses. Their judgments rely on past experience, training, cultural biases, current trends, personal values, idiosyncratic preferences. Thus, whether an idea or product is creative or not does not depend on its own qualities, but on the effect it is able to produce in others who are exposed to it. Therefore it follows that what we call creativity is a phenomenon that is constructed through an *interaction between producer and audience*. Creativity is not the product of single individuals, but of social systems making judgments about individuals' products.

A second strategy that has been used to accommodate the fact that social judgments are so central to creativity is not to deny their importance, but to separate the process of creativity from that of persuasion, and then claim that both are necessary for a creative idea or product to be accepted (Simonton, 1988, 1991, 1994). However, this strategem does not resolve the epistemological problem. For if you cannot persuade the world that you had a creative idea, how do we know that you actually had it? And if you do persuade others, then of course you will be recognized as creative. Therefore it is impossible to separate creativity from persuasion; the two stand or fall together. The impossibility is not only methodological, but epistemological as well, and probably ontological. In other words, if by creativity we mean the ability to add something new to the culture, then it is impossible to even think of it as separate from persuasion.

Of course, one might disagree with this definition of creativity. Some will prefer to define it as an intrapsychic process, as an ineffable experience, as a subjective event that need not leave any objective trace. But any definition of creativity that aspires to objectivity, and therefore requires an intersubjective dimension, will have to recognize the fact that the audience is as important to its constitution as the individual to whom it is credited.

AN OUTLINE OF THE SYSTEMS MODEL

Thus, starting from a strictly individual perspective on creativity, I was forced by facts to adopt a view that encompasses the environment in which the individual operates. This environment has two salient aspects: a cultural, or symbolic, aspect which here is called the domain; and a social aspect called the field. Creativity is a process that can be observed only at the intersection where individuals, domains, and fields interact (Figure 16.1).

The domain is a necessary component of creativity because it is impossible to introduce a variation without reference to an existing pattern. "New" is meaningful only in reference to

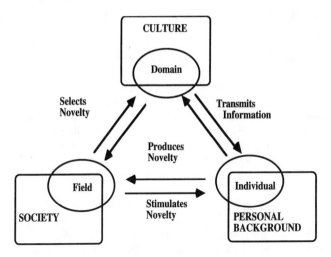

Figure 16.1. The systems view of creativity. For creativity to occur, a set of rules and practices must be transmitted from the domain to the individual. The individual must then produce a novel variation in the content of the domain. The variation then must be selected by the field for inclusion in the domain.

the "old." Original thought does not exist in a vacuum. It must operate on a set of already existing objects, rules, representations, or notations. One can be a creative carpenter, cook, composer, chemist, or clergyman because the domains of woodworking, gastronomy, music, chemistry, and religion exist and one can evaluate performance by reference to their traditions. Without rules there cannot be exceptions, and without tradition there cannot be novelty.

Creativity occurs when a person makes a change in a domain, a change that will be transmitted through time. Some individuals are more likely to make such changes, either because of personal qualities or because they have the good fortune to be well positioned with respect to the domain – they have better access to it, or their social circumstances allow them free time to experiment. For example, until quite recently the majority of scientific advances were made by men who had the means and the leisure: Clergymen like Copernicus, tax collectors like Lavoisier, or physicians like Galvani could afford to build their own laboratories and to concentrate on their thoughts. And, of course, all of these individuals lived in cultures with a tradition of systematic observation of nature and a tradition of record keeping and mathematical symbolization that made it possible for their insights to be shared and evaluated by others who had equivalent training.

But most novel ideas will be quickly forgotten. Changes are not adopted unless they are sanctioned by some group entitled to make decisions as to what should or should not be included in the domain. These gatekeepers are what we call here the field. The term *field* is often used to designate an entire discipline or kind of endeavor. In the present context, however, I want to define the term in a more narrow sense and use it to refer only to the social organization of the domain – to the teachers, critics, journal editors, museum curators, agency directors, and foundation officers who decide what belongs to a domain and what does not. In physics, the opinion of a very small number of leading university professors was enough to certify that Einstein's ideas were creative. Hundreds of millions of people accepted the judgment of this tiny field and marveled at Einstein's creativity without understanding what it was all about. It has been said that in the United States 10,000 people in Manhattan constitute the field in modern art. They decide which new paintings or sculptures deserve to be seen, bought, included in collections – and therefore added to the domain.

Psychologists involved in creativity research also constitute a field in this sense. This field usually consists of teachers or graduate students who judge the products of children or other students. It is they who decide which test responses, mosaics, or portfolios are to be considered creative. So it is true that creativity tests can measure creativity – as long as it is recognized that what is meant by *creativity* is not a real objective quality, but refers only to the acceptance by a particular field of judges. Such creativity, while part of the domain of creativity research, may have nothing to do with creativity in any other domain outside of it. At every level, from considering Nobel Prize nominations to considering the scribbles of 4-year-olds, fields are busy assessing new products and deciding whether or not they are creative – in other words, whether they are enough of an improvement to deserve inclusion in the domain.

The systems model is analogous to the model that scholars have used to describe the process of evolution. Evolution occurs when an individual organism produces a variation which is selected by the environment and transmitted to the next generation (see, e.g., Campbell, 1976; Csikszentmihalyi, 1993; Mayr, 1982). The variation that occurs at the individual level corresponds to the contribution that a person makes to creativity; the selection is the contribution of the field, and the transmission is the contribution of the domain to the creative process (cf. Simonton, 1988; Martindale, 1989). Thus, creativity can be seen as a special case of evolution; specifically, it is to cultural evolution as the mutation, selection, and transmission of genetic variation is to biological evolution.

In biological evolution it makes no sense to say that a beneficial step was the result of a particular genetic mutation alone, without taking into account environmental conditions. For instance, a genetic change that improved the size or taste of corn would be useless if at the same time it made the corn more vulnerable to drought or disease. Moreover, a genetic mutation that cannot be transmitted to the next generation is also useless from the point of view of evolution. The same considerations apply to creativity when the latter is seen as the form that evolution takes at the cultural level: To be creative, a variation has to be adapted to its social environment, and it has to be capable of being passed on through time.

THE CULTURAL CONTEXT

What we call creativity always involves a change in a symbolic system, a change that in turn will affect the thoughts and feelings of the members of the culture. A change that does not affect the way we think, feel, or act will not be creative. Thus, creativity presupposes a community of people who share ways of thinking and acting, who learn from each other and imitate each other's actions. It is useful to think about creativity as involving a change in memes – the units of imitation that Dawkins (1976) suggested were the building blocks of culture. Memes are similar to genes in that they carry instructions for action. The notes of a song tell us what to sing; the recipe for a cake tells us what ingredients to mix and how long to bake it. But whereas genetic instructions are transmitted in the chemical codes that we inherit on our chromosomes, the instructions contained in memes are transmitted through learning. By and large we learn memes and reproduce them without change; when a new song or a new recipe is invented, then we have creativity.

Memes seem to have changed very slowly in human history. One of the earliest memes was the shape that our ancestors gave to the stone tools they used for chopping, carving, scraping, and pounding. The shape of these flint blades remained almost unchanged during the Paleolithic, or Old Stone Age, for close to a million years – which is roughly $\frac{199}{200}$ of human history. It is not until about 50,000 years ago, during the Upper Paleolithic era, that humans began to use new tools: blades specialized for performing specific functions, and even tools for making other tools. The first change in the meme of the tool took almost a million years to develop; once this first step was taken, however, new shapes followed each other in increasingly rapid succession. For thousands of generations, men looked at the stone blades they held in their hands, and then reproduced ones exactly like them, which they passed on to their children. The meme of the tool contained the instructions for its own replication. But then someone discovered a more efficient way of chipping stone blades, and a new meme appeared that started reproducing itself in the minds of men, and generating offspring – that is, new tools that had not existed before – which were increasingly different from their parents.

The meme of a flint scraper or a flint axe is part of the domain of technology, which includes all the artifacts that humans use to achieve control over their material environment. Other early domains were those of language, art, music, religion – each including a set of memes related to each other by rules. Since the recession of the last Ice Age about 15,000 years ago, memes and corresponding domains have of course proliferated to an extent that would have been impossible to foresee only a few seconds earlier in evolutionary time. Nowadays the single domain of technology is subdivided into so many subdomains that no single individual can master even a minute fraction of it.

Cultures as a Set of Domains

It is useful in this context to think about cultures as systems of interrelated domains. This is not to claim that culture is nothing but a system of interrelated domains – after all, there are over a hundred different definitions of culture being used by anthropologists, and no single definition can be exhaustive. The claim is simply that in order to understand creativity, it is useful to think of culture in this way. Table 16.1 presents some questions and hypotheses that follow from this definition of culture, and which have a bearing on the understanding of creativity.

Cultures differ in the way that memes (i.e., technical procedures, kinds of knowledge, styles of art, belief systems) are stored. As long as they are recorded orally and can be transmitted only from the mind of one person to another, traditions must be strictly observed so as not to lose information. Therefore, creativity is not likely to be prized, and it would be difficult to determine in any case. Development of new media of storage and transmission (e.g., books, computers) will have an impact on rates of novelty production and its acceptance.

Another dimension of cultural difference is the accessibility of information. With time, people who benefit from the ability to control memes develop protective boundaries around their knowledge, so that only a few initiates at any given time will have access to it. Priestly castes around the world have evolved to keep their knowledge esoteric and out of reach of the masses. Even in the times of the Egyptian civilization, craft guilds kept much of their technical knowledge secret. Until recently in the West, knowledge of Latin and Greek was used as a barrier to prevent the admittance of the masses to professional training. The more such barriers, the less likely it becomes that potentially creative individuals will be able to contribute to a domain.

Similarly, how available memes are also bears on the rate of creativity. When knowledge is concentrated in a few centers, libraries, or laboratories, or when books and schools are rare, most potentially creative individuals will be effectively prevented from learning enough to make a contribution to existing knowledge.

Cultures differ in the number of domains they recognize and in the hierarchical relationship among them. For example, in Western cultures philosophy tended to develop out of religion, and then the other scholarly disciplines separated out of philosophy. For a long time

Table 16.1. *Questions and Hypotheses Concerning How Culture Affects the Incidence of Creativity*

1. How is information stored (e.g., oral vs. written records)?

   The more permanent and accurate the storage, the easier it is to assimilate past knowledge, and hence to be well positioned for the next step in innovation.

2. How accessible is the information (e.g., are there restrictions based on esoteric language, limited training, or inherited status)?

   The more accessible the information, the wider the range of individuals who can participate in creative processes.

3. How available is the information (e.g., is diffusion restricted because of material or social constraints)?

   See Question 2.

4. How differentiated is the culture (i.e., how many separate domains such as religion, philosophy, and mathematics does it contain)?

   The more differentiated the domains that the culture contains, the more specialized the information; hence, advances should be made more readily.

5. How integrated is the culture (i.e., can the contents of the various domains be translated into each other's terms; e.g., is science consistent with religion)?

   The more integrated the culture, the more relevant an advance in one domain will be to the culture as a whole. This may make it more difficult for an innovation in any one domain to be accepted, but once accepted, it will be diffused more readily.

6. How open is the culture to other cultures?

   The more exposed the culture is to information and knowledge from other cultures, the more likely it is that innovation will arise.

religion was the queen of disciplines, and it dictated which memes could be included in different domains; now scholarly domains are much more autonomous, although it could be claimed that mathematics has become the benchmark by which other domains are judged.

The multiplication and gradual emancipation of domains has been one of the features of human history. For a long time almost every aspect of cultural thought and expression was unified in what we would call a religious domain. Art, music, dance, narrative, protophilosophy and protoscience were part of an amalgam of supernatural beliefs and rituals. Now every domain strives to achieve independence from the rest and to establish its own rules and legitimate sphere of authority.

Cultures in which the separate domains are clearly related to each other – and these tend to be the simpler ones – are likely to resist novelty in any one area, since it would involve a readjustment of the entire culture. On the other hand, once a change is accepted in one domain of such a culture, the effect of that change is likely to reverberate across the entire system.

New memes most often arise in cultures that, either because of geographical location or economic practices, are exposed to different ideas and beliefs. The Greek traders collected information from Egypt, the Middle East, the north coast of Africa, the Black Sea, Persia, and even from Scandinavia, and this disparate information was amalgamated in the crucible of the Ionian and Attic city-states. In the Middle Ages, the Sicilian court welcomed techniques and knowledge from China and Arabia, as well as from Normandy. Florence in the Renaissance was a center of trade and manufacture, and so was Venice; later the maritime trade of the Iberian Peninsula, the Netherlands, and Great Britain moved the center of

Table 16.2. *Questions and Hypotheses Concerning How the Domain Affects the Incidence of Creativity*

1. How is information recorded?

   The more clear and accurate the system of notation, the easier it is to assimilate past knowledge, and hence to take the next step in innovation.

2. How well integrated is the information in the domain?

   If the information is very tightly integrated, it might be difficult to change it; but if it is too loosely organized, it will be difficult to recognize valuable innovations.

3. How central is the domain to the culture?

   At different times, one or another domain will take precedence in the culture (e.g., religion in the Middle Ages, physics in the early part of the twentieth century), and it will attract the more talented minds to it, thereby making creativity more likely.

4. How accessible is the domain?

   When because of accident or planning a domain becomes identified with an elite, it becomes more difficult to introduce innovation within it.

5. How autonomous is the domain from the rest of the culture?

   At different times, one domain may achieve hegemony over the others (e.g., religion or politics over arts or the sciences), in which case it is more difficult to produce variations in the subordinate domain.

information exchange to those regions. Even now, when the diffusion of information is almost instantaneous, useful new ideas are likely to arise from centers where people from different cultural backgrounds are able to interact and exchange ideas.

The Role of the Domain in the Creative Process

Cultures are made up of a variety of domains: music, mathematics, religion, various technologies, and so on. Innovations that result in creative contributions do not take place directly in the culture, but in one of such domains. Table 16.2 presents some considerations that are relevant to understanding the role of domains in this process.

It is usually the case that, with time, a domain develops its own memes and system of notation. Natural languages and mathematics underlie most domains. In addition there are formal notation systems for music, dance, and logic, as well as other less formal ones for instructing and assessing performance in a great variety of different domains. For instance Jean Piaget (1965) gave a detailed description of how rules are transmitted in a very informal domain, that of the game of marbles played by Swiss children. This domain has endured over several generations of children, and it consists of specific names for marbles of different sizes, color, and composition. Furthermore, it contains a variety of arcane rules that children learn from each other in the course of play. So even without a notation system, domains can be transmitted from one generation to the next through imitation and instruction.

One obvious factor is the stage of development that the domain has attained. There are times when the symbolic system of a domain is so diffuse and loosely integrated that it is almost impossible to determine whether a novelty is or is not an improvement on the status quo. Chemistry was in such a state before the adoption of the periodic table, which integrated and rationalized knowledge about the elements. Earlier centuries may have had many potentially creative chemical scientists, but their work was too idiosyncratic to be evaluated against a common standard. Or, conversely, the symbolic system may be so tightly organized that no new development seems possible; this resembles the situation in physics at the end of the preceding last century, before the revolution in thinking brought about by quantum theory. Both of these examples suggest that creativity is likely to be more difficult before a paradigmatic revolution. On the other hand, the need for a new paradigm makes it more likely that if a new viable contribution does occur despite the difficulty, it will be hailed as a major creative accomplishment.

At any given historical period, certain domains will attract more gifted young people than at other times, thus increasing the likelihood of creativity. The attraction of a domain depends on several variables: its centrality in the culture, the promise of new discoveries and opportunities that it presents, the intrinsic rewards accruing from working in the domain. For instance, the Renaissance in early-fifteenth-century Florence would have not happened without the discovery of Roman ruins, which yielded a great amount of new knowledge about construction techniques and sculptural models and motivated many young people, who otherwise would have gone into the professions, to become architects and artists instead. The quantum revolution in physics at the beginning of this century was so intellectually exciting that, for several generations, some of the best minds flocked to physics or applied its principles to neighboring disciplines such as chemistry, biology, medicine, and astronomy. Nowadays similar excitement surrounds the domains of molecular biology and computer science.

As Thomas Kuhn (1962) remarked, potentially creative young people will not be drawn to domains where all the basic questions have been solved and which, therefore, appear to be boring – that is, offer few opportunities to obtain the intrinsic and extrinsic rewards that follow from solving important problems. A domain in which novelty can be evaluated objectively, and which has clear rules, a rich and complex symbolic system, and a central position in the culture will be more attractive than one lacking such characteristics.

Domains also vary in terms of their accessibility. Sometimes rules and knowledge become the monopoly of a protective class or caste, and others are not admitted to it. Creative thought in Christianity was renewed by the Reformation, which placed the Bible and its commentaries in reach of a much larger population, which earlier had been excluded by an entrenched priestly caste from perusing it directly. The enormously increased accessibility of information on the Internet might also bring about a new peak in creativity across many different domains, just as the printing press did over four centuries ago.

Finally, some domains are easier to change than others. This depends in part on how autonomous a domain is from the rest of the culture or social system that supports it. Until the seventeenth century in Europe it was difficult to be creative in the many branches of science that the Church had a vested interest in protecting – as the case of Galileo illustrates. In Soviet Russia, the Marxist-Leninist dogma took precedence over scientific domains, and many new ideas that conflicted with it were not accepted. The most notorious case, of course, was Lysenko's application of the Lamarckian theory of evolution to the development of new strains of grain, because this theory was more "Marxist" than the Darwinian-Mendelian paradigm. Even in our time, some topics in the social (and even in the physical and biological) sciences are considered less politically correct than others and are given scant research support as a consequence.

Creativity is the engine that drives cultural evolution. The notion of evolution does not imply that cultural changes necessarily follow some single direction or that cultures are getting any better as a result of the changes brought about by creativity. Following its use in biology, evolution in this context means increasing complexity over time. In turn, complexity is defined in terms of two complementary processes (Csikszentmihalyi, 1993, 1996). First, it means that cultures tend to become differentiated over time; that is, they develop increasingly independent and autonomous domains. Second, the domains within a culture become increasingly integrated, that is, related to each other and mutually supportive of each others' goals, which is analogous to the differentiated organs of the physical body that help each others' functioning.

In this sense creativity does not always support cultural evolution. It generally contributes to differentiation, but it can easily work against integration. New ideas, technologies, or forms of expression often break down the existing harmony between different domains, and thus might, at least temporarily, jeopardize the complexity of a culture. The separation of physics from the tutelage of religion that was accomplished by Galileo's discoveries ushered in an era of tremendous differentiation in science, but at the expense of a corresponding loss of integration in Western culture. Presumably – if the evolution of culture is to continue – creative insights will in the future restore the relationship between the currently divergent domains, this integration thus temporarily restoring the complexity of the culture, at least until new steps in differentiation again break it apart.

THE SOCIAL CONTEXT

Even the most individually oriented psychologists agree that in order to be called creative, a new meme must be socially valued. Without some form of social valuation it would be impossible to distinguish ideas that are simply bizarre from those that are genuinely creative. But this social validation is usually seen as something that follows the individual's creative act and can be – at least conceptually – separated from it. The stronger claim made here is that there is no way, even in principle, to separate the reaction of society from the person's contribution: The two are inseparable. As long as the idea or product has not been validated, we might have originality, but not creativity.

Nowadays everyone agrees that van Gogh's paintings show that he was a very creative artist. It is also fashionable to sneer at the ignorant bourgeoisie of his period for failing to recognize van Gogh's genius and letting him die alone and penniless. The implication, of course, is that we are much smarter, and if we had been in their place we would have loved van Gogh's paintings. But we should remember that a hundred years ago those canvases were just the hallucinatory original works of a sociopathic recluse. They became creative only after a number of other artists, critics, and collectors interpreted them in terms of new aesthetic criteria and transformed them from substandard efforts into masterpieces.

Without this change in the climate of evaluation, van Gogh would not be considered creative even now. But would he have been creative anyway, even if we didn't know it? In my opinion, such a question is too metaphysical to be considered part of a scientific approach. If the question is unanswerable in principle, why ask it? The better strategy is to recognize that in the sciences as well as in the arts, creativity is as much the result of changing standards and new criteria of assessment, as it is of novel individual achievements.

Societal Conditions Relevant to Creativity

The second main element of the systems model is society, or the sum of all fields that operate within a time–space framework. Fields are made up of individuals who practice a given domain and have the power to change it. For example, all the accountants who practice by the same rules comprise the field of accountancy, and it is they who have to endorse a new way of keeping accounts if it is to be accepted as a creative improvement. A society can then be defined as the sum of the individuals in its interrelated fields – from architects to zookeepers, from mothers to consumers of computer peripherals.

Table 16.3 suggests some of the ways a society might influence the frequency and intensity of new memes. Again, as in the previous tables, the list should be useful both as a heuris-

Table 16.3. *Questions and Hypotheses Concerning How Society Affects the Incidence of Creativity*

1. Is surplus energy available?

   A society where all of the physical and mental energy must be invested in survival tasks is less likely to encourage or recognize innovation.

2. Does society value and encourage creativity?

   Regardless of material conditions, societies differ in terms of how much value is placed on innovation.

3. Is the social and economic organization conducive to change?

   Certain types of economies (e.g., rentier) have no interest in allowing change to occur; mercantile societies might be more open to change.

4. How much mobility and conflict is there?

   Both the external threats to and internal strife of a society seem to encourage the generation and the acceptance of novelty; the same might be true of social mobility.

5. How complex is the social system?

   Both differentiation and integration within society affect the rate of generation and adoption of novelty.

tic device to familiarize the reader with some of the implications of the systems perspective, and as a source of hypotheses for further study that might enrich the field of creativity research.

Other things being equal, a society that enjoys a material surplus is in better position to help the creative process. A wealthier society is able to make information more readily available, allows for a greater rate of specialization and experimentation, and is better equipped to reward and implement new ideas. Subsistence societies have fewer opportunities to encourage and reward novelty, especially if it is expensive to produce. Only societies with ample material reserves can afford to build great cathedrals, universities, scientific laboratories. Even the composition of music, the writing of poetry, or the painting of pictures require a market where subsistence needs are not primary. But it seems that there is often a lag between social affluence and creativity; the impact of wealth may take several generations to manifest itself. So the material surplus of the nineteenth-century United States was first needed to build a material infrastructure for society (canals, railroads, factories), before it was invested in supporting novel ideas such as the telephone or the mass production of cars and planes.

But it is not enough to have the material resources to implement new ideas – it is also important to be interested in them. Societies that had great resources and were located at the confluence of trade routes have sometimes shunned new ideas. In Egypt, for example, after a unique burst of creativity that resulted in astonishing accomplishments in architecture, engineering, art, technology, religion, and civic administration, the leaders of society apparently agreed that the best policy was to leave well enough alone. Thus, most of Egyptian art for thousands of years was produced in a few central workshops supervised by priests or bureaucrats and was done by relying on universally binding rules, common models, and uniform methods. The sociologist of art Arnold Hauser (1951) writes that "originality of subject-matter was never very much appreciated in Egypt, in fact was generally tabooed; the whole ambition of the artist was concentrated on thoroughness and precision of execution" (p. 36).

Whether a society is open to novelty or not depends in part on its social organization. A farming society with a stable feudal structure, for instance, would be one where tradition counts more than novelty. Societies based on commerce, with a strong bourgeois class trying to be accepted by the aristocracy, have on the other hand been usually favorable to novelty. Whenever the central authority tends toward absolutism, it is less likely that experimentation will be encouraged (Therivel, 1995). Ancient Chinese society is a good example of a central authority supported by a powerful bureaucracy that was able to resist for centuries the spread of new ideas. Despite enormous early cultural advances and a great number of creative individuals, Chinese society believed that the use of gunpowder for weapons and that of movable type for the printing of books were bad ideas. Of course, they might have been right; nevertheless, currently China is trying to catch up as fast as possible with the new ideas that in the past it had politely ignored.

Rentier societies, where the ruling classes lived off the profits of land rent, pensions, or stable investments, have been historically reluctant to change because any novelty was seen to potentially threaten the status quo that provided the livelihood of the oligarchy. This condition might become relevant again as the United States moves more toward an economy where pensions and retirement plans are a major source of income for an increasing number of people.

A different and more controversial suggestion is that egalitarian societies are less likely to support the creative process than those where relatively few people control a disproportionate amount of the resources – especially in artistic domains. Aristocracies or oligarchies may be better able to support creativity than democracies or socialist regimes, simply because when wealth and power are concentrated in a few hands, it is easier to use part of it for risky or "unnecessary" experiments. Also, the development of a leisure class often results in a refinement of connoiseurship that in turn provides more demanding criteria by which a field evaluates new contributions.

Societies located at the confluence of diverse cultural streams can benefit more easily from that synergy of different ideas that is so important for the creative process. It is for this reason that some of the greatest art, and the earliest science, developed in cities that were centers of trade. The Italian Renaissance was in part due to the Arab and Middle Eastern influences that businessmen and their retinues brought into Florence and the seaports of Venice, Genoa, and Naples. The fact that periods of social unrest often coincide with creativity (Simonton, 1991) is probably due to the synergy resulting when the interests and perspectives of usually segregated classes are brought to bear on each other. The Tuscan cities supported creativity best during a period in which noblemen, merchants, and craftsmen fought each other bitterly and when every few years, as a different political party came to power, a good portion of the citizenry was banished into exile.

External threats also often mobilize society to recognize creative ideas that otherwise might not have attracted much attention. Florence in the fifteenth century spent so many resources on the arts in part because the leaders of the city were competing against their enemies in Siena, Lucca, and Pisa and tried to outdo them in the beauty of their churches and public squares (Heydenreich, 1974). The reason that high-energy physics became such an important field after World War II is that practically every nation wished to have the technology to build its own nuclear arsenal.

Finally, the complexity of a society also bears on the rates of innovation it can tolerate. Too much divisiveness, as well as its opposite, too much uniformity, are unlikely to generate novelty that will be accepted and preserved. Ideal conditions for creativity would be a social system that is highly differentiated into specialized fields and roles, yet is held together by what Durkheim (1912/1967) called the bonds of "organic solidarity."

The Role of the Field

The recognition that culture and society are as involved in the constitution of creativity as the individual may set the course of investigation on the right footing, but it certainly does not answer all the questions. In fact, it brings a host of new questions to light. New ideas often arise in the process of artistic or scientific collaboration (Csikszentmihalyi & Sawyer, 1995; Dunbar, 1993), and peers play an important role in supporting the creativity of individuals (Mockros & Csikszentmihalyi, in press).

Perhaps the major new question this perspective brings to light is: Who is entitled to decide what is creative? According to the individual-centered approach, this issue is not problematic. Since it assumes that creativity is located in the person and expressed in his or her works, all it takes is for some "expert" to recognize its existence. So if some kindergarten teachers agree that a child's drawing is creative, or a group of Nobel Prize physicists judge a young scientist's theory creative, then the issue is closed, and all we need to find out is how the individual was able to produce the drawing or the theory.

But if it is true, as the systems model holds, that attribution is an integral part of the creative process, then we must ask, What does it take for a new meme to be accepted into the domain? Who has the right to decide whether a new meme is actually an improvement, or simply a mistake to be discarded? How are judgments of creativity influenced by the attributional process (Kasof, 1995)?

In the systems model, the gatekeepers who have the right to add memes to a domain are collectively designated the field. Some domains, such as Assyrian languages and literature, may have a very small field consisting of a dozen or so scholars across the world. Others, such as electronic engineering, may include many thousands of specialists whose opinion would count in recognizing a viable novelty. For mass-market products such as soft drinks or motion pictures, the field might include not only the small coterie of product developers and critics, but the public at large. For instance, if New Coke is not a part of the culture, it is because although it passed the evaluation of the small field of beverage specialists, it failed to pass the test of public taste.

Table 16.4 presents some of the ways in which fields influence the likelihood that novelty will be produced and accepted. The first issue to be considered is the field's access to economic resources. In some domains it is almost impossible to do novel work without access to capital. To build a cathedral or to make a movie requires the collaboration of people and materials, and these must be made available to the would-be creative artist. Even to publish poetry, surely one of the least expensive domains, requires access to a press, paper, and distribution outlets. Not surprisingly, creativity in the arts and sciences has flourished historically in societies that had enough surplus capital to finance experimental work. The masterpieces of Florence were built with the profits that the city's bankers made throughout Europe; the masterpieces of Venice were the fruit of that city's seagoing trade. Dutch painters and scientists blossomed after Dutch merchants began to dominate the sea-lanes; then it was the turn of France, England, Germany, and, finally, the United States. As resources accumulate in one place, they lay down the conditions that make innovation possible.

A field is likely to attract original minds to the extent that it can offer scope for a person's experimentations and promises rewards in case of success. As we shall see, even though individuals who try to change domains are in general intrinsically motivated – that is, they enjoy

Table 16.4. *Questions and Hypotheses Concerning How the Field Affects the*
Incidence of Creativity

1. Is the field able to obtain resources from society?

    A field is likely to stagnate if it cannot provide either financial or status rewards to its practitioners.

2. Is the field independent of other societal fields and institutions?

    When a field is overly dependent for its judgments on religious, political, or economic considerations, it is unlikely to select the best new memes. On the other hand, being completely independent of the rest of society also reduces the field's effectiveness.

3. How much does the domain constrain the judgments of the field?

    When the criteria of a domain do not specify which novelty is an improvement, the field has more discretion in determining creativity. It is likely that both too little and too much freedom for the field are inimical to creativity.

4. How institutionalized is the field?

    A certain amount of internal organization is needed for a field to exist. Too much energy invested in self-preservation usually results in a field that becomes highly bureaucratic and impervious to change.

5. How much change does the field support?

    Criteria that are too liberal for accepting novelty may end up debasing the domain; criteria that are too narrow result in a static domain.

---

working in the domain for its own sake – the attraction of extrinsic rewards such as money and fame are not to be discounted.

Leonardo da Vinci, one of the most creative persons on record in terms of his contributions to the arts and the sciences, constantly moved during his lifetime from one city to another, in response to changing market conditions. The leaders of Florence, the dukes of Milan, the popes of Rome, and the king of France waxed and waned in terms of how much money they had to devote to new paintings, sculptures, or cutting-edge scholarship; and as their fortunes changed, Leonardo moved to wherever he could pursue his work with the least hindrance.

The great flowering of Impressionism in Paris was due in part to the willingness of the new middle classes to decorate their homes with canvasses; this in turn attracted ambitious young painters from every corner of the world. It is true that the first beneficiaries of the new affluence were academic painters; but as their craft became so perfect that it became boring – and especially as the new photographic techniques made lifelike pictures no longer unique – the painters who benefited were those who broke the tradition and introduced new memes.

The centrality of a field in terms of societal values will also determine how likely it is to attract new persons with an innovative bent. In this particular historical period, bright young men and women are attracted to the field of computer sciences because it provides the most exciting new intellectual challenges; others to oceanography because it might help to save the planetary ecosystem; some to currency trading because it provides access to financial power; and some to family medicine, because it is the medical specialty most responsive to societal needs. Any field that is able to attract a disproportionate number of bright young persons is more likely to witness creative breakthroughs.

Every field needs a certain degree of autonomy in order to make its assessments purely in terms of excellence within the domain instead of extraneous considerations, but the amount of autonomy might vary considerably. Occasionally fields become extensions of political power, responsible to society at large rather than to the domain. For instance, the works of Renaissance artists were not evaluated by a separate aesthetic field, but had to pass muster from ecclesiastical authorities. When Caravaggio painted his vigorously original portrait of St. Matthew in a relaxed pose, it was not accepted by the prior of the church that had commissioned it because it looked too unsaintly. In the Soviet Union, specially trained party officials had the responsibility of deciding which new paintings, books, music, movies, and even scientific theories were acceptable, based on how well they supported political ideology.

The autonomy of a field is to a certain extent a function of the codification of the domain it serves. When the domain is arcane and highly codified, like Assyriology or molecular biology, then the decision as to which new meme is worth accepting will be made by a relatively small field that is committed to following the traditions and rules of the domain. On the other hand, in the domains of movies or popular music, which are much more accessible to the general public, the specialized field is notoriously unable to enforce a decision as to which works will be creative. For the same reasons, creativity is more ephemeral in the arts than in the sciences. Works of art that seemed to shine with originality to audiences at the beginning of this century may seem trite and pointless to us. It is instructive to compare the list of Nobel Prize winners in literature with those in the sciences; few of the writers from years past are now recognized as creative compared with the scientists.

In order to establish and preserve criteria, a field must have a minimum of organization. However, it is often the case that instead of serving the domain, members of the field devote most of their energies to serving themselves, making it difficult for new ideas to be evaluated on their merits. It is not only the Church that has hindered the spread of new ideas for fear of losing its privileges. Every industry faces the problem that better ideas that require changing the status quo will be ignored, because so much effort and capital has been invested in existing production methods.

Another important dimension along which fields vary is the extent to which they are ideologically open or closed to new memes. The openness of a field depends in part on its internal organization, in part on its relation to the wider society. Highly hierarchical institutions, where knowledge of the past is greatly valued, generally see novelty as a threat. For this reason churches, academies, and certain businesses based on tradition seek to promote older individuals to leadership positions as a way of warding off excessive change. Also, creativity is not welcome in fields whose self-interest requires keeping a small cadre of initiates performing the same routines, regardless of efficiency; some of the trade unions come to mind in this context.

But caution is important for a field, and it is not always dictated by self-interest. When a field is too open and accepts every novelty indiscriminately, the domain risks losing its credibility, and its internal structure is likely to get confusing and unmanageable. It requires an adroit balancing act for those responsible for evaluating novelty to decide which new ideas are worth preserving. If a historical period is stagnant, it is probably not because there were no potentially creative individuals around, but because of the ineptitude of the relevant fields.

It might be objected that some of the most influential new ideas or processes seem to occur even though there is no existing domain or field to receive them. For instance, Freud's ideas had a wide impact even before there was a domain of psychoanalysis or a field of analysts to evaluate them. Personal computers were widely adopted before there was a tradition and a group of experts to judge which were good, which were not. But the lack of a social context in such cases is more apparent than real. Freud, who was immersed in the already-existing domain of psychiatry, simply expanded its limits until his conceptual contributions could stand on their own as a separate domain. And the first field of psychoanalysis was composed of medical men who met with Freud to discuss his ideas and were convinced by them to the point of identifying themselves as practitioners of the new domain. Without peers and without disciples, Freud's ideas might have been original, but they would not have had an impact on the culture, and thus would have failed to be creative. Similarly, personal computers would not have been accepted had there not been a domain – computer languages that allowed the writing of software and, therefore, various applications – and an embryonic field – people who had experience with mainframe computers, with video games, and so on who could become "experts" in this emerging technology.

In any case, the point is that how much creativity there is at any given time is not determined just by how many original individuals are trying to change domains, but also by how receptive the fields are to innovation. It follows that if one wishes to increase the frequency of creativity, it may be more advantageous to work at the level of fields than at the level of individuals. For example, some large organizations such as Motorola, where new technological inventions are essential, spend a large quantity of resources in trying to make engineers think more creatively. This is a good strategy as far as it goes, but it will not result in any increase in creativity unless the field – in this case, management – is able to recognize which of the new ideas are good and has ways for implementing them, that is, including them in the domain. Whereas engineers and managers are the field who judge the creativity of new ideas within an organization such as Motorola, the entire market for electronics becomes the field that evaluates the organization's products once these have been implemented within the organization. Thus, at one level of analysis the system comprises the organization, with innovators, managers, and production engineers as its parts; but at a higher level of analysis the organization becomes just one element of a broader system that includes the entire industry.

THE INDIVIDUAL IN THE CREATIVE PROCESS

When we get to the level of the person, we are immediately on more familiar ground. After all, the great majority of psychological research assumes that creativity is an individual trait, to be understood by studying individuals. For example, a recent analysis of doctoral dissertations on the topic found that 6 out of 10 theses written by psychology Ph.D.'s in 1986 were focused on individual traits (Wehner, Csikszentmihalyi, & Magyari-Beck, 1991), and none dealt with the effects of culture and social groups. Cognitive processes, temperament, early experiences, and personality were the most frequently studied topics.

The systems model makes it possible to see the contributions of the person to the creative process in a theoretically coherent way. In the first place, it brings to attention the fact that before a person can introduce a creative variation, he or she must have access to a domain, and must want to learn to perform according to its rules. This implies that motivation is important – a topic already well understood by scholars in the field of creativity. But it also suggests a number of additional factors that are usually ignored, for instance, that cognitive and motivational factors interact with the state of the domain and the field.

Second, the system model reaffirms the importance of individual factors that contribute to the creative process. Persons who are likely to innovate tend to have personality traits that favor breaking rules and early experiences that make them want to do so. Divergent thinking, problem finding, and all the other factors that psychologists have studied are relevant in this context.

Finally, the ability to convince the field about the virtue of the novelty one has produced is an important aspect of personal creativity. The opportunities that one has to get access to the field, the network of contacts, the personality traits that make it possible for one to be taken seriously, the ability to express oneself in such a way as to be understood, are all part of the individual traits that make it easier for someone to make a creative contribution.

But none of these personal characteristics are sufficient, and probably they are not even necessary. Conservative and unimaginative scientists have made important contributions to science by stumbling on important new phenomena, and primitive painters like Rousseau le Douanier or Grandma Moses, who were trying to be traditional but could not quite paint realistically enough, have been seen as having contributed to the history of art. At the same time, it is probably true that persons who can master a domain, and then want to change it, will have a higher proportion of their efforts recognized as creative. So we shall review briefly now what the characteristics of such persons are, starting with a consideration of the background factors that have a bearing on the production of novelty.

The Background of Creative Individuals

One of the first issues to consider is whether an individual is born in an environment that has enough surplus energy to encourage the development of curiosity and interest for its own sake (Table 16.5). Even though it is said that necessity is the mother of invention, too much deprivation does not seem to lead to innovative thinking. When survival is precarious – as it has been and still is in most of the world – there is little energy left for learning and experimenting. The lack of books, schooling, and intellectual stimulation will have obvious detrimental effects. It is not impossible for a talented person to emerge from a ghetto or a third-world country, but much potential is lost for lack of access to the basic tools of a domain.

Ethnic groups, and families within them, differ in the amount of importance they place on different domains. Jewish tradition has emphasized the importance of learning, and Asian-American families have instilled strong academic and artistic motivation in their children (Kao, 1995). Some cultural groups emphasize musical abilities, others focus on engineering or technology. Such traditions help to focus a child's interest on a particular domain, thus providing the preconditions for further innovation.

Cultural capital consists in the educational aspirations of one's parents, the nonacademic knowledge one absorbs in the home, the informal learning that one picks up from home and community. Moreover, it involves the learning opportunities that include schooling, the availability of mentors, exposure to books, computers, museums, musical instruments, and so forth. Even in very poor families, when the parents read books to children, this seems to help the latter to become involved in intellectual pursuits and to break away from their destitute conditions (Beattie & Csikszentmihalyi, 1981). Parental expectations for educational attainment are also an important component of a child's cultural capital.

Another important aspect of personal background that has bearing on creativity is whether the child will have access to the field. In many domains it is indispensible for a young person to be trained by experts as soon as possible (Bloom, 1985). To study physics or music long enough to be able to innovate in it depends in part on whether there are laboratories or conservatories in which one can practice and learn state-of-the-art knowledge in the particular domain. Parents have to be able to afford tutors, as well as have the time and resources needed to drive the child back and forth to lessons and competitions. The careers of creative individuals are often determined by chance encounters with mentors who will open doors for them, and such encounters are more likely in places where the field is more densely represented – certain university departments, laboratories, or centers of artistic activity.

It has been observed that many creative individuals grew up in atypical conditions, on the margins of the community. Many of them were orphaned early, had to struggle against relative poverty and prejudice, or were otherwise singled out as different from their peers (Csikszentmihalyi & Csikszentmihalyi, 1993). For example, all seven of the creative geniuses

Table 16.5. *Questions and Hypotheses Concerning How Personal Background Affects the Incidence of Creativity*

1. Do the family and community have surplus energy available?

   A child is likely to be discouraged from expressing curiosity and interest if the material conditions of existence are too precarious.

2. Is there a tradition of respect for learning and culture in the child's environment?

   Ethnic and family traditions can have a very important role in directing the child's interest toward specific domains.

3. Is the family able to introduce the child to a domain?

   Cultural capital (i.e., home learning, schooling) is essential for a child to develop expertise in a domain.

4. Is the family able to connect the child with the field?

   Tutors, mentors, and connections are often indispensable for advancing far enough to have one's ideas recognized.

5. Do early conditions support conformity or innovation?

   Marginality (social, ethnic, economic, religious) seems to be more conducive to wanting to break out of the norm than a conventional, middle-class background.

of this century described by Gardner (1993) were outsiders to the societies in which they worked: Einstein moved from Germany to Switzerland, Italy, and the United States; Gandhi grew up in South Africa; Stravinsky left Russia; Eliot settled in England; Martha Graham as a child moved from the South to California, where she became exposed to and influenced by Asian art. Freud was Jewish in Catholic Vienna; and Picasso left Spain for France. It seems that a person who is comfortably settled in the bosom of society has fewer incentives to change the status quo.

Personal Qualities

Having the right background conditions is indispensible but certainly not sufficient for a person to make a creative contribution. He or she must also have the ability and inclination to introduce novelty into the domain. These are the traits that psychologists have most often studied, and it is to these that we shall now turn (Table 16.6). Because the individual traits of creative people have been so widely studied, I shall touch on them only briefly and without being able to do them justice.

Talent, or innate ability, refers to the fact that it is easier to be creative if one is born with a physical endowment that helps to master the skills required by the domain. Great musicians seem to be unusually sensitive to sounds even in their earliest years, and artists seem to be sensitive to color, light, and shapes even before they start practicing their craft. If we extend the definition of creativity to domains such as basketball – and in principle there is no reason for not doing so – then it is clear that a creative player like Michael Jordan benefits from unusual physical coordination. At this point, we know very little about the relationship between brain organization and the ability to perform in specific domains. It would not be surprising, however, to find that interest or skill in certain domains can be inherited. Howard Gardner's (1983, 1993) postulate of seven or more separate forms of intelligence also seems to support the notion that each of us might be born with a propensity to respond to a different slice of reality, and hence to operate more effectively in one domain rather than another. Many creative individuals display unusual early abilities that are almost at the

Table 16.6. *Questions and Hypotheses Concerning How Individual Qualities Affect the Incidence of Creativity*

1. Does the person have special talents?

   In certain domains (e.g., music, mathematics), genetic inheritance may play an important role in directing interest to the domain and in helping to master it.

2. Is the person curious, interested, intrinsically motivated?

   A great deal of intrinsic motivation is needed to energize the person to absorb the relevant memes and to persevere in the risky process of innovation.

3. Is the person a divergent thinker interested in discovery?

   Cognitive abilities such as fluency, flexibility, and discovery orientation seem necessary to engage successfully in the process of generating novelty.

4. Does the person have the relevant personality traits?

   To be able to innovate successfully, a person needs to have appropriate traits – which may vary depending on the field and the historical period. In general, one must persevere and be open to experience, as well as adopt apparently contradictory behaviors.

level of the child prodigies described by Feldman (1986). On the other hand, a roughly equal number who have achieved comparable creative contributions appear to have had rather undistinguished childhoods and were not recognized as exceptional until early adulthood.

Clearly very little is known as yet about the relationship of central nervous system structures and creativity, although many claims are being made these days with limited support. For instance, cerebral lateralization research has led many people to claim that left-handers or ambidextrous individuals, who are presumed to be using the right side of their brains more than right-handers, are more likely to be creative. Left-handers are apparently over-represented in such fields as art, architecture, and music; many exceptional individuals from Alexander the Great to Leonardo, Michelangelo, Raphael, Picasso, Einstein, and the three presidential candidates of the 1992 election – Clinton, Bush, Perot – were all left-handers (Coren, 1992; Paul, 1993). Suggestive as such trends might be, there is also evidence that left-handed persons are much more prone to a variety of unusual pathologies (Coren, 1992 pp. 197–220); thus, whatever neurological difference handedness makes might not be directly linked to creativity, but rather to deviancy from the norm that can take either a positive or a negative value.

Perhaps the most salient characteristic of creative individuals is a constant curiosity, an ever renewed interest in whatever happens around them. This enthusiasm for experience is often seen as part of the "childishness" attributed to creative individuals (Csikszentmihalyi, 1996; Gardner, 1993). Without this interest, a person would be unlikely to become immersed deeply enough in a domain to be able to change it. Another way of describing this trait is that creative people are intrinsically motivated. They find their reward in the activity itself, without having to wait for external rewards or recognition. A recurring refrain among them goes something like this: "You could say that I worked every day of my life, or with equal justice you could say that I never did any work in my life." Such an attitude greatly helps a person to persevere during the long stretches of the creative process when no external recognition is forthcoming.

The importance of motivation for creativity has long been recognized. Cox (1920) advised that if one had to bet on who is more likely to achieve a creative breakthrough, a highly intelligent but not very motivated person, or one less intelligent but more motivated, one should always bet on the second. Because introducing novelty in a system is always a risky and usually an unrewarded affair, it takes a great deal of motivation to persevere in the effort. One recent formulation of the creative person's willingness to take risks is the "economic" model of Sternberg and Lubart (1995).

Probably the most extensively studied attributes of the creative cognitive style are divergent thinking (Guilford, 1967) and discovery orientation (Getzels & Csikszentmihalyi, 1976). Divergent thinking – usually indexed by fluency, flexibility, and originality of mental operations – is routinely measured by psychological tests given to children; such tests show modest correlations with childish measures of creativity, such as the originality of stories told or pictures drawn (Runco, 1991). Whether these tests also relate to creativity in "real" adult settings is not clear, although some claims to that effect have been made (Milgram, 1990; Torrance, 1988). Discovery orientation, or the tendency to find and formulate problems where others have not seen any, has also been measured in selected situations, with some encouraging results (Baer, 1993; Runco, 1995). As Einstein and many others have observed, the solution of problems is a much simpler affair than their formulation. Anyone who is technically proficient can solve a problem that is already formulated; but it takes true originality to formulate a problem in the first place (Einstein & Infeld, 1938).

Some scholars dispute the notion that problem finding and problem solving involve different thought processes; for example the Nobel Prize–winning economist and psychologist Herbert Simon (1985, 1989) has claimed that all creative achievements are the result of normal problem solving. However, the evidence he presents, based on computer simulation of scientific breakthroughs, is not relevant to the claim, since the computers are fed preselected data, preselected logical algorithms, and a routine for recognizing the correct solution – all of which are absent in real historical discoveries (Csikszentmihalyi, 1988a, 1988c).

The personality of creative persons has also been exhaustively investigated (Barron, 1969, 1988). Psychoanalytic theory has stressed the ability to regress into the unconscious while still maintaining conscious ego controls as one of the hallmarks of creativity (Kris, 1952). The widespread use of multifactor personality inventories suggest that creative individuals tend to be strong on certain traits, such as introversion and self-reliance, and low on others, such as conformity and moral certainty (Csikszentmihalyi & Getzels, 1973; Getzels & Csikszentmihalyi, 1976; Russ, 1993).

There is a long tradition of associating creativity with mental illness, or genius with insanity (Jacobson, 1912; Lombroso, 1891). Recent surveys have added new credence to this tradition by demonstrating rather convincingly that the rate of various pathologies such as suicide, alcoholism, drug addiction, and institutionalization for nervous diseases is much higher than expected in certain "creative" domains, such as drama, poetry, and music (Jablow & Lieb, 1988; Jamison, 1989; Martindale, 1989; Richards, 1990). These results, however, demonstrate only that some fields, ones that in our culture get little support, are associated with pathology either because they attract persons who are exceptionally sensitive (Mitchell, 1972; Piechowski, 1991) or because they can offer only depressing careers. They may have little or nothing to say about creativity itself.

One view I have developed on the basis of my studies is that creative persons are characterized not so much by single traits, as by their ability to operate through the entire spectrum of personality dimensions. So they are not just introverted, but can be both extroverted and introverted, depending on the phase of the process they happen to be involved in at the moment. When gathering ideas, a creative scientist is gregarious and sociable; when starting to work, he or she might become a secluded hermit for weeks on end. Creative individuals are sensitive and aloof, dominant and humble, masculine and feminine, as the occasion demands (Csikszentmihalyi, 1996). What dictates their behavior is not a rigid inner structure, but the demands of the interaction between them and the domain in which they are working.

In order to want to introduce novelty into a domain, a person should first of all be dissatisfied with the status quo. It has been said that Einstein explained why he spent so much time developing a new physics by saying that he could not understand the old physics. Greater sensitivity, naiveté, arrogance, impatience, and higher intellectual standards have all been adduced as reasons why some people are unable to accept the conventional wisdom in a domain and feel the need to break out of it.

Values also play a role in developing a creative career. There are indications that if a person holds financial and social goals in high esteem, it is less likely that he or she will continue for long to brave the insecurities involved in the production of novelty, and will tend to settle instead for a more conventional career (Csikszentmihalyi, Getzels, & Kahn, 1984; Getzels & Csikszentmihalyi, 1976). A person who is attracted to the solution of abstract problems (theoretical value) and to order and beauty (aesthetic value) is more likely to persevere.

How these patterns of cognition, personality, and motivation develop is still not clear. Some may be under heavy genetic control, while others develop under the conscious direction of the self-organizing person. In any case, the presence of such traits is likely to make a person more creative if the conjunction with the other elements of the system – the field and the domain – happen to be propitious.

INTERNALIZING THE CREATIVE SYSTEM

In order to function well within the creative system, one must internalize the rules of the domain and the opinions of the field, so that one can choose the most promising ideas to work on, and do so in a way that will be acceptable to one's peers. Practically all creative individuals say that one advantage they have is that they are confident that they can tell which of their own ideas are bad, and thus they can forget the bad ones without investing too much energy in them. For example Linus Pauling, who won the Nobel Prize twice, was asked at his 60th birthday party how he had been able to come up with so many epochal discoveries. "It's easy," he is said to have answered. "You think of a lot of ideas, and throw away the bad ones." To be able to do so, however, implies that one has a very strong internal representation of which ideas are good and which are bad, a representation that matches closely the one accepted by the field.

An extremely lucid example of how a person internalizes the system is given by the inventor Jacob Rabinow, who has over 200 patents on a variety of very different inventions (Csikszentmihalyi, 1996). In addition to being a prolific inventor himself, he is also prominent in the field because he works for the Patent Office, and hence decides which inventions by other individuals deserve recognition. In describing what it takes to be an original thinker, Rabinow mentions first the importance of the domain:

So you need three things to be an original thinker. First, you have to have a tremendous amount of information – a big database if you like to be fancy. If you're a musician, you should know a lot about music, that is, you've heard music, you remember music, you could repeat a song if you have to. In other words, if you were born on a desert island and never heard music, you're not likely to be a Beethoven. You might, but it's not likely. You may imitate birds but you're not going to write the Fifth Symphony. So you're brought up in an atmosphere where you store a lot of information.

So you have to have the kind of memory that you need for the kind of things you want to do. And . . . you get better and better by doing the things you do well, and eventually you become either a great tennis player or a good inventor or whatever, because you tend to do those things which you do well and the more you do, the easier it gets, and the easier it gets, the better you do it, and eventually you become very one-sided but you're very good at it and you're lousy at everything else because you don't do it well. This is what engineers call positive feedback. The small differences at the beginning of life become enormous differences by the time you've done it for 40, 50, 80 years as I've done it. So anyway, first you have to have the big database. (p. 48)

Next Rabinow brings up what the person must contribute, which is mainly a question of motivation, or the enjoyment one feels when playing (or working?) with the contents of the domain:

Then you have to be willing to pull the ideas, because you're interested. Now, some people could do it, but they don't bother. They're interested in doing something else. So if you ask them, they'll, as a favor to you, say: "Yeah, I can think of something." But there are people like myself who like to do it. It's fun to come up with an idea, and if nobody wants it, I don't give a damn. It's just fun to come up with something strange and different. (p. 48)

Finally he focuses on how important it is to reproduce in one's mind the criteria of judgment that the field uses:

And then you must have the ability to get rid of the trash which you think of. You cannot think only of good ideas, or write only beautiful music. You must think of a lot of music, a lot of ideas, a lot of poetry, a lot of whatever. And if you're good, you must be able to throw out the junk immediately without even saying it. In other words, you get many ideas appearing and you discard them because you're well trained and you say, "that's junk." And then you see the good one, you say, "Oops, this sounds interesting. Let me pursue that a little further." And you start developing it. . . . And by the way, if you're not well trained, but you've got ideas, and you don't know if they're good or bad, then you send them to the Bureau of Standards, National Institute of Standards, where I work, and we evaluate them. And we throw them out. (p. 49)

CONCLUSION

It is certain that psychologists interested in the phenomenon of creativity will continue to focus on the individual and his or her thought processes. After all, the unique qualities of creative geniuses are so attractive that we can't curb our curiosity about them. What the present chapter seeks to accomplish, however, is to point out that creativity cannot be recognized except as it operates within a system of cultural rules, and it cannot bring forth anything new unless it can enlist the support of peers. If these conclusions are accepted, then it follows that the occurrence of creativity is not simply a function of how many gifted individuals there are, but also of how accessible the various symbolic systems are and how responsive the social system is to novel ideas. Instead of focusing exclusively on individuals, it will make more sense to focus on communities that may or may not nurture genius. In the last analysis, it is the community and not the individual who makes creativity manifest.

NOTE

This chapter was prepared in part with support from the Spencer Foundation.

REFERENCES

Baer, J. (1993). *Creativity and divergent thinking.* Hillsdale, NJ: Erlbaum.
Barron, F. (1969). *Creative person and creative process.* New York: Holt, Rinehart, & Winston.
Barron, F. (1988). Putting creativity to work. In R. J. Sternberg (Ed.), *The nature of creativity* (pp. 76–98). Cambridge University Press.
Beattie, O., & Csikszentmihalyi, M. (1981). On the socialization influence of books. *Child Psychology and Human Development, 11*(1), 3–18.
Bloom, B. (1985). *Developing talent in young people.* New York: Ballantine.
Campbell, D. T. (1976). Evolutionary epistemology. In D. A. Schlipp (Ed.), *The library of living philosophers: Karl Popper.* La Salle, IL: Open Court.
Coren, S. (1992). *The left-handed syndrome: The causes and consequences of left-handedness.* New York: Free Press.
Cox, C. (1926). *The early mental traits of three hundred geniuses.* Stanford, CA: Stanford University Press.

Csikszentmihalyi, M. (1988a). Motivation and creativity: Toward a synthesis of structural and energistic approaches to cognition. *New Ideas in Psychology, 6*(2), 159–176.
Csikszentmihalyi, M. (1988b). Society, culture, person: A systems view of creativity. In R. J. Sternberg (Ed.), *The nature of creativity* (pp. 325–339). Cambridge University Press.
Csikszentmihalyi, M. (1988c). Solving a problem is not finding a new one: A reply to Simon. *New Ideas in Psychology, 6*(2), 183–186.
Csikszentmihalyi, M. (1990). The domain of creativity. In M. A. Runco & R. S. Albert (Eds.), *Theories of creativity* (pp. 190–212). Newbury Park, CA: Sage.
Csikszentmihalyi, M. (1993). *The evolving self: A psychology for the third millennium.* New York: HarperCollins.
Csikszentmihalyi, M. (1996). *Creativity: Flow and the psychology of discovery and invention.* New York: HarperCollins.
Csikszentmihalyi, M., & Csikszentmihalyi, I. S. (1993). Family influences on the development of giftedness. In *The origins and development of high ability* (pp. 187–206). Chichester: Wiley (Ciba Foundation Symposium 178).
Csikszentmihalyi, M., & Getzels, J. W. (1973). The personality of young artists: An empirical and theoretical exploration. *British Journal of Psychology, 64*(1), 91–104.
Csikszentmihalyi, M., & Getzels, J. W. (1988). Creativity and problem finding. In F. G. Farley & N. R. W. (Eds.), *The foundations of aesthetics, art, and art education* (pp. 91–106). New York: Praeger.
Csikszentmihalyi, M., Getzels, J. W., & Kahn, S. P. (1984). *Talent and achievement: A longitudinal study of artists* (A report to the Spencer Foundation). Chicago: University of Chicago.
Csikszentmihalyi, M., Rathunde, K., & Whalen, S. (1993). *Talented teenagers: The roots of success and failure.* Cambridge University Press.
Csikszentmihalyi, M., & Sawyer, K. (1995). Shifting the focus from individual to organizational creativity. In C. M. Ford & D. A. Gioia (Eds.), *Creative action in organizations* (pp. 167–172). Thousand Oaks, CA: Sage.
Dawkins, R. (1976). *The selfish gene.* Oxford: Oxford University Press.
Dunbar, K. (1993). Scientific reasoning strategies for concept discovery in a complex domain. *Cognitive Science, 17,* 397–434.
Durkheim, E. (1912/1967). *The elementary forms of religious life.* New York: Free Press.
Einstein, A., & Infeld, L. (1938). *The evolution of physics.* New York: Simon & Schuster.
Feldman, D. (1986). *Nature's gambit: Child prodigies and the development of human potential.* New York: Basic.
Feldman, D., Csikszentmihalyi, M., & Gardner, H. (1994). *Changing the world: A framework for the study of creativity.* Westport, CT: Praeger.
Gardner, H. (1983). *Frames of mind: The theory of multiple intelligences.* New York: Basic.
Gardner, H. (1993). *Creating minds.* New York: Basic.
Getzels, J. W., & Csikszentmihalyi, M. (1976). *The creative vision: A longitudinal study of problem finding in art.* New York: Wiley.
Gruber, H. (1988). The evolving systems approach to creative work. *Creativity Research Journal, 1*(1), 27–51.
Guilford, J. P. (1967). *The nature of human intelligence.* New York: McGraw-Hill.
Harrington, D. M. (1990). The ecology of human creativity: A psychological perspective. In M. A. Runco & R. S. Albert (Eds.), *Theories of creativity* (pp. 143–169). Newbury Park, CA: Sage.
Hauser, A. (1951). *The social history of art.* New York: Vintage.
Heydenreich, L. H. (1974). *Il primo rinascimento.* Milano: Rizzoli.
Jablow, H. D., & Lieb, J. (1988). *The key to genius: Manic-depression and the creative life.* Buffalo, NY: Prometheus.
Jacobson, A. C. (1912). Literary genius and manic depressive insanity. *Medical Record, 82,* 937–939.
Jamison, K. R. (1989). Mood disorders and patterns of creativity in British writers and artists. *Psychiatry, 52,* 125–134.
Kao, G. (1995). Asian Americans as model minorities? A look at their academic performance. *American Journal of Education, 103,* 121–159.
Kasof, J. (1995). Explaining creativity: The attributional perspective. *Creativity Research Journal, 8*(4), 311–366.
Kris, E. (1952). *Psychoanalytic explorations in art.* New York: International Universities Press.
Kuhn, T. S. (1962). *The structure of scientific revolutions.* Chicago: University of Chicago Press.
Lombroso, C. (1891). *The man of genius.* London: Walter Scott.
Magyari-Beck, I. (1988). New concepts about personal creativity. *Creativity and Innovation Yearbook, 1.* Manchester: Manchester Business School, pp. 121–126.

Martindale, C. (1989). Personality, situation, and creativity. In R. R. J. Glover & C. R. Reynolds (Eds.), *Handbook of creativity* (pp. 211–232). New York: Plenum.

Maslow, A. H. (1963). The creative attitude. *Structuralist, 3*, 4–10.

Mayr, E. (1982). *The growth of biological thought.* Cambridge, MA: Belknap.

Milgram, R. M. (1990). Creativity: An idea whose time has come and gone? In M. A. Runco & R. S. Albert (Eds.), *Theories of creativity* (pp. 215–233). Newbury Park, CA: Sage.

Mitchell, A. R. (1972). *Schizophrenia: The meaning of madness.* New York: Taplinger.

Mockros, C., & Csikszentmihalyi, M. (in press). The social construction of creative lives. In R. Purser & A. Montuori (Eds.), *Social creativity.* Creskill, NY: Hampton.

Paul, D. (1993). *Left-handed helpline.* Manchester: Dextral.

Piaget, J. (1965). *The moral judgment of the child.* New York: Free Press.

Piechowski, M. J. (1991). Emotional development and emotional giftedness. In N. Colangelo & G. A. Davis (Eds.), *Handbook of gifted education* (pp. 285–306). Boston: Allyn & Bacon.

Richards, R. (1990). Everyday creativity, eminent creativity, and health. *Creativity Research Journal, 3,* 300–326.

Runco, M. A. (1991). *Divergent thinking.* Norwood, NJ: Ablex.

Runco, M. A. (Ed.). (1995). *Problem finding.* Norwood, NJ: Ablex.

Russ, S. W. (1993). *Affect and creativity.* Hillsdale, NJ: Erlbaum.

Simon, H. A. (1985). *Psychology of scientific discovery.* Keynote presentation at the 93rd annual meeting of the American Psychological Association, Los Angeles, CA.

Simon, H. A. (1988). Creativity and motivation: A response to Csikszentmihalyi. *New Ideas in Psychology, 6*(2), 177–181.

Simonton, D. K. (1988). *Scientific genius.* Cambridge University Press.

Simonton, D. K. (1990). Political pathology and societal creativity. *Creativity Research Journal, 3*(2), 85–99.

Simonton, D. K. (1991). Personality correlates of exceptional personal influence. *Creativity Research Journal, 4,* 67–68.

Simonton, D. K. (1994). *Greatness: Who makes history and why.* New York: Guilford.

Stein, M. I. (1953). Creativity and culture. *Journal of Psychology, 36,* 311–322.

Stein, M. I. (1963). A transactional approach to creativity. In C. W. Taylor & F. Barron (Eds.), *Scientific creativity* (pp. 217–227). New York: Wiley.

Sternberg, R. J., & Lubart, T. I. (1995). *Defying the crowd: Cultivating creativity in a culture of conformity.* New York: Free Press.

Therivel, W. A. (1995). Long-term effect of power on creativity. *Creativity Research Journal, 8,* 173–92.

Torrance, E. P. (1988). The nature of creativity as manifest in its testing. In R. J. Sternberg (Ed.), *The nature of creativity* (pp. 43–75). Cambridge University Press.

Wehner, L., Csikszentmihalyi, M., & Magyari-Beck, I. (1991). Current approaches used in studying creativity: An exploratory investigation. *Creativity Research Journal, 4*(3), 261–271.

PART V

Special Topics in Creativity

17   Creativity Across Cultures

TODD I. LUBART

Creativity does not occur in a vacuum. When we examine a creative person, creative product, or creative process, we often ignore the environmental milieu. We decontextualize creativity. The environment, however, is always present and can have a profound effect on creative expression. The environment may be involved in stimulating and supporting creativity as well as defining and evaluating it.

In this vein, recent theories have acknowledged that a confluence of environment-centered variables and person-centered variables (intelligence, knowledge, cognitive styles, personality, and motivation) is necessary for creativity (Amabile, 1983; Arieti, 1976; Csikszentmihalyi, 1988; Gruber, 1989; Sternberg & Lubart, 1991, 1995). Concerning the environment, we can identify a set of interrelated contexts that influence creativity. These include the physical setting, the family, the school or workplace, the field of endeavor, and the culture. This chapter focuses on the effect of the cultural environment on creativity.

Culture refers to a shared system of cognitions, behaviors, customs, values, rules, and symbols concerning the manner in which a set of people interact with their social and physical environment (Reber, 1985; Triandis, 1996). Culture is learned and socially transmitted from generation to generation. Cultural groups are often identified at the societal level, following geopolitical boundaries. Within these cultural groups there may be identifiable sub-cultures based on age (e.g., teen culture), socioeconomic class, religion, or other characteristics. In this chapter, twentieth-century cultures, defined at the societal level, will be examined. Because cultures are dynamic and change over time, the studies of diverse cultures presented here should be considered as snapshots of a particular culture at a particular point in time. These snapshots will show the main ways in which creativity varies across cultures. There are effects on the conception of creativity, the creative process, the direction of creativity toward certain domains of activity or certain social groups, and the extent to which creativity is nutured.

CONCEPTIONS OF CREATIVITY

Creativity from a Western perspective can be defined as the ability to produce work that is novel and appropriate (Barron, 1988; Jackson & Messick, 1967; Lubart, 1994; MacKinnon, 1962; Ochse, 1990; Stein, 1953). Novel work is original, not predicted, and distinct from previous work. Appropriate work satisfies the problem constraints, is useful, or fulfills a need. Creativity can occur in virtually any domain, including the visual arts, literature, music, business, science, education, and everyday life.

An important feature of Western creativity seems to be its relationship to an observable product (Hughes & Drew, 1984). This product can be assessed by an appropriate group of judges, either peers or experts. Amabile (1983) proposes that the creativity of a product is, to a large extent, a social judgment. Consistent with the conception of creativity already proposed, when raters assess products such as poems or drawings for creativity, the qualities of novelty and appropriateness to the topic play an important role in their judgments (Amabile, 1982; Lubart & Sternberg, 1995).

The widely used Torrance Tests of Creative Thinking also provide evidence of a product-oriented, originality-based definition (Torrance, 1974). Creativity is assessed through tasks such as the generation of questions about a scene, the construction of a picture using a certain colored shape, and the generation of unusual uses for a common object. The tasks are scored for fluidity (the number of ideas), flexibility (the diversity of ideas), and originality (the rarity of ideas), which together indicate the level of creative performance.

In contrast to the Western conception of creativity, it is possible to distinguish an alternative, Eastern view. The Eastern conception of creativity seems less focused on innovative products. Instead, creativity involves a state of personal fulfillment, a connection to a primordial realm, or the expression of an inner essence or ultimate reality (Chu, 1970; Kuo, 1996; Mathur, 1982). Creativity is related to meditation because it helps one to see the true nature of the self, an object, or an event (Chu, 1970; Onda, 1962). This conceptualization is similar to humanistic psychology's conception of creativity as part of self-actualization (see Sarnoff & Cole, 1983). Krippner and Arons (1973) state:

> The [Western] creative worker is predatory: he grabs the insight for a [specific] purpose. . . . Robert Louis Stevenson reported that he was able to control his dreams for creative purposes, his short story, "The Strange Case of Dr. Jekyll and Mr. Hyde" being the best-known of this ability. . . . A process-oriented, rather than product-oriented creative person would use insight-producing states to . . . obtain "enlightenment." (p. 121)

An anthropological field study of 155 traditional painters in India offers further support for an Eastern view of creativity. In this study, the creative artist is one who contacts the "psychic reality within the depths of himself, . . . strive[s] to make it manifest, . . . to become one with it, integrating it through differentiation, meditation, and self-realization. In a very real sense, the artist is enjoined to re-create, or reactivate, what is already latent in his unconscious" (Maduro, 1976, p. 135).

In Hinduism, creativity is seen as spiritual or religious expression rather than as an innovative solution to a problem (see Aron & Aron, 1982; Sherr, 1982). Hallman (1970) regards the reduced emphasis on originality as the greatest difference between Hindu and Western definitions of creativity. In Hindu cosmology, time and history are seen as cyclical. "To create is to imitate the spiritual, . . . to make traditional truths come alive and become operative in daily affairs" (Hallman, 1970, p. 373). Thus, in the Eastern view, creativity seems to involve the reinterpretation of traditional ideas – finding a new point of view – whereas in the Western approach, creativity involves a break with tradition (Kristeller, 1983).

Given the divergent conceptions that different cultures may have for the same term, it is interesting, however, that creativity is generally viewed as a positive construct (Chu, 1970; Joncich, 1964). Evidence of this positive view of creativity in the West can be found in the desire of schools to promote creativity and in the large number of creativity self-help books in the popular press (Adams, 1974/1986; Walberg, 1988). In non-Western settings, gods of originality are worshiped and creative individuals are praised. For example, creative architectural geniuses among West African Hausa are admired and emulated by builders (Saad, 1985). In the Benin culture, the deity Olokun, god of inspiration and idealism, is revered (Ben-Amos, 1986). Olokun can influence artists through dreams and enhance their originality. Similarly, the Hindu god Vishvakarma, spirit of the creative process, was described with great significance and stature by Indian artists (Maduro, 1976). However, as described later, cultures vary in the relative importance given to creativity. Also, Wonder and Blake

(1992) argue that the Eastern view centers on artistic, poetic, and everyday life domains of creative activity because people can draw upon their own experiences in these domains.

Given the different Western and Eastern views of creativity, the question of their origin can be raised. Modern conceptions of creativity may derive from cultures' creation myths (Mason, 1988; Sinclair, 1971). In other words, creation myths may provide a prototype for framing implicit conceptions of human creativity (von Franz, 1995). The Eastern view of cosmic creation can be characterized as "an ongoing process – a developing, an unfolding" (Sinclair, 1971, p. 83). The Eastern concept of creativity stresses similar themes of development and progress toward the realization of the nature of the universe. If Eastern creation (and human creativity) can be characterized as a circular movement in the sense of successive reconfigurations of an initial totality, then the Western view of both creation and human creativity seems to involve a linear movement toward a new point (see von Franz, 1995). Judeo-Christian views of cosmic creation involve the "production of the universe . . . by an uncreated being who brings order to the formless void" (Sinclair, 1971, p. 84). The Book of Genesis states that creation took six days of labor and each day resulted in observable progress (such as the formation of land). The contemporary Western concept of creativity fits this view in the sense that creativity is viewed as an insightful production achieved by an individual engaged in a working process with a finite beginning and end (Mason, 1988; Wonder & Blake, 1992).

Offering further support for the creation myth–conception of creativity link, some creation myths view the Creator in terms of a craftsman (potter, weaver, blacksmith, carpenter, etc.), and human creativity involves following this divine craft (Ben-Amos, 1986; von Franz, 1995). Taking an African creation myth as an example, Nommo, a primordial being, wove together four elements to make the universe; contemporary weavers, by drawing threads from the spindles of a loom, are viewed as symbolically reenacting the creation event (Ben-Amos, 1986). In summary, modern views of creativity seem to echo cultural creation myths and may derive from them.

CULTURAL VARIATION IN THE CREATIVE PROCESS

In addition to culturally based conceptions of creativity, descriptions of the creative process exist for both the Western and Eastern views of creativity. The most widely cited Western description of the creative process involves four stages: preparation, incubation, illumination, and verification (Hadamard, 1945; Poincaré, 1921; Ribot, 1906; Rossman, 1931; Wallas, 1926). Preparation consists of preliminary analysis of a problem and initial conscious work on the task. Incubation follows and may involve active unconscious work on the problem, automatic spreading of activation in memory, associative play, or simply forgetting unimportant problem details and resting mentally. Illumination occurs when a promising idea suddenly becomes consciously available. Metaphorically a lightbulb goes off in a person's head. Ideas may break into consciousness because of their aesthetic value or cognitive coherence. The creative idea is then evaluated, developed, and refined during the verification stage. Although the validity of this four-stage process is debatable, introspective accounts by Western creators and think-aloud protocols of Western painters and poets at work have often been viewed as supportive of this framework (Ghiselin, 1952/1985; Patrick, 1935, 1937). For our analysis, the most important feature of the Western process model is its cognitive problem-solving orientation, which fits well with a product-oriented definition of creativity.

Evidence for an alternative process model congruent with the Eastern definition of creativity comes, in part, from Maduro's (1976) study of Indian painters, which was mentioned earlier. The painters describe a four-stage model based on the Yoga Sutras. The first stage is preparatory but differs from the Western model: "The artist attempts to contact by self-will and ceaseless effort the subjective region of his mind. . . . The artist removes himself symbolically from the normal world by burning incense . . . to deities [and] . . . prays for inspiration from Vishvakarma [the patron of creativity]" (Maduro, 1976, p. 143). The second stage is achievement of an internal identification with the subject matter of the painting. As one artist describes for a religious painting, "Only after becoming the deity in his feelings can the artist paint creatively" (p. 146). The third stage is one of insight similar to illumination. However, the insights seem to be more personal- than product- or subject-oriented. The last stage involves the social communication of personal realizations and is similar to the verification stage of the Western model.

In another description of the Eastern creative process, Chaudhuri (quoted in Chu, 1970) explains that literary creators and visual artists begin with meditation, which results in "an unbroken flow of sense impressions and images relating to their object." This flow can lead to "a flash of aesthetic insight into the heart of the object." "The artist experiences intimate oneness, the spirit of the object. . . . [which] causes creative inspiration" (pp. 40–41). In contrast to the Western process description, emotional, personal, and intrapsychic elements are emphasized in the Eastern creative process.

CULTURE AS A CHANNEL FOR CREATIVITY

Beyond the conception of creativity, culture influences the manifestation of creativity in terms of the forms and domains of creativity, the limitation of creativity to certain social groups, and the effects of language on creativity.

Forms and Domains of Creativity

Culture encourages creativity in some situations and for some topics but discourages it for others. For example, Mar'i and Karayanni (1983) observed that many Arab students' responses to the question, "What would happen if mules and other animals which help us plow the farm cease to exist?" were elaborate and original. However, a religious question – "What would happen if worship places cease to exist?" – yielded shallow responses or those that rejected the question. For the Ashanti, an African group, creativity is encouraged in the carving of secular objects but discouraged for objects depicting religious motifs (Silver, 1981). For traditional Indian painters, Pichwai paintings of the Shri Nathji idol or other religious topics are the most important genre. Depiction of a fundamental motif is not open to change, but creativity can play a role in the depiction of subthemes. In landscape paintings, a greater degree of stylistic variation is permitted. Paintings produced for popular calendars, a third genre, are seen as a leisure-time form of painting and show the most creativity (Maduro, 1976).

Taken together these instances of selectivity for creativity suggest that the level of creativity permitted on a topic is often inversely related to the topic's role in the maintenance of deep cultural patterns. Ludwig (1992) draws on Margaret Mead's studies of Bali to illustrate this idea. In Bali, "The more serious the art form, like sculptures of gods or ritual dances, the less the permitted change, and the less serious the art form, like carvings of kitchen gods, the theatrical performances of clowns, the playing of instruments or the weaving of containers, the greater the originality can be" (p. 456). In general, although creativity is possible for topics such as social organization, economics, and religion, it may be relatively rare because these topics are involved in maintaining basic cultural patterns (Bascom, 1969).

Within a culturally selected domain, the expression of creativity may be further specified. Consider Samoan dance as an example:

Each Samoan is expected to create his or her individual style within the basic framework of three larger styles: the women's, the boys', and the comedians'. But a dancer, no matter how original, does not compose new steps, nor does the over-all order of the positions change. . . . There are no fundamental structural changes in the dance in Samoan culture. Creativity occurs [in minute changes] on the surface level because the culture [allows and rewards it on that level]. (Colligan, 1983, p. 42)

In Yoruba figure carvings, the ear and human face are treated in a standardized fashion; creative variation occurs in the objects held in the hand of the figure, ritual items and costume associated with the figure, and the arrangement of figures in relationship to each other (Bascom, 1969). Further examples of limitations on the scope of creativity within a domain can be found in Yurok-Karok basket weaving and Pueblo Indian pottery (Biebuyck, 1969). In both cases, aspects of craft design are rigid but decoration is open to variation.

Social Structure and Creativity

Several examples of musical creativity illustrate how cultures can restrict creativity based on social structure. In the Omaha Indian culture, tradition demands that there is "but one way to sing a song"; if a religious song is sung to an incorrect tune, ritual weeping occurs (Colligan, 1983). New melodies can be introduced, however, by elite males who are part of a medicine society and conceive songs on vision quests. In general, musical creativity is inhibited. For a certain social group, however, creativity is allowed.

Musical creativity in Bali is restricted in a different manner. Innovation in musical composition is seen as a group endeavor. Groups of musicians are expected to differ in style from each other. Individual musicians, however, are expected to be stereotyped, anonymous contemporaries with regard to creativity (Colligan, 1983; Gaines & Price-Williams, 1990). This type of channeling effect on creativity may derive from a culture's position on an individualism–collectivism dimension, which will be discussed later.

Finally, the Kaluli of Papua New Guinea illustrate another way that musical creativity depends on social structure. In this case the focus is on gender-based groups. Men and women can both be creative but in different musical genres. For women, songs that express the personal emotions of the singer are valued, such as songs in which an individual's sorrow for a loved one's death is expressed. For men, songs that provoke a collective emotional response are valued, such as those that incite the audience to cry or even to attack the singer (Brenneis, 1990). Concerning other domains than music, diverse gender-based differences occur. For example for the !Kung San who live in southern Africa, creativity in healing ceremonies is a male endeavor, creativity in bead weaving is reserved for women, and creative storytelling or musical performance is found for both men and women (Shostak, 1993). For the Pueblo Indians in the American Southwest, storytelling is a male activity and pottery making is traditionally associated with women (Babock, 1993).

In addition to gender-based differences in the kind of creative activities, differences in the quantity or quality of creativity are possible. The empirical findings are mixed; studies using the Torrance Tests of Creative Thinking or similar measures administered to children and adults in a variety of cultures show that sometimes males outperform females, sometimes females outperform males, and sometimes there are no significant differences. Mar'i and Karayanni (1983) have argued that in Arab cultures males tend to perform better than females on creativity tasks, which may be attributed to females' submissive social roles, limited occupational choices, and/or limited schooling opportunities. Differential opportunities for schooling may be particularly important to consider when examining gender-based differences in creativity because schools familiarize students with testing situations. In the United States, stable male–female differences are not observed (Barron & Harrington, 1981; Kogan, 1974). This may be attributed to an increasing trend toward equality between the sexes. Perhaps in a matriarchal culture, females will be more creative in general than males.

It is important to note that contradictory findings often exist for studies conducted within a single culture. For example, Khaleefa, Eados, and Ashria (1996) examined gender differences on creativity in Sudan. Three hundred subjects (aged 15–20 years old) from three major cities and several types of schools completed two divergent-thinking tests, a creative activities questionnaire, and a creative personality test. On one task (alternative uses) and the creative personality test, males showed significantly higher scores than female. On the creative activities list, females scored significantly higher than males. No differences occurred for the other divergent-thinking task (consequences). Thus, the existence of gender-based differences on the quantity or quality of creative work remains an open question.

Culture, Language, and Creativity

Related to the effects of culture on creativity, described earlier, is the channeling influence of language on creativity. Whorf (1956) proposed that language shapes thought. Language structures categories and expresses a culture's understanding of the world (Lakoff & Johnson, 1980). Language, as a vehicle of culture, can therefore be expected to shape creativity. Several studies have assessed the effect that language has on creativity by contrasting monolingual and bilingual groups. A recent review of 24 studies concluded that a majority of the studies show a positive link between bilingualism and creativity (Ricciardelli, 1992). In these studies, bilinguals spoke English and either French, Spanish, Italian, Greek, Chinese or other languages. Creativity measures were mainly the Torrance Tests of Creative Thinking although some other creative-thinking tasks were also used. It should be noted that the creativity advantage for bilinguals was not found in all the studies reviewed and did not occur consistently on the diverse creativity tasks. Ricciardelli (1992) proposed that there may be a threshold of bilingual proficiency that must be passed before an advantage for creativity will occur.

The existence of a bilingual advantage suggests that language as an integral part of culture may restrict the ways that people can creatively conceive of a problem. There are several possible reasons for a bilingual advantage. First, bilinguals may have a more flexible approach to the world due to a dual linguistic perspective (see Lambert, 1977). This flexibility may derive, in part, from a greater metalinguistic awareness of arbitrary, nonphysical aspects of words and the effect of context on the meaning of words (Ben-Zeev, 1977; Mohanty & Babu, 1983). Thus, bilinguals may find it easier to encode and access knowledge in diverse ways. Second, bilinguals may have a greater diversity of associations to the same concept because it is situated in two different linguistic conceptual networks. Third, bilinguals may have a greater tolerance for ambiguity because they are comfortable with situations in which one basic idea may have different nuances depending on the linguistic community (Ricciardelli, 1992). Tolerance of ambiguity is considered a valuable trait for creativity because there is often a phase in which incompatible, ill-defined elements coexist during problem solving. A final reason for a bilingual advantage concerns the living conditions of bilinguals: They often participate in activities of two cultural groups, as opposed to monolinguals, who have activities focused essentially on one cultural group. Thus, given the complexity of studying linguistic cultural influences on creativity, bilingualism may involve nonlinguistic benefits of biculturalism.

THE NURTURANCE OF CREATIVITY

In addition to culture's role in channeling creativity toward certain domains or social groups, culture may influence the overall level of creative activity. Creativity may be stimulated or hindered by cultural features such as worldview and the value placed on conformity or tradition.

Worldview refers to a culture's broad conception of the nature of the world and people's role in the world (Sadowsky, Maguire, Johnson, Ngumba, & Kohles, 1994). For example, the U.S. worldview has been characterized, in part, as emphasizing individualism, a work ethic of accomplishment and achievement, and a belief in progress and a better future (Spindler & Spindler, 1983). Consider each component with regard to creativity.

Cultures characterized by individualism, such as North American and Western European ones, define the self as autonomous from the collective. Collectivist cultures, in contrast, define the self within a social context such as the family, with its norms and obligations (Triandis, 1996). According to Triandis et al. (1993), individualist cultures value independance, self reliance, and creativity, whereas collectivist cultures emphasize obedience, cooperation, duty, and acceptance of an in-group authority. In related work at the person level rather than the cultural level, the traits of individuality and individuation – the willingness of a person to differentiate him- or herself from others – have been linked to creative activities and behaviors such as offering a new, original opinion as opposed to a majority view (Maslach, 1974; Sternberg & Lubart, 1995; Whitney, Sagrestano, & Maslach, 1994).

Concerning a work ethic of accomplishment and achievement, we have already seen how the Western definition of creativity focuses on tangible creative products. The value placed on being active and productive should foster creativity as measured by Western standards. It is worth highlighting that Western creativity tests such as those developed by Torrance specifically note fluidity – the number of ideas produced in response to a problem – as one aspect of creativity.

With regard to a belief in progress and optimism toward the future, theorists have proposed that cultures with such beliefs empower people to work on improving the world (Arieti, 1976; Trachtman, 1975). These beliefs imply a cultural acceptance of change, growth, and movement from the status quo. Those cultures that do not maintain faith in progress and have a pessimistic view of the future are believed to stifle creativity in general.

In addition to varying worldviews and related to the individualism–collectivism dimension, cultures vary on the extent to which they value conformity and tradition (Mann, 1980). Some cultures more than others accept deviation (at least in certain domains). For example, Silver (1981) reports that Ashanti "wood carvers refrain from overtly criticizing their peers. In general they praise attempts at anything new under the assumption that the innovation may prove popular, while at worst it may fail harmlessly" (p. 105). Of course, there is a range of permissiveness across cultures (Berry, Poortinga, Segall, & Dasen, 1992). A few cross-cultural studies show links between levels of conformity or dogmatism/open-mindedness and creativity (see Aviram & Milgram, 1977; Marino, 1971; Straus & Straus, 1968). The previously mentioned study of traditional Indian painters also provides evidence on the link between conformity to tradition and creativity (Maduro, 1976). Interviews with the painters revealed that the level of conformity to tradition demanded by their *jati* (subgroup) had a conscious impact on creativity. One subgroup of painters, the Adi Gaur *jati*, follows the traditions, restrictions, and orthodox customs of the priestly Brahmin caste. The second group of painters, the Jangira *jati,* identifies with the supreme creator Vishvakarma and shows greater flexibility and tolerance in its practices. Seventy percent of the painters ranked creative by the whole artistic community were Jangiras even though there were twice as many Adi Gaurs in the community.

In addition to the value placed on conformity and tradition, numerous other cultural characteristics may influence creativity. For example, perseverance, tolerance of ambiguity, and risk taking have often been identified as important for creativity, and research indicates that cultures vary on these dimensions (Berry et al., 1992; Blinco, 1992; McDaniels & Gregory, 1991). Additionally, cultures may possess beliefs or attitudes that can foster or hinder creativity. For example, Krippner (1967) and Adams (1986) identify several culturally held beliefs that may work against creativity, including: "Fantasy and reflection are a waste of time," "Playfulness is for children only" (Adams, 1986, pp. 53–64); "There is a right answer," "Reason, logic, numbers, utility, and success are *good* – intuition, emotions, qualitative thinking, and failure are *bad*" (Krippner, 1967, pp. 144–156).

A given culture, of course, may contain some elements that foster creativity and others that stifle it, yielding an overall influence that may be positive, negative, or neutral. Also, cultural features may not operate to the same extent in all domains of endeavor; for example, a culture may emphasize conformity in musical expression but allow diversity in the visual arts.

DISCUSSION

Given that much of the research on creativity has been conducted in a few countries, especially the United States, it is potentially valuable to look across cultures (Raina, 1993). By moving beyond a single culture's perspective on creativity, we can observe the influence of the cultural environment. This chapter focuses on twentieth-century cultures. With the globalization of media access, particularly television, it may become increasingly difficult to study creativity in isolated cultures. However, cultural variables can also be studied historically. In this regard, Simonton (1984, 1990) and others have conducted a series of investigations of the effect of political, economic, and geographic variables on creativity by looking at one or several cultures over long periods of time. Political fragmentation (measured by the prevalance of independent nations), for example, had a catalyzing effect on creativity across historical periods in Western, Islamic, and Indian civilizations. However, this effect did not hold for literary creativity in China. Political instability indicated by coups d'état, revolts, and assassinations seemed to assert a negative influence on creativity in science, philosophy, literature, and music in the generation following the instability (Simonton, 1990). Political fragmentation and political instability may relate to cultural diversity in general, and therefore to creativity. A certain degree of affluence in a society and physical proximity to one or more larger cultural centers are other conditions that have been linked to creativity (Csikszentmihalyi, 1988; Kavolis, 1964; Silver, 1981; Simonton, 1988). To the extent that a culture embodies or maintains these political, economic, and geographic conditions, that culture should be more conducive to creativity.

Another point of discussion concerning cultural variation on creativity is the practical issue of how to measure creativity in diverse settings. Translated versions of the Torrance Tests of Creative Thinking are used often in cross-cultural research (e.g., Tanwan, 1977). However, it is difficult to determine whether creativity as embodied in the Torrance tests is congruent with the actual definitions of creativity in the cultures studied. The Torrance tests seem to fit with the Western conception of creativity more than with the Eastern conception. Given this, the extent to which the Torrance tests capture the Western conception of creativity is also debatable. The Torrance tests offer a score of originality, but the appropriateness criterion for creativity is not explicitly taken into account in the scoring system.

Furthermore, the use of brief paper-and-pencil creativity tasks, such as the Torrance tests, for cross-cultural comparisons raises numerous technical issues. For example, the images and objects that are the basis of the test questions seem to be culturally bound. Rudowicz, Lok, and Kitto (1995) in a study of a Chinese version of the Torrance tests with a Hong Kong sample noted that "stimuli, in the form of pictures, presented in the verbal forms seem to relate to stories that are more familiar to American and European children than to Asian children" (p. 424). In one of the tasks, subjects are asked how to improve an elephant toy to make it more amusing. It seems likely that cultures vary on their exposure to stuffed animals as toys in general and elephants in particular. Poor performance of a cultural sample on a creativity task may be due to a lack of familiarity with the content of a task, rejection of the task as useless, a lack of test-taking practice, or a misinterpretation of the task (see Rogoff & Chavajay, 1995). Future research on creativity may benefit from an analysis of the relevance of the Torrance tests (or other creativity measures) in diverse settings. In this regard, Ngub'usim (1988) proposed a creativity task based on a popular traditional African riddle game. Riddles such as "Who (or what) does not speak, does not breath, does not gain weight, does not grow, and does not move but is alive?" are given and the subject responds with as many ideas as possible. This task is scored for fluency, flexibility, and originality like the Torrance tests, but the problem content is culturally relevant for the subjects.

Finally, the culture-specific nature of originality (or novelty) also poses a difficult issue for comparative studies. An unusual response in one culture may be mundane in another (see Vernon, 1967). If raters or norms from one culture are used to assess creativity in another culture, the results will probably be biased. However, statistical-frequency-based measures of originality that lump together the responses of different cultural groups tend to inflate the originality score of responses common in one group and to diffuse culture-specific originality (Jones & Shea, 1974). The analysis of creativity in a culture with raters or norms from that culture is probably the best method, although the groups will not share a common reference point.

CONCLUSION

The analysis of creativity in diverse cultures shows that creativity is context dependent. Culture is involved in defining the nature of creativity and the creative process. The Western definition of creativity as a product-oriented, originality-based phenomenon can be compared with an Eastern view of creativity as a phenomenon of expressing an inner truth in a new way or of self-growth. Culture acts in a second fashion by channeling creativity. Culture promotes creativity in certain forms and domains and in certain segments of the population. Creativity occurs in dance in Samoa, in group settings for Bali music, and in secular carving for the Ashanti. Finally, culture provides a set of facilitating and inhibiting conditions for creativity that influence the general level of creative activity. For example, some cultures emphasize conformity more than others. In sum, when we look beyond our own doorstep, we discover how deeply creativity is bound to cultural context.

NOTE

I thank Jacques Lautrey, Marie-Hélène Lavallard, Chantal Pacteau, and Sophie Von Gestel for helpful comments on this chapter. This chapter is based on an earlier article that appeared in the *International Journal of Psychology*. Correspondence should be sent to Todd I. Lubart, Université René Descartes (Paris V), Laboratoire Cognition et Développement, 28 Rue Serpente, 75006 Paris, France.

REFERENCES

Adams, J. L. (1986). *Conceptual blockbusting: A guide to better ideas* (3rd ed.). New York: Addison-Wesley. (Original work published 1974)

Amabile, T. M. (1982). Social psychology of creativity: A consensual assessment technique. *Journal of Personality and Social Psychology, 43*(5), 997–1013.

Amabile, T. M. (1983). *The social psychology of creativity.* New York: Springer-Verlag.

Arieti, S. (1976). *Creativity: The magic synthesis.* New York: Basic.

Aron, E. N., & Aron, A. (1982). An introduction to Maharishi's theory of creativity: Its empirical base and description of the creative process. *Journal of Creative Behavior, 16*(1), 29–49.

Aviram, A., & Milgram, R. M. (1977). Dogmatism, locus of control, and creativity in children educated in the Soviet Union, the United States, and Israel. *Psychological Reports, 40*(1), 27–34.

Babock, B. A. (1993). At home, no womens are storytellers: Ceramic creativity and the politics of discourse in Cochiti Pueblo. In S. Lavie, K. Narayan, & R. Rosaldo (Eds.), *Creativity/Anthropology* (pp. 70–99). Ithaca, NY: Cornell University Press.

Barron, F. (1988). Putting creativity to work. In R. J. Sternberg (Ed.), *The nature of creativity* (pp. 76–98). Cambridge University Press.

Barron, F., & Harrington, D. M. (1981). Creativity, intelligence, and personality. *Annual Review of Psychology, 32*, 439–476.

Bascom, W. (1969). Creativity and style in African art. In D. P. Biebuyck (Ed.), *Tradition and creativity in tribal art* (pp. 98–119). Berkeley: University of California Press.

Ben-Amos, P. (1986). Artistic creativity in Benin Kingdom. *African Arts, 19*(3), 60–63.

Ben-Zeev, S. (1977). Mechanism by which childhood bilingualism affects understanding of language and cognitive structures. In P. A. Hornby (Ed.), *Bilingualism: Psychological, social, and educational implications* (pp 29–55). New York: Academic.

Berry, J. W., Poortinga, Y. H., Segall, M. H., & Dasen, P. R. (1992). *Cross-cultural psychology: Research and applications.* Cambridge University Press.

Biebuyck, D. P. (Ed.), (1969). *Tradition and creativity in tribal art.* Berkeley CA: University of California Press.

Blinco, P. M. (1992). A cross-cultural study of task persistence of young children in Japan and the United States. *Journal of Cross-Cultural Psychology, 22*(3), 407–415.

Brenneis, D. (1990). Musical imaginations: Comparative perspectives on musical creativity. In M. A. Runco (Ed.), *Theories of creativity* (pp. 170–189). Norwood, NJ: Ablex.

Chu, Y-K. (1970). Oriental views on creativity. In A. Angoff & B. Shapiro (Eds.), *Psi factors in creativity* (pp. 35–50). New York: Parapsychology Foundation.

Colligan, J. (1983). Musical creativity and social rules in four cultures. *Creative Child and Adult Quarterly, 8*(1), 39–47.

Csikszentmihalyi, M. (1988). Society, culture, and person: A systems view of creativity. In R. J. Sternberg (Ed.), *The nature of creativity* (pp. 325–339). Cambridge University Press.

Gaines, R., & Price-Williams, D. (1990). Dreams and imaginative processes in American and Balinese artists. *Psychiatric Journal of the University of Ottowa, 15*(2), 107–110.

Ghiselin, B. (1985). *The creative process.* Berkeley: University of California Press. (Original work published 1952)

Gruber, H. E. (1989). The evolving systems approach to creative work. In D. B. Wallace & H. E. Gruber (Eds.), *Creative people at work* (pp. 3–24). New York: Oxford University Press.

Hadamard, J. (1945). *An essay on the psychology of invention in the mathematical field.* Princeton, NJ: Princeton University Press.

Hallman, R. J. (1970). Toward a Hindu theory of creativity. *Educational Theory, 20*(4), 368–376.

Hughes, A. O., & Drew, J. S. (1984). A state creative? *Papers in the Social Sciences, 4,* 1–15.

Jackson, P. W., & Messick, S. (1967). The person, the product, and the response: Conceptual problems in the assessment of creativity. In J. Kagan (Ed.), *Creativity and learning* (pp. 1–19). Boston: Houghton Mifflin.

Joncich, G. (1964). A culture-bound concept of creativity: A social historian's critique, centering on a recent American research report. *Educational Theory, 14,* 133–143.

Jones, J., & Shea, J. (1974). Some problems in the comparison of divergent thinking scores across cultures. *Australian Psychologist, 9*(3), 47–51.

Kavolis, V. (1964). Economic conditions of artistic creativity. *American Journal of Sociology, 70,* 332–341.

Khaleefa, O. H., Eados, G., Ashria, I. H. (1996). Gender and creativity in an Afro-Arab Islamic culture: The case of Sudan. *Journal of Creative Behavior, 30*(1), 52–60.

Kogan, N. (1974). Creativity and sex differences. *Journal of Creative Behavior, 8*(1), 1–14.

Krippner, S. (1967). The 10 commandments that block creativity. *Gifted Child Quarterly, 11*(3), 144–156.

Krippner, S., & Arons, M. (1973). Creativity: Person, product or process? *Gifted Child Quarterly, 17*(2), 116–123, 129.

Kristeller, P. O. (1983). "Creativity" and "tradition." *Journal of the History of Ideas, 44,* 105–114.

Kuo, Y-Y. (1996). Taoistic psychology of creativity. *Journal of Creative Behavior, 30*(3), 197–212.

Lakoff, G., & Johnson, M. (1980). *Metaphors we live by.* Chicago: University of Chicago Press.

Lambert, W. E. (1977). The effect of bilingualism on the individual: Cognitive and social consequences. In P. A. Hornby (Ed.), *Bilingualism: Psychological, social and educational implications.* New York: Academic.

Lubart, T. I. (1994). Creativity. In R. J. Sternberg (Ed.), *Thinking and problem solving* (pp. 289–332). New York: Academic.

Lubart, T. I., & Sternberg, R. J. (1995). An investment approach to creativity: Theory and data. In S. M. Smith, T. B. Ward, & R. A. Finke (Eds.), *The creative cognition approach* (pp. 271–302). Cambridge, MA: MIT Press.

Ludwig, A. M. (1992). Culture and creativity. *American Journal of Psychotherapy, 46*(3), 454–469.

MacKinnon, D. W. (1962). The nature and nurture of creative talent. *American Psychologist, 17,* 484–495.

Maduro, R. (1976). *Artistic creativity in a Brahmin painter community.* Research monograph 14. Berkeley: Center for South and Southeast Asia Studies, University of California.

Mann, L. (1980). Cross-cultural studies of small groups. In H. C. Triandis & R. W. Brislin (Eds.), *Handbook of cross-cultural psychology: Vol. 5. Social psychology* (pp. 155–210). Boston: Allyn & Bacon.

Mar'i, S. K., & Karayanni, M. (1983). Creativity in Arab culture: Two decades of research. *Journal of Creative Behavior, 16*(4), 227–238.

Marino, C. (1971). Cross-national comparisons of Catholic–Protestant creativity differences. *British Journal of Social and Clinical Psychology, 10,* 132–137.

Maslach, C. (1974). Social and personal bases of individuation. *Journal of Personality and Social Psychology, 29*(3), 411–425.

Mason, J. H. (1988). The character of creativity: Two traditions. *History of European Ideas, 9*(6), 697–715.

Mathur, S. G. (1982). Cross-cultural implications of creativity. *Indian Psychological Review, 22*(1), 12–19.

McDaniels, T. L., & Gregory, R. S. (1991). A framework for structuring cross-cultural research in risk and decision taking. *Journal of Cross-Cultural Psychology, 22*(1), 103–128.

Mohanty, A. K., & Babu, N. (1983). Bilingualism and metalinguistic ability among Kond tribals in Orissa, India. *Journal of Social Psychology, 121,* 15–22.

Ngub'usim, M-N. (1988). The psychometric function of traditional African riddles. *International Journal of Psychology, 23*(4), 489–503.

Ochse, R. (1990). *Before the gates of excellence.* Cambridge University Press.

Onda, A. (1962). Zen and creativity. *Psychologia, 5,* 13–20.

Patrick, C. (1935). Creative thought in poets. In R. Woodworth (Ed.), *Archives of Psychology, 178,* 1–74.

Patrick, C. (1937). Creative thought in artists. *Journal of Psychology, 4,* 35–73.

Poincaré, H. (1921). *The foundations of science.* New York: Science Press.

Raina, M. K. (1993). Ethnocentric confines in creativity research. In S. G. Isaksen, M. C. Murdock, R. L. Firestein, & D. J. Treffinger (Eds.), *Understanding and recognizing creativity: The emergence of a discipline* (pp. 435–453). Norwood, NJ: Ablex.

Reber, A. S. (1985). *The Penguin dictionary of psychology.* New York: Penguin.

Ribot, T. A. (1906). *Essay on the creative imagination.* Chicago: Open Court.

Ricciardelli, L. A. (1992). Creativity and bilingualism. *Journal of Creative Behavior, 26*(4), 242–254.

Rogoff, B., & Chavajay, P. (1995). What's become of research on the cultural basis of cognitive development? *American Psychologist, 50*(10), 859–877.

Rossman, J. (1931). *The psychology of the inventor.* Washington, DC: Inventors Publishing.

Rudowicz, E., Lok, D., & Kitto, J. (1995). Use of Torrance Tests of Creative Thinking in an exploratory study of creativity in Hong Kong primary school children: A cross-cultural comparison. *International Journal of Psychology, 30*(4), 417–430.

Saad, H. T. (1985). The role of individual creativity in traditional African art: The *gwani* (genius) amongst master builders of Hausaland. *Nigeria Magazine, 53*(4), 3–16.

Sadowsky, G. R., Maguire, K., Johnson, P., Ngumba, W., & Kohles, R. (1994). World views of white American, mainland Chinese, Taiwanese, and African students. *Journal of Cross-Cultural Psychology, 25*(3), 309–324.

Sarnoff, D. P., & Cole, H. P. (1983). Creativity and personal growth. *Journal of Creative Behavior, 17*(2), 95–102.

Sherr, J. (1982). The universal structures and dynamics of creativity: Maharishi, Plato, Jung, and various creative geniuses on the creative process. *Journal of Creative Behavior, 16*(3), 155–175.

Shostak, M. (1993). The creative individual in the world of the !Kung San. In S. Lavie, K. Narayan, & R. Rosaldo (Eds.), *Creativity/Anthropology* (pp. 54–69). Ithaca, NY:Cornell University Press.

Silver, H. R. (1981). Calculating risks: The socioeconomic foundations of aesthetic innovation in an Ashanti carving community. *Ethnology, 20,* 101–114.

Simonton, D. K. (1984). *Genius, creativity, and leadership.* Cambridge, MA: Harvard University Press.

Simonton, D. K. (1988). Creativity, leadership, and chance. In R. J. Sternberg (Ed.), *The nature of creativity* (pp. 386–426). Cambridge University Press.

Simonton, D. K. (1990). Political pathology and societal creativity. *Creativity Research Journal, 3*(2), 85–99.

Sinclair, E. C. (1971). Towards a typology of cultural attitudes concerning creativity. *Western Canadian Journal of Anthropology, 2*(3), 82–89.

Spindler, G. D., & Spindler, L. (1983). Anthropologists view American culture. *Annual Review of Anthropology, 12,* 49–78.

Stein, M. I. (1953). Creativity and culture. *Journal of Psychology, 36,* 311–322.

Sternberg, R. J., & Lubart, T. I. (1991). An investment theory of creativity and its development. *Human Development, 34,* 1–31.

Sternberg, R. J., & Lubart, T. I. (1995). *Defying the crowd: Cultivating creativity in a culture of conformity.* New York: Free Press.

Straus, J. H., & Straus, M. A. (1968). Family roles and sex differences in creativity of children in Bombay and Minneapolis. *Journal of Marriage and Family, 30,* 46–53.

Tanwan, R. S. (1977). Measurement of creativity thinking and their use in India. *Indian Psychological Review, 14*(2), 59–62.

Torrance, E. P. (1974). *Torrance Tests of Creative Thinking: Norms-technical manual.* Lexington, MA: Ginn.

Trachtman, L. E. (1975). Creative people, creative times. *Journal of Creative Behavior, 9*(1), 35–50.

Triandis, H. C. (1996). The psychological measurement of cultural syndromes. *American Psychologist, 51*(4), 407–415.

Triandis, H. C., McCusker, C., Betancourt, H., Sumiko, I., Leung, K., Salazar, J. M., Setiadi, B., Sinha, J. B. P., Tozard, H., & Zaleski, Z. (1993). An etic-emic analysis of individualism and collectivism. *Journal of Cross-Cultural Psychology, 24*(3), 366–383.

Vernon, P. E. (1967). A cross-cultural study of "creativity tests" with 11-year-old boys. *New Research in Education, 1,* 135–146.

von Franz, M-L. (1995). *Creation myths* (rev. ed.). Boston: Shambhala.

Walberg, H. J. (1988). Creativity and talent as learning. In R. J. Sternberg (Ed.). *The nature of creativity* (pp. 340–361). Cambridge University Press.

Wallas, G. (1926). *The art of thought.* New York: Harcourt, Brace.

Whitney, K., Sagrestano, L. M., & Maslach, C. (1994). Establishing the social impact of individuation. *Journal of Personality and Social Psychology, 66*(6), 1140–1153.

Whorf, B. L. (1956). *Language, thought, and reality: Selected writings of Benjamin Lee Whorf* (J. Carroll, Ed.). Cambridge, MA: MIT Press.

Wonder, J., & Blake, J. (1992). Creativity East and West: Intuition vs. logic. *Journal of Creative Behavior, 26*(3), 172–185.

18   *Computer Models of Creativity*

MARGARET A. BODEN

Computational psychology uses ideas from artificial intelligence (AI) to formulate its theories about how the mind works, and sees AI models as tests of the coherence and power of those theories. In addition, it compares empirical evidence about human psychology with the performance and internal processing of the models. Among the many psychologically motivated AI models, some aim to throw light on creativity.

Creativity is the generation of ideas that are both novel and valuable. *Ideas,* here, is intended in a very broad sense to include concepts, designs, theories, melodies, paintings, sculptures, and so on. The novelty may be defined with reference either to the previous ideas of the individual concerned or to the whole of human history. The former definition concerns P-creativity (P for psychological), the latter H-creativity (H for historical) (Boden, 1990, chap. 3). H-creativity presupposes P-creativity, for if someone has a historically novel idea, then it must be new to that person as well as to others.

The idea may not be recognized immediately (even by its originator) as valuable, or even as new. Historians of science and of art have described many self-doubts, and many more social disputes, over what are now regarded as important creative insights. Even something so apparently straightforward as the discovery of dinosaurs was negotiated by the relevant (international) scientific peer group for many years before agreement could be reached on just what, if anything, had been discovered (Schaffer, 1994). (Notice that *discovery,* like *creativity,* is an honorific term.) As for novelty, this may be mistakenly ascribed because of scholars' ignorance of earlier work. In short, H-creativity is not a psychological category, but a historical-sociological one (Brannigan, 1981). For theoretical psychologists, P-creativity is the more fundamental notion.

Even P-creativity is not a purely scientific concept, since a creative idea (by definition) must be valuable in some way, and values cannot be justified by science: One cannot derive an *ought* from an *is.* Value is not found by science, but negotiated by social groups (sometimes involving seesawing judgments with the passage of time). But science – and computer modelers – can take account of the evaluative aspects of creativity. We can ask what aesthetic (and moral) values certain groups of people have and whether any are human universals (some psychologists posit universal aesthetic preferences for types of landscape and tree shapes, grounded in our evolutionary origins in the African savannah [Heerwagen & Orians, 1993; Orians & Heerwagen, 1992]. Moreover, values can be included within psychological theories of creativity and within computer models of it. This is easier said than done: It is difficult to specify aesthetic values (historians of art do so with limited success, and there is no unproblematic definition of mathematical "elegance" or scientific "simplicity"), and even more difficult to translate these values into computational terms. It is, however, possible.

It is widely assumed – even regarded as obvious – that computational theory cannot deal with social interaction, motivation, emotion, or personality. If that were true, a comprehensive computational psychology of creativity would be impossible, for each of these aspects of humanity is involved in creativity (Boden, 1994). Although any creative idea can arise only in the mind of some individual, its generation is often a group effort. It always arises within some culturally familiar domain (what I later call a "conceptual space"). And the emerging idea, or notions very close to it, may already be a topic of discussion (Schaffer, 1994). Even if it is not, one person's musings about related matters may trigger another individual to formulate it anew (which is why brainstorming can encourage creativity). Motivation, emotional involvement, and self-confidence are needed too, if someone is to acquire the necessary expertise and to risk experimenting with unusual ideas. Thus, we see a characteristic personality type of highly creative individuals, many of whom are driven, and in turn drive their associates even unto death: Florence Nightingale, lying on her sickbed, dictated (in both senses) to her male helpers, some of whom sickened and died under the strain (for seven twentieth-century examples, see Gardner, 1993).

This common assumption (that computational psychology can study only individual cognition) is encouraged by the widespread use of the misleading term *cognitive science*. But it is mistaken. In principle, computational psychology has a wider remit. Indeed, much of the earliest AI work was concerned with social psychology and motivation, and even personality (Boden, 1972, 1977/1987, chaps. 2–4), and some recent AI research also addresses such issues (e.g., Beaudoin & Sloman, 1993; Sloman, 1987; Wright, Sloman, & Beaudoin, in press).

In practice, however, most computationalists have focused on cognitive (as opposed to social or dynamic) psychology. With respect to creativity, computer modelers have asked what sorts of novelties can arise in individual minds, and what cognitive processes make this possible. In this chapter, we shall see how computational concepts and AI models can be used to clarify, and even to answer, such questions.

AI models of creativity fall into two broad groups, because creativity itself is of two types. On the one hand, there is what we may call "combinational" creativity. Here, the novel idea consists of an unusual combination of, or association between, familiar ideas. Poetic imagery, metaphor, and analogy fall into this class. On the other hand, there is *exploratory-transformational* creativity, grounded in a richly structured conceptual space. A *conceptual space* is an accepted style of thinking in a particular domain – for instance, in mathematics or biology, in various kinds of literature, or in the visual or performing arts. A conceptual space is defined by a set of enabling constraints, which make possible the generation of structures lying within that space – for instance, limericks or theories in organic chemistry. If one or more of these constraints is altered (or dropped), the space is transformed. Ideas that previously were *impossible* (relative to the original conceptual space) become conceivable.

For each of these types, there are some computer models *of* creativity and many more merely *relevant to* creativity. Even today, computer models of creativity are relatively few. But countless AI models are somehow relevant, including some of the earliest AI work (Boden, 1977/1987, chap. 11). This is partly because associative processes and analogy are often modeled without any declared intent to model creativity. The explicit focus, instead, may be on "pattern matching," "problem-solving," "reminding" or "case-based reasoning" (Kolodner, 1993; Schank, 1990; Schank & Childers, 1988), and the like. Moreover, many AI programs map conceptual spaces (domains of thought), which could be used within models of creativity as such. One example is work on the structure of human motivation, such as that inspired by Robert Abelson and Roger Schank (e.g., Abelson, 1973; Dyer, 1983; Schank & Abelson, 1977). Story plots cannot be generated, or assessed, without some understanding of motivational structure. A more specialized example is work on the structure of music, including not only tonality and meter (Longuet-Higgins, 1987), but also expressiveness

(Longuet-Higgins, 1994). This chapter concentrates on computational models *of* creativity – but the relevance of other computational research should be borne in mind.

Exploratory-transformational creativity can itself be divided into two types: exploratory and transformational. ET-creativity, one might say, includes both E-creativity and T-creativity. The vast majority of current computer models concerned with ET-creativity actually model only the E-type. This is no accident. There are two reasons why T-creativity is harder to model (and to achieve) than E-creativity.

First, T-creativity involves some transformation of one or more of the (relatively fundamental) dimensions defining the conceptual space concerned. In other words, it demands more than merely following the usually accepted ways of thinking in this space, and more than the mere minimal "tweaking" of superficial dimensions.

The distinction between tweaking and transformation is to some extent a matter of degree. As we shall see in the section titled "Exploring Conceptual Spaces," a computer program initially capable of drawing only two-armed acrobats might later be able, after tweaking (substituting) the numerals included within its generative model of human bodies, to draw figures with one, six, or 26 arms. One might be tempted to say that its conceptual space had been "transformed": After all, it can now depict a variety of imaginary humanoid figures, whereas at first it could not. But if the only generative change involved were substituting one arm/numeral for another, these novel pictures would all be drawn in the same general style as the first ones. The number of arms would surprise us, but the overall style would not. A change more deserving of the term *transformation* would be to alter some relatively fundamental aspects of the general drawing style so as to produce figures of an essentially different, though related type. What counts as a fundamental dimension depends on the "generative grammar" of the conceptual space concerned (see the discussion of the "prairie house" in the section titled "Exploring Conceptual Issues").

The second reason for the difficulty of modeling (and, again, of achieving) T-creativity is that the values satisfied by the nontransformed cases may not be fully satisfied by the new, transformed, cases. This means that, in order to avoid generating unacceptable structures, the system (program or person) must adjust the old values and/or adopt new ones that accept the new structural types. The values within almost all current computer programs are "frozen," which limits their ability to model, or to appreciate, T-creativity. A system capable of generating T-products but not of evaluating them would not be T-creative in the sense that artists and scientists are. At best, it could produce T-novel ideas whose value might be recognized and developed by others. This holds whether the system concerned is a computer model (such as some of those discussed in the section titled "Transformational Creativity") or a human being (e.g., a schizophrenic generating word salad or paintings in an uncontrolled, uncritical way). Small wonder, then, that there are (as yet) very few convincingly T-creative computer models.

Before discussing any specific examples, we should note that the prime question for psychologists is not, "Are these computer models *really* creative?" (a philosophical problem I have discussed elsewhere; Boden, 1990, chap. 11), but rather, "What light do they throw on how human creativity is possible?" This (scientific) inquiry may be advanced not only by their apparent successes but also by their failures. As Karl Popper (1963) pointed out, science advances not by the formulation of unchallengeable truths, but by successive conjectures and refutations. To know what theories do not work, and why, is a preliminary to discovering the correct one. So if most of the models we shall discuss do not measure up to human performance (even in E-creativity), that is not to deny their theoretical interest. In a creativity competition between people and computers, people will win every – well, almost every – time. Here, however, our aim is not competing, but understanding.

COMPUTER MODELS OF ASSOCIATION AND ANALOGY

Association and analogy are examples of combinational creativity. In some cases of poetic imagery, for instance, a novel association is made, communicated, and then dropped. Or the association may be retained and reinforced, either by repetition (as when a poetic image is closely followed by several others, each making essentially the same association) or by a systematic comparison of the internal structures of the two ideas associated. The latter case covers analogies that are sustained and explored for purposes of rhetoric or problem solving. Sometimes, the associations are entirely unexpected: when an image or analogy comes (unbidden) to mind. Other times, they are less spontaneous: when one tries to think of an image for x or an analogy for y.

"Connectionist" computer models, which (learn to) recognize and discriminate input patterns, suggest ways in which such associative thinking can happen. A connectionist model, or artificial neural network, consists of many simple computational units functioning in parallel, each connected to its neighbors by excitatory and inhibitory links. One form of connectionism that has received significant attention from psychologists is PDP (parallel distributed processing; Rumelhart & McClelland, 1986), in which different concepts are represented by distinct equilibrated activity patterns defined over the network as a whole. The system's "knowledge" is stored not as bits located in numbered memory registers; but as the (variable) weights, or strengths, of the myriad connections.

PDP systems have certain "natural" properties (resulting from their basic structure) characteristic of associative thinking. For example, they can regenerate a familiar activity pattern if they are given only part of it; they can recognize that two input patterns are similar, though different; and they can recognize a familiar input in the presence of noise. These capabilities remind us of various skills of the creative thinker. Such skills include the abilities to remember something given only a small part as a trigger ("Good night, sweet ladies . . ."), to see similarities between things that are different (the sun as a lamp), to recognize something partly obscured by noise (a lost Rembrandt touched up by a modern amateur), to be reminded of one thing by another (a metal crown called to mind by a human body displacing water in a bath), and to think of and/or appreciate analogies ("The heart is a pump").

Analogy, of course, is more than association. Analogical thinking involves some more or less sustained comparison between the internal structure of the two ideas concerned. Analogies can be explored, developed, assessed – and then confirmed or rejected ("Is the heart really a pump, and how can we decide?"). Current connectionism, in general, does not offer extended structural comparisons. Moreover, powerful connectionist systems were not available before the 1980s. Much of the AI work on analogy (of which there is a great deal) therefore does not use connectionist methods – or, if it does, it combines associative connectionism (providing conceptual links within semantic networks) with structured thinking modeled by methods characteristic of classical AI (Holyoak & Barnden, 1994).

The earliest AI model of analogy compared the structures of previously given geometrical patterns like those presented in IQ tests (Evans, 1968). Recent approaches focus on more "open" problems, where the program is required to find (and to assess) the analogous item for itself. However, this description is problematic, as we shall see. The concepts and problem descriptions concerned are often provided to the program in a form that encourages, even invites, the desired comparison. Providing concepts in some suitable form is of course unavoidable: The two concepts must be linked and/or structured such that the analogy can, eventually, be drawn. But the ease and directness with which this is done may be unrealistically increased by deliberately prestructuring the relevant items. In such cases, what seems to be an open search is comparable to the IQ test, in which one must pick the best analogy from a closed set of carefully predesigned items.

An analogy model that has been applied within various domains is SME (Structure-Mapping Engine; Falkenhainer, Forbus, & Gentner, 1989). SME is based on Dedre Gentner's (1989) theory of analogy, which stresses structural similarities enabling objects and relations in one concept to be mapped systematically onto their equivalents in the other. This shared internal structure outweighs differences in superficial features, and higher-order relations (between relations) are preferred over lower-order ones (between objects). In the analogy between the heart and the pump, the forceful expulsion of liquid and its circulation around a closed loop are mapped across both heart and pump, but irrelevant properties (such as color) are ignored.

SME constructs and evaluates various global matches between its concepts or other inputs (graphics, for instance). The matches can suggest *candidate inferences,* wherein a predicate applying to one concept is hypothetically applied to the other. (William Harvey, who showed that the heart is a pump, postulated then-invisible capillaries linking arteries and veins, because a closed hydraulic system has connected channels.) Partly because of this power to "transfer" knowledge from one area to another (the prime feature of case-based reasoning in general), SME has been used in the computer modeling of scientific explanation (Falkenhainer, 1990). SME has also been used as the second stage in a dual-process model of similarity-based retrieval (Forbus, Gentner, & Law, 1994). The MAC/FAC system models the fact that human subjects rely primarily on merely superficial similarities when retrieving concepts from long-term memory, but rely more on structural commonalities in making similarity judgments between items in working memory. Accordingly, the first stage of retrieval uses surface similarities, and the second uses SME to assess deeper similarities.

The SME system does not include the thinker's plans and goals as a central criterion for all analogical matches, but can include these pragmatic criteria if appropriate in context. Gentner and colleagues criticize computational models in which analogy depends crucially on current goals, such as the PI system (Holyoak & Thagard, 1989, 1994, chap. 10; Thagard, 1992). In PI, there are three general constraints on analogy: pragmatic centrality, semantic similarity, and structural consistency – the first taking precedence. It is a (nondistributed) connectionist system that does inductive problem solving by means of multiple constraint satisfaction. PI contains two modules, ARCS and ACME, for generating and interpreting analogies, respectively, and a large semantic network (WordNet) whose units are linked by features like *super/subordinate, part, synonym,* and *antonym.*

PI uses multiple constraint satisfaction to judge the strength of different analogies. It prefers mappings wherein it has been specifically informed of a correspondence between two items, or where some element is so central to the parent structure that some mapping for it must be found. For example, ACME was asked to interpret Socrates' analogy between *philosopher* and *midwife.* The item *baby* is so central to the concept of *midwife* that ACME must find a match for it – even though an idea is semantically very dissimilar from a baby. The generation of analogies (by ARCS) is heavily constrained by pragmatics, which counts very heavily in assessing the "nearest" match given a large retrieval set of similar concepts. The examples cited by ARCS's programmers include outline plots of Aesop and Shakespeare, and the problem of how to use X-rays to destroy a tumor without damaging the surrounding tissues. The SME team, however, claims that MAC/FAC solves these problems in a more efficient, and a more psychologically realistic, way.

Case-based reasoning (e.g., Kolodner, 1993) is a form of analogical problem solving that notes similarities between the current problem situation and some familiar instance, and that transfers (with some creative modification, if necessary) aspects of the latter to the former. A computer model of story generation, for example, can transform the idea of one character killing another into an episode in which a person commits suicide (Turner, 1994).

Most current computer modals of analogy focus on the retrieval and mapping of preexisting concepts, rather than the creative construction of new ones. Admittedly, someone might say that the storytelling program just mentioned constructed a genuinely new concept: suicide. But its concept of suicide is semantically very close to its initial concept of murder: The "slots" for killer and victim are merely filled by the same individual instead of two different ones. No fundamental restructuring of the initial concept takes place. This lack of conceptual fluidity is seen by Douglas Hofstadter as a serious problem, one that characterizes classical AI (and much connectionism) in general (Hofstadter & FARG, 1995). Human conceptualization, he insists, is inherently fluid, and analogy involves not only comparisons between, but (often) also restructuring of, previously existing concepts. He criticizes analogy models such as SME and PI for relying on (formal, meaningless) structural features that are carefully preassigned so that the intended conceptual mapping should take place. Moreover, their representations of concepts are fixed, remaining unaltered after the analogy has been drawn. Similarly, scientific discovery programs (see the section titled "Exploring Conceptual Spacor") use ready-made concepts and principles of inference provided by the programmer, and so model conscious (and unadventurous) scientific reasoning rather than novel analogical insights. Hofstadter's own approach is significantly different.

He stresses the essential "fluidity" (changeability, reconfigurability) of all our concepts and the intimate links between perception and analogy. Not only does perception involve analogy (the recognition of similarity) and vice versa, but our concepts – and therefore our perception – may be significantly altered by analogical thinking. The initial (perceptual) description may be adapted, or even destroyed, during the recognition of the analogy. (He compares this process with conceptual revolutions in science: The initial interpretation is discarded, and a fundamentally different interpretation is substituted for it.) He draws on detailed accounts of his own conscious phenomenology during both "normal" and "creative" thinking – which he sees as fundamentally similar. The difference between them, he argues, lies in the extent to which the fluidity of concepts is encouraged, the degree to which the concepts concerned are allowed to "slip" from their normal constraints in order that some relatively far-fetched similarity should be recognized. Similarity being multidimensional, the question arises of *which* similarities will be noticed in a particular case. Hofstadter suggests various ways in which different types and levels of similarity may be encouraged, discovered, and compared.

His theory has been implemented in a set of broadly connectionist (but not PDP) systems applied to several different domains (for an overview, see Hofstadter & FARG, 1995): "Copycat" finds analogies between alphabetic letter strings (see also Hofstadter, 1994; Mitchell, 1993); "Tabletop" considers the layout of eating utensils (see also French, 1995); and "Letter Spirit" recognizes alphabetic letters in various fonts (see also McGraw, 1995). (Letter Spirit is the first step within an ambitious project to implement the creative design of a very wide range of letter fonts: Each letter must resemble not only all its cross-font cousins, all Bs for instance, but also all 25 of its own-font siblings – constraints that are complex, subtle, and to some extent in conflict.)

These programs are nondeterministic parallel processors, combining a multitude of competitive bottom-up processes with (changing) top-down influences. The lowest-level processes concern tiny details; but as processing proceeds, patterns of low-level activity develop that in effect act as larger-scale agents. Each program simultaneously considers many different descriptions, on various levels, of its concepts or perceptual inputs. Their representations are built up dialectically, each step being influenced by (and also influencing) the type of analogical mapping that the current context seems to require. If a partially built interpretation seems to be mapping well onto the developing analogy, it is maintained and developed further; otherwise, it is dropped and an alternative is tried, using different features of the target concept.

The range of possible interpretations depends on the descriptors available. Some mark relatively superficial features, others concern the inner structure of a concept or conceptual neighborhood. The closeness of the match between the potential analogy and its target is assessed for each set of descriptors, and the probability of focusing on a particular match varies – and may be influenced by top-down guidance. These models can therefore draw analogies in a fairly rigid way or in a more "creative" fashion, by allowing less or more conceptual slippage, respectively.

Hofstadter's complaint that most analogy programs map prestructured concepts, the programmer having already done the really creative work, invites the riposte that he, too, has to provide the descriptors, and the processes of comparison and "choice," used by his programs. His criticism that other models are oversimplified draws the reply that he himself restricts his models to "toy" domains, each equipped with a carefully chosen set of domain-specific descriptors. It remains to be seen whether his approach can be applied to larger-scale conceptual networks without running into the sands of the combinatorial explosion. And his charge that other models of analogy work only with prestructured concepts looks stronger when applied to PI than to SME, which has been applied to automatically generated structures as well as to predesigned ones.

These disagreements are reminiscent of the conflict between connectionist and traditional AI (Boden, 1991). The brain is, at base, some sort of "connectionist" engine. No psychological theory incompatible with this fact would be acceptable, and theories that try to build higher-level processing from connectionist roots should be taken seriously. Phenomenological evidence, too, suggests that many of our thought processes are relatively fleeting, fluid, and chaotic. But (as the high priests of PDP connectionism themselves allow), our more "logical" thinking is not like this and seems to be closer to the serial processing characteristic of classical AI. The systematic exploration of analogy (whether for problem solving or sustained rhetorical exposition) is arguably nearer to SME and PI than to Copycat and its computational cousins. On the other hand, the initial discovery of analogies, especially where no problem discipline has already been established, is better modeled by Hofstadter's approach. As in other areas of AI, then, the competing approaches have different and largely complementary strengths. Future models of human thought must somehow combine the two.

Sustained analogical thinking is the type of combinational creativity that is closest to exploratory-transformational creativity for both share a concern with conceptual structure. However, analogy focuses on the structure of individual concepts or thoughts, whereas exploratory-transformational creativity is grounded in structured conceptual domains, or styles of thinking. The next two sections consider this type of creativity.

EXPLORING CONCEPTUAL SPACES

A computer model of E-creativity must define the conceptual space concerned and provide ways of moving through it so as to reach P-novel, or even H-novel, locations. The domains that have been studied in AI research include (for example) physics and chemistry, story-telling, drawing and architecture, and music. In these AI systems, the evaluation sometimes occurs as post hoc self-criticism, but more often it is tacitly included within the defining constraints and/or pathfinding processes. This lack of reflective self-criticism is clearly a weakness of (most) current programs, insofar as they are intended as models of human creativity.

A related limitation of exploratory (and transformational) programs is that they ignore the social nature of evaluation. As noted in the first section, even the discovery of dinosaurs required lengthy social negotiation to be recognized (or socially constructed) as a "discovery" (Schaffer, 1994). Computer models of scientific discovery employ (tacit or explicit) criteria of evaluation that are not newly negotiated, but taken for granted. To the charge that this falsifies the nature of "real" creativity, AI modelers can reply, first, that they are primarily interested in how certain novel ideas can be generated in the mind and, second, that the evaluative criteria they use were negotiated by scientists in the past and are now generally accepted.

Models of scientific discovery include one of the earliest "expert systems" (DENDRAL), which searched the space of a tiny corner of organic chemistry and proposed new (including H-novel) molecular structures accordingly (Lindsay, Buchanan, Feigenbaum, & Lederberg, 1980). This was a case of "brute force" discovery: The computational power of the computer enabled the program to search the predefined space exhaustively, which human chemists cannot do. A later version of the same program (meta-DENDRAL) was also able to suggest new hypotheses by noticing previously unknown patterns in the chemical data. For example, if it discovered that (in certain experimental conditions) molecules of a certain type break at particular points, it would search for a smaller structure located near the broken bonds; if such a structure were found, meta-DENDRAL would suggest that breakpoints near this substructure might happen in molecules of other types, too. Unlike DENDRAL, which could generate only chemically possible structures, meta-DENDRAL took the risk of creative mistake: Although all of its hypotheses were plausible, some turned out to be false. Nevertheless, the creativity of this program was strictly limited, and possible only in this highly circumscribed domain of chemical expertise.

A model of scientific creativity that is intended to have a more general application is the BACON family of programs (Langley, Simon, Bradshaw, & Zytkow, 1987; Langley & Shrager, 1990; Simon, 1995). BACON, BLACK, GLAUBER, STAHL, and DALTON – as their names suggest – focus on the discovery of basic principles of physics and chemistry. These include mathematically expressed laws of functional dependency or conservation (e.g., Kepler's law, Boyle's law, Ohm's law, and Black's law), qualitative distinctions (e.g., acid and alkali), componential analyses (e.g., water is composed of hydrogen and oxygen), and structural hypotheses (e.g., there are two hydrogen atoms in each water molecule).

These programs use heuristic searches to find the simplest way of describing the input data. For instance, BACON uses mathematical heuristics to seek simple linear relationships first, followed by more complex ones. (It can accommodate noisy data, up to a point, by taking the best-fit equation and ignoring extraneous, or missing, data points.) So it asks whether the data measurements under investigation are directly or inversely proportional, and if so whether any constants are involved in the equation relating them. If no such function is found, other heuristics suggest new theoretical concepts defined in terms of the relevant measurements (e.g., their arithmetical product, ratio, or cube or square). Then, the program looks for a simple mathematical relationship involving the newly defined concept. Perhaps it is a constant? Or perhaps it is systematically related to some third concept – which may itself be a new theoretical construct, defined in terms of observables? BACON can define concepts in terms of the slope and intercept of graphs constructed on the basis of the initial measurements. Up to a point, it can use mathematical symmetry as a criterion for preferring one form of equation over another (mathematically equivalent) one. It can even introduce a new unit of measurement, by taking one object as the standard (human scientists often choose water).

The BACON family is still being developed by Herb Simon and colleagues. The early models named above are now integrated (the output of one contributing to the input of another), and combined with AI studies of qualitative physics and knowledge representation, in IDS (Integrated Discovery System; Langley & Shrager, 1990, chap. 4). IDS can P-create hierarchical taxonomies, qualitative laws, and quantitative laws; it can plan experiments and (by incorporating the closely related KEKADA [Kulkarni & Simon, 1988]) will take surprising results as a cue to the formulation of new hypotheses, for which it then plans new experimental tests; and it can design new measuring instruments, which it then assumes in planning further experiments (Langley & Shrager, 1990, chaps. 8–10). This work is closely related to research in machine learning and knowledge representation (Simon, 1995; Zytkow, 1995).

Simon believes that his programmed principles of discovery – the ways of generating and evaluating P-new ideas – have general application. Accordingly, he has applied them to data both ancient and modern. Given data mentioning "calx of iron," "muriatic acid," and "phlogiston," STAHL's inferences about chemical reactions will be couched in similarly old-fashioned (and partly misguided) vocabulary. This is intended not as an amusing stroll through past quaintness and folly, but as a study in the historical psychology of science. Simon's team cite the original notebooks of past scientists and claim to be uncovering the historical development of new ideas – including new forms of scientific argument (such as the search for conservation laws) – that are available to any high school student today.

Many other machine discovery (and machine learning) systems have been described. Some of these, too, have been applied to the history of science (one, for instance, suggests how chemists' successive structural models of solutions have developed, and how they have affected their discoveries [Gordon, Edwards, Sleeman, & Kodratoff, 1994]). All of these scientific programs, however, can be criticized as sidestepping important – some would say, the most important – questions.

To be sure, BACON and similar programs can find linear (and other) relationships between measurements. But they have a built-in expectation that such relationships may be there to be found. In the history of science, the mere idea of asking such a question was a very creative (very significant) step. Moreover, these programs do not have to decide *which* properties to measure – yet, in the history of science, this was by no means obvious. It is true that most human scientists are engaged in the "puzzle solving" of "normal science" (Kuhn, 1962) and do not pioneer new types of questions, or even discover new "laws": They inherit their heuristics and expectations from their forerunners, whose names have entered the history books. But to name programs after such luminaries as BACON and DALTON is to invite such comparisons.

Again, connectionists criticize such models for assuming an unrealistic rigidity of argument and conceptualization (Churchland, 1989; Hofstadter & FARG, 1995). If they model scientific discovery at all, such critics say, they capture only certain aspects of conscious, deliberate, problem solving – as opposed to the shifting perceptions and conceptualizations involved in insightful discovery. Perhaps some form of hybrid system, incorporating both associative and deliberative thinking, would be a better model of human creativity. (A hybrid model of cancer diagnosis, for example, combines connectionist pattern matching with the induction of symbolically expressed explanatory rules [Downs, Harrison, & Cross, 1995].) And, of course, such models have no sense of the real world, or of actual experimental procedure.

The success of programs for scientific discovery, limited though it is, is not matched by programs for producing poems or (especially) stories. The reason is that the relevant conceptual spaces – broadly speaking, the spaces of human motivation, world knowledge, and natural language – are so much richer, and even less well understood at the theoretical level. This, no doubt, is largely why Simon's model building has favored scientific domains. However, Simon (1994) argues that his computational theory is also relevant to the creation and understanding of literature and other arts.

Simon's account of literary criticism involves a controversial ("internalist") approach to meaning, which – along with his remarks about specific literary examples – has been criticized not only by literary scholars but also by people working in AI (Franchi & Guzeldere,

1995; Guzeldere & Franchi, 1994). And his account of cognition in general has been simi-larly challenged, on the grounds that we cannot properly ascribe meaning to any conceivable computer program (which must be "all syntax and no semantics"), or even to robots (Drey-fus, 1992; Searle, 1980). This is not the place for a rehearsal of those philosophical argu-ments, since our concern here is the extent to which computer models in various domains can at least *appear* to be creative (but see Boden, 1990, chap. 11). They are, however, a forceful reminder of the fact that literature places huge demands on our abilities to inter-pret texts in the light of our experience of the natural and cultural world.

Poetry (or rather, certain types of poetry) presents somewhat less of a challenge to the AI modeler than does connected prose, because human readers are accustomed to projecting meaning into relatively unconstrained poetic texts. Even by the 1960s, a very simple haiku program had produced stanzas to which humans could ascribe some acceptable sense (Mas-terman, 1971; Masterman & McKinnon Wood, 1968). The apparent success of this program was due almost entirely to the hermeneutic generosity of the human reader. To a lesser though significant extent, the same is true of late-twentieth-century story-writing programs.

Story-writing programs are not primarily concerned with the delicacies of linguistic expression (some ignore it entirely). In only one AI model are syntactic structure and prepo-sitional choice subtly related to the semantic content of the "story" – which concerns the competing strategies in a game of naughts and crosses (tic-tac-toe) (Davey, 1978). Rather, automatic story writers are primarily concerned with plot generation. This involves problem solving (planning) based largely on "scripts" describing stereotypical behavior, and on rep-resentations of motivational concepts (including help, friendship, competition, revenge, and betrayal) (Boden, 1977/1987, chaps. 4 and 11; Schank & Riesbeck, 1981). In other words, the prime aesthetic criteria applied by story-writing programs are the motivational plausi-bility and interest of the plot.

Usually, these are the only such criteria used by the program. Most automatic storytellers pay little attention to the rhetorical problems involved in constructing a convincing and/or interesting narrative (Ryan, 1991). Instead, the focus is entirely on the activities of the char-acters in the story. So the pioneering TALE-SPIN (Meehan, 1976, 1981) represented plan-ning as occurring only in the heads of the characters (humanoid animals, similar to those fea-tured in Aesop's fables). However, a more recent program, MINSTREL (Turner, 1994), makes a clear distinction between the (rhetorical) goals of the author and the goals of the characters. Character goals may be rejected, or their expression suppressed in the final nar-rative, for reasons of narrative interest or consistency. The results are not aesthetically excit-ing, but neither are they negligible: People answering "blind" questionnaires (without know-ing that the author is a program) credit MINSTREL with the storytelling abilities of an early high school student.

MINSTREL models creativity in two senses: It generates stories (normally regarded as an example of creativity), and in so doing it sometimes constructs novel methods for solving familiar problems. To do this, it relies on 25 creative heuristics called TRAMS (Transform, Recall, Adapt Methods). These include "ignore motivations" and "generalize actor" (both used very often by MINSTREL) and "ignore subgoal" and "thwart via death" (both used only rarely). For example (as mentioned in the preceding section), MINSTREL generates the concept of suicide from that of killing. This transformation is not effected by mere ran-dom reflexiveness (switching from "other" to "self"), but by a character's reasoned search for self-punishment, in which previous (successful) encounters with dragons or other enemies are transformed into a fight that is deliberately lost. Over time, as its uses of TRAMs accu-mulate, the program comes to generate stories that are significantly different from its initial efforts.

Even within MINSTREL's highly limited world, its TRAM-heuristics can lead to problems of consistency and/or combinatorial explosion. Some TRAMs are more troublesome than others. For instance, both "limited recall" and "ignore neighbors" drop connections to previous problem descriptions, so that many more remembered episodes will match the current problem requirements. The first of these – which removes only the *distant* connections – is often helpful, because the most important results of the remembered action are retained; but the second usually leads MINSTREL to suggest "solutions" so unconstrained as to be nonsensical.

In the language of exploration and transformation used throughout this chapter, we may say that MINSTREL explores, even tweaks, its story space, but not that it truly transforms it. For when it does attempt a fundamental transformation of story space, it loses so much of the initial structure that the results are (usually) unmanageable. The changes to motivation space effected by "ignore neighbors," for instance, are almost always too great to be compensated for. Accordingly, the program is limited to exploring story space by means of relatively minor changes (generating suicide from murder, or more generally substituting one actor for another). What MINSTREL's programmer terms "transformations" are (if successful) relatively superficial changes: They do not fundamentally alter the structure of the story space that MINSTREL inhabits.

Current computer models of the visual arts are like TALE-SPIN rather than MINSTREL, in the sense that their built-in aesthetic assumptions are applied only in generating new structures, not in evaluating and amending them at successive stages. (Occasionally, there are no built-in aesthetics at all, the program relying entirely on interactive evaluation by a person: see Sims's program in the upcoming section.) Nevertheless, these models differ in interesting ways, as is evident by comparing three examples: two concerned with architectural design, one with line drawing.

Let us consider, first, a program that generates plans and "matching" facades for Palladian villas (Hersey & Freedman, 1992). The Palladian villa has a rectangular outline and preferred numerical proportions and dimensions. Its internal walls divide the plan into smaller rectangles, and the rooms are positioned and proportioned only in certain ways. Palladio designed many variations on his basic theme, which survive as actual buildings or as drawings. He also left some remarks describing his design technique, such as his habit of "splitting" rectangles vertically or horizontally. But art historians have long disagreed about just what are the underlying rules. The Palladian program is an attempt to clarify them. Its success must be judged on three criteria: its ability to generate, or closely approximate, designs *actually produced* by Palladio; its ability to come up with new designs recognizable as Palladian, which he *might have* thought of, but didn't; and its ability to avoid non-Palladian designs, structures that Palladio *would not* have produced.

The last two criteria require aesthetic judgment as well as historical evidence. However, many such judgments are noncontentious. Some unarguably non-Palladian features occur in houses built by his imitators, and others were produced by early versions of the program. These include bays (even rectangular ones) jutting out from the rectangular perimeter; internal corridors; long, thin rooms; too many rooms; rooms of greatly disparate size; many internal (windowless) rooms; and the largest room's lying off the central axis. Other "departures" are more debatable. For instance, Palladio almost never built cylindrical rooms, and only rarely abandoned mirror-image symmetry. Should we say that an architect (or program) who does so is faithful to Palladio's inspiration, or not? When does tweaking amount to transformation? Whatever our answer, the grounds of judgment have been made explicit. So there is more chance of fruitful debate, and even of agreement.

This program has been criticized, however, for providing a relatively unprincipled model of Palladian design. As already noted, in early versions it produced many unacceptable designs, each of which prompted a "fix" ensuring that the unacceptable design feature did not arise again. Some critics offer, instead, a Palladian *shape grammar,* by which unaccept-able designs (compare: ungrammatical word strings) simply cannot be generated (Stiny & Mitchell, 1978). (Shape grammars are often described as paper-and-pencil rule-following exercises, but can be expressed as computer programs.)

Another architectural shape grammar describes Frank Lloyd Wright's Prairie Houses (Koning & Eizenberg, 1981). The three-dimensional structures it generates include "re-peats" of examples designed by Lloyd Wright and H-new houses within the same style (Kon-ing & Eizenberg, 1981). A world expert on Lloyd Wright's work, having devoted an entire chapter to the Prairie Houses, declared their architectural balance to be "occult" (cited in Koning & Eizenberg, 1981, p. 322). We are presumably meant to infer both that their styl-istic unity is a mystery accessible only to aesthetic intuition, and that only the intuitive genius of Lloyd Wright could have designed them. However, to say that we do something intuitively does not mean that some power of intuition is involved: It means, rather, that we do not know how we do it. "Intuition" is the name of a question, not of an answer. Moreover, it is a question that can sometimes be answered with the help of computer models.

The dimensions of the Prairie House conceptual space are clearly identified within this architectural grammar as *more* or *less* fundamental. Decisions about the existence, number, and nature of balconies are made very late, so cannot affect the design of the house as a whole. Accordingly, added balconies are seen as stylistically (as well as literally) superficial. By contrast, decisions about the fireplace (or fireplaces) must be made very early, other design decisions depending on them. Consequently, to "add" a fireplace is to make a funda-mental alteration to the overall structure of the building. But if the grammar is followed, it will still be recognizable as an (unusual) form of Prairie House.

Since the grammar allows a range of choices at each point of choice, one can move into various regions of the conceptual space, differing from neighboring regions in more or less fundamental ways. Distinct "families" of houses inhabit different regions of the space, and our intuitive sense of similarity and dissimilarity can be specified accordingly. The principle of unity is no longer occult, but has been made explicit.

The third visual example is AARON, a program (more accurately, a series of programs) for generating line drawings (McCorduck, 1991) and, recently, for coloring those drawings (Cohen, 1995). Unlike computer graphics in general, AARON is not focused primarily on surfaces. Rather, it generates some representation of a three-dimensional core, and then draws a line around it. Those versions of the program that can draw a wide range of idio-syncratic portraits use 900 control points to specify the three-dimensional core, of which 300 specify the structure of the face and head. AARON was written by Harold Cohen (already an acclaimed painter in the 1960s), and its drawings have been exhibited in the Tate and other galleries worldwide. They are aesthetically pleasing, even interesting: In other words, they are not shown merely for their curiosity value. The art curator Eugene Schwartz has said: "Now we find that there is a new kind of artistic intelligence working alongside of us. . . . [AARON] will send first a chill, and then a burst of energy through the art world. Its effect on tomorrow's art may equal the invention of the camera" (quoted in Simon, 1994, p. 145).

Until very recently, colored images of AARON's work were hand painted by Cohen him-self, as he had not yet built a coloring program that satisfied him. But in 1995 he exhibited a coloring program at the Boston Computer Museum. This incarnation of AARON chooses colors by tonality (light/dark) rather than hue, although it can decide to concentrate on a par-ticular family of hues. It draws outlines using a paintbrush, but colors the paper by applying five round "paint blocks" of differing sizes. Some characteristic features of the resulting painting style are due to the physical properties of the dyes and painting blocks rather than to the program guiding their use. Like drawing-AARON, painting-AARON is still under continuous development.

The drawings are individually unpredictable (because of random choices), but all the drawings produced by a given version of AARON will have the same style. For instance, one version draws acrobats, using built-in knowledge of human anatomy (head, trunk, arms, legs) and of how body parts appear from different viewpoints or in different attitudes. AARON's powers of evaluation are limited and not self-corrective. Some evaluative criteria (about aesthetic balance, for instance) are built into its generative processes, and it may consider what it has already done in deciding what to do next. But AARON cannot reflect on its own productions, nor adjust them so as to make them better.

AARON's drawing capacities, though initially impressive, are strictly circumscribed. It cannot draw one-armed acrobats, for instance (although it can draw acrobats with only one arm visible because the second arm is occluded). The relevant conceptual space does not allow for the possibility of one-armed people: To this program, they are unimaginable. If AARON could "drop" one of the limbs, as a composer may ignore a current stylistic constraint, it could draw one-armed figures (though the realism of AARON's style could be maintained only by additional changes in the bodily balance rules).

A more powerful transformation might be made if the numeral 2 were used within the program to denote the number of arms. Given a heuristic that enabled the program on occasion to substitute one numeral for another, 2 might sometimes be replaced by 1 – or by some other number. (Chemists after Kekulé did this in asking whether any ring molecules could have five atoms.) A program that (today) drew one-armed acrobats for the first time by employing a "substitute-the-numeral" (or "vary-the-variable") heuristic *could* (tomorrow) draw seven-legged acrobats as well. A program that merely "dropped the left arm" *could not*. This example is reminiscent of work in developmental psychology suggesting that increasing flexibility and imaginativeness is made possible by the development of explicit representations (on successive levels) of existing skills (Karmiloff-Smith, 1992).

You may feel that architecture, if not line drawing, is relatively easy to discuss in computational terms. After all, the aesthetics of the Palladian style have always been described in terms of mathematical regularity and proportion, and Lloyd Wright presented his Prairie Houses as examples of a single, minimalist, architectural paradigm. Perhaps we should consider something more spontaneous, less "cut and dried"?

What about jazz improvisation? This is normally regarded as one of the peaks of spontaneous creativity, and to many people appears less constrained than even the most undisciplined architecture. The former view is justified, but the latter is not. The conceptual space of jazz improvisation has been partially mapped by two programs, each of which was written in an attempt to understand how the human musician does it.

One is a program designed to teach people to improvise jazz (Boden & Hodgson, in preparation; Hodgson, 1990; Waugh, 1992). It clearly defines various dimensions of the musical space and various ways of traveling through it. The program can be left to wander through the space by itself, in which case it will improvise – on a given melody, harmony, and rhythm – by making (random) choices on many dimensions simultaneously. Quite often, when it is working in this fashion, it creates novel musical ideas that a professional jazz musician finds interesting and may wish to develop in his or her own playing. Alternatively, the human user can make the program concentrate on one (or more) dimension at a time and explore it (or them) in a very simple way. This is why it can help jazz novices, who can focus on the aspect of jazz that is currently causing them difficulty.

Many dimensions of musical space are explored by this jazz improviser. For instance, the program can produce fragments (of random length) of ascending or descending scales, ensuring that the scale chosen is the one relevant to the harmony at that particular point. It can provide "call" and "reply" over two or more bars. It can replace the current melody note by another note drawn from the same scale, or provide a chromatic run between this melody note and the next. It can "cut and paste" a library of melodic and rhythmic patterns, or play fractionally ahead of or behind the beat. If the library of musical patterns is drawn from the style of a specific jazz musician, the music sounds strongly reminiscent of that artist. Providing this data enables the program to explore the space not only of jazz in general, but of Charlie Parker or Louis Armstrong in particular.

Because the thematic melody, harmony, and meter – and the library of musical patterns – are all provided to this program at the start, it is not limited to jazz. It can cope with other forms of tonal music. Give it "seeds" from Bach or Mozart, or a Latin American bossa nova, and it will improvise accordingly. In a sense, that is a strength. But it is also a weakness, for the program cannot compose its own seeds. Not only is it incapable of constructing a Bach invention or Debussy prelude: It cannot compose a jazz theme, either.

Another program, however, can do so – not only improvising an acceptable melody, but composing the basic chord sequence too (Johnson-Laird, 1991). (For the record, yet another program, which *can* imitate Bach or Debussy, or any other Western or non-Western composer, does not do so "from scratch": It starts by analyzing a database of music written by the composer it is imitating [Cope, 1993].)

The second jazz program, because it does start from scratch, has an even more challenging task (or rather, its programmer – Johnson-Laird – does). It plays merely at the level of a moderately competent beginner, whereas the first can sometimes sound like a highly skilled professional jazz musician. But it tells us even more about the conceptual space concerned and suggests some specific ways in which human musicians move through it.

For instance, it distinguishes between creative journeys that can be made very quickly and journeys that take more time. Human short-term memory is very limited, yet good jazz musicians can improvise as fast as they can play. This implies that the rules they use for improvisation put very little load on their memory. Accordingly, when this program improvises the melody, harmony, meter, chord, and passing notes (all of which must be mutually consistent), it never looks back beyond the immediately preceding note or chord. By contrast, people cannot compose chord sequences very fast (they are agreed on before the improvisation starts). The reason is that jazz chord sequences can have a complex, hierarchically nested structure – rather like sentences. A simple chord sequence may be comparable to "The dress is purple," but interesting ones are more like "The dress that the girl the cat the dog bit last Saturday scratched sewed is a very deep shade of purple." This last sentence does not trip easily off the tongue: It takes some time (and thought) to produce. The program that generates jazz from scratch is therefore made up of two parts. One composes complex chord sequences, using significant time and memory to do so. Its output is then fed as input to the other part, which improvises on it in real time, using rules requiring very little memory.

In jazz as in architecture, then, a computational psychology can help us understand what goes on in creative minds. And as in jazz, so in other forms of music: Research on the computer composition and analysis of music is increasing (for a useful collection of reviews, see Smoliar, 1995). Science can help humanist scholars to define the conceptual spaces concerned, and it can tell us something about how, in practice, they can be explored.

But what about transformations? None of the programs I've mentioned transforms one style into another – although one of them can "mix" styles, by mixing databases (of Bach and Scott Joplin, for example) (Cope, 1991). And the BACONian programs that "discovered" a host of scientific laws did not originate the idea of looking for linear relationships or for conservation principles: Those styles of scientific inquiry were provided to them for free. Perhaps this is no accident? Perhaps it is in principle impossible for a computer model to transform its way of working?

TRANSFORMATIONAL CREATIVITY

As yet, only very few computer models have a plausible, let alone convincing, claim to transformational creativity. All these programs can make changes in their own rules, and some can also evaluate the novel results. Most use genetic algorithms (GAs): general methods of iterative self-modification, inspired by genetic mutations and crossover in biology, which involve automatic (or sometimes interactive) selection at each "generation." But a handful of apparently T-creative programs employ self-modifying heuristics designed to foster transformations within the conceptual space concerned.

Heuristics for psychological T-creativity were designed by Doug Lenat (1977, 1983), in his programs AM and EURISKO. Both programs include heuristics for altering concepts, and EURISKO also includes heuristics for altering its own heuristics (so as to improve its own processing style).

AM's task is to play around with about 100 very simple mathematical concepts, so as to come up with new ideas (which are added to the pool). The most interesting new ideas are identified, and then further altered and elaborated. The types of conceptual change involved include generalizing, specializing, inverting, exemplifying, and combining concepts. These are domain-neutral notions, but the program's (approximately 300) heuristics also include many specifically mathematical ones. What counts as "interesting" to AM is decided by heuristics such as "If the union of two sets possesses a property that was possessed by each original set, that is interesting" and "If the union of two sets possesses a property that was lacking in each original set, that is interesting." Again, these two heuristics are domain-neutral (noting conservation and emergence, respectively). But specifically mathematical criteria are provided also.

Lenat describes AM as creative, for it has generated many undeniably interesting P-novel ideas. Starting from 100 set-theoretic concepts, the program generated many arithmetic ideas – including addition, multiplication, prime numbers, and Goldbach's conjecture. It has even suggested a minor H-novel theorem (in an area of mathematics, maximally divisible numbers, previously unknown to Lenat).

However, the creativity of Lenat's program is problematic (Rowe & Partridge, 1993). For one thing, AM has picked out an enormous number of ideas that human mathematicians regard as boring, or even valueless. Creative humans have silly ideas too, of course, but not so many – and they are usually able to reject them on closer evaluation. Again, critics (Ritchie & Hanna, 1984) have claimed (though Lenat in Lenat & Seely-Brown, [1984], denies) that a rarely used heuristic employed just before AM's discovery of prime numbers was included in the 300 because of its potential for aiding the development of this important idea. Third, AM's processing is sometimes partly interactive, for a human can direct AM to explore a P-novel concept whose potential interest is obvious to human mathematicians, but not to the program. Fourth, the syntax of the LISP programming language, in which AM is written, tacitly constrains the structure of AM's P-novel ideas in such a way that they are highly likely to be mathematically intelligible (whether or not they are also interesting). Strictly, these intelligibility constraints should have been made explicit. And finally, AM is unable to change its own values: Its criteria of what is "interesting" never vary.

EURISKO is fundamentally similar to AM, but it allows for transformation of heuristics as well as concepts. For example, one metaheuristic lowers the probability-of-use of any heuristic that, having been used several times already, has never led to an interesting result. Another looks out for heuristics that have been helpful only rarely and specializes them in several different ways. Other metaheuristics generalize heuristics or create new ones by analogy with old ones (various methods are used for constructing generalizations or analogies: EURISKO monitors their success and favors the most useful). Many of these heuristics can be applied reflexively. For instance, the specializing heuristic can be applied to itself, because it is sometimes useful and sometimes not.

EURISKO has come up with H-novel ideas in various domains. One such – a three-dimensional unit for a computer chip, carrying out two logical functions simultaneously – was awarded a U.S. patent, normally regarded as recognizing creative innovation. Another was so successful against its human rivals in a national competition (playing war games with battleships) that it prompted a defensive rule change; when that proved insufficient to make EURISKO lose, an extra rule was added: *No programs* are allowed to compete! Despite these successes, EURISKO is not widely used. A prime reason for this is that its power lies largely in the domain-specific heuristics, whose identification and expression require considerable effort and expertise.

Genetic algorithms originated within AI, where they are used for problems involving optimization and classification (Holland, Holyoak, Nisbett, & Thagard, 1986). They are also widely used within artificial life (A-Life). A-Life studies the spontaneous emergence of new forms of order, often (though not always) of increasing complexity (Boden, 1996; Langton, 1995).

One common way of using GAs is to start with an initial rule set, or program, which performs the relevant task badly – if at all (sometimes, the initial rules are randomly composed and/or chosen). To produce the next generation, the GA makes random changes to one or more of the initial rules. These may be point mutations (substitutions at one or more points within one rule) or crossovers of more or less complexity (wherein sequences of fixed or random length are swapped between two rules). The daughter program then attempts to solve the problem, and its performance is automatically evaluated so as to assess how much each individual rule contributes to its overall success (however limited that success may be). The relatively helpful rules are then used in "breeding" the granddaughter program. After many iterations of this variation selection cycle, the evolved program may be highly efficient or even optimal. Another way of using GAs is to start with many identical copies of the initial program, make random variations in each one, and use the most successful (least unsuccessful) descendants as "parents" of the next generation. Here, the evaluation picks out entire programs (not individual rules) and may be either automatic or interactive.

GA programs in general are *relevant to* T-creativity (and E-creativity also), for they all modify some initial style of processing so as eventually to produce another one. That is, they all gradually transform their problem space, increasing their value (efficiency) as they do so. The extent to which they may properly be seen as models *of* creativity is debatable. They are not usually so described (or intended) when applied for relatively humdrum purposes, such as optimization and classification. Even in these contexts, however, their designers sometimes stress their likeness to processes of inductive classification and theory formation in science (Holland et al., 1986). They are more likely to be described as models *of* creativity when applied to artistic domains, normally regarded as involving human creativity. And GA studies of evolution as such could also be regarded as models *of* creativity, although they are rarely described in these terms. Examples mentioned later include the automatic evolution of computer-animated creatures, and the evolution of novel anatomies and behaviors in robots (real and simulated).

Examples of GAs as *models of* creativity include two in the domain of graphic art. Karl Sims (1991) and William Latham (Todd & Latham, 1992) have developed GA programs for generating infinitely many colored images (of two-dimensional patterns and three-dimensional forms, respectively). The selection is interactive: At each stage, a human being chooses the (one or two) most attractive or interesting image/s to breed the next generation. Both programs satisfy the "novelty" criterion for creativity, coming up with H-novel images on every run. And both seem to be acceptable from the evaluative point of view: Sims's model generates many attractive patterns, and the products of Latham's system, though not to everyone's taste, are sold in art galleries around the world.

Inspection of the images produced by these programs may suggest that Latham's program (like AARON, discussed in the preceding section) engages only in E-creativity, whereas Sims's system has achieved T-creativity. Put another way, Sims's program can seem "more creative" than Latham's. If one asks a group of people which program is the more creative, many (in my experience, usually most) choose the Sims model.

The main reason for this judgment is that Sims's model generates more, and deeper, surprises than Latham's does. One cannot predict even the general form (never mind the details) of the next generation. Even more to the point, it is sometimes impossible to see any family resemblance between a Sims-pattern and its parent/s. Being able to inspect the relevant code does not always help: Sims himself cannot always explain why the visible differences between parent and daughter images result from the code differences between the mini programs that generated them. In other words, the Sims model sometimes *transforms the image space* so profoundly that the daughter images appear to bear almost no relation to their parent/s. Latham's program, by contrast, produces images all of which are instantly recognizable as "Latham forms," and each of which bears a very strong family resemblance to its parents and siblings. Another reason why many people regard Sims's model as "more creative" is that it always comes up with at least some patterns they regard as attractive, whereas Latham's may not. Indeed, quite a few people find Latham's images, which resemble mollusks and snakes, strongly repellent.

However, we have seen (in the section titled "Creativity and Computers") that both E-creativity and T-creativity arise within some structured conceptual space, whose constraints enable only certain types of ideas to be generated. Moreover, the "value" we ascribe to ET-novelties depends on the evaluative criteria we apply to that particular conceptual space. These may be partly extrinsic (so a scientific hypothesis should tally with the empirical data) but are always largely intrinsic, in that we evaluate a new idea partly in terms of its relation to (previous ideas in) *the relevant space.* That is, ET-creativity (unlike combinatorial creativity) involves not only the appearance of novelty, but also its development. The creative artist or scientist thinks in a disciplined manner, even if he or she sometimes rejects certain aspects of the familiar thinking style and/or relies on chance to suggest some new notions. Such thinkers may be playful, but are not merely playing around. When something of (potential) interest turns up as a result of their playfulness, they focus on it – accepting, amending, and developing it in disciplined ways. Only when it fails, or when the limits of its potential are glimpsed, do they turn to other things.

This aspect of human creativity gives grounds to deny the T-creative superiority of Sims's program. For this program is, in effect, just playing around. It is not even playing around within an aesthetically structured space, for it has no built-in criteria guiding it to generate one sort of image rather than another. The appearance of T-creativity arises because, at each generation, Sims's program can make random changes within the very heart of the code defining the parental image space. It may, for instance, nest an entire image-generating program within another or concatenate two unrelated (and already complex) programs. The resulting image may be deeply surprising to human beings watching the program run, but this image is not "captured," to be focused on (explored) for a while. Although it can be used to breed the next generation, the breeding process may transform it just as drastically as before. At present, there is no way in which one can instruct the program to make one sort of change rather than another. The human evaluator, who selects the parent/s at each stage, rapidly becomes bored on finding that any "interesting" feature of a chosen image may disappear immediately, and certainly cannot be incrementally developed or systematically explored.

Latham – who, unlike Sims, is a professional artist – allows his GAs only to tweak the parameters of the current program, not to transform it at its heart. His reward is that he can use the program to explore a specific type of conceptual space, which he finds aesthetically interesting, in specific directions – often reaching places that (he says) he could not possibly have reached unaided. The price is that there can be no truly fundamental surprises. Latham's own aesthetic "voice" speaks through all his program's images – which is why it is possible for some people to be repelled (and others attracted) by virtually all of its products.

Life forms were Latham's inspiration for aesthetic, not biological, reasons. But many GA researchers aim to throw light on biological evolution. GAs have been used to evolve (for example) the "brains" – sensorimotor morphology, behavior, and hardware – of actual mobile robots (Cliff, Harvey, & Husbands, 1993; Thompson, 1995), and predator–prey behaviors in simulated robots (Cliff & Miller, 1997; Miller & Cliff, 1997). They have also evolved the anatomy and "lifelike" behavior of combative jointed creatures, simulated in a virtual world with physics similar to ours (Sims, 1994).

Biological evolution can be thought of as a form of T-creativity. Its products are not ideas, but morphologies and/or behaviors. Its evaluations are effected not by negotiation between social groups, but by natural selection within some environmental niche. And changes within biological space (the space of possible genotypes and phenotypes) are always "accidental" and "blind," whereas the exploration and transformation of conceptual spaces is often deliberately pursued and sometimes consciously guided.

Accordingly, computer models of evolution raise various points relevant to psychological creativity. For instance, two of the "creature-evolving" examples cited earlier display a form of serendipity: Flaws in the actual (Thompson, 1995) or the simulated (Sims, 1994) physics were not merely compensated for, but positively exploited, enabling the resulting creatures to do (task-efficient) things that would not be possible in a physically perfect system.

Again, work in A-Life has confirmed Darwin's suggestion that coevolution, in which two (or more) species evolve alongside and in response to each other, can enable a species to evolve both farther and faster than it would have done in isolation (Ray, 1992, 1994). Modeling the ways in which this can happen may help us in thinking about the effects of criticism, competition, and cooperation in fostering – and preventing – human creativity.

Finally, these computer models provide an example wherein a system's criteria of evaluation (its fitness function) are not fixed, but evolve in response to the changing environment. Human creativity, too, involves alterations in the evaluation function. Sometimes these occur for chance reasons unrelated to the structure of the space, so that we speak of an isolated "change" rather than a progressive "evolution." An example would be a sudden, and "structureless," change in the fashion for headgear triggered by photographs of a world-renowned pop star's wearing a particular hat. But sometimes the changes in evaluative criteria are more gradual and more closely related to the structure of the space concerned. One example would be the way in which single-key tonal music gradually became boring and modulations – of increasing harmonic unexpectedness – then became preferred. A-Life work on the evolution of fitness functions might help us to understand some of the changes we see in evaluations carried out by human social groups.

CONCLUSION

Some readers of this volume may have started this chapter – or avoided it altogether – in the common belief that computer models are irrelevant to creativity. The preceding sections have argued that this belief is false. But they have not mentioned a widespread assumption that underlies it. This is the view that creativity cannot be brought within the domain of science because it is essentially unpredictable.

Briefly (for a fuller discussion, see Boden, 1990, chap. 9), science does not necessarily involve prediction, or even detailed post hoc explanation. Its aim is to understand how events in the natural world are possible, what are the underlying structures generating superficially observable phenomena, and how those phenomena are interrelated – in short, to discover structural possibilities. Detailed predictions and explanations after the fact are possible only in some fields. They are not in general available for nonlinear systems and evolution – yet these are proper topics for science and have been much illuminated by the relevant theories within physics and biology.

With respect to creativity, there are many reasons for expecting that – in the general case – detailed prediction and explanation will not be possible. This is especially clear with respect to combinational creativity, but ET-creativity, too, is largely unpredictable (and H-creativity is by definition unpredicted). Although one can sometimes deliberately lead someone else to make a specific P-creative move (good teachers do this often), this is usually impossible. Chance factors such as serendipity cannot be foreseen. When they happen, their effect may be mysterious (even to the individual concerned) because of the idiosyncratic, and largely unconscious, complexity of human minds. ET-creativity can sometimes be explained post hoc, and may even seem in retrospect to have been inevitable. The reason for this is that the constraints defining any conceptual space offer specific possibilities for exploration, tweaking, and transformation. But why individuals focused on *this* constraint rather than *that* one, and why they made *just this* change rather than some other, will not usually be explicable. We can understand, nonetheless, how the old and new spaces are related, and why the P-creative idea could not have occurred before the creative transformation. (Analogously, we can see how various fossil species are related, and why a given anatomical change makes a particular behavioral adaptation possible. But that is not to say that we can explain just how modern horses arose out of *Eohippus*, or what will happen to them in future.)

In sum, a psychological science of creativity is a reasonable aim. It would integrate cognitive, social, motivational, and personality factors. It would enable us to understand how creativity is possible, and even (up to a point) how it can be fostered and encouraged. But predicting creative ideas, or even explaining them in detail, will not in general be possible.

REFERENCES

Abelson, R. P. (1973). The structure of belief systems. In R. C. Schank & K. M. Colby (Eds.), *Computer models of thought and language* (pp. 287–340).

Beaudoin, L. P., & Sloman, A. (1993). A study of motive processing and attention. In A. Sloman, D. Hogg, G. Humphreys, D. Partridge, & A. Ramsay (Eds.), *Prospects for artificial intelligence* (pp. 229–238). Amsterdam: IOS.

Boden, M. A. (1972). *Purposive explanation in psychology.* Cambridge, MA: Harvard University Press.

Boden, M. A. (1987). *Artificial intelligence and natural man* (2nd. ed.). New York: Basic. (Original work published 1977)

Boden, M. A. (1990). *The creative mind: Myths and mechanisms.* London: Abacus; New York: Basic.

Boden, M. A. (1991). Horses of a different color? In W. Ramsey, S. P. Stich, & D. E. Rumelhart (Eds.), *Philosophy and connectionist theory* (pp. 3–19). Hillsdale, NJ: Erlbaum.

Boden, M. A. (Ed.). (1994). *Dimensions of creativity.* Cambridge, MA: MIT Press.

Boden, M. A. (Ed.). (1996). *The philosophy of artificial life.* Oxford: Oxford University Press.

Boden, M. A., & Hodgson, P. W. (in preparation). *Creativity: An interactive experience* (provisional title of CD-ROM).

Brannigan, A. (1981). *The social basis of scientific discoveries.* Cambridge University Press.

Churchland, P. M. (1989). *A neurocomputational perspective: The nature of mind and the structure of science.* Cambridge, MA: MIT Press.

Cliff, D., Harvey, I., & Husbands, P. (1993). Explorations in evolutionary robotics. *Adaptive Behavior,* 2, 71–108.

Cliff, D., & Miller, G. F. (1997) Co-evolution of pursuit and evasion.: Part 2, Simulation methods and results. Submitted for publication.

Cohen, H. (1995). The further exploits of AARON painter. In S. Franchi & G. Guzeldere (Eds.), *Constructions of the mind: Artificial intelligence and the humanities.* Special edition of *Stanford Humanities Review,* 4(2), 141–160.

Davey, A. (1978). *Discourse production: A computer model of some aspects of a speaker.* Edinburgh: Edinburgh University Press.

Downs, J., Harrison, R. F., & Cross, S. S. (1995). A neural network decision-support tool for the diagnosis of breast cancer. In J. Hallam (Ed.), *Hybrid problems, hybrid solutions* (pp. 51–60). Oxford: IOS Press.

Dreyfus, H. L. (1992). *What computers still can't do.* Cambridge, MA: MIT Press.

Dyer, M. G. (1983). *In-depth understanding: A computer model of integrated processing for narrative comprehension.* Cambridge, MA: MIT Press.

Evans, T. G. (1968). A program for the solution of a class of geometric analogy intelligence test questions. In M. L. Minsky (Ed.), *Semantic information processing* (pp. 271–353). Cambridge, MA: MIT Press.

Falkenhainer, B. (1990). A unified approach to explanation and theory formation. In J. Shrager & P. Langley (Eds.), *Computational models of discovery and theory formation* (pp. 157–196). San Mateo, CA: Morgan Kaufmann.

Falkenhainer, B., Forbus, K. D., & Gentner, D. (1989). The structure-mapping engine: Algorithm and examples. *Artificial Intelligence, 41,* 1–63.

Forbus, K. D., Gentner, D., & Law, K. (1994). MAC/FAC: A model of similarity-based retrieval. *Cognitive Science, 119,* 141–205.

Franchi, S., & Guzeldere, G. (Eds.). (1995). *Constructions of the mind: Artificial intelligence and the humanities.* Special edition of *Stanford Humanities Review, 4*(2) 1–345.

French, R. (1995). *The subtlety of sameness.* Cambridge, MA: MIT Press.

Gardner, H. (1993). *Creating minds: An anatomy of creativity seen through the lives of Freud, Einstein, Picasso, Stravinsky, Eliot, Graham, and Gandhi.* New York: Basic.

Gentner, D. (1989). The mechanisms of analogical learning. In S. Vosniadou & A. Ortony (Eds.), *Similarity and analogical reasoning* (pp. 199–241). Cambridge University Press.

Gordon, A., Edwards, P., Sleeman, D., & Kodratoff, Y. (1994). Scientific discovery in a space of structural models: An example from the history of solution chemistry. *Proceedings of the Sixteenth Annual Conference of the Cognitive Science Society,* pp. 381–386. Hillsdale, NJ: Erlbaum.

Guzeldere, G., & Franchi, S. (Eds.). (1994). *Bridging the gap: Where cognitive science meets literary criticism. (Herbert Simon and respondents).* Special supplement of *Stanford Humanities Review,* 4(1), 1–164.

Heerwagen, J. H., & Orians, G. H. (1993). Humans, habitats, and aesthetics. In S. R. Kellart & E. O. Wilson (Eds.), *The biophilia hypothesis* (pp. 138–172). Washington, DC: Shearwater.

Hersey, G., & Freedman, R. (1992). *Possible Palladian villas (plus a few instructively impossible ones).* Cambridge, MA: MIT Press.

Hofstadter, D. R. (1994). How could a COPYCAT ever be creative? In T. Dartnall (Ed.), *Artificial intelligence and creativity: An interdisciplinary approach* (pp. 405–424). Dordrecht: Kluwer Academic.

Hofstadter, D. R., & FARG (Fluid Analogies Research Group). (1995). *Fluid concepts and creative analogies: Computer models of the fundamental mechanisms of thought.* New York: Basic.

Holland, J. H., Holyoak, K. J., Nisbett, R. E., & P. R. Thagard. (1986). *Induction: Processes of inference, learning, and discovery.* Cambridge, MA: MIT-Press.

Holyoak, K. J., & Barnden, J. A. (Eds.). (1994) *Advances in connectionist and neural computation theory: Vol. 2. Connectionist approaches to analogy, metaphor, and case-based reasoning.* Norwood, NJ: Ablex.

Holyoak, K. J., & Thagard, P. R. (1989). Analogical mapping by constraint satisfaction. *Cognitive Science, 13,* 295–356.

Holyoak, K. J., & Thagard, P. R. (1994). *Mental leaps: Analogy in creative thought.* Cambridge, MA: MIT Press.

Johnson-Laird, P. N. (1993). Jazz improvisation: A theory at the computational level. In P. Howell, R. West, and I. J. Cross (Eds.), *Representing musical structure* (pp. 291–326). London: Academic.

Karmiloff-Smith, A. (1992). *Beyond modularity: A developmental perspective on cognitive science.* Cambridge, MA: MIT Press.

Kolodner, J. (1993). *Case-based reasoning.* San Mateo, CA: Morgan Kaufman.

Koning, H., & Eizenberg, J. (1981). The language of the prairie: Frank Lloyd Wright's Prairie Houses. *Environment and Planning B, 8,* 295–323.

Kuhn, T. S. (1962). *The structure of scientific revolutions.* Chicago: Chicago University Press.

Kulkarni, D., & Simon, H. A. (1988). The processes of scientific discovery: The strategy of experimentation. *Cognitive Science, 12,* 139–175.

Langley, P., & Shrager, J. (Eds.). (1990). *Computational models of discovery and theory formation.* San Mateo, CA: Morgan Kaufmann.

Langley, P., Simon, H. A., Bradshaw, G. L., & Zytkow, J. M. (1987). *Scientific discovery: Computational explorations of the creative process.* Cambridge, MA: MIT Press.

Langton, C. J. (Ed.). (1995). *Artificial life: An overview.* Cambridge, MA: MIT Press.

Lenat, D. B. (1977). The ubiquity of discovery. *Artificial Intelligence, 9,* 257–286.

Lenat, D. B. (1983). The role of heuristics in learning by discovery: Three case studies. In R. S. Michalski, J. G. Carbonell, & T. M. Mitchell (Eds.), *Machine learning: An artificial intelligence approach* (pp. 243–306). Palo Alto, CA: Tioga.

Lenat, D. B., & Seely-Brown, J. (1984). Why AM and EURISKO appear to work. *Artificial Intelligence Journal, 23,* 269–294.

Lindsay, R., Buchanan, B. G., Feigenbaum, E. A., & Lederberg, J. (1980). *DENDRAL.* New York: McGraw-Hill.

Longuet-Higgins, H. C. (1987). *Mental processes: Studies in cognitive science.* Cambridge, MA: MIT Press.

Longuet-Higgins, H. C. (1994). Artificial intelligence and musical cognition. *Philosophical Transactions of the Royal Society of London, Series A, 349,* 103–113. (Special issue on "Artificial intelligence and the Mind: New breakthroughs or dead ends?" ed. M. A. Boden, A. Bundy, & R. M. Needham.)

McCorduck, P. (1991). *Aaron's code.* San Francisco: Freeman.

McGraw, G. E. (1995). *Letter spirit: Part 1. Emergent high-level perception of letters using fluid concepts.* Unpublished doctoral dissertation, Indiana University, Bloomington, IN.

Masterman, M. (1971). Computerized haiku. In J. Reichardt (Ed.), *Cybernetics, art, and ideas* (pp. 175–183). London: Studio Vista.

Masterman, M., & McKinnon Wood, R. (1968). Computerized Japanese haiku. In J. Reichardt (Ed.), *Cybernetic serendipity* (pp. 54–55). London: Studio International.

Meehan, J. (1976). *The metanovel: Writing stories by computer.* Unpublished doctoral dissertation, technical report 74, Yale University, New Haven, CT.

Meehan, J. (1981). TALE-SPIN. In R. C. Schank & C. J. Riesbeck (Eds.), *Inside computer understanding: Five programs plus miniatures* (pp. 197–226). Hillsdale, NJ: Erlbaum.

Miller, G. F., & Cliff, D. (1997) Co-evolution of pursuit and evasion. Part 1, Biological and game-theoretic foundations. Manuscript submitted for publication.

Mitchell, M. (1993). *Analogy-making as perception.* Cambridge, MA: MIT Press.

Orians, G. H., & Heerwagen, J. H. (1992). Evolved responses to landscapes. In J. Barkow, L. Cosmides, & J. Toobey (Eds.), *The adapted mind: Evolutionary psychology and the generation of culture* (pp. 555–580). Oxford: Oxford University Press.

Popper, K. R. (1963). *Conjectures and refutations: The growth of scientific knowledge.* London: Routledge & Kegan Paul.

Ray, T. S. (1992). An approach to the synthesis of life. In C. G. Langton, C. Taylor, J. Doyne Farmer, & S. Rasmussen (Eds.), *Artificial life* (Vol. 2, pp. 371–408). Redwood City, CA: Addison-Wesley. (Reprinted in M. A. Boden [Ed.], *The philosophy of artificial life* [pp. 111–145]. Oxford: Oxford University Press, 1996)

Ray, T. S. (1994). An evolutionary approach to synthetic biology: Zen and the art of creating life. *Artificial Life, 1,* 179–210.

Ritchie, G. D., & Hanna, F. K. (1984). AM: A case study in AI methodology, *Artificial Intelligence Journal, 23,* 249–263.

Rowe, J., & Partridge, D. (1993). Creativity: A survey of AI approaches. *Artificial Intelligence Review, 7,* 43–70.

Rumelhart, D. E., & McClelland, J. L. (1986). *Parallel distributed processing: Explorations in the microstructure of cognition* (2 vols.). Cambridge, MA: MIT Press.

Ryan, M.-L. (1991). *Possible worlds, artificial intelligence, and narrative theory.* Bloomington: Indiana University Press.

Schaffer, S. (1994). Making-up discovery. In M. A. Boden (Ed.), *Dimensions of creativity* (pp. 13–51). Cambridge, MA: MIT Press.

Schank, R. C. (1990). *Tell me a story: A new look at real and artificial memory.* New York: Scribner's.

Schank, R. C., & Abelson, R. P. (1977). *Scripts, plans, goals, and understanding.* Hillsdale, NJ: Erlbaum.

Schank, R. C., & Childers, P. (1988). *The creative attitude: Learning to ask and answer the right questions.* New York: Macmillan.

Schank, R. C., & Riesbeck, C. (Eds.). (1981). *Inside computer understanding: Five programs plus miniatures.* Hillsdale, NJ: Erlbaum.

Searle, J. R. (1980). Minds, brains, and programs. *Behavioral and Brain Sciences, 3,* 473–497. (Reprinted in M. A. Boden [Ed.], *The philosophy of artificial intelligence* [pp. 67–88]. Oxford: Oxford University Press, 1990)

Simon, H. A. (1994). Literary criticism: A cognitive approach. In G. Guzeldere & S. Franchi (Eds.), *Bridging the gap: Where cognitive science meets literary criticism (Herbert Simon and Respondents).* Special supplement of *Stanford Humanities Review, 4*(1), 1–27.

Simon, H. A. (1995). Machine discovery [Special issue]. *Foundations of Science, 1*(2), 171–200.

Sims, K. (1991). Artificial evolution for computer graphics. *Computer Graphics, 25*(4), 319–328.

Sims, K. (1994). Evolving 3D morphology and behavior by competition. *Artificial Life, 1,* 353–372.

Sloman, A. (1987). Motives, mechanisms, and emotions. *Journal of Emotion and Cognition, 1,* 217–233. (Reprinted in M. A. Boden [Ed.], *The philosophy of artificial intelligence* [pp. 231–247]. Oxford: Oxford University Press, 1990)

Smoliar, S. (Ed.). (1995). The music collection. *Artificial Intelligence, 79,* 341–398.

Stiny, G., & Mitchell, W. J. (1978). The Palladian grammar. *Environment and Planning, B, 5,* 5–18.

Thagard, P. R. (1992). *Conceptual revolutions.* Princeton, NJ: Princeton University Press.

Thompson, A. (1995). Evolving electronic robot controllers that exploit hardware resources. In F. Moran, A. Moreno, J. J. Merelo, & P. Chacon (Eds.), *Advances in artificial life: Proceedings of the Third European Conference on Artificial Life* (pp. 641–657). Berlin: Springer.

Todd, S., & W. Latham (1992). *Evolutionary art and computers.* London: Academic.

Turner, S. R. (1994). *The creative process: A computer model of storytelling and creativity.* Hillsdale, NJ: Erlbaum.

Wright, I. P., Sloman, A., & Beaudoin, L. P. (in press). The architectural basis for grief. *Philosophy, Psychiatry, & Psychology.*

Zytkow, J. M. (1995) Creating a discoverer: Autonomous knowledge seeking agent [Special issue]. *Foundations of Science, 1*(2), 253–283.

19   *Organizational Creativity*

WENDY M. WILLIAMS AND LANA T. YANG

Before you build a better mousetrap, it helps to know if there are any mice out there.
>> Mortimer B. Zuckerman

He who builds a better mousetrap these days runs into material shortages, patent-infringement suits, work stoppages, collusive bidding, discount discrimination – and taxes.
>> H. E. Martz

Individual creativity and group creativity are two different beasts. Consider the mad but brilliant scientist, long deprived of food, sleep, soap, and water, pacing the hallways until the "aha" insight hits at 4 a.m. Say he has just solved a fundamental problem in modern physics concerning the behavior of subatomic particles. If he can demonstrate through a mathematical proof his logic – and if his logic predicts observable data – his tenure worries are probably behind him. True, he must be able to convince one journal to publish his idea. However, even if his idea is not well received by his immediate colleagues, as long as it is recognized by eminent members of the scientific community, his future is relatively secure.

Now imagine an equally gifted budding genius who works for a corporation. She has a significant insight that could revolutionize the business. Unlike the physicist, whose major challenge was to record and publish his mathematical proof, the corporate scientist faces the additional challenges of dealing with co-workers and superiors in the hierarchy who may or may not support her idea (or who may wish to steal or suppress it for nefarious reasons), demonstrating the utility and profitability of her idea to skeptics, proving that the idea can be tested on a small scale, showing that this test will not adversely affect business or alienate customers, and generally shepherding her idea through the quagmire of the business environment. It is clear from this example that building a better mousetrap in an organizational setting requires more than simply an awareness of the existence of mice.

This volume on creativity explores many approaches and aspects of what, exactly, creativity is and the factors that influence its expression. The goal of this chapter is to discuss organizational creativity and to show why creativity within an organizational setting is not simply individual creativity that happens at work. We begin by discussing classic views of organizations, showing how the structure of organizations affects employee creativity. Next, we review formal theories of creativity and approaches to understanding creativity from the perspectives of the individual, the environment or system, and the organization, with an emphasis on using these approaches to understand organizational creativity. We close with a discussion of how organizational creativity can be increased.

ORGANIZATIONAL CHARACTERISTICS AFFECTING CREATIVITY

The heightened competition within today's business climate has forced organizations to reexamine the assumptions of traditional theories of organizational structure and operation.

373

Established formulas for decision making have become less applicable, because these formulas were based on principles promoting and reflecting the stability of a prior era. Traditional procedures for routinizing problem-solving processes through the use of hierarchical and bureaucratic systems are being challenged and shown to be inefficient. As a result, the limitations of policies based on traditional conceptions of organizations are being exposed. Often, these shortcomings stem from the failure of older theories to incorporate the flexibility and adaptability required by organizations in the current era, in which shifting international markets and new products, technologies, and ideas are constantly transforming industries.

Given the challenges faced by today's organizations, the relevance of creativity to problem solving, decision making, and research and development is clear. To remain competitive, businesses can no longer follow time-tested formulas of precedent; they must be able to produce and be receptive to innovation, which is synonymous here with creativity in an organizational context.

How can research on the nature of organizations help us to understand organizational influences upon creativity? Consider first traditional models of organizational structure and behavior. These models responded to the uncertainty in organizational environments and interpersonal relationships by emphasizing rational thinking and decision making. In these models, the goal of organizations is one of reducing uncertainty and supplanting it with routine. Consequently, procedures and regulations designed to maximize predictability and order have been seen as positive influences on organizations. Roles within organizations are strictly defined according to specific functions and jurisdictions in order to avoid overlap, maximize productivity and efficiency, and make it easier to evaluate performance. Hierarchies are established to ensure the accountability of each worker to a supervisor who has a better sense of the bigger picture of the workings of the organization and who understands how to utilize workers' abilities to the fullest to further organizational goals.

In general, traditional organizational views see the effective use of *control* as the way to get the most out of an organization. We will return often in this chapter to the issue of what makes an organization a conducive environment for the expression of creativity. In short, however, traditional concepts of organizations that so heavily emphasize *control* have had the effect of *minimizing* employee creativity.

What was the origin of these traditional views of organizations and their optimal functioning? An important early influence on thinking about the optimal structure of organizations was the work of Adam Smith (1776/1996), who, in 1776, revolutionized productivity by proposing the concept of division of labor. Division of labor is so familiar to us today that it can be easy to forget that it was once a revolutionary idea. Division of labor increased work output by assigning specific work roles to each employee, instead of having each worker complete an entire complex task, which had been the norm before Smith. By concentrating all the efforts of a single worker on one aspect of the task, the time that would have been lost in switching from task to task was saved. Workers benefited by developing specialized experience and knowledge, which enabled them to gain dexterity in their assigned task and consequently become more productive.

Many years later, Smith's early thinking on restructuring the organization was complemented by Weber (1922/1996), whose classic conceptualization of bureaucracy laid the foundation for traditional organizational theories. Weber characterized the functioning of an organizational machine as guided by principles of "fixed and jurisdictional areas . . . generally ordered by rules . . . laws or administrative regulations" (p. 80). Work roles were strictly defined, and a system of levels of graded authority operated to ensure "supervision of the lower offices by the higher ones" (p. 80). The regulation and control of all relationships was impersonal and was reduced to a set of prior, established rules. In Weber's conceptualization, an official of the bureaucracy should be "devoted to impersonal and functional purposes" (p. 82) in return for the security of lifelong tenure, a fixed salary, and an expected old-age pension. The career of a bureaucrat generally followed the hierarchical order of upward movement from lower to higher positions, and this movement was usually based on seniority.

Thus, Weber elaborated upon the work of Smith by defining the optimal organization as a highly controlled, rigid, hierarchical environment in which each worker knew his or her place and performed clearly defined and explicitly assigned duties. Once again, it is clear that this traditional view of organizations, which still describes the structure and functioning of many organizations today, depicts an environment inhospitable for the expression of creativity. But how, exactly, does the traditional organization hinder creativity? We will consider two types of obstacles to creativity and innovation within the organizational setting – *structural* and *personal.*

Structural Obstacles to Creativity and Innovation

Inadvertently, Smith and Weber contributed to many of the structural obstacles that hinder the process of innovation and creativity in organizational contexts. The structures they proposed encourage rigid adherence to rules and regulations. This emphasis encourages conservative thinking and can hinder effective problem solving and information flow. Constant, open communication between segments of an organization is an essential ingredient for creative production (Kanter, 1988). However, the rigidly divided, territorial structure of labor advocated by Smith and Weber tends to create a situation in which "task" and "rank" overshadow the development of new concepts and approaches to problem solving. The organizational environment proposed by Smith and Weber nurtures established patterns of thinking that *reject* unfamiliar, and potentially creative, ideas.

In fact, innovative concepts produced by subordinates may be rejected by supervisors as a direct consequence of the structure of the traditional organization, because the supervisors are unfamiliar with the subordinates' areas of specialization. This unfortunate side effect of specialization was recognized early: Despite stressing the increases in efficiency resulting from task specialization and a hierarchy of authority, Simon (1946) noted that authority based on the unity of command is "incompatible with the principle of specialization" (p. 114) because the knowledge of each supervisor is limited to his or her area of concentration. Consequently, potentially valuable ideas may not be given a chance to prove their worth. Supervisors who lack their subordinates' intimate knowledge of a task area may veto valuable ideas because these ideas seem risky. In general, the value of creative ideas may not be apparent to management in a classically structured organization.

In addition to the consequences to creativity resulting from greater specialization in the modern business world, there are also consequences to creativity resulting from the need for workers to switch tasks often. Today, workers must adapt quickly as they switch from performing one specialized task to performing another equally specialized task. As Hunter and Schmidt (in press) have noted: "Currently, product life cycles are much shorter than worker life cycles – most manufactured products now undergo fundamental redesign in 5 to 10 years (6 to 12 months in high-technology industries). This means that workers must abandon old strategies and learn new ones that are often incompatible" (p. 5). It may be difficult for workers to develop and advance creative ideas when most of their time and mental energy is spent simply becoming familiar with the basics of their jobs. Some workers describe this common situation as requiring them constantly to sprint up the learning curve.

Personal Barriers to Creativity and Innovation

In addition to these structural barriers to creativity, traditional organizations are also characterized by distinct, inefficient patterns of thinking. The result are personal barriers to innovation and creativity. Merton (1957) provides a contrast to the Weberian analysis of bureaucracy in a classic examination of what he calls the *bureaucratic personality*. (Despite this research being 40 years old, the type of person described is undoubtedly familiar to each one of us!) Individuals with a bureaucratic personality are concerned mostly with attaining the security of tenure and salary. This need for security motivates their hostility toward change. In fact, concepts such as innovation threaten the stability that ensures these individuals' future in the organization.

Merton noted that bureaucratic individuals' long tenure in the organization breeds the tendency to sanctify bureaucratic symbols and status, which glorify their own position and seniority within the organization. Their long tenure also increases the likelihood that counterproductive thinking will result from excessive rule-boundedness. Mindless adherence to familiar rules and regulations was seen to result in *goal displacement* – a situation in which rules become ends in themselves, or terminal values, rather than instrumental vehicles that enforce the larger objectives of the organization (such as commercial competitiveness). As a result, bureaucratic individuals often present the greatest obstacle to the introduction and development of innovation in their organizations.

An illustration of the impact of personal barriers to innovation can be found in Mitroff's (1987) study of a traditionally structured organization that attempted to move toward a more team-based design. This change was initiated when it was revealed that the old structure had hindered responsiveness to new market trends and had hastened the organization's decline. Despite these problems with the old structure, the organization's attempt to shift toward a fluid structure with a lateral rather than vertical design was stalled, due to extreme resistance by those in the organization who feared loss of control. These individuals defended the status quo by attributing the company's problems to "weak individuals" rather than to the organization's structure.

It soon became clear that change was only possible in the long run if the company recruited different types of workers who could think integratively, and retrained its current employees to think across traditional lines of responsibility. In addition, the company's informational structure had to be revised to remove barriers between parts of the organization. As Mitroff (1987) concludes, "More businesses appear to be facing the fact that they can no longer afford to separate their internal management systems from the final product" (p. 271).

In Defense of Hierarchies

Are traditionally structured organizations uniformly bad? Absolutely not. Our focus in this chapter is on organizational creativity and the factors that hinder versus enhance it. From our perspective, traditional structures and hierarchies are elements of organizations that tend to hinder creativity. However, these traditional structures have advantages in terms of meeting other organizational goals. For example, Jaques (1990) defends managerial hierarchy and declares that searching for an alternative to hierarchical organization is misguided. He describes the main complaints against hierarchies as consisting of (a) excessive bureaucratic layering, (b) the insignificance of added value contributed by managers to subordinates' work, and (c) the greed and insensitivity displayed by career bureaucrats.

Jaques believes that hierarchies ensure an indispensable accountability of each worker and supervisor to their tasks and to the organization. While Jaques presents a valid point, evidence presented later in this chapter suggests that hierarchies perform better under certain conditions than others. For our purposes in understanding organizational creativity, the conclusion is that traditional organizational structures and hierarchies are limited in their encouragement and acceptance of creativity.

Do Formal Organizational Theories Explain Organizational Creativity?

Creativity in the context of traditional organizational theories has been seen as a dark interloper of irrationality and a disruptive force that destabilizes the security of rule-bound thinking. In the context of classic theories, creativity occurs only by chance. Consider the "garbage can" model of organizational problem solving (March & Olsen, 1976). In this classic model, input flows consisting of problems, participants, solutions, and choice opportunities mix together in the organizational environment. This mix results in conclusions being drawn and decisions being made. These outcomes are seen as satisfying the people involved more by *coincidence* than by design as a function of a reason-based system. In the garbage can model, decision making occurs without systematic adherence to overarching organizational goals. This model of organizational functioning is one of the few in the traditional organizational literature through which creative problem solving can operate. However, the name of this model provides insight into how it is perceived, how it is seen to operate, and how highly its processes are valued.

More recent views of organizational functioning and decision making emphasize more strongly the role of "nonrational" factors and resources. There is a growing awareness that, in modern business environments, established principles and procedures are not as effective as they once were. Thus, employees' ability to draw on nonrational resources is becoming increasingly important. Creativity in synthesizing complex information becomes more essential as rapidly changing organizational life requires individuals to tolerate ambiguity, instead of perpetuating conservative decision making (Krantz, 1990). Consequently, creative problem solving is generally seen by today's organizations as desirable, and attempts are made to develop creativity in employees as a necessary skill in today's corporate environment. Modern organizational theories recognize that the potential offered by the "irrational" creative process can and should be harnessed (Krantz, 1990). Indeed, Kanter (1988) compares innovation to wildflowers, emphasizing innovation's organic nature and potential to be nurtured and cultivated to produce abundant rewards.

But what, exactly, is known about the causes of organizational creativity? What theories have been offered that can help us understand organizational creativity – either focusing broadly on general creativity or focusing specifically on organizational creativity? We turn now to these questions.

THEORIES OF CREATIVITY AND THEIR APPLICATIONS TO ORGANIZATIONS

Research on creativity has sprung from many academic disciplines, including psychology, organizational behavior, education, history, and sociology. This volume profiles many of these traditions in the study of creativity. In fact, the development of scientific thinking about creativity has followed a trajectory similar to that of research on intelligence: an early emphasis upon isolated individuals and their internal traits and capabilities, followed by a developing focus upon the interaction between the individual and the environment. The original "individual" views have been elaborated on in later "systems" views. Thus, research on creativity has sought to understand (a) what creativity is (its components within the mind of the individual), (b) how creativity works at the interface of the individual and the environment, and (c) the systems consisting of groups of individuals collaborating on creative products within organizations. Work continues on individual-based and systems-based approaches simultaneously. In fact, each approach offers its own insights about the nature of creativity.

The major focus in creativity research has been on the *individual creator* and her or his personality, traits, abilities, experiences, and thought processes. Within this focus, creativity is often seen as the product of a special individual in an isolated moment of insight. Creativity is generally viewed as being difficult to train and cultivate, since creative products are spontaneous and specific to the person and occurrence. The loci of creativity are within the individual, and their expression in creative products is influenced by random acts of chance. Later research focused on the *individual in context.* These systems views are based on analyses of creative individuals within their social and historical contexts. Thus, these views incorporate environmental influences on creativity. Some researchers have chosen to focus instead on the *thought processes* that lead to creative outcomes. These researchers have attempted to model the specific processes and inputs required for creative thinking. Still other researchers have attempted to model *organizational creativity* directly, as a part of macro-level analyses of organizational functioning.

As you can see, these types of approaches are wide ranging and their levels of analysis widely discrepant. Given that this volume presents many of these approaches in detail, we will touch upon them only briefly here. Our goal is to illustrate the significance of the major approaches to the study of creativity in our developing understanding of organizational creativity.

Individual Views of Creativity

Consider first a strictly individual-based approach to the study of creativity, the psychometric perspective. In the psychometric perspective, researchers measure creativity in laboratory tests and link it to personality and intelligence variables. The originator of this focus was Guilford (1956), who developed tests of divergent thinking. Later work by Torrance (1987, 1988) elaborated on the tests used to measure creativity and showed that performance on these creativity tests predicted creative real-world performances years later (see also Plucker & Renzulli, Chapter 3, this volume). What are the implications for organizational creativity of research from the psychometric perspective? This highly individual-oriented focus can yield data on what types of personality and other individual characteristics are most closely related to creative performance on laboratory tasks. Thus, some might conclude that organizational creativity needs could be met by hiring individuals with the right levels of intelligence combined with other aspects of personality, for example.

However, the problems with drawing such conclusions are, first, that the individual in an organization must function within a group-oriented organizational culture, and so may not express creativity as it was expressed in the lab. This failure to express latent talent is what Hunt (1995) refers to as the "can" versus "will" distinction. Second, when drawing conclusions based on laboratory data, we do not know the extent of the relation between such performance and real-world creativity in organizational settings. For example, Gruber (1988) has questioned whether scoring high on a creativity test has anything to do with meaningful creative accomplishments later in life. In general, the contributions to understanding organizational creativity derived from psychometric approaches have been modest.

Others have modeled creative thinking through the use of computer simulations. In these simulations, a computer is supplied with relevant information, and it then attempts to duplicate creative insights (Kulkarni & Simon, 1988). Such demonstrations are interesting in that they duplicate creative discoveries and may provide some idea of the exact steps involved in the creative thought process. However, implications for understanding organizational creativity are unclear at this point. One possibility is that explicit training in creative-thinking styles can be initiated based on the understanding of the exact steps involved. Some research has suggested that creativity can be trained through direct intervention and teaching of thinking strategies (Davidson & Sternberg, 1984). But considering that different creative discoveries may involve unique processes combined in original ways, it is unclear whether meaningful increases in creative thinking could result from training based on computer simulations.

Systems Views of Creativity

The psychometric and computer-simulation-based approaches to studying creativity focus on the individual and on specific traits, abilities, and thought processes associated with creativity. However, a problem with these individually oriented approaches is that they often neglect the cyclical relationship that can develop between the individual and the environment, and that can result in the individual's modification of external conditions to increase creativity. Classic studies in the fields of history and anthropology (e.g., Kroeber, 1944; Toynbee, 1936/1954; see also Csikszentmihalyi, 1994) support the idea that environments can be manipulated to stimulate cultures, which subsequently yield a large number of both abstract and concrete innovations. (Unfortunately, though, in institutional contexts, the goal of creating an environment receptive to new ideas clashes with fundamental beliefs based on traditional organizational theories, as discussed earlier. Traditional organizations seek to establish fixed procedures and rules rather than to introduce "irrational" elements into organizational functioning. The result is that creativity can be stifled.)

Thus, in response to the shortcomings of individual views of creativity, researchers began examining creativity from a more systems-oriented perspective. This approach has been called holistic, in contrast to "more atomistic views of creativity" (Gardner, 1988a, p. 299; see also Gardner, 1994). Within a systems-based view, creativity can still be seen as an "individualized phenomenon" (Lubart & Sternberg, 1988, p. 63; see also Sternberg and Lubart, 1991, 1995a, 1995b); however, the creative process is perceived as taking place within the context of a particular environment rather than in a vacuum. Obviously, systems-oriented views are relevant to understanding organizational creativity, since the organization is, by definition, a system. Systems views can help us to conceptualize the multiple factors that influence creative performance within an organizational setting.

In the view of systems theorists, creative individuals are stimulated by elements such as their circle of friends, progress in their field of research, and the dynamics of the society in which they live. Creative products, then, are made possible by this closely intertwined and interacting system of social networks and fields of study or enterprise. This system is seen as compelling the creative individual toward answers to gaps in existing knowledge. Gruber (1988) in particular calls this approach "pluralistic" and "experientially sensitive" (p. 33), in light of its attention to multiple influences on creativity and to the contributions of past work in a discipline, and in light of its focus on the unique experiences of each creative individual within the context of his or her social and emotional world.

Gruber (1981, 1986) was one of the founders of the evolving systems approach to studying creativity, which prompted further development of the systems-based paradigm. Csikszentmihalyi, Gardner, and Simonton are among the theorists who have continued research based on the systems approach. Csikszentmihalyi (1988, 1994) provides a definition of creativity within this paradigm as an attribute of ideas or products that are original (in that they are statistically infrequent and unpredictable), valuable to a culture or field, and carried to a useful completion. He sees creativity as a product of interactions between three components: a *person* who makes changes in the contents of a *domain* that are acceptable to a *field*. Thus, Csikszentmihalyi recognizes the role of the members of a person's field as judges of the person's creative endeavors. Within organizations, most people are surrounded by members of their field who exert considerable influence as judges. The types of judgments other individuals are expected to make, and the criteria on which they make these judgments, are two areas open to organizational influence. Organizations that encourage the optimal types of judging behaviors and attitudes will thus encourage creativity.

Gardner's understanding of creative processes is expressed on four levels of cognitive analyses: (a) the *subpersonal* level of genetic and neurobiological factors, (b) the *personal* level of development in some form of human intelligence, (c) the *extrapersonal* level of progress or development in bodies of knowledge or domains, and (d) the *multipersonal* level of a social context of a field of inquiry that is created through interactions among colleagues in a domain (Gardner, 1988, 1994). Like Csikszentmihalyi, Gardner recognizes the role of multipersonal input in the creative process, which (as stated earlier) is an aspect of organizational environments that is at least partly under organizational control (see also Policastro & Gardner, Chapter 11, this volume).

In a similar vein, Gruber (e.g., 1981, 1986, 1988) has completed detailed studies of the lives of great creators. Gruber examined exceptional individuals such as Charles Darwin, in order to trace the mental processes and influences over Darwin's lifetime that led him to formulate his theory of evolution, for example. The study of creative geniuses or prodigies appeals to our desire to understand how some individuals achieve impressive accomplishments (e.g., Gruber, 1981; Howe, Chapter 21, this volume). The lives of the great creators are often filled with early obstacles that were circumvented and extraordinary feats of effort and inspiration. Insights into organizational influences upon creativity can sometimes be drawn from elaborate and well-documented case studies.

The study of the life course of creative individuals is sometimes referred to as the historiometric approach (Simonton, 1984, 1988, 1989, and Chapter 6, this volume). Historiometric research adopts a systems perspective by examining the creative individual within the natural historical context. Consequently, this approach can provide insights about creative thinking of individuals who work in organizations and, through extrapolation, can provide insights about the qualities of organizational environments that foster or hinder creativity.

What are the unfortunate implications of systems-oriented theories for creative performance in organizations, provided that the goal is to enhance organizational creativity? Many systems theorists believe that creativity occurs only when the appropriate mix of social, individual, and problem-solving elements ignite. Consequently, many sharing this view (as well as proponents of individual-based perspectives) do not believe that creative processes can be improved upon or trained in individuals who do not already possess creative proclivities. However, as is the case for IQ, creativity has been shown to increase as a result of practice (Sternberg, 1987).

Interestingly, when we consider organizational views of employee characteristics, we find a similar evolution of perspective. In the 1870s, people were seen as limited by innate capacities: Ideas about employees were based on the concept of internally located failure. By the 1930s, however, employee failure was seen as the result of inadequate handling by employers; the view was one of externally located failure. Similarly, views of creativity have evolved to conceptualize creativity both as a trait that is innate in gifted individuals, and as a trait that is trainable through techniques such as modeling and through environmental stimulation (Sternberg & Williams, 1996).

Thinking Process Views of Creativity

Now that we have reviewed individual-focused and systems-oriented perspectives on creativity, we will consider theories of creativity that emphasize the *thinking processes* that result in creative performances. A more substantial recognition of the role of context or environment in creative functioning came about when researchers focusing on creative thought processes were forced to deal explicitly with the issues of contexts that encourage or hinder creative thinking.

Rubenson and Runco (1992) proposed a psychoeconomic model of the creative process. This model views creativity as a product resulting from economic decisions, made by individuals and systems, regarding how much human and material capital and time they are willing to invest in creative potential. These decisions are guided by the supply and demand parameters of the society and the era, a concept that supports the systems view of creative production. These supply and demand characteristics influence the external reinforcements, consisting of either rewards or penalties, that are available for innovators. As Amabile (1988) notes, and as will be discussed later, these supply and demand characteristics define environmental conditions that can make extrinsic rewards for innovation either more or less likely.

Amabile (1983, 1988, 1996; see also Amabile & Hennessey, 1987) has found evidence that such extrinsic benefits can undermine intrinsic motivation (which is itself central to the quality and quantity of innovation), although she acknowledges that, in some cases, extrinsic and intrinsic motivators can combine additively to enhance motivation. The psychoeconomic model suggests more forcefully the additive role of extrinsic and intrinsic motivators: "The simultaneous increase in external [and internal] demand implies that the individual's total demand for creative activity might still increase" (Rubenson & Runco, 1992, p. 136).

Implications of the psychoeconomic model for organizational creativity are broad. Specifically, organizations conceptualizing employees' creative outputs as the result of a system of rewards and penalties can enact specific guidelines encouraging and rewarding creative behavior. By defining an environment conducive to innovation, management can make structural and policy changes that engender creativity. For example, management can make seed money available for risky projects and can eliminate negative performance evaluations for employees who propose ideas that do not succeed, despite the early promise of these ideas.

Another model presented through an economic metaphor is Sternberg and Lubart's (1995) investment theory of creativity, which is based on research in cognitive psychology. The theory postulates that six resources must coincide for creative production: intellectual processes, knowledge, intellectual style, personality, motivation, and environmental context. This theory asserts that creative thinkers, like good investors, buy low and sell high – not in the world of finance, but in the world of ideas. Specifically, creative people generate ideas that are like undervalued stocks. Initially, others often view these ideas as bizarre, useless, and foolish, and the ideas are rejected. The authors believe that the ideas are rejected because the creative innovator defies the crowd and makes people uncomfortable by standing up to vested interests. The majority do not maliciously or even willfully reject creative notions: Rather, they do not realize or admit that the ideas represent valid and often superior alternatives.

According to Sternberg and Lubart, there is evidence that creative ideas are, in fact, often rejected. For example, initial reviews of major works of literature and of art are often negative. Influential scientific papers are often rejected not by one but by several journals before they are eventually published and later hailed as classics – a well-known example being

McClintock's Nobel Prize–winning research that was originally rejected by top biology journals. According to the investment theory, the creative person buys low by coming up with an idea that is likely to be rejected and derided. The person then attempts to convince other people of the value of that idea, thereby increasing the perceived value of the investment. Having convinced others of the worth of the idea, the creative person sells high, leaving the idea to others, and moves on to the next unpopular idea. Although people tend generally to want others to appreciate their ideas, universal applause for a new idea usually means that the idea is not very creative.

The implications of the investment theory for organizational creativity are also broad. First, this theory suggests that organizations should actively encourage employees to buy low and sell high in the world of ideas, and reward employees who do so. Second, organizations should create environments in which employees feel secure in offering their new ideas. Third, organizations should not seek to stifle their outspoken and adversarial members, but rather should work to harness these individuals' ideas for the organization's benefit. Fourth, organizations should recognize that creative performance sometimes has more to do with employees having the right attitude than with employees having been born with the right profile of abilities. And finally, organizations should be mindful of the fact that many creative individuals never attempt to share their creative insights with others, let alone try to persuade others of the merit of these insights. An organizational climate that offers incentives for creative production (e.g., "creative idea of the month" contests) may prod such individuals.

Organizational Views of Creativity

We turn now to models of creativity focusing on the macro level of the *organization*. These models discuss the resources necessary for creative output within organizational settings. We consider first the influential work of Amabile (e.g., 1983, 1988, 1996; Collins & Amabile, Chapter 15, this volume), whose definition of organizational innovation as "the successful implementation of creative ideas within an organization" (Amabile, 1988, p. 126) highlights the central roles played by both utility and action in such creative innovation. In Amabile's view, action must be taken by management to foster innovation and resources allocated for its development and implementation. She also delineates specific conditions and qualities that inhibit and encourage innovation, at the level of both the individual and the organizational environment.

Amabile (1988, 1996) recognizes that different environmental models can serve either to promote or to inhibit creativity. She discusses these environmental conditions in depth and expands upon her theory of creativity at the level of the individual to formulate a model of the "creativity intersection." Using three interlocking circles to represent each of the three components of creativity (domain-relevant skills, creativity-relevant processes, and intrinsic task motivation), she illustrates that the area of overlap between the elements conveys "the area of highest creativity for individuals and highest innovation for organizations" (1988, p. 157). It is in this area of greatest overlap that people's domain-relevant skills overlap with their strongest intrinsic interests and creative-thinking processes. The key for organizations, then, is to identify this creativity intersection for each individual, and also to enable the concurrent development of the skills, processes, and motivation central to creative performance.

Amabile proposes four criteria for models of organizational innovation: (a) the entire process of individual creativity must be incorporated, (b) all aspects of organizations' influencing innovation should be considered, (c) the phases in the organizational innovation process should be profiled, and (d) the influence of organizational creativity on individual creativity should be described. Based on this conceptualization of organizational creativity, Amabile's research has revealed that organizational environments fostering creativity share the following characteristics (in descending order of importance): considerable freedom (in deciding what to do and how to do it), good project management, sufficient resources, encouragement, an atmosphere of cooperation and collaboration, ample recognition, sufficient time for creative thinking, a sense of challenge, and internally generated pressure to accomplish important goals.

Kanter, the final organizational theorist we will discuss, works within the business and organizational behavior domains (e.g., Kanter, 1983, 1984, 1985, 1986, 1988). Her work on innovation within organizations examines in depth the structural, collective, and social conditions necessary for innovation to occur. In Kanter's (1988) view, innovation begins with individuals completing tasks, working either alone or in groups. Next, macro-level conditions within the organization work to enhance or diminish organizational innovation. Kanter believes that some structural and social factors are more important at certain stages than at others; the goal of her model is to elucidate these structural and social factors and their impact upon innovation at different stages in the innovation process. She tries to connect tasks in the innovation process to those structural arrangements and social patterns that facilitate each task. The stages she examines consist of idea generation, coalition building, ideal realization, and transfer or diffusion. In particular, her model emphasizes flexibility and integration within the organization.

Kanter notes that the innovation process is uncertain and unpredictable, that it is knowledge intensive, that it is controversial, and that it crosses boundaries. Thus, innovation is seen as being most likely to flourish under conditions of flexibility, quick action and intensive care, coalition formation, and connectedness. Kanter states that innovation is most likely in organizations that (a) have integrative structures, (b) emphasize diversity, (c) have multiple structural linkages inside and outside the organization, (d) have intersecting territories, (e) have collective pride and faith in people's talents, and (f) emphasize collaboration and teamwork. Organizations producing innovation have "more complex structures that link people in multiple ways and encourage them to do what needs to be done within strategically guided limits, rather than confining themselves to the letter of their job" (1988, p. 172).

Kanter notes also that different kinds of innovations characterize different kinds of companies at different stages of development. For example, product innovations are more likely in new organizations, and process innovations in established organizations. In short, Kanter believes that, although innovation stems from individual talent and creativity, it is the *organizational context* that mediates this individual potential and channels it into creative production.

ENHANCING CREATIVITY IN ORGANIZATIONS

In any discussion of methods for enhancing organizational creativity, it is important to recognize the feedback cycle linking organizational culture or atmosphere, individual creativity, and organizational innovation. For example, an organization that penalizes rather than rewards those who offer unorthodox approaches to problem solving may find that few innovators or *intrapreneurs* (i.e., entrepreneurs working within an existing organization; see Pinchot, 1985) can be counted among its ranks. Whether this paucity of creativity is a result of the employees that such companies attract – or fail to attract – or of the policies that make innovators less likely to exercise their creative potential is a matter of debate. What is indisputable is the effect of this low level of creative performance on maintaining a stable but stagnant organization.

Gaining Acceptance of Innovation

As discussed earlier, some of the most potent obstacles to changing organizational structures stem from psychological resistance to dramatic, fundamental shifts in the operation of these organizations. Organizations are filled with members who earn their livelihood – and in some cases, their status in society – from these organizations. Consequently, ego investment in maintaining rank inequalities may motivate the most vocal opponents of organizational change.

Consider the shrewd plan followed by the Japanese emperor, who, at the turn of the twentieth century, implemented a dramatic change in government. By giving key roles in the new structure to the powerful samurai warriors who presented the greatest obstacles to his administration, the emperor transformed the Japanese power structure without bloodshed. Such cooptation of potential enemies to radical changes anticipated and subdued resistance. Modern innovators who seek to introduce dramatic change in their organizations should consider such wise examples; hence the saying, "Keep your friends close, and your enemies closer." Of course, the potential downside of this strategy is that coopted enemies may overthrow organizational leaders and seize control for themselves.

Selznick's (1948) classic analysis of how to gain acceptance of innovation echoes the lesson of the Japanese emperor. Selznick viewed the organization as a system of formal structures and informal cliques, which operate as cooperative systems and adaptive social structures. He believed that changes or internal tensions develop as a result of conflicts between formal authority and social power. According to Selznick, by giving rebellious elements within the organization recognition and concessions, the organization reduces their threat to the stability of the system and increases receptivity to change.

In another classic study, Coch and French (1948) provided additional support for this concept. They found that group participation in planning reduced worker resistance to changes and facilitated transitions. According to this theory, much resistance to change stems from motivational barriers rather than from unfamiliarity with or unwillingness to acquire new skills. As a result, the authors recommended the use of group meetings with workers and management, where the need for change is communicated and participation in the planning process is stimulated, with the goal of increasing motivation.

In contrast to the obstacles caused by *lack of familiarity* with a given area, other types of barriers may stem from *excessive familiarity* or knowledge of a field. Excessive familiarity can create rigid mindsets that are unreceptive to innovation. Sternberg (1997) discusses how these costs of expertise can result in inferior performance in flexible problem solving, due to people's overreliance on often-rehearsed procedural knowledge. Experts may also become married to certain mental frameworks at the expense of others, because of the experts' intellectual and emotional investment in the views they customarily endorse (Frensch & Sternberg, 1989).

In fact, Kanter (1988) refers to what sociologists call *trained incapacity*, a symptom of focusing exclusively on a certain area, as an example of a barrier to the cross-fertilization of ideas and interdisciplinary exchange central to creative insights. The marriage of formerly separate concepts or fields can often produce an innovation of more utility and value than anything developed by focusing on any one field alone. In order to achieve this conceptual exchange, constant communication between levels, specialties, and departments is necessary.

So how, exactly, can organizations increase receptivity to innovation? As discussed earlier, the introduction of an emphasis on creativity and divergent thinking in an organizational setting may be viewed with suspicion by those who have become accustomed to fixed patterns of thinking. So how do new ideas become accepted? Sternberg and Lubart (1992) and Hollander (1958) suggest different, although complementary paths toward acceptance. Sternberg and Lubart's investment theory of creativity holds that successful ideas that gain legitimacy are those that are not only novel, but also appropriate for the situation at hand, and that can result in a high-quality product. Smart "investors," the creative individuals in this paradigm, are seen as knowing how to take sensible risks in order to maximize returns on underappreciated but promising ideas.

In Hollander's (1958) classic analysis, the process of new idea acceptance is seen as operating through *idiosyncrasy credit*. On this view, an individual wishing to introduce innovative but unfamiliar ideas must first establish social status through prior conformity to group norms. Only then can the individual attempt to convince others to accept dramatic changes. Once leadership, power, and influence are attained, the capacity to propose change is created. Although using status in this manner may put the individual at risk for losing status altogether, this model holds that only those who demonstrate the respectability of prior group membership or leadership can exert the influence necessary for change to be approved. (Of course, this claim assumes a hierarchical organizational structure.)

Encouraging Creative-Thinking Styles

What do we know about individual styles of thinking that foster or inhibit creativity? Sternberg's (1988, 1997) "thinking styles" model, which integrates intelligence, intellectual style, and personality, can be used to explain how individuals differ in the cognitive approaches they take toward innovation. Sternberg proposes three types of thinking style functions: legislative, executive, and judicial. According to his model, innovators are likely to have a legislative style, which is reflected by their greater tendency to formulate problems and create new, often global perspectives and systems of rules. Legislative types contrast with executive individuals, who enjoy implementing systems of rules (perhaps a less extreme aspect of Merton's bureaucratic personality discussed earlier), and with judicial individuals, who prefer evaluating systems, rules, and people.

According to Sternberg's theory, in order to encourage creative-thinking styles, employees must be enabled to use thinking styles that lead more often to creative outputs. Employees must also be rewarded, as opposed to punished (which is, unfortunately, the norm in many organizations), for attempts at creative thinking, even if unsuccessful. Obviously, this approach will be more successful with employees naturally oriented toward creative styles, but still, it is possible to encourage rather than discourage these styles in any employee. In addition, organizations may wish to consider evidence of past creative accomplishments, and tendencies toward creative-thinking styles, when making hiring and promotion decisions.

Should Organizations Focus on Training Creativity?

How, exactly, can employees be encouraged to be more creative? Is formal training in creative-thinking skills effective? Modern theories of organizational behavior support the potential success of innovation training and a shift toward internal work incentives. As illustrated in Perrow's (1972) classic work on complex organizations, the employee has come to be conceptualized as a malleable element of the organization. As described earlier in this chapter, employees of the past were seen as having more agency in determining work behavior. Consequently, employee *failures* were attributed to inherent deficiencies. Since the 1930s, however, the employee has been seen more as a force to be coaxed. This perspective shifts responsibility for the effectiveness of employee performance to the *trainer,* rather than blaming shortcomings on the employees' personal limitations.

However, seeing people more as "sculpture" than "sculptors" in the organization (Bell & Staw, 1989) underestimates the importance of employee agency. In organizations that view employees as material to be molded, a need for self-efficacy (i.e., employees' beliefs that they are capable of achieving what they desire to achieve) and employee empowerment is sometimes ignored. But such needs for self-efficacy and empowerment are directly related to workers' intrinsic motivation and involvement in the institution, two factors that are positively associated with creative performance. Thus, too-strident attempts at training can backfire.

The evolution of conceptions of worker trainability can be understood through a classic paradigm presented by McGregor (1960). He labels management's conventional, "carrot-and-stick" view of workers "Theory X." He then contrasts this Theory X view of workers with his Theory Y view, which reflects different assumptions about the complexity of human nature and motivation. Rather than seeing the average worker (in terms of Theory X) as naturally lazy, lacking ambition, preferring to be led, resistant to change, and not very bright, McGregor suggests that management often focuses on extrinsic incentives at the exclusion of other incentives. This tendency results in the neglect of other components of worker motivation, such as psychological requirements based on safety needs, social needs, ego needs, and self-fulfillment needs.

Theory Y considers motivators such as the need for association and belonging, achievement and status, and realization of one's potential. This view sees the role of management not as one of creating incentives based on external factors such as economic or coercive relations, but rather as one of *recognizing* and *tapping* the internal motivations that already exist. McGregor proposed that increasing employee self-direction through decentralized forms of organizations that operate through delegation of authority would increase participation and hence satisfy social and ego needs. In addition, emphasizing self-evaluation and personal goal setting, rather than an assembly-line style of performance appraisal by management, also increases egoistic and self-fulfillment needs.

Zuboff (1988) adds force to McGregor's advocacy of the shift to intrinsic rewards in her analysis of the limits of hierarchy in technologically oriented organizations. She notes that as work becomes more abstract and intellectual, rather than physical and observable, internal motivation and commitment become increasingly significant in production quality and quantity. This observation is especially true of such highly intellectual products as innovations and creative performances. The invisibility of intellectual work hinders performance appraisals of subordinates in a hierarchy, so day-to-day operations are largely self-regulated. However, organizations often recognize only begrudgingly that tangible evidence of daily progress is not possible for creative goals and performances. Formal recognition of the amount of time and effort required for creative output – which cannot be charted by specific day-to-day accountability – is necessary if organizations are to enable and enhance employee creativity.

Modifying Organizational Structure to Enhance Creativity

Can organizations be designed to encourage employee creativity? Can traditional organizational structures and rigid hierarchies be abandoned without sacrificing productivity and accountability? In general, redesigning organizations to encourage creativity is a process that involves a radical change in organizational structure and philosophy. Conventional wisdom as espoused by classical organizational theorists established bureaucratic institutions as the models for organizational structure. However, a growing body of research reveals the drawbacks of traditional organizational structures, which have become increasingly unwieldy in today's marketplace.

For example, Williamson (1970) provides mathematical evidence that hierarchies contain inherent inefficiencies. This analysis demonstrates that both effective control of organizational functioning and the potency of organizational purpose and commitment *diminish* as the distance between the production line and the top of the bureaucracy increases. Thus, large bureaucracies not only perpetuate sluggish communication and flabby control, but also result in high costs due to high personnel maintenance expenditures. Organizational purpose, a key ingredient in increasing worker motivation, may be lost due to layers of bureaucracy. Communication delays, enhanced by increasing red tape, prevent the information flow necessary for the "cross-fertilization" of knowledge that fuels innovation (Kanter, 1988).

Consequently, increasing communication in the corporate climate may necessitate a restructuring of the organization, from a hierarchical structure to a flat structure where teamwork rather than rank is emphasized. Networking between employees increases and creative ideas are explored more seriously when divisive barriers between organizational levels are eliminated. The removal of barriers means that all employees have an opportunity to contribute and experiment with new ideas. Open discussion must be encouraged and intrinsic rewards such as mutual support between workers must be established, with the goal of replacing traditional, external motivators such as career advancement and job security.

However, intrinsic motivation cannot be generated without a supportive external environment that reflects the organization's dedication to, and even expectation of, employee innovation. Kanter (1988) shows that these expectations can be manifested through tangible resources reserved for innovative endeavors. Coalition support among employees, as well as the sponsorship of the "top brass," must be secured for the organization to commit itself to creative production. This organizational commitment is represented both by capital and by time – and often by patience – devoted to an often-frustrating process that results in few immediate rewards.

What alternative organizational models exist, and how do these structures impact employee creativity? A classic theory by Burns and Stalker (1961) explored the relative value of hierarchical and alternative forms of organizations. The authors examined two organizational forms, a mechanistic model based on stable conditions and an organic model reflecting more dynamic conditions. They argued that either model can be appropriate, depending on the specific conditions faced by an organization.

In traditional situations characterized by stable environments, mechanistic models based on traditional, vertical, hierarchical structures, as well as on formalized regulations and decision making, provide greater security. Organic models introduce more environmental uncertainty. However, organic models deal more efficiently with conditions in which the environment changes rapidly and there is a need for increased worker input and less reliance on rigid rules and authority-focused relationships. In the past, mechanistic models served organizational purposes adequately. However, in today's uncertain business world, stimulated by constantly advancing technologies, organic forms of organizations better handle organizational demands. Such organic forms are also more supportive of the "innovative wildflowers" and creative idea production described by Kanter (1988).

Kast and Rosenzweig (1972) supported the analysis of Burns and Stalker in their general systems theory of organizations, which viewed organizations as capable of operating either in open or closed systems. In closed systems, equilibrium and the maintenance of stability are overarching goals. Objectives are clear-cut and unified. On the other hand, open systems such as biological and social systems (and, now, global market systems) operate in dynamic equilibrium due to a constant inflow of materials, energy, and information. Open systems are turbulent and unstable and strive toward multiple goals that arise out of different necessities. Both sets of authors (Kast and Rosenzweig; Burns and Stalker) recognize the oversimplification that results from labeling the approach of either system as good or bad, and assert the appropriateness of each system for certain types of conditions. Their theories were prescient, given the evolution that has characterized the global marketplace as we approach the millennium.

What specific techniques can be used to restructure organizations to enhance creativity? Orsburn, Moran, Musselwhite, Zenger, and Perrin (1990) advocate "self-directed work teams" that differ from conventional work groups, in that they are composed of highly trained employees who perform many supervisory functions themselves. These work teams rely on a reward/penalty system based on demonstrated skill acquisition as well as skill erosion. The authors describe the increases in productivity, flexibility, quality, worker commitment, customer satisfaction, and streamlining capacity that result from implementing a system of self-directed work teams.

Orsburn, Moran, Musselwhite, and Zenger (1994) recommend that organizations formally recognize and reward teams and take steps to build team spirit. The authors recommend that organizations accomplish these goals by providing special T-shirts (and the like), having teams compete in company athletic events, and holding celebrations to mark key events in the team's development. However, the drawback of a system based on self-directed work teams is the length of time (two to five years) it takes for employees to become skilled and mature enough to become members of a self-directed team. Between the start-up and final self-directed team state, there are three transition stages: confusion, leader-centered teams, and tightly formed teams. During this transition period, successful acquisition of three areas of skills in particular (technical, administrative, and interpersonal) are emphasized.

As another alternative to traditional bureaucracies, Peters and Waterman (1982) advocate "loose–tight organizations." In the optimal case, these organizations allow for the "co-existence of firm central direction and maximum individual autonomy" (p. 508). The authors found this situation in companies such as Hewlett-Packard, Marriott, and Proctor & Gamble. In a similar vein, Ouchi (1981) proposes what he calls "Z organizations," modeled after Japanese companies, as another alternative. In such organizations, the attainment of greater status is deemphasized, and consensual, participative decision making is considered crucial because the input of all workers is valued. Collective commitment is therefore highly visible, and the organization is perceived by its workers as having a holistic orientation toward its objectives and employees.

Egalitarian relationships are strongly fostered by the atmosphere of Z companies. Dehumanizing, authoritarian relationships are discouraged, partly as a consequence of the lack of segmentation of the organizational structure. Rather than differentiating strictly between "my" duties and "yours," workers are encouraged to cooperate in an environment of mutual trust and goal congruence. Some hierarchical control is used, but self-direction is the main motivator – making Z organizations more like "clans" than bureaucracies. However, Ouchi does consider drawbacks, such as the loss of professionalism in Z organizations as a function of their deemphasis of specialized skills, and the tendencies of these organizations to be racist and sexist because of the homogeneity that is implicitly valued in groups that work so closely together.

CONCLUSION

Given the changing needs of today's organizations and the growing demand for flexibility in dynamic business environments, creativity in problem solving and decision making has never been more important. The management consulting industry has blossomed as a direct result of the recognition of companies' need for restructuring to maintain competitiveness. With the acknowledgment that adaptive organizations are the ones who survive, companies are looking increasingly to the input of their workers as a means of gaining an edge over rival companies. Consequently, attempts at restructuring have highlighted the need for more employee autonomy, intrinsic motivation, and commitment, and have called into question the applicability of traditional organizational theories in today's business world. The marketplace is now, literally, the world, and organizational structures must reflect the impact of this developing emphasis.

Senge's (1990) concept of a "fifth discipline" of holistic, systems thinking that integrates other disciplines, and that focuses on a vision for the future rather than on short-term returns, embodies the goals that today's organizations must pursue. Senge believes that companies need team learning and a shared vision. These advances can only be achieved with a shift of mind that departs dramatically from the perspective of organizations in the past, which relied on fixed, predictable principles. Instead, Senge advocates "learning organizations" that are responsive and adaptive to the constant inflows of information and resources characteristic of open systems.

However, as Senge notes, the creative personality working within an organizational setting may find him- or herself distanced from other people within the organization, functioning in an isolated, highly motivated, driven state that tends to become self-focused. Senge states that the type of intellectual activity required for creative production can be at odds with the more team-oriented type of thinking needed in organizational settings. He sees creative people as tending to focus on ideas, at times even obsessively so.

Thus, once again, we see the tug of war between the creative thinker whose ideas are fostered through solitary, focused work (on the one hand), and the team-oriented, organizational leader who focuses squarely on working with others within the system (on the other hand). The challenge for organizations is to achieve a balance between these two types of thinking and performing, so that creative ideas are available and are cultivated within the organizational setting. As Hisrich (1990) notes, experimentation should be encouraged and mistakes and failures allowed. Only through such attitude and policy changes will creativity become the norm instead of the exception in organizational life. To remain competitive, organizations must recognize that success depends upon their economic and spiritual investment in open experimentation and in projects exploring innovation and change.

REFERENCES

Amabile, T. M. (1983). *The social psychology of creativity.* New York: Springer-Verlag.
Amabile, T. M. (1988). A model of creativity and innovation in organizations. In B. M. Staw, & L. L. Cummings (Eds.), *Research in organizational behavior* (vol 10, pp. 123–167). London: JAI.
Amabile, T. M. (1996). *Creativity in context: Update to the social psychology of creativity.* Boulder, CO: Westview.
Bell, N. E., & Staw, B. M. (1989). People as sculptors versus sculpture: The roles of personality and personal control in organizations. In M. B. Arthur, D. T. Hall, B. S. Lawrence (Eds.), *Handbook of career theory* (pp. 232–251). Cambridge University Press.
Burns, T., & Stalker, G. M. (1961). *The management of innovation.* London: Tavistock.
Coch, L., & French, J. R. P., Jr., (1948). *Human relations.* New York: Plenum.
Csikszentmihalyi, M. (1988). Society, culture, and person: A systems view of creativity. In R. J. Sternberg (Ed.), *The nature of creativity* (pp. 325–339). Cambridge University Press.
Csikszentmihalyi, M. (1994). Creativity. In R. J. Sternberg, *Encyclopedia of human intelligence* (pp. 298–306). New York: Macmillan.
Davidson, J. E., & Sternberg, R. J. (1984). The role of insight in intellectual giftedness. *Gifted Child Quarterly, 28,* 58–64.
Frensch, P. A., & Sternberg, R. J. (1989). Expertise and intelligent thinking: When is it worse to know

better? In R. J. Sternberg (Ed.), *Advances in the psychology of human Intelligence* (Vol. 5, pp. 157–188). Hillsdale, NJ: Erlbaum.

Gardner, H. (1988a). Creative lives and creative works: A synthetic scientific approach. In R. J. Sternberg (Ed.), *The nature of creativity: Contemporary psychological perspectives* (pp. 298–321). Cambridge University Press.

Gardner, H. (1988b). Creativity: An interdisciplinary perspective. *Creativity Research Journal, 1*, 8–26.

Gardner, H. (1994). *Creating minds.* New York: Basic.

Gruber, H. E. (1981). *Darwin on man: A psychological study of scientific creativity* (2nd ed.). Chicago: University of Chicago Press. (Original work published 1974)

Gruber, H. E. (1986). The self-construction of the extraordinary. In R. J. Sternberg & J. E. Davidson (Eds.), *Conceptions of giftedness* (pp. 247–263). Cambridge University Press.

Gruber, H. E. (1988). The evolving systems approach to creative work. *Creativity Research Journal, 1*, 27–51.

Guilford, J. P. (1956). Structure of intellect. *Psychological Bulletin, 53*, 267–293.

Hisrich, R. D. (1990). Entrepreneurship/intrapreneurship. *American Psychologist, 45*(2), 209–222.

Hollander, E. (1958). Conformity, status, and idiosyncrasy credit. *Psychological Review, 65*, 117–127.

Hunt, E. B. (1995). *Will we be smart enough? A cognitive analysis of the coming workforce.* New York: Russell Sage.

Hunter, J. E., & Schmidt, F. L. (in press). Intelligence and job performance: Economic and social implications. *Psychology, Public Policy, and Law.*

Jaques, E. (1990). In praise of hierarchy. *Harvard Business Review, 68* (January–February), 127–133.

Kanter, R. M. (1983). *The change masters.* New York: Simon & Schuster.

Kanter, R. M. (1984). Innovation: Our only hope for times ahead? *Sloan Management Review, 25*, 51–55.

Kanter, R. M. (1985). Supporting innovation and venture development in established corporations. *Journal of Business Venturing, 1*, 47–60.

Kanter, R. M. (1986). Creating the creative environment. *Management Review, 75*, 11–12.

Kanter, R. M. (1988). When a thousand flowers bloom: Structural, collective, and social conditions for innovation in organizations. In B. M. Staw & L. L. Cummings (Eds.), *Research in organizational behavior* Vol. 10, pp. 123–167. London: JAI.

Kast, F. E., & Rosenzweig, J. E. (1972). General systems theory: Applications for organization and management. *Academy of Management Journal, 15*(4), 447–465.

Krantz, J. (1990). Lessons from the field. An essay on the crisis of leadership in contemporary organizations. *Journal of Applied Behavior Science, 26*(1), 49–64.

Kroeber, A. L. (1944). *Configurations of culture growth.* Berkeley: University of California Press.

Kulkarni, D., & Simon, H. A. (1988). The process of scientific discovery: The strategy of experimentation. *Cognitive Science, 12*, 139–175.

Lubart, T. I., & Sternberg, R. J. (1988). Creativity: The individual, the systems, the approach. *Creativity Research Journal, 1*, 63–67.

March, J. G., & Olsen, J. P. (1976). *Ambiguity and choice in organizations.* Bergen: Universitetsforlaget.

McGregor, D. M. (1960). *The human side of enterprise.* New York: McGraw-Hill.

Merton, R. K. (1957). *Social theory and social structure.* New York: Free Press.

Mitroff, I. I. (1987). *Business NOT as usual: Rethinking our individual, corporate, and industrial strategies for global competition.* New York: Jossey-Bass.

Orsburn, J. D., Moran, L., Musselwhite, E., & Zenger, J. H. (1994). Rewarding work teams. *Personnel Journal, 73*(10), 43.

Orsburn, J. D., Moran, L., Musselwhite, E., Zenger, J. H., & Perrin, C. (1990). *Self-directed work teams: The new American challenge.* New York: Irwin.

Ouchi, W. G. (1981). *Theory Z: How American business can meet the Japanese challenge.* New York: Addison-Wesley.

Perrow, C. (1972). *Complex organizations.* Glenview, IL: Scott, Foresman.

Peters, T. J., & Waterman, R. H, Jr. (1982). Simultaneous loose–tight properties. In T. J. Peters (Ed.), *In search of excellence: Lessons from America's best-run companies* (pp. 85–115). New York: Harper-Collins.

Pinchot, G. (1985). *Intrapreneurship.* New York: Harper & Row.

Rubenson, D. L., & Runco, M. A. (1992). The psychoeconomic approach to creativity. *New Ideas in Psychology, 10*, 131–147.

Selznick, P. (1948). Foundations of the theory of organization. *American Sociological Review, 13*, 25–35.

Senge, P. M. (1990). *The fifth discipline.* New York: Doubleday.

Simon, H. A. (1946). The proverbs of administration. *Public Administration Review, 6*, 53–67.

Simonton, D. K. (1984). Artistic creativity and interpersonal relationships across and within generations. *Journal of Personality and Social Psychology, 46*(6), 1273–1286.

Simonton, D. K. (1988). Quality and purpose, quantity and chance. *Creativity Research Journal, 1,* 68–74.

Simonton, D. K. (1989). Multiple discovery and invention: Zeitgeist, genius, or chance? *Journal of Personality and Social Psychology, 37*(9), 1603–1616.

Smith, A. (1996). Of the division of labour. In J. M. Shafritz & J. S. Ott (Eds.), (1996), *Classics of organization theory,* (4th ed., pp. 40–45). Belmont, CA: Wadsworth. (Original work published 1776)

Sternberg, R. J. (1987). Teaching intelligence: The application of cognitive psychology to the improvement of intellectual skills. In J. B. Baron & R. J. Sternberg (Eds.), *Teaching thinking skills: Theory and practice* (pp. 182–218). New York: Freeman.

Sternberg, R. J. (1988). Mental self-government: A theory of intellectual styles and their development. *Human Development, 31,* 197–224.

Sternberg, R. J. (1997). *Thinking styles.* Cambridge University Press.

Sternberg, R. J. & Lubart, T. I. (1991). An investment theory of creativity and its development. *Human Development, 34,* 1–31.

Sternberg, R. J., & Lubart, T. I. (1992). Buy low and sell high: An investment approach to creativity. *Current Directions in Psychological Science, 1*(1), 1–5.

Sternberg, R. J., & Lubart, T. I. (1995a). *Defying the crowd: Cultivating creativity in a culture of conformity.* New York: Free Press.

Sternberg, R. J., & Lubart, T. I. (1995b). Ten tips toward creativity in the workplace. In C. M. Ford & D. A. Gioia (Eds.), *Creative action in organizations: Ivory tower visions and real world voices* (pp. 173–180). London: Sage.

Sternberg, R. J., & Williams, W. M. (1996). *How to develop student creativity.* Alexandria, VA: Association for Supervision and Curriculum Development.

Torrance, E. P. (1987). *The blazing drive: The creative potential.* Buffalo, NY: Bearly.

Torrance, E. P. (1988). Creativity as manifest in testing. In R. J. Sternberg (Ed.), *The nature of creativity* (pp. 43–75). Cambridge University Press.

Toynbee, A. J. (1936–1954). *A study of history* (Vol. 1–10). Oxford: Oxford University Press.

Weber, M. (1996). Bureaucracy. In J. M. Shafritz & J. S. Ott (Eds.), *Classics of organization theory.* (4th ed., pp. 80–85). Belmont, CA: Wadsworth. (Original work published 1922)

Williamson, O. (1970). *Corporate control and business behavior.* Englewood Cliffs, NJ: Prentice-Hall.

Zuboff, S. (1988). The limits of hierarchy in an informated organization. In S. Zuboff (Ed.), *In the age of the smart machine: The future of work and power* (pp. 165–190). New York: Basic.

20 Enhancing Creativity

RAYMOND S. NICKERSON

I find the following assumptions about creativity to be plausible if not compelling: (1) Both nature and nurture are important determinants of creative expression; (2) debate over which has the greater effect is generally not very useful; (3) essentially all people of normal intelligence have the potential to be creative to some degree; (4) few people realize anything close to their potential in this regard; (5) creative expression is generally desirable, because it usually contributes positively to the quality of life of the individual who engages in it and often enriches the lives of others as well; (6) the search for ways to enhance creativity – to help people develop more of their potential – is a reasonable quest in the absence of compelling evidence that such a search is futile; (7) the evidence, although somewhat tenuous, suggests that creativity can be enhanced; and (8) *how* to enhance creativity is not well understood, but there are possibilities that merit exploration.

This chapter deals with two questions that relate directly to the last two assumptions: Can creativity be enhanced, and, if so, how? In stating the assumptions, I have revealed that my answer to the first question is a cautious yes, and that I believe that something useful may be said in connection with the second. I confess at the outset that much of what I have to say is speculative. Much of the literature to which I will refer is speculative as well. Although creativity has been a focus of research for a considerable time, relatively few empirical studies have directly addressed the question of whether and, if so, how creativity might be enhanced. I will mention studies of which I am aware that bear most directly on this question, but I will also note opinions that various researchers and thinkers have expressed on the topic, and will venture some of my own.

First, I will comment briefly on several topics that relate to the question of what constitutes creativity. Some of these topics are discussed more extensively in other chapters of this book. Here I wish only to provide an immediate frame of reference for the discussion of whether creativity can be enhanced, and if so, how.

WHAT IS CREATIVITY?

Creativity is typically defined in terms of the results of activity: Creative people are people, it is said, who characteristically produce creative products. Although not everyone considers it possible to articulate clear objective criteria for identifying creative products, novelty is often cited as one of their distinctive characteristics, and some form of utility – usefulness, appropriateness, or social value – as another. "Creativity is reflected in the generation of novel, socially valued products" (Mumford, Reiter-Palmon, & Redmond, 1994, p. 3). "Creative products, be they poems, scientific theories, paintings or technological advances, are both novel and acknowledged to be valuable or useful in some way" (Gilhooly, 1982, p. 123). "In my view, creativity is best described as the human capacity regularly to solve problems

392

or to fashion products in a domain, in a way that is initially novel but ultimately acceptable in a culture" (Gardner, 1989, p. 14).

Bruner (1962) emphasizes the element of surprise: "An act that produces *effective surprise* – this I shall take as the hallmark of a creative enterprise" (p. 3). But he too notes that surprise is not enough; what is produced must be useful as well as surprising. Perkins (1988) defines a creative person as one who fairly routinely produces creative results, creative results being results that are both original and appropriate. Amabile and Tighe (1993) say that, in order to be considered creative, a "product or response cannot merely be different for the sake of difference; it must also be appropriate, correct, useful, valuable, or expressive of meaning" (p. 9). Others offer similar definitions (Albert, 1975; Besemer & Treffinger, 1981; Bowers, Farvolden, & Mermigis, 1995; Ghiselin, 1963; Jackson & Messick, 1973; MacKinnon, 1962; Sternberg, 1985, 1988).

I want to argue that however we conceive of creativity we should not make its existence dependent on its being recognized as such. By definition, we are not aware of creativity that goes unnoticed, but we have every reason to believe that it exists. Much of the work in science and art that has been recognized as extraordinarily creative has not received this recognition until long after it was done; many products that have eventually been judged by society to be valuable or useful were considered worthless or worse when first produced. We cannot rule out the possibility that for every creative product that is eventually recognized as such there are others that go unnoticed indefinitely.

With respect to novelty or originality as a criterion of creativity, it is important to note that even the most original or novel of those products or ideas that have been widely recognized as unusually creative have not represented complete breaks with the past but have built upon preceding products and ideas (Ward, 1995; Weisberg, 1995). For an activity or product to be perceived as creative in science, it must be novel, but not too great a departure from prevailing ideas; if it does not connect with existing theory, it is likely to be ignored. As a matter of historical fact, never has a major scientific figure produced a theory that was independent of the work and thinking of his or her predecessors. "Everything that a scientist does is a function of what others have done before him: the past is embodied in every new conception and even in the possibility of its being conceived at all" (Medawar, 1979, p. 30). The principle that scientists invariably build on the work of their predecessors holds even when they are producing advances that come to be regarded in time as revolutionary; Einstein acknowledged that he could not have conceived the theory of relativity without the benefit of the discoveries of the great physicists who had come before him (Holton, 1981).

A similar principle applies in the arts as well. Simonton (1980) has shown, for example, that musical compositions that are seen as creative tend to be original in the sense of departing somewhat from prevailing norms, but that they do not depart as much as many innovations that do not become widely acclaimed. As Ward (1995) puts it, "Creative thinking moves beyond what has been done only slowly, and when it does, it is more as a modification of the past than rejection of it" (p. 71). One may reasonably doubt that the music of Stravinsky would have been evaluated as kindly by society had it followed hard on the heels of that of Bach without the benefit of the work of intervening innovators over 200 years. Of course it is also doubtful that the one *could* have followed the other directly, not only because some of the instruments that Stravinsky used did not exist at the time of Bach, but because Stravinsky's thinking was influenced by the work of all his predecessors. The point I want to emphasize, however, is that by the time Stravinsky composed, what he produced was not as great a departure from the music of the time as it was from the music of Bach, and was, therefore, less likely to be rejected as too far removed from the prevailing norms.

An alternative to defining creativity in terms of novel and useful *products* is to consider it a property of thinking. Sometimes creativity is seen as the ability to get lots of ideas, especially new and original ideas (Cropley, 1992; Feldhusen & Treffinger, 1986; Gallagher, 1975). Cropley (1992) suggests that to be creative means to be daring and innovative in one's thinking. He distinguishes between the connotation of creativity that involves end products that are perceived by knowledgeable people as creative and the connotation (often given by teachers) that emphasizes a tendency to be inventive, original, and innovative. Koestler (1964) defines creativity in terms of the capacity to make connections – to bring together previously unconnected "frames of reference."

I like this connotation, especially with the qualification that originality should be understood to mean original or novel to the individual involved, so that a thought would be considered creative if it is novel to the one who produces it, irrespective of how many others may have entertained that thought. Thus, one who *re*discovers the Pythagorian theorem, say, is being creative, despite the fact that the discovery is not new to the world. Moreover, the connotation admits the possibility of being more creative, or less so, in many aspects of daily life. It admits, for example, the possibility of reading a story in more or less creative ways, or that of viewing commonplace events or objects from more or less novel perspectives, or that of being more or less inventive in the use of one's time.

Creativity and Problem Solving or Finding

The relationship between creativity and problem solving is a very close one in the minds of many investigators. Guilford (1964) has argued that the terms refer to essentially the same mental phenomena. Some investigators have taken the position that creativity is a special form of problem solving. Newell, Shaw, and Simon (1962), for example, describe creative activity as "a special class of problem-solving activity characterized by novelty, unconventionality, persistence, and difficulty in problem formulation" (p. 66), and express the opinion that the data available as of the time of their writing show no particular differences between the processes involved in creative thinking and those involved in noncreative thinking. Mumford et al. (1994) also refer to creative thought as a form of problem solving. Feldhusen and Treffinger (1986) combine creativity and problem solving into "a single complex concept," arguing that "creative abilities such as fluency, flexibility, and originality . . . are in reality indispensable components of realistic and complex problem solving behavior" (p. 2).

Many writers have proposed conceptual models of problem solving, sometimes explicitly referred to as creative problem solving, that characterize it as a phased or step-wise process (e.g., Bransford & Stein, 1984; Dewey, 1910; Hayes, 1989; Johnson, 1955; Noller, 1977; Parnes, Noller, & Biondi, 1977; Polya, 1945/1957; Rossman, 1931; Torrance, 1988; Torrance & Myers, 1970; Wallas, 1926/1945). Generally these models recognize from four to six phases of the process, beginning with those dealing with finding, recognizing, defining, or refining the problem, moving through some having to do with seeking possible solutions or ways of making progress toward a solution, and ending with evaluating the alternatives, settling on the best among them, and, sometimes, reflecting on the process or looking for ways to apply the results.

Laboratory investigations of problem solving typically begin with the presentation to participants of well-defined problems. For this reason, some writers have expressed skepticism as to whether such studies shed light on how people respond in real-world contexts in which the problems that have to be solved are often not well structured and perhaps have to be discovered and formulated (Getzels, 1982; Mumford et al., 1994). Csikszentmihalyi and Getzels (1971) distinguish between *presented* and *discovered* problems and associate creativity especially with the second kind. Kay (1994) defines creative thought as "a p[rocess by which] the individual finds, defines, or discovers an idea or problem not predeterm[ined by the sit]uation or task" (p. 117).

Many researchers have emphasized the importance of problem finding an[d def]inition or formulation – as distinct from problem solving – as an important [creative] activity (Campbell, 1960; Getzels & Csikszentmihalyi, 1975, 1976; Mackworth, [1965]; Runco, & Berger, 1991; Runco, 1994; Runco & Nemiro, 1994; Starko, 1989). [There is] some evidence that the quality of artwork is predictable to an extent from the exploratory behavior in which the artists engage before doing their more explicitly creative work (Csikszentmihalyi & Getzels, 1970, 1971; Getzels & Csikszentmihalyi, 1976; Kay, 1991). There is evidence too that students who have been taught to explore different ways to define problems may engage in more creative problem solving over the longer term (Baer, 1988).

Closely related to the distinction between problem finding and problem solving are the distinctions between hypothesis generation and hypothesis testing, and between idea generation and exploration. The distinction between hypothesis generation and hypothesis testing is important in science. Hypothesis testing has received more attention from researchers and is the better understood of the two processes. It involves the checking of hypothesized dependencies and other relationships among variables of interest against the results of observation and controlled experimentation. Scientists are generally agreed on how this is to be done, and the basic rule is that testing procedures be public and replicable. Hypothesis generation is a much more private affair and not well understood. Where hypotheses come from and how to evoke them are challenging questions for creativity research.

The distinction between idea generation and exploration is basic to the Geneplore model of creativity proposed by Finke, Ward, and Smith (1992). "Geneplore" comes from a blending of *generate* and *explore*. Finke et al. argue that creative thinking employs generative and exploratory cognitive processes in a cyclic fashion. During the generative phase of a cycle, "one constructs mental representations called preinventive structures, having various properties that promote creative discovery. These properties are then exploited during an exploratory phase in which one seeks to interpret the preinventive structures in meaningful ways. These preinventive structures can be thought of as internal precursors to the final, externalized creative products and would be generated, regenerated, and modified throughout the course of creative exploration" (p. 17). Finke et al. note that the Geneplore model, as they conceive it, admits of the possibility that people can be creative in different ways.

I see the question of the relationship between creativity and problem solving as dependent, to a large degree, on how one conceives of problem solving. If one's conception of problem solving is sufficiently broad to include solving problems algorithmically or by the application of well-known or memorized procedures, then some instances of problem solving would be seen as creative, but not all. If one recognizes as instances of true problem solving only those that require some original thinking, then, by definition, all problem solving is creative. According to the latter view, creativity is not required when experts solve problems by applying algorithmic techniques with which they are familiar by virtue of their expertise, but it is likely to be necessary when the same experts attempt to solve problems outside their areas of expertise where the techniques with which they are familiar do not apply.

Problem finding involves, one might say, thinking about what to think about. To borrow a metaphor from Sternberg and Lubart (1991), it means deciding where to invest one's cognitive capital. One can hardly doubt that deliberately devoting time to problem finding is likely to increase the chances of producing creative results. Unfortunately, problem finding has not been a major focus of education (Getzels, 1982; Houtz, 1994); students are typically given problems to solve and are seldom taught to search out problems for themselves.

Creativity and Insight

Insight – the experience of suddenly realizing the solution to a problem or of grasping a familiar situation in a new and more productive way – is often associated with creativity. Insight is a form of discovery, its distinguishing characteristic being the suddenness of its occurrence. Exactly how insight and creativity relate – the question of the extent to which one is essential to the other – is a matter of some debate. Some investigators play down the importance of sudden illuminations that appear to result from processes that occur below the level of awareness and argue that all problems involve essentially the same incremental approach to solution (Perkins, 1981; Weisberg, 1986, 1993; Weisberg & Alba, 1981); others argue that problems that require insight for solution evoke different solution strategies than do those that do not (Metcalfe, 1986a, 1986b; Schooler & Melcher, 1995).

The subjective experience of insight is compelling. At a given point in time, one "sees" the solution of a problem or one does not. One is not likely to feel that one is getting incrementally closer to the solution before having the insight that is necessary to yield the solution; when the solution "announces itself," as it were, it does so suddenly without much warning. Feeling-of-warmth judgments tend to increase with time when people work on problems that do not require an insight for solution, but not when they work on problems that do (Metcalfe, 1986b; Metcalfe & Weibe, 1987). The experience of insight is often described as an "Aha!" experience. Schooler and Melcher (1995) argue that approaches to insight and analytic problems probably share some mental processes but not all.

Creativity and Intelligence

The relationship between creativity and intelligence is also controversial. No one, to my knowledge, claims that intelligence is a sufficient condition for creativity, although some investigators see it as a necessary one (Amabile, 1983; Getzels & Jackson, 1962). Perkins (1988) distinguishes between characteristics that *enable* creativity and those that *promote* it, and between those that enable or promote creativity in particular and those that enable or promote achievement more generally. The modest correlation that has typically been reported between general intelligence and creativity, and the fact that the correlation appears to be quite weak at higher levels of intelligence, indicate, Perkins suggests, that intelligence may enable creativity to some degree, but it does not ensure it.

My own view – similar to that of Perkins – is that highly intelligent people are more likely to be creative than are people with lower intelligence, but that high intelligence is neither a necessary nor a sufficient condition for creativity. Although many very creative people are also highly intelligent, it appears that a sizable percentage are not (Cropley, 1967; Torrance, 1962), and clearly there are many highly intelligent people who are not unusually creative. Highly intelligent people may have the potential to develop higher levels of creativity than less intelligent people, on average, or to express their creativity in more spectacular ways, but this does not preclude the possibility that many people at all levels of intelligence have a greater creative potential than they are likely to develop spontaneously.

Creativity and Ethics

Creativity, like intelligence, can be seen both as an intrinsic good and as a means to other ends. Other things being equal, more intelligence and more creativity are preferable to less. But both intelligence and creativity can serve bad ends as well as good. Criminals can be intelligent and creative. The considerable attention that is being attracted by the speed with which innovative antisocial and criminal uses of computer networking technology have made their appearance is a recent and compelling reminder of this fact. Success in making people more creative is not the same as success in making them better in an ethical sense.

Some investigators rule out the possibility of creativity serving bad ends by definition. McLeod and Cropley (1989), for example, list ethical desirability among five elements that they consider to be necessary for creativity. According to this view, any act that is ethically undesirable should not be considered creative; as Cropley (1992) puts it, "The positive social value associated with the term *creativity*, along with the presence of an ethical element in education, make it repugnant to speak of the creativity of a cheat, a mass murderer, or an evil demagogue" (p. 49).

Whether or not one makes ethical desirability an aspect of creativity by definition is an issue of semantics. The more substantive issue, in my view, is the importance of recognizing the possibility of learning to be clever without learning to be good. I believe that creativity, at least as it is generally implicitly represented in tests of creativity, can serve either good or bad ends, and that, consequently, attempting to enhance creativity in a value-free way is a bit like teaching a child how to aim and fire a gun without providing guidance regarding what, and what not, to shoot at.

Creative Versus Critical Thinking

Creative thinking and critical thinking are often contrasted. Creative thinking is expansive, innovative, inventive, unconstrained thinking. It is associated with exploration and idea generation. It is daring, uninhibited, fanciful, imaginative, free-spirited, unpredictable, revolutionary. Critical thinking is focused, disciplined, logical, constrained thinking. It is down to earth, realistic, practical, staid, dependable, conservative. Sometimes creativity and criticalness are seen as polar opposites. From this perspective, a move toward one of these characteristics means necessarily a move away from the other. In terms of the focus of this chapter, it would mean that the enhancement of creativity would necessarily involve the diminution of criticalness.

I prefer to think of creativity and criticalness as independent dimensions (Nickerson, 1990) and to believe it is reasonable to assume that the thinking of a given individual could be characterized by both properties to a high degree. Indeed, I believe not only that it is possible to promote both creative and critical thinking in the same individuals, but that not to attempt to do so would be unwise.

It is important here to distinguish between abiding traits and temporary mindsets that may be adopted for specific purposes. One may wish to adopt an especially *un*critical frame of mind for a while in order, say, to facilitate the generation of a large set of ideas that are relevant to some objective (see later comments on brainstorming), or one might want to become unusually critical when it is time to evaluate the ideas in order to select a course of action from among them. When I say that I believe a person can be both creative and critical, I am referring to creativity and criticalness as traits that characterize one's thinking over extended periods of time.

Presumably there are people who are relatively creative and not very critical, some who are relatively critical and not very creative, some who are neither creative nor critical and some who are both creative and critical. The question of whether creativity and criticalness are correlated (positively or negatively) or relatively independent in the population is an empirical one. I know of no data that rule out the possibility that the correlation is very low and that all parts of the creativity–criticalness space are more or less equally occupied. Or it could be that people who tend to be highly creative – in the sense of habitually engaging in creative thought – tend not to be highly skilled as critical thinkers, and conversely. None of these possibilities rules out the reasonableness of aspiring to be good at both types of thinking or of trying to help students grow intellectually in both ways.

It can be argued that the ability to think *well* requires both creative and critical capabilities, that neither type of thinking can be effective without the other. The kind of creativity that generates total abandon – no sense of appropriateness to the situation – is probably not very useful. Guilford (1983) argued the need for the involvement of convergent as well as divergent thinking in creativity. Others have stressed the importance of evaluation in creative thinking as well (Basadur, 1994; Farnham-Diggory, 1972; Runco & Chand, 1994). Lundsteen (1968) put the matter this way: "The ability at will to make creative thinking coordinate with more logical reasoning may make the difference between lunacy and creativity" (p. 133).

Conversely, it is not likely that one can be effectively critical without being creative in the process. Critiquing a proposed new strategy or method for accomplishing some objective, for example, is likely to involve imaging the various ways in which the proposed approach could fail or cause unanticipated consequences. It would be easy to find many examples of well-intentioned innovations that went wrong in ways that no one had the imagination to foresee.

We usually do not associate creativity with deduction, but creativity often plays a significant role in the development of mathematical proofs. The point is illustrated by Georg Cantor's (1915/1955) ingenious proof that the set of real numbers is not only infinite but, unlike the set of rational fractions, uncountable. To construct the proof, Cantor invented the concept of a *diagonal number.* Suppose, he argued, that there were a finite number of decimals between 0 and 1. Imagine that we listed them all, in no particular order, as follows:

.77358436 · · ·
.84663925 · · ·
.16486902 · · ·
.53992175 · · ·
.35487250 · · ·
.94882604 · · ·
.04327489 · · ·
.36498105 · · ·

A new (diagonal) number may be composed from this set of numbers by making its first digit correspond to the first digit of the first number in the set (7), its second digit to the second digit of the second number (4), and, in general, making the nth digit in the diagonal number correspond to the nth digit of the nth number in the set. Thus, the first eight digits of the diagonal number defined on the above set is

.74497685 · · ·

Now, suppose we construct a new number that differs with respect to the diagonal number with respect to every digit, say by incrementing every digit by 1 and changing 9 to 0. We can be sure that the resulting number, in this case

.85508796 · · ·

differs from *every* number in the original set with respect to at least one digit and so is not a member of that set. Inasmuch as it would always be possible to define such a number, no matter how many numbers there were in the original set, the supposition that there are a finite number of decimals between 0 and 1 must be false. Cantor's proof is deductive, but construction of it required a spectacular creative insight; the same may be said of many deductive proofs.

In short, creative and critical thinking are two sides of the same coin. Good thinking requires both and requires that there be a balance between their contributions. Creative thinking, at its best, generates original ideas, unusual approaches to problems, novel perspectives in terms of which to view situations; critical thinking evaluates what creative thinking offers, subjects the possibilities to criteria of acceptability, and selects among them some for further consideration. Idea generation and evaluation are going on more or less simultaneously and continuously in any instance of extended creative activity. An appropriate metaphor of the process is that of an ongoing dialogue between two agents, one of which puts forth ideas without restraint and the other of which evaluates those ideas. Different individuals might play the roles of the different agents in specific situations, but a reasonable goal of education is that of enhancing the ability of the same individuals to play both roles.

Types and Degrees of Creativity

Creativity is sometimes treated as an all-or-none entity – one is either creative or not – but many investigators have expressed a different view. Amabile (1983) recognizes the possibility of degrees of creativity, as do Cattell and Butcher (1968), Taylor (1975), Gruber, Terrell, and Wertheimer (1982), and Lubart and Sternberg (1995), among others. Some researchers make the assumption that creativity can be expressed by nearly anyone, although not necessarily in the same way or to the same degree (Amabile, 1983; Cropley, 1992; Treffinger, Isaksen, & Dorval, 1994).

Csikszentmihalyi (1996) distinguishes three types of people who are often described as *creative*: (1) those who express unusual thoughts, (2) those who experience the world in novel and original ways, and (3) those who effect significant changes in their culture. He sees the first group as *brilliant* (interesting and stimulating), the second as *personally creative*, and the third as *creative unqualifiedly*. The third meaning of creativity, he argues, is not just a more developed form of the first two, but qualitatively different; all three types are seen as relatively unique – "actually different ways of being creative, each to a large measure unrelated to the others" (p. 26). Csikszentmihalyi defines the third type of creativity as "any act, idea, or product that changes an existing domain, or that transforms an existing domain into a new one," and a creative person as "someone whose thoughts or actions change a domain or establish a new domain" (p. 28).

Gardner (1993b) contrasts "'little C' creativity – the sort which all of us evince in our daily lives – and 'big C' creativity – the kind of breakthrough which occurs only very occasionally" (p. 29). Big C creativity is seen in people like T. S. Eliot, Albert Einstein, Pablo Picasso, and others whose work has played a significant role in shaping the ideas and standards of their culture. Little C creativity can be expressed in small departures from daily routines.

In a similar vein, Boden (1991) distinguishes between psychological (P) and historical (H) creativity:

The psychological sense concerns ideas (whether in science, needlework, music, painting, literature . . .) that are fundamentally novel with respect to *the individual mind* which had the idea. If Mary Smith has an idea which she could not have had before, her idea is P-creative – no matter how many people may have had the same idea already. The historical sense applies to ideas that are fundamentally novel with respect to *the whole of human history*. Mary Smith's surprising idea is H-creative only if no one has ever had that idea before her. (p. 32)

H-creative ideas are a subset of P-creative ideas in this view.

A P-creative person, Boden suggests, is someone who has the capacity to produce

P-creative ideas on a more or less sustained basis. Whether a P-creative idea becomes identified by society as H-creative depends on factors external to its originator, including historical accident and social fashion. P-creativity and H-creativity can be seen as marking the ends of a continuum that has exemplars all along it: A P-creative idea is novel to the individual who has it, while an H-creative idea is new to humanity, but there are many ideas that fall between these extremes, being novel with respect to some subset of humanity greater than one. Mandler (1995) captures this notion of degree of novelty: "A particular act may be novel for all humanity, for a specific social-cultural unit, or for an individual" (p. 10).

H-creativity is a socially determined quality. For at least two reasons, it is impossible to answer the question of whether some of the P-creative ideas and products that have been ignored by society were equally as worthy as those that became recognized as H-creative: (1) By hypothesis, P-creative ideas of the past that were ignored by posterity are, for the most part, lost, and (2) H-creativity changes the standards. Theoretically, eminence should be an indication of H-creativity, but, in fact, the relationship is not simple, because, especially with respect to science, posterity tends to credit individuals with developments that were due to the combined contributions of many people.

Usually, when we think of creativity, we tend, I suspect, to think of people – Pythagoras, Archimedes, Michelangelo, Leonardo, Mozart, Newton, Dostoyevsky, von Neumann – who have become famous as a consequence of their creative (H-creative) work that has become part of the valued heritage of humankind. There can be no doubt that the creative products that we associate with such people have been instrumental in determining the kind of world in which we live. There can be no doubt either that the world sorely needs people who can come up with creative approaches to the problems it faces today. Among the reasons for wanting to know how to enhance creativity is the hope of enabling and evoking, here and there, the kind of creativity that can benefit society as a whole. One wonders how many great works of art or science the world has missed because the potential that individuals had to produce them was never developed.

But the expression of creativity in more modest ways is important as well. The ability to look at mundane things from an unusual perspective, to see connections that are not apparent to the casual observer, can add color and excitement to one's daily life. One can get a great deal of satisfaction from writing a poem even if no one reads it but oneself, from having an insightful thought even if one discovers that one was not the first person to have it. Csikszentmihalyi (1996) stresses the satisfaction that can come from being engaged in creative work: "When we are involved in it, we feel that we are living more fully than during the rest of life" (p. 2). I find it easy to believe that we have an innate drive to create and that we get satisfaction from the *act* of creating, whether what we are creating is something that fits the stereotype of a creative product – a poem, a painting, a scientific hypothesis – or something more private and less tangible – an inventive approach to a problem of personal significance, a novel way of looking at a familiar situation, the perception of humor where it is not easily found.

CAN CREATIVITY BE ENHANCED?

The belief that creativity can be enhanced through training has many adherents (Amabile, 1983; Amabile & Tighe, 1993; Cropley, 1992; Dominowski, 1995; Finke, Ward, & Smith, 1992; Guilford & Tenopyr, 1968; Hennessey, Amabile, & Martinage, 1989; Stein, 1974, 1975; Sternberg & Lubart, 1996). Amabile (1983) argues that anyone with normal cognitive abilities can reasonably aspire to produce work that is creative to some degree in some domain. Cropley (1992) contends that all students, regardless of IQ, are capable of thinking both divergently and convergently, although they may be disposed, as a result of experience, to think one way (most likely convergently, in his view) more than the other. Guilford and Tenopyr (1968), who consider it unlikely that people with low verbal intelligence will be highly creative, admit the possibility that their creative abilities can be improved to some extent. Perkins (1990) argues that, independently of empirical evidence on the question, theoretical considerations support the assumption that creative thinking can be taught.

There have been several attempts to develop approaches to the enhancement of creativity in the classroom. In some cases, the enhancing of creativity has been a subgoal in an effort to improve thinking more generally. A few attempts have progressed to the point of providing materials for use in the classroom and some have been used at least on an experimental basis. The approaches described in what follows are among these.

Brainstorming and Creative Problem Solving

One of the earliest attempts to develop a structured approach to the enhancement of creativity started with promotion of the process of brainstorming by Osborn (1953, 1963). This technique, designed specifically for use by groups, involves attempting to evoke ideas by providing a social context that gives free reign to imagination and reinforces the use of it. The rules encourage participants to express ideas, no matter how strange or wild they may seem and forbid criticism during the brainstorming session. It is assumed that people's imaginations will be stimulated by the ideas expressed by others and that they, in turn, will be able to express their own in relatively uninhibited fashion.

Whether brainstorming increases creativity or simply increases the expression of ideas by lowering the standards for what is expressed – lowering the normal level of self-criticism – is debatable (Parloff & Handlon, 1964). The approach is intended to lower one's tendency to be self-critical during the idea elicitation stage – to disinhibit the expression of "far-out" ideas; the assumption is that among the ideas that are expressed as a consequence of this relaxing of conventional restraints, some will prove to be solid when later subjected to critical evaluation. Moreover, the hope is that *more* good ideas will be generated by this process than by one in which people express only ideas that they have already evaluated critically.

It is easy to imagine why this might be the case. The expression of an idea by one member of a group, no matter how bizarre or unpromising it may be, can stimulate the thinking of other members of the group, and as a consequence of this stimulation, ideas may be evoked that would not have emerged otherwise. Even if only a small fraction of all the ideas evoked have merit on reflection, the process still may yield a net benefit. Evidence that brainstorming can be effective comes from studies showing that groups using it have, at least sometimes, generated more and better ideas than control groups not using it (Meadow, Parnes, & Reese, 1959; Parnes & Meadow, 1963).

Brainstorming has been incorporated as a major element in a multistep process referred to as creative problem solving (Isaksen & Treffinger, 1985; Osborn, 1963; Parnes, 1981; Treffinger, McEwen, & Wittig, 1989). The process is composed of three major components: understanding the problem, generating ideas, and planning for action. The first of these components is composed of three stages: mess finding, data finding, and problem finding. The second component has a single stage: idea finding; and the third has two: solution finding and acceptance finding. Each of the stages involves a brainstorming type of activity intended to identify many possibilities for consideration, which is to be followed by a more evaluative phase aimed at selecting from among the possibilities generated those that are worthy of further consideration.

Although the term *brainstorming* usually connotes a group process, individuals can do something similar to it by themselves. One is brainstorming, in a sense, whenever one attempts to generate a set of possible courses of action or approaches to a problem, reserving criticism and evaluation of the list until it is relatively complete. When applied on an individual basis, the approach is sometimes referred to as the principle of deferred judgment (Parnes, 1963). There is evidence that brainstorming sometimes works better with nominal groups – pooled results from individual brainstormers – than with actual ones (Diehl & Stroebe, 1986; Dunnette, 1964; Dunnette, Campbell, & Jastaad, 1963; Stein, 1975; Taylor, Berry, & Block, 1958). In keeping with the two-phase distinction of their Geneplore model of creative thinking, Finke, Ward, and Smith (1992) recommend a form of brainstorming in which individuals generate ideas in the absence of group influence and then subject those ideas to exploration and evaluation in group settings.

Brainstorming can be thought of as a *search* process, the target of the search being innovative and useful ideas. Many investigators of decision making and problem solving have stressed the importance of search as essential to identifying one's decision alternatives or one's options for trying to find a problem solution. Several investigators have emphasized *insufficient* search as a common failing of human thinking (Baron, 1985, 1994; Kanouse, 1972; Perkins, Farady, & Bushey, 1991; Pyszczynski & Greenberg, 1991).

The Productive Thinking Program

The Productive Thinking Program (Covington, Crutchfield, Davies, & Olton, 1974) is a self-instructional program, packaged in a series of fifteen booklets, designed for use by fifth and sixth graders. The aim of the program is to improve thinking generally, but much attention is given to the enhancement of inventiveness or creativity. Specific goals include, for example, increasing one's production of ideas, and especially of unusual ideas.

Efforts to evaluate the effectiveness of the program have produced mixed results (Mansfield, Bussé, & Krepelka, 1978; Torrance, 1987). Success has varied with such factors as class size and teacher enthusiasm. Not surprisingly, the combination of small classes and enthusiastic teachers appears to produce the greatest gains. Some evaluation studies have shown that participants in the program have increased their ability to solve extended problems similar to those addressed in the training material, which often require the exploration of multiple possibilities and the consideration of several hypotheses, but evidence of transfer to qualitatively different problems has not been easy to obtain (Olton & Crutchfield, 1969; Treffinger, Speedie, & Bruner, 1974; Waldrop et al., 1969).

The limitation of the gains to problems similar to those encountered in the program material was found also, in most – though not all – cases, on tests intended to measure divergent thinking in particular (Ripple & Dacey, 1967; Treffinger & Ripple, 1969, 1971). One plausible explanation for this outcome is the relatively small amount of training that the program provides and restriction of the learning context to that of solving mysteries (Nickerson, Perkins, & Smith, 1985).

The CoRT Program

CoRT stands for the Cognitive Research Trust, a British organization founded and directed by Edward de Bono, who has written several books on the topic of enhancing thinking – "lateral thinking" in particular. De Bono (1970, 1992) distinguishes lateral thinking from vertical thinking; the distinction is similar in many respects to the distinction that is commonly made between creative and critical thinking.

The CoRT Program, as described in de Bono (1973), is composed of six units, each of which contains several lessons. Each lesson is intended to fit within a single class session. One of the six units (CoRT 4) is focused explicitly on creativity and offers suggestions of strategies that may be used to help one generate ideas that might not normally be brought to mind.

Like the other units, the one on creativity presents a structured approach to problem solving that makes use of specified "operations" or mnemonics to remind one to ask oneself specific questions about a situation. The questions are intended to get one to consider possibilities and to take perspectives about a situation that one otherwise would be unlikely to consider or to take. Objective data on the effectiveness of the CoRT Program, and in particular on the effectiveness of CoRT 4 in enhancing creativity, are sparse.

An adaptation of the CoRT Program was tested in Venezuela in the early 1980s as one of several experimental educational innovations undertaken under the auspices of the Venezuelan government. Venezuelan students, mostly 10- and 11-year-olds when the study began, were given the adapted lessons (two class periods per week); all of the students participated for at least one year and some for two or three. Evaluation data showed that students who received the CoRT training for a year did better than controls, who did not receive the training, in generating pertinent ideas during problem solving; those who received the training for three years also showed gains as judged by the abstractness and elaborateness of the ideas they generated (de Sanchez & Astorga, 1983; for a brief summary, see Nickerson, Perkins, & Smith, 1985).

Project Intelligence

A study of moderate scale that produced modest positive results involved a structured effort to enhance several aspects of thinking through classroom instruction. The core of Project Intelligence, also conducted under the auspices of the Venezuelan government, was a one-year course that was designed to engage seventh-grade students in discussion and thought-provoking classroom activities around a few major themes emphasizing generic capabilities such as observation and classification, critical and careful use of language, deductive and inductive reasoning, problem solving, inventive thinking, and decision making. The course was developed, taught, and evaluated by a team of researchers and educators from the United States and Venezuela. Much of the material was subsequently adapted for use in the United States and published under the title *Odyssey* (M. J. Adams, 1986).

Part of the course (about 60 out of about 100 lessons) was given to 463 students in Barquisimeto, Venezuela, during the school year 1982–1983. The effectiveness of the course was evaluated with a battery of tests composed of the Otis-Lennon School Ability Test (Otis & Lennon, 1977), the Cattell Culture-Fair Intelligence Test (Cattell & Cattell, 1961), a group of general abilities tests (Manuel, 1962), and about 500 test items constructed specifically to assess competence with respect to the particular skills the course was intended to enhance. The latter tests were referred to as target abilities tests; a unique subset of them was associated with each of the major themes of the course. Tests were given before, during, and immediately following participation in the course. Results were generally positive in the sense that participating students showed larger gains on all test measures than did a matched group of controls who had not participated in the course. Details on the project may be found in Herrnstein, Nickerson, de Sanchez, and Swets (1986), Nickerson (1994a), and Perkins (1995).

Most relevant to the theme of this chapter is the section of the course that dealt most directly with creativity – a section on inventive thinking, development of which was led by David Perkins and Catalina Laserna (Perkins & Laserna, 1986). This section was composed of two units centered on the idea of design. The first unit contained nine lessons and the second six. (Each lesson was intended to occupy a one-hour class session.) Only the first unit – nine lessons – was given during the year. These lessons progressed from analysis of designs of common objects (e.g., a pencil), with a view to understanding the functionality of design features, to the inventing of new designs that would meet specified functional objectives.

No effort was made to determine the relative contributions of the various course units to improvements in performance on the standardized tests. The target abilities tests, however, showed greater gains by students in the experimental groups, relative to those by students in matched control groups, for all themes. In order to obtain a further indication of the effectiveness of the inventive-thinking lessons, students were given an open-ended design problem (to design a table for an apartment that was too small to accommodate one of typical size). Solutions were evaluated in terms of 14 variables assessed independently by two judges who were unaware of the students' group affiliations. The designs produced by the participating students were rated as significantly better than those produced by the controls with respect to all 14 variables.

A serious limitation of these results is that they represent only short-term effects of the classroom instruction; the circumstances in which the study was conducted did not permit the determination of longer-term effects. As far as they go, however, the results support the idea that creativity can be enhanced by a modest amount of classroom instruction that has been carefully prepared with that objective in mind.

Other Efforts

Several investigators have suggested structured aids to idea generation. Attribute listing (Crawford, 1954) and morphological synthesis (involving the listing of dimensions or attributes of objects and considering the possibility of novel combinations of them; Allen, 1962; Koberg & Bagnall, 1974) are cases in point. Feldhusen and Treffinger (1986), Finke, Ward, and Smith (1992) and Starko (1995) discuss these and other approaches – including the forced combining of concepts and the use of metaphor – to facilitate the elicitation of novel ideas.

Synectics, a technique developed by Gordon (1961, 1966, 1981) to stimulate idea generation, emphasizes the use of analogies and metaphors; it is similar to brainstorming in that people are encouraged to give their imaginations free rein and to be noncritical during the idea generation phase of problem solving. The approach has been spelled out in a series of guidebooks (Gordon & Poze, 1972, 1975, 1979, 1984). Sanders and Sanders (1984) have proposed an approach to teaching creativity built entirely around the use of metaphor.

Some aspects of brainstorming and related techniques have been promoted recently in the context of an effort to increase the productivity of industrial and other organizations with an approach referred to as total quality management (TQM) or total quality control (TQC). The approach appears to have grown out of an introduction by U.S. engineers, notably W.E. Deming and J. M. Juran, of quality control techniques to Japanese industry in the early 1950s. It involves adherence to specific "steps for improvement": identification of the problem, collection and analysis of facts, identification of main causes, planning and implementation of improvements, confirmation of effects, standardization of the process, and review of the activities and planning for future work. These steps are sometimes grouped to comprise a "plan, do, check and act" cycle.

A variety of procedures have been identified or developed to help accomplish these steps or to help management evaluate the effectiveness of attempts to improve quantity or quality of output. These include check sheets, Pareto diagrams, cause–effect diagrams, affinity diagrams, and process decision program charts (Shiba, 1989). Some of the procedures for group participation in problem solving are very similar to those proposed by Osborn, Gordon, and others, in that they are designed to encourage first the relatively unconstrained generation of ideas and then the critical winnowing of the ideas through structured group exercises in order to arrive at a group consensus on a plan of action to be followed. The approach has been embraced by many U.S. companies and by the U.S. Department of Defense. How effective it has been is not clear: Opinions abound but objective data are lacking.

The Purdue Creative Thinking Program, developed by Feldhusen (1983), is a program packaged as a set of 32 audiotaped lessons, accompanying worksheets, and a teacher's manual. Each taped lesson, which is about 15 minutes in duration, focuses on a key idea or principle for creative thinking that is illustrated by a story of a historical figure. Students' worksheets contain exercises – three or four for use following each audio lesson – intended to help students practice originality, flexibility, fluency, and elaboration in their thinking.

Sternberg and Williams (in press) had high school students participate in a college-level psychology course that was taught to some of them in such a way as to encourage creativity – by having them generate theories, design experiments, conduct thought experiments, and so on – and to others in such a way as not to encourage creativity. Students who had scored high on a test of creativity and who were in the group that was taught so as to encourage creativity did better in the course than did those who had not scored high on creativity.

The Philosophy for Children Program (Lipman, 1991; Lipman, Sharp, & Oscanyan, 1980), established in the early 1970s, is usually thought of as focused on the development of critical thinking, but among the many skills it targets are those involving constructing hypotheses, discovering alternatives, formulating questions, dealing with ambiguities, making connections, and working with analogies. This is in keeping with founder-director Lipman's view that it is impossible to engage in effective critical thinking that is devoid of creativity or, more generally, to think well without using both creative and critical skills. "Higher-order thinking involves constant shuttling back and forth, a constant dialogue, between rationality and creativity" (Lipman, 1991, p. 216). I find much in the approach to admire, but believe there is need for more data on the question of its effectiveness in realizing its goals (Nickerson, 1993).

The approaches and programs mentioned in the foregoing paragraphs are representative of the efforts that have been made to facilitate the enhancement of creativity, but are not an exhaustive list of them. Much other work has been done (J. L. Adams, 1974; Allen, 1962; Bransford & Stein, 1984; Cropley, 1992; Eberle, 1977; Feldhusen & Treffinger, 1986; Isaksen & Treffinger, 1985; Parnes et al., 1977; Ruggiero, 1984; Sanders & Sanders, 1984; Torrance, 1972; Treffinger, 1979; F. Williams, 1972). Several of the programs or structured approaches for enhancing creativity, sometimes as one among other objectives related to improving thinking generally, are described in Nickerson et al., (1985), Chance (1986), Perkins (1995), and Starko (1995).

Effectiveness of Structured Approaches

Hard data on the question of whether creativity can be enhanced are not as abundant as one would like. One reason for this is that research on the question is fraught with conceptual and practical difficulties. What one is likely to accept as evidence that creativity has been enhanced must depend in part on what one will take as evidence of creativity or as instances of creative behavior, and this is a matter of some debate. Most of the measures that might be considered appropriate for the task are not very precise, so results are likely to be open to more than one interpretation. The behavior that efforts to increase creativity are target-ing is behavior in real-world (nonlaboratory) situations – spontaneous behavior and typically unobserved behavior. Such behavior is difficult to measure directly, and the extent to which formal tests of creativity measure the ability or tendency to be creative outside the test situ-ation is questionable.

Training aimed at improving performance on specific tasks like those used in some tests of creativity has often been effective in raising scores on those tests, but evidence that what has been learned generalizes to situations unlike those involved in training, or even that it persists for very long, is seldom obtained. Cropley (1992) has noted the possibility that short-term efforts to teach creativity will have a long-term effect precisely opposite to the desired one:

> Children can become aware in the course of training that certain kinds of behavior are preferred by the teacher and can alter their behavior accordingly. Although children may be encouraged by the training to work hard on the various tasks which they are presented, they can learn that it is easy to give "origi-nal" answers if one engages in hair splitting, gives rambling answers without regard to accuracy or rele-vance, or offers banalities in the name of creativity. In this way, "creativity" can quickly degenerate to a special form of conformity. (p. 91)

It must be acknowledged, too, that creative talent, as evidenced by school tests and activ-ities does not guarantee creative productivity in adulthood (Nicholls, 1972; Renzulli, 1986). There are many possible explanations of this. Perhaps the factors that contribute to unusual creative productivity in adulthood are not tapped by many of the tests of creativity that are commonly used in schools (Dudek & Côté, 1994).

The aim of education with respect to creativity is, of course, to increase people's long-term ability and tendency to be creative, and one would like to be able to determine whether, or the extent to which, this objective has been realized. One hopes that efforts to foster cre-ativity during childhood will increase the creativity of individuals when they become adults, but few investigators are willing or able to do studies with sufficient longevity to obtain direct evidence on this question. The question of what to use as a control group, and that of what would constitute appropriate baseline measures against which change can appropriately be assessed, are difficult ones in life span research.

It is important to note that, although data supporting the assumption that creativity can be enhanced to nontrivial degrees are sparse, so are data that support the assumption that this cannot be done. In fact, the question has not been very extensively researched. There is, however, enough positive evidence to justify the belief that enhancement of at least some types of creative expression is possible. Moreover, among people doing research on creativ-ity, the belief that nontrivial enhancement is possible is quite strong. And nothing we know about cognition generally or about the determinants of creativity in particular represents a serious challenge to this belief.

Much research on creativity has centered on the identification of personality characteris-tics that distinguish more creative persons from those who are less creative (Eysenck, 1993; Lubart, 1994; MacKinnon, 1965). (See Amabile [1983] for a list of characteristics that have been identified as important to the development of creativity.) Discussions of specific per-sonality characteristics that are associated with creativity generally do not make clear whether the relationship is assumed to be one of cause and effect, in contrast to one of non-causal association or correlation, and, if so, which is cause and which effect. We might be convinced, for example, that creative people tend to be unusually inquisitive, and be left wondering whether they are creative because they are inquisitive, inquisitive because they are creative, or inquisitive and creative for other reasons. In short, although numerous per-sonality characteristics have been associated with creativity, no single constellation of such characteristics has been identified as constituting necessary and sufficient conditions for creativity (Stein, 1968).

If it were clear that certain personality traits were causes of creativity, we would still be left with the question of the extent to which those particular traits were genetically determined or shaped by environmental circumstances. The evidence does not give us very precise answers to the general question of the relative importance of nature and nurture in determining personality traits, but it leaves little room for doubt that both factors play some role. This being the case, it seems reasonable to attempt to cultivate those traits that are associated with creativity. But focusing on traits should not be done to the extent of overlooking the importance of situational determinants of creativity. It is just such a concentration of research on the creative person to the neglect of creative situations (circumstances conducive to creativity), Amabile (1983) has argued, that has encouraged the belief that creativity or the determinants of creative potential are largely innate.

Amabile points out that there is considerable informal evidence, in first-person accounts, of the importance of situational factors on the creative development and productivity of people judged by society to be creative to an unusual degree. While acknowledging that some aspects of the skills and personality styles that are important to creativity are innate, Amabile and Tighe (1993) contend that a considerable amount of development is possible through education and experience.

In my view, neither belief – that some people are born with the capacity to be creative and others are not, that relatively few people are genetically endowed with great creative potential and most are endowed with very little – has a very firm objective basis. An equally plausible belief is that creative potential is a relatively common endowment, or even that just about everyone has the potential to be creative to some nontrivial degree. This is not to argue that there is no such thing as creative genius that is dependent, at least in part, on unusual genetic makeup – it would be difficult to believe that all of us have the potential to be a Mozart, or a Gauss, or a Newton – but it is to suggest that most of us fail to realize the potential we have – which may be great – primarily because of lack of exposure to circumstances and conditions that are supportive of its development.

If the evidence regarding whether creativity can be enhanced is less than compelling either way, should we try to enhance it? One way to think of this question is to consider the two possible ways to be wrong: Which would be the more serious error – to try to enhance creativity if success is impossible, or to fail to try to enhance it if it really can be enhanced? In my view, the latter would be the more regrettable mistake. And because I believe that enhancement is possible and that the challenge is to discover more effective approaches of bringing it about, I see efforts to enhance creativity as opportunities to learn more about how to do it well.

HOW CAN CREATIVITY BE ENHANCED?

A clear, unequivocal, and incontestable answer to the question of how creativity can be enhanced is not to be found in the psychological literature. Some investigators have gone so far as to say that there is little to be learned about creativity from reading the current cognitive literature (Finke et al., 1992). Although this seems to me an overly harsh assessment of the state of knowledge about creativity, I believe that most of what can be said about how to enhance creativity in practically significant and lasting ways rests on evidence that is largely indirect and/or in need of further substantiation.

The literature on creativity points to many variables – including abilities, interests, attitudes, motivation, general intelligence, knowledge, skills, habits, beliefs, values, and cognitive styles – that are believed by investigators to play some role in determining how creative an individual is likely to be. Guilford (1950), who is generally credited with spurring interest in research on creativity in his presidential address to the American Psychological Association, distinguished between creative potential and the realization of that potential, and suggested that creative abilities determine whether one can exhibit creative behavior to a noteworthy degree, but that whether one will actually do so will also depend on other factors.

In general there appears to be considerable agreement among recent and current investigators of creativity on the point that creativity is the product of the combined effects of many factors, including personal traits and characteristics, as well as social, cultural, and environmental factors (Amabile, 1983; Csikszentmihalyi, 1988; Perkins, 1981; Simonton, 1984, 1990; Sternberg & Lubart, 1991, 1995; Williams, 1972). In the aggregate, the literature supports the assumption not only that different people express creativity in different ways, but also that personality traits and situational factors that determine creative expression differ from person to person.

The recommendations for enhancing creativity that follow are built around such traits and factors. They are offered as suggestions only. In most cases, incontrovertible evidence that they will work cannot be given, but encouraging evidence can be. I believe that all are consistent with what is known about creativity and its development and, in particular, with what has been learned from efforts to teach creativity in the classroom.

Establishing Purpose and Intention

Purpose is essential to creative expression – nobody carves a statue without intending to do so. Moreover, there is some evidence that people can sometimes behave more creatively – produce more creative responses – than they otherwise would if only they are asked to do so, even in the absence of instructions as to how to do this (Ironson & Davis, 1979). But I wish to suggest the importance of something stronger than a momentary intention to engage in a creative activity. By purpose I mean here a deep and abiding intention to develop one's creative potential – a long-term interest in some form of creative expression.

Dudek and Côté (1994) have stressed the importance of this factor: "The creative vision is more likely to be the result of a slow personal development on both cognitive and emotional levels. To achieve a novel point of view may necessitate years of continuing development which has nothing to do with divergent skills or fast information processing" (p. 132). Others who have noted the importance of purpose in this long-term sense include Perkins (1981) and Hidi (1990).

Some people believe that searching for creative ideas is not fruitful. Henle (1962), for example, argues that we cannot find creative ideas by intentionally looking for them; she also argues, however, that if we are not receptive to them, they will not come – that their occurrence requires an appropriate attitude on our part. So even from this point of view, the intention to be creative is seen as important for creative activity.

I suspect that few people will question the malleability of purposes and intentions. How best to get students to intend to be creative – to take creative behavior as a goal – is a legitimate question, and some of what follows speaks to it, but creativity is a sufficiently valued asset in modern society that many students will find it easy to take enhanced creativity as a goal if only they are convinced of its attainability.

Building Basic Skills

A solid grounding in the skills that are generally considered fundamental to a basic education is conducive, if not essential, to the development of creative potential. Some conceptual models of creativity explicitly recognize various levels of creative activity and see the higher-level abilities resting on the lower-level ones (Feldhusen & Kolloff, 1978; Renzulli, 1977; Treffinger, 1979).

Feldhusen and Kolloff (1978), for example, have proposed a conceptual model of creativity that distinguishes three levels, or stages, of creativity development. And they have designed a program, for use primarily with gifted students, that includes activities considered to be appropriate for each of these levels. At the first level, the activities are aimed at strengthening basic language and mathematical skills and encouraging the use of one's imagination. Second- and third-level activities build on the basic skills and involve first the learning of various structured approaches to creative problem solving, such as some of those described later in this chapter, and eventually the performance of independent self-directed projects.

Encouraging Acquisition of Domain-Specific Knowledge

Knowledge of a domain does not always lead to creativity, but such knowledge does appear to be a relatively necessary condition for it; people who do noteworthy creative work in any given domain are almost invariably very knowledgeable about the domain. One cannot expect to make an impact in science as a consequence of new insights unless one has a thorough understanding of what is already known, or believed to be true, in a given field. The great innovators in science have invariably been thoroughly familiar with the science of their day. Serendipity is widely acknowledged to have played a significant role in many scientific discoveries; but it is also widely acknowledged that good fortune will be useful only to one who knows enough to recognize it for what it is. In mathematics there may be rare exceptions to the rule that familiarity with one's field is a necessary condition for creative work – Ramanujen, for example – but to the extent that such exceptions exist, they truly are exceptions to a principle that applies nearly universally.

The same principle holds true in the arts. As a rule great artists have mastered the prevailing techniques of their art form before they have begun to innovate and to influence its further development. Hayes (1985) has presented evidence that classical composers who today are recognized for their creative influence on music seldom produced masterworks until they had been composing for at least 10 years. Every form of art is part craft; and successful performance as an artist requires mastery of the tools and techniques through which the art form is expressed. Such mastery involves both declarative and procedural knowledge, the acquisition of which requires study and practice over an extended time. Artistic expression can rest on knowledge in another sense as well. One cannot write poetry – or prose for that matter – that expresses deep insights about life unless one has deep insights to express. As Wakefield (1994) has put it: "Turning a poet's thoughts inward does not necessarily make better poetry. Something needs to be learned about life first, and something needs to be learned about poetry" (p. 114).

In my view, the importance of domain-specific knowledge as a determinant of creativity is generally underestimated, even though investigators have given it considerable emphasis (Cropley, 1992; Csikszentmihalyi, 1996; Gardner, 1993a; Necka, 1986; Weisberg, 1988, 1993). Some have argued that any given individual is more likely to express creativity in certain domains than in others. Runco (1987) found this to be the case with gifted children, for example. On the basis of extensive interviews with 91 unusually creative people from many domains, Csikszentmihalyi (1996) concluded that "a person who wants to make a creative contribution not only must work within a creative system, but must also reproduce that system within his or her own mind" (p. 47). Before one can reasonably hope to change a domain, in other words, one must master the domain as it exists.

There is a caveat. Some investigators have argued that very high levels of domain-specific knowledge can, in some instances, work against creativity. The idea is that experts in an area can become so committed to a standard or "correct"way of approaching problems in their area of expertise that they are unlikely to consider the possibility of alternative approaches (Frensch & Sternberg, 1989; Simonton, 1984). The point is well taken, in my view, and there is such a thing as being blinded to new possibilities by one's expertise; but I believe that, on balance, the evidence is that too little knowledge is far more likely to be problematic than is too much.

Stimulating and Rewarding Curiosity and Exploration

Investigators have suggested that creative children tend to be more playful than their less creative peers (Lieberman, 1965; Wallach & Kogan, 1965). Finke and his colleagues have demonstrated the importance of playing with combinations of pictorial parts in the generation of creative visual patterns (Finke, 1990; Finke & Slayton, 1988; Finke, Ward, & Smith, 1992). Intellectual playfulness – finding pleasure in playing with ideas – appears often to be a characteristic of creative adults as well. There is a great deal of whimsy and play, for example, in much of the thinking that scientists do – a considerable amount of toying with ideas and fantasizing – imagining oneself, for example, riding on a photon at the head of a beam of light. Again the emphasis is on curiosity as an *abiding* trait, on attitudes that are so deeply ingrained that they determine one's lifestyle.

The type of curiosity that evokes the expression of creativity is seen in a persistent reluctance to take things for granted, a deep desire for explanations, and skepticism of "obvious" explanations. As Bruner (1962) has put it, "A willingness to divorce oneself from the obvious is surely a prerequisite for the fresh combinatorial act that produces effective surprise" (p. 12). The ability to see things from different perspectives, especially novel or unusual perspectives, and the willingness and ability to change one's perspective – to reformulate a problem on which one is making little progress – have been stressed by many investigators as important aspects of creative thinking (Gilhooly & Green, 1989; Perkins, 1990; Sternberg & Lubart, 1992).

An attitude akin to childlike naïveté is not unknown among great scientists. Einstein attributed his formulation of the theory of relativity in part to the fact that he kept asking himself questions about space and time that only children wonder about (Holton, 1973). Bertrand Russell (1955/1984) speaks of Einstein as having "the faculty of not taking familiar things for granted" and illustrates the fact by referring to Einstein's expression of "'surprised thankfulness' that four equal rods can make a square, since, in most of the universes he could imagine, there would be no such things as squares" (p. 408). In keeping with evidence of the importance of curiosity as a determinant of creativity, Csikszentmihalyi (1996) has argued that "the first step toward a more creative life is the cultivation of curiosity and interest, that is, the allocation of attention to things for their own sake" (p. 346).

Is it possible to stimulate curiosity – one's own or that of others – about the world? I believe (1) that it is possible to increase one's own curiosity about the world simply by training oneself to be more observant, to pay closer attention to aspects of daily experience to which we tend to be largely oblivious, (2) that curiosity is contagious, and (3) that there is little a teacher can aspire to do that will be more important to the quality of the intellectual lives of his or her students throughout their adulthood than to foster in them a deep sense of wonder about the world and existence.

It may be that some people are naturally more curious about the world than others. It could be, too, that all children are curious and that whether they maintain their curiosity into adulthood depends to a large degree on the extent to which it is encouraged or inhibited in early life. Whether or not it is possible to stimulate or enhance curiosity, squelching it appears to be all too easy to do. It should not be surprising if children who are constantly rebuffed for being inquisitive, or who standardly receive "just because" answers to their "why" questions, become less interested in exploring the mysteries of their existence as a consequence.

We need to take seriously the possibility that children are naturally curious and that they have to learn not to be. I alluded to the fact that Einstein characterized his own thought processes as childlike in a significant way. Might a reason why there are not more people with the creative capability of Einstein be that the educational process stifles in many the curiosity with which all of us begin to experience the world? How else can we account for the rather amazing lack of curiosity that most of us show about the incredible world in which we live? Children pose questions that adults would be embarrassed to ask. It appears that, in achieving adulthood, we learn not to ask questions that would reveal our sophistication as the mask for ignorance that it is.

Csikszentmihalyi (1996) says this on the subject:

Each of us is born with two contradictory sets of instructions: a conservative tendency, made up of instincts for self-preservation, self-aggrandizement, and saving energy, and an expansive tendency made up of instincts for exploring, for enjoying novelty and risk – the curiosity that leads to creativity belongs to this set. We need both of these programs. But whereas the first tendency requires little encouragement or support from outside to motivate behavior, the second can wilt if it is not cultivated. If too few opportunities for curiosity are available, if too many obstacles are placed in the way of risk and exploration, the motivation to engage in creative behavior is easily extinguished. (p. 11)

The idea that children are naturally curious and that early educational experiences can stultify their curiosity is a very disturbing one. The first article of the Hippocratic oath – do no harm – is as appropriate and as important for education as it is for medicine. If only we knew how to follow that advice in this context. I find it very thought provoking that Amabile (1983) begins the penultimate chapter of a book about how social factors affect creativity with the retrospective observation that, although it had not been her intention, most of her research had uncovered methods for destroying creativity. There appear to be many ways of doing that. Determining the extent to which specific educational practices stifle creativity is an objective that deserves much attention.

If it is not clear what determines what will capture a child's interest, it seems reasonable to assume that whatever the answer to this question is, children who are exposed to lots of creative products in stimulating and pleasurable ways are more likely to find something that will genuinely interest them deeply than will children who do not have comparable exposure. Moreover, curiosity has the interesting property that the more it is indulged, the more it grows. When one finds some aspect of life sufficiently interesting to attempt to learn something new about it, one is likely to discover that what one has learned has whetted one's appetite to learn more. One now knows enough to ask questions that one could not even conceive before.

Building Motivation

How much does motivation have to do with creativity? How important is perspiration relative to inspiration? Some investigators of creativity believe that motivation counts a great deal (Amabile, 1983; Golann, 1963; Nicholls, 1972). "Passion" is often used to describe the attitude of productive scientists and artists about their work. Perkins (1994) points out that creative breakthroughs usually occur following concerted efforts that, in many cases, have been made over several years.

Biographers of great mathematicians have often described them as being obsessed with mathematics. Bell (1937/1956) put Gauss's preoccupation with mathematical ideas this way: "As a young man Gauss would be 'seized' by mathematics. Conversing with friends he would suddenly go silent, overwhelmed by thoughts beyond his control, and stand staring rigidly oblivious to his surroundings" (p. 326). Gauss himself attributed his prodigious output to the constancy with which he thought about mathematics, and he made the not easily believed claim that if others reflected on mathematical truths as deeply and continuously as did he, they would make the same discoveries.

Keynes (1942/1956) suggested that Newton's peculiar gift was the ability to concentrate intently on a problem for hours, days, or weeks, if necessary, until he had solved it. Newton himself claimed that during the time of his greatest discoveries in mathematics and science (when he was in his early twenties) he thought constantly about the problems on which he was working. Ulam (1976) stresses the importance for mathematical creativity of what he refers to as "'hormonal factors' or traits of character: stubbornness, physical ability, willingness to work, what some call 'passion'" (p. 289). What may be said of creative mathematics, in this regard, appears to be equally true of creative work in other arenas as well. Many writers have stressed the "hard work" aspect of creativity, among them Roe (1952, 1953), McClelland (1962), and Golann (1963). The importance of motivation is implicit in many of the other factors considered here.

Especially Internal Motivation

The distinction between motivation that is internally generated and that which comes from sources outside oneself has received much emphasis in the literature. There seems to be a broad consensus among researchers that internal, or intrinsic, motivation is a more effective determinant of creativity than is external, or extrinsic, motivation (Amabile, 1983, 1990; DeCharms, 1968; Deci, 1975, 1980; Golann, 1962; Hennessey & Amabile, 1988); some have claimed that external motivation can actually undermine creativity under certain conditions (Deci, 1971, 1972a, 1972b; Greene & Lepper, 1974; Kruglanski, Friedman, & Zeevi, 1971; Lepper, Greene, & Nisbett, 1973).

There is some evidence that external reward may decrease the internal motivation of children whose internal motivation is initially high and increase that of children whose internal motivation is initially low (Loveland & Olley, 1979), although the possibility of a regression-to-the-mean effect must be considered here. There is also evidence that the effect that external reward has on internal motivation depends somewhat on how the reward is perceived by those who receive it. If the reward is perceived as the *reason* for having engaged in the activity, its receipt may have an adverse effect on internal motivation, but if it is not perceived in this way, it may help sustain interest (Amabile, 1983; Calder & Staw, 1975; Kruglanski et al., 1971; Lepper, Sagotsky, Dafoe, & Greene, 1982).

The difference between internal and external motivation, according to one view, is a matter, at least in part, of perceived locus of control. One is externally motivated when one considers one's involvement in some activity to be under someone else's control. This has implications for the effectiveness of external evaluation of creative activities: "If the evaluation conveys external control over task engagement, then internal motivation can be expected to decrease. If it conveys positive competence information, then internal motivation can be expected to increase" (Amabile, 1983, p. 114). In other words, the point is not that efforts to be creative should never be evaluated, but that there is a need for caution in the way evaluations are done in classroom situations in which the goal is to increase students' internal motivation to be creative.

A centrist view on the relationship between internal and external motivation has been expressed by Crutchfield (1962). Characterizing external motivation as that in which "the achievement of the creative solution is a *means* to an ulterior end, rather than an end in itself" and internal motivation as that in which "the creative act is an *end*, not a means" (p. 121), he admits the possibility of each type of motivation yielding creative activity, but argues that internal motivation – that which causes people to engage in creativity for the pleasure of doing so – is likely to be important in higher levels of creative productivity. Others who have recognized the possibility of creativity being externally motivated to good effect include Osborn (1963), Torrance (1965), Ochse (1990), and Lubart and Sternberg (1995).

Lubart and Sternberg (1995) suggest that the effect of motivation on creativity follows a Yerkes-Dodson principle, according to which an intermediate degree of motivation is better than either a very low or very high degree. With respect to the difference between internal and external motivation, they argue that what is important is whether the motivator focuses attention on the task or the goal; internal motivators typically focus attention on the task, whereas external ones typically focus it on the goal, and creativity suffers in the latter case. The inverted-U relationship between motivation and creativity results, Lubart and Sternberg suggest, from the fact that with very high levels of motivation, one becomes too focused on the goal to concentrate effectively on the creative work itself.

In short, the importance of motivation in creativity is well documented. One who strongly wishes to be creative is far more likely to be so than one who lacks this desire. In the absence of strong motivation, one's creative potential is unlikely to be developed very fully, because the hard work required will not be sustainable. Creativity researchers are generally agreed not only that motivation is essential to creativity, but that internal motivation is a more effective determinant of creative productivity than is external motivation. In my view, motivation – including internal motivation – is fueled, in part, by the desire for recognition of accomplishment. There can be no question of the importance that scientists, including the most creatively productive of them, attach to recognition and acclaim for their discoveries. Artists are equally desirous of public recognition of the worth of their work. However, in keeping with Lubart and Sternberg's notion of the inverted-U relationship, desire for recognition, if too strong, can work against creative productivity; and is unlikely to be effective in any case in the absence of an intrinsic interest in the creative activity for its own sake.

The question of exactly how external motivators should be used is a continuing challenge for research. I know of no one who claims they should never be used, but many urge caution in their use, noting that they can, if used injudiciously, become demotivating in the long run. I want to argue that, used with discretion, external motivators (enticements, recognition, rewards) can be effective in evoking and maintaining creative behavior. By being used with discretion, I mean that external motivators should be used in such a way as to encourage the expression of natural abilities and to reinforce internal motivation, to the extent that it exists. I do not have in mind attempting to motivate people to engage in activities for which they have no intrinsic interest or natural talent. Whether it it possible to instill internal motivation where none exists is an open question; however, the evidence supports the assumption that where there is some internal motivation, it can be reinforced and helped to grow. The goal should be to reinforce and strengthen internal motivation and to use external motivators to that end.

Encouraging Confidence and a Willingness to Take Risks

Timidity is not conducive to creativity. Fear is seen as a major reason why children hesitate to express their ideas, especially perhaps unconventional ones (Freeman, 1983). Fear of failure, fear of exposing one's limitations, and fear of ridicule are powerful deterrents to creative thinking, or at least to public exposure of products of creative efforts. People who are highly susceptible to pressures to conform tend not to be creative (Crutchfield, 1962).

Confidence comes with successful experiences. Especially for people who may have had few such experiences in the past, what is required is an environment that encourages and rewards creative effort per se; even when it is not highly successful, effort itself must be rewarded. The importance of an environment that is generally supportive of creative thinking has been emphasized by many investigators (Cropley, 1992; Feldhusen & Treffinger, 1986; Rogers, 1954/1970; Treffinger, Isaksen, & Firestein, 1983; E. E. Williams, 1976).

Researchers have stressed the role of success as a motivator for further effort, and of failure as a demotivator (Deci, 1975; Deci & Ryan, 1980). This does not mean that students should never be allowed to experience failure, but it suggests that they should be encouraged to work toward goals that are within their reach, especially when their confidence is weak, and that failures resulting from genuine effort should be treated as opportunities to learn and not as occasions for embarrassment.

Building confidence requires care. It is important to recognize the naïveté, and possibly damaging effects, of the assumption that all people can be whatever they wish to be. Expectations should be high but not impossible. Also, the line between self-confidence and arrogance is a fuzzy one, as is that between a willingness to take reasonable risks and irrational disregard for possible consequences of actions. As Crutchfield (1962) points out, it is possible to carry nonconformity, or counterconformity, to an excess that can impair creativity. More generally, it may sometimes be difficult to draw the line between intellectual independence and complete disregard for authority, between a willingness to be unconventional and a compulsion to be a nonconformist for the sake of nonconformity, between inquisitiveness and out-of-control impulsiveness, but these lines must be drawn.

The tendency to be guided by inner as opposed to externally imposed goals and standards is sometimes viewed as a distinctive characteristic of creative people (Houtz, Jambor, Cifone, & Lewis, 1989). Creative people tend to be somewhat underwhelmed by authority and more than willing to hold unconventional views (Barron, 1969; Dellas & Gaier, 1970; MacKinnon, 1962, 1965; Perkins, Jay & Tishman, 1993); they are often seen as nonconformists (Barron, 1968; MacKinnon, 1962), probably for good reason. And they are not risk averse (Glover, 1977).

Creative children may be less easy to manage than children who are not so creative, and thus represent a greater challenge to both teachers and parents (Getzels & Jackson, 1962; Getzels & Smilansky, 1983). "Creative students are often unconventional, individualistic, nonconforming, and typically viewed as 'difficult,' but these seemingly difficult tendencies may be functionally tied to creative behavior" (Runco & Nemiro, 1994, p. 239). Failure to promote creativity in the classroom may well be due sometimes to recognition of the increased challenge that creatively expressive children can represent to classroom order and teacher authority.

Focusing on Mastery and Self-Competition

Evidence shows that people who take it as a goal to improve their performance, and hence compare their current performance with past performance, are likely to be more willing to accept challenging tasks and to persist if they experience failure than are people who set their sights on outperforming others and "winning" in the conventional sense (Grieve, Whelan, Kottke, & Meyers, 1994; Nicholls, 1984; Orlick, 1986). This is not to suggest that outcomes – winning the prize for best entry in the contest, getting one's poems published, having a successful one-person exhibit – are unimportant and should be considered of no consequence, but it is to suggest that the greater emphasis should be on mastery and self-competition. An outcome orientation may work for individuals who have unusual native ability and who do, in fact, often win competitive events, but it is not as likely to be effective for the more typical individual whose native talents are less outstanding and who seldom, if ever, carry away the grand prize from a competition.

In addition to the experimental evidence that mastery orientation works better than outcome orientation in keeping people motivated to improve at targeted tasks, one also sees compelling illustrations of the fact outside the laboratory. The vast majority of people who compete – many of whom compete regularly – in marathons, for example, have no hope of ever winning a race. The possibility of bettering one's "personal best," however, is a powerful incentive for many runners. Others get great satisfaction out of simply being able to complete the course within some specified time – or at all. Few students who would like to be able to write poetry will ever win a Pulitzer Prize for doing so – although some will – but pleasure can be obtained from the act of composing and from being able to produce better poems with increasing experience. Students need to understand the difference between mastery orientation and outcome orientation and to be able to derive satisfaction from competing against themselves.

Promoting Supportable Beliefs About Creativity

The importance of beliefs as determinants of the quality of one's thinking and intellectual performance more generally has been emphasized by several writers (Andrews & Debus, 1978; Baron, 1991; Deci & Ryan, 1985; Dweck, 1975; Reid, 1987). Beliefs sometimes become self-fulfilling prophecies. This is true of beliefs that people hold about the determinants of their own capabilities and of beliefs that teachers hold about the extent to which students' capabilities can or cannot be enhanced as a consequence of what is done in the classroom.

Of particular relevance to the goal of enhancing creativity is the not surprising fact that the belief that one's intellectual capabilities are genetically determined and not subject to improvement by other influences can be demotivating, whereas the contrary belief that one's capabilities can be enhanced through learning can motivate effort (Dweck & Eliot, 1983; Stevenson, Chen, & Lee, 1993; Torgeson & Licht, 1983). It follows that to the extent that creativity is determined by motivation, the demotivating belief that creativity cannot be increased by effort becomes self-fulfilling.

An extreme illustration of the power of beliefs to affect behavior is the phenomenon of learned helplessness, the acquired conviction that effort is pointless because one's fate is determined by circumstances beyond one's control (Peterson, Maier, & Seligman, 1993). Fortunately, optimism appears to be learnable as well (Seligman, 1991; Seligman, Reivich, Jaycox, & Gillham, 1995).

Students need to believe that creativity is determined by motivation and effort to a significant degree. They need to understand that creative products are seldom produced without intent and effort, that there is considerable evidence to support the belief that most people have potential they never realize, and that persistent effort to develop that potential is likely to be successful. It is hard to imagine a belief that is more important to creativity than the belief that how one's mind is developed and used is one's personal responsibility.

Students need to know too that, although there are reasons to believe that modest effort would probably suffice to increase the degree of creativity most of us exhibit in our daily lives, truly outstanding creative works in science and art have often taken many years –

sometimes the better part of a lifetime – to produce. Kepler discovered his laws of planetary motion as the result of over 20 years of incessant calculation in the face of one failed attempt after another. Goethe took about 20 years to write *Faust;* Napier spent a similar amount of time working out the properties of logarithms. Charles Babbage spent 40 years attempting to perfect his analytical engine. One could generate a long list of such examples of creative persistence.

I am not suggesting that examples like these should be held up to students as evidence that unless they are prepared to commit decades to an objective, they have no hope of being creative, but they do need to know that few creative products of lasting value have been generated quickly and with little effort, and that many have required extraordinary persistence over remarkably long periods of time. They need to understand that if one really wants to be creative in a substantive way, one must be prepared to work at it.

Providing Opportunities for Choice and Discovery

The evidence is fairly compelling, and not surprising, that people are more interested in – more internally motivated to engage in – activities they have chosen for themselves than activities that have been selected for them by others, or in which they are obliged to engage for reasons beyond their control (Dudek & Côté, 1994; Kohn, 1993). This appears to be more than a matter of being able to choose activities that one enjoys and to avoid those that one dislikes. Specific activities that are enjoyable when people elect to engage in them may not be enjoyable to the same individuals when forced upon them.

In school settings, students typically work on problems of someone else's choosing; seldom are they challenged to find problems of their own on which to work. Presumably one reason for this is the fact that having students work on "set" problems poses far less formidable challenges of administration and evaluation than does having them work on problems that they themselves find. I do not mean to discount the practical importance of this consideration or to argue that students should work *only* on problems of their own choosing; the suggestion is that, if they are to have a good chance of developing their creative potential, they need to have some experience in problem finding and selection, as well as in problem solving.

They also need opportunities to make real discoveries – to learn, from personal experience, how gratifying the experience of discovery can be. The history of science contains many accounts of the feeling of elation experienced by scientists upon making a discovery. The same feeling – perhaps on a smaller scale – can be experienced by anyone upon discovering something genuinely new to him- or herself. The importance of providing people with the opportunity to make real discoveries – to generate ideas that they have not thought of before – as a means of enhancing creativity has been stressed by Finke, Ward, and Smith (1992).

Developing Self-management (Metacognitive) Skills

An important aspect of the growing interest in metacognition in recent years has been an increasing emphasis on the role of self-management (intentional monitoring and guiding of one's own behavior) in human performance (Jausovec, 1994; Kitchener, 1983). Studies have shown that people can learn to exercise better control over their performance in various contexts than they tend to exercise spontaneously. Runco (1990) has stressed the importance of self-evaluative skills and metacognition more generally to creative thinking.

Self-management involves becoming an *active* manager of one's cognitive resources. It is, in part, a matter of paying attention to one's own thought processes and of taking responsibility for one's thinking. It involves learning of one's own strengths and weaknesses as a creative thinker and finding ways to utilize the strengths and to mitigate or work around the weaknesses. It means making an effort to discover conditions that facilitate one's own creative work.

Many creative people have found that they can be most productive when working in particular environments or under specific conditions. Perkins (1981) gives numerous examples. The conclusion I draw from these examples is not that for every person there is only one particular environment or set of conditions that is conducive to that person's creativity, but that creative expression is a matter of habit and routine more than one might assume.

Creative pursuits are time consuming. If one wants to write poetry or compose music, one must find time – lots of time – to write or compose. It is not surprising to discover that many eminently creative people have structured their lives so as to ensure the availability of time for their creative activities on a regular basis. Time management can be learned. And learning it is probably quite important for anyone who desires to become more proficient at some creative endeavor. Without skill at time management, it is easy to find oneself continually in react mode or frequently engaged in activities that have no purpose other than that of "killing time."

Teaching Techniques and Strategies for Facilitating Creative Performance

A variety of techniques (strategies, heuristics) have been proposed to aid thinking and problem solving generally. A brief description of several of them – creating subgoals, working backwards, hill climbing, means–ends analysis, forward chaining, considering analogous problems, specialization and generalization, and considering extreme cases – is given in Nickerson (1994b). These strategies have been identified primarily through observing how successful problem solvers approach problems. They were not designed to enhance creativity, but as already noted, some investigators see creativity as a form of problem solving, and certainly problems can be solved in more and less creative ways. Many suggestions have been made regarding things one can do to stimulate creative thinking specifically – for example, to break a set, to increase the flow of novel ideas, or to gain a new perspective or point of view on a problem that is proving to be difficult to solve.

The use of acronyms as mental checklists—reminders to ask specific questions or to perform specific operations – is among the simpler and more familiar of the techniques that have been proposed to aid creativity. Eberle (1977) organized questions of the sort recommended by Osborn (1953) so as to be prompted by the acronym SCAMPER, which is intended to bring to mind questions having to do with Substitution, Combination, Adaptation, Modification (especially Magnification and Minification), Putting to other uses, Elimination, and Rearrangement. De Bono (1983) makes use of acronyms as reminders to perform certain operations: CAF is intended to remind one, for example, to Consider All Factors; PNI is a prompt to list all Positive, Negative, and Interesting aspects of a situation. The acronym IDEAL, used by Bransford and Stein (1984), identifies the steps in their approach to problem solving and creativity: Identify the problem, Define and represent the problem, Explore possible strategies, Act on the strategies, and Look back and evaluate the effects of your activities.

Another simple technique to enhance creative productivity that has received considerable attention in the literature is that of laying aside, temporarily, a problem or task on which one is failing to make headway despite a concerted effort to do so. Some investigators have noted that insights or "breakthroughs" – major advances toward an objective – have often been reported to occur unexpectedly after a period of intense effort that seems to lead nowhere, followed by a period of rest or engagement in unrelated activities. There are many accounts in the literature of unusually creative people being inspired with novel and productive ideas at unpredictable times, when not actively thinking about the subject of the inspiration, but after having labored on it without much success for lengthy periods (Ghiselin, 1952). This phenomenon led to the idea, first put forward by Wallas (1926/1945), that creative work typically involves a period of "incubation," during which one does not consciously think about the task but the mind continues to work on it below the level of consciousness.

The idea that an incubation period generally precedes insight experiences has not been accepted by all psychologists (Ericsson & Simon, 1980; Perkins, 1981; Simon, 1966; Weisberg, 1986). Moreover attempts to obtain evidence of incubation in the laboratory have not been very successful (Dominowski & Jenrick, 1972; Murray & Denny, 1969). Some objections to the concept are based on rejection of the assumption that the mind continues working on a problem of interest below the level of awareness when one is not consciously focusing on the problem. There are other explanations, however, of why performance on any cognitively demanding task might be improved as a consequence of taking a break from the task.

One possibility that has been suggested is that progress on a problem can be blocked by fixation on ideas that are not getting one closer to a solution and an inability to free oneself from that fixation. Ceasing to think about the problem provides an opportunity for the dissipation of such fixation and, consequently, greater accessibility to knowledge that is likely to lead to a solution (Finke et al., 1992; Smith, 1995). Woodworth and Schlosberg (1954) made a similar suggestion. Whatever the explanation of its effectiveness, the strategy of putting a recalcitrant problem aside for a while has many advocates (Poincaré, 1924, 1952; Simon, 1966, 1986; Smith & Blankenship, 1989).

Other techniques have been mentioned in preceding sections of this chapter in connection with specific programs or structured approaches to creativity. Morphological synthesis and the listing of attributes are cases in point. Other examples of teachable strategies and of activities aimed at enhancing creativity, for use in the classroom or by oneself, may be found in many books on creative thinking or problem solving. A partial list of sources includes J. L. Adams (1974), Bransford and Stein (1984), Finke et al. (1992), Hayes (1989), Levine (1987), Michael (1968), Mitchell, Stueckle, and Wilkens (1976), Parnes et al., (1977), Polya (1945/1957), Renzulli and Callahan (1973), Ruggiero (1984), Sanders and Sanders (1984), Treffinger (1979), Wicklegren (1974), and F. Williams (1972).

Providing Balance

Children need to be able to engage in creative expression in the classroom without fear of ridicule or reprimand. This does not mean that in the interest of not stifling creativity, children should be allowed to do whatever they wish. The need for structure, discipline, self-restraint, and respect for tradition and convention is as real and important as the need for freedom, spontaneity, innovativeness, and risk taking. Although creativity can be stifled by a repressive environment, it is not necessarily fostered by total lack of constraint (Marjoram, 1988); too little structure can be as inhibiting of creativity as too much (Runco & Okuda, 1993). The challenge is to find the proper balance – to teach children to recognize and respect rules, bounds, and limits without stifling their creativity. This means teaching not only what the rules are, but why rules are necessary and why particular rules make sense.

Finding the right balance between demand and support is also a challenge. Children need to have goals that stretch their capabilities, but they also need a supportive environment that rewards effort even when it is not successful. There is reason to believe that environments that are both demanding and supportive are more conducive to the development of creativity than those that have much of one of these characteristics but little of the other (Knapp, 1963; Thistlewaite, 1963).

TEACHING BY EXAMPLE

The relative importance of attitudes and values for creative thinking and for effective thinking more generally has been stressed by many writers (Barell, 1991; Baron, 1985, 1994; Ennis, 1985, 1987; Mumford, Connelly, Baughman, & Marks, 1994; Newmann, 1991; Schrag, 1987; Tishman, Jay, & Perkins, 1993). Perkins (1988, 1990) distinguishes among potencies (native abilities, talents), plans (or patterns of thinking), and values as possible determinants of creativity and argues that the evidence suggests that although potencies may enable creativity, plans and, especially, values are more likely to promote it. "The clearest evidence of all demonstrates the connection between creative thinking and values broadly construed – a person's commitments and aspirations" (Perkins, 1990, p. 421). "Much more than we usually suppose," Perkins argues, "creating is an intentional endeavor shaped by the person's values" (p. 422).

Fair-mindedness, openness to evidence, a desire for clarity, respect for others' opinions, inquisitiveness, and reflectiveness are among the attitudinal qualities – habits of mind – that have been widely associated with good thinking and taken as goals of efforts to teach thinking. "Mindfulness" captures the idea that good thinking depends on a habitual tendency to approach problems in a thoughtful and nonimpulsive way (Langer, 1989).

In my view, attitudes and values that are critical to the development and use of creative potential are best taught by example. I doubt that it is possible to teach them effectively if one does not have them. It is hard to imagine, for example, how one might get students to be curious about the world if one is not deeply curious about it oneself, to be open to new ideas if one's own mind is closed, to value reflectiveness if one gives no evidence of being reflective, and so on. The objective of enhancing creativity demands a great deal of the classroom teacher.

SUMMING UP

To recap, numerous characteristics, competencies, traits, attitudes, and other factors have been associated with creativity. In addition to general intelligence, I have mentioned purpose and intention, basic skills, domain-specific-knowledge, curiosity and inquisitiveness, motivation, self-confidence and a willingness to take risks, mastery orientation and self-competition, beliefs, choice and the opportunity to discover, self-management skills, and specific creativity-aiding techniques. I might have also mentioned a tolerance for ambiguity and unconventionality (Barron & Harrington, 1981; Golann, 1963; MacKinnon, 1962), the ability to think analogically and to make remote associations (Gentner & Grudin, 1985; Mednick, 1962; Polya, 1954; Rothenberg, 1990), flexibility of thought (Guilford & Hoepfner, 1971; Wallach, 1970), facility with visualization and the manipulation of mental images (Koestler, 1964; Mansfield & Bussé, 1981), as well as other factors (Tardif & Sternberg, 1988).

I do not mean to suggest that all these factors contribute to any instance of creative thinking or action to the same degree, or even that all of them are always involved to some extent. It would be useful to be able to identify a set of determinants that would be considered necessary and sufficient. I cannot do that. It seems likely to me that people are creative in different ways, to different degrees, and for different reasons. Sternberg and Lubart (1991, 1992; Lubart & Sternberg, 1995) capture this idea in their investment metaphor, according to which people invest various cognitive and conative resources in creative enterprises, and creative products can result from different confluences of these resources.

This being said, it also seems to me that assuming a modicum of intelligence and creative potential, the most basic determinants of the extent to which one is likely to realize one's potential are affective or conative (attitudinal, motivational) and not cognitive. Desire, internal motivation, and commitment are more important, in my view, than either domain-specific knowledge or knowledge of specific creativity-enhancing techniques or heuristics. With sufficient motivation, one is likely to obtain the necessary knowledge and to discover useful heuristics; without it, knowledge of any kind is unlikely to do much good.

CONCLUDING COMMENTS

I began this chapter by stating several assumptions about creativity. I believe all of them are consistent with the results of research on creative persons and creative behavior and that some are strongly supported by these results. It would be difficult to accept these assumptions without believing in the desirability and reasonableness of attempting to enhance creativity – the caveat about the possibility of learning to be clever without learning to be good notwithstanding. In my view, this objective can be justified in many ways, but especially by the belief that creative expression generally contributes positively to the quality of life of individuals who engage in it and often enriches the lives of others as well The quality of one's life is as much a matter of perspective as of anything else; enhancing one's ability to think creatively – assuming it is possible to do so – seems a reasonable way to broaden that perspective.

I have noted several approaches to the enhancement of creativity that seem to me to be suggested by the assumptions and thinking of many researchers in the field. In most cases, direct and compelling experimental evidence of their effectiveness is lacking; the claim I want to make is that what is known about creativity suffices to make the approaches worth trying. The likelihood that they will work, if used with good judgment, is high, in my view, and the chance that they will do harm is small.

To my knowledge, there is no easy, step-wise method that is guaranteed to enhance creativity to a nontrivial degree. The following observation was made by Rubin (1968) almost 30 years ago: "The research evidence unfortunately does not suggest that by using a prescribed scheme we can produce creativeness at will. What it suggests, rather, is that virtually everyone has more creativity than he makes use of, that different conditions flush it forth in different individuals, and that a given procedure tends to nurture a part, but not the whole, of one's creative capacity" (p. 88). I believe this observation to be consistent not only with the research evidence that existed at the time, but with what has accrued since it was made. Creativity and how to foster it remain less well understood than we would like. On the other hand, research has revealed many promising leads as to what is worth trying and much useful guidance to those who wish to enhance creativity – their own or others – and are prepared to work at it persistently over a long period of time.

This chapter has focused primarily on the possibility of enhancing creativity through instruction and in-school experiences. It was not my intent by this focus to discount the importance of home life, including during preschool years, to the development of one's creative potential. Longitudinal data suggest that child-rearing practices during children's preschool years influence the creative potential they show during adolescence. The significance of early home experiences in the shaping of the character and capabilities of people who have achieved eminence as adults is also well documented (Goertzel, Goertzel, & Goertzel, 1978). Many of the preceding suggestions for enhancing creativity are probably as applicable in the home setting as in the classroom, but apparently even simply reading to children regularly can enhance their ability to be imaginative (Singer & Singer, 1976). Surely it would be hard to overstate the importance of the principle of teaching by example in the context of the home.

Finally, some mention must be made of the fact that development of tools, the use of which would augment intellectual performance, has been a goal of many technologists for some time. Computer software packages are now commercially available that are intended to help people write, compose music, prove mathematical theorems, design devices, and perform other intellectually demanding tasks, including many that are usually considered creative. Can we assume that such tools – at least the best of them – will facilitate creativity? And if so, will the facilitation be largely a matter of increasing creative output, or could it mean improved quality of output as well?

Would a good word processor have improved Shakespeare's work? Would sophisticated computer aids for composing or doing mathematics have helped Mozart or Gauss? Suppose the answer to these questions is no. It would not follow that such tools cannot facilitate creativity. It is conceivable that they are more effective in enhancing the creativity of people with less extraordinary potential than that of a Shakespeare, a Mozart, or a Gauss. I doubt that that is the case, but it could be. I doubt it because I suspect that people who are productively creative without the help of powerful tools are generally likely to be even more so with it. We are in the realm of conjecture here, because the question of the potential for technological aids to enhance creativity has not yet received much attention from researchers; this situation seems likely to change as more and more tools that are designed for this purpose are forthcoming and put to use.

REFERENCES

Adams, J. L. (1974). *Conceptual blockbusting: A guide to better ideas.* San Francisco: Freeman.
Adams, M. J. (Coordinator). (1986). *Odyssey: A curriculum for thinking.* Watertown, MA: Mastery Education Corporation.
Albert, R. S. (1975). Toward a behavioral definition of genius. *American Psychologist, 30,* 140–151.
Allen, M. S. (1962). *Morphological creativity.* Englewood Cliffs, NJ: Prentice-Hall.
Amabile, T. M. (1979). Effects of external evaluation on artistic creativity. *Journal of Personality and Social Psychology, 37,* 221–233.
Amabile, T. M. (1983). *The social psychology of creativity.* New York: Springer-Verlag.
Amabile, T. M. (1990). Within you, without you: Towards a social psychology of creativity, and beyond. In M. A. Runco & R. S. Albert (Eds.), *Theories of creativity* (pp. 61–91). Newbury Park, CA: Sage.
Amabile, T. M., & Tighe, E. (1993). Questions of creativity. In J. Brockman (Ed.), *Creativity* (pp. 7–27). New York: Simon & Schuster.
Andrews, G. R., & Debus, R. I. (1978). Persistence and the causal perception of failure: Modifying cognitive attributions. *Journal of Educational Psychology, 70,* 154–166.
Baer, J. M. (1988). Long-term effects of creativity training with middle-school students. *Journal of Early Adolescence, 8,* 183–193.
Barell, J. (1991). *Teaching for thoughtfulness: Classroom strategies to enhance intellectual development.* New York: Longman.
Baron, J. (1985). *Rationality and intelligence.* Cambridge University Press.
Baron, J. (1991). Beliefs about thinking. In J. F. Voss, D. N. Perkins, & J. W. Segal (Eds.), *Informal reasoning and education* (pp. 169–186). Hillsdale, NJ: Erlbaum.
Baron, J. (1994). *Thinking and deciding* (2nd ed.). Cambridge University Press.
Barron, F. (1968). *Creativity and personal freedom.* Princeton, NJ: Van Nostrand.
Barron, F. (1969). *Creative person and creative process.* New York: Holt, Rinehart, & Winston.
Barron, F., & Harrington, D. M. (1981). Creativity, intelligence, and personality. *Annual Review of Psychology, 32,* 439–476.
Basadur, M. (1994). Managing the creative process in organizations. In M. A. Runco (Ed.), *Problem finding, problem solving, and creativity* (pp. 237–268). Norwood, NJ: Ablex.
Bell, E. T. (1956). The prince of mathematicians. In J. R. Newman (Ed.), *The world of mathematics* (pp. 295–339). New York: Simon & Schuster. (Original work published 1937)

Besemer. S. P., & Treffinger, D. J. (1981). Analysis of creative products: Review and sysnthesis. *Journal of Creative Behavior, 15*, 158–178.

Boden, M. A. (1991). *The creative mind: Myths and mechanisms*. New York: Basic.

Bowers, K. S., Farvolden, P., & Mermigis, L. (1995). Intuitive antecedents of insight. In S. M. Smith, T. B. Ward, & R. A. Finke (Eds.), *The creative cognition approach* (pp. 27–51). Cambridge, MA: MIT Press.

Bransford, J. D., & Stein, B. S. (1984). *The ideal problem solver: A guide for improving thinking, learning, and creativity*. New York: Freeman.

Bruner, J. S. (1962). The conditions of creativity. In H. Gruber, G. Terrell, & M. Wertheimer (Eds.), *Contemporary approaches to creative thinking* (pp. 1–30). New York: Atherton.

Calder, B., & Staw, B. (1975). Self-perception of intrinsic and extrinsic motivation. *Journal of Personality and Social Psychology, 31*, 599–605.

Campbell, D. (1960). Blind variation and selective retention in creative thought as in other knowledge processes. *Psychological Review, 67*, 380–400.

Cantor, G. (1955). *Contributions to the founding of the theory of transfinite numbers*. (P. Jourdain, Trans.). New York: Dover. (Originally work published 1915)

Cattell, R. B., & Butcher, H. J. (1968). *The prediction of achievement and creativity*. Champaign, IL: Institute for Personality and Ability Testing.

Cattell, R. B., & Cattell, A. K. S. (1961). *Culture fair intelligence test* (Scale 2, Forms A & B). Champaign, IL: Institute for Personality and Ability Testing.

Chance, P. (1986). *Thinking in the classroom*. New York: Teachers College Press.

Covington, M. V., Crutchfield, R. S., Davies, L., & Olton, R. M. (1974). *The productive thinking program: A course in learning to think*. Columbus, OH: Merrill.

Crawford, R. P. (1954). *Techniques of creative thinking*. New York: Hawthorn.

Cropley, A. J. (1967). *Creativity*. London: Longmans.

Cropley, A. J. (1992). *More ways than one: Fostering creativity*. Norwood, NJ: Ablex.

Crutchfield, R. S. (1962). Conformity and creative thinking. In H. Gruber, G. Terrell, & M. Wertheimer (Eds.), *Contemporary approaches to creative thinking* (pp. 120–140). New York: Atherton.

Csikszentmihalyi, M. (1988). Society, culture, and person: A systems view of creativity. In R. J. Sternberg (Ed.), *The nature of creativity* (pp. 325–339). Cambridge University Press.

Csikszentmihalyi, M. (1996). *Creativity: Flow and the psychology of discovery and invention*. New York: HarperCollins.

Csikszentmihalyi, M., & Getzels, J. W. (1970). Concern for discovery: An attitudinal component of creative productions. *Journal of Personality, 38*, 91–105.

Csikszentmihalyi, M., & Getzels, J. W. (1971). Discovery-oriented behavior and the originality of creative products: A study with artists. *Journal of Personality and Social Psychology, 19*, 47–52.

de Bono, E. (1970). *Lateral thinking: Creativity step by step*. New York: Harper & Row.

de Bono, E. (1973). *CoRT thinking*. Blanford, England: Direct Educational Services.

de Bono, E. (1983). The Cognitive Research Trust (CoRT) thinking program. In W. Maxwell (Ed.), *Thinking: The expanding frontier*. Philadelphia: Franklin Institute Press.

de Bono, E. (1992). *Serious creativity: Using the power of lateral thinking to create new ideas*. New York: HarperCollins.

DeCharms, R. (1968). *Personal causation*. New York: Academic.

Deci, E. (1971) Effects of externally mediated rewards on intrinsic motivation. *Journal of Personality and Social Psychology, 18*, 105–115.

Deci, E. (1972a). Intrinsic motivation, extrinsic reinforcement, and inequity. *Journal of Personality and Social Psychology, 22*, 113–120.

Deci, E. (1972b). The effects of contingent and noncontingent rewards and controls on intrinsic motivation. *Organizational Behavior and Human Performance, 8*, 217–229.

Deci, E. (1975). *Intrinsic motivation*. New York: Plenum.

Deci, E. (1980). *The psychology of self-determination*. Lexington, MA: Heath.

Deci, E., & Ryan, R. M. (1980). The empirical exploration of intrinsic motivational processes. In L. Berkowitz (Ed.), *Advances in experimental social psychology* (pp. 39–80). New York: Academic.

Deci, E. L., & Ryan, R. M. (1985). *Intrinsic motivation and self-determination in human behavior*. New York: Plenum.

Dellas, M., & Gaier, E. L. (1970). Identification of creativity: The individual. *Psychological Bulletin, 73*, 55–73.

de Sanchez, M. A., & Astorga, M. (1983). *Provecto aprender a pensar: Estudios de sus efectos sobre una muestra de estudiantes venezolanos*. Caracas, Venezuela: Ministerio de educacion.

Dewey, J. (1910). *How we think*. Boston: Heath.

Diehl, M., & Stroebe, W. (1986). Productivity loss in brainstorming: Toward the solution of a riddle. *Journal of Personality and Social Psychology, 53,* 497–509.

Dominowski, R. L. (1995). Productive problem solving. In S. M. Smith, T. B. Ward, & R. A Finke (Eds.), *The creative cognition approach* (pp. 73–95). Cambridge, MA: MIT Press.

Dominowski, R. L., & Jenrick, R. (1972). Effects of hints and interpolated activity on solution of an insight problem. *Psychonomic Science, 26,* 335–338.

Dudek, S. Z., & Côté, R. (1994). Problem finding revisited. In M. A. Runco (Ed.), *Problem finding, problem solving, and creativity* (pp. 130–150). Norwood, NJ: Ablex.

Dunnette, M. D. (1964). Are meetings any good for solving problems? *Personnel Administration, 27,* 12–29.

Dunnette, M. D., Campbell, J., & Jastaad, K. (1963). The effects of group participation on brainstorming effectiveness for two industrial samples. *Journal of Applied Psychology, 47,* 10–37.

Dweck, C. S. (1975). The role of expectations and attributions in the alleviation of learned helplessness. *Journal of Personality and Social Psychology, 45,* 165–171.

Dweck, C. S., & Eliot, E. S. (1983). Achievement motivation. In P. H. Mussen (Ed.), *Handbook of child psychology* (Vol. 4). New York: Wiley.

Eberle, R. E. (1977). *SCAMPER.* Buffalo, NY: DOK.

Ennis, R. H. (1985). Critical thinking and the curriculum. *National Forum, 65,* 28–31.

Ennis, R. H. (1987). A taxonomy of critical thinking dispositions and abilities. In J. B. Baron & R. J. Sternberg (Eds.), *Teaching thinking skills: Theory and practice* (pp. 9–26). New York: Freeman.

Ericsson, K. A., & Simon, H. A. (1980). Verbal reports as data. *Psychological Review, 87,* 215–251.

Eysenck, H. J. (1993). Creativity and personality: A theoretical perspective. *Psychological Inquiry, 4,* 147–178.

Farnham-Diggory, S. (1972). *Cognitive processes in education.* New York: Harper & Row.

Feldhusen, J. F. (1983). The Purdue Creative Thinking Program. In I. S. Sato (Ed.), *Creativity research and educational planning* (pp. 41–46). Los Angeles: Leadership Training Institute for the Gifted and Talented.

Feldhusen, J. F., & Kolloff, M. B. (1978). A three-stage model for gifted education. *Gifted Child Today, 1,* 3–5, 53–58.

Feldhusen, J. F., & Treffinger, D. J. (1986). *Creative thinking and problem solving in gifted education.* Dubuque, IO: Kendall/Hunt.

Finke, R. A. (1990). *Creative imagery: Discoveries and inventions in visualization.* Hillsdale, NJ: Erlbaum.

Finke, R. A., & Slayton, K. (1988). Explorations of creative visual synthesis in mental imagery. *Memory and Cognition, 16,* 252–257.

Finke, R. A., Ward, T. B., & Smith, S. M. (1992). *Creative cognition: Theory, research, and applications.* Cambridge, MA: MIT Press.

Freeman, J. (1983). Emotional problems of the gifted child. *Journal of Child Psychology and Psychiatry, 24,* 481–485.

Frensch, P. A., & Sternberg, R. J. (1989). Expertise and intelligent thinking: When is it worse to know better? In R. J. Sternberg (Ed.), *Advances in the psychology of human intelligence* (Vol 5, pp. 157–188). Hillsdale, NJ: Erlbaum.

Gallagher, J. J. (1975). *Teaching the gifted child* (2nd ed.). Boston: Allyn & Bacon.

Gardner, H. (1989). *To open minds.* New York: Basic.

Gardner, H. (1993a). *Creating minds.* New York: Basic.

Gardner, H. (1993b). Seven creators of the modern era. In J. Brockman (Ed.), *Creativity* (pp. 28–47). New York: Simon & Schuster.

Gentner, D., & Grudin, J. (1985). The evolution of mental metaphors in psychology: A ninety-year retrospective. *American Psychologist, 40,* 181–192.

Getzels, J. W. (1982). The problem of the problem. In R. M. Hogarth (Ed.), *Question forming and response consistency* (pp. 37–44). San Francisco: Jossey-Bass.

Getzels, J. W., & Csikszentmihalyi, M. (1975). From problem solving to problem finding. In I. A. Taylor & J. W. Getzels (Eds.) *Perspectives in creativity* (pp. 90–116). Chicago: Aldine.

Getzels, J. W., & Csikszentmihalyi, M. (1976). *The creative vision: A longitudinal study of problem finding in art.* New York: Wiley.

Getzels, J. W., & Jackson, P. (1962). *Creativity and intelligence: Explorations with gifted students.* New York: Wiley.

Getzels, J. W., & Smilansky, J. (1983). Individual differences in pupil perceptions of school programs. *British Journal of Experimental Psychology, 53,* 307–316.

Ghiselin, B. (Ed.). (1952). *The creative process.* Los Angeles: University of California Press.

Ghiselin, B. (1963). Ultimate criteria for two levels of creativity. In C. W. Taylor & F. Barron (Eds.), *Scientific creativity: Its recognition and development* (pp. 30–43). New York: Wiley.

Gilhooly, K. J. (1982). *Thinking: Directed, undirected and creative.* New York: Academic.

Gilhooly, K. J., & Green, A. J. K. (1989). Learning problem-solving skills. In A. M. Colley & J. R. Beech (Eds.), *Acquisition and performance of cognitive skills.* Chichester: Wiley.

Glover, J. A. (1977). Risky shift and creativity. *Social Behavior and Personality, 5,* 317–320.

Goertzel, M. G., Goertzel, V., & Goertzel, T. G. (1978). *Three hundred eminent personalities.* San Francisco: Jossey-Bass.

Golann, S. E. (1962). The creativity motive. *Journal of Personality, 30,* 588–600.

Golann, S. E. (1963). Psychological study of creativity. *Psychological Bulletin, 60,* 548–565.

Gordon, W. J. (1961). *Synectics.* New York: Harper.

Gordon, W. J. (1966). *The metaphorical way of learning and knowing.* Cambridge, MA: Porpoise Books.

Gordon, W. J. (1981). *The new art of the possible: The basic course in Synectics.* Cambridge, MA: Porpoise Books.

Gordon, W. J., & Poze, T. (1972). *Teaching is listening.* Cambridge, MA: SES Associates.

Gordon, W. J., & Poze, T. (1975). *Strange and familiar.* Cambridge, MA:SES Associates.

Gordon, W. J., & Poze, T. (1979). *The metaphorical way of learning and knowing.* Cambridge, MA:SES Associates.

Gordon, W. J., & Poze, T. (1984). *Presenter's manual for the SES seminar for teaching.* Cambridge, MA:SES Associates.

Greene, D., & Lepper, M. (1974). Effects of extrinsic rewards on children's subsequent intrinsic interest. *Child Development, 45,* 1141–1145.

Grieve, F. G., Whelan, J. P., Kottke, R., & Meyers, A. W. (1994). Manipulating adults' achievement goals in a sport task: Effects on cognitive, affective, and behavioral variables. *Journal of Sport Behavior, 17,* 1–17.

Gruber, H. E., Terrell, G., & Wertheimer, M. (1982). Preface. In H. Gruber, G. Terrell, & M. Wertheimer (Eds.), *Contemporary approaches to creative thinking* (pp. ix–xiv). New York: Atherton.

Guilford, J. P. (1950). Creativity. *American Psychologist, 5,* 444–454.

Guilford, J. P. (1964). Creative thinking and problem solving. *Education Digest, 29,* 21–31.

Guilford, J. P. (1983). Transformation: Abilities or functions. *Journal of Creative Behavior, 17,* 75–86.

Guilford, J. P., & Hoepfner, R. (1971). *The analysis of intelligence.* New York: McGraw-Hill.

Guilford, J. P., & Tenopyr, M. L. (1968). Implications of the Structure-of-Intellect model for high school and college students. In W. B. Michael (Ed.), *Teaching for creative endeavor: Bold new venture* (pp. 25–45). Bloomington: Indiana University Press.

Hayes, J. R. (1989). *The complete problem solver* (2nd ed.). Hillsdale, NJ: Erlbaum.

Hayes, J. R. (1985). Three problems in teaching General skills. In S. F. Chipman, J. W. Segal, & R. Glaser (Eds.), *Thinking and learning skills: Vol 2. Research and open questions* (pp. 391–405). Hillsdale, NJ: Erlbaum.

Henle, M. (1962). The birth and death of ideas. In H. Gruber, G. Terrell, & M. Wertheimer (Eds.), *Contemporary approaches to creative thinking* (pp. 31–62). New York: Atherton.

Hennessey, B. A., & Amabile, T. M. (1988). The conditions of creativity. In R. J. Sternberg (Ed.), *The nature of creativity* (pp. 11–38). Cambridge University Press.

Hennessey, B. A., Amabile, T. M., & Martinage, M. (1989). Immunizing children against the negative effects of reward. *Contemporary Educational Psychology, 14,* 212–227.

Herrnstein, R. J., Nickerson, R. S., de Sánchez, M., & Swets, J. A. (1986). Teaching thinking skills. *American Psychologist, 41,* 1279–1289.

Hidi, S. (1990). Interest and its contribution as a mental resource for learning. *Review of Educational Research, 60,* 549–571.

Holton, G. (1973). *Thematic origins of scientific thought.* Cambridge, MA: Harvard University Press.

Holton, G. (1981). Einstein's search for the Weltbild, *Proceedings of the American Philosophical Society, 125,* 1–15.

Houtz, J. C. (1994). Creative problem solving in the classroom: Contributions of four psychological approaches. In M. A. Runco (Ed.), *Problem finding, problem solving, and creativity* (pp. 153–173). Norwood, NJ: Ablex.

Houtz, J. C., Jambor, S. O., Cifone, A., & Lewis, C. D. (1989). Locus of evaluation control, task directions, and type of problem effects on creativity. *Creativity Research Journal, 2,* 118–125.

Ironson, G. H., & Davis, G. A. (1979). Faking high or low creativity scores on the adjective check list. *Journal of Creative Behavior, 13,* 139–145.

Isaksen, S. G., & Treffinger, D. J. (1985). *Creative problem solving: The basic course.* Buffalo, NY: Bearly.

Jackson, P. W., & Messick, S. (1973). The person, the product, and the response: Conceptual problems in the assessment of creativity. In M. Bloomberg (Ed.), *Creativity: Theory and research.* New Haven, CT: College and University Press.

Jausovec, N. (1994). Metacognition in creative problem solving. In M. A. Runco (Ed.), *Problem finding, problem solving, and creativity* (pp. 77–95). Norwood, NJ: Ablex.

Johnson, D. M. (1955). *The psychology of thought and judgment.* New York: Harper & Brothers.

Kanouse, D. E. (1972). Language, labeling, and attribution. In E. E. Jones, D. E. Kanouse, H. H. Kelley, R. E. Nisbett, S. Valins, & B. Weiner (Eds.), *Attribution: Perceiving the causes of behavior* (pp. 121–136). Morristown, NJ.: General Learning Press.

Kay, S. (1991). The figural problem solving and problem finding of professional and semiprofessional artists and nonartists. *Creativity Research Journal, 4,* 233–252.

Kay, S. (1994). A method for investigating the creative thought process. In M. A. Runco (Ed.), *Problem finding, problem solving, and creativity* (pp. 116–129). Norwood, NJ: Ablex.

Keynes (1956). Newton, the man. In J. R. Newman (Ed.), *The world of mathematics* (pp. 277–285). New York: Simon & Schuster. (Original work published 1942)

Kitchener, K. S. (1983). Cognition, metacognition, and epistemic cognition. *Human Development, 26,* 222–232.

Knapp, R. H. (1963). Demographic, cultural and personality attributes of scientists. In C. W. Taylor & F. Barron (Eds.), *Scientific creativity: Its recognition and development* (pp. 205–216). New York: Wiley.

Koberg, D., & Bagnall, J. (1974). *The universal traveler: A soft-systems guidebook to creativity, problem solving and the process of design.* Los Altos, CA: Kaufmann.

Koestler, A. (1964). *The act of creation.* London: Hutchinson.

Kohn, A. (1993). Choices for children: Why and how to let students decide. *Phi Delta Kappan, 75,* 8–20.

Kruglanski, A. W., Friedman, I., & Zeevi, G. (1971). The effects of extrinsic incentives on some qualitative aspects of task performance. *Journal of Personality, 39,* 606–617.

Langer, E. (1989). *Mindfulness.* Reading, MA: Addison-Wesley.

Lepper, M., Greene, D., & Nisbett, R. (1973). Undermining children's intrinsic interest with extrinsic rewards: A test of the "overjustification" hypothesis. *Journal of Personality and Social Psychology, 28,* 129–137.

Lepper, M. R., Sagotsky, G., Dafoe, J. L., & Greene, D. (1982). Consequences of superfluous social constraints: Effects of young children's social inferences and subsequent intrinsic interest. *Journal of Personality and Social Psychology, 42,* 51–65.

Levine, M. (1987). *Effective problem solving.* Englewood Cliffs, NJ: Prentice-Hall.

Lieberman, J. N. (1965). Playfulness and divergent thinking: An investigation of their relationship at the kindergarten level. *Journal of Genetic Psychology, 107,* 219–224.

Lipman, M. (1991). *Thinking in education.* Cambridge University Press.

Lipman, M., Sharp, A. M., & Oscanyan, F. (1980). *Philosophy in the classroom.* Philadelphia: Temple University Press.

Loveland, K., & Olley, J. (1979). The effect of external reward on interest and quality of task performance in children of high and low intrinsic motivation. *Child Development, 50,* 1207–1210.

Lubart, T. I. (1994). Creativity. In R. J. Sternberg (Ed.), *Thinking and problem solving* (pp. 289–332). San Diego, CA: Academic.

Lubart, T. I., & Sternberg, R. J. (1995). In S. M. Smith, T. B. Ward, & Ronald A. Finke (Eds.), *The creative cognition approach* (pp. 271–302). Cambridge, MA: MIT Press.

Lundsteen, S. W. (1968). Language arts in the elementary school. In W. B. Michael (Ed.), *Teaching for creative endeavor: Bold new venture* (pp. 131–161). Bloomington: Indiana University Press.

MacKinnon, D. W. (1962). The nature and nurture of creative talent. *American Psychologist, 17,* 484–495.

MacKinnon, D. W. (1965). Personality and the realization of creative potential. *American Psychologist, 20,* 273–281.

Mackworth, N. H. (1965). Originality. *American Psychologist, 20,* 51–66.

Mandler, G. (1995). Origins and consequences of novelty. In S. M. Smith, T. B. Ward, & R. A. Finke (Eds.), *The creative cognition approach* (pp. 9–25). Cambridge, MA: MIT Press.

Mansfield, R. S., & Bussé, T. V. (1981). *The psychology of creativity and discovery.* Chicago: Nelson-Hall.

Mansfield, R. S., Bussé, T. V., & Krepelka, E. J. (1978). The effectiveness of creativity training. *Review of Educational Research, 48,* 517–536.

Manuel, H. T. (1962). *Tests of general ability: Inter-American series* (Spanish, Level 4, Forms A & B). San Antonio, TX: Guidance Testing Associates.

Marjoram, T. (1988). *Teaching able children.* London: Kogan Page.

McClelland, D. C. (1962). On the psychodynamics of creative physical scientists. In H. Gruber, G. Terrell, & M. Wertheimer (Eds.), *Contemporary approaches to creative thinking* (pp. 141–174). New York: Atherton.

McLeod, J., & Cropley, A. J. (1989). *Fostering academic excellence.* Oxford: Pergamon.

Meadow, A., Parnes, S. J., & Reese, H. (1959). Influence of brainstorming instruction and problem sequence on a creative problem solving test. *Journal of Applied Psychology, 43,* 413–416.

Medawar, P. B. (1979). *Advice to a young scientist.* New York: Basic.

Mednick, S. A. (1962). The associative bias of the creative process. *Psychological Review, 69,* 220–232.

Metcalfe, J. (1986a). Feelings of knowing in memory and problem solving. *Journal of Experimental Psychology: Learning, Memory, and Cognition, 12,* 288–294.

Metcalfe, J. (1986b). Premonitions of insight predict impending error. *Journal of Experimental Psychology: Learning, Memory, and Cognition, 12,* 623–634.

Metcalfe, J., & Weibe, D. (1987). Intuition in insight and non-insight problem solving. *Memory and Cognition, 15,* 238–246.

Michael, W. B. (Ed.). (1968). *Teaching for creative endeavor: Bold new venture.* Bloomington: Indiana University Press.

Mitchell, B., Stueckle, A., & Wilkens, R. F. (1976). *Conceptual planning for creative learning.* Dubuque, IO: Kendall-Hunt.

Mumford, M. D., Connelly, M. S., Baughman, W. A., & Marks, M. A. (1994). Creativity and problem solving: Cognition, adaptability, and wisdom. *Roeper Review, 16,* 241–246.

Mumford, M. D., Reiter-Palmon, R., & Redmond, M. R. (1994). Problem construction and cognition: Applying problem representations in ill-defined domains. In M. A. Runco (Ed.), *Problem finding, problem solving, and creativity* (pp. 3–39). Norwood, NJ: Ablex.

Murray, H. G., & Denny, J. P. (1969). Interaction of ability level and interpolated activity in human problem solving. *Psychological Reports, 24,* 271–276.

Necka, E. (1986). On the nature of creative talent. In A. J. Cropley, K. K. Urban, H. Wagner, & W. H. Wieczerkowski (Eds.), *Giftedness: A continuing worldwide challenge* (pp. 131–140). New York: Trillium.

Newell, A., Shaw, J., & Simon, H. (1962). The processes of creative thinking. In H. Gruber, G. Terrell, & M. Wertheimer (Eds.), *Contemporary approaches to creative thinking* (pp. 63–119). New York: Atherton.

Newmann, F. M. (1991). Higher order thinking in the teaching of social studies: Connections between theory and practice. In J. F. Voss, D. N. Perkins, & J. W. Segal (Eds.), *Informal reasoning and education* (pp. 381–400). Hillsdale, NJ: Erlbaum.

Nicholls, J. G. (1972). Creativity in the person who will never produce anything original and useful: The concept of creativity as a normally distributed trait. *American Psychologist, 27,* 717–727.

Nicholls, J. G. (1984). Achievement motivation: Conceptions of ability, subjective experience, task choice, and performance. *Psychological Review, 49,* 529–538.

Nickerson, R. S. (1990). Dimensions of thinking: A critique. In B. F. Jones & L. Idol (Eds.), *Dimensions of thinking and cognitive instruction: Implications for educational reform* (Vol. 1, pp. 495–509). Hillsdale, NJ: Erlbaum.

Nickerson, R. S. (1993). Communities of inquiry: A vision of what reflective education could be. (Review of *Thinking in education,* by M. Lipman, *American Journal of Psychology, 106,* 620–632)

Nickerson, R. S. (1994a). Project Intelligence. In R. Sternberg, S. J. Ceci, J. Horn, E. Hunt, J. D. Matarazzo, & S. Scarr (Eds.), *Encyclopedia of intelligence* (pp. 857–860). New York: Macmillan.

Nickerson, R. S. (1994b). The teaching of thinking and problem solving. In R. J. Sternberg (Ed.), *Thinking and problem solving,* Vol. 12 of E. C. Carterette & M. Friedman (Eds.), *Handbook of perception and cognition* (pp. 409–449). San Diego, CA: Academic.

Nickerson, R. S., Perkins, D. N., & Smith, E. E. (1985). *The teaching of thinking.* Hillsdale, NJ: Erlbaum.

Noller, R. B. (1977). *Scratching the surface of creative problem solving: A bird's eye view of CPS.* Buffalo, NY: DOK.

Ochse, R. (1990). *Before the gates of excellence: The determinants of creative genius.* Cambridge University Press.

Okuda, S. M., Runco, M. A., & Berger, D. E. (1991). Creativity and the finding and solving of real-world problems. *Journal of Psychoeducatinal Assessment, 9,* 45–53.

Olton, R. M., & Crutchfield, R. S. (1969). Developing the skills of productive thinking. In P. Mussen, J. Langer, & M. Covington (Eds.), *Trends and issues in developmental psychology* (pp. 68–91). New York: Holt, Rinehart, & Winston.

Orlick, T. (1986). *Psyching for sport: Mental training for atheletes.* Champaign, IL: Leisure Press.

Osborn, A. (1953). *Applied imagination.* New York: Scribner's.

Osborn, A. (1963). *Applied imagination: Principles and procedures of creative thinking.* New York: Scribner's.

Otis, A. S., & Lennon, R. T. (1977). *Otis-Lennon school ability test* (Intermediate Level 1, Form R). New York: Harcourt, Brace, Jovanovich.

Parloff, M. D., & Handlon, J. H. (1964). The influence of criticalness on creative problem solving. *Psychiatry, 27,* 17–27.

Parnes, S. J. (1963). The deferment-of-judgment principle: Clarification of the literature. *Psychological Reports, 12,* 521–522.

Parnes, S. J. (1981). *Magic of your mind.* Buffalo, NY: Bearly.

Parnes, S. J., & Meadow, A. (1963). Development of individual creative talent. In C. W. Taylor & F. Barron (Eds.), *Scientific creativity: Its recognition and development* (pp. 311–320). New York: Wiley.

Parnes, S. J., Noller, R. B., & Biondi, A. M. (1977). *A guide to creative action.* New York: Scribners.

Perkins, D. N. (1981). *The mind's best work.* Cambridge, MA: Harvard University Press.

Perkins, D. N. (1988). Creativity and the quest for mechanism. In R. J. Sternberg & E. E. Smith (Eds.), *The psychology of thought* (pp. 309–336). Cambridge University Press.

Perkins, D. N. (1990). The nature and nurture of creativity. In B. F. Jones & L. Idol (Eds.), *Dimensions of thinking and cognitive instruction* (pp. 415–443). Hillsdale, NJ: Erlbaum.

Perkins, D. N. (1994). Creativity: Beyond the Darwinian paradigm. In M. A. Boden (Ed.), *Dimensions of creativity* (pp. 119–142). Cambridge, MA: MIT Press.

Perkins, D. N. (1995). *Outsmarting IQ: The emerging science of learnable intelligence.* New York: Free Press.

Perkins, D. N., Farady, M., & Bushey, B. (1991). Everyday reasoning and the roots of intelligence. In J. F. Voss, D. N. Perkins, & J. W. Segal (Eds.), *Informal reasoning and education* (pp. 83–106). Hillsdale, NJ: Erlbaum.

Perkins, D. N., Jay, E., & Tishman, S. (1993). Beyond abilities: A dispositional theory of thinking. *Merrill-Palmer Quarterly, 39,* 1–21.

Perkins, D. N., & Laserna, C. (1986). Inventive thinking. In M. J. Adams (Coordinator), *Odyssey: A curriculum for thinking.* Watertown, MA: Mastery Education Corporation.

Peterson, C., Maier, S. F., & Seligman, M. E. P. (1993). *Learned helplessness: A theory for the age of personal control.* New York: Oxford University Press.

Poincaré, H. (1924). *The foundations of science.* New York: Science Press.

Poincaré, H. (1952). Mathematical discovery. In *Science and method* (pp. 46–63). Essays collected and translated by F. Maitland. New York: Dover. (Original publication date not given)

Polya, G. (1954). *Mathematics and plausible reasoning: Vol. 1. Induction and analogy in mathematics.* Princeton, NJ: Princeton University Press.

Polya, G. (1957). *How to solve it: A new aspect of mathematical method.* Garden City, NY: Doubleday. (Original work published 1945)

Pyszczynski, T., & Greenberg, J. (1991). Toward an integration of cognitive and motivational perspectives on social inference: A biased hypothesis-testing model. In *Advances in experimental social psychology* (pp. 297–340). New York: Academic.

Reid, W. A. (1987). Institutions and practices: Professional education reports and the language of reform. *Educational Researcher, 16*(8), 10–15.

Renzulli, J. S. (1977). *The enrichment triad model.* Mansfield Center, CT: Creative Learning Press.

Renzulli, J. S. (1986). The three-ring conception of giftedness: A developmental model for creative productivity. In R. J. Sternberg & J. E. Davidson (Eds.), *Conceptions of giftedness* (pp. 53–92). Cambridge University Press.

Renzulli, J. S., & Callahan, C. M. (1973). *New directions in creativity.* New York: Harper & Row.

Ripple, R. E., & Dacey, J. (1967). The facilitation of problem solving and verbal creativity by exposure to programmed instruction. *Psychology in the Schools, 4,* 240.

Roe, A. (1952). A psychologist examines sixty-four eminent scientists. *Scientific American, 187*(5), 21–25.

Roe, A. (1953). *The making of a scientist.* New York: Dodd, Mead.

Rogers, C. (1970). Toward a theory of creativity. In P. E. Vernon (Ed.), *Creativity* (pp. 137–151). New York: Penguin. (Original work published 1954)

Rossman, J. (1931). *The psychology of the inventor.* Washington, DC: Inventors Publishing.

Rothenberg, A. (1990). *Creativity and madness.* Baltimore, MD: Johns Hopkins University Press.

Rubin, L. J. (1968). Creativity and the curriculum. In W. B. Michael (Ed.), *Teaching for creative endeavor: Bold new venture* (pp. 74–89). Bloomington: Indiana University Press.

Ruggiero, V. R. (1984). *The art of thinking: A guide to critical and creative thought.* New York: Harper & Row.

Runco, M. A. (1987). The generality of creative performance in gifted and nongifted children. *Gifted Child Quarterly, 31*, 121–125.

Runco, M. A. (1990). Implicit theories and ideational creativity. In M. A. Runco & R. S. Albert (Eds.), *Theories of creativity* (pp. 234–252). Newbury Park, CA: Sage.

Runco, M. A. (Ed.). (1994). Problem finding, problem solving, and creativity, Norwood, NJ: Ablex.

Runco, M. A., & Chand, I. (1994). Problem finding, evaluative thinking, and creativity. In M. A. Runco (Ed.), *Problem finding, problem solving, and creativity* (pp. 40–76). Norwood, NJ: Ablex.

Runco, M. A., & Nemiro, J. (1994). Problem finding, creativity, and giftedness. *Roeper Review, 16*, 235–241.

Runco, M. A., & Okuda, S. M. (1993). Reaching creatively gifted children through their learning styles. In R. M. Milgram, R. Dunn, & G. E. Price (Eds), *Teaching and counseling gifted and talented adolescents: An international learning style perspective* (pp. 103–115). New York: Praeger.

Russell, B. (1984). The greatness of Albert Einstein. In M. Gardner (Ed.), *"The sacred beetle" and other great essays in science.* New York: New American Library. (Original work published 1955)

Sanders, D. A, & Sanders, J. A. (1984). *Teaching creativity through metaphor: An integrated brain approach.* New York: Longman.

Schooler, J. W., & Melcher, J. (1995). The ineffability of insight. In S. M. Smith, T. B. Ward, & R. A. Finke (Eds.), *The creative cognition approach* (pp. 97–133). Cambridge, MA: MIT Press.

Schrag, F. (1987). Thoughtfulness: Is high school the place for thinking? *Newsletter of the National Center on Effective Secondary Schools, 2*, 2–4.

Seligman, M. E. P. (1991). *Learned optimism.* New York: Knopf.

Seligman, M. E. P., Reivich, K., Jaycox, L., & Gillham, J. (1995). *The optimistic child: How learned optimism protects children from depression.* New York: Houghton Mifflin.

Shiba, S. (1989, July). Lessons in quality. *Look Japan*, pp. 32, 33.

Simon, H. A. (1966). Scientific discovery and the psychology of problem solving. In R. G. Colodny (Ed.), *Mind and cosmos: Essays in contemporary science and philosophy* (pp. 22–40). Pittsburgh, PA: Pittsburgh University Press.

Simon, H. A. (1986). The information processing explanation of Gestalt phenomena. *Computers in Human Behavior, 2*, 241–255.

Simonton, D. K. (1980). Thematic fame, melodic originality, and musical Zeitgeist: A biographical and transhistorical content analysis. *Journal of Personality and Social Psychology, 38*, 972–983.

Simonton, D. K. (1984). *Genius, creativity, and leadership.* Cambridge, MA: Harvard University Press.

Simonton, D. K. (1990). *Psychology, science, and history: An introduction to historiometry.* New Haven, CT: Yale University Press.

Singer, J. L., & Singer, D. L. (1976). Imaginative play and pretending in early childhood: Some experimental approaches. In A. Davids (Ed.), *Child personality and psychopathology* (Vol. 3, pp. 69–112). New York: Wiley.

Smith, S. M. (1995). Fixation, incubation, and insight in memory and creative thinking. In S. M. Smith, T. B. Ward, & R. A. Finke (Eds.), *The creative cognition approach* (pp. 135–156). Cambridge, MA: MIT Press.

Smith, S. M., & Blankenship, S. E. (1989). Incubation effects. *Bulletin of the Psychonomic Society, 27*, 311–314.

Starko, A. J. (1989). Problem finding in creative writing: An exploratory study. *Journal for the Education of the Gifted, 12*, 172–186.

Starko, A. J. (1995). *Creativity in the classroom: Schools of curious delight.* New York: Longman.

Stein, M. I. (1968). Creativity. In E. F. Borgatta & W. W. Lambert (Eds.), *Handbook of personality theory and research* (pp. 900–942). Chicago: Rand McNally.

Stein, M. I. (1974). *Stimulating creativity* (Vol. 1). New York: Academic.

Stein, M. I. (1975). *Stimulating creativity* (vol. 2). New York: Academic.

Sternberg, R. J. (1985). Implicit theories of intelligence, creativity, and wisdom. *Journal of Personality and Social Psychology, 49*, 607–627.

Sternberg, R. J. (1988). *The nature of creativity: Contemporary psychological perspectives.* Cambridge University Press.

Sternberg, R. J., & Lubart, T. I. (1991). An investment theory of creativity and its development. *Human Development, 34*, 1–31.

Sternberg, R. J., & Lubart, T. I. (1992). Buy low and sell high: An investment approach to creativity. *Current Directions in Psychological Science, 1*, 1–5.

Sternberg, R. J., & Lubart, T. I. (1995). *Defying the crowd: Cultivating creativity in a culture of conformity.* New York: Free Press.

Sternberg, R. J., & Lubart, T. I. (1996). Investing in creativity. *American Psychologist, 51,* 677–688.

Sternberg, R. J., & Williams, W. M. (in press). *How to develop student creativity.* Alexandria, VA: Association for Supervision and Curriculum Development.

Stevenson, H. W., Chen, C., & Lee, S-Y. (1993). Mathematics achievement of Chinese, Japanese, and American children: Ten years later. *Science, 259,* 53–58.

Tardif, T. Z., & Sternberg, R. J. (1988). What do we know about creativity. In R. J. Sternberg (Ed.), *The nature of creativity* (pp. 429–440). Cambridge University Press.

Taylor, D. W., Berry, P. C., & Block, C. H. (1958). Does group participation when using brainstorming facilitate or inhibit creative thinking? *Administrative Science Quarterly, 3,* 23–47.

Taylor, I. A. (1975). An emerging view of creative actions. In I. A. Taylor & J. W. Getzels (Eds.), *Perspectives in creativity* (pp. 297–325). Chicago: Aldine.

Thistlewaite, D. L. (1963). The college environment as a determinant of research potentiality. In C. W. Taylor & F. Barron (Eds.), *Scientific creativity: Its recognition and development* (pp. 265–271). New York: Wiley.

Tishman, S., Jay, E., & Perkins, D. N. (1993). Teaching thinking dispositions: From transmission to enculturation. *Theory Into Practice, 32,* 147–153.

Torgeson, J. K., & Licht, B. G. (1983). The LD child as an inactive learner: Retrospects and prospects. In K. D. Gadow & I. Bialer (Eds.), *Advances in learning and behavioral disabilities.* Greenwich, CT: JAI.

Torrance, E. P. (1962). *Guiding creative talent.* Englewood Cliffs, NJ: Prentice-Hall.

Torrance, E. P. (1965). *Rewarding creative behavior: Experiments in classroom creativity.* Englewood Cliffs, NJ: Prentice-Hall.

Torrance, E. P. (1972). Can we teach children to think creatively? *Journal of Creative Behavior, 6,* 114–143.

Torrance, E. P. (1987). Can we teach children to think creatively? In S. G. Isaksen (Ed.), *Frontiers of creativity research: Beyond the basics.* Buffalo, NY: Bearly.

Torrance, E. P. (1988). *The nature of creativity as manifest in its testing.* In R. J. Sternberg (Ed.), *The nature of creativity,* Cambridge University Press.

Torrance, E. P., & Myers, R. (1970). *Creative learning and teaching.* New York: Dodd, Mead.

Treffinger, D. J. (1979). *Encouraging creative learning for the gifted and talented.* Ventura, CA: LTI.

Treffinger, D. J., Isaksen, S. G., & Dorval, K. B. (1994). Creative problem solving: An overview. In M. A. Runco (Ed.), *Problem finding, problem solving, and creativity* (pp. 223–256). Norwood, NJ: Ablex.

Treffinger, D. J., Isaksen, S. G., & Firestein, R. I. (1983). Theoretical perspective on creative learning and its facilitation. *Journal of Creative Behavior, 17,* 9–17.

Treffinger, D. J., McEwen, P., & Wittig, C. (1989). *Using creative problem solving in inventing.* Honeoye, NY: Center for Creative Learning.

Treffinger, D. J., & Ripple, R. E. (1969). Developing creative problem solving abilities and related attitudes through programmed instruction. *Journal of Creative Behavior, 3,* 105–110.

Treffinger, D. J., & Ripple, R. E. (1971). Programmed instruction in creative problem solving: An interpretation of recent research findings. *Educational Leadership, 28,* 667–675.

Treffinger, D. J., Speedie, S. M., & Bruner, W. D. (1974). Improving children's creative problem solving ability: The Purdue Creativity Project. *Journal of Creative Behavior, 8,* 20–30.

Ulam, S. M. (1976). *Adventures of a mathematician.* New York: Scribner's.

Wakefield, J. F. (1994). Problem finding and empathy in art. In M. A. Runco (Ed.), *Problem finding, problem solving, and creativity* (pp. 99–115). Norwood, NJ: Ablex.

Waldrop, J. L., Olton, R. M., Bodwin, W. L., Covington, M. V., Klausmeier, H. J., Crutchfield, R. S, & Ronda, T. (1969). The development of productive thinking skills in fifth-grade children. *Journal of Experimental Education, 37,* 67–77.

Wallach, M. A. (1970). Creativity. In P. H. Mussen (Ed.), *Carmichael's manual of child psychology* (Vol. 1, pp. 1211–1266): New York: Wiley.

Wallach, M. A., & Kogan, N. (1965). *Modes of thinking in young children.* New York: Holt, Rinehart, & Winston.

Wallas, G. (1945). *The art of thought.* London: C. A. Watts. (Original work published 1926)

Ward, T. B. (1995). What's old about new ideas? In S. M. Smith, T. B. Ward, & R. A. Finke (Eds.), *The creative cognition approach* (pp. 157–178). Cambridge, MA: MIT Press.

Weisberg, R. W. (1986). *Creativity, genius and other myths.* New York: Freeman.

Weisberg, R. W. (1988). Problem solving and creativity. In R. J. Sternberg (Ed.), *The nature of creativity* (pp. 148–176). Cambridge University Press.

Weisberg, R. W. (1993). *Creativity: Beyond the myth of genius.* New York: Freeman.

Weisberg, R. W. (1995). Case studies of creative thinking: Reproduction versus restructuring in the real world. In S. M. Smith, T. B. Ward, & R. A Finke (Eds.), *The creative cognition approach* (pp. 53–72). Cambridge, MA: MIT Press.

Weisberg, R. W., & Alba, J. W. (1981). An examination of the alleged role of "fixation" in the solution of several "insight" problems. *Journal of Experimental Psychology, 110,* 169–192.

Wicklegren, W. A. (1974). *How to solve problems.* San Francisco: Freeman.

Williams, E. E. (1976). Intellectual creativity and the teacher. In W. R. Lett (Ed.), *Creativity and education.* Melbourne: Australian International Press and Publications.

Williams, F. (1972). *A total creativity program for individualizing and humanizing the learning process.* Englewood Cliffs, NJ: Educational Testing Service.

Woodworth, R. S., & Schlosberg, H. (1954). *Experimental psychology.* New York: Hold.

21   *Prodigies and Creativity*

MICHAEL J. A. HOWE

Most of the questions people ask concerning child prodigies have to do with either the antecedents or the likely consequences of being a prodigy. For example, in order to become a highly creative adult, is it necessary to have been a child prodigy? If not, is it usually helpful, or can it be a disadvantage? To become a child prodigy in the first place, is it essential to have experienced a stimulating and supportive early background? These questions all deserve attention, since they raise important issues relating to the causes of creative accomplishments. Knowing about child prodigies is important because it can help us to understand why and how certain people become capable of impressive creative achievements (Feldman, 1986; Howe, 1982, 1997; Radford, 1990). There is no invariant relationship that links being a prodigy with becoming a creative adult, but there are some illuminating connections between early progress and mature attainments.

I shall examine some of the possible relationships between the state of being a child prodigy and the events that precede and follow it. Rather than addressing questions in a piecemeal fashion, it is advantageous to take a more systematic approach, introducing a general framework that helps structure the discussion. In order to explore the various links and connections, I attempt to identify instances of individuals who fall into each of the categories that are formed by the various possible combinations of the following circumstances:

1. The individual's early family background conditions (stimulating and supportive backgrounds versus unstimulating and unsupportive ones) that are widely known to affect a child's early learning and development
2. Exceptional childhood progress (being a prodigy or a nonprodigy)
3. Mature accomplishments (creative achievements versus their absence)

Combining the possible states yields eight distinct categories of people. One category, consisting of those men and women who did not have a stimulating and supportive early upbringing, were not child prodigies, and were incapable of creative achievements in maturity, is of little interest here. Of the other seven categories, the most common one, comprising the many individuals who did have a stimulating and supportive upbringing, but did not become prodigies and were not capable of creative adult achievements, is relatively uninformative. But with each of the other six categories, information about people who belong within them – is likely to be illuminating.

The remaining six categories are as follows:

1. People who enjoyed a stimulating and supportive early upbringing, were prodigies in childhood, and, as adults, were capable of creative accomplishments
2. People who enjoyed a stimulating and supportive early upbringing, were child prodigies, but were not, as adults, capable of creative achievements
3. People who enjoyed a stimulating and supportive early upbringing, but were not child prodigies and yet, as adults, were capable of creative achievements
4. People who did not have a stimulating and supportive early upbringing, but become prodigies in childhood and, as adults, were capable of creative achievements

431

    5. People who did not have a stimulating and supportive early upbringing, but became prodi-
       gies in childhood and were not, as adults, capable of any creative achievements
    6. People who did not have a stimulating and supportive early upbringing and were not prodi-
       gies in childhood, but, as adults, were nevertheless capable of creative achievements

Although assigning people to these six categories may seem a rather crude procedure, if
only because it ignores gradations that are present in each of the three factors involved, it
cannot by any means be an entirely objective one. There are a number of problems. For
example, there do not exist either the straightforward measures or the agreed cutoff points
that would be necessary in order to make unchallengeable decisions about whether or not
an individual is a prodigy or whether or not a particular individual's early childhood was stimulating and supportive, or even whether someone's achievements as an adult deserve to be
described as creative. There are some instances in which universal agreement might be
expected: Few would deny that Einstein was creative, that John Stuart Mill had a stimulating early upbringing, or that the young Mozart was a child prodigy. But in many cases these
decisions are more blurred, and placing individuals within categories has to be to some
extent a matter of judgment.

    Two particular considerations need mentioning. The first concerns the factors that have
to be taken into account in order to decide whether a child is a prodigy or not. In principle,
it ought to be a relatively simple matter of ascertaining whether a child does or does not
meet specified criteria. In practice, doing that would be difficult, because of the virtual
impossibility of making comparisons across skill and knowledge domains. How, for instance,
do we compare the merits of an exceptional 12-year-old violinist with those of an outstanding 10-year-old mathematician?

    Another problem is that there is a very imperfect relationship between the extent to which
a young person's attainments were actually exceptional and the chances of that individual
having been labeled a child prodigy. The main reason for that is that some kinds of capabilities are more visible than others, in the sense of being likely to come to the attention of
other people. For instance, in the case of a young performing musician, a chess player, or
tennis player who regularly takes part in competitions, if the child's capabilities are genuinely
exceptional, it will be difficult for teachers and other adults who know the child not to be
aware of that. And once the superior abilities are at all widely identified and recognized, it
will be very likely that the child will be labeled a prodigy. It is different with a young scientist such as Einstein, or a child whose precocity takes the form of superior philosophical
understanding. Here, because the intellectual activities associated with the individual's
superior abilities may be relatively private ones, rarely displayed to others and even then
unrecognizable as being exceptional to all but a small number of unusually knowledgeable
individuals, it is less likely that other people will become aware that the young person is
exceptional. Consequently, the likelihood of such a child being called a prodigy will be correspondingly small. The outcome, in brief, is that a substantial number of those individuals
who are designated prodigies may be less exceptional than some of the individuals who are
not so labeled. So whether or not someone has been called a prodigy is a very inexact indication of the actual extent to which a young person is genuinely outstanding.

    Awareness of this limitation can help us to avoid the distortions it may create. For
instance, in the case of an individual like Einstein we may assume that it is legitimate to place
him in the prodigy category providing that evidence exists – as it does – that the books he
was reading and the thoughts he was expressing as a young teenager indicate that by that age
his scientific understanding was genuinely exceptional (R. W. Clark, 1979), despite the fact
that the young Einstein was not generally acknowledged by his teachers to have been a
prodigy.

    The second consideration that requires attention before we turn to examining particular individuals within each of the six categories relates to the first of the three phenomena to be considered, namely the experience of having (or not having) a stimulating and supportive early upbringing. The word *stimulating* will raise few eyebrows, there being nothing surprising or controversial about the suggestion that a stimulating early environment is a desirable if not essential early influence in the life of a creative individual. Up to a point, the more the opportunities to learn and the greater the encouragement for acquiring new skills and extending one's knowledge, the better, as far as intellectual development is concerned. There exists a large body of empirical evidence testifying to the value of early stimulation and encouragement to learn (Howe, 1990).

However, the view that a child's early upbringing must also be a supportive one would not gain universal agreement. Some experts would argue that what matters is the degree to which a child's mind is stimulated, with supportiveness being a secondary and less crucial factor. My reasons for insisting on a degree of supportiveness and structure as a necessary element of a child's early environment, with the implication that a stimulating background on its own may not be enough, stem from some research findings obtained by Mihalyi Csikszentmihalyi and his coresearchers (Csikszentmihalyi & Csikszentmihalyi, 1993; Csikszentmihalyi, Rathunde & Whalen, 1993). They wanted to know why some able youngsters, but not others, were capable of concentrating on the kinds of learning activities that are essential for a young person to make substantial progress in a difficult area of accomplishment. These researchers had noticed that many young people find it hard to do effortful things on their own, especially when these require sustained concentration, with studying and practicing being about the least favored of all activities for many youngsters, even highly able ones.

Csikszentmihalyi's approach involved identifying those adolescents who could practice and study on their own and discovering how they differed from those who could not. The young participants who took part in the investigation were divided into four groups on the basis of information about their family backgrounds. These were rated as being more or less stimulating (referring to the extent to which parents provided opportunities to learn and had high educational expectancies) and more or less supportive. This latter dimension referred to the amount of support and structure available within the family background. For instance, a family in which there were clear rules and clearly allotted tasks, and in which individuals could depend upon one another, was rated as being supportive. People knew what they had to do and got on with it. A family in which structured support was unavailable or unreliable tended to be one in which young people spent a lot of their energy complaining, arguing, negotiating, and saying things like "Its not fair" or "It's not my turn."

Each young person's family background fell into one of the following four categories: neither stimulating nor supportive, supportive but not stimulating, stimulating but not supportive, or both supportive and stimulating. When the researchers observed how the young people felt and behaved in situations that did not involve learning and studying, such as talking with friends or watching television, it was found that those aspects of the family background made little difference. But when the participants were asked to report how they were experiencing learning and studying activities, there was an interesting finding. In three of the categories, responses were generally very negative: The young people did not enjoy these activities and their level of alertness was low. But one category of respondents was very different. That was the group whose family backgrounds were both supportive and stimulating. These adolescents, but not the others, were often positive about studying. They enjoyed it more than the others did, and when they were engaged in learning on their own they reported being much more attentive and alert than the other young people.

So the way youngsters experience the activities that make them unusually competent is closely related to their family backgrounds. Young people from families that are both stimulating and supportive seem to have acquired the habit of getting on with the job of learning, and that yields them rich benefits. Compared with them, the others are at a disadvantage, temporarily at least. Now we will consider some individuals in each of the six categories and discuss the issues they raise.

> *Category 1.* People who enjoyed a stimulating and supportive early upbringing, were prodigies in childhood, and, as adults, were capable of creative achievements

A substantial proportion of the individuals who we regard as having been creative geniuses fit within this category, as do a number of Nobel Prize winners (Zuckerman, 1977). The name of Mozart is often the first to come to mind. Other well-known examples are Yehudi Menuhin, the great violinist, John Stuart Mill, one of the greatest nineteenth-century thinkers, and Norbert Wiener, the mathematician who started the science of cybernetics. The latter two both wrote autobiographies in which they describe their early lives at some length.

It is significant that both Mozart and Menuhin are musicians. A number of the world's great musicians belong in this category, and many of the great composers were highly accomplished performers by the time they reached adolescence. Even today, it is rare for someone to become a professional classical musician at all, let alone an exceptionally creative one, unless that person has made substantial progress while still a child. One reason for this is that since there is so much to be learned in order to gain the necessary expertise, requiring a large investment in time and motivation, someone who delayed their musical education until adulthood would find it hard to devote sufficient time to the necessary training and practice. Such a person would be unlikely to maintain the single-minded long-term devotion that would be needed in order to catch up with those individuals who acquire their serious interest in music during childhood. To reach the standard of a reasonably good amateur instrumentalist takes about 3,000 hours, and to be a professional instrumentalist demands something on the order of 10,000 hours of training and practice, assuming that the young musician is able and committed and is receiving expert instruction (Ericsson, Krampe, & Tesch-Römer, 1993; Sloboda, Davidson, Howe, & Moore, 1996). The sacrifices that such an investment demands are heavy enough even for someone who begins when young and makes considerable progress while still a child.

Because it is so beneficial for musicians to make a good early start, and because the activity of musical performance is one that can hardly remain hidden from others, when a young musician is unusually able it is very likely that other people will be aware of it. Hence, it is not surprising that musicians are relatively numerous among child prodigies. But it would be quite wrong to assume that all highly successful adult musicians were prodigies in childhood. That is apparent from the findings of a study by Lauren Sosniak (1985, 1990), who enquired into the early progress of a sample of 25 exceptional U.S. pianists. At the time she talked to them and their parents, when the pianists were in their early 30s, they were on the brink of careers among the ranks of successful concert pianists.

The individuals who participated in Sosniak's study were some exceptionally successful individuals among the much larger number of highly competent musicians. For every person who succeeds at making a career as a concert pianist, there are hundreds of promising young performers with similar aspirations. One of Sosniak's aims was to discover what set apart the few who succeeded from the less successful others. It might have been expected that the very best performers began to distinguish themselves at a very early age, but Sosniak discovered that in most cases that did not happen. Most of the pianists in her highly selected and exceptionally able sample did not begin to set themselves apart from others until relatively late. Even by the time they had reached adolescence and had already been playing the piano for around seven or eight years, and were clearly doing well, their progress was in most cases no better than that of hundreds of other young pianists. For the majority of those who, by the time they reached 30, had become exceptionally successful, there had been no obvious very early indications to signal the fact that they would be the ones who would eventually draw ahead of their peers. Other studies of the early progress of successful young musicians have observed a similar absence of very early signs of exceptionality in the majority of those performers who were eventually the most successful (Howe, Davidson, Moore, & Sloboda, 1995; Sloboda & Howe, 1991). And when exceptional individuals do draw ahead of their rivals, there does not seem to be one particular reason why: Many different factors, including sheer luck and good fortune, seemed to have played parts in determining which few individuals were ultimately most successful.

How important is the family background of a musician? Among the autobiographical accounts of composers, there are a few reports of individuals who have succeeded in the face of parental opposition, but that is rare. In the group of exceptional musicians investigated in Lauren Sosniak's study and in the much larger sample of young musicians studied in other recent investigations conducted by John Sloboda, Jane Davidson, and myself (Davidson, Howe, Moore, & Sloboda, in press; Howe et al., 1995; Sloboda et al., 1996) no cases were identified of individuals reaching very high standards without substantial early support and encouragement. In the vast majority of instances, this was largely provided by the child's own family. By no means all of the parents of the young people who participated in these investigations had musical expertise themselves, and some of them had no serious interest in music. Nevertheless, they were almost without exception conscientious and supportive, taking pains to ensure that the child had opportunities to learn and practice and maintaining a close interest in their child's progress. Compared with the parents of children who had music lessons but were less successful, these parents were more likely to exchange information with the teacher and more willing to give help and encouragement when the child was practicing.

This close parental involvement in the learning process clearly paid off, and some of our findings (Sloboda & Howe, 1991) show that, in its absence, very few of the young people would have become good musicians. For example, having established that devoting a fair amount of time to practice is absolutely essential in order for a young person to acquire competence as a performing musician and that almost all of the parents of our successful young musicians took a keen interest in their child's practice, we asked the children what they thought would have happened had their parents not encouraged them to practice when they were young. The majority of the children we questioned told us that in the absence of parental encouragement they would have either practiced infrequently or ceased doing so altogether. Had that happened, of course, these children would never have turned into the successful young musicians they had become by the time we talked to them.

The picture that emerges from research into the progress of musicians is one of close dependencies, with the exceptional early expertise that might lead to an individual being labeled a prodigy depending on the stimulation provided by opportunities to learn and the support offered by conscientious parents who take seriously their responsibility to help their child and with the high degree of early progress that may be signified by the prodigy label being a necessary if not sufficient precondition for becoming a creative adult musician. We shall never know how Mozart would have progressed in the absence of the intense regime of instruction and practice imposed by his father, but prodigious musical skills in the absence of strong parental encouragement are at best extremely rare. It would not be too great an exaggeration to assert that one cannot become a musical prodigy in the absence of a stimulating early background and that one cannot be a creative musician unless one has been highly skilled and committed, if not a prodigy, while still a child.

As we shall see, in some other spheres of creative achievement the aforementioned three stages tend to be less closely interlinked. All the same, a substantial number of individuals who make creative achievements did have stimulating and supportive early backgrounds and by mid-childhood already possessed the kinds of exceptional abilities for which they would be called a prodigy. Mozart clearly belongs in this category.

The life of John Stuart Mill also exemplifies this pattern. Born in 1806, Mill was the first of nine children of a phenomenally diligent self-made father, James Mill, who set out to make his eldest son a genius (Mill, 1873/1971; Packe, 1954). In the spaces between the scholarly labors that established his own reputation and were eventually rewarded by a prestigious governmental position, James Mill gave his eldest son a superb intellectual grounding that is described in some detail in the son's *Autobiography*. Another account of the early life of a child prodigy was written by Norbert Wiener, the mathematician, whose exceptionality in childhood was partly the outcome of the intensive early education that his father provided for him (Wiener, 1953). Wiener's father translated into English an account of the early life of a scholar, Karl Witte, another creative individual whose parents set out to make their son into an outstandingly able individual (Witte, 1914/1975). It is interesting to note that in none of these cases did the parents regard their child as being inherently exceptional. Mill recorded that "if I thought anything about myself, it was that I was rather backward in my studies, since I always found myself so, in comparison with what my father expected from me" (Mill, 1873/1971, p. 35). The elder Witte was also convinced that his son's basic aptitudes were only mediocre, and Wiener's father similarly regarded his son as an essentially average boy whose unusual abilities were the result of exceptional training.

> *Category 2.* People who enjoyed a stimulating and supportive early upbringing, were child prodigies, but were not, as adults, capable of achievements

There are many reasons why not every highly promising young person has a fulfilling and productive adult life, let alone one filled with creative achievements. Certainly, there is no guarantee that a child prodigy will develop the qualities that exceptional mature accomplishments depend upon. A musician may be technically outstanding but lack some of the emotional or intellectual resources that contribute to a performance being distinctive and original, or a mathematician may be exceptionally well equipped with mental skills and knowledge but not have the drive needed to fuel the lengthy and concentrated intellectual efforts required to make progress in the face of difficulties and obstacles.

In certain circumstances, some of the influences that contribute to a young person's progress being sufficiently exceptional to justify that individual's being labeled a prodigy may actually have the effect of reducing the likelihood of the individual eventually becoming capable of creative mature accomplishments. For example, imagine a situation in which a father, who perhaps has been disappointed by events in his own life and career, is anxious to ensure that his child will not fail and determines to give the child an early start that will provide him or her with exceptional capabilities. This kind of scenario is not especially uncommon, and when it happens there is a large element of parental identification with the child's success.

In circumstances like this, while there is much to be said for having a good start in life, as far as the child is concerned there are also likely to be costs, some of which may have effects that tend to reduce the likelihood of young people being able to make the best of their abilities. One possible ill-effect is that the overenthusiastic parent may inadvertently deprive the child of important experiences. A child whose early years are filled with learning sessions may have insufficient time to play with other children and learn how to make friends. A child who misses out on ordinary activities such as watching television may end up lacking the points of contact and shared knowledge that help people to get on with others. A child whose activities are largely determined by a parent's bidding may be overconscious of the necessity to please other people and may fail to develop personal enthusiasms and interests.

In particular, those whose exceptional early progress has been largely directed by a parent may fail to gain the independence and the sense of having their own direction and knowing what they want to do with their life that are characteristic of those who make substantial creative achievements. Young people who are deprived of opportunities to make choices and decisions for themselves, and choose their own friends and make their own mistakes, or who do not learn to look after themselves and survive life outside home and away from the family may enter adulthood without a sense of purpose and with none of the confidence and single-mindedness that are likely to be found in those who have been encouraged to take on responsibilities and acquire the various qualities and skills that make people independent, self-aware, and confident enough to pursue their goals.

Even among creative individuals who have had good reasons to be grateful for their parents' efforts to help develop their intellects, a number have suffered from the shadows cast by the more negative effects that too often arise when the parent is intent on making the child outstandingly able. John Stuart Mill, who was the first to acknowledge the positive aspects of his early education, endured a period of depression and acute mental crisis in his early twenties, in which he was aware of his lack of deep feeling and strong sense of purpose that creative work requires. He also knew that some of his acquaintances had regarded him as a manufactured man, capable only of reproducing opinions stamped on him by others. John Ruskin, whose parents were demanding and controlling, experienced severe problems in later life that were probably a consequence of that. Norbert Wiener found life very difficult as a young man, largely because his overprotective parents had made it hard for him to become fully independent and strike out on his own.

Mill and Wiener eventually managed to get through the crises induced by the unnaturally intensive "hothouse" regimes of their early years. Someone who did not was an acquaintance of Wiener named William Sidis (Wallace, 1986). Like Wiener, Sidis was the son of Russian Jewish immigrants to the United States who went to enormous pains to give their son a magnificent early education. Both of their fathers were energetic, full of intellectual enthusiasm, and somewhat domineering. Like Wiener, the young William Sidis was an exceptionally clever child, but unlike him he never fulfilled his early promise; his short adult life was unhappy and unproductive, and he never made proper use of his remarkable abilities.

The defects of Sidis's early upbringing were essentially those of Wiener's, somewhat intensified. Although the father of William Sidis was in many respects an enlightened educator and claimed to avoid any compulsion and pressure, his concern was only with intellectual development, and neither of Sidis's parents paid much attention to the emotional needs of their son. The young Wiener was encouraged to have plenty of outdoor interests, and he went on long walks with his father, but the parents of William Sidis regarded all nonintellectual pursuits as silly or wasteful. The father, keen to publicize his achievements as a manufacturer of superior children, drew the media's attention to his son's spectacular intellectual feats, but neither parent helped their son deal with the public attention that came his way.

Whereas Wiener's struggle to detach from his controlling parents and create a life for himself was eventually successful, Sidis never really succeeded in making the transition. He had few social skills and found it hard to dress himself or keep himself clean. He was dependent on his parents, but deeply resented that dependence and eventually came to loathe his mother and refused to attend his father's funeral. William Sidis died at the age of 46, an unhappy man, his intellectual powers largely unused. He had little confidence in himself and had developed a resentment against science, mathematics, and all that his parents stood for.

> *Category 3.* People who enjoyed a stimulating and supportive early upbringing, but were not child prodigies and yet, as adults, were capable of creative achievements

As we have seen, there are certain areas of achievement – such as music – in which it is extremely unlikely that someone will be outstandingly successful unless considerable progress has already been made by the end of childhood, but that is certainly not true of all fields of endeavour. The novelist Tolstoy and the psychologist William James are examples of individuals who provided few early indications of the exceptional creativity they were to display as adults. Charles Darwin provides a particularly striking instance of a person whose childhood abilities were entirely unexceptional despite having an advantaged early education in a wealthy and enlightened family, but who nevertheless went on to have an exceptionally creative adult career.

As a schoolboy, the most remarkable thing about Darwin was the extent to which he was unremarkable, considering that his grandfathers (Erasmus Darwin, who was well known for his botanical poems, and Josiah Wedgwood, the innovative industrialist and manufacturer of pottery) had been among the most original men of their generation, and his father, a physician with an unusually inquiring mind, gave him plenty of attention, as did his devoted older sisters (Bowlby, 1990; Browne, 1995; Desmond & Moore, 1991). He won no prizes at school and never distinguished himself at sports. Anyone believing in the notion that human intelligence is fixed would have ridiculed the suggestion that Charles Darwin the very average schoolboy could ever become Charles Darwin the great scientist.

Yet Darwin's school friends did notice that in contrast to his mediocre performance at lessons, he knew a great deal about natural history and was good at identifying the objects they brought to him. By the time he left school at the age of 16, Darwin had acquired an intense interest in natural history and had become a keen amateur collector. Darwin began to be interested in natural history well before he was 10 years old, and he stayed enthusiastic throughout his childhood and adolescence. Like many young boys, he collected things enthusiastically but indiscriminately at first, and the life that the young Darwin enjoyed within his wealthy family provided him with opportunities that helped to prepare him for his eventual career. He became especially interested in collecting beetles, a passion that endured. He was also a keen collector of butterflies, moths, and other insects. Even at 10, he had known enough to notice that there were moths to be seen on the Welsh coast that were not found in Shropshire. He was also an enthusiastic bird-watcher. Throughout his childhood there were always opportunities for collecting, and there were plenty of books on natural history at home. There was no need for him to be a solitary naturalist, since curiosity about the natural world was almost a family trait, and it was never difficult for Darwin to find friends who shared his interests.

There seems to have been no point in his childhood at which Darwin was not interested in natural history. The nature of his collecting activities altered as his knowledge increased and his observational skills were sharpened, but there was no abrupt change from indiscriminate collector to informed naturalist, or from a strictly amateur naturalist to a serious biologist. The alterations in his activities and interests were gradual, reflecting a steadily deepening knowledge: The same butterflies and beetles that had excited him at 10 still fascinated him at 20, but for different reasons. By the end of adolescence, what had begun as a child's hobby was starting to become a way of life. He was gradually turning into an expert, but without ever having had to make a conscious commitment to studying natural history as an academic subject.

Darwin was strongly influenced by his elder brother, Erasmus. When Charles was only 13, he and Erasmus (who was then studying at Cambridge) set up a simple chemistry laboratory in a toolshed in the Darwins' garden. Ostensibly, Erasmus was in charge and giving the orders, with Charles a mere assistant, but the actual day-to-day arrangements for setting everything up and running the laboratory experiments were left entirely in Charles's hands. It is clear from the letters between the brothers that survive that Erasmus never doubted that his younger brother was sufficiently responsible to make all the necessary arrangements.

Darwin's progress demonstrates that it is not always necessary for a creative person to have been precocious in childhood. Despite the fact that Darwin was never a child prodigy, there is nothing particularly mysterious or inexplicable about his eventual emergence as a major biologist. His progress was unhurried, gradual but steady. Partly because of his financially comfortable circumstances, it was possible to build up the knowledge and skills he needed over a period of many years. As a child he did not have to be competitive or rely on winning honors or prizes. There was no science taught at school, and his headmaster regarded Darwin's interests in natural history and chemistry as a complete waste of time. That probably helped, by ensuring that biological pursuits were free of unpleasant associations with school.

> *Category 4.* People who did not have a stimulating and supportive early upbringing, but were prodigies in childhood and, as adults, were capable of creative achievements

Up to now, all the individuals who have been mentioned enjoyed the stimulation and support of good family backgrounds, with the parents having played a constructive role in giving their child a good start in life. The absence of such a beginning is clearly a disadvantage to a young person and conceivably enough of a handicap to rule out the chances of becoming a highly creative adult. In actuality, however, it is possible to identify individuals who have created major achievements despite having had no special advantages in their early years.

In written accounts that depict eminent individuals' early lives as disadvantaged or deprived, a degree of skepticism is sometimes necessary, particularly when those accounts are autobiographical. Some successful people are overanxious to emphasize any "rags to riches" aspects of their lives and depict themselves of having risen to a great height from the direst beginnings. For instance, although George Bernard Shaw's descriptions of his early life stress the poverty of those years and suggest that his mother rejected and neglected him, in reality his childhood was, by most people's standards, a lively and stimulating one. Similarly, where the author H. G. Wells reports, accurately enough, that his working-class parents were poor and in debt and often quarreled and the family home was damp and squalid, we have to balance that with other equally pertinent information, such as the fact that his father was an excellent cricket player and something of a local celebrity, as well an avid reader of books, and the knowledge that his mother, although hardly well educated, did keep a diary and conscientiously taught him to read at an early age (MacKenzie & MacKenzie, 1973).

However, it is possible to identify a few individuals who belong in the category of people who, despite not having had a stimulating and supportive early upbringing, were nevertheless prodigies in childhood and who, as adults, did produce creative achievements. The scientific genius Michael Faraday, whose many attainments included the discovery of electromagnetic induction, which made electric engines possible, belongs in this category. He certainly came from a poor family, with no special advantages, and indisputably produced major creative achievements (Cantor, 1991; Pearce Williams, 1965). As a child he was very bright and curious, even though it may be stretching things a little to describe the young Faraday as a prodigy. But despite the poverty of his origins, which made it necessary for him to leave school at the age of 13, Faraday was able to educate himself and eventually became a great scientist. He achieved this largely through his own efforts, and it took immense discipline and determination, as well as an enormous capacity for hard work.

It also took a certain amount of luck, starting when he became apprenticed to a bookseller and bookbinder. This man happened to be a kindly and sympathetic individual who helped a number of his apprentices to achieve successful careers. For a young person who is a keen reader and intellectually curious, a bookshop is not a bad working environment, and it is clear that Faraday profited from the contact with books that his work made possible and from the opportunities he had there to listen to the conversations of lively and educated people.

Faraday took good advantage of his opportunities. He read voraciously and also went to lectures and classes. For a would-be scientist, his lack of formal schooling after the age of 13 would not have been quite as much of a disadvantage as it would be today, because at the time even good schools like the one Darwin attended taught no science. Although he was partly self-taught, Faraday's efforts to make progress were helped by an excellent eighteenth-century how to study book, *The Improvement of the Mind,* by Isaac Watts (1801). From it he learned about effective study skills and how to make the best use of books, as well as how to organize and plan learning activities.

Considering how hard he worked at his studies, Faraday does not seem to have learned faster than other enthusiastic students. What was most impressive about him, and helps to account for his swift progress, was his enormous energy, self-discipline, and remarkable capacity to persevere at his studies. He submitted himself to a grinding routine and never seems to have relaxed his efforts. It is not entirely clear what caused him to be so immensely determined, disciplined, and single-minded while still a teenager. He was clearly excited by science, although the likelihood of a scientific career must have seemed remote.

His family background provides one possible clue to the sources of his determination. Although his parents were poor and not well educated, they were members of a religious sect in the which mutual support played a prominent role. As a result, the quality of supportiveness that Csikszentmihalyi's research has shown to be a necessary quality of the backgrounds of adolescents who make good progress at their studies was clearly present in large measure. Faraday's family were probably ill equipped to provide the other necessary element, intellectual stimulation, but as soon as he started on his apprenticeship the stimulating and lively atmosphere of his workplace would have compensated for that deficit (Howe, 1996). As a result, for at least some of his formative years Faraday would have experienced that combination of intellectual stimulation and family support that was not available during his early childhood.

George Bidder, a prominent nineteenth-century British engineer, provides an equally interesting, although less famous, example of an individual who became a child prodigy and went on to have a creative career despite coming from a disadvantaged early background (E. F. Clark, 1983). Bidder, who was born in Devonshire to a family of stonemasons, became intrigued by mental arithmetic at the age of 6, and his skill at this soon began to attract people's attention. His father perceived that he could make money from George's feats and started displaying the child at local fairs, so that by the time George Bidder was 9 he was being exhibited up and down the country. He became known throughout England as the Calculating Boy. At that time it was not uncommon for wealthy individuals to sponsor the education of a promising youngster, and Bidder's feats eventually brought him to the attention of people who were willing to pay for him to receive a better education than would otherwise have been available to the child of a poor artisan family. John Stuart Mill's father, James Mill, had benefited from a similar arrangement, enabling him to go to Edinburgh University. Coincidentally, Bidder also completed his education at Edinburgh, after which he went on to have a very successful career as an engineer.

> *Category 5.* People who did not have a stimulating and supportive early upbringing, but became prodigies in childhood and were not, as adults, capable of any creative achievements

Predictably, information about individuals who belong in this category is far from common. One rare example is someone who as a boy entered into a competition with George Bidder. He was an American named Zerah Colburn, who was born in Vermont, and their encounter occurred when Bidder was 12 and Colburn probably 14 (Howe, 1990). Like Bidder, Colburn was a talented mental calculator in his childhood, attracting attention from the age of 6 when his father heard him repeating multiplication tables to himself. Colburn, like Bidder, traveled round giving public demonstrations, thereby earning a substantial amount of money. As a young child, Colburn seems to have been even more precocious than Bidder, and it was reported that at the age of 6 he could solve problems such as squaring 1,449, multiplying 12,225 times 1,223, and saying how many seconds there are in 2,000 years.

Unhappily, although Colburn was reputed to have been an outgoing, personable, and intelligent man, and had an interesting life during which he worked as an actor, teacher, minister, and a mathematician employed to make astronomical calculations, prior to his premature death at the age of 35, he was neither prosperous nor happy, and despite his remarkable early promise he never produced any lasting creative achievements.

> *Category 6.* People who did not have a stimulating and supportive early upbringing and were not prodigies in childhood, but, as adults, were nevertheless capable of creative achievements

Like the preceding category, this one does not overflow with exemplars, and it would hardly be surprising to discover that in the absence of either the advantages of a good early background or early indications of promise leading to a young person being labeled a prodigy, the chances of someone producing major adult creative achievements are effectively nil. Nevertheless, this sixth category is not entirely empty. In it belongs a British genius, George Stephenson, who had an enormous role in making steam travel a practical possibility (Davies, 1975; Rolt, 1960).

Born in 1781, George Stephenson grew up in considerable poverty. His father worked as a poorly paid laborer in a mining region near Newcastle in the northeast of England. The parents brought up their six children in one room of a small cottage, and because there was never sufficient money to send any of the children to school, George Stephenson did not begin to learn to read and write until he was 18 and finally able to spare a few pennies for lessons.

Despite these severe handicaps, George was a lively child and was fascinated by the steam engines that were used to pump water from the coal mines in the neighborhood and lift tubs of coal to the surface. At the age of 11 or 12, he was making ingenious models of mine engines and machinery out of waste materials such as clay, corks, twine, and pieces of wood. By the age of 18 he had a relatively skilled job as a "plugman," or engineman responsible for keeping a pump engine working and fixing minor defects. By then he was regarded by his workmates as an unusually resourceful young man. When an engine suffered a serious breakdown the engineman's usual response would be to send for the chief engineer. But according to Samuel Smiles (1857/1881), Stephenson's first biographer, he applied himself so assiduously and successfully to the study of the engine and its gearing – taking the machine to pieces in his leisure hours for the purpose of cleaning it and understanding its various parts – that he soon acquired a thorough practical knowledge of its construction and mode of working, and very rarely needed to call the engineer of the colliery to his aid. His engine became a sort of pet with him, and he was never wearied of watching it and inspecting it with admiration. (p. 9)

Stephenson's constant close interest in the detailed working of machines and his delight in persistently giving close attention to their operation, hour after hour, never tiring of observing how the different parts work together, are typical of those individuals who become mechanical inventors, even today. He also continued his earlier interest in model building. Sometimes he would carry out small experiments of his own to test ideas that came to him when he was told about scientific findings. For a nineteenth-century engineer, practical activities of this kind would have been crucial to his growing competence, and the outcome of regularly and frequently engaging for lengthy periods of time in them would have been in some respects not unlike the result of constant practice that musicians have to do or the lengthy training and preparation activities that are necessary in order to move ahead in other areas of expertise. Samuel Smiles (1857/1881), who was very aware of how important these undramatic background activities were for acquiring special skills, observed:

The daily contemplation of the steam-engine, and the sight of its steady action, is an education of itself to an ingenious and thoughtful man. And it is a remarkable fact, that nearly all of that has been done for the improvement of this machine has been accomplished, not by philosophers and scientific men, but by labourers, mechanics, and enginemen. Indeed, it would appear as if this were one of the departments of practical science in which the higher powers of the human mind must bend to mechanical insight. (p. 10)

But Stephenson still had a long way to go before he could be more than a skilled workman. A major limitation was that he was totally illiterate: At 18 he could not even write his own name. By this time he had heard about the new improvements to steam engines that had been made by James Watt and others, but because he was unable to read he had no access to the information that he was so anxious to acquire. Even simple arithmetic would have been beyond him. He would have been unable to decipher the diagrams and plans that are essential to the work of an engineer, and he knew nothing about the physical sciences.

Although his long working hours gave him very little leisure time, and despite his being barely able to afford the fourpence a week that it cost him to have lessons, at the age of 18 George Stephenson began learning to read, write, and do simple arithmetic, going to classes in a neighboring village three nights a week. He did all this with enormous determination. One of his friends explained why Stephenson "took to figures so wonderful":

George's secret was his perseverance. He worked out the sums in his by-hours, improving every minute of his spare time by the engine-fire, there studying the arithmetical problems set him upon his slate by the master. In the evenings he took to Robertson the sums which he had "worked," and the new ones were "set" for him to study out the following day. Thus his progress was rapid. (Smiles, 1857/1881, p. 11)

Eventually, the determination and hard work invested in his plans to educate himself brought rewards. After demonstrating to his employers on a number of occasions that he had the initiative and competence they were looking for to make their mines operate better and more economically, at the age of 32 Stephenson was made responsible for introducing new transport systems in the mines where he was employed. By 1814, a time when there were no obvious reasons for believing that locomotives could ever be other than cumbrous and inefficient machines, Stephenson had become convinced that reliable and economical railway travel was possible. He was also sure that he would play a large part in making that happen. "I will," he accurately predicted soon after he had been elevated from a workman to an engineer, "do something in coming time which will astonish all England." At that time there was a fair amount of interest in the possibility of steam locomotion, and steam locomotives had already been invented. But they were clumsy and unreliable, and enormous developments still needed to be made in order to make passenger travel a practical possibility.

It took Stephenson a long time to reach the point of being prepared to make a real contribution as an inventor. By then he was well over 30. By that age Charles Darwin had pieced together the theory of evolution by natural selection, and Charles Dickens, who had written *Pickwick Papers* when he was only 24, had already been famous for several years. Schubert had died before reaching the age of 32. In the majority of cases the preparatory years of individuals who create major accomplishments broadly correspond with the years of childhood and adolescence, but George Stephenson was an exception.

CONCLUSION

Broadly speaking, child prodigies are individuals who have made an unusually good start in life. As far as the likelihood of someone eventually becoming capable of mature creative accomplishments is concerned, the fact that one was a prodigy in childhood is significant not because it points to some inherent special quality of the person, but simply because it provides an indication of significant progress already having been made while the person was still young. Making exceptional early progress does not guarantee that someone will eventually become capable of exceptional creative achievements, but in many cases it undoubtedly helps to make that possible. That is especially true in areas of achievement in which mastery depends upon an individual undergoing lengthy and concentrated training in order to build up the combination of knowledge and skills that an expert in the field has to be able to draw upon. So it is hardly surprising that in such fields of attainment – music, mathematics, and chess, for instance – it is not unusual for exceptional adult achievers to have been prodigies or near-prodigies while they were children. Moreover, for reasons we mentioned earlier, it is entirely possible for creative individuals working in those fields to have been exceptionally able as children without ever having been identified as being prodigies.

In some other areas of achievement, mature accomplishments are not so dependent upon the individual having acquired a particular or specific corpus of knowledge and basic skills. Take literature for example. Undoubtedly it is necessary for an individual to be highly imaginative, knowledgeable, "good with words," and so on, but there is no particular form of training in a defined set of experiences that either is essential for the necessary qualities to be acquired or guarantees that the person will be qualified for a successful creative career. That is not to say that creative writers share no early experiences: The majority of novelists report spending many childhood hours reading, and many describe their enjoyment of storytelling events in their early years. But the connections between early learning and mature achievements are less straightforward than with musicians and mathematicians, and compared with them the early lives of novelists and playwrights have been far more diverse. The young Trollope was a daydreamer; the young Charles Dickens was keenly alert to the world he perceived; George Eliot as a girl was studious and somewhat prudish, and closer to our image of a child prodigy than the others; the Brontë children created shared imaginary worlds that depended upon the close relationships that existed within a family consisting of intelligent and well-informed individuals.

As we have seen, however, the very circumstances that help to give a child the kind of good early start that is characterized by precocious progress in a particular field or domain can sometimes have negative effects. Although for many creative adults the early progress that was acknowledged by their being regarded as prodigies was clearly beneficial if not essential, as far as their mature accomplishments were concerned, it is also true that a number of those individuals who were prodigies in childhood experienced personal difficulties that were at least partly attributable to the unusual circumstances of their childhoods. In some cases, among which that of William Sidis is well documented, the pressures of a rigorous training regime in childhood and the parental failure to ensure that their intellectually precocious child was given opportunities to acquire some of the nonintellectual capabilities that people depend upon in order to enjoy an independent and self-directed life, had unhappy consequences. In the case of Sidis, for example, the adult ex-prodigy was ill equipped to make effective use of the undoubtedly exceptional mental abilities he had acquired during his early years.

Unhappy consequences are particularly likely when a parent's commitment to a child's success is excessive. Such a parent may fail to appreciate that young people have to enjoy the kinds of experiences that make someone into an independent adult, and that creative people need to have their own personal sense of direction. The parent of a prodigy may also fail to perceive that many of the qualities individuals must call upon to enjoy fulfilling lives are ones that a child brought up in the unusual hothouse atmosphere of an early life dedicated to gaining exceptional skills or knowledge of a particular kind may have few opportunities to acquire. For these and other reasons, including the possible consequences of submitting a child to too much pressure to succeed, the chances are that numerous individuals whose early experiences have furnished them with impressive skills will never succeed in putting them to productive use in later years.

It is definitely not essential to have been a prodigy to become capable of creative mature achievements. With a stimulating and supporting early family background, it is sometimes possible for someone to eventually become a genius without having displayed any precocious abilities during childhood. In the case of Charles Darwin, a well-known example who is widely acknowledged to have been a genius but without having seemed at all remarkable as a child, it is significant that his childhood interests provided him with a fund of knowledge and skills that he was able to build upon later.

Perhaps surprisingly, a few people make outstanding creative achievements despite neither having experienced particularly stimulating and supportive home backgrounds nor having been a child prodigy. In some cases an individual from an apparently unpromising background has nevertheless displayed an exceptional ability in childhood. Sometimes, as with George Bidder, this was instrumental in enabling the young person to access educational opportunities that would otherwise not have been available. Occasionally, as in George Stephenson's case, someone who has received virtually no formal education prior to adulthood has nevertheless become a creative genius.

That is not to say that there are no limits to what can be achieved in the absence of a good early start. Stephenson was able to make himself into a great engineer because a large proportion of the skills an engineer needed at the beginning of the nineteenth century were practical ones that could be acquired and practiced in everyday life. Modern-day equivalents of George Stephenson are fairly rare, although the ranks of exceptional jazz and other nonclassical musicians have included a number of individuals who have had little education or formal training. Even in his time, someone with Stephenson's total lack of school education could never have become a great scientist like Faraday or Darwin, because science is not something that can be learned from everyday experience: It requires deliberate learning from books. Even a career like Faraday's is hard to imagine today. He was able to succeed as a scientist despite his lack of schooling, but that would probably not be possible now, when science education is made available in schools and young scientists have to acquire a substantial body of knowledge and skills in order to become prepared for making original contributions.

More often than not, it is helpful for someone to have been exceptionally able at a young age, which shows that substantial progress has already been made and demonstrates that the individual has acquired some of the working habits that substantial attainments are built on and is also capable of the hard and sustained effort that creative achievements demand. But for great creative accomplishments to be possible, events have to turn out well on a number of different fronts. The progress that leads to someone being labeled a child prodigy is not sufficient to ensure that this will happen, and circumstances that increase a young person's chances of being a child prodigy can sometimes act to diminish rather than increase the likelihood of the same individual striking out with sufficient independence and self-motivation to reach the very highest levels of creative accomplishment. Those individuals who have the best beginnings, do not always end up making the highest ascents.

REFERENCES

Bowlby, J. (1990). *Charles Darwin: A biography.* London: Hutchinson.

Browne, J. (1995). *Charles Darwin: Voyaging.* London: Pimlico.

Cantor, G. (1991). *Michael Faraday: Sandemanian and scientist.* Basingstoke, England: Macmillan.

Clark, E. F. (1983). *George Parker Bidder: The calculating boy.* Bedford: KSL Publications.

Clark, R. W. (1979). *Einstein: The life and times.* London: Hodder & Stoughton.

Csikszentmihalyi, M., & Csikszentmihalyi, I. S. (1993). Family influences on the development of giftedness. In G. R. Bock and K. Ackrill (Eds.), *CIBA Foundation Symposium No. 178: The Origins and Development of High Ability* (pp. 187–201). Chichester, England: Wiley.

Csikszentmihalyi, M., Rathunde, K., & Whalen, S. (1993). *Talented teenagers: The roots of success and failure.* Cambridge University Press.

Davidson, J. W., Howe, M. J. A., Moore, D. G., & Sloboda, J. A. (in press). The role of family influences in the development of musical ability. *British Journal of Developmental Psychology.*

Davies, H. (1975). *George Stephenson.* London: Weidenfeld & Nicolson.

Desmond, A., & Moore, J. (1991). *Darwin.* London: Michael Joseph.

Ericsson, K. A., Krampe, R. T. & Tesch-Römer, C., (1993). The role of deliberate practice in the acquisition of expert performance. *Psychological Review, 100,* 363–406.

Feldman, D. H. (1986). *Nature's gambit: Child prodigies and the development of human potential.* New York: Basic.

Howe, M. J. A. (1982). Biographical evidence and the development of outstanding individuals. *American Psychologist, 37,* 1071–1081.

Howe, M. J. A. (1990). *The origins of exceptional abilities.* Oxford: Blackwell.

Howe, M. J. A. (1996). The childhoods and early lives of geniuses: Combining psychological and biographical evidence. In K. A. Ericsson (Ed.), *The road to excellence: The acquisition of expert performance in the arts and sciences, sports and games* (pp. 255–270). New York: Erlbaum.

Howe, M. J. A. (1997). Beyond psychobiography: Towards more effective syntheses of psychology and biography. *British Journal of Psychology, 88,* 235–248.

Howe, M. J. A., Davidson, J. W., Moore, D. G., & Sloboda, J. A (1995). Are there early childhood signs of musical ability? *Psychology of Music, 23,* 162–176.

MacKenzie, N., & MacKenzie, J. (1973). *The life of H. G. Wells: The time traveller.* London: Weidenfeld & Nicholson.

Mill, J. S. (1971). *Autobiography.* London: Oxford University Press. (Original work published 1973)

Packe, M. St. J. (1954). *The life of John Stuart Mill.* London: Secker & Warburg.

Pearce Williams, L. (1965). *Michael Faraday: A biography.* London: Chapman & Hall.

Radford, J. (1990). *Child prodigies and exceptional early achievement.* London: Harvester.

Rolt, L. T. C. (1960). *George and Robert Stephenson.* London: Longmans.

Sloboda, J. A., Davidson, J. W., Howe, M. J. A, & Moore, D. G. (1996). The role of practice in the development of performing musicians. *British Journal of Psychology, 87,* 287–309.

Sloboda, J. A., & Howe, M. J. A. (1991). Biographical precursors of musical excellence: An interview study. *Psychology of Music, 19,* 3–21.

Smiles, S. (1881). *Life of George Stephenson* (Centenary ed.). London: Murray. (Original work published 1857)

Sosniak, L. A. (1985). Learning to be a concert pianist. In B. S. Bloom (Ed.), *Developing talent in young people* (pp. 149–164). New York: Ballantine.

Sosniak, L. A. (1990). The tortoise, the hare, and the development of talent. In M. J. A. Howe (Ed.), *Encouraging the development of exceptional abilities and talents* (pp. 149–164). Leicester: British Psychological Society.

Wallace, A. (1986). *The prodigy.* New York: Dutton.

Watts, I. (1801). *The improvement of the mind.* London: J. Abraham.

Wiener, N. (1953). *Ex-prodigy: My childhood and youth.* New York: Simon & Schuster.

Witte, K. H. G. (1975). *The education of Karl Witte* (Leo Wiener, Trans.). New York: Arno. (Original work published 1914)

Zuckerman, H. (1977). *Scientific elite: Nobel laureates in the United States.* New York: Free Press.

PART VI

Conclusion

RICHARD E. MAYER

Approximately 50 years ago, Guilford (1950) revived interest in what was then the neglected field of creativity research by offering a compelling rationale and research agenda. In many ways, the *Handbook of Creativity* represents a progress report on how the field of creativity research has developed over the past 50 years. Within its 20 substantive chapters, the *Handbook* contains summaries by leading creativity researchers representing a seemingly chaotic diversity of research methodologies and questions.

How is creativity different from intelligence? How can we measure a person's creativity? Which cognitive processes are involved in creative thinking? How does a creative product happen? Which life experiences produce a creative person? What are the characteristics of creative people? What motivates creative people? What are the biological and evolutionary bases of creativity? How do social and cultural contexts affect creativity? Is creativity the dominion of an elite few or can everyone be creative? How does creativity develop? Can people learn to become more creative? These are the kinds of questions addressed in this volume.

These are deep questions that require creative research methodologies. Although the *Handbook* summarizes some important steps in answering these questions, the ongoing challenge for creativity researchers is to create new and useful research methodologies. In this chapter I explore two research issues underlying an agenda for creativity research – what to study and how to study.

WHAT TO STUDY

A logical starting place for creativity research is to define what is meant by creativity. In short, it is reasonable to ask: What is it that we are trying to study? Among the *Handbook* authors who offered introductory definitions of creativity, the majority endorse the idea that creativity involves the creation of an *original* and *useful* product. Gruber and Wallace (Chapter 5) state: "What do we mean by creative work? Like most definitions of creativity, ours involves novelty and value: The creative product must be new and must be given value according to some external criteria." Martindale (Chapter 7) states, "A creative idea is one that is both original and appropriate for the situation in which it occurs." Lumsden (Chapter 8), in summarizing the literature, states that "creativity is a kind of capacity to think up something new that people find significant." Feist (Chapter 14) notes that "psychologists and philosophers who study the creative process, person, and product are in consensus about what is creative: novel and adaptive solutions to problems." Lubart (Chapter 17) states that "creativity from a Western perspective can be defined as the ability to produce work that is novel and appropriate." Boden (Chapter 18) states that "creativity is the generation of ideas that are both novel and valuable." Nickerson (Chapter 20) notes that "although not everyone considers it possible to articulate clear objective criteria identifying creative products,

Table 22.1. *Two Defining Features of Creativity*

Author (Chapter)	Feature 1: Originality	Feature 2: Usefulness
Gruber & Wallace (5)	novelty	value
Martindale (7)	original	appropriate
Lumsden (8)	new	significant
Feist (13)	novel	adaptive
Lubart (16)	novel	appropriate
Boden (17)	novel	valuable
Nickerson (19)	novelty	utility

novelty is often cited as one of their distinctive characteristics, and some form of utility – usefulness, appropriateness, or social value – as another." In summary, there appears to be consensus that the two defining characteristics of creativity are originality and usefulness, as summarized in Table 22.1.

In spite of agreement on a basic definition of creativity, there are several clarifying questions for which *Handbook* authors – reflecting the diversity of the field – have different answers. First, is creativity a property of *people, products,* or *processes?* Authors who view creativity as a property of people tend to focus on individual differences in people's creativity (e.g., Plucker & Renzulli, Chapter 3) or on the distinctive characteristics of creative people (e.g., Simonton, Chapter 6; Feist, Chapter 14; Policastro & Gardner, Chapter 11). Authors who view creativity as a property of products tend to focus on case studies of creative production (e.g., Gruber & Wallace, Chapter 5) or on computer simulations of creative production (e.g., Boden, Chapter 18). Authors who view creativity as a property of cognitive processing tend to focus on analyzing the steps involved in creative thinking (e.g., Runco & Sakamoto, Chapter 4; Ward, Smith, & Finke, Chapter 10) or in teaching creative cognitive processing (e.g., Nickerson, Chapter 20).

The overarching definition of creativity seems to favor the idea that creativity involves the creation of new and useful products, including ideas as well as concrete objects; however, from this definition, it follows that creative people are those who create new and useful products, and creative cognitive processes occur whenever a new and useful product is created. Even if one takes the perspective that creativity is a property of people, it is possible to focus on the life events of a creative person such as the relation between childhood experiences and adult creativity (Howe, Chapter 21) or the cognitive processes of a creative person during the creative episode (Gruber & Wallace, Chapter 5). Overall, the *Handbook* authors represent all three views.

Second, is creativity a *personal* or *social* phenomenon? According to the personal view, creativity involves producing something new and useful with respect to the person doing the creating (e.g., Runco & Sakamoto, Chapter 4; Ward, Smith, & Finke, Chapter 10). For example, Ward, Smith, and Finke (Chapter 10) argue that "creative capacity is an essential property of normative human cognition" so that seemingly ordinary events such as constructing "concepts from an ongoing stream of otherwise discrete experiences" are acts of personal creativity. According to the social view, creativity involves producing something new and useful with respect to the social or cultural environment (e.g., Csikszentmihalyi, Chapter 16; Lubart, Chapter 17). For example, Csikszentmihalyi (Chapter 16) takes the position that creativity means "the ability to add something new to the culture" such that a creation by an individual must be "sanctioned by some group entitled to make decisions as to what should or should not be included in the domain." A possible reconciliation is that both "person-centered" and "environment-centered" considerations (Lubart, Chapter 17) are essential for understanding human creativity. Unfortunately, scientifically valid examples of this kind of reconciliation are difficult to find in the *Handbook* or in the larger creativity literature.

Third, is creativity *common* or *rare?* On one side, some creativity researchers view creative thought as a common aspect of everyday cognition so that all humans are capable of creativity (Runco & Sakamoto, Chapter 4; Ward, Smith, & Finke, Chapter 10; Weisberg, Chapter 12). The goal of this research is often to examine the cognitive processes of normal people as they solve problems that require creativity. On the other side, some researchers view creative thought as a rare event that occurs only within a very small group of unique individuals (Gruber & Wallace, Chapter 5; Simonton, Chapter 6; Howe, Chapter 21). The goal of this research is often to understand the unique characteristics of the creative person and the unique prerequisites for the creative episode. Although the dominant view in the *Handbook* seems to be that there are important differences between creative and noncreative people (consistent with the rare view), the *Handbook* also contains many examples of creativity in normal people (consistent with the common view).

Fourth, is creativity *domain-general* or *domain-specific?* According to the domain-general view, creativity is a general skill or trait or characteristic that can be applied to a wide variety of situations. The domain-general view is implicit in the classic psychometric studies of creativity in which the goal is to measure the level of creativity in people by using a battery of tests (Plucker & Renzulli, Chapter 3). In contrast, the domain-specific view of creativity is that different kinds of creative ability are required in different domains, for example, the creativity involved in artistic production is different from that involved in scientific discovery (Gruber & Wallace, Chapter 5; Policastro & Gardner, Chapter 11). Similarly, Weisberg (Chapter 12) provides evidence for the domain-specific view by showing how domain knowledge is related to creative accomplishment. Although the dominant view among cognitive scientists (Gardner, 1983, 1994) is that cognitive ability is at least partially domain-specific, the *Handbook* reflects both views.

Fifth, is creativity *quantitative* or *qualitative?* The quantitative view is that creativity consists of one or more factors of which people may have varying amounts. The quantitative view is a basic tenet of the research that uses psychometric tests of creativity (Plucker & Renzulli, Chapter 3). In contrast, the qualitative view is that creativity always manifests itself in a unique way in each creative person or each creative episode. For example, Gruber and Wallace (Chapter 5) point to "the necessary uniqueness of the creative person" and argue for "efforts to understand each case as a unique functioning system." Although the quantitative view predominates, the *Handbook* contains a rich sampling of both views.

In summary, there is some consensus in the creativity research community concerning what to study: Creativity occurs when someone creates an original and useful product. However, there is a lack of consensus on such basic clarifying issues as whether creativity refers to a product, process, or person; whether creativity is personal or social; whether creativity is common or rare; whether creativity is domain-general or domain-specific; and whether creativity is quantitative or qualitative.

HOW TO STUDY

Perhaps the most contentious issue concerns how to study creativity. The *Handbook* highlights a representative sampling of creativity research approaches: *psychometric, experimental, biographical* (including case study and historiometric), *biological, computational,* and *contextual* (including cultural and evolutionary). Reviews of the history of creativity research (e.g., Albert & Runco, Chapter 2; Runco & Sakamoto, Chapter 4) suggest that the three most widely used approaches are the psychometric – the original approach that Guilford (1950) trumpeted 50 years ago; the experimental – the tried-and-true method at the heart of classic research in cognitive psychology (Albert & Runco, Chapter 2; Runco & Sakamoto, Chapter 4); and the biographical – including qualitative analyses such as what Gruber and Wallace (Chapter 5) call the case study method and quantitative analyses such as what Simonton (Chapter 6) calls the historiometric perspective. Although the biological (or cognitive neuroscience), computational (or artificial intelligence), and contextual approaches (including cultural and evolutionary) are not as well developed as the "big three" approaches, they constitute potentially important approaches for the future.

In addition, each of these six approaches may focus on each of three research paradigms: *describing* the nature of creativity (such as determining how to measure creativity, analyzing the cognitive processes involved in solving a creativity problem, or describing creative episodes of creative people), *comparing* creativity and noncreativity (such as comparing people who score high versus low on a creativity test, comparing the cognitive processes involved in creative and noncreative problem-solving tasks, or comparing the characteristics of creative and noncreative people), and relating factors to creativity (such as determining the relation between scores on tests of creativity and other cognitive measures, determining manipulations that facilitate or hinder creative production, or identifying life events that foster or inhibit the development of creative people).

A creativity research matrix of 18 different research methodologies is generated by crossing six research approaches with three research paradigms. Table 22.2 gives examples of each of these 18 methodologies along with corresponding chapter numbers in which the methodology is described.

Psychometric Methodologies

Psychometric approaches to the study of creativity are those in which creativity is viewed as a mental trait that can be quantified by appropriate measurement instruments. The underlying view is of creativity as a mental trait: Creativity is best understood as a measurable human factor or characteristic. The most important characteristics of this approach are *quantitative measurement,* so that the creativity of a person can be summarized as a number, *controlled environments,* so that testing takes place in artificial contexts, and *ability-based analyses,* so that human creativity depends on the level of the component abilities of the reasoner.

The starting point for all psychometric measures of creativity are Guilford's (1950, 1967) tests of divergent thinking, which were later refined by Torrance (1974). Divergent-thinking tests are so central to creativity research that Sternberg and O'Hara (Chapter 13) assert, "Guilford almost single-handedly created psychometric interest in the study of creativity." These tests involve what Sternberg and O'Hara (Chapter 13) describe as "the generation of numerous novel solutions to problems as opposed to one single correct answer." Examples include listing possible uses for a common object, such as a brick, or listing possible consequences of a given situation, such as people having six fingers instead of five. Scoring may be based on the originality and fluency of the responses, as well as flexibility and elaboration (as described by Plucker & Renzulli, Chapter 3).

When focusing on describing creativity, the psychometric approach deals mainly with the development of instruments to measure the amount of creative ability possessed by individuals. A milestone achievement involves the Torrance Tests of Creative Thinking (Torrance,

Table 22.2. *Descriptions of Six Research Approaches to Three Research Paradigms*

Approach and Paradigm	Description (Chapter)
Psychometric	
Describe	Develop a test to measure creativity (3)
Compare	Compare people who score high and low in creativity (3, 13)
Relate	Determine relations between creativity measures and other measures (1, 3, 13)
Psychological	
Describe	Describe the cognitive processes involved in creative thinking (10)
Compare	Compare the cognitive processes in creative and noncreative thinking (10)
Relate	Determine factors that affect or improve creative thinking (10, 14, 19)
Biographical	
Describe	Provide a qualitative narrative of a case history of a creative person (5, 9)
	Provide a quantitative analysis of a case history of a creative person (12)
Compare	Provide a qualitative description of commonalties of case histories of creative people (11)
	Provide a quantitative analysis of commonalties of case histories of creative people (6)
Relate	Identify life events in a case history that foster the development of a creative person (5)
	Provide a quantitative analysis of events in case histories that foster the development of creative people (6, 9, 20)
Biological	
Describe	Describe the biological correlates of creative thinking (7)
Compare	Compare the biological characteristics of creative and noncreative people (7)
Relate	Determine how biological impairments affect creativity
Computational	
Describe	Produce computer code that simulates creative production (17)
Compare	Compare computer programs that are creative and noncreative
Relate	Determine how changes in a program affect creativity
Contextual	
Describe	Describe creativity in social and cultural contexts (15)
Compare	Describe conceptions of creativity in different cultures (16)
Relate	Identify techniques to overcome barriers to creativity in a social context (18)
	Identify the evolutionary processes that shape human creativity (8)

1974), which is "the most commonly used test of divergent thinking" (Plucker & Renzulli, Chapter 3).

When focusing on making comparisons, the psychometric approach compares people who score low versus high on tests of creativity. For example, Plucker and Renzulli (Chapter 3) and Feist (Chapter 14) review research showing that creative people tend to display different personality characteristics – as measured by psychometric tests of personality – than do noncreative people.

When focusing on discovering relationships, the psychometric approach examines the relation between measures of creativity and other measures. For example, Sternberg and

O'Hara (Chapter 13) review research concerning the relation between scores on tests of creativity and scores on tests of intelligence, whereas Plucker and Renzulli (Chapter 3) and Feist (Chapter 14) examine the degree to which certain personality traits are related to creativity.

On the positive side, the family of psychometric research methods listed in Table 22.1 represents the most well-developed branch on the tree of creativity research methods. For example, Plucker and Renzulli (Chapter 3) point out that "a majority of work dealing with creativity relies on psychometric methods" and note that "the quest to quantify the creative process, primarily through the use of divergent-thinking batteries, has been the lightning rod for the psychometric study of creativity." On the negative side, a purely psychometric approach to creativity may unnecessarily restrict a fuller understanding of human creativity. Critics argue that divergent-thinking tests do not really measure or predict creative thinking, are too task specific, and have added little to cognitive theory or educational practice (Plucker & Renzulli, Chapter 3). On balance, its seems most reasonable to recognize both the strengths and weaknesses of the psychometric approach, while seeking to use it where appropriate as one of several viable methodologies.

Experimental Methodologies

Experimental approaches to the study of creativity focus on the cognitive processes involved in solving creativity problems. The underlying view is of creativity as cognitive processing: Creativity is best understood by analyzing the cognitive processes of people as they engage in creative thinking on a given creativity problem. Three important characteristics of the experimental approach are *controlled environments,* in which researchers present creativity problems to people in artificial contexts, *quantitative measurement,* in which researchers make quantitative measurements, and *cognitive task analysis,* in which researchers analyze the component processes involved in creative-thinking tasks.

Some of the earliest experimental studies of creativity focused on the nature of insight (Sternberg & Davidson, 1995), including the effects of brainstorming on creative production (Runco & Sakamoto, Chapter 4; Nickerson, Chapter 20) and the teaching of creative-thinking skills (Nickerson, Chapter 20). The classic Gestalt psychology interpretations of insight (Mayer, 1995) include the idea that creative thinking occurs when a person is able to reformulate (or reorganize) the problem in a more productive way, so that creative thinking involves a series of discrete phases. The search for the phases in creative thinking remains a challenge for current creativity researchers, as summarized in by Ward, Smith, and Finke (Chapter 10).

When focusing on describing creativity, the experimental approach uses cognitive task analysis to specify the component processes in creative thinking. For example, Ward, Smith, and Finke (Chapter 10) show that creative thinking can be analyzed into two basic subprocesses: *generative processes,* such as retrieving or transforming existing knowledge, and *exploratory processes,* such as searching for a potential function or evaluation.

When focusing on making comparisons, the experimental approach compares the cognitive processes involved in creative and noncreative thinking. For example, Ward, Smith, and Finke (Chapter 10) summarize research demonstrating differences in students' creative and noncreative thinking, such as Metcalfe's (1986; Metcalfe & Weibe, 1987) finding that students can predict how near they are to the solution for noninsight problems but not for insight problems or Schooler & Melcher's (1995) finding that asking students to verbalize as they were thinking hurt performance on insight problems but not on noninsight problems.

When focusing on discovering relationships, the experimental approach examines factors that contribute to or inhibit creative thinking. For example, Nickerson (Chapter 20) reviews many valiant attempts to teach people how to think creatively, including brainstorming (Osborn, 1953), the Productive Thinking Program (Covington, Crutchfield, Davies, & Olton, 1974), the CoRT Program (de Bono, 1973), and Project Intelligence (Nickerson, 1994). In these studies, the goal is to determine whether learning how to use creative thinking strategies enhances people's creative problem-solving performance. Collins and Amabile (Chapter 15) review research showing that intrinsic motivation fosters creative problem solving, whereas extrinsic motivation hurts it. For example, Collins and Amabile (Chapter 15) review research showing that people produce less creative products when they expect to be evaluated than when they do not.

On the positive side, the experimental approach provides for internal validity, that is, research that is well-enough controlled to allow for valid inferences. By focusing on how people solve a specific creativity problem posed by the researcher, experimental approaches "reduce the complexity surrounding creativity and thereby allow sound inferences about causality" (Runco & Sakamoto, Chapter 4). On the negative side, the experimental approach may lack external validity, that is, lack research results that can generalize to real creative thinking. Runco and Sakamoto (Chapter 4) point out: "This trade-off between control . . . and generalizability . . . is inherent in all experimental research, but the problem is especially acute in studies of creativity. This is because creativity may depend on spontaneity, which is contrary to control." The resolution to this dilemma may involve using a variety of methods that all converge on the same phenomenon.

Biographical Methodologies

Biographical approaches to the study of creativity are based on analyzing the case histories of creative people. The underlying view is creativity as a life story: Creativity is best understood by examining the events in the life of a creative person, including a detailed examination of creative episodes. In short, biographical researchers "examine those creative individuals whose status as creators is unquestionable" (Simonton, Chapter 6). In contrast to the controlled environments used in psychometric and experimental methodologies, a distinguishing characteristic of biographical methodologies is the study of creativity in authentic environments. In contrast to the ubiquitous use of quantitative measurement in psychometric and experimental methodologies, biographical researchers may rely on qualitative descriptions (described as case studies by Gruber & Wallace, Chapter 5) or on quantitative measurements (such as the historiometric approach described by Simonton, Chapter 6).

A major schism in the biographical approach concerns the relative merits of individual qualitative descriptions and grouped quantitative descriptions of creative people. On the side of individual qualitative descriptions, Gruber and Wallace (Chapter 5) argue that "the creative person is unique" rather than "conveniently far out along some well-charted path," so it is not possible "to reduce psychological description to a fixed set of dimensions." Csikszentmihalyi (Chapter 16) emphasizes the role of social and cultural context in the description of case histories of creativity. In contrast to the quantitative analyses of the psychometric and experimental approaches, Gruber and Wallace (Chapter 5) call for a "detailed analytic and sometimes narrative description of each case." On the side of grouped quantitative descriptions, Simonton (Chapter 6) argues for a historiometric approach based on quantitative analyses in which case studies of creative people are collated in an attempt to discover "general laws and statistical relationships that transcend the particulars of the historic record."

Biographical methodologies have a rich history dating back to Galton's (1869) *Hereditary*

Genius, which examined common features of the lives of people who produced outstanding accomplishment. Simonton (Chapter 6) reviews Terman's (1925) famous longitudinal studies of gifted individuals and Cox's (1926) famous retrospective studies of well-known gifted individuals, which are recognized as the starting place for modern creativity research in the biographical tradition.

When focusing on describing creativity, the biographical approach may offer detailed narrative descriptions of the case history of a creative person. Examples of qualitative biographical research include Wallace and Gruber's (1989) collection of 12 case studies and Gardner's (1993) collection of 7 case studies, as described in Chapters 5 (Gruber & Wallace) and 11 (Policastro & Gardner), respectively.

When focusing on making comparisons, the biographical approach includes quantitative summaries of commonalities among a collection of case histories of creative people. Examples of quantitative biographical research include the finding that "creative output tends to be a curvilinear, inverted backwards-J function of age" (Simonton, Chapter 6), and the first major creative output generally does not occur until the creator has had at least 10 years of experience in a field (Hayes, 1989; as described in Weisberg, Chapter 12). Taking a more qualitative approach, Policastro and Gardner (Chapter 11) were able to categorize case histories into four different kinds of creative people.

When focusing on discovering relationships, the biographical approach seeks to identify either life events in a case history that foster the development of a creative person or quantitative analyses of events in a collection of case histories that foster the development of creative people. For example, an important question is: "In order to become a highly creative adult, is it necessary to have been a child prodigy?" (Howe, Chapter 21). By examining cases of child prodigies who became creative adults, child prodigies who did not become creative adults, nonprodigies who became creative adults, and nonprodigies who did not become creative adults, Howe (Chapter 21) was able to conclude, "There is no invariant relationship that links being a prodigy with becoming a creative adult." Similarly, Feldman (Chapter 9) reviews case studies demonstrating that "being a stellar student is clearly not a prerequisite to the production of great creative work."

The strength of the biographical approach rests in its richness and authenticity. By carefully documenting the life histories of creative people, the biological approach provides a level of detail and authenticity that cannot be matched by the psychometric and experimental approaches. However, the weakness of the biographical approach rests in its lack of control and representativeness. How can we build a coherent theory of creativity from the highly detailed case histories of a few selected individuals? Simonton's (Chapter 6) historiometric approach represents a compromise between the rich but uncontrolled database provided by case histories and the narrow but controlled database of more quantitative methodologies. On balance, the biographical approach provides a useful adjunct to other approaches, but one that needs to meet the criteria for scientific investigation.

Biological Methodologies

Biological (or cognitive neuroscience) approaches to creativity seek to determine the physiological correlates of creative problem solving. The underlying view is of creativity as a measurable physiological trait: Creativity can best be understood as physiological changes that accompany creative problem solving. The distinguishing characteristic of this approach is a focus on physiological measures, such as EEG measures of cortical activation and PET measures of brain glucose metabolic rate, as described by Martindale (Chapter 7).

When focusing on describing creativity, the biological approach examines brain activities of people as they engage in creative thinking. Martindale (Chapter 7) summarizes evidence that "creative inspiration occurs in a mental state where attention is defocused, thought is associative, and a large number of mental representations are simultaneously activated" as indicated "by low levels of cortical activation, more right- than left-hemisphere activation, and low levels of frontal-lobe activation." When focusing on making comparisons, the biological approach compares the brain activities of creative and noncreative people as they engage in creative thinking. Martindale (Chapter 7) presents converging evidence that "creative people do not exhibit all of these traits in general but only while engaged in creative activity." For example, Martindale (Chapter 7) shows how "creative people tend to be deficient in cognitive inhibition" as is indicated by "lower levels of frontal-lobe activation in creative as compared with uncreative people" when they were engaged in creative thinking. When focusing on discovering relationships, the biological approach focuses on how biological factors – such as a brain injury – affect creativity. This issue is not directly addressed in the *Handbook*.

The strengths of the biological (or cognitive neuroscience) approaches to creativity rest in providing converging evidence that could not be obtained through other methodologies. The weaknesses rest in the long-debated assumption that cognitive activity can be reduced entirely to physiological activity. Another way to state this critique is to say that a complete description of brain activity during creative thinking would not constitute a complete theory of creativity. On balance, it appears that the results of biological research on creativity can augment but not replace the results of more mainline methods.

Computational Methodologies

Computational approaches to creativity are based on the idea that a person's creative thinking can be formalized as a computer program, using the techniques of artificial intelligence. The underlying view is of creativity as mental computation: Creativity can best be represented as a runnable computer program. The distinguishing characteristic of this approach is a focus on formal modeling, as described by Boden (Chapter 18).

When focusing on describing creativity, the computational approach seeks to produce computer code that simulates creative production. In reviewing research on artificial intelligence, Boden (Chapter 18) notes that "computer models of creativity are relatively few," but there are some models based on "combinatorial creativity" – that is, creating unusual connections between ideas – and "exploratory-transformational creativity" – that is, searching and manipulating a "richly structured conceptual space." The reviewed programs range from those that can make scientific discoveries to those that can create jazz improvisations. When focusing on making comparisons, the computational approach seeks to model the thinking processes of creative and noncreative people. When focusing on discovering relationships, the computational approach focuses on how features of a formal model – such as the way the program is organized – affect creativity. These issues are not emphasized in the *Handbook*.

The strengths of the computational approach are that it brings a level of precision that is rare in creativity research and that it offers an objective test of theories of creativity through computer simulation. That is, by running a computer program it is possible to assess the degree to which it models real creative thinking. The weaknesses of the computational approach include its assumption that cognition can be reduced to mathematics and the difficulty of including noncognitive factors in creativity. On balance, computational methodologies seem to offer a unique source of evidence that can be used in conjunction with other creativity research methodologies.

Contextual Methodologies

Contextual approaches to creativity focus on creativity in its social, cultural, or evolutionary context. The underlying view is of creativity as a context-based activity: Creativity cannot be dissociated from its social, cultural, or evolutionary context. The distinguishing characteristic of this approach is a focus on context, which goes beyond a simple focus on creative thinking in individuals.

When focusing on describing creativity, the contextual approach seeks to describe creative thinking in its social, cultural, or evolutionary context. For example, Csikszentmihalyi (Chapter 16) proclaims that creativity "is as much a cultural and social as it is a psychological event." Further, Csikszentmihalyi argues for a systems model of creativity that includes a culture (or domain), society (or field), and the individual. In the systems model, "for creativity to occur, a set of rules must be transmitted from the domain to the individual, the individual must then produce a novel variation in the context of the domain," and "the variation then must be selected by the field for inclusion in the domain."

When focusing on making comparisons, the contextual approach may compare conceptions of creativity in different cultures. For example, Lubart (Chapter 17) examines "the cultural environment of creativity" by showing how "the Eastern conception of creativity seems less focused on innovative products" than the Western conception of creativity. In particular, Lubart shows how "creativity involves a state of personal fulfillment" in some Eastern views.

When focusing on discovering relationships, the contextual approach focuses on overcoming barriers to creativity in a social context or on identifying evolutionary processes that shape human creativity. For example, Williams and Yang (Chapter 19) show how organizations can create barriers to creativity, and offer some suggestions for overcoming them. Taking an evolutionary perspective, Lumsden (Chapter 8) is concerned with the ways that evolution might have shaped human creativity, including the idea that creativity may be domain-specific.

A major strength of contextual approaches is a broadening of the study of creativity. The narrow focus on cognition epitomized by the psychometric and experimental approaches should be widened to recognize the social, cultural, and evolutionary context of creative cognition. Lubart (Chapter 17) summarizes this point in his simple but powerful observation: "Creativity does not occur in a vacuum." A major weakness of contextual approaches is the lack of rigorous data. Lumsden (Chapter 8) points to this weakness by "demanding of evolution what we demand of any science, historical or otherwise, namely conjectures that can be tested in the hard light of new data." Although the call for broadening the study of creativity is welcome, a major obstacle to its implementation is the need for cultural and evolutionary studies of creativity to be based on testable theories and solid empirical evidence.

Overall, the approaches differ with respect to their emphasis on quantitative measurement (as reflected in the psychometric and experimental research) versus qualitative measurement (as reflected in some kinds of biographical research), their use of controlled environments (as reflected in much of the psychometric and experimental research) versus authentic environments (as reflected in biographical research), and their focus on life stories of creative people (as reflected in biographical approaches) versus single acts of creative thinking (as reflected in the experimental approach).

THE PAST AND FUTURE OF CREATIVITY RESEARCH

Although creativity researchers have managed to ask some deep questions, they have generally not succeeded in answering them. Feldman (Chapter 9) notes that "the amount of research on creativity has increased during the past two decades but still lags far behind most mainstream topics in psychology." Nickerson (Chapter 20) confesses at the outset that much of what he has to say is speculative. He also notes that much of the literature on which he draws is speculative. In summary, readers of the *Handbook* are sometimes confronted by speculation that is only loosely related to empirical data, by sweeping generalizations that are not tightly supported by research evidence, and by a level of theorizing that is too vague to yield testable predictions.

An important challenge for the next 50 years of creativity research is to develop a clearer definition of creativity and to use a combination of research methodologies that will move the field from speculation to specification. First, the classic definition of creativity as the construction of novel and useful products needs to be clarified and broadened beyond its psychometric origins. Is creativity a property of products or processes or people? Is creativity a personal or social phenomenon? Is creativity common to all people or a unique characteristic of a select few? Is creativity a domain-general activity that is essentially the same in all contexts or a domain-specific activity that depends on the context under consideration? Is creativity best conceived as a set of characteristics along which people may vary or as uniquely manifested in each creative individual? In clarifying the definition of creativity, the makings of a new research agenda is likely to emerge.

Second, creativity research needs to be based on the creative use of research methodologies that converge on an empirically tested theory of creativity. The three classical approaches – psychometric, experimental, and biographical – each have their strengths and weaknesses. At times it appears that the psychometric and experimental approaches can be too hard – by emphasizing precise measurements of creativity in contrived settings – whereas the biographical approach can be too soft – by emphasizing qualitative descriptions of a few highly selected cases in authentic settings. What is needed is a methodology that combines the scientific respectability of the psychometric and experimental approaches with the authenticity of the biographical approach. The newer approaches – biological, computational, and contextual – have not yet had a major impact on the field, but may provide useful converging evidence in the future. Although no single approach may be able to provide a complete theory of creativity, what is needed is a creative combination or amalgamation that addresses the unique needs of creativity research.

Creativity was at the heart of the cognitive psychology proposed by Gestalt psychologists in the 1930s and 1940s (Duncker, 1945; Kohler, 1929; Wertheimer, 1959). The motivating question for these researchers involved understanding the nature of insight, that is, where creative ideas come from (Mayer, 1995). The focus on insight, however, was lost when cognitive psychology opted for the precision of the information-processing approach in the 1960s (Mayer, 1996). In spite of this shift, creativity research has always had a foothold on the field of cognitive psychology, albeit a small and tenuous one. For example, Albert and Runco (Chapter 2) report that only about 0.01% of the recent psychological literature deals with creativity. This *Handbook* will have served an important historic role if it rekindles interest in the great unanswered questions concerning how people produce creative solutions to real problems.

REFERENCES

Covington, M. V., Crutchfield, R. S., Davies, L., & Olton, R. M. (1974). *The productive thinking program.* Columbus, OH: Merrill.

Cox, C. (1926). *The early mental traits of three hundred geniuses.* Stanford, CA: Stanford University Press.

de Bono, E. (1973). *CoRT thinking.* Blanford, England: Direct Educational Services.

Duncker, K. (1945). On problem solving. *Psychological Monographs, 58*(5), Whole No. 270.

Galton, F. (1869). *Hereditary genius: An inquiry into its laws and consequences.* London: Macmillan.

Gardner, H. (1983). *Frames of mind: The theory of multiple intelligences.* New York: Basic.

Gardner, H. (1993). *Creating minds.* New York: Basic.

Gardner, H. (1994). Multiple intelligences theory. In R. J. Sternberg (Ed.), *Encyclopedia of human intelligence* (pp. 740–742). New York: Macmillan.

Guilford, J. P. (1950). Creativity. *American Psychologist, 5,* 444–454.

Guilford, J. P. (1967). *The nature of human intelligence.* New York: McGraw-Hill.

Hayes, J. R. (1989). Cognitive processes in creativity. In J. A. Glover, R. R. Ronning, & C. R. Reynolds (Eds.), *Handbook of creativity* (pp. 135–145). New York: Plenum.

Kohler, W. (1925). *The mentality of apes.* New York: Harcourt, Brace, Jovanovich.

Mayer, R. E. (1995). The search for insight: Grappling with Gestalt psychology's unanswered questions. In R. J. Sternberg & J. E. Davidson (Eds.), *The nature of insight* (pp. 3–32). Cambridge, MA: MIT Press.

Mayer, R. E. (1996). Learners as information processors: Legacies and limitations of educational psychology's second metaphor. *Educational Psychologist, 3–4,* 151–162.

Metcalfe, J. (1986). Feelings of knowing in memory and problem solving. *Journal of Experimental Psychology: Learning, Memory, and Cognition, 12,* 288–294.

Metcalfe, J., & Weibe, D. (1987). Intuition in insight and non-insight problem solving. *Memory & Cognition, 15,* 238–246.

Nickerson, R. S. (1994). Project intelligence. In R. J. Sternberg (Ed.), *Encyclopedia of human intelligence* (pp. 857–860). New York: Macmillan.

Osborn, A. (1953). *Applied imagination.* New York: Scribner's.

Schooler, J. W., & Melcher, J. (1995). The ineffibility of insight. In S. M. Smith, T. B. Ward, & R. A. Finke (Eds.), *The creative cognition approach* (pp. 97–133). Cambridge, MA: MIT Press.

Sternberg, R. J., & Davidson, J. E. (Eds.). (1995). *The nature of insight.* Cambridge, MA: MIT Press.

Terman, L. M. (1925). *Mental and physical traits of a thousand gifted children.* Stanford, CA: Stanford University Press.

Torrance, E. P. (1974). *The Torrance Tests of Creative Thinking.* Bensenville, IL: Scholastic Testing Service.

Wallace, D. B., & Gruber, H. E. (Eds.). (1989). *Creative people at work: Twelve cognitive case studies.* New York: Oxford University Press.

Wertheimer, M. (1959). *Productive thinking.* New York: Harper & Row.

Author Index

Italicized numbers indicate pages on which full citations appear.

461

Subject Index

479